The Beauty Therapy Fact File

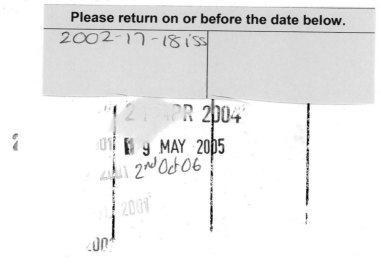

*This book is dedicated to my father for his advice,
inspiration and encouragement*

The Beauty Therapy Fact File

Third Edition

Susan Cressy

Lecturer in Beauty Therapy, South Trafford College, Manchester

Butterworth-Heinemann
Linacre House, Jordon Hill, Oxford OX2 8DP
225 Wildwood Avenue, Woburn, MA 01801—2041
A division of Reed Educational and Professional Publishing Ltd

 A member of the Reed Elsevier plc group

OXFORD AUCKLAND BOSTON
JOHANNESBURG MELBOURNE NEW DELHI

First published 1993
Reprinted 1994 (twice)
Second edition 1996
Reprinted 1996 (twice), 1997
Third edition 1998
Reprinted 1998, 1999 (twice), 2000

British Library Cataloguing in Publication Data
Cressy, Susan
 Beauty Therapy Fact File – 3rd ed
 1. Beauty culture
 I. Title
 646.7'2

ISBN 0 7506 3835 4

Composition by Scribe Design, Gillingham, Kent
Printed and bound in Great Britain

Contents

Preface

Having been in the beauty business as a student, practitioner, lecturer and assessor for twenty-five years, I have become aware of the need to provide a book which includes all subjects covered by the beauty therapy syllabus of all awarding bodies. These subjects include facial and body treatments, exercise, diet and nutrition, manicure and pedicure, epilation and depilation as well as business management.

Because it is important for the student to become commercially competent and familiar with the constantly changing trends in beauty therapy, this third edition includes a detailed section on arometherapy which is extensively used in beauty establishments for facial, body and holistic therapy. Other new and popular treatments such as ultrasound, glycolic acid treatment, anti-ageing 'non-surgical facelift' treatment, bodywrapping, crystal exfoliation, natural nail care and semi-permanent make-up have also been included.

It has been my intention to produce a book which will appeal to all ages and levels of ability, providing a comprehensive and factual source of reference for students, teachers and practising beauty and holistic therapists. In fact anyone who has an interest in the world of health and beauty.

This book has been written in easy to read sections to include the detailed anatomy and physiology required for NVQ Levels 2 and 3 and the scientific facts relevant to the therapist, the salon and treatments carried out.

The business management section provides the necessary information for NVQ Levels 2 and 3 as well as a useful insight into the setting up and management of a business. This is becoming increasingly more important as the opportunities within the health and beauty industry are constantly expanding.

This book is the only one of its kind to cover all NVQ levels of beauty therapy as well as much additional material to expand and reinforce the therapist's knowledge. It is intended, therefore, to assist students in their studies, to aid in revision for assessment and to provide an easy source of reference for those returning to the profession or refreshing their technical knowledge.

Acknowledgements

I wish to thank the following people for their contributions to this textbook:

Crystal Clear International Limited, 28 Rodney Street, Liverpool L2 TQ, for supplying the photograph of equipment.

Doctor W. J. Cunliffe of the Leeds Foundation for Dermatological Research, the University of Leeds, for supplying the photographs of skin disorders and diseases.

Depilex Limited, 61–71 Hallam Road, Nelson, Lancashire, for supplying the photographs of electrical equipment.

Elemis Limited, 57–65 The Broadway, Stanmore, Middlesex HA7 4DU, for supplying the photographs in Chapter 12.

M. D. Formulations for supplying the photograph of their products.

Totally UK Ltd, Spelthorne Lane, Ashford Common, Middlesex TW15 1UX, for supplying the photographs of ultrasound, body brushing and body wrapping.

Helen Stewart, Lorraine Jones and Diane Towey for proofreading.

Simon Edward, Leslie Fletcher and Lorraine Connaughton for the photographs of manual techniques.

Karon Holmes, Top to Toe Beauty Salon, Cheshire, for supplying literature and illustrations for the business management section.

My family for their patience and support during the writing of this book.

Susan Cressy

Part One Facial Treatments

1 Facial anatomy and physiology

Cells

The human body is composed of millions of cells which differ in size, shape, structure and function. Each cell is made up of many parts which are called *organelles* (small organs). It is in these parts that chemical reactions take place contributing to the living processes in the cell. See Figure 1.1.

Despite their differences, all body cells have some common characteristics:

○ They have the ability to absorb nutrients which may be used for growth and repair.
○ They have the ability to utilize oxygen and nutrients to release heat and energy and, as a result, produce carbon dioxide and water.
○ They have the ability to increase in size and multiply in number.
○ They have the ability to respond to environmental change such as light and temperature.

Cell structure

Cells contain protoplasm, a colourless jelly-like substance, enclosed by a cell membrane which is semipermeable, allowing soluble substances to enter or leave the cell.

Each cell contains a nucleus or dense mass of protoplasm in the centre, which is important for cell reproduction and is surrounded by its own nuclear membrane. The nucleus is surrounded by cytoplasm which contains the nutrients necessary for growth and repair.

The mitochondria in the cell provides the energy required by the cell for its activities.

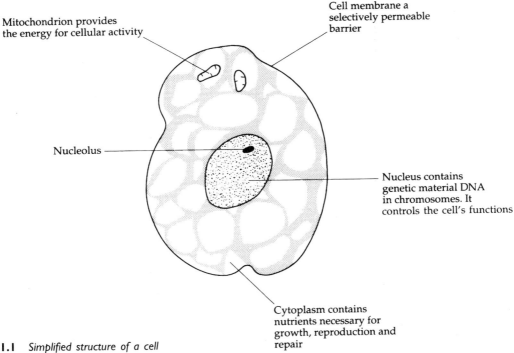

Mitochondrion provides the energy for cellular activity

Cell membrane a selectively permeable barrier

Nucleolus

Nucleus contains genetic material DNA in chromosomes. It controls the cell's functions

Cytoplasm contains nutrients necessary for growth, reproduction and repair

Figure 1.1 *Simplified structure of a cell*

Cellular respiration takes place. This is when the cell takes up oxygen that we breathe in and glucose (produced by the digestion of the food we have eaten) which are then converted to carbon dioxide and water in a chemical reaction that gives off energy, that is:

Glucose + oxygen → carbon dioxide + water + energy

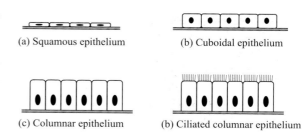

Figure 1.2 *Types of epithelium tissue*

Mitosis

Mitosis is the process of cell division or reproduction which, after a series of changes within the cell, produces two new identical cells. This occurs in human tissue, including the hair and skin.

Groups of similar cells form body tissues, which have specific functions and they may be classified as follows:

Epithelial, connective, nerve, muscular and blood.

Epithelial tissue

This tissue provides a protective covering for surfaces inside and outside the body. The skin, the lining of the heart, blood and lymphatic vessels and the digestive and respiratory organs are all made up of epithelial tissue. The skin is made up of stratified epithelium which means it has many layers.

Epithelial tissue may be:

○ *Simple* – single layer of cells.
○ *Compound* – several layers of cells.

Classification of simple epithelial

Squamous
Cells which fit closely together like flat stones, provides a smooth lining for the heart, blood and lymph vessels and the alveoli in the lungs (Figure 1.2(a)). They are found in areas of the body which have little wear and tear.

Cuboidal
Cube-shaped cells lying on a basement membrane which are actively involved in secre-

tion and absorption (Figure 1.2(b)). They are found in the tubules of the kidney and some glands.

Columnar
Rectangular in shape on a basement membrane with a nucleus near its base, they are found lining the ducts of glands, the gall bladder, and the organs of the alimentary tract, where some cells secrete mucous and others absorb the products of digestion (Figure 1.2(c)).

Ciliated
These are columnar cells with fine hair-like processes on their free surface, they are found on wet surfaces (Figure 1.2(d)). The hairs are called cilia and their function is to move the contents of the tubes they line, in one direction only. They are found in respiratory passages and uterine tubes.

Classification of compound epithelium

Stratified (Figure 1.3(a))
Composed of at least two layers of cells, it is durable and protects underlying structures. In the more superficial layers the cells are flat but in the deeper layers the cells are cuboidal or columnar. The basal cells are continually multiplying, producing new cells which flatten the cells above, pushing them outwards. These cells may be:

○ *Keratinized*, which are found on dry surfaces such as skin, nails and hair, providing protection to and preventing drying out of the underlying cells.

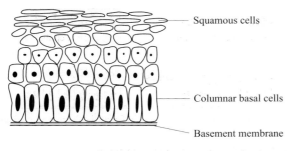

Squamous cells

Columnar basal cells

Basement membrane

(a) Stratified epithelium

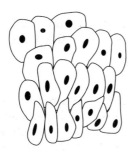

(b) Transitional epithelium

Figure 1.3 *Stratified and transitional epithelium*

○ *Non-keratinized*, which are found on wet surfaces that may be subjected to wear and tear such as the lining of the mouth, the oesophagus and the conjunctiva of the eyes.

Transitional (Figure 1.3(b))
Similar to non-keratinized epithelium but the cells in the outer layer tend to be large and rounded rather than flat. This type of epithelium lines hollow structures that are subjected to expansion from with, for example the urinary bladder. The function of these cells is to prevent rupture of the organ.

Connective tissue

Connective tissue takes various forms and provides support for, and protects and binds together, other body tissues. It includes bone, cartilage and adipose tissue.

Collagen is a fibrous connective tissue which is non-elastic and found in bundles throughout many organs and other structures. It is important in the subcutaneous layer of the skin as it provides support which, when broken down, contributes to the wrinkling which occurs, particularly after exposure to ultraviolet radiation.

Also present in the subcutaneous layer of the skin is *elastic fibrous connective tissue*. As the name implies these fibres help to maintain the elasticity of the skin and provide support helping to maintain a youthful skin. With age and exposure to the elements these fibres become less effective therefore contributing to the formation of wrinkles.

Cells of connective tissue are:

○ *Fibroblasts* – large flat cells which form collagen and elastin helping with tissue repair.
○ *Macrophages* – irregular in shape and they engulf bacteria by the process of phagocytosis thus defending the body from bacterial invasion.
○ *Plasma* – developed from B lymphocytes they give rise to antibodies providing a defence mechanism in the blood.
○ *Mast* – similar to *basophil leucocytes*, they are found in abundance along the blood vessels. They produce heparin, an anticoagulant which helps the passage of protective substances from the blood to the affected tissues and histamine released when cells are damaged.

Cartilage

This is much firmer tissue capable of enduring a lot more stress than other connective tissue. It has no blood vessels or nerves and it is a dense network of collagen and elastin fibres surrounded by the perichondrium. There are three kinds:

1 Hyaline cartilage, found at joints or over the end of long bones and forming the nose larynx, trachea, bronchi and bronchial tubes and it provides support and flexibility.
2 Fibrocartilage found in the discs between the vertebrae it provides strength and rigidity.
3 Elastic cartilage provides strength and maintains the shape of certain organs.

Nerve tissue

Nerve tissue is sensitive to stimulation and carries messages to and from the brain.

Muscular tissue

Muscular tissue provides the body with the power of movement as it is contractile tissue. There are three main types of muscle tissue and they are:

1 *Skeletal*, muscles under our conscious control.
2 *Visceral*, involuntary muscle not under our conscious control.
3 *Cardiac*, not under our conscious control, the heart muscle is responsible for the constant pumping action of the heart.

Blood

The cells of the blood circulate in blood vessels carrying food, waste products and hormones around the body.

Red blood cells – erythrocytes

These contain millions of molecules of a substance called haemoglobin and in the lungs oxygen breathed in combines with the haemoglobin and this gives the cells their bright red colour. This oxygenated blood is carried in the arteries to the tissues. Carbon dioxide and water, waste products of cellular activity, are carried from the tissues by the red blood cells to the lungs via the veins.

Red blood cells are manufactured in bone marrow and the body needs iron for their production. The body has the ability to control the number of red cells according to its needs, for example when there is a large blood loss the bone marrow immediately begins to increase red cell production.

White blood cells – leucocytes

These are larger than the red cells and they are irregular in shape. White blood cells are involved in the body's defence against disease. Some white blood cells are manufactured in the bone marrow and lymphocytes are formed in the spleen, tonsils and lymph glands. They are classified as polymorphs, lymphocytes and monocytes.

Polymorphs
There are three types of polymorphs:

1 Neutrophils which engulf and destroy bacteria.
2 Eosinophils which combat bacterial invasion and reduce the effects of histamine which is released into the tissue when antigens or foreign substances enter the body.
3 Basophils which are essential to life because they release a substance called heparin that works to stop the blood from clotting inside the vessels.

Lymphocytes
These make up about 25 per cent of the blood's white cells and they provide the body with its natural immunity to disease. They make antitoxins to combat the toxins or chemicals produced by some bacteria and antibodies to destroy antigens.

Monocytes
These form up to 8 per cent of the white cells and the larger monocytes engulf bacteria and also remove the cell debris which results from bacterial invasion.

The activities of polymorphs and monocytes is called an inflammatory response.

The activities of the lymphocytes is called an immune response.

Both these responses may be activated at the same time. Inflammation is the body's response to injury or invasion at a local level.

Platelets or thrombocytes

Platelets are made in the bone marrow. They are the tiniest cells in the body (one millilitre of blood contains about 250 million platelets), disc-shaped and without a nucleus. Their one basic function is to make blood clot when bleeding has to be stopped. When platelets come into contact with the damaged blood vessel they begin to enlarge, their shape becomes irregular and they become sticky, causing them to adhere to the collagen fibres. More platelets are produced and these stick to the existing platelets. This accumulation of platelets makes a *platelet plug* which will prevent blood loss from small wounds. The plug tightens and becomes more secure as it is reinforced by *fibrin* threads which are formed during the coagulation process.

Structure of the skin

The skin is the largest organ of the body. It provides a protective outer covering to the underlying structures and prevents the invasion of bacteria.

The skin has three main layers:

1 *The epidermis*, the surface of the skin.
2 *The dermis*, which supports the epidermis and provides contour and elasticity.
3 *The hypodermis*, which is sometimes referred to as the subcutaneous layer, and is made up of adipose tissue containing fat cells, muscles and veins.

The epidermis

This is the most superficial layer of the skin, composed of stratified epithelium (layered cells). See Figure 1.4. The thickness varies from one part of the body to another, the thinnest being on the eyelids and the thickest on the soles of the feet and the palms of the hands. This layer is free from nerve endings of pain but is extremely sensitive to touch. There are two distinct regions which consist of five different layers:

The active area of cell renewal	Stratum germinativum Stratum spinosum
The upper area where cells are changing from living to dead	Stratum granulosum Stratum lucidum Stratum corneum

Cell renewal is the change of living cells containing a nucleus (the vital body in a cell, essential for its growth and reproduction), into dead, horny flat cells with no nucleus which are constantly shed from the surface of the skin.

Stratum germinativum – basal layer
This is the deepest layer of the epidermis and its lower surface is attached to the dermis, from

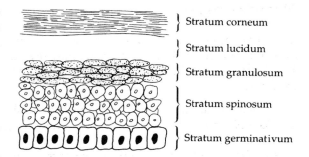

Figure 1.4   *The layers of the epidermis*

which it receives nutrient fluid from the blood vessels. It is in this layer that the development of new cells (mitosis) occurs. This leads to a gradual displacement of the older cells towards the surface.

Melanin-forming cells called *melanocytes* are formed in this layer. Melanin is the skin's natural protection against the harmful effects of ultraviolet light and is responsible for the change in skin colour when exposed to the sun.

Stratum spinosum – prickle cell layer
This consists of the cells immediately above the basal layer. Each cell connects with the next by means of fine threads or filaments through which they receive nourishment from the tissue fluid or protoplasm.

Towards the upper part of this layer, chemical changes take place and the *keratinization* process has begun. Keratinization is the change of living cells containing a nucleus into layers of flat cells composed of the hard durable protein keratin.

Stratum granulosum – granular layer
The final stages of keratinization take place in this layer. The cells become flattened and the nucleus begins to disintegrate, there is a loss of fluids which contributes to the transformation of cells into keratin, a tough fibrous protein.

Stratum lucidum – transparent layer
This is made up of small, tightly packed transparent cells with no nucleus. This layer is thought to be the barrier zone controlling the transmission of water through the skin. It lies between the outer horny layer and the inner

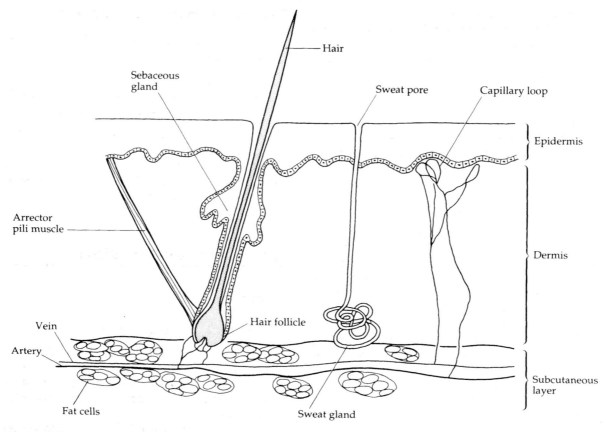

Figure 1.5 *Structure of the skin*

granular layer. It is more evident in the thickest areas of skin, the soles of the feet and the palms of the hands.

Stratum corneum – horny layer

This consists of several layers of keratinized epithelial cells tightly packed together. As they contain the protein keratin they are very tough and horny and they have no nucleus. The superficial layers are constantly being shed and the cells beneath contain an epidermal fatty substance resembling bees' wax which keeps them waterproof and helps prevent the skin from cracking and becoming open to bacterial infection.

The dermis

This is the chief supportive section of the visible surface skin or epidermis. It is composed of dense connective tissue which is tough, highly elastic and flexible, and it creates the strength, contour, elasticity and smoothness of the skin. The tissue is highly sensitive and fibrous, and comprises:

1 *Collagen*, which provides support to the skin.
2 *Elastin*, which gives the skin its elasticity and resilience.
3 *Fibroblast cells*, which are responsible for the manufacture of collagen and to a lesser degree elastin.

It also contains:

○ Blood and lymph vessels.
○ Nerve endings.
○ Hair follicles.
○ Sweat and sebaceous glands.
○ Papillary muscles.

The dermis has a higher water content than any other region of the skin and it provides nourishment to the epidermis. It has two layers: the upper papillary layer and the deep reticular layer.

The superficial papillary layer

This is irregular in shape with protrusions into the epidermis called papillae (Figure 1.5). There are several nerve endings in this layer including touch, which end in rounded bodies, and pain, cold and heat, which have delicate branched nerve endings.

Fine capillaries are found here, bringing oxygen and nourishment to the skin and carrying away waste products. This is a highly active and important area of the skin.

The deep reticular layer

This layer is situated below the papillary layer. The tough and elastic collagen fibres, interwoven with elastic fibres in this layer, are responsible for the elasticity and general tone of the skin. Sweat and sebaceous glands are present as well as the arrector pili muscles, small bundles of involuntary muscle fibres which are attached to the hair follicles.

There are many fine veins and arteries passing through this area which link up with the papillary capillaries. The lymph vessels also form a network through the dermis allowing the removal of waste from the skin.

(a) Adipose tissue

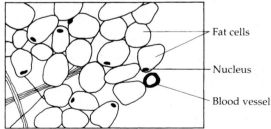

Fat cells

Nucleus

Blood vessel

(b) Areolar tissue

Elastic fibres

Fibroblasts

Collagen fibres

Figure 1.6 *Adipose and areolar tissue*

The hypodermis – subcutaneous layer

This layer (Figure 1.6) is an area for the formation and storage of fat, a combination of:

o *Adipose tissue*, containing fat cells.
o *Areolar tissue*, containing elastic fibres, which makes this layer elastic and flexible.

It is thicker in women than men, thus giving a more rounded appearance to their contours. As fat is a poor conductor of heat, the hypodermis helps to reduce the loss of heat through the skin and so keep the body warm.

Functions of the skin

Protection

The skin performs many functions:

o It is a protective cover for the underlying internal organs.
o The stratum corneum, as long as it remains intact, acts as a barrier against bacterial invasion.
o The sebum produced by the sebaceous glands has slight antiseptic properties and keeps the skin supple.
o Melanin is the skin's natural protection against ultraviolet light.
o The sensory nerve endings in the skin prevent the body from further injury by reflex action to a painful stimulus.
o It is waterproof and prevents the absorption of water and the loss of essential body fluids.

Temperature control

Blood carries heat and the normal body temperature is 36.8°C. The centre for the regulation of heat and sweating is in the brain (the hypothalamus). Loss of body heat is mainly controlled by the blood supply and sweat glands of the skin.

A great deal of the body's heat is distributed by the circulatory system around the body. When the body temperature rises, the capillaries in the skin dilate and heat from the extra blood which has been brought to the surface is lost by:

○ *Radiation* (heat moves away from the body).
○ *Conduction* (the clothes we are wearing absorb the heat).
○ *Convection* (cool air touches the body, heats and rises, and is replaced by more cool air).

When the body temperature lowers the capillaries in the skin constrict and keep the heat within the body.

Evaporation of sweat from the skin's surface helps to regulate body temperature, because when the temperature rises, the sweat glands are sent a message by the brain and are stimulated to produce sweat which then evaporates on the skin's surface and cools the body.

Sensation

The skin contains sensory nerve endings which when stimulated by external stimuli send messages to the brain which in turn responds via the motor nerves.

The nerve receptors are located at different levels in the skin and some messages are interpreted before reaching the brain when reflex action occurs. See Figure 1.7.

The sensory nerve endings in the skin react to:

○ Heat.
○ Cold.
○ Touch.
○ Pressure.
○ Pain.

Motor nerves supply the arrector pili muscle which is attached to the hair follicle and causes it to stand on end. Secretory nerve fibres innervate the sweat and oil glands of the skin.

Absorption

Since the skin acts as a waterproof barrier very little absorption takes place. The very superficial layers of the stratum corneum absorb small amounts of special conditioning creams used to improve very dry skin conditions.

There is a passage via the hair follicles to some fatty substances.

Minute amounts of water may be absorbed over a large surface area.

Excretion and secretion

Perspiration is excreted by the sweat glands removing waste from the skin.

Secretion is the production of sebum from the sebaceous glands and this is the skin's natural moisturiser which helps to keep it soft, supple and intact.

Appendages to the skin

The sebaceous glands

The sebaceous glands are situated in the dermis opening into the hair follicle and are found all over the body. They are more numerous in the scalp and on the face particularly around the forehead, nose, cheeks and chin.

Although the glands secrete sebum, the skin's natural moisturiser, it can attract dirt, trapping it on the skin and causing blackheads, papules and pustules.

In cases when too little sebum is produced dry patches and irritation may occur. This condition is called *asteatosis*. When there is an over-production of sebum and the skin takes on a very oily appearance this condition is called *seborrhoea*.

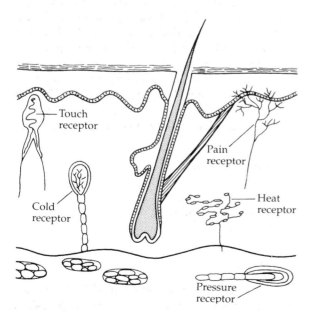

Figure 1.7 *Sensory nerves of the skin*

The sebaceous glands are affected by the endocrine system and during puberty can become overactive.

The male sex hormone *testosterone* causes the gland to enlarge. The female sex hormone *oestrogen* decreases the size of the gland.

The sudoriferous or sweat glands

These glands consist of a coiled base emanating from the deeper layers of the dermis, a tube-like duct which rises through the epidermis ending at the skin's surface to form a sweat pore.

There are two kinds of sweat glands:

The eccrine glands
They are found all over the body, having a duct and a pore through which secretions are brought to the skin's surface.

The apocrine glands
They are connected with hair follicles and are found chiefly in underarm, breast and genital areas of the body. As well as water and salt, fatty substances are secreted from these glands and react with the air to cause body odour.

Disorders of the sudoriferous glands

Anhidrosis
Lack of perspiration, partially or complete.

Hyperhydrosis
Over-secretion of perspiration, localized or general, most affected are the axillae, palms of the hand and soles of the feet.

Bromhidrosis
Foul smelling perspiration caused by decomposition of retained sweat in covered areas of the body, an intake of strong smelling foods or a chronic bacterial infection of the sweat glands.

Miliaria rubra
A combination of sensitive skin, exposure to a hot atmosphere and excessive sweating.

The bones of the skull

The skull is divided into two parts:

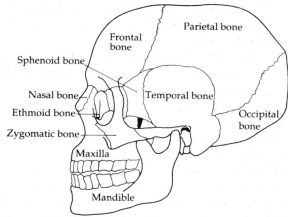

Figure 1.8 *Bones of the skull*

1   The cranium.
2   The face.

It is part of the *axial skeleton*, which constitutes the central bony core of the body and consists of:

○   Skull.
○   Vertebral column.
○   Ribs.
○   Sternum.

The cranium

The cranium provides a bony protection for the brain and is formed by a number of flat irregular bones (Figure 1.8). There is a protective lining to the cranium called the *periosteum* and it also provides attachment to muscles and tendons.

The joints between the bones are immovable and the bones themselves have numerous perforations through which nerves, blood and lymph vessels pass.

The cranium consists of the following bones:

○   One frontal bone
○   Two parietal bones
○   Two temporal bones
○   One occipital bone
○   One sphenoid bone
○   One ethmoid bone

The face

The shape of the face is determined by the bones which support the muscles of facial expression. There are fourteen bones of the face:

- *Two zygomatic*. More commonly known as the cheek bones.
- *Two maxillae*. Two bones originally, but fusion takes place before birth, forming the upper jaw, the front of the roof of the mouth, the side walls of the nasal cavities and part of the floor of the orbital cavities.
- *Two nasal*. Two flat bones which form the bridge of the nose.
- *One mandible*. This is the only movable bone of the skull and forms the lower jaw.

The following bones are the internal facial bones which do not affect the contour of the face:

- *Two palatine*. The bones which form the back part of the roof of the mouth and part of the side walls of the nose.
- *Two lacrimal*. One in each eye socket or orbit.
- *Two turbinate*. Bones inside the nose.
- *One vomer*. A thin flat bone which forms the main part of the nasal septum.

The muscles of the face

The function of muscles is to produce movement of the body with the help of the skeletal and nervous systems. The muscles of the face are made up of voluntary muscle tissue which is controlled by the will.

Muscle tissue consists of cells which are capable of contraction. Over the years lines and wrinkles will form as a result of the constant use of the muscles of facial expression.

The *origin* of a muscle is the end which usually remains fixed during contraction. The *insertion* of a muscle is the end which moves during a contraction.

Frontalis

Origin: Epicranial aponeurosis
Insertion: Skin and fascia of eyebrows.
Action: Raises the eyebrows and wrinkles the forehead.

Occipitalis

Origin: Occipital bone.

Insertion: Epicranial aponeurosis
Action: Moves the scalp.

Corrugator

Origin: Bone below the inner part of the eyebrow.
Insertion: Attaches to skin and fascia at base of the nose.
Action: Draws eyebrows together causing vertical furrows.

Procerus

Origin: Nasal bone.
Insertion: Skin between the eyebrows and the muscle fibres of frontalis.
Action: Depresses the eyebrow and causes wrinkles across the bridge of the nose.

Orbicularis occuli

Origin: Inner parts of the eye orbit.
Insertion: Skin around the eye.
Action: Closes eyes tightly.

Levator palpebrae

Origin: Roof of eye orbit.
Insertion: The upper lid.
Action: Opens the upper lid.

Nasalis

Origin: Maxillae.
Insertion: Fascia at the bridge of the nose.
Action: Compresses the nasal openings.

Dilator naris

Origin: Maxillae.
Insertion: Fascia and skin in the nose.
Action: Dilates nasal opening.

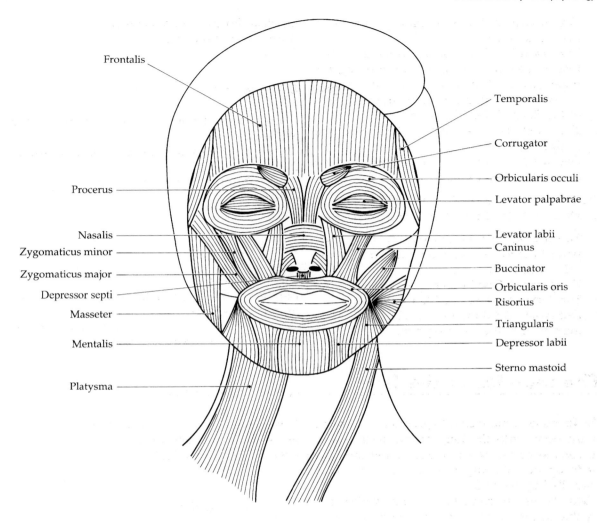

Figure 1.9 *Muscles of facial expression*

Depressor septi

Origin: Depression in front of maxilla.
Insertion: Fascia and skin in the nose.
Action: Contracts septum and helps dilate the nose.

Caninus

Origin: Maxillae.
Insertion: Skin at the angle of the mouth.
Action: Raises the angle of the mouth as in a snarl.

Levator labii

Origin: Maxillae.
Insertion: Skin and fascia of the upper lip.
Action: Raises the upper lip.

Zygomaticus – major and minor

Origin: Zygomatic bone.
Insertion: Skin and fascia at the angle of the mouth.
Action: Raises the lips as in laughing.

Risorius

Origin: The fascia of the parotid gland.
Insertion: Skin and fascia at the corner of the mouth.
Action: Draws the corners of the mouth out and back as in grinning.

Buccinator

Origin: Maxilla and mandible.
Insertion: Skin and fascia at the corner of the mouth.
Action: Compresses the cheeks and aids in mastication.

Orbicularis oris

Origin: A sphincter muscle around the mouth with no bony attachment.
Insertion: Fascia and skin around the mouth.
Action: It closes the mouth and causes the lips to wrinkle. Also puckers the lips as in kissing.

Triangularis

Origin: The mandible.
Insertion: Skin and fascia at the corner of the mouth.
Action: Pulls the corner of the mouth down.

Depressor labii

Origin: The mandible.
Insertion: Skin and fascia of the lower lip.
Action: Pulls the lower lip down and to one side.

Mentalis

Origin: Middle of the mandible.
Insertion: Skin and fascia of the lower lip.
Action: Pushes up the lower lip, wrinkling the chin.

Temporalis

Origin: Temporal bone.
Insertion: Coronoid process of the mandible.
Action: Raises the lower jaw and draws it backwards, it helps with chewing.

Masseter

Origin: Zygomatic arch.
Insertion: Outer part of the mandible.
Action: Raises the jaw, helps with chewing.

Pterygoids

Origin: The sphenoid bone.
Insertion: The mandible.
Action: Raises the jaw, opens the mouth and helps in chewing.
   See Figure 1.9.

Muscles of the neck and shoulder

Platysma

Origin: Fascia over pectoralis major and deltoid.
Insertion: The mandible and the fascia below the chin.
Action: Helps draw down the mandible and lower lip and wrinkles the skin of the neck.

Sternomastoid

Origin: Sternum and clavicle.
Insertion: Mastoid process.
Action: Both sides together flex the neck. One side alone bends the head sideways.

Trapezius

Origin: Occipital bone and all thoracic vertebrae.
Insertion: Clavicle and spine of scapula.
Action: Elevates and braces the shoulder and rotates the scapula.

Deltoid

Origin: Clavicle, acromion process and spine of scapula.
Insertion: The humerus.
Action: Front, draws arm forwards. Back, draws arm back. Middle, abducts the arm.

The muscles of the face are in constant use all our lives and with age wrinkles and dropped contours occur.

Wrinkles occur because the muscles are constantly contracting during normal facial movements and with age the skin loses its elasticity and the natural moisture in the skin slows down.

Dropped contours occur when certain muscles lose their tone by over stretching and lengthening. Common problems include:

○ *Frontalis*: causes horizontal lines on the forehead.
○ *Corrugator*: Causes vertical lines to develop between the eyebrows.
○ *Orbicularis occuli*: Causes overhanging lids when it loses tone and fine lines under the eyes.
○ *Procerus*: Causes horizontal lines on the bridge of the nose.
○ *Levator labii*: Causes naso labial folds with loss of tone.
○ *Orbicularis oris*: Fine vertical lines around the mouth are caused through constant puckering, for example smoking.
○ *Triangularis*: Causes jowls to form when tone is lost.
○ *Platysma*: Causes a crepey neck condition and dropped contour of the chin.
○ *Digastric*: This is deeply situated under platysma and when it loses tone causes a double chin condition.

The facial nerves

The central nervous system consists of:

○ The *brain*
○ The *spinal cord*

The brain and the spinal cord receive messages via the sensory fibres from the body's sense organs and receptors. They then filter and analyse them and send signals along the motor fibres which produce an appropriate response in the muscles and glands.
○ *Sensory nerves* carry messages into the brain.
○ *Motor nerves* carry messages from the brain.
○ *Cranial nerves* originate from nuclei in the brain and there are twelve pairs.

○ *Spinal nerves* are connected to the spinal cord and there are thirty-one pairs. Eight of these pairs are in the neck area and are called the cervical nerves, as they are named and grouped, according to the vertebrae with which they are associated.

The cranial nerves and the spinal nerves together make up the *peripheral nervous system*.

The cranial nerves are as follows:

1 Olfactory – sensory.
2 Optic – sensory.
3 Oculomotor – motor.
4 Trochlear – motor.
5 Trigeminal – mixed.
6 Abducent – motor.
7 Facial – mixed.
8 Vestibulocochlear – sensory.
9 Glossopharyngeal – mixed.
10 Vagus – mixed.
11 Accessory – motor.
12 Hypoglossal – motor.

They serve sense organs, the muscles and most of the skin of the head. The most important nerves beauty therapists should consider are:

○ 5th cranial nerve – *trigeminal*
○ 7th cranial nerve – *facial*
○ 11th cranial nerve – *accessory*.

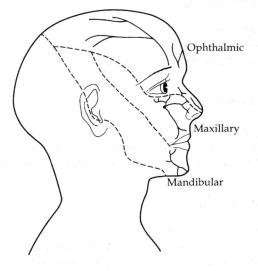

Figure I.10 *5th cranial nerve*

Ophthalmic

Maxillary

Mandibular

5th (trigeminal) nerve

This is the largest cranial nerve (Figure 1.10). It is the chief sensory nerve of the face and the motor nerve of mastication.

It is divided into three branches:

1 *Mandibular branch*
   Sensory: Teeth and gums of lower jaw, mouth and cheeks.
   Motor: Masseter and temporalis.
2 *Maxillary branch*
   Sensory: Upper jaw, cheeks, lower eyelids and sides of forehead.
3 *Ophthalmic branch*
   Sensory: Tear glands, skin of forehead, nose and upper eyelids.

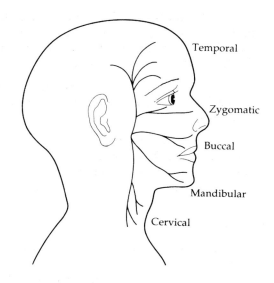

Figure 1.11 *7th cranial nerve*

7th (facial) nerve

Mainly a motor nerve of facial expression, it has a small sensory part which conveys impulses from the taste buds (Figure 1.11).

It is divided into five branches:

1 *Temporal branch*. Innervates the auricular muscles, orbicularis occuli and frontalis.
2 *Zygomatic*. Innervates orbicularis occuli.
3 *Buccal branch*. Innervates buccinator, upper lip, risorius and the side of the nose.
4 *Mandibular branch*. Innervates the lower lip and mentalis.
5 *Cervical branch*. Innervates platysma.

11th (accessory) nerve

This is a motor nerve and moves sternomastoid and trapezius muscles. Therefore, its main function is to move the head.

The blood supply to the neck and head

Blood consists of *plasma* and *corpuscles*.

Plasma is the liquid portion and accounts for about 55 per cent of the volume and it contains the following:

○ Water.
○ Salts.
○ Food substances.
○ Blood proteins.
○ Waste materials.
○ Gases.
○ Hormones.
○ Antibodies.
○ Antitoxins.
○ Enzymes.

Corpuscles are cells in the blood and account for about 45 per cent of the volume, they are divided into:

○ Red corpuscles which give the blood its red colour and transport oxygen in the blood.
○ White corpuscles which provide the body with protection.
○ Platelets which make the blood clot when bleeding has to be stopped.

Functions of the blood

Blood:

○ Transports food and oxygen to the tissues.
○ Removes waste products from the tissues.
○ Transports hormones via the endocrine system to other parts of the body.
○ Transports the white corpuscles to the source of infection.

○ Protects by means of the white corpuscles fighting invading organisms and helping wounds to heal and by clotting, to prevent bleeding and forming a barrier to germs.

When performing any facial treatments the blood supply to the area increases, this results in the following:

○ Improvement in skin colour.
○ Increased warmth in the tissues.
○ Nutrients are carried to the area.
○ Waste products are removed from the area.

Blood vessels

The blood is pumped from the heart in the arteries which lead to smaller vessels called arterioles. It is then passed through the tissues via the capillaries. Blood is then carried back to the heart via the venules and then the veins.

Arteries

Carry blood from the heart, they have thick walls and are muscular and elastic. They vary in size from one inch in diameter to a fraction of an inch and they are placed deep in the tissues.

Veins

These are thin walled elastic blood vessels which contain valves to prevent backflow. They carry blood from the body back to the heart and are found near the surface of the skin.

Capillaries

These are minute thin walled blood vessels running through the tissues and they connect the smaller arteries with the veins. They have extremely thin walls allowing substances to cross from the blood to the tissue fluids.

The dermis contains an extensive network of capillaries which arise from arteries in the subcutaneous layer. The dermal papillae are supplied with blood via the capillary loops, providing nourishment to the new cells in the basal layer of the epidermis.

Arteries supplying the head and neck

External carotid artery

This artery supplies the superficial tissues of the head and neck. The branches are:

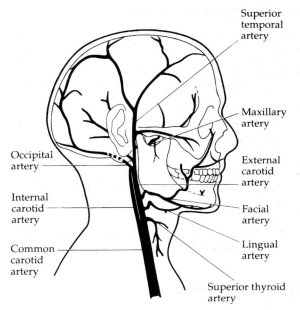

Figure 1.12 *Main arteries of the right side of the head and neck*

○ Thyroid artery, supplying the thyroid gland and adjacent muscles.
○ Lingual artery, supplying the tongue, mouth and throat.
○ Facial artery, supplying the muscles of facial expression and the mouth.
○ Maxillary artery, supplying the jaw area and interior of the skull.
○ Occipital artery, supplying the occipital part of the scalp.
○ Temporal artery, supplying the frontal, parietal and temporal areas of the scalp.

Internal carotid artery

This artery supplies the brain, the eyes, forehead and nose (Figure 1.12).

Venous return from the head and neck

Venous blood is returned from the face and scalp by means of the superficial and deep veins. The superficial veins have the same names as the branches of the external carotid artery and they unite to form the *external jugular*

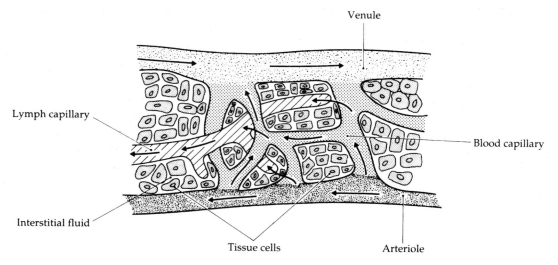

Figure 1.13 *Exchange of tissue fluid. Nutrients and oxygen pass from the blood through the capillary walls and into the tissue fluid. Waste products pass from the cells into the tissue fluid, back into the lymph capillaries*

vein. Venous blood from the brain is collected in the *venous sinuses.*

Deep sinuses

They include:

○ Superior sagittal sinus.
○ Inferior sagittal sinus.
○ Straight sagittal sinus.
○ Transverse sagittal sinus.

These empty into the internal jugular vein.

The lymph–vascular system

This is a system that carries lymph, a watery fluid derived from blood plasma, around the body. It deals with waste products and works in conjunction with the blood, in particular with the white blood cells, or lymphocytes, that are important to the body in its defence against disease.

Small lymph vessels run alongside the arteries and veins collecting lymph from the tissues.

Lymph vessels convey excess fluid, foreign particles and waste materials from the tissues and cells of the body. Fluid escapes from the blood capillaries by diffusion and filtration into the lymphatics (Figure 1.13).

Some lymph vessels contain:

○ An involuntary muscle which contracts in one direction and drives the lymph forwards.
○ Valves to prevent backflow.

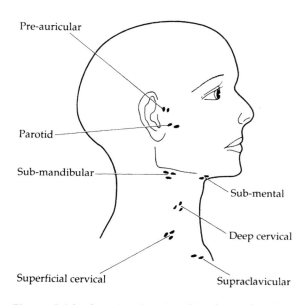

Figure 1.14 *Some lymph nodes of the face and neck*

There are lymph glands (or lymph nodes) at various points in the system, and are numerous around major arteries, for example the groin, armpits and neck. Their functions are:

o To filter the lymph preventing bacteria and other foreign substances from entering the blood stream.
o To produce white corpuscles, a defence against bacteria.
o Bacteria which may be present in the lymph are filtered and destroyed in the lymph glands. For this reason these glands may become inflamed, swollen and painful.

Lymph vessels become larger as they join together and eventually form two large ducts:

1 The thoracic duct.
2 Right lymphatic duct.

These drain into the subclavian veins.

There is an efficient network of lymphatic vessels in the dermis which become lymph capillaries in the subcutaneous layer, helping to remove waste products from the skin (Figure 1.14).

2 Sterilization

Beauty therapists have a duty to their clients to ensure that their premises, equipment and all materials used are kept clean and germ free and all sanitary precautions are taken. They must prevent cross-infection within the salon by using appropriate methods of sterilization.

Terminology

Antiseptic: A chemical agent which inhibits the growth and multiplication of bacteria.
Asepsis: Being free from bacteria and other microorganisms that could cause disease.
Bacteria: Are minute unicellular microorganisms found nearly everywhere. There are two general types of bacteria: non-pathogenic and pathogenic.
Disinfectant: A chemical agent which completely destroys bacteria.
Fungi: Are simple vegetable life which include yeasts, moulds and mushrooms.
Non-pathogenic: Harmless or actually beneficial to man.
Pathogenic: Disease producing and harmful.
Sanitize: To make clean and sanitary.
Sepsis: Being infected with bacteria.
Sterilization: Is the complete destruction of bacteria and their cause.
Virus: A microorganism smaller than bacteria. Viruses can only live and reproduce within living cells. They cause diseases such as the common cold, measles and poliomyelitis.

Bacteria

Bacteria enter the body in the following ways:

○ Airborne through respiration.
○ Contaminated food.
○ Contaminated objects which have been handled by an infected person.

○ Direct contact, touching an infected person.
○ In the salon infection may occur when unsterilized equipment is used or therapists work unhygienically and pass on infection.

Therapists must not work on any person who has visible signs of infection.

Classification of bacteria

Figure 2.1 shows the different types of bacteria and the following chart gives their characteristics.

Name	Shape	Characteristics
Cocci	Round	Singly or in groups
Diplococci	Round, grow in pairs	Causes pneumonia
Streptococci	Round, grow in chains	Pus-forming, found in blood poisoning
Staphylococci	Round, grow in bunches or clusters	Pus-forming and are present in abscesses, pustules and boils
Bacilli	Rod-shaped	Many are spore producers, and produce diseases such as influenza, tetanus and typhoid
Spirilla	Curved or corkscrew	Subdivided into other groups including spirochaetal organisms

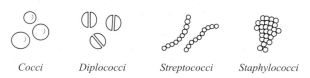

Cocci   *Diplococci*   *Streptococci*   *Staphylococci*

Bacilli   *Spirilla*

Figure 2.1 *Types of bacteria*

Growth movement and reproduction of bacteria

Bacteria will grow in an environment which is warm, dark, damp and where sufficient food is present. When the conditions are ideal, bacteria grows and multiplies rapidly, but when favourable conditions cease to exist, bacteria will stop multiplying and die.

Bacilli and *spirilla* move easily as they have flagella or cilia (hair-like projections) which move the bacteria, because of their whip-like motion, through a liquid.

General infection occurs when the body cannot cope with the bacteria and the build-up of toxins and a localized infection may be transported around the body in the blood.

Viruses

Viruses are living organisms which are so small they are only visible with an electron microscope. They are many and varied and become active when they are inside the right type of living cell. They are responsible for such things as influenza, chicken pox and measles and, more seriously, AIDS (acquired immune deficiency syndrome) which is caused by the HIV (human immunopathic virus) and Hepatitis B.

Fungi

These are microscopic plant organisms consisting of many cells, for example moulds, mildew and yeast. They are totally incapable of manufacturing their own food and are parasitic (obtaining food from other living organisms) or saprophytic (obtaining food from dead plants or animal matter). They can be single-celled yeasts, a network of branching threads, or much larger, formed from interwoven hyphae, for example mushrooms and toadstools. An example of a parasitic fungus is ringworm.

There are, however, some useful fungi which are beneficial in different ways:

○ Mushrooms are a popular food with many varieties enjoyed by many.
○ Penicillin is an effective treatment for illness.

○ Some are contained in food such as blue cheese or used as a raising agent for bread.
○ Used to produce alcohol.

The body will defend itself from infection in several ways:

1 The bacteria may be killed by enzymes present in the mouth, nose, tears, sweat and even sebum.
2 The skin is a defence against bacterial invasion as long as it is intact.
3 Macrophage cells will engulf bacteria and destroy them.
4 White blood cells will destroy bacteria or produce antibodies.
5 The lymphatic system will deal with the invading bacteria or virus in the lymph nodes.

Methods of sterilization and sanitization

Ultraviolet (UV) radiation

This is one of the most convenient and commonly used methods of sanitization used in beauty salons today. The UV cabinet only has disinfectant properties and is efficient in storing previously sterilized equipment.

Small instruments, brushes, ventouses, electrodes, etc., are sanitized by shortwave ultraviolet radiation. All instruments with a fine cutting edge should be wiped first with spirit, for example isopropyl alcohol or surgical spirit.

UV radiation is damaging to the eyes so most modern units have a safety switch built in, to switch off the lamp when the door is opened.

This method of sterilization is only effective on the surfaces the rays touch, so the items must be turned during sanitization which will take twenty minutes.

Autoclave

This method boils water under pressure and is suitable for small metal instruments. The autoclave is a proven method of sterilization and is used in health and beauty salons. The

Figure 2.2 *Autoclave sterilizing unit*
Courtesy Depilex Limited

vessel itself looks rather like a pressure cooker. It is easy to use and cheap to run. It consists of two chambers: an upper chamber in which the instruments are placed; and a lower chamber for the water.

The higher the pressure, the hotter the water has to be to boil, for example at atmospheric pressure water boils at 100°C which is not hot enough to sterilize.

Using the autoclave at 15 lb per square inch, it boils at 121°C, which is hot enough to sterilize.

For sterilization to be complete this procedure would take fifteen minutes. The automatic autoclave shown in Figure 2.2 is recommended as it has an automatic timer and a pressure gauge. The whole sterilization process is, therefore, automatic once the start button has been pressed.

Disinfectant

Disinfectants currently available are either prepared and ready for use or need to be diluted. The manufacturers' instructions should be followed for disinfectants which have to be diluted.

A good disinfectant should be:

○ Easy to use.
○ Non-corrosive.

○ Quick-acting.
○ Non-irritating.
○ Odourless.

The quickest method of sanitization is cleaning with alcohol, either by immersion, or by wiping the exposed surface of the implement with the alcohol before placing it in a dry sterilizer. Alcohol impregnated wipes, which are easy to use, are available commercially and are ideal for use in the salon.

Containers which are used for disinfecting with alcohol, should be washed on a regular basis in hot soapy water. The alcohol should be discarded after one use as it will be unsterile.

All equipment should be cleaned first, before sterilization, to remove surface debris. This may be achieved in the following manner:

1 Wash implements in hot soapy water.
2 Rinse with plain water.
3 Dry thoroughly.
4 Use chosen method of sterilization.

After use the outer surface of all pieces of electrical equipment should be wiped over with an alcohol such as isopropyl alcohol.

Salon hygiene

Beauty therapists must ensure that their salons are hygienic at all times.

○ All surfaces and curtains must be washed.
○ The salon must have up-to-date, effective sterilizing units.
○ Clean bed linen should be used for each client or the couch should be covered with paper sheeting.
○ Clean towels must be used for each client.
○ Waste must be placed in closed containers.
○ Hands must be washed before and after each client.
○ Lids should be kept on jars and bottles containing creams and lotions to prevent contamination.
○ Spatulas must be used to remove cream from containers.
○ Salon surfaces must be washed daily with disinfectant.
○ Therapists must wear a clean overall.

Personal hygiene

When working in such close proximity as thera-pists do to their clients, it is extremely important to pay special attention to personal hygiene.

○ Take a daily bath or shower.
○ Use an effective antiperspirant.
○ Teeth should be brushed regularly and mouthwash used if necessary.
○ Hair should be kept clean and tied back off the face.

○ Overalls and shoes should be spotlessly clean.
○ Shoes should be comfortable to prevent aching backs.
○ Hands should be clean and nails kept short.
○ Nail enamel should not be worn as clients could have an allergy to it. It may also chip during treatment which would look unpro-fessional.

The first impression therapists make will be a lasting one. Therefore, it must be a good one, so a clean salon and a professionally turned out therapist will instil confidence in the client.

3 The skin

Skin analysis

Before carrying out any facial treatment it is important to have analysed the client's skin thoroughly, because it will allow the therapist to:

○ Recognize the skin type.
○ Recognize any contraindications to treatment.
○ Recognize any disorder which may be treated.
○ Choose the correct products to use for treatment.
○ Recognize which electrical treatments will be most beneficial.
○ Advise the client on home treatment.

Different skin types and their characteristics

There are four basic skin types:

1 Normal.
2 Dry.
3 Sensitive.
4 Greasy.

Normal skin

This is the most rare skin type as once hormones begin changing the body at puberty, the skin will become more greasy and with age it becomes drier.

○ Skin looks clear.
○ Has an even colour.
○ Feels neither tight nor greasy.
○ Soft and supple to the touch.
○ The epidermis is of an average thickness.
○ Skin has a high degree of elasticity.

Dry skin

○ Pale in colour.
○ Thin epidermis.
○ Tightens after washing.
○ Often looks flaky.
○ Underactive sebaceous glands.
○ Fine lines appear around the eyes, prematurely.
○ Has a tendency to broken capillaries.

Sensitive skin

○ Often accompanies dry skin.
○ Thin epidermis.
○ Has a translucent appearance.
○ Feels very tight after washing.
○ Reacts to external stimuli by becoming red and blotchy.
○ Prone to dry flaky patches and broken capillaries.
○ Wrinkles prematurely.

Greasy skin

○ Sallow complexion.
○ Thick epidermis.
○ Overactive sebaceous glands causes a shiny appearance.
○ Open pores, particularly down the centre panel.
○ Comedones and pustules often present.

Combination skin

From the age of approximately fifteen years onwards many clients will have characteristics from more than one of the four mentioned. This type of skin is referred to as a *combination* and it must be taken into consideration when choosing treatment.

Determining skin type

To determine skin type, therefore, the following should be noted:

The skin colour: The paler the more sensitive.
The skin texture: Very dry skin has a rough surface and greasy skin feels smoother.
The pore size: Greasy skin has open pores because of the constant production of sebum.
The signs of sebaceous gland activity: The sebum present on the skin indicates greasy areas.
Evidence of any previous skin type: Large open pores, for example, on a mature skin would indicate a previously greasy skin or scarring or pitting would indicate an acnefied skin.
The elasticity: Evidence of lines on the face indicate whether the skin is ageing naturally or prematurely.
The muscle tone: Dropped contours indicates maturity.
Any blemishes present: Broken capillaries would indicate sensitivity; pustules would indicate blemished skin, etc.

Asking clients questions about their lifestyle, general health and skin care routine will be helpful by providing additional information about probable causes of skin problems. The required information would be:

Occupation: They could work in an environment which is dehydrating their skin, for example central heating, air conditioning, or outdoor work. The atmosphere could be dusty and dirty causing skin blockages and pustules. They may work in different climates thus exposing their skin to extremes of climatic conditions.

Lifestyle: They may be too busy to spend time on their own skin because they are busy mothers or working housewives with little time to themselves. Or their social life may be hectic and they are going straight out from work and probably have little sleep.

Health: They may suffer poor health and this is often reflected in their skin or they may be on medication which can also affect their skin badly.

Skin care: What is their regime at the moment. Do they bother using the correct products or do they use incorrect products which may be harming their skin? Do they spend any length of time at all on skin care?

Skin blemishes and disorders

A skin blemish is a mark on the skin which may be temporary or permanent, but it will not contraindicate facial treatment.

A skin disorder is a condition of the skin which may be treated by beauty therapists.

Dermatological terms

Erythema: Reddening of the skin, due to the dilation of blood vessels, as a reaction to an external stimulus, or an infection.
Keloid: An overgrowth of an existing scar which grows much larger than the original wound (see Figure 3.1).
Lesion: Is a structural or functional change in skin tissue caused by disease, injury, or vascular and pigmentary changes.
Macule: A discoloration of the skin, either red or pigmented, which is not raised above the skin's surface.
Naevus: Birthmark.
Objective lesions: Are changes which can be seen clearly on the surface of the skin.
Oedema: Swelling of the tissue.
Papule: Small, superficial, raised area of the skin, solid and lacking in fluid.
Pustule: A papule which develops at the mouth of the hair follicle. It becomes infected with bacteria, becoming purulent in the centre with a red, inflamed surrounding area.
Scale: An accumulation of epidermal flakes, which may be dry or greasy; they are indicative of an abnormal process of keratinization.
Scar: Special tissue which forms after the healing of a wound or injury.
Subjective lesions: Are a burning or itching sensation which can be felt but not seen.
Vesicle: A tiny elevation in the skin which contains fluid.

Disorders of the sebaceous glands

Comedone

This is caused by excess sebum in the follicle and an accumulation of dead skin cells which turns black on exposure to the air.

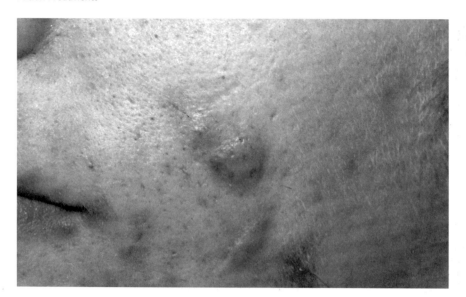

Figure 3.1 *Keloid scar Courtesy Leeds Foundation for Dermatological Research*

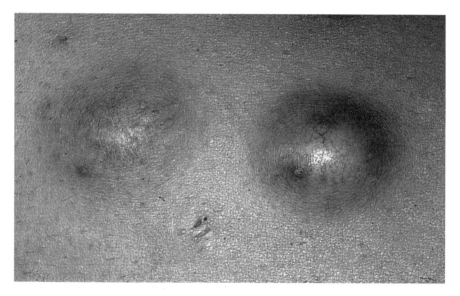

Figure 3.2 *Sebaceous cyst Courtesy Leeds Foundation for Dermatological Research*

Milium

More commonly called a whitehead, it forms when sebum is trapped in the follicle but there is no surface opening, due to an overgrowth of epidermal skin tissue at the mouth of the follicle. Milia (more than one) are most common on a dry skin and normally appear below the eye and along the cheekbone.

Sebaceous cyst

This is caused by an overgrowth of surface skin tissue which blocks the sebaceous duct, causing a retention of sebum in the follicle and gland. This gradually distends and forms a skin-coloured raised lump, semiglobular in shape, usually with a shiny surface. See Figure 3.2.

Pigmentary disorders of the skin

Lentigo

This is a freckle, a tiny yellow to brown macule which appears on areas exposed to sunlight and is most common on a fair skin. (Plural *lentignes*.)

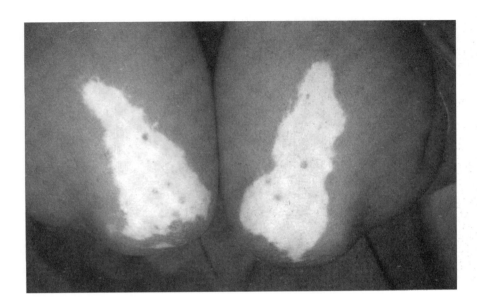

Figure 3.3 *Vitiligo Courtesy Leeds Foundation for Dermatological Research*

Chloasma

Usually irregular areas of increased pigmentation, not raised above the skin's surface, and may be caused by the contraceptive pill, sunburn, pregnancy, or disorders of the abdominal organs.

Vitiligo

These are areas of the skin devoid of pigment, caused by the basal layer of the epidermis no longer manufacturing melanin (see Figure 3.3).

Leucoderma

An area of the skin with less pigmentation than the surrounding tissue and which therefore appears lighter in colour.

Portwine stain

Can vary in size and is found on the face and neck area. It is a birthmark, pink to purple in colour, and is not raised above the skin's surface.

Strawberry mark

This develops before or shortly after a baby is born but normally disappears spontaneously before the child reaches the age of ten. It is raised above the skin and has a cleft surface.

Broken capillaries

Minute thin-walled blood vessels close to the surface of the skin which dilate and break. They are usually found on the nose and cheek area and are caused by extremes of temperature or over-stimulation of the tissues. Sensitive skin is more susceptible to this condition. It often appears blue because of the congestion in the area and transparent skin.

Hypertrophic disorders

Xanthoma

Only slightly raised from the skin surface, it is a buff-coloured growth which appears at the inner corner of the eye. It has a texture similar to chamois leather and is caused by inflammation of the deeper layers of skin followed by fat deposits (in some cases this is due to an excess amount of cholesterol in the blood). They can be surgically removed although they do not contraindicate facial treatment.

Verruca filiformis

Skin tag is the common name given to this condition, a wart which is commonly found on the face and neck. It is a long, thin flexible growth, greyish in colour. It is a benign growth, easily treated with diathermy.

Seborrhoeic wart

Soft and greasy lesions, pigmented with a cleft surface, affects middle aged and elderly people. Very common and benign.

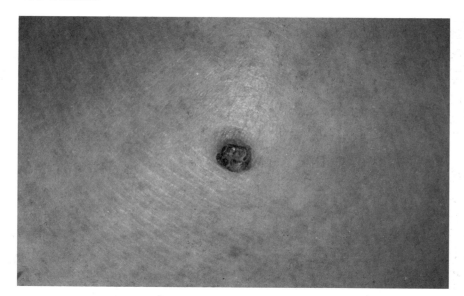

Figure 3.4 *Malignant melanoma*
Courtesy Leeds Foundation for Dermatological Research

Benign melanoma

An irregular pigment formation usually light to dark brown, flat or raised, sometimes with abnormal hair growth and enlarged sebaceous glands. They can have a rough warty texture. Common term is a mole.

Malignant melanoma

It usually appears as a blue-black mole which gradually increases in size (see Figure 3.4). A relatively rare tumour, there has however been an increase over the last twenty years, thought to be due to increased exposure to sunlight.

It may occur anywhere on the skin's surface but the legs have a higher incidence than other parts of the body. It does not always arise in the pre-existing mole. However, if the following should occur it is advisable to seek medical help:

○ Increase in size of pigmented lesion.
○ Alteration in pigmentation of the lesion.
○ Ulceration or bleeding of a pigmented or non-pigmented lesion.

Contraindications to facial treatment

Therapists must be able to recognize when not to perform any treatment. These include when:

○ A skin disease is present.

○ A skin disorder may temporarily prevent treatment.
○ A medical condition is present, for which medical approval must be sought.

A skin disease is an infection of the skin with characteristics that can be seen. An infectious disease must not be treated, to avoid the spread of infection from one person to another.

The presence of pus is a sign of infection and *staphylococci* are the most common pus-forming bacteria.

Bacteria is harmful when it is *pathogenic* and invades the body by way of:

○ A break in the skin.
○ Breathing.
○ Dirt in the eyes and ears.

Types of infection

Boils

A boil is an infection of a hair follicle by staphylococci bacteria which begins as a small red nodule gradually increasing in size and becoming inflamed. It is sometimes referred to as a *furuncle* and when several adjacent follicles are infected it is called a *carbuncle*.

Impetigo

This is bacterial infection of the epidermis and a pus-filled blister is the first sign. When this

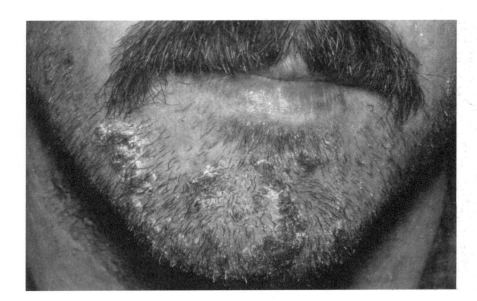

Figure 3.5 *Impetigo*
Courtesy Leeds Foundation for Dermatological Research

ruptures the infection spreads and the weeping blisters form a crust. This is more common in children and is highly contagious and therefore must be medically treated (Figure 3.5).

Herpes simplex

This is a viral infection which occurs around the nose and mouth. Its characteristics are a group of blisters on a red area of skin. A tingling or burning sensation precedes the appearance of the blisters and this condition may occur repeatedly and usually at the same site each time.

This infection can be precipitated by an illness with a high fever, exposure to the sun or when generally run down. Its common name is a cold sore.

Ringworm

The common term for fungal infections is ringworm and the fungi causing skin disease generally live in keratin. It affects the skin on different parts of the body and the disorders the fungi cause are referred to as tineas, qualified by a word describing the part of the body affected:

○ *Tinea pedis* – ringworm of the feet.
○ *Tinea corporis* – ringworm of the body.
○ *Tinea capitis* – ringworm of the scalp.
○ *Tinea unguium* – ringworm of the nails.
○ *Tinea versicolor* – ringworm of the upper trunk and sometimes the neck and upper arms.

The fungus produces enzymes which break down the keratin and ringworm may appear as single or multiple ringed lesions in the skin varying in severity from mild scaling to inflamed itchy areas. The primary lesion is a small red maculae which spreads outwards.

Basal cell carcinoma

Also known as a rodent ulcer (Figure 3.6), the most common site is below the eyes or the side of the nose. This condition is much more common in countries like South Africa and Australia. Probably induced by over-exposure to ultraviolet light. It occurs more frequently in fair skinned people and rarely on negroid skin, therefore the degree of pigmentation is a contributory factor. It is usually a condition of middle aged and elderly people and is normally slow to grow so if a doctor is consulted soon enough there should be a cure. It is only when it remains untreated it may prove fatal after many years. It comes in several forms:

1 *Ulcer*. This begins as a small papule and spreads outwards leaving a central ulcer.
2 *Cyst*. This begins as a papule which enlarges to form a cystic pearl shaped lesion with an irregular surface.
3 *Pigmented*. Sometimes an ulcer or a cyst becomes pigmented and it is then difficult to distinguish it from a malignant melanoma.

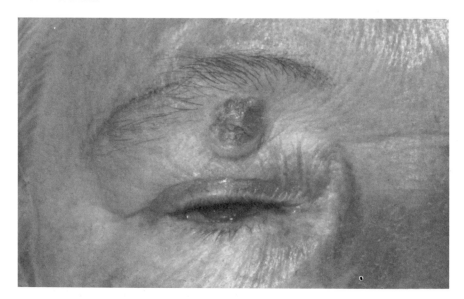

Figure 3.6 *Rodent ulcer or bascal cell carcinoma Courtesy Leeds Foundation for Dermatological Research*

Temporary disorders

Temporary disorders include:

○ Sunburn.
○ Cuts and abrasions on the face.
○ Bruising.
○ Severe acne vulgaris.
○ Allergic reaction which sensitizes the skin. Urticaria is an acute allergic reaction causing red wheals of varying size on the surface of the skin. The attack may be local or widespread and lesions can subside after several hours.

Cleansing the skin

The aim of cleansing is to remove:

○ All makeup.
○ Surface dirt.
○ The top layer of dead skin cells.
○ Unblock congested pores.

In the process, skin tissues and circulation are stimulated thus improving skin colour and cell regeneration. As cleansing is a preliminary to all treatments it allows the client to become accustomed to the therapist's touch.

Cleansing should be effective without irritating the skin and to achieve this the most appropriate products must be chosen. The following points must be considered:

○ Skin type.
○ Skin allergies.
○ Age of client.
○ Skin problems present.

Cleansing preparations

Most cleansers are mixtures of oil and water, which do not mix. Therefore, a third ingredient – *an emulsifier* – is added, which stabilizes the oils and forms an emulsion.

Depending on the amount of water present, a cleanser can vary from liquid to semi-solid.

Cleansing milk

This is an oil-in-water emulsion and can have up to 90 per cent water. It is a free-flowing milky liquid which is ideal for a younger skin as it feels cool and grease free. It may also contain a detergent element, which helps to control bacteria and grease, but would be drying on an older skin.

Cleansing lotion

Recommended only for oily and congested skins as they contain alcohol, an astringent which reduces sebum and leaves the face feeling stripped after use.

Cleansing creams

They vary greatly in texture and consistency and are mainly water-in-oil emulsions, so are suitable for dry and mature skins as they are more greasy.

The water content, which is small, evaporates and cools the skin and the oil content removes the grease and dirt.

The most suitable type for a mature skin is the consistency of a mousse, as it does not drag the skin.

Liquefying cleanser

This cleanser melts quickly on contact with the skin but does not penetrate the epidermis. As it is made mostly of oily material and removes makeup quickly and effectively, it is ideal for a skin which requires the minimum amount of manipulation. It closely resembles petroleum jelly and toning must be thorough as it leaves the skin feeling very greasy.

Soapless cleansers

These are ideal for clients who prefer to use water on their face but do not want the tight stripped feeling from soap. It is a rich but light emulsion applied to the face with dampened hands and rinsed off with water. Gentle in action it deep cleanses without over-drying the skin and is suitable for normal, greasy and combination skins.

Complexion soaps

These are bars of soap in a form which does not leave the skin feeling tight or with an altered pH. Often an oily, blemished skin may also be sensitive so these soaps are ideal for removing grease without irritating the skin.

Facial scrubs

A facial scrub is a soft creamy texture containing very fine exfoliating particles that cleanse the skin gently, by removing dead cells and impurities, which make the skin look dull and lifeless. They may be used several times a week on greasy skin but less often on dry sensitive skin. They are applied with the fingertips and mixed with a small amount of water, massaged in and rinsed off with water.

Toning the skin

Skin toners are necessary:

○ After cleansing to ensure complete removal from the skin of all cleansing preparations.
○ After a face mask to remove all traces of the face mask and refine skin texture.
○ Before makeup to refresh the skin and close the pores.

They vary in strength and action but all have a tightening and cooling effect on the skin. They are as follows:

Astringent

This is the strongest acting of the toners and its strength is due to the alcohol content, which irritates the skin causing swelling around the pores, so that they look temporarily less obvious. They are too strong for dry or sensitive skin as they dry out the oils on the skin's surface.

Some astringents contain antiseptic substances which kill surface bacteria and are useful in treating a blemished skin as they help to dry and heal pustules and prevent the formation of blackheads.

Skin tonics and fresheners

These may vary in strength, achieving a toning and cooling effect, without any harsh stinging.

The mildest tonics are based on *rosewater* with added glycerine and may be used on dry, dehydrated or mature skin. The slightly stronger fresheners may contain *alkalis* which are added to produce stimulating and cooling effects and will act to degrease the surface sebum.

Constituents of toning lotions

Rosewater Orangewater Camomile }	Flower waters, the mildest ingredients.
Witch hazel	A solution of alcohol and water plus extract from the bark of the witch hazel.
Glycerine	A humectant and skin softener.
Ethyl alcohol Isopropyl alcohol }	Alcohols are astringent because of their cooling effect on the skin, which results from their evaporation.
Zinc sulphate	Extremely mild astringent.
Menthol Camphor Sage }	Cooling and refreshing, they are astringent through an irritant effect, triggering the cold sense nerve endings in the skin, which produces a cool sensation.
Hexachlorophene	Antiseptic.

Moisturizing the skin

To remain smooth and supple the skin needs to maintain an adequate moisture level but it is constantly losing natural moisture through evaporation and is particularly affected by:

○ Exposure to the elements, sun, wind, cold.
○ Excessive use of degreasing products on the skin.
○ Central heating and air conditioning.
○ Sebum flow slowing down with age.

It is necessary therefore to prevent further moisture loss and plump out the tissues by using the appropriate moisturizer. They come in the form of creams from thick to light and fluffy, or very lightweight oil in water emulsions, probably containing a humectant.

Humectants

These are substances which attract particles of moisture from the air and into the skin, for example glycerine urea and rosewater, which work well to augment the skin's own moisture level. There are circumstances, however, when the humectant ingredient will do the opposite:

○ In winter when the weather is very cold and dry or in centrally heated homes when the air becomes very dry.
○ If there is no moisture in the air for the humectant to attract then it will draw water from the skin to its surface causing evaporation and subsequent dehydration of the skin.

To prevent dehydration, a water in oil cream is ideal, made up from a small percentage of water and humectant, blended with oils and made into a liquid or cream. The general rule is the drier the skin and its environment, the richer the moisturizer.

Occlusives

These are moisturizers which trap moisture in the skin preventing evaporation, normally a water in oil emulsion. They form a thin protective layer on the surface helping to preserve the moisture level.

Special creams

These may be classified as:

○ Night creams.
○ Neck creams.
○ Eye creams.
○ Nourishing creams.
○ Skin foods.

All these names are used to describe a rich moisturizing cream, using different proportions of oils, waxes, water and other ingredients to create different textures.

A night cream is not necessary before the mid-twenties and even when required, very heavy creams tend to clog the pores and cause puffiness particularly around the eye area.

The neck and eyes do in fact show signs of ageing earlier than other areas because the tissues are finer and more delicate and there are no underlying sebaceous glands to provide natural lubrication.

Eye gels are made from gentle plant and herb extracts such as camomile and cornflower, suitable for eyes prone to puffiness as they have a decongestant and tightening effect and leave the area grease free.

Neck creams may be much richer, a water-in-oil emulsion, as the skin is much drier and less sensitive and used in moderation will help counteract a crepey neck.

There are many claims by cosmetic companies that their creams have anti-ageing properties because they contain:

○ *Collagen*: Fibres in the dermis which give the skin structural support, provide strength, and allow the skin to stretch and contract.
○ *Elastin*: A protein which gives the skin its elasticity.

However applied to the skin, these creams do not have much effect on natural ageing but do have humectant properties, plumping out the skin with retained moisture.

Skin conditions

The ageing skin

Ageing of the skin may occur naturally with age or it can be premature, caused by environmental conditions, or ill health or just poor treatment of the skin.

The skin shows the signs of age faster because it is exposed to the environment and constant wear and tear. Other factors to be considered are hereditary, health and physical. Taking care of the skin, therefore, should begin at an early age because it is harder to improve a neglected skin or undo the damage already done.

Certain changes take place in the skin as we become older:

○ It becomes thinner.
○ It becomes drier.
○ It loses its firmness.
○ Expression lines form.
○ Discoloration occurs.
○ Areas of dilated arterioles appear.
○ Elasticity is lost.

The reasons for these physical characteristics occurring are:

1 Blood circulation slows down.
2 Metabolism slows down.
3 Chemical changes take place.
4 Sebaceous glands diminish in number and size.
5 Collagen production breaks down.
6 Altered or reduced hormone production.
7 Environmental factors.
8 Self-inflicted abuse.

Blood circulation slows down
Essential nutrients the skin requires to remain healthy are not brought to the skin quite as quickly and the removal of toxins from the area slows down, affecting the general appearance of the skin.

Metabolism slows down
The skin's cell renewal process becomes less efficient and it may appear sluggish and lose its healthy glow.

Chemical changes take place
Tissue repair and cell regeneration slows down.

Sebaceous glands diminish in number and size
The amount of natural moisture present in the skin is reduced.

Collagen production breaks down
The skin becomes thinner and fragmented and loses its flexibility.

Altered or reduced hormone production
This is particularly a problem during the menopause.

Environmental factors
Ultraviolet A rays penetrate deep into the dermis causing premature ageing, collagen breaks down producing lines and wrinkles.

Sun damaged skin also has a thick epidermis caused by accelerated cell renewal, another defence mechanism of the skin against ultraviolet B rays. This occurs to protect the skin from further damage, therefore the skin becomes tough-looking, with an uneven texture and pigmentation.

Air pollution from industry, car fumes, etc., harms the skin and causes dehydration.

Self-inflicted abuse

Smoking deprives the skin of nutrients and oxygen (essential for keeping it healthy) and vitamin C (which is necessary for the support of healthy collagen). Carbon monoxide, present through smoking, adversely affects the oxygen carrying capacity of the red blood cells' haemoglobin for many hours.

Alcohol is not harmful to the skin in moderation but large amounts dilate the blood vessels and over a long period of time weakens the capillary walls. This causes redness and broken capillaries. Alcohol also dehydrates the skin by drawing water from the tissues robbing the body of vitamin B and vitamin C required for a healthy skin.

Crash dieting causes premature sagging and wrinkling of the skin because when weight is lost too rapidly the skin does not have enough time to adjust to the sudden change. This is often noticeable in the face. Essential nutrients may be eliminated from the diet when crash dieting, therefore the health of the skin is affected.

Lack of exercise can contribute to poor skin conditions. Exercise will stimulate the flow of blood, supplying the skin with oxygen and nutrition, and stimulate the metabolism, encouraging cell renewal and collagen and elastin synthesis.

Lack of sleep causes slackness in the skin, tension in the face, frown lines and makes the skin look lifeless. Cells reproduce most actively between midnight and 4 a.m. A good night's sleep is a rejuvenating treatment for the skin.

Prolonged and incorrect use of cosmetics can create sensitivity in the skin if the products used are too harsh and can cause excessive dryness which may lead to premature ageing.

Stress causes tension in facial muscles and restricts blood vessels. Therefore interchange of blood slows down.

Rosacea

Also known as *acne rosacea* (Figure 3.7), this is a chronic hypersensitivity of the face normally affecting the nose and cheeks. The characteristics are:

○ Excessive oiliness.
○ Redness, which sometimes takes on a butterfly shape across the cheeks and nose.
○ Papules and pustules.
○ Lumpy appearance.

This condition usually appears in middle age and is more common in women than men but more severe for a man when rhinophyma may occur (a large, bulbous purple veined nose). The cause is unknown but the condition is aggravated by:

○ Eating highly spiced food.
○ Alcohol.
○ Extremes of temperature.
○ Very hot tea and coffee.
○ Sunlight.
○ Emotional stress.
○ Digestive disorders.

All the above cause the already weakened and congested blood vessels to dilate even more and the sensitive skin to become even more inflamed. This condition should be treated by a doctor particularly in its most severe form but the therapist may be able to help by giving soothing treatments and advising the client about diet and camouflage makeup.

Icthyosis vulgaris

The term *icthyosis* comes from the Greek word for fish because the appearance of the skin in this condition looks like the scales of a fish. It is a condition of abnormal keratinization and is usually hereditary.

The characteristics are dry, scaly skin which looks as though it has cracked and is darker than normal. It is more common on the extensor surfaces of the body. The condition often improves with age, often disappearing in adulthood and in a warm humid climate.

Psoriasis

This is a fairly common skin disorder which affects about 2 per cent of caucasians at some

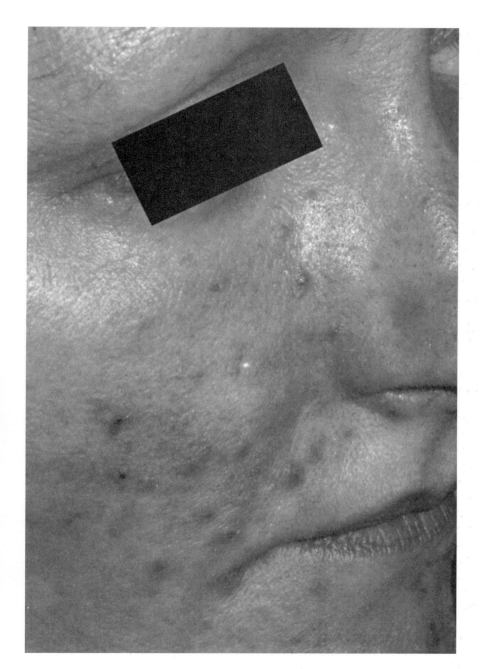

Figure 3.7 *Acne rosacea
Courtesy Leeds Foundation
for Dermatological Research*

time during their lives. Its exact cause is unknown but it is thought that there is an inherited defect in the skin, which causes psoriasis and is precipitated by certain factors:

1 Infection. Sometimes psoriasis appears two to three weeks after a streptococcal infection.
2 Trauma to the skin can induce lesions.
3 Mental stress. This is not a cause but it is

known that worry or anxiety can trigger the appearance of psoriasis.

It may appear at any time but the most common age at which it develops is between the ages of 15 and 30 and is more likely to occur in someone who has one or both parents with the disorder. The most common sites affected by psoriasis are the elbows,

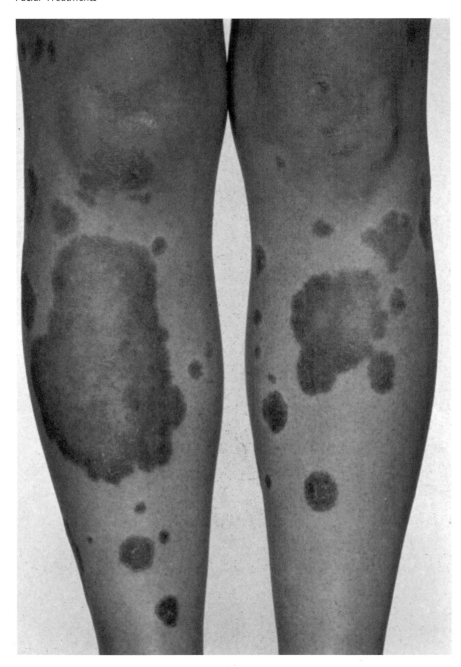

Figure 3.8 *Psoriasis Courtesy Leeds Foundation for Dermatological Research*

knees and back, usually areas with less underlying flesh.

The characteristics are:

o Dull, red papules.
o Round or oval in shape.
o Well-defined margins.
o Covered in silvery scales.

See Figure 3.8.

The attacks of psoriasis are quite erratic; there may be long periods of time when the skin is clear of any sign and when it does appear the length of time it is present varies greatly.

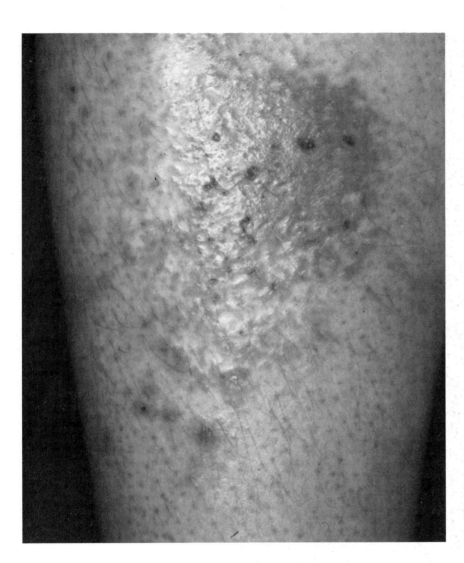

Figure 3.9 *Eczema*
Courtesy Leeds Foundation for
Dermatological Research

The excessive scaling and flaking is caused by a rapid production of skin cells and a tendency of these cells to cling together. A dermatologist can help to control and improve this condition. The patches can lessen or disappear temporarily when the skin is exposed to natural sunlight. Fortunately when it does clear it leaves no marks or scars on the skin.

If stress, depression or worry are linked with an outbreak it would be advisable to find a relaxation technique to counteract these problems.

Eczema

This is a skin condition from which many people suffer and it is a sequence of inflammatory changes triggered by the skin's intolerance to a sensitizer.

The characteristics are:

○ Red rash.
○ Itchiness.
○ Scaling of the skin which may be loose and thin or thick depending upon how the normal process of keratinization has been affected.
○ Blisters.
○ Weeping may occur.
○ Skin may crack.

The appearance of eczema may include one, two or several of the above features and therefore one person's eczema may vary greatly from the next.

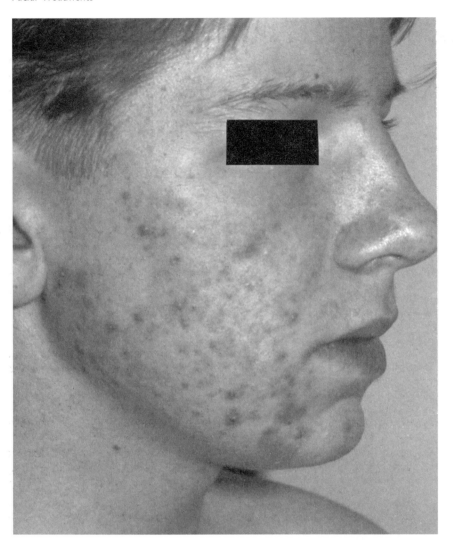

Figure 3.10 *Acne vulgaris Courtesy Leeds Foundation for Dermatological Research*

Types of eczema

There are two types of eczema:

1 *Endogenous*: Caused by an internal stimulus via the bloodstream.
2 *Exogenous:* This is caused by external contact with a primary irritant to which the skin is allergic. This condition is often referred to as contact dermatitis. See Figure 3.9.

Some primary irritants are:

○ Cosmetics.
○ Detergents.
○ Soaps.
○ Rubber.
○ Dyes.

If the factor which causes the exogenous eczema is identified then the avoidance of that substance will effect a cure.

Two common forms of eczema are:

1 *Atopic:* Seen in childhood and often associated with a family history of hay fever and asthma.
2 *Seborrhoeic:* This occurs where the skin is very greasy due to over-activity of the sebaceous glands.

Seborrhoea

This condition is a functional disorder of the sebaceous glands, characterized by an over-production of sebum which gives the face a shiny, greasy appearance. Because of this the follicles will appear large and open and the skin looks coarse. The condition often appears during puberty when there is a glandular disturbance and sometimes accompanies acne vulgaris.

Acne vulgaris

Affects adolescents between the ages of 14 and 20 and is an inflammatory condition of the sebaceous glands. It has been known to flare up in women in their thirties or forties who have never suffered from skin problems before. Its characteristics are:

○ Greasy shiny skin with enlarged pores.
○ Inflammation in and around the sebaceous glands.
○ Comedones.
○ Papules.
○ Pustules.
○ Cysts and nodules (in severe cases).

In most cases it has cleared up by the age of 25. However, it is important to control this condition at a very early age as the longer it remains the more stubbornly it resists treatment. It is advisable for the client suffering from acne to seek medical advice before treatment. The incidence of acne in both sexes is similar. See Figure 3.10.

The stages of acne

1 Acne begins to develop when there is an increase in hormone production during puberty which stimulates the sebaceous glands.
2 A blackhead forms in the sebaceous duct, caused by an increase rate of sebum which blocks the mouth of the follicle preventing the free flow of sebum and this plug of sebum turns black when exposed to the air.
3 Hyperkeratinization, an accelerated cell production within the basal cells lining the follicle, takes place.
4 A papule may be caused by the distension and inflammation of the sebaceous gland, which is caused by the excess sebum leaking through the weakened walls of the sebaceous duct into the surrounding tissue.
5 A pustule is formed when the papule becomes infected with bacteria and dead skin cells.

6 Nodules may then form which are deeper and more painful lesions.

Inflamed cysts are characteristic of the more severe cases of acne. They look very much like boils and are usually found on the back of the neck. As the name infers, they are very painful and slow to heal.

Causes of acne

Acne can be hereditary and the hormones which influence the production of sebum and cell activity are *testosterone* and *progesterone*. Anxiety or stress can worsen the condition and an increase in fatty acids has been found in sebum during periods of stress.

Poor hygiene can lead to secondary infection in acne sufferers, therefore skin must be kept scrupulously clean. Faces must be dried with a tissue which must then be discarded.

Treatment

Spots must not be picked as scarring may occur.

Sunlight is beneficial to this condition for several reasons:

○ The initial erythema and subsequent tanning have a camouflaging effect and this is psychologically beneficial.
○ The bactericidal effects penetrate the lower as well as the upper epidermis so may have an effect on the bacteria found deeper in the sebaceous duct.
○ The increase in desquamation refines skin texture.

Severe acne must be treated by a doctor but the beauty therapist can treat milder forms by deep cleansing, skin peeling and offering home care advice on skin care and diet.

Home care advice

Skin must be kept scrupulously clean, removing the excess sebum and the dirt, which it attracts and holds on the surface of the skin.

A gentle pH-balanced soap is ideal as it will cleanse the skin without overstimulating or drying it out excessively. The temptation is to use very harsh products on the skin but in the long term, the chemicals contained in these products may have an adverse reaction.

The face must never be dried with a towel as this provides a harbouring ground for bacteria. It is preferable to use tissues and discard them or a flannel which is used only once and then washed.

The face should be steamed gently, twice a week, to open the pores and eliminate waste matter which has collected in the follicles. A few herbs can be added to the water, for example camomile and sage for their restorative properties.

Diet should be altered to omit foods high in fat and sugar. Plenty of fresh fruit and vegetables should be eaten since they contain vitamins which are responsible for maintaining a healthy skin. If necessary a daily vitamin supplement can be taken and plenty of roughage, for example, wholemeal bread and salads, should be eaten to aid elimination.

Exercise, particularly in the fresh air, will help to increase circulation, bringing essential nutrients to the skin and removing waste more quickly. It also creates a feeling of well being and counteracts stress which often aggravates this condition.

Allergies

Many people suffer from an allergic reaction to products which are used in facial therapy and are more often turning to hypoallergenic or natural products to overcome this problem.

Allergic reaction can happen at any time, even if the substance causing the allergy has been used for many years without causing any adverse reactions.

The skin can be irritated by:

○ Something being applied directly onto the skin.
○ Something being absorbed systemically into the body.

The skin reacts to the irritant by producing massive amounts of histamine, part of the body's defence mechanism, and usually turns red and blotchy. Other characteristics are eyes watering and stinging, tissues swelling and the nose starts to run.

The intensity of the reaction depends upon the amount of irritant applied to the skin.

The best way to deal with an allergy is to locate and remove the cause and this can be done in three ways:

1 See a dermatologist, recommended by your doctor, who will determine by means of patch tests the cause of the allergy.
2 Eliminate one product after another, week-by-week, to determine the cause yourself. This is feasible only if you already suspect the cause of the problem.
3 In the case of a cosmetic product, for example makeup, do not use anything for a week and then each week reintroduce one product at a time until the allergic reaction returns, enabling you to eliminate the cause.

Sensitization

This is when the body's immune system actually recognizes an allergen as alien and the white blood cells react against it causing the unpleasant symptoms of a severe allergic reaction the next time the allergen is used on the skin.

A completely non-allergenic range of products is not possible as there is always someone somewhere allergic to something. A hypoallergenic range of products only guarantees to be less allergy producing than others by omitting as many known allergens as possible.

Common irritants

Common irritants include:

○ Perfume.
○ Detergents in cleansers.
○ Eosin, stain in lipsticks.
○ Lanolin.
○ Sulphur.
○ Para-amino benzoic acid, in sunscreen products.
○ Mercury formaldehyde, in nail enamel.

Skin and the sun

Sunbathing in moderation and with adequate protection is very therapeutic as it promotes

Figure 3.11 *MD Formulations facial products*

relaxation and induces a feeling of well being. However, the sun ages the skin and as the face is exposed more than any other part of the body the effects are easily seen.

Most cosmetic companies are now producing skin care ranges, as well as makeup, which have protection against ultraviolet (UV) rays incorporated into the products.

UVA rays are absorbed deep into the dermis and are responsible for ageing of the skin, because of the damage caused to the collagen and elastin fibres. UVB rays are the burning rays and are absorbed into the epidermis.

To protect the face from premature ageing due to exposure to UV rays, the following advice should be followed:

○ Use sunscreen products which filter out both UVA and UVB rays.
○ Use a total sunblock on particularly sensitive skin or parts of the face, that is, lips, eyes, nose, cheekbones.
○ Wear a large-brimmed hat.
○ Do not sunbathe between the hours of 11 a.m. and 4 p.m. as the sunlight is at its strongest.

The suntan is the skin's natural defence mechanism against the harmful effects of ultraviolet radiation and the technical term for suntanning is *melanogenesis.*

When the skin is exposed to the UVA and UVB rays an enzyme present in the melanocytes, called *tyrosinase,* is activated causing the amino acid *tyrosin* to produce the pigment *melanin.* This moves upwards to the surface of the skin giving it a golden suntan.

Ultraviolet radiation is described in detail in Chapter 16.

Alpha hydroxy acids

These are mild organic acids that are found in many common fruits and food such as:

○ *Glycolic acid* from sugarcane.
○ *Citric acid* from citrus fruits.
○ *Malic acid* from apples.
○ *Tartaric acid* from grapes.
○ *Lactic acid* from sour milk.

The action on the skin of these fruit acids, or AHAs as they are more commonly termed, is to loosen or break up the thick horny outer layer of skin where an excessive build up of dead skin cells occurs. This causes a sloughing of the dead skin cells which improves the texture and condition of the skin. They also increase the skin's natural moisture-holding capability and improve the appearance of fine lines and wrinkles.

The use of these acids dates back thousands of years. Cleopatra used to bathe in sour milk (lactic acid) and other women of her day applied red wine (tartaric acid) to their faces. This made their skin appear fresher and smoother. Today, cosmetic companies provide effective AHA treatments in more stable and elegant cosmetic preparations that will provide excellent results (Figure 3.11).

Glycolic acid has the smallest molecular weight of all the alpha hydroxy acids and therefore by virtue of its smaller molecular size it has greater penetration than other AHAs.

Functions of glycolic acid

○ It weakens the intercellular bonds that hold the skin cells together, and therefore enhancing natural exfoliation.
○ It helps to rehydrate the skin.
○ It stimulates collagen production helping to restructure the dermis and epidermis.
○ The stratum corneum is made more permeable to other products and treatments.

Indications for use of glycolic acid

○ Dry or dehydrated skin.
○ Mature skin showing signs of age.
○ Sun-damaged skin.
○ Acne or spotty skin and congested areas.
○ Superficial scarring from an acne condition.
○ Hyperpigmentation.
○ Ingrowing hairs.

The effects of use

The appearance of the skin is greatly improved, it becomes smoother, lines and wrinkles are less noticeable and the skin is softer. The deep cleansing action of glycolic acid helps to eliminate blockages in the sebaceous follicle caused by a build-up of dead skin cells and therefore helps to control an acne condition.

Safety in use

The action on the skin can be quite strong and the glycolic acid in retail products is combined with a *buffer*, an ingredient which reduces the irritation to the skin.

The best treatment products to use are those that are pH balanced as they are most effective and the least irritating to the skin.

The concentrations of glycolic acid vary between professional products used by the therapist in a salon treatment and the retail products sold for homecare. Professional products have a concentration of around 40 per cent because the application is controlled by an expert and will be applied for the correct amount of time and as often as the therapist feels the client requires treatment.

A client record card must be filled in at the initial consultation to document medical history and the skin care products already in use, and to check for contraindications.

Provide detailed instructions on homecare so the client understands how to use the products correctly.

After a professional treatment with glycolic acid, sunblock should be applied to the skin and it is advisable for the client to wear a sunblock on a daily basis to prevent further sun damage occurring.

Tingling may occur during treatment, this is a normal reaction which usually lasts for as long as the product is on the skin. If the reaction is severe and the skin becomes very red or stings then treatment must be discontinued. It is important to monitor the client at all times during treatment.

Contraindications

○ Any client on Roaccutane, a medical treatment for acne.
○ Any client undergoing radiation treatment or chemotherapy.
○ Sunburn.
○ Cut or broken skin.
○ Irritated skin.
○ Recent scar tissue.
○ Keloid scars.
○ Active eczema, psoriasis or herpes.
○ Forty-eight hours before or after:
  —electrolysis
  —waxing
  —using depilatories
  —bleaching.

Skin terminology

Alpha hydroxy acids (AHA)

These are natural acids found in fruit, milk and sugar which help loosen dead skin cells on the skin's surface, increasing the speed at which they are removed and renewed. These acids are incorporated into treatment creams, cleansers and moisturizers. AHA treatment products do not always have hydrating properties, therefore those used in the morning should be followed by a lightweight moisturizer that also contains a sunscreen to prevent future damage. At night follow the application of the AHA with a good nightcream with added ingredients such as antioxidants.

Anti-oxidants

These are derived from vitamins such as A, C and E, and form part of the body's natural defence and balance system. Anti-oxidants protect the skin by attaching themselves to free radicals, thus preventing them from doing as much harm to the skin.

Ceramides

These are lipids which are naturally present in the skin and they make up a moisture barrier over the surface. Ceramides added to skin products will help to strengthen this seal allowing the skin to stay moisturized longer.

Collagen

This is a strong fibrous protein which forms connective tissue in the dermis and provides the support and strength to the skin.

Elastin

This is a highly elastic protein which makes up the elastic fibres in the dermis providing suppleness and smoothness to the skin making it more resilient.

Enzymes

These are protein molecules naturally present in our bodies and they can be helpful or destruc-tive. They are catalysts which work by speeding up chemical changes that take place in our cells – some help the skin's natural renewal process and others break it down. When added to skin creams the beneficial enzymes may block the action of skin ageing enzymes and prevent the collapse of collagen.

Free radicals

These are harmful, highly unstable molecules, created by oxidation (in simple terms, this is what happens when a sliced apple turns brown), which are activated by stress, the release of adrenaline in our bodies, pollution, smoking and ultraviolet light. They are molecules which have lost an electron and travel round the body colliding with other molecules trying to replace their lost electron. Unchecked they attach themselves to the skin's surface eventually permeating down to the collagen. These reactive molecules cause skin cells to oxidize and damage the skin by making it less firm and can cause sagging skin, wrinkles, premature ageing and changes in pigmentation.

Hyaluronic acid

This forms part of the tissue which surrounds the collagen and elastin fibres. It is a natural moisturizing ingredient responsible for the skin's plumpness and moisture content, and it has the ability to attract and bind hundreds of times its weight in water. As we age the amount produced in the skin decreases leaving it less resilient and pliable. It is often added to moisturizers by skin care companies.

Liposomes

These are tiny spheres or lipids made up of water and fat and filled with active ingredients. The liposomes are the transportation system which carries the active ingredients to where the skin needs them. Liposome spheres are smaller than a skin cell, therefore ingredients held inside the liposomes can accurately be delivered into the skin and released precisely as needed.

Nanospheres

These are smaller versions of liposomes which are supposed to penetrate deeper into the skin because of their smaller size.

Photoageing

This is the effect on the skin caused by exposure to ultraviolet light, the single greatest cause of wrinkles and ageing skin. Most of the damage occurs from casual exposure on a daily basis, although UVB rays are more intense in the summer UVA rays are the same intensity all year round and are far more damaging as they penetrate deep into the dermis and destroy collagen, elastin and other connective tissue. The result is fine lines, wrinkling, leathery appearance, hyperpigmentation and loss of elasticity.

Retinoic acid

This is a derivative of vitamin A which was originally prescribed for the treatment of acne. It does refine the skin reducing wrinkles but the side effects are extreme sensitivity to sunlight, increased reddening of the skin and peeling. Its action is to speed up cell renewal and boost collagen synthesis.

SPF (sun protection factor)

SPF is a guide to the effectiveness of sunscreen in screening out UVB rays. For example, a sunscreen with an SPF of 10 will allow the skin to be protected for ten times longer (100 minutes of exposure for a skin which normally burns after 10 minutes) from the sun before it starts to burn.

Tocopherol

This is the technical term for vitamin E. It has healing properties and helps to repair sun-damaged skin. It is the most important anti-oxidant.

Skin care advice

When clients regularly have facial treatments at the salon, it is advisable to recommend that they also use appropriate skin care products at home to reinforce the treatments. It is important to tell clients how to look after their skin at home to prevent premature ageing. Advice should include:

- To drink at least six to eight glasses of water a day to keep moisture levels high, an important factor in cell renewal and hydrating the skin to prevent wrinkle formation. It also helps to detoxify and remove waste.
- To have at least eight hours of sleep a night. While we are sleeping new cells are formed, waste is removed and the skin prepares itself for the day ahead. If sleeping is a problem, advise clients to have a relaxing aromatherapy bath before bed, or listen to a relaxation tape or have a hot mug of milk last thing at night before retiring to bed as it contains a sleep-inducing amino acid.
- To use a sunscreen every day as damage caused by exposure to ultraviolet rays is the single greatest cause of wrinkles and ageing skin. Many skin care products now incorporate a sunscreen but if they do not, a sunblock could be used under a moisturizer.
- To eat a healthy diet. Skin must be fed from the inside with all the necessary vitamins, minerals and nutrients for a healthy skin. Vitamin A keeps skin healthy and prevents it from becoming dry and flaky. Vitamin C is important for the production of collagen and Vitamin E helps to rehydrate the skin and speed up the healing process.
- To use an effective cleanser to remove makeup, dirt and skin blockages caused by a build-up of sebum in the pores.
- To handle the skin gently and use cotton wool or cotton buds to remove makeup. Tissues are too harsh and may scratch or stretch the surface. Use appropriate products which are gentle on the skin and clean without upsetting the skin's pH balance.
- To take regular exercise, preferably on a daily basis to increase circulation and lymphatic flow which helps to improve skin condition and colour, making the skin look younger.
- To keep alcohol intake to a minimum as it dehydrates the skin.
- To avoid smoking. Cigarettes reduce the necessary nutrients and oxygen required for a healthy skin and cause a dull lifeless

looking skin. It activates harmful free radicals and weakens collagen and elastin fibres causing premature wrinkling of the skin.

Effects on the skin through vitamin deficiency

Vitamin A
A lack of vitamin A causes dry flaky skin because one of its functions is to regulate the size and function of the sebaceous glands.

Vitamin B
A lack of one or more of this group results in redness, tenderness and cracks at the corner of the mouth and tiny lines in the skin around the mouth. It also interferes with the transportation of oxygen to the cells and the efficiency of waste removal.

Vitamin C
A lack of vitamin C causes the collagen fibres to break down and show signs of early wrinkling. It also causes the tiny capillaries that supply nutrients to the skin to become fragile.

Vitamin E
This vitamin is essential to the health of the skin and deficiency causes dry, rough and tired looking skin and allows free radicals to cause damage.

Effects on the skin through mineral deficiency

Zinc
Skin wrinkles and sags and stretchmarks form more easily. In more severe cases, skin healing slows down.

Sulphur
The hair and nails will become weaker and the skin will scale as keratin in the hair, nails and skin is normally rich in sulphur.

Selenium
This mineral is important in maintaining tissue elasticity. Therefore, a deficiency would contribute to premature ageing of the skin.

Silicon
A lack of silicon causes flabbiness of the skin, weak nails and dull hair.

Sources of vitamins and minerals

Vitamin A: Spinach, cabbage, carrots, eggs, fish-liver oils, liver, butter.
Vitamin B: Raw fruits and vegetables, whole grains, liver, brewer's yeast, milk, wheatgerm.
Vitamin C: Citrus fruits, tomatoes, raw green vegetables, potatoes, spinach, broccoli, strawberries.
Vitamin E: Wheatgerm, seeds, green leafy vegetables, whole grains.
Zinc: Seafood, meat, liver, nuts, whole grains, oysters, cheese.
Sulphur: Fish, eggs, cabbage, sprouts, onions, lean beef, dried beans.
Selenium: Wholemeal bread, cheddar cheese, cod, crab, shrimps, garlic.
Silicon: Avocado, apples, honey.

4 Face masks

Face mask treatments

The application of face masks reinforces the beneficial effects of the facial cleanse. A mask is a preparation which contains various ingredients to which active substances are added to form a paste or gel. They have different actions depending on their formulations.

Actions on the skin

They can be:

○ Deep cleansing.
○ Desquamating.
○ Stimulating.
○ Refining.
○ Nourishing.
○ Soothing.

The choice of mask depends on an accurate skin analysis and a sound knowledge of the effects of the ingredients used. There are several types of mask:

Setting masks
These include clay, peeling and astringent masks.

Non-setting masks
These include biological masks which are based on fruit, plant, herbal and vegetable extracts. Natural masks made from eggs, fruit, honey and oatmeal.

Specialized masks
These include gel, wax, thermal and oil masks.

General effects of face masks on the skin

○ Cools the skin due to evaporation of water content.

○ Increased circulation improves skin colour.
○ Increased circulation draws more fluid to the skin and it appears to plump out, temporarily, helping to minimize wrinkles. This is known as *turgence*.
○ Toning and refining, pores appear smaller.
○ Moisturizing effects of some ingredients.
○ Relaxing and therapeutic as the client has to rest.

Setting masks

Clay masks

These are useful to the therapist because of their range of actions and low cost. They absorb oil, dirt and surface impurities, leaving the skin cleansed, refined, and with an improved colour.

It is important to analyse the client's skin well before mixing a clay mask and to understand that skin conditions can change. Therefore, each mask must be mixed specifically for the individual client and therapists must have a good understanding of the effects of the ingredients they are using.

Ingredients
Fuller's earth:
○ Has a fast vascular response causing erythema.
○ Deep cleanses.
○ Aids desquamation.
○ Has a slight bleaching effect.
Kaolin:
○ Deep cleanses.
○ Draws out impurities.
○ Aids desquamation.
○ Stimulates circulation and lymph flow.
Magnesium carbonate:
○ Gently stimulating.
○ Refining.

Figure 4.1 *Face mask*

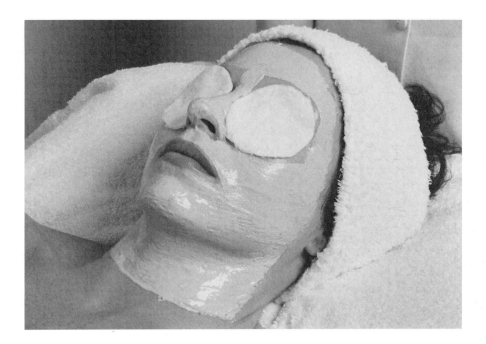

- ○ Softening.
- ○ Cleansing.

Calamine:
- ○ Soothes.
- ○ Reduces vascularity.
- ○ Cleanses.

The clays come in dry powder form and have to be mixed with active ingredients to form a paste for easy application:

Rose water and *orange flower water*: Mildly stimulating and toning.
Witch hazel: Stimulating and drying, refining the pores.
Almond oil: Slightly stimulating and nourishing.
Glycerine: Soothing and moisturizing.

Suggested clay mask recipes
- ○ **Normal skin:**
  One part magnesium.
  One part calamine.

  Mix with rose water to form a smooth paste.
  Effects: To cleanse, refine and soften the skin since there are no skin problems present.

- ○ **Dry skin:**
  One part calamine.

One part magnesium.

Mix with almond oil to form a smooth paste.
Effects: Stimulates blood and lymph flow and improves skin colour. Deep cleanses and aids desquamation and improves skin texture.

- ○ **Sensitive skin:**
  One part calamine.
  One part magnesium.

Mix with glycerine to form a smooth paste.
Effects: Soothes and reduces any vascularity present. Cleanses and softens the skin. The glycerine has humectant properties and therefore prevents the skin from over drying.

- ○ **Greasy skin:**
  Fuller's earth

Mix with witch hazel to form a smooth paste.
Effects: Has a very fast vascular response causing an erythema which can improve a sallow complexion. It is deep cleansing and drying and tightens open pores as well as having a slight bleaching effect on the skin.

Clay masks should not be left on any skin for too long. They should be removed when the mask begins to dry or no longer than 8 to 10 minutes. Even a greasy skin does not require any longer because Fuller's earth has a rapid effect on the skin.

When using more than one mask at a time, for a combination skin, the mask should be applied to the area requiring more treatment first, as it has to remain on the skin longer for maximum effect. Both masks can then be removed at the same time.

Astringent masks

These are any masks which incorporate the use of an astringent, for example camphor or menthol, often plant-based, to refresh the skin, boosting circulation, tightening the pores and giving it a healthy glow.

They are an excellent pep-up for tired skin but should not be used often as they can have a drying, irritating effect.

Peeling masks

These masks are based on rubber, wax or some type of plastic. When they have hardened on the skin they are peeled off in one piece taking surface dirt and dead skin cells with them. They normally contain a softening ingredient and they form an occlusive layer on the skin preventing moisture loss.

Non-setting masks

Biological masks

The constituents of these masks are:

o Fruit.
o Plants.
o Herbs.
o Natural products.

Actions on the skin
The trace elements in the ingredients create increased cellular activity in the basal layer of the epidermis. This results in refinement of skin texture because of the improvement in respiration and elimination.

Plant enzymes trigger a beneficial reaction in the skin's cells even in the deeper layers.

Ingredients
Fruits and plants:
o Have a stabilizing action on the skin's pH.
o Balance the skin's water content.
o Astringent.
o Moisturizing.
o Increases cellular regeneration.
o Soothing.
Vegetables and herbs:
o Regenerating.
o Moisturizing.
o Evens out skin colour.
o Stimulates.
o Brightens.
o Encourages elimination of waste.
o Antiseptic.
o Diuretic.

Indications for use of biological masks
Biological masks should be used for the following skin types:

Hypersensitive skin conditions: May be used when other forms of treatment have been contraindicated, as the action is gentle. Freshens and refines the skin while keeping the acid/alkali balance constant and improving cell renewal.
Dehydrated and dry skin conditions: Those skins lacking in surface moisture and natural oils, benefit from the use of biological masks as stimulation is possible without further loss of moisture. The skin is left fresh and soft, free from dead skin cells and with a fine texture.
Mature skins requiring regeneration: The active ingredients aid in regeneration without irritating or reducing moisture.
Oily, blemished skin but sensitivity present: The main benefits are deep cleansing and desquamating. Oil and adhesions are removed from the skin's surface and because bacteria thrive on this oily film the skin is left more able to protect itself.
Unstable skin conditions where the pH requires stabilizing: Over-use of predominantly alkaline products on the skin progressively destroys the acid mantle and retards its renewal process, thus allowing the skin to become more susceptible to

infection and dehydration. Biological masks help to stabilize the skin's pH.
Skin congestion: Due to ill health or incorrect care.

○ **Normal skin:**
One ripe banana.
One tablespoon honey.
One beaten egg.

Mash the banana and add the honey and egg. Push through a sieve and apply to the face and neck. Leave on for 10–15 minutes.
Effects: Moisturizes and softens the skin.

○ **Dry skin 1:**
One egg yolk.
A few drops of almond oil.

Mix thoroughly and apply thinly over the face and leave on for 10 minutes.
Effects: Softens and refines skin texture.

○ **Dry skin 2:**
Two tablespoons oatmeal.
Half cup of milk.
Two teaspoons of elderflower water.

Mix the oatmeal and milk and heat gently until soft, remove from the heat and add the elderflower water and beat together. Apply to the face and leave on for 15–20 minutes.
Effects: Cleanses, refines and softens the skin.

○ **Sensitive skin:**
Warm olive oil.
Ground almonds.

Mix to form a thick paste. Apply to the face and neck and leave on for 15–20 minutes.
Effects: Soothes, softens and moisturizes.

○ **Greasy skin 1:**
One egg white.
A few drops of lemon juice.

Whisk together and apply evenly to the face and neck.
Effects: Stimulating and tightening, mildly bleaching with antiseptic properties.

○ **Greasy skin 2:**
Half a cucumber.
Fresh orange or lemon juice.

Mash the cucumber and mix with the juice and apply to the face between two pieces of gauze. May be left for 15–20 minutes.
Effects: Toning and refining.

These masks may be applied with a brush, or because of their consistency between two layers of gauze.
Removal should be thorough using tepid water and sterile sponges.

Specialized masks

Wax mask

This is made from a combination of waxes and oils:

○ Beeswax.
○ Paraffin wax.
○ Petroleum jelly.
○ Mineral oil.

It is applied to the skin after it has been warmed to a temperature of 49°C and the face and neck have been covered with nourishing cream.
This mask is most beneficial to dry, dehydrated or ageing skin since it is hydrating and allows the penetration of nourishing creams without over stimulation of the tissues.
A congested skin also benefits, as the stimulation of the sudoriferous glands causes the skin to perspire, ridding itself of impurities and aiding desquamation.

Actions on the skin
○ The circulation is increased.
○ The warmth of the mask opens the pores and softens the skin.
○ The nourishing cream is absorbed into the epidermis.
○ The skin perspires removing waste.

Effects on the skin
○ Improves skin colour.
○ Refines skin texture.
○ Cleanses the skin.
○ Moisturizes the skin.
○ Fine lines are temporarily plumped out.

Gel masks

There are products on the market, consisting of active fluids of natural extracts, which when mixed with a gelling agent, create a mask specifically for a particular skin type or condition. This provides a unique skin care programme for the client, as massage and moisturizing creams can be made from the same products, to complement each other.

Ingredients
Aloe: Moisturizing.
Camphor: Stimulating and detoxicating.
Ginseng: Regenerative.
Carrot: Stimulates cell reproduction.
Azulene: Anti-reddening.
Horse chestnut: Decongestant.
Witch hazel: Astringent.
Rosemary: Normalizes oil production.
Propolis: Purifies an oily skin.

Oil masks

Oil masks are usually combined with heat treatment to increase the skin's capacity to absorb the oil. They may be used on the following skin types:

○ Dehydrated.
○ Crepey.
○ Mature.
○ Over exposed to ultraviolet light.

The action on the skin is soothing and softening due to the moisturizing properties of the oil and the heat produced in the tissues. Respiration and elasticity are also improved.

Hypersensitive and extremely vascular complexions are contraindicated to this type of mask, where heat is used. In this case the oil mask could be used without the addition of heat.

Olive oil and ground almonds
○ Olive oil
○ Ground almonds

Mix together to form a smooth paste. This mixture should be applied between two pieces of gauze and may be left on the skin for 20 minutes. Once removed the oil on the skin should be massaged lightly in and the excess removed and the skin toned with rose water.

Hot oil mask
○ Almond oil

The oil should be warmed to a moderate temperature and a piece of gauze to fit the face immersed in it. The eyes should be protected and the gauze applied to the face before positioning the heat lamp in place. The position of the lamp will vary according to the skin sensitivity, intensity of the lamp and previous skin reaction.

Timing of the treatment can vary from 5 to 20 minutes for the same reasons as above.

After removal of the mask the oil may be used for massage when indicated. The excess oil must then be removed.

Thermal masks

This is a thick paste applied to the skin, over a cream, which has been specially formulated to work with the mask for maximum benefit. There are usually a range of creams for different skin types so again it is important to analyse the skin type accurately before treatment and if necessary use different creams for different areas of the face and neck.

A chemical reaction occurs in the mask causing heat to be produced, which stimulates the skin, improving cellular regeneration and increasing the effectiveness of the skin in absorbing the special cream.

The heat develops as the mask hardens and then gradually subsides after about 20 minutes. The mask becomes rigid and is removed in one piece. The contraindications are:

○ Highly strung client.
○ Highly vascular complexion.

Ready-made masks

Most companies provide a variety of ready-made masks using different ingredients for a specific purpose and also recommend the use of more than one mask in the same facial treatment to achieve the best results. Ingredients include old favourites such as clays, plants and herbs and also essential oils, marine-based products as well as anti-ageing ingredients.

Several masks may be involved in a specialized multi-level manual facial and these can include:

o A mask to cleanse and exfoliate dead skin cells.
o A mask to rehydrate the skin.
o A mask to introduce special products such as collagen into the skin.
o A balancing mask to maintain the skin's pH and minimize signs of ageing.

There are also many more scientific masks available such as:

o Enzyme masks with active ingredients designed to stimulate skin function at a cellular level and which are antioxidant in effect.
o A mask which lowers skin temperature and improves lymphatic drainage.
o Marine masks containing spirulina and alginate with lipo cell complex skin serum which helps the active ingredients to be transported to the lower layers of the epidermis.
o Anti-ageing masks containing fruit acids, sunflower seeds and juniper oil.

General contraindications to all masks

o Skin diseases.
o Cuts and abrasions.
o Bruises.
o Undiagnosed lumps and bumps.

Bleaching facial hair and skin

There are commercial products available to buy over the counter for bleaching and as long as the manufacturers' instructions are followed precisely they should be safe to use.

These preparations are used to:

o Lighten dark hairs.
o Fade areas of hyperpigmentation.
o To lighten discoloured areas, for example elbows and knees. ·
o Remove nicotine stains.

When bleaching the skin, the effect is only evident on the top superficial layers of the epidermis and when the superficial layers are shed the hyperpigmentation or discoloration returns.

Hyperpigmentation occurs when there is an uneven distribution of melanin caused by:

o Ultraviolet rays stimulating uneven melanin production.
o Hormonal changes occurring during pregnancy and oestrogen therapy.
o Chloasma from the contraceptive pill.
o Hereditary factors, such as dark areas around the eyes.

Cosmetic companies are producing professional products which will help to reduce hyperpigmentation of the skin effectively. They may contain ingredients such as *hydroquinone* which can have an irritating effect on the skin. Therefore it is important to carry out a skin test prior to use. Apply a small amount of the preparation on the inner arm twice a day for three days to make sure there is no adverse reaction.

Face masks which have slight bleaching properties, for example equal proportions of fullers earth and magnesium may be used for the following reasons:

o To brighten a sallow complexion.
o To even out a fading suntan.

Contraindications to bleaching

o Broken skin.
o Skin infections.
o Highly sensitive skin.
o Very dry, flaky skin.
o Sunburn.
o Pustular acne.

5 *Facial massage*

Facial massage is the most relaxing and therapeutic part of facial treatment, benefiting all clients, no matter what their skin type. When incorporated into a facial it may also be combined with electrical procedures to increase its effectiveness. Care must be taken in performing the massage manipulations not to over-stretch or over-stimulate the tissues.

To ensure total relaxation it is essential to consider the following points:

o The room should be warm and quiet.
o There should be adequate bed covering.
o Ensure the client is comfortably positioned.
o Have all treatment products prepared in advance and close by.
o Refrain from talking unnecessarily.
o Warm the massage medium in your hands before applying to the client's skin.
o Do not lose contact with the client's skin before completion of the massage.
o All movements should be rhythmical and flowing.
o Indicate to the client the end of the massage with a gentle but firm pressure on completion of the final movement.

Contraindications to facial massage

o Skin disease.
o Cuts or abrasions.
o Bruising.
o Allergy prone skin.
o Highly vascular skin.

Aims of facial massage

o To relax the client.
o To nourish the skin.
o To improve skin texture.
o To improve muscle tone.
o To encourage cellular regeneration.

Massage mediums

Oil

As well as allowing ease of movement and deeper massage, oil nourishes and softens the skin. The oil itself must be light, non-sticky and easily absorbed. Olive and almond oils are most commonly used.

Essential oils

Essential oils are used quite extensively in body treatment but can also be very effective in treating different skin conditions. They are very concentrated oils extracted from plants and mixed with a suitable carrier oil. Depending upon the effects which are to be achieved, essential oils can be mixed to obtain the required results.

A carrier oil should penetrate the skin easily to allow the essential oils to be absorbed and ideally should have little or no smell; grapeseed, avocado, almond and wheatgerm are excellent carrier oils.

Some of the more relaxing essential oils are:

o Camomile.
o Cypress.
o Ylang-Ylang.
o Sandlewood.
o Patchouli.
o Rose.
o Neroli.
o Lavender.

Massage creams

There are creams available for facial massage which contain specific ingredients and are of different textures to suit all skin types. As facial massage should be performed for no less than 20 minutes, one of the most important properties of the cream is that it is not absorbed into the skin too quickly, requiring the therapist to reapply before the end of the massage.

Sensitive skin would benefit from essential oils formulated specifically to treat the accompanying problems or a soothing massage cream.

Dry/mature skin would benefit from a rich cream to nourish the skin but of a light consistency to prevent dragging the tissues, or essential oils.

Normal skin would benefit from all massage mediums provided they were not too heavy.

Greasy skin would benefit from the therapeutic effects of essential oils or a massage cream with a higher water to oil ratio.

Classification of massage manipulations

Effleurage

This is a soothing, stroking, surface movement used at the beginning and end of the facial massage and used during the massage as a linking movement between manipulations.

It can be firm or light without dragging the skin and it is performed either with the palmar surface of the hand or the padded parts of the fingertips. The hand should be completely relaxed and moved over the face and the neck with a gentle but even pressure.

Petrissage

These are pressure movements which are deeper and compress the muscle tissue intermittently against underlying structures. These movements are performed with the padded palmar surface of the fingers and thumbs. When performing these manipulations the hands should be moulded to the area being treated and movements should be slow and rhythmical.

Knuckling is a method of kneading using the knuckles to knead and lift the tissues in an upward circular movement.

Scissoring is a movement only performed over a flat bony area and the pressure exerted is very gentle. The index and middle fingers of both hands are placed opposite and inside each other and gentle pressure is exerted with both sets of fingers working towards each other lifting and releasing the tissues.

Tapotement

These are stimulating movements such as tapping and digital hacking performed with the palmar surfaces of the fingertips. Digital hacking to the face is an upward movement with the fingers, rapidly, one after the other, lifting the tissues and immediately releasing them. The hands must be relaxed when performing this movement. Tapping is a more rigid movement usually performed using two fingers together and working along the jawline.

Vibrations

Using the palmar surface of the hands and the fingertips on the area to be treated, the muscles of the therapist's arms and hands are contracted and relaxed rapidly creating a fine trembling movement which promotes relaxation.

Effects of massage manipulations

Effleurage

○ Increases circulation: The skin is nourished.
○ Increases lymph flow: Waste products are removed.
○ Aids desquamation: Improves skin texture.
○ Causes an erythema: Improves skin colour.
○ Soothes nerves.
○ Relaxes the client.

Petrissage

○ Increases circulation and lymph flow: The skin is nourished.

53

○ Aids desquamation: Improves skin texture.
○ Stimulates the skin: Improves colour, texture and cellular regeneration.
○ Increases muscle tone: Improves facial contours.
○ Eases away tension nodules: Relaxes muscles.

Tapotement

○ Produces an erythema.
○ Stimulates the nerve endings revitalizing the skin tissues.

Vibrations

○ Relaxes the client.
○ Gently stimulating.

Facial massage is incorporated into a facial after all the cleansing and electrical treatments have been carried out, except for those treatments which, for maximum effect, have to be performed as the concluding treatment.

A basic facial would be as follows:

1 Superficial cleanse.
2 Deep cleanse.
3 Facial massage.
4 Face mask.

The effects of facial massage

Physical	Physiological	Psychological
The therapist's hands warm the area	Increase in blood flow nourishes the tissues and increases cellular regeneration	The client feels relaxed
The pores relax and open	Oxygen is carried to the area, carbon dioxide is carried away	Skin feels rejuvenated
Skin becomes more receptive to absorption of nourishing and hydrating products	Lymph flow is increased, waste products are carried away, reinforcing the external cleansing of the skin	Sense of well being and good health is induced
Puffiness may be removed with massage manipulations	Heat and warmth is increased in the tissues because of the stimulation of blood supply	Client feels pampered
Relaxes tense muscles	Increase in sebum and sweat which helps to remove dirt and grease and maintains the moisture balance in the skin	Stress levels are reduced
Aids desquamation	Stimulates and nourishes underlying muscle tissue	Increases self-confidence
Softens and lubricates the skin	Stimulates or soothes the nerve endings	Essential oils if used have a beneficial effect on the nervous system, calming, uplifting and soothing
Eases tension lines	Essential oils if used have a beneficial effect on the body's systems	
Removes tension nodules in the muscles		
Erythema is produced		

○ Physical effects are those that can be seen or felt on the surface of the skin.
○ Physiological effects are those that occur in the body under the surface of the skin.
○ Psychological effects are those that the client feels.

6 Eye treatments

Eyebrow shaping

The eyes are the focal point of the face and the natural shape of the eyebrows normally enhances the features. The shape should not be altered drastically, just improved by plucking the stray hairs, which gives a cleaner line, allowing successful application of eyeshadow.

The thickness of the eyebrows helps in balancing facial features. Therefore, it is important not to overpluck. The following points must be taken into consideration before shaping begins:

○ The face shape.
○ Spacing of the eyes.
○ State of the existing eyebrow.
○ Client's own wishes.
○ Age.
○ Fashion.

Contraindications

○ New scar tissue.
○ Highly strung or nervous client.
○ Skin disease.
○ Bruising.
○ Eye disorders.

Eyebrow shaping should be carried out after the cleansing routine and before the soothing massage. If steaming is to be included as part of the facial, it could be applied at this stage, allowing the pores to open, making the treatment less painful.

To cause the least discomfort to the client:

○ Place warm pads of cotton wool over the brows to open the pores.
○ Hold the skin taut when plucking.
○ Always pluck in the direction of growth.

Figure 6.1 *Eyebrow shaping*

○ Start on the bridge of the nose as this area is less sensitive.
○ Apply a cooling soothing lotion to the area on completion of treatment. See Figure 6.1.

Determining correct eyebrow width

1 Rest an orange stick against the widest part of the nose and the inner corner of the eye. The eyebrow should not extend beyond this line.
2 Move the orange stick so that it makes a diagonal line from the nose across the outer corner of the eye and up to the eyebrow. It should not extend past this point. (See Figure 6.2.)

Eyebrow shapes

There are certain shapes which are more suited to a particular face shape and these should be considered before reshaping (Figure 6.3).

High forehead
The arch of the eyebrow should be slightly elevated to create the illusion of a lower forehead.

Low forehead
The arch should be as low as possible to give more height to the forehead.

Wide set eyes
The eyes will appear closer by leaving the brows unplucked on the inner corners.

Close set eyes
To make the eyes appear wider apart pluck more from the inner corners and extend the outer corner.

Round face
Arched eyebrows narrow the face.

Oblong face
The eyebrows should be almost horizontal.

Square face
The eyebrow should have a wide, high arch to create an oval impression.

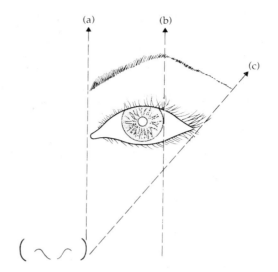

Figure 6.2 *How to determine eyebrow shape
(a) Hair between the eyebrows to the left of this point should be removed; (b) A line passing the outer edge of the iris through the eyebrow indicates the highest point of the eyebrow; (c) A line from the corner of the nose, passing the outer corner of the eye to the eyebrow and any hairs to the right of this point should be removed*

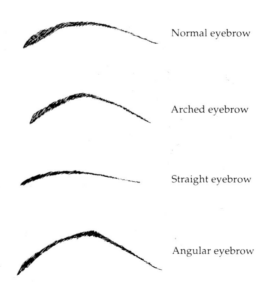

Normal eyebrow

Arched eyebrow

Straight eyebrow

Angular eyebrow

Figure 6.3 *Eyebrow shapes*

Pear-shaped face
Extra width is needed at the forehead, eyebrows should be arched and extended at the outer corners.

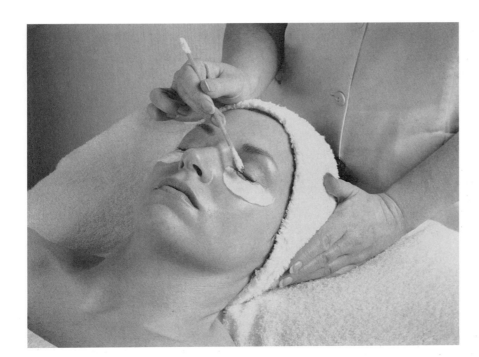

Figure 6.4 *Eyelash tinting*

Eyebrow and eyelash tinting

This is a very popular salon treatment and can be very effective in accentuating the eyes which are for most women one of their best features.

The tinting procedure usually lasts for up to six weeks but can be repeated more often, if the client does not have an allergy to the tint. The tinting products available are vegetable dyes but when mixed with hydrogen peroxide a chemical reaction occurs, which changes the character of the tint. It is essential, therefore, that a skin sensitivity test be carried out on the client at least 48 hours before treatment.

A small amount of the tint should be mixed according to the manufacturer's instructions and applied to the skin, in an unobtrusive position, such as behind the ear or on the inside of the elbow. This should then be covered with a plaster. See Figure 6.4.

Positive reaction

The skin will become red in the area of the patch test and there will be severe itchiness and in some cases swelling of the tissue. The treatment is therefore *contraindicated*.

Negative reaction

If the client experiences no discomfort or irritation then the treatment may proceed.

It is important to remember that the skin may become sensitive to a particular product even after many years of use and an allergic reaction may occur. Regular testing for allergy is important as the dye is being used on a highly sensitive area.

Even if clients have had a negative reaction to the test it is possible that they may experience irritation or discomfort during the treatment and the procedure must be immediately halted and the tint removed.

Reasons for use

o   To enhance the general appearance of the eyes.
o   For those sensitive to eye makeup.
o   To emphasize the colour intensity of those with blond or red hair.
o   When taking part in a sport such as swimming.
o   For those with no time to apply makeup.

○ Contact lens wearers irritated by fibres from mascara.
○ For those with fine or thin eyebrows.

Contraindications

○ Skin disorders.
○ Skin diseases.
○ Eye disorders.
○ Excessively dry or flaky skin.
○ Immediately after eyebrow shaping.
○ Clients who are unable to keep their eyes still for any reason.
○ History of sensitivity to eye makeup.

Eye disorders

Conjunctivitis (pink eye)

This is inflammation of the conjunctiva, the thin transparent membrane that covers the white of the eye. The characteristics are eyes becoming sore, gritty and watering continually, then becoming red and bloodshot.

The causes are allergy, irritation or infection. Where infection is present it may be treated by the doctor with antibiotic eye drops.

Stye – hordeolum

This is an infection in the hair follicle of an eyelash. The eye becomes red and sore and blinking is extremely painful. A small papule forms, swelling occurs and pus is present. It may become itchy but rubbing or scratching will increase the irritation and spread the infection. It may occur when the client is run down and it must be treated by a doctor.

Watery eye – epyphora

The function of the tear duct is to bathe and wash the eye with tears which then drain away into the nasal cavity. When some irritation occurs preventing this function, the over-secretion of tears overflows onto the face.

Black eye

This is bruising, normally caused by a blow which breaks the blood capillaries under the skin. The area will be painful and swollen but if steps are taken to reduce the temperature in the area with a cold compress the result may not be quite so bad.

Healthy eyes

Good health is reflected in the eyes, as it is in the skin, and it is important to look after the eyes and the skin surrounding them.

For sparkling eyes as well as healthy teeth fluoride is an essential part of your diet. Foods rich in fluoride are seafood, watercress, spinach, cabbage, egg yolk and porridge oats.

The skin under the eyes is thinner here than on the rest of the face and there are very few sebaceous glands. As a result this area is prone to dryness and crows' feet, or expression lines appearing.

Crows' feet

Caused by constant facial expressions, they are more commonly called laughter lines and are found particularly on a fairly dry skin. They appear with age and may be aggravated by poor eyesight or rough handling when applying or removing cosmetics.

Treatment
Use a good eye cream which plumps out the tissue temporarily, but care must be taken not to apply too much, as this may cause swelling and irritate the eyes. Always apply with the ring finger, using a gentle tapping movement, to prevent stretching of the skin. A gel is very soothing and cools the eye area if there is any sensitivity present.

When cleansing the eye makeup, use a non-oily, special eye makeup remover and protect the skin under the eye with a small piece of damp cotton wool. Then gently remove the eye makeup onto the cotton wool and not the skin.

When performing facial massage be particularly careful that movements are gentle and always from the outer corner to the inner corner of the eye. Slight pressure on the inside corner of the eye relieves tired eyes and removes tension.

Dark circles

There are several causes:

- Anaemia.
- Tiredness due to lack of sleep.
- Poor elimination, creating a build-up of toxins in the system.
- Too much sugar and starch in the diet.
- Lack of fresh air and exercise.

Treatment
Recommend a diet to help detoxify the system and reduce starch, that is, cakes, bread, cereals and sweets, which encourage carbon dioxide and lowers the oxygen content of the blood. The dark colour of the blood shows up under the thin skin underneath the eyes and camouflage makeup can be used to disguise this problem.

Swollen eyes

- This could indicate a medical condition which causes fluid retention.
- The skin around the eyes may have been overstretched and the contours dropped.
- A night cream may have been used which is too heavy.
- The client may be suffering from an allergic reaction.
- The problem could be hereditary.

Treatment
If you suspect a medical condition then refer the client to a doctor. Use cold compresses on the eyes to cool and soothe.

7 Facial electrical treatments

There are several pieces of equipment which may be incorporated into a facial treatment to obtain specific results which may not be obtained by manual methods. Not all the treatments pass an electrical current through the body but instead use the current to work the machine, producing the required effect.

Choice of equipment

It is important for therapists to recognize when it is appropriate to incorporate a piece of electrical equipment into a facial routine. Most pieces of equipment achieve one or more of the following effects:

○ Cleansing.
○ Toning.
○ Stimulating.
○ Relaxing.
○ Nourishing.

Some skin conditions may be improved or corrected more quickly by use of the appropriate equipment. It is important, therefore, to analyse the skin correctly and have a complete understanding of the effects of all equipment.

It is also very important to understand how each piece of equipment works, how to use it safely and effectively.

Circuits and currents

To make an electric current flow along a given path, a supply of energy is needed, for example a battery or the mains supply. The supply of energy will allow the current to flow if there is a conductor along which the current can flow.

○ A conductor is any material which allows electricity to flow through it.

○ An insulator will not allow electricity to flow through it.

Examples

Conductors	Insulators
Copper	Wood
Iron	Glass
Aluminium	Polythene
Carbon	Rubber
Sea water	Paraffin
Sulphuric acid	Propanone

An electric current is a flow of charged particles called electrons. The flow of current can be changed by:

○ A resistor which will reduce the current flow.
○ A variable resistor (rheostat) which can change current flow in a circuit.
○ A switch which will direct where the current is able to flow.
○ A capacitor or condenser is a device which stores electrical charges.
○ A potentiometer varies the voltage in an electrical circuit thus allowing the intensity of a current to be turned up from zero.

An electric current requires a complete circuit to flow along, if there is a break then current flow will stop.

Electrical current is measured in amperes (amps). Resistance is a term used to describe something which opposes the flow of an electrical current and this resistance is measured in ohms.

Effects of electrical current

There are three main effects:

1 Magnetic force.
2 Heating.
3 Chemical.

An alternating current is a flow of current which constantly changes direction many times per second and it is produced by large scale generators that provide electricity for the mains supply.

A direct current is produced using either electrical cells (batteries) or a rectified, smoothed alternating current and it flows in one direction only, from positive to negative.

Equipment	Current
Faradism	Interrupted or surged direct
High frequency	Alternating
Desincrustation	Direct
Iontophoresis	Direct

An electrical circuit is the movement of an electrical current from its source, through the conductors and back to the original source. For example, from the equipment through the wires to an active electrode, through the body and back to the equipment via an indifferent electrode.

A fuse is a safety device which blows when an excessive current flows in a circuit. This can be caused by a fault or because the circuit is dangerously overloaded. Fuses in plugs have different current ratings:

3 amp: For use with appliances up to 700 watts.
5 amp: For use with appliances between 700 and 1000 watts.
13 amp: For use with appliances between 1000 and 3000 watts.

Wiring a plug (Figure 7.1)

When wiring a plug it is important to follow certain safety procedures:

○ Never use frayed wire – trim the end neatly.
○ Do not use wires with split or cracked insulation.
○ Cut insulation using wire strippers.
○ Do not use excessive lengths of wire.
○ Do not use a fuse of the incorrect value.

Power appliances are fitted with a three-pin plug and the three wires are colour-coded.

Live	**L**	Brown
Neutral	**N**	Blue
Earth	**E**	Green and yellow

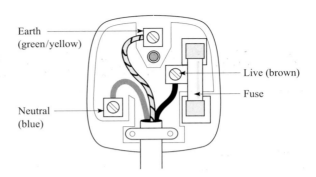

Figure 7.1 *Wiring a mains plug*

Terminology

Alternating current: Is a flow of current moving in one direction and then in the opposite direction, 50 cycles per second, and comes from the mains supply.
Ampere: Is a unit of electrical strength.
A *circuit:* Is the movement of an electrical current from its source, through the conductors (wire, electrode, body) and back to the original source.
A *conductor:* Is a substance which allows electricity to pass through it, for example metals, water and carbon.
Direct current: Is a constant flow of current travelling in one direction and is supplied by batteries.
An *electric current:* Is a stream of *electrons* or negatively charged particles which flow along a conductor.
A *fuse:* Is a safety device which blows when an excessive current flows in a circuit. This can be caused by a fault or because the circuit is dangerously overloaded.
An *insulator:* Is a substance that resists the passage of an electric current, for example plastics and rubber.
Ohm: Is a unit of electrical resistance.
A *rectifier:* Converts an alternating current into a direct current.
A *switch:* Is used to complete or break a circuit.
Volt: Is a unit of electrical pressure.

How to choose and maintain electrical equipment

There must be a demand for any piece of equipment bought, a machine lying idle is a waste of money for the salon.

The machine must be sturdy if it is to be in constant use.

Ensure the machine is of good quality and does not break down, as it will cost the salon money while it is out of use being repaired.

Shop around and make sure you obtain the machine at a reasonable price and with a guarantee.

If possible advertise the machine within the salon, offer a discounted price on the treatments if a course is booked in advance. With a good response the machine could be paid for before you receive it.

Consider the size of the salon and the space available for storage. It may be advisable to buy a piece of equipment which combines several different units in one.

If the business is mobile then it is advisable not only to purchase the combined unit but also to ensure that it is in a protective case.

Take out a service contract with a good local electrician who will regularly service all equipment, preferably one who is familiar with the type of equipment used and who may even provide a replacement while your own is being repaired.

Make sure that all machines are wired up correctly and any continental machines have been checked as the wiring may be different.

Store the equipment and all accessories safely and neatly after they have been cleaned and sterilized.

Handle all leads carefully to prevent loose connections.

General contraindications to electrical treatment

○ Any skin disease.
○ Recent scar tissue.
○ Heart disease. A weak heart may not be able to maintain an increase in blood pressure caused by a dilation of the blood vessels, an effect of an electrical current flowing through the body.
○ Arteriosclerosis. More commonly referred to as hardening of the arteries. The arteries are unable to open up to allow the increased flow of blood, which is a natural response to stimulation of the circulation and fainting may occur.

○ Hypersensitive skin. Irritation or itchiness may occur as this skin type is very easily stimulated. Broken capillaries can worsen due to the increased dilation of the capillaries in response to the increase in circulation.
○ During pregnancy. It is not advisable to use electrical equipment which allows a flow of electrical current to pass through the body.
○ Epilepsy.
○ Cuts, abrasions or bruising.
○ Metal pins or plates.

Safety precautions when using electrical equipment

○ Check plugs and machine for loose wires.
○ Make sure:
  —there are no trailing leads.
  —all the controls are at zero at the commencement and conclusion of treatment.
  —the machine is not positioned near water.
  —the machine is easily accessible during treatment.
○ Do not allow the client to touch *any* machine.
○ Always check a machine with a thermostat; do not assume it is working correctly.
○ Test the machine on yourself before using it.
○ Check for contraindications
○ Test the client for skin sensitivity when necessary.

Facial steaming

The facial steamer is one of the most versatile treatments. It is beneficial to all skin types and can be incorporated into most skin care routines.

There are free-standing models with a height-adjusting facility and an adjustable head, allowing accurate placement of the steam vapour, as well as a control of steam pressure. Most new models are easy to empty and have an indicator that emits a beeping noise when the water reservoir is almost empty (Figure 7.2).

To prevent calcium and mineral deposits within the machine it is advisable to use distilled water in the steamer instead of tap water.

Some models produce ozone which has an antibacterial effect on the skin, promotes healing and

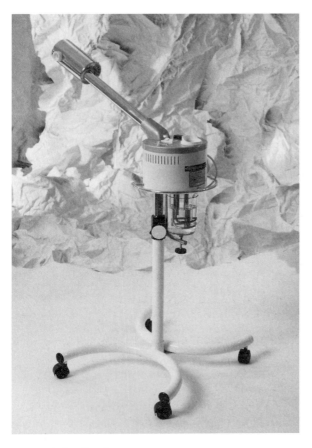

Figure 7.2 *Facial steamer*
Courtesy Depilex Limited

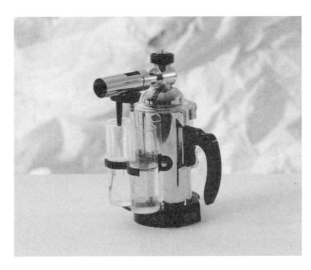

Figure 7.3 *Hand-held steamer*
Courtesy Depilex Limited

helps to destroy bacteria. These models contain a high pressure mercury vapour lamp, over which the vapour passes and ozone is produced.

It should be noted here that although most steamers on the market have a facility for the use of ozone, there has been recent legislation proposed to reduce or remove the use of ozone in facial steam therapy. The principle of this is that the concentration of ozone being emitted by these units could exceed the specified safety levels of between 100–120 micrograms per cubic metre and the ozone produced is inhaled directly into the lungs.

Some examining bodies have preempted any official legislation by removing the use of ozone in steam therapy, although it is still common practice within the industry.

The small hand-held model is a specialized steamer which emits a very fine spray to the face, carrying plant extracts, herbal solutions or skin fresheners. On the side of the steamer are two glass beakers, one to hold the special solution which is drawn up and mixed with the distilled water in the main reservoir of the steamer. The other beaker catches drips of water produced by the vapour. See Figure 7.3.

Effects of steaming

○ Opens the pores.
○ Stimulates the sudoriferous glands to produce sweat helping to eliminate waste.
○ Grease deposits in the follicles are softened and comedones are removed more easily.
○ Sebaceous glands are stimulated, helping to lubricate the skin.
○ Softens dead skin cells aiding desquamation.
○ Increased circulation causes an erythema, improving skin colour.
○ Prepares the skin for further treatment.
○ Relaxing.
○ Increase in circulation brings nutrients to the skin and carries away waste products.

Uses of steaming

Steaming is, in effect, a gentle cleansing treatment suitable for all skin types and would be performed after the superficial and deep cleanse.

Dry skin
○ Deep cleanses.
○ Desquamates the dead skin cells.
○ Hydrates.
○ Improves colour.

Sensitive skin
○ Gently cleanses.
○ Hydrates.

Any area of high colour should be protected with cotton wool pads.

Mature skin
○ Increases cellular regeneration.
○ Desquamates the dead skin cells.
○ Hydrates.
○ Improves skin colour.

Normal skin
○ Maintains the function and texture.
○ Cleanses.
○ Hydrates.

Greasy skin
○ Unblocks congestion.
○ Deep cleanses.
○ Improves skin colour.

The general rule for placement of the steamer is the greasier the skin, the closer the vapour and the more sensitive the skin, the further away the steamer should be placed.

The length of time the steamer is used for would depend upon the skin type and condition. The average time within a facial routine would be 5 minutes, less if the skin was very sensitive or mature and longer if it was very congested.

Specific contraindications

○ Sunburn.
○ Acne rosacea.
○ Extreme vascularity.

Exfoliation

This is a method by which skin cells are removed from the outermost layer of the epidermis.

It may be achieved in varying degrees by:

○ Manual cleansing.
○ Brush cleansing.
○ Pore grains.
○ Oatmeal scrubs.
○ Abrasive sponges
○ Abrasive masks.
○ Biological peels.
○ Chemical peels.
○ Fruit acids.

The effects of exfoliation are:

○ To improve skin texture and colour by removing dead skin cells.
○ To help in the removal of skin blockages.
○ To increase cellular regeneration.
○ To increase the absorption of creams into the epidermis.

With modern technology a new system has been developed which exfoliates the dead skin cells and also fine lines and wrinkles to achieve a smooth and rejuvenated skin.

Crystal clear micro-epidermal skin exfoliation system

This is a 'state of the art' therapeutic method of skin abrasion providing more than the standard

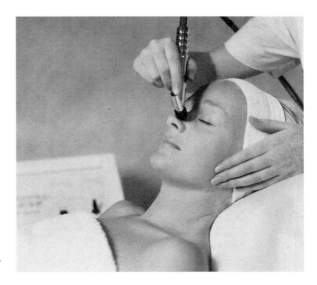

Figure 7.4 *Crystal Clear facial treatment. Courtesy Crystal Clear International Limited*

skin peeling treatment. The unit is composed of a compressor and a suction pump which delivers a controlled stream of micronized aluminium oxide crystals to the skin through a disposable sterilized nozzle (Figure 7.4). The used crystals and exfoliated skin cells are then removed by the controlled vacuum action of the unit leaving the skin instantly smooth and fresh, promoting new skin and collagen growth.

The pressure used to deliver the stream of crystals is fully adjustable which allows the therapist to treat many different skin types and conditions on the face and body. It is a completely painless treatment and is very simple to operate.

It works on three different levels:

Level 1: This is the most superficial of the treatments and is often used as an introduction to the client in preparation for the higher levels. This will exfoliate the skin and help in the removal of milia and comedones.

Level 2: This is a more concentrated procedure and is particularly good for the treatment of fine lines and wrinkles, pigmentation and acne scarring. This level complements the use of microcurrent, electrical, neuromuscular stimulation (non-surgical facelift) treatment.

Level 3: This is the level which focuses on the treatment of scars, stretchmarks and lip and frown lines.

Body exfoliation will be achieved by using the body nozzle to remove dead skin cells and stimulate blood circulation. It will help in the treatment of cellulite to eliminate the orange peel effect which appears on the thighs and other parts of the body.

It is also an excellent treatment to prepare the skin for a false tan application.

For the treatment of lines, wrinkles and scars, a course of ten treatments is recommended once a week and this should be followed by monthly maintenance treatments.

Contraindications

○ Hyper sensitive skin.
○ Eczema.
○ Psoriasis.
○ Broken capillaries.
○ Bruising.

○ New scar tissue.
○ Skin diseases.
○ Skin disorders.
○ Asthma.
○ Hepatitis.

Benefits

○ Removal of skin congestion.
○ Improved skin colour.
○ Clearer, brighter complexion.
○ Increased cellular regeneration.

Cosmetic brush treatments

This treatment can be used in two different ways:

1 Brush cleansing.
2 Brush massage for the application of specialized products.

The machines themselves vary in size from small hand-held units to a large individual machine or, in a combined unit, with other equipment.

The brushes come in various sizes and textures, made from natural hair or bristle.

The machines have a controllable brush speed and can be rotated clockwise and anticlockwise. See Figure 7.5.

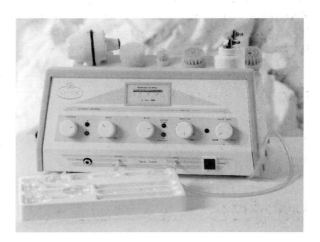

Figure 7.5 *Brush massage machine*
Courtesy Depilex Limited

Brush cleansing

Brush cleansing reinforces the manual cleanse. This method desquamates by gently removing the dead surface skin cells and helps to remove skin blockages. It stimulates circulation and improves skin colour and cellular regeneration.

The skin should be thoroughly cleansed and steamed first to soften the skin, so that the dead cells can be removed more easily. Depending upon the skin type a cleansing medium should be applied with a mask brush:

○ Soap – greasy/blemished skin.
○ Cream and water cleanser – greasy skin.
○ Facial scrub – congested skin.
○ Cleansing lotion – normal/combination skin.
○ Cleansing cream – dry skin.

The correct brush size must be used for the area to be treated, for example the neck would need a larger size than the sides of the nose. The brush should always be moistened with water before use to soften the bristles.

Slower speeds should be used on the dry/sensitive skin for a more gentle effect and the faster speeds on the coarser skins with a thicker epidermis. Pressure and speed should be reduced over bony areas. The brushes must be guided over the skin. It is not necessary to rotate the brush at all since the machine does it for you.

It is advisable to apply damp cotton wool pads to the client's eyes during treatment to prevent any of the cleansing medium going into the eyes.

The cleansing medium should be removed with damp cotton wool pads and the facial routine continued, or apply the appropriate moisturizer.

Brush massage

With this method special moisturizing and regenerating creams are used and the brush massage aids desquamation preparing the skin to absorb the nutrient properties of these creams.

Circulation is increased bringing nourishment to the area and encouraging cell renewal. The lymph flow is increased removing waste products and the skin colour is improved.

The face is prepared as for brush cleansing by cleansing and steaming the face, the regenerating cream is then applied to a moist skin. The brush massage is then performed with a soft haired applicator for approximately 5–10 minutes. The excess cream is then removed and a nourishing face mask applied.

Mature skin benefits from this treatment as cell renewal slows down with age and as the dead epidermal cells are not being shed as quickly, the skin may look dull and lifeless.

Brush massage, therefore, removes the dead skin cells and increases the circulation so improving skin colour and encouraging cell renewal. The regenerating cream applied to the skin helps to maintain the correct moisture level and makes the skin feel soft and supple.

Contraindications to brush massage and cleansing

○ Acne to avoid irritation and spread of infection.
○ Sensitive skin with broken capillaries.
○ Skin disease.
○ Bruising.

The brushes must be throughly cleansed in hot soapy water and then disinfected to ensure that they are completely clean after use and then stored in a dry sterilizer.

Vibratory massage treatment

The two methods used in facial treatment are:

1 Percussion vibration.
2 Audio-sound vibration.

The percussion method produces vibrations of low penetration while the audio-sound method has a deeper effect on the tissues without irritating the skin.

Effects

○ Increases the circulation.
○ Increases the lymphatic flow.

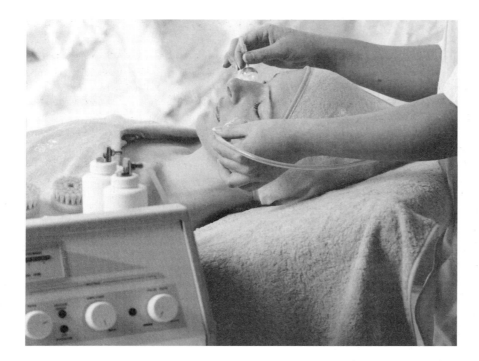

Figure 7.6 *Vacuum suction treatment Courtesy Depilex Limited*

○ Causes an erythema.
○ Increases warmth in the tissues.
○ Encourages cell renewal.
○ Relaxing.

Contraindications

○ Infection or irritation of the skin.
○ Bony face.
○ Sinus trouble.
○ Recent scar tissue.

Sensitive skin would be a contraindication to the percussion method because of the direct, superficial application. The audio-sound method could be used because the effect is deep in the tissues and does not cause dilation of surface blood vessels.

Each method has several different applicators and variable intensity to allow treatment of different skin conditions and density of skin tissue.

The face may be treated indirectly during a facial massage by placing the percussion vibrator over the therapist's hand. This produces a gentler effect and also makes it more comfortable for a client with little subcutaneous tissue.

Timing of treatment would depend entirely on skin reaction.

Vacuum suction

This is a mechanical method of lymphatic drainage, the removal of waste products from the skin via the lymphatic system.

The machine itself contains an electrically-driven vacuum pump connected to a perspex or glass ventouse by a flexible plastic tube. The pump draws air from the ventouse, causing the air pressure beneath to be reduced and forms a partial vacuum which lifts the underlying skin tissue into the ventouse.

There is a control valve which sets the degree of suction and a gauge which indicates the vacuum within the ventouse.

The ventouses come in different sizes and shapes, the larger apertures for lymphatic drainage and the smallest for comedone extraction. Some have a small hole on the side, which is covered by a finger to create the vacuum and at the end of each stroke, the finger is lifted away from the hole to release the vacuum. For those ventouses without a hole the little finger should be used to break the suction at the end of each stroke.

Vacuum suction machines with a pulsating action are beneficial to mature wrinkled skin, as the vacuum is intermittent and less stimulating. In this case two ventouses are used one on either side of the face working in unison. The frequency and the pulse width can be adjusted to suit all skin types and different areas of the face. See Figure 7.6.

Precautions

o Before using the equipment check all electrical precautions.
o Select correct size ventouse.
o Test vacuum on yourself first.
o Use the necessary lubrication for the skin type:
   –greasy, use cleansing lotion
   –dry/mature/sensitive, use oil or massage cream.
o Ensure the vacuum is not excessive, that is, tissue should not be lifted into the ventouse more than 20 per cent.
o Always break the suction before removing the ventouse from the face, using your little finger or unblocking the hole on the ventouse.
o All strokes should be towards the lymph nodes.

Benefits of treatment

o Waste products are removed via the lymphatic system improving elimination and absorption.
o Deep cleansing to the skin, helping in the removal of skin blockages and congestion.
o Cleansing action is improved with the application of a special cleansing medium.
o Desquamates the dead skin cells improving skin texture.
o Nourishing because the increase in circulation bring nutrients and oxygen to the area.
o Skin colour is improved due to the increase in circulation.
o Hydrating or moisturizing when a rich lubricant is used.

Aim of treatment

The aim of the treatment is to increase the lymphatic circulation and remove waste products from the skin of the face and neck to the superficial lymph nodes. Manual massage will be performed after vacuum suction to remove the waste from the lymph nodes to be absorbed back into the main system for elimination.

Drainage is performed:

o From the neck to the superficial and deep cervical nodes or submandibular nodes.
o From the chin and jawline to the submental and submandibular nodes.
o Across the lower cheek area to the buccal nodes and parotid nodes.
o From the nose to the buccal nodes.
o Across the upper cheek area to the preauricular nodes.
o From the forehead to the preauricular nodes.

Care of the machine

Ventouses and tubes should be washed in warm soapy water, dried thoroughly and then placed in a UV sterilizing cabinet. Check ventouses regularly for chips or cracks.

Contraindications

o Sensitive skin with dilated capillaries as the suction could worsen the condition.
o Thin over-stretched skin as the loose tissue would be sucked into the ventouse causing discomfort.
o Recent scar tissue.
o Skin disease.
o Bruised skin.
o Bony areas where treatment would be ineffective.
o Acne rosacea.

High frequency

This is a rapidly alternating current with a frequency of 200,000 cycles per second; it is so rapid it does not stimulate motor or sensory nerves.

The current produces heat in the tissues and depending upon the method of application used, the physiological effects are stimulating or soothing.

The two methods of high frequency are:

1 Direct.
2 Indirect.

The machine has an on/off switch, an intensity control and an ebonite handle, connected to the machine by an extendable cord. Each machine has a selection of glass electrodes which fit into the handle and come in different shapes and sizes:

Saturator electrode: This electrode is used for indirect high frequency and is held by the client to complete the circuit.

Mushroom-shaped electrode: This is the most frequently used electrode and normally comes in two sizes to suit all areas of the face and neck.

Horse shoe-shaped electrode: This is shaped to fit the neck or across the shoulders.

Fulgurator electrode: This is long and thin with a tiny pointed end used to spark pustules.

The roller electrode: Often used over a special cream and gauze in direct high frequency.

Contraindications

o   Headaches/migraine.
o   Highly nervous clients.
o   Epilepsy.
o   Pregnancy.
o   Skin disease.
o   Excessive number of dental fillings.
o   Metal pins or plates.
o   High or low blood pressure/heart disease.
o   New scar tissue/cuts or bruises.

Direct high frequency

Using the appropriate glass electrode in the ebonite handle, the high frequency current is passed directly into the client's skin, using small circular movements and starting on the neck area. The lighter the contact the more stimulat-

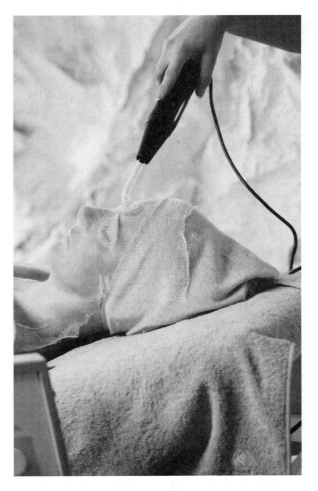

Figure 7.7 *Direct high frequency*
Courtesy Depilex Limited

ing the treatment. Talc should be used as a lubricant to allow the electrodes to move smoothly over the skin (Figure 7.7).

For the skin to gain maximum benefit from this treatment it should be performed at the end of a facial and makeup should not be worn.

The effects are:

o   Increase in circulation. Produces heat in the tissues, bringing nutrients to the area and removing waste.
o   Produces an erythema. Improves skin colour.
o   Aids desquamation. Refines the skin.
o   Dries the skin. Helps to heal pustules.

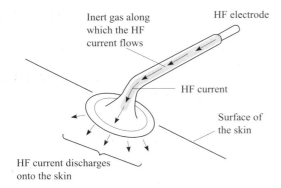

Inert gas along which the HF current flows

HF electrode

HF current

Surface of the skin

HF current discharges onto the skin

Figure 7.8 *How ozone is produced. When the high frequency current mixes with the oxygen between the electrode and the skin, ozone is produced*

○ Cleansing. Due to the increase in sebum flow and perspiration.
○ Germicidal. Due to ozone formation which kills bacteria.

How ozone is produced
The glass electrodes are partial vacuums, that is, hollow tubes with a low density of air and inert gas which in most machines produces a blue light. This provides a passage along which the current flows and the high frequency energy is discharged into the skin where the electrode makes contact.

When the high frequency current is passed through oxygen, it produces ozone (Figure 7.8). This occurs between the electrode and the skin and more intensely when the electrode is lifted very slightly off the face to 'spark' pustules.

This method, therefore, is most beneficial to:

○ Oily and blemished skin to dry and heal.
○ Sallow skin to improve colour.
○ Sluggish skin to stimulate and encourage cell renewal.

Indirect high frequency

This is a treatment which is combined with the facial massage and is performed after all cleansing treatments have been carried out.

With this method of high frequency the saturator electrode is placed in the ebonite handle and given to the client to hold. The therapist then performs a facial massage and the high frequency current discharges from the client to the therapist's hands at the point of contact.

Depending upon the client's skin type, oil, massage cream or special creams may be applied to the skin. Whichever medium is chosen, it must not disappear into the skin too quickly as this treatment must not be interrupted to apply further applications.

All massage manipulations may be used apart from tapotement as at least one hand must remain in contact with the client's skin at all times.

The effects of this method are:

○ Relaxation. Warmth is created by the energy produced and a sedative effect is achieved.
○ Removes tension. A combination of the massage and the warmth in the area relieves muscular tension.
○ Produces a mild erythema.
○ Improves circulation. Brings nourishment, removing waste and warming the tissues.
○ Nourishing. The creams applied to the skin are absorbed more readily when high frequency is applied indirectly.

This method, therefore, is most beneficial for:

○ Muscular tension to ease aches and pains.
○ Sensitive skin to gently decongest areas with thread veins.
○ Dry/mature skin to gently stimulate and nourish.
○ Tense clients to promote relaxation.

Precautions when using high frequency

Explain to the client about the loud buzzing noise the electrode makes when it is in use, as this can sound quite alarming.

Remove all jewellery.

Check all electrical precautions.

Do not allow the client to come into contact with anything metal.

The electrode or one hand, depending upon which method is used, should be placed on the face before switching on the current. Alternatively, place your finger on the electrode, switch on the machine, when the electrode is in contact with the client's skin you may remove your finger and the high frequency current will be discharged into the client's skin.

Do not touch the client with your other hand when performing direct high frequency.

Timing of treatment would depend upon the skin type being treated, the reaction of the skin and the client's tolerance to treatment. The following may be used as a guide:

Direct:
○ Oily or blemished skin, 5–10 minutes.
○ Dry or sensitive skin, no more than 5 minutes.
Indirect:
○ A normal 20 minute massage unless the skin has an adverse reaction.

After use the electrodes should be cleaned and sterilized and put away safely. It is also essential to clean the machine itself and the ebonite holder with surgical spirit. When residues of grease or talc remain, this acts as a conductor to the high frequency current and the therapist may feel electric shocks in her hand.

Facial faradic or electrical muscle stimulation

The facial faradic machine is used to stimulate muscles and is classed as a passive exercise treatment. There are special facial units available, or faradic machines designed for the body with a facial outlet.

The facial unit has an on/off switch, a pulse indicator switch, an intensity control and a single output with a facial electrode attachment. The positive and negative electrodes are both built in to the facial attachment to complete the circuit.

The *Faradic current* is an interrupted or surged direct current, that is, a direct current that is rapidly switched on and off. There is a 'stimulating' period while the current flows and the muscle contracts and a 'rest' period when the current does not flow and the muscle relaxes.

The contraction should resemble normal facial exercises. Because the current has no chemical effect on tissue it will not scar or burn the skin.

This treatment is used for:

○ Increasing tone of muscles and improving facial contours.
○ Stimulating an exhausted skin and improving colour.
○ Delaying the effects of ageing by increasing cellular regeneration.

Effects of the faradic current

○ The sensory nerve endings in the skin are stimulated and the client will feel a pins and needles sensation.
○ The muscle contracts when the motor point is stimulated and this increases tone, improving facial contours.
○ The circulation to the area is increased bringing nourishment.
○ The contractions cause a pumping action on blood and lymph flow therefore the elimination of waste is speeded up.
○ An erythema occurs in the area of the working electrode.

To obtain a good contraction the electrode should be:

1 Moistened with saline solution.
2 Applied to a clean and grease free skin.
3 Positioned correctly over the motor point of the muscle – where the nerve enters the muscle.

Treatment time is usually about 15 minutes to exercise the facial muscle in a general toning routine. Each muscle may be contracted five times but as treatment progresses the number of contractions may be increased depending upon client tolerance and reaction of muscles to treatment.

The treatment may be given several times a week and if incorporated into a facial routine should be performed after the cleanse, when the area is clean and grease free and before the massage to relax the client.

A skin sensitivity test must be performed before treatment.

How to determine skin sensitivity

To prevent any injury to the facial muscles therapists must carry out a sensitivity test before

71

treatment. For this test clients are required to close their eyes while a sharp object (such as the pointed end of an orange stick) and a piece of cotton wool are placed randomly on their face and neck. If they can differentiate between the two then they have good sensitivity and treatment may proceed. If they cannot the treatment is contraindicated.

The most common method is to work on individual muscles, starting on the neck, as this is the least sensitive area and the muscles are much longer and respond well to stimulation.

A general sequence beginning on the neck:

1 Sternomastoid.
2 Platysma.
3 Masseter.
4 Orbicularis oris.
5 Risorius.
6 Zygomaticus.
7 Orbicularis occuli.
8 Frontalis/corrugator if not contraindicated.

Clients should be in a fairly upright position for comfort and to allow therapists to work with ease.

All the superficial muscles of facial expression may be exercised together by stimulating the facial nerve. This can be activated in front of the ear where it enters the cheek. The branches of this nerve innervate different areas of the face.

Precautions

○ Check all electrical precautions.
○ Position electrode before turning on the current.
○ Turn current up on a contraction.
○ If it is necessary to reposition the electrode always turn down the intensity before moving the electrode.
○ Avoid working in the mouth area if the client has a lot of metal fillings as this will be very uncomfortable for the client.
○ Always check with clients that they are comfortable.

Contraindications

○ Muscular disorders.
○ Highly strung nervous client.

○ Skin disease.
○ Recent scar tissue.
○ Fatigue or muscle tremor.
○ Hypersensitive skin due to irritation of the sensory nerve endings.
○ Lack of skin sensitivity.
○ Epilepsy.

Galvanism

A galvanic current is a *constant direct current* which may be used in facial treatment in two ways:

1 *Desincrustation*, to deep cleanse the skin by removing oil and skin blockages.
2 *Iontophoresis*, to introduce active water soluble substances into the skin for specific effects.

Useful terminology

Active electrode: Working electrode which is applied to the face during treatment.
Anaphoresis: Movement of negative ions to the positive pole.
Anions: Ions with a negative charge.
Anode: Positive pole.
Cataphoresis: Movement of positive ions to the negative pole.
Cathode: Negative pole.
Cations: Ions with a positive charge.
Indifferent electrode: Non-working electrode which the client holds to complete the circuit.
Ion: An atom carrying an electrical charge.
Ionization: Use of active ions or electrically charged elements in treatments.
Milliamp meter: Measures the amount of galvanic current being used and indicates the level of the skin's resistance.
Saponification: 'Soaping' or cleansing of the skin using a negative charge with saline solution or desincrustation lotion.

How galvanism works

The current which flows through the skin forms a circuit between the active and indifferent electrodes and the active substances pass into the epidermis on the galvanic charge (Figure 7.9).

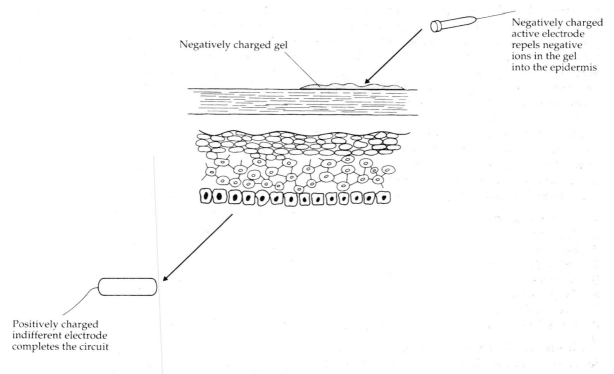

Negatively charged gel

Negatively charged active electrode repels negative ions in the gel into the epidermis

Positively charged indifferent electrode completes the circuit

Figure 7.9 *Penetration of ions into the epidermis*

The active electrode can be either negative or positive. The active substances to be introduced into the skin are either negatively or positively charged.

The polarity selected for the active electrode, must be the same as the polarity indicated on the active substances to be used, if they are to penetrate the epidermis, as **like charges repel.**

The effects on the skin of the chosen polarity

Positive pole (anode)
○ Hardens the skin.
○ Closes the pores.
○ Decreases circulation.
○ Soothes nerve endings.
○ Produces an acid reaction.

Negative pole (cathode)
○ Softens the skin.
○ Opens the pores.
○ Increases circulation.

○ Stimulates nerve endings.
○ Produces an alkaline reaction.

Uses of the positive pole

○ To close the pores after facial treatment.
○ To decrease vascularity.
○ To refine skin tissue by firming and tightening.
○ To prevent inflammation due to previous stimulating treatment.
○ To introduce acid pH solution, for example astringent, into the skin.
○ To soothe the nerve endings.
○ To introduce active substances into the skin for a specific purpose, for example moisturizing, soothing.

Uses of the negative pole

○ To open pores and aid cleansing.
○ To soften and moisten the tissues.
○ To remove surface oil.

73

○ To dissolve sebum and ingrained dirt.
○ To introduce an alkaline solution, for example desincrustation fluid into the skin for cleansing.
○ To stimulate an exhausted skin condition.
○ To introduce water soluble substances into the skin for a specific purpose.

The galvanic machine

The machine may be an independent piece of equipment or part of a combined unit. The features comprise:

1 A pilot light.
2 An intensity control.
3 A polarity changer.
4 A milliamp meter.
5 A socket for the electrode.

As galvanic units operate from the mains the alternating current is converted into the smooth direct current used for galvanism by the following devices contained within the machine:

○ The *transformer*, which reduces the voltage of the alternating mains current.
○ The *rectifier*, which changes the alternating current to a direct current.
○ The *capacitor*, which smooths out any irregularities in the direct current.

Modern machines are safe to use but manufacturers' instructions must be closely adhered to and treatment must not exceed 10 minutes. In fact, 6 minutes is adequate time to carry out effective treatment.

The electrodes

The *active* or working electrode which introduces water soluble substances into the skin takes different forms:

○ Metal rollers.
○ Metal ball electrodes.
○ Tweezers.
○ Rod with a round, flat applicator head.

The tweezer electrode is used for desincrustation and must be covered by sixteen thicknesses of lint. The flat applicator head must also be covered with lint but it is not necessary to use more than one thickness as the surface area of this electrode is much larger.

The *indifferent* electrode which the client holds to complete the circuit comes in the form of a metal rod which must be covered with viscose sponge, or a small metal plate, similarly covered and placed behind the client's shoulder.

Both electrodes are attached to the galvanic machine by leads. The skin must be kept moist during treatment to aid the flow of current.

General effects of the galvanic current

○ Tonic. Increases in circulation.
○ Relaxing. Warmth produced in the tissues.
○ Soothing. Fluid in the tissues is drawn to the negative pole. This is called *Electro-osmosis*. Therefore, when the positive pole is used over an area, tissue fluids and waste products will be directed away from the area so relieving tension.

Safety precautions

○ Check client for contraindications.
○ Remove all jewellery from the client.
○ Check all electrical precautions.
○ Ensure that all wires are securely attached to the electrodes.
○ Ensure all dials are at zero.
○ Test the client for skin sensitivity.
○ When lint is used make sure it is folded without any creases to prevent concentration of current.
○ Lint must be evenly damp not dripping wet.
○ Warn clients that they may feel a slight tingling sensation and experience a metallic taste in their mouth, particularly if they have a lot of metal fillings.
○ The area to be treated must be clean and grease free.
○ Turn the current up slowly and watch the milliamp meter for a lowering of the skin's resistance.
○ Always apply a firm even pressure.
○ Turn the current down slowly on completion of treatment.

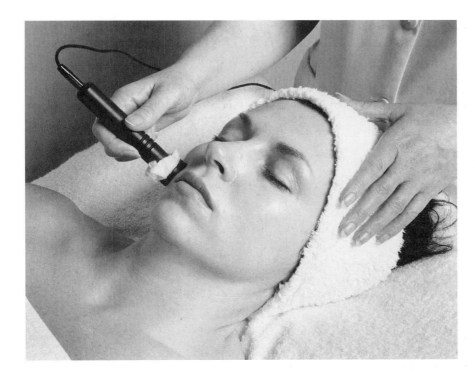

Figure 7.10
Desincrustation

Contraindications to galvanic treatment

○ Lack of skin sensation.
○ Skin infections.
○ Highly vascular skin or sensitive skin.
○ Metal pins or plates.
○ Heart condition.
○ Bruising.
○ Cuts or abrasions
    (could be covered with petroleum jelly to prevent a concentration of current in the area).

The skin sensitivity test must be carried out prior to treatment using the orange stick and cotton wool as described on page 72.

Desincrustation

This is a deep cleansing treatment especially for oily congested skins. It would be used after cleansing and if appropriate after facial steaming. The negative pole is used and a negatively charged alkaline desincrustation gel is applied to the skin (Figure 7.10).

Because the negative pole is used:

○ The circulation increases.
○ The skin will be softened.
○ Pores will open.
○ Sebum in the follicles will liquefy.
○ An alkaline is formed on the skin's surface.

In addition, the alkaline solution which is applied will help to dissolve dirt and remove the congestion in the skin.

The electrode must be moved over the face in small circular movements and the skin should remain evenly moist throughout the treatment. Depending upon the area being treated, timing should be between 3 and 5 minutes which is normally sufficient time for the effects of the pole to work and the active substances to penetrate the epidermis. For a small area such as the centre panel the treatment should take about 3 minutes and the whole face should take approximately 5 minutes.

The desincrustation fluid must then be thoroughly removed after lowering the current and switching off the machine. Some

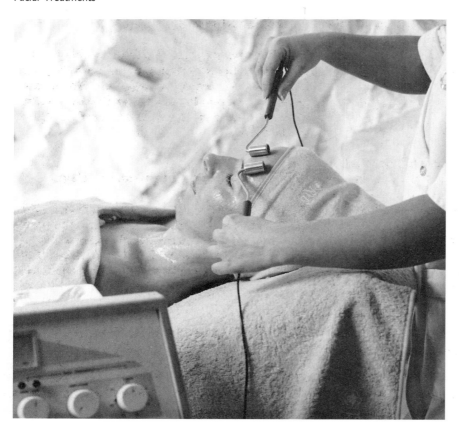

Figure 7.11 *Iontophoresis*
Courtesy Depilex Limited

manufacturers recommend the use of a cleanser to ensure complete removal of the fluid and then wiping over the skin with the appropriate toning lotion.

The polarity of the machine should then be reversed to positive to neutralize the effects of the negative pole, which are all stimulating and the new lint should be evenly soaked in an astringent before applying to the face for half the length of time that desincrustation was performed.

This treatment would actually stimulate the sebaceous glands and produce more sebum if performed too often. Therefore, the treatment should not be repeated within two weeks.

Iontophoresis

This is the passing of active substances through the skin on a galvanic charge. It is normally carried out at the end of a facial and the active elements stay in the skin and continue working after treatment. See Figure 7.11.

The introduction of active substances into the skin by iontophoresis is quicker and more intensive in effect and results in deeper penetration than by manual applications.

The active substances are gradually absorbed into the bloodstream through interchange of blood and tissue fluids. It is not necessary for a galvanic current of high intensity to be used to pass active substances into the skin. All that is necessary are:

○ An uninterrupted flow of current.
○ The electrodes in good contact.
○ The skin evenly moist.

The skin should be thoroughly cleansed and a massage performed, possibly with a cream, which complements the active substances used for iontophoresis.

For this treatment to work efficiently the creams applied to the face must be water soluble (oil-in-water), as a water-in-oil cream will leave an oily film on the skin preventing penetration of the active substances.

Treatment time should take approximately:

3 minutes for one part of the face.
6 minutes for the whole face and neck.

Little time is needed to allow full penetration of the products into the skin. Sensitive skin may require even less time, or to set the machine at the lowest possible intensity, to avoid irritation of the skin.

The polarity used to introduce these substances into the skin should be the same as that indicated by the manufacturer. Normally the positive pole is used as the substances used for iontophoresis are positively charged.

Polarity is normally indicated clearly on the product itself or on the container pack. In the case of a product labelled positive and negative, always begin on negative and reverse the polarity to positive.

The skin should be left free from makeup after iontophoresis for the skin to gain maximum benefit from the treatment.

When to use electrical equipment

Once beauty therapists have learnt to analyse the skin correctly and understand the uses of all available electrical equipment they will instinctively know when to use the machines at the most appropriate time during the facial routine. The following is a simple guide for therapists:

○ Facial steaming.
○ Brush cleansing.
○ Desincrustation.
○ Vacuum suction.

These treatments all reinforce the general cleansing of the skin and prepare it for further treatment. Therefore, they will be used after the deep cleanse. The skin must be totally clean and grease free before application.

Facial faradism

As this treatment may be uncomfortable for the client it should be carried out immediately prior to a relaxing facial massage. The treatment, however, responds more readily to warm relaxed muscles so it can be beneficial to steam the face first.

High frequency – indirect method

This treatment is always performed with the facial massage. The use of the current, combined with manual massage, increases the warmth of the skin tissues by stimulating circulation. The effect also helps the skin absorb the nourishing products being used.

Vibratory massage

This treatment either replaces or reinforces the facial massage and therefore will be performed after the cleanse and other appropriate treatments.

High frequency – direct method

Because this treatment has a bactericidal effect on the skin it is advisable to use it after all other treatments have been carried out. The skin will gain maximum benefit if nothing is applied after the high frequency.

Iontophoresis

This treatment is nourishing and the effects of the positive pole are to:

○ Close the pores.
○ Harden the tissues.
○ Reduce vascularity.
○ Soothe nerve endings.

This treatment should conclude a facial as any further manipulations will only serve to counteract these effects. The client should also be advised not to wear any makeup for at least eight hours after treatment.

MENS

This is a treatment which is often referred to as the 'non-surgical or knifeless facelift', a sometimes misleading term used to advertise an electrical treatment which is rejuvenating to the skin. The initials stand for:

Micro current
Electrical
Neuromuscular
Stimulation

The origins of this treatment are medical with physiotherapists using the current to stimulate soft tissue and muscle damage from injury or illness, for example torn ligaments and Bells palsy. The effects of the MENS current used in healing have been well-documented, with the recovery of the facial profile improving dramatically in six to twelve weeks in Bells palsy sufferers and athletes treated with the MENS current have recovered from ruptured ligaments and tendons in six months instead of the usual eighteen months.

This success led a pioneering doctor to apply the current cosmetically to:

○ Correct sagging muscles.
○ Rejuvenate skin tissues.
○ Refine lines and wrinkles.

The treatment works by using a low frequency micro current which is a thousand times smaller than the current used in conventional electro-therapy equipment. This minute current gently stimulates the area being treated, it is pleasant, relaxing and painless it has no side effects and it is suitable for both men and women of all ages, to treat the face and the body. Micro current equipment will imitate the body's own bio-electrical impulses to stimulate the regenerative processes of the skin and muscle.

Effects of treatment

○ Speeds up the circulation increasing oxygen and nourishment to the area.
○ Speeds up lymphatic flow, draining away toxins leaving skin fresher, clearer and smoother in texture.

○ Speeds up mitotic activity improving cellular regeneration.
○ Speeds up collagen production.
○ Activates, regenerates and rejuvenates the skin and muscles.
○ Flattens deep lines and wrinkles.
○ Reduces a double-chin.
○ Re-educates muscle tone shortening muscle fibres when slack.
○ Lifts the eyebrows and overhanging lids.
○ Lifts the corners of the mouth.
○ Revives the skin's ability to store moisture.

Contraindications

○ Clients who have a pacemaker.
○ Skin diseases.
○ Epilepsy.
○ Metal pins or plates.
○ Pregnancy.
○ Heart disease.
○ Sunburn.
○ Pustular acne.
○ New scar tissue.

Laser therapy

The laser is one of the newest forms of treatment being introduced into salons and, although it is not widely used, it is becoming increasingly more popular and may be found in some beauty salons with many more investigating the potential of this treatment.

The word originates from the initial letters of the phrase:

Light
Amplification
Stimulated
Emission
Radiation

There are many types of laser but all have the ability to produce a very particular type of light energy. The light is highly concentrated with a beam that is capable of travelling in a narrow and precise straight line over enormous distances. The laser however is very versatile because of its ability to produce these beams in different concentrations of frequency and intensity.

Depending upon the effect and intensity of energy required, any part of the light spectrum can be used, from the blue–green high intensity beam of the argon laser, to the invisible white and red cool beams of the gallium arsenide and helium neon lasers. The former is used in medicine to cauterize blood vessels, responsible for producing a bleeding stomach ulcer, for example. The latter is used in many beauty salons to rejuvenate the skin, smooth wrinkles, firm sagging facial muscles and reduce stretch marks.

Those used for medical and dermatological reasons can be hot or cold, some with deep penetration and others which bathe the surface of the skin with a gentle light. The four main types used in clinics and hospitals are:

1   The argon laser.
2   The ruby laser.
3   The carbon dioxide laser.
4   The helium neon laser.

The argon laser

This produces a blue–green light which causes a reaction in red objects only and is used in the treatment of port wine stains and dilated blood vessels. The beam coagulates the blood vessels under the skin leaving the area lighter in colour.

The blue–green beam can be passed through the clear cornea, lens and vitreous humor of the eye without causing any damage but it is absorbed by the pigmented retina allowing eye surgeons to treat detached retinas in less than two milliseconds.

The ruby laser

This laser has a pure red light and is absorbed by tissues which contain pigment, leading to its use in destroying melanomas and also to remove port wine stains.

The carbon dioxide (CO_2) laser

This can be finely tuned to produce either a powerful beam capable of penetrating almost anything in its path or a low-powered beam that merely pricks the surface of the skin. The low-powered version is used to remove tatoos, warts and skin tags.

This beam is invisible so helium is incorporated into the laser tube to produce a red beam that will guide the operator.

The helium neon (cold beam) laser

This is the laser used by beauty therapists because it has a very gentle beam of low wattage which will not burn or vaporize tissue. The light excites the cells on which it is directed thus stimulating them electrically and biochemically, minimizing fine lines, stimulating muscles and improving skin tone.

How the laser works in facial treatment

A mixture of gases, usually helium and neon, are placed in a tube, through which a light source which has been energized by an alternating current is passed. The light rays then bombard the molecules of gas, further radiation is produced and added to the existing light producing an intense beam of light.

This laser beam is passed through a fibre optics cable to an applicator head which is then placed over the facial acupuncture points one at a time and circulation to the whole face is increased.

Effects of treatment

Heat is transferred to the skin tissues and therefore has a soothing effect. The blood supply is stimulated which encourages the acceleration of tissue repair improving skin texture.

An increase in cell activity helps the synthesis of collagen and elastin, improving elasticity. The skin is revitalized and brightened.

It is said that these combined effects reduce lines and improve muscle tone. For maximum effect a course of ten to fifteen treatments is recommended. For example:

Three treatments per week for two weeks.

79

Two treatments per week for two weeks.
One treatment per week for two weeks.

Each treatment should not last more than 25 minutes.

Precautions

Laser therapy should always be applied in an enclosed area.

Any equipment in the immediate area with a reflective surface should be removed or covered.

A permanent sign should be placed on the door of the treatment room to advise that a laser is in operation.

Clients should not be left alone with the equipment.

Special matt black goggles supplied with the laser must always be worn during treatment. No other goggles will do because those provided have been specially treated to prevent exposure to the beam.

Glasses are also supplied for the operator and must be worn during treatment.

Eye contact with the beam must be avoided at all costs.

Use of the laser machine must be restricted to those specially trained in its use.

All staff must be aware of the dangers of laser equipment and to avoid any interruption during laser treatment.

Equipment must be locked away when not in use to prevent unauthorized use.

A record of treatment must be kept for each client.

Contraindications

○   Infectious skin disorders.
○   Infectious eye disorders.
○   Heart or blood pressure problems.
○   During pregnancy.
○   On the thyroid gland area.

8 *Makeup application and uses*

Most facial treatments carried out in a salon require that makeup should not be worn for several hours or more afterwards to allow the skin to benefit from the effects of the treatment.

The separate application of makeup, therefore, is a service offered in all salons and makeup lessons have proved to be a very popular addition to the treatments offered by salons.

Makeup is required for different reasons:

o Wedding makeup.
o Camouflage makeup.
o Makeup lessons.
o Photographic makeup.
o Evening makeup.
o Demonstrations.

To offer this service therapists must have:

1 A large mirror.
2 Lighting above and on the sides of the mirror.
3 A comfortable and adjustable chair.
4 An attractive and well-stocked makeup display.
5 A set of makeup brushes.
6 Cosmetic sponges.
7 Tissues.
8 Cotton wool.
9 Tweezers.
10 Headband.
11 Makeup palette.

Makeup brushes

Brushes made from natural hair are the most attractive and they last much longer, maintain their shape and provide easy application. The most commonly used brushes are sable, pony, squirrel and goat. They come individually or as sets and are usually presented in a wallet or pouch with compartments for each brush. This will protect the brushes and keep them clean if they are being carried around but when in constant use an upright container is more convenient to use.

Types of brushes

Powder brush
This is the largest brush in the set. Very full and round in shape, it is used for the application and removal of loose powder.

Blusher brush
Half the size or less of the powder brush and slightly more flat in shape, it is more flexible, allowing the therapist to apply the blusher evenly and in the correct position.

Contour brush
The contour brush is similar in shape to the blusher brush but the end is straight and it is used for shaping the face and blending the blushers and shaders.

Eyeliner brush
This is the smallest brush with a fine tapered end. It is made from a natural hair such as sable so that it holds the point well, allowing the finest of lines to be drawn around the eye.

Concealer brush
This is shaped like a very small flat paintbrush and is very useful when concealing blemishes or areas of pigmentation and blending eyeliners to soften the line.

Angled eyeshadow brush
This brush is similar in shape to the concealer brush but with the tip cut off at an angle. This is to allow the greatest control over the placement of eyeshadow on the lids and in the socket area.

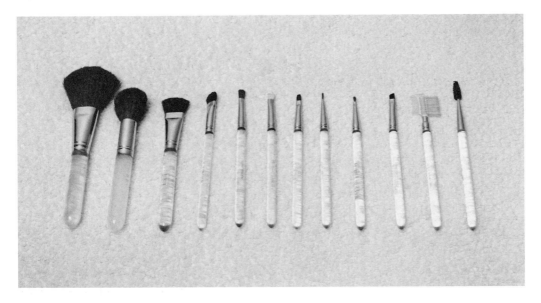

Figure 8.1 *Set of makeup brushes*

Eyeshadow brush

This is a tiny version of the blusher brush and is most useful for blending eyeshadows or allowing a very light application of colour.

Eyeshadow sponge

Using a sponge applicator gives more coverage and depth of colour, is ideal for blending and applies the eyeshadow more cleanly than a brush, which if very soft sometimes flicks the eyeshadow on the surrounding area.

Eyebrow brush

Looks like a very thin toothbrush and is used to remove any trace of powder in the eyebrow, as well as brushing them into shape.

Lipstick brush

This is a small, flat fairly stiff brush with a straight edge, used to outline the lips or correct their shape, as well as applying the colour for a lasting effect.

See Figure 8.1.

Care of makeup brushes

They must be washed regularly in a mild detergent or in alcohol if they are made from natural hair. To dry they should be laid flat and if possible left with the air circulating around them.

Other makeup items required

In addition to brushes, therapists need the following essential items:

- ○ Cosmetic sponges for applying foundation and other cream products.
- ○ Tissues for protecting the face when applying eye makeup and lipstick.
- ○ A makeup palette to mix and blend colours, for example foundations and lipsticks.
- ○ Tweezers to remove any stray eyebrows which would spoil the eyeshadow application.
- ○ A pencil sharpener, preferably a special one used for makeup pencils which are very soft and quite often larger or smaller in size then a normal pencil.

Reasons for use of makeup

1 It provides protection from the elements. Worn in cold weather it is a barrier which

will help prevent loss of moisture. In the summer there are products which provide protection against the harmful effects of ultraviolet light.

2　Makeup highlights good features and masks imperfections.
3　Birthmarks or other pigmentary disorders can be camouflaged with skilfully applied makeup.
4　In certain cases it can be used to improve looks.
5　To change an image.
6　To follow fashion.
7　For special occasions when something a little out of the ordinary is required.

Selection of makeup

No two makeups are ever the same; each one is personal to the individual so before selection there are various points which must be considered:

o　Skin type.
o　Skin colour.
o　Skin texture.
o　Blemishes on the skin.
o　Bone structure.
o　Face shape.
o　Age of the client.
o　Personality of the client.
o　What they will be wearing.
o　The occasion.
o　Under what lighting conditions the makeup will be worn.

Decisions may then be made about the type of makeup to be used, the amount of corrective work to be undertaken and the colours to be applied.

Everything should be placed close to hand and stored neatly with each item easily accessible – preferably in a special makeup box which has adequate sized compartments.

Application of makeup

The skin must be thoroughly cleansed and toned before applying moisturizer. It should then be rested for about five minutes to allow the skin to absorb the moisturizer and then the excess moisturizer blotted with a tissue. When foundation is applied immediately over moisturizer some of it will be absorbed into the skin and may cause a blotchy effect.

Order of work

1　*Colour correction.* The products for this are similar in texture to a moisturizer and come in two shades:
　　–*green* to tone down a highly coloured area caused by sensitivity or dilated capillaries.
　　–*purple* to brighten a sallow skin.
2　*Concealer.* To cover blemishes or areas of uneven pigmentation often found around the eyes and lips and any other shadows on the face.
3　*Foundation.* To even out skin texture and colour and to provide a base for the rest of the makeup.
4　*Cream or gel blushers and shaders.* Cream products must always be applied before any powder product is used.
5　*Cream eye makeup.*
6　*Loose powder.* To set the makeup already applied and to provide an ideal base for the powder products still to be used.
7　*Powder blushers and shaders, powder eyeshadows.*
8　*Mascara.*
9　*Eyebrow pencil.*
10　*Lip pencil, lipstick or lipgloss.*

Makeup products

Concealer

This is often an essential item required for covering imperfections and it is important to choose the right shade, texture and formulation for a natural look. When concealing a spot the aim is to find a concealer which will hide it, dry it out and stay in place. A good product combined with a good application technique will ensure the flaw does not look worse after application than before.

Some concealers are more than just camouflage, they contain ingredients that help to heal blemishes such as salicyclic acid, which are waterproof, or provide a sunfilter. They are now available in different shades to match skin tone and in a variety of formulations:

o Stick or pot concealers offer the greatest coverage because they are thicker and contain more pigment.
o Tubes, wands and pens are less opaque, lighter in texture and easier to blend which makes them more suitable for clients who do not wear very much makeup or a tinted moisturizer.

When choosing a concealer, apply it along the jawline and look at it in natural light to make sure that it is a good match for the skin tone. Concealer may be applied in several ways:

o Wedge-shaped sponges may be used to evenly conceal dark under eye circles. Too much concealer can make the skin look crepey and it is best to use a creamy formula that is not too matt to cake on dry skin and not too greasy to slide off the skin. Using a moisturizer first will make the application easier and prevents the concealer settling in the fine lines around the eyes.
o A cotton bud or washable applicator is more hygienic than using fingers and both are ideal for applying over a tiny blemish or spot.
o A small firm bristled brush is ideal for camouflaging small scars and thread veins.

Set the concealer with a yellow-based pressed powder as pink tones emphasize redness and this will also guarantee a longer lasting cover.

Foundations

The main purpose of foundation is to even out the skin's texture and colour and to cover minor imperfections. Today, the colour range is extensive from flat white to the deepest mahogany but colour should always match the skin tone. They come in several forms.

Liquids
These provide only a light protective film as they have a high percentage of water and a low percentage of oil. Because of the low percentage of oil they are suitable for a greasy skin but not a blemished skin as they do not provide adequate cover.

Gels
Basically these are liquids with special gelling agents added. The purpose of a gel foundation is to give a natural tanned look to the skin and they are most effective on a clear skin.

Creams
These are thicker and heavier with a higher oil content which makes them more suitable for a drier skin type. They are usually waterproof and give extra protection to dry skins, particularly in the winter.

Cream mousse
These are suitable for most skin types and are very popular because they are light in texture and give a good cover without feeling heavy on the face. They normally come in an aerosol can.

All-in-one foundation
These are made from a mixture of cream and powder and require a damp sponge for application because they can be difficult to apply. They are not suitable, therefore, on a dry or sensitive skin.

Block foundation
These consist of an emulsion of fats and waxes in water with plasticizing agents and pigments compressed into a solid cake form. They provide excellent cover for a discoloured or blemished skin but they can dry it out and therefore are not suitable to use on a dry skin.

To apply any foundation successfully, a damp sponge should be used to give a natural look and to help blend it in around the hairline. A dry sponge will give a heavier coverage when this is required (Figure 8.2). Foundation should also be applied to the eyes and lips to provide a base for longer lasting eyeshadow and lipstick. If, however, the foundation feels too heavy on the eyelids a special eyeshadow base may be used to prevent creasing of the eyeshadow during the day.

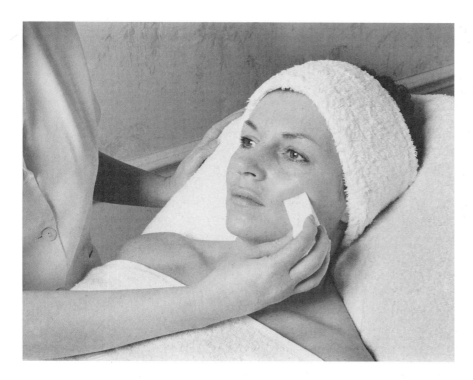

Figure 8.2 *Application of foundation*

Contour cosmetics

These cosmetics are used to accentuate and enhance good features or to minimize not so good features! They consist of the following:

Blushers which add warmth and shape to the cheeks.
Shaders which are darker than the foundation and are used to shape the face.
Highlighters which are lighter than the foundation and are used to accentuate good features.

As with foundation they are available in several forms:

Creams which will add moisture as well as colour and are used over the foundation but before the face powder.
Powders which are always applied after the face powder.
Gels which are transparent for a natural look, applied over foundation but never covered with face powder.
Sticks are solid creams and are applied over foundation but need to be well blended.

Points to remember
The following points are useful tips:

○ Light colours will highlight a feature.
○ Dark colours recede or fade out.
○ Bright colours attract attention.
○ Always blend blushers upwards and outwards and never apply too near the eyes or nose.
○ Never overdo the use of contours as the effect should be natural for normal use.

Shaders
Areas for correction with shaders are:

○ A square jawline.
○ A double chin.
○ A wide nose.
○ Below the cheekbone to create a hollow.

Highlighters
Highlighters can erase deep lines such as the nasolabial folds. Used above the cheekbones it will emphasize good bone structure and used on the eyes it will highlight and draw attention to them.

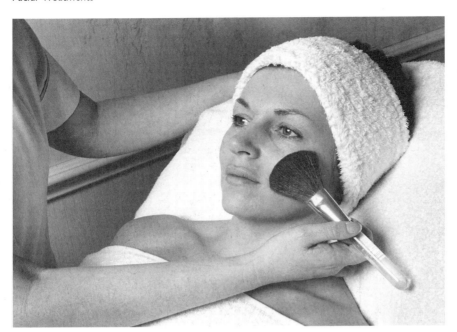

Figure 8.3 *Application of face powder*

Blushers

Blusher gives the face a healthy glow if applied correctly: it draws attention to the eyes and emphasizes good bone structure. For those with colour already in the cheeks, blusher evens out the natural skin tones.

A good selection of colours should be available, and blusher can be matched up to clothes and makeup and not just the skin tone.

The finish on a blusher can be matt (suitable for day wear) or slightly sparkled (suitable for evening makeup).

Blushers come in the same forms as foundation:

○ Powder.
○ Cream.
○ Gel.
○ Liquid.
○ Mousse.

The same principle applies when applying the blusher. Creams, liquids and gels are applied before the face powder and the powder blusher applied afterwards.

Face powder

Face powder is essential to help set the makeup, keeping it fresh looking all day and providing a surface suitable for powder blushers and shaders, which if placed directly onto foundation would go streaky. It also removes the shiny appearance leaving a matt finish and a smooth complexion.

Probably the best powder to use is a translucent one. Translucent powder is always used by makeup artists because it is semi-transparent and allows the light to shine through. Coloured powder tends to give the face an unnatural or heavily made up look and often they change colour when oils are absorbed from the skin. See Figure 8.3.

Face powder comes in two forms:

1 Loose.
2 Pressed.

Loose powder

This usually comes in a large container with a removable lid. There are also smaller containers rather like talcum powder shakers which enable the therapist to dispense the face powder more economically. For professional use the larger container if used economically and hygienically is more appropriate and the smaller shaker is suitable to be carried around without fear of spillage.

Figure 8.4 *Application of eyeshadow*

Pressed powder

This is the traditional face powder which comes in a compact with a powder puff, carried easily in a handbag or pocket and may be used to touch up the makeup or remove shine during the day. This type of powder does have its drawbacks. The powder puff needs to be washed frequently because the oils from the face will be transferred onto the pressed powder after each use causing the surface of the powder to harden. Bacteria may also be transferred to the powder so it is advisable, therefore, to use small disposable cotton wool pads to apply the powder and then discard them for a fresh one.

Matt powder is ideal for everyday use, but for a special effect irridescent powder may be used for an evening makeup, with touches of silver or gold in it.

Properties of face powder
○ The main constituent of powder is talc.
○ The irridescent or glittery effect is produced by adding fine aluminium powder, guanine or mica coated with titanium dioxide.
○ Zinc oxide is incorporated to mask blemishes.
○ Magnesium stearate determines the cling of the powder and the degree to which it is waterproof.

○ Magnesium carbonate contributes to the smoothness of the powder and absorbs any perfume added.

Eyeshadow

The skilful use of eye makeup draws attention to one of the best facial features. It can enhance already beautiful eyes and it can make quite ordinary eyes look glamorous. Eyeshadow adds colour and dimension and comes in several forms:

○ *Cream*: Oil-based, it spreads easily and blends well but it needs to be set with powder as it tends to crease.
○ *Powders*: Compressed powder with added moisture to provide cling, its staying power is good but it may feel taut on very dry skins.
○ *Gels*: They are easy to apply but add gloss rather than depth of colour so may require several coats to obtain a good colour.
○ *Water colours*: A cake eyeshadow applied with a wet brush to give a long lasting finish, with a depth of colour stronger than powder.
○ *Crayons and pencils*: Soft wax pencils which are easy to apply without dragging but need to be blended well (Figure 8.4).

Eyeliner

Eyeliner is used for defining the eye shape and making the eyelashes look longer. There are many colours available in the form of a pencil to complement the colour of the eyeshadow but a colour to match the natural hair colour can be more complementary. Eyeliner may be applied in different ways:

○ Liquid which is oil-based in water and applied with a fine sable brush.
○ Cakes or blocks of water colour powder applied with a fine dampened brush and easier to control than the liquid.
○ Crayon or pencil which is a wax stick and easier to use when it is kept sharp.

Eyebrow pencil

This is a wax crayon but of a harder consistency to define eyebrows when necessary. Colours should always blend with the natural colour of the eyebrow and the hair colour. An eyebrow powder may be used instead if the effect of the pencil is too harsh.

False eyelashes

The application of false eyelashes is a procedure which goes in and out of fashion with many people but the application of makeup will sometimes include using false eyelashes to enhance the finished result. They may be used:

○ For photographic makeup.
○ For glamour makeup.
○ For catwalk modelling.
○ For theatre and film.
○ To thicken sparse eyelashes.
○ To add length to short lashes.
○ To add curl to straight eyelashes.
○ To follow fashion.
○ At the client's request.

There are two types of false eyelashes – temporary strip lashes and semi-permanent individual lashes. The modern false eyelashes are made from synthetic fibres which hold a permanent curl and they vary from very realis- tic lightweight lashes to very thick, dark, heavier lashes.

Contraindications

○ Eye disorders such as styes, bruises, swellings, eczema, psoriasis and conjunctivi- tis.
○ Watery eyes.
○ Sensitive eyes.
○ Cuts and abrasions.
○ Hay fever.
○ Allergy to adhesive. A skin test must be performed twenty-four hours before applica- tion of the lashes. A small amount of adhesive should be applied in an unobtru- sive spot and covered. Watch for a reaction. If there is an allergy to the glue the skin may become red, itchy or inflamed.

Individual lashes

For a more natural effect, individual lashes are more appropriate. They may be single or in groups of varying lengths and may be trimmed to suit the client. They are applied directly to the lashes using a semi-permanent glue to maintain their appearance but they do have to be replaced as they fall off. They will become detached through rough handling, by using an oily eye makeup remover or they will fall out when the natural lash to which they are attached falls out. Because the glue is stronger in effect than that used for strip lashes, great care must be taken with its application so that none of the glue enters the eye.

Temporary strip lashes

Strip lashes will appear heavier and quite long but some strips are fairly sparse or trimmed very effectively to look as natural as possible. To achieve a more natural effect the length of strip can be trimmed, the lashes can be thinned out or reduced in length. Always trim the outside longer edge of the strip to fit the client's eye, never the inner corner or you will distort the natural shape.

Figure 8.5 *Application of mascara*

Safety precautions

○ Check clients for contraindications.
○ Carry out a patch test particularly if clients have sensitive eyes.
○ Sit clients in a comfortable semi-reclining position.
○ Remove all traces of eye makeup and grease.
○ Use tweezers to hold the false lashes.
○ Do not apply glue directly on to the eye, apply to the false lash first.
○ Use the minimum amount of glue to apply the lashes.
○ Have a sterile eye bath ready to bathe the eye if glue gets into it.
○ Use a special eyelash solvent for removing the semi-permanent lashes.
○ Recommend a special cleanser for the client to use at home to clean the eyes to prevent removing the semi-permanent lashes.

Mascara

The purpose of mascara is to colour, lengthen and thicken eyelashes. See Figure 8.5. A good mascara ideally should be:

○ Easy to apply.
○ Runproof.
○ Waterproof.
○ Long lasting.
○ Hypoallergenic.
○ Lash thickening.

There are different types on the market all with different qualities.

The *block* is the oldest and most economical variety of mascara and although not as popular as the more convenient wand with a brush, it is still in use and it has to be applied with a wet brush.

The *cream* mascara is applied and removed easily but is not runproof or waterproof.

The *automatic liquid mascara* is probably the most popular having most of the ideal qualities required from a mascara. It is easy to apply and contains filaments to thicken and lengthen lashes, it is long lasting and given the correct cleanser is easy to remove. However, it is not always runproof and waterproof. There are some on the market with these qualities but they are often resistant to cleansing and can be difficult to remove.

Lipsticks

The purpose of a lipstick is to add balance and colour to the face. They come in several forms:

1 Conventional stick which provides excellent coverage.
2 A tube with a sponge applicator which provides a creamy and glossy finish.
3 Crayons and pencils which are excellent for outlining the lips and providing a longer lasting matt colour. They are made with harder wax and less oil than a lipstick.
4 Colour or gloss in a pot which adds sheer colour to the lips or gloss over a lipstick.

There are many requirements for an ideal lipstick which makes a good one hard to produce and these are:

o They should be easy to apply providing an even coverage.
o They must adhere well to the lips.
o The colour should not change once applied.
o Their appearance should be attractive.
o They should feel and taste pleasant.
o The physical properties of the lipstick should not change.
o The texture should be firm but not brittle and they must not bend during use.

See Figures 8.6 and 8.7.

Making a lipstick
This is a two-stage process where all the ingredients are blended into a base and the mixture is then moulded into sticks. The ingredients consist of a mixture of fats, waxes and oils.

The waxes encourage the lipstick to set and allow it to be formed into a stick. The more wax that is used the harder the lipstick will be but too much wax will make it difficult to apply.

The oils moisturize, lubricate and soften the lips but the balance must be right to prevent the lipstick from becoming too greasy.

Waxes most commonly used are *carnauba* from Brazilian palm trees, *gandelilla* from plants grown in Mexico and *beeswax*.

Oils most commonly used are *castor oil*, used in more expensive lipsticks, and *mineral oil*.

Other ingredients are then added to this base:

Emollients for soothing and softening are added so that lipsticks can then be sold as 'lipcare' rather than just as a cosmetic product. These include almond oil, wheatgerm oil and more recently a sun filter for protection against UV rays.

Colour in the form of dyes and pigments which must be safe to use as they are being applied to the lips.

Pigments are much more difficult to add to the base as they are insoluble and they have to be ground into a paste first. Because they add colour without actually dyeing the skin they come off with the lipstick. Natural organic pigments are used to produce the bright shades of pink, red and orange. For a frosted finish, tiny particles coated with the light reflecting titanium dioxide are added.

Dyes are used less frequently than pigments. They are soluble and therefore mix more easily with the base. They also give a longer lasting effect but are more likely to cause an allergic reaction.

Perfumes are added to some lipsticks in the form of essential oils with light floral scents.

When the extra ingredients have been added to the base the mixture is heated and any air trapped in the mixture rises to the surface preventing the formation of unsightly bubbles. The finished product is then poured into stainless steel moulds to harden and then tested for consistency and texture before being packaged.

Problems with lipsticks
Bleeding of the lips. This occurs when the lipstick is applied and it spreads outwards causing an unsightly messy outline. This happens when:

1 The formula is very creamy and glossy and even normal body temperature causes it to melt slightly.
2 Fine vertical lines are present around the lips and they allow the lipstick to seep into them. This problem can be rectified by applying foundation and powder to the lips and outlining them with a pencil before applying the lipstick.

The lipstick changes colour. This happens particularly with the darker shades and the blue tones in the lipstick are emphasized. To prevent this happening the lips can be prepared as detailed above with the foundation creating a barrier between the lips and the lipstick.

Figure 8.6 *Drawing a lip line*

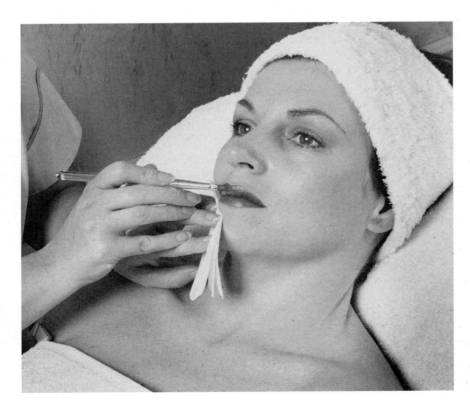

Figure 8.7 *Application of lipstick*

Alternatively a white cream fixative can be applied.

Lipstick drying the lips. This is usally caused by the use of frosted shades or an overuse of fillers and binders in the ingredients. Avoid using frosted shades and moisturize the lips well, particularly in the winter.

Contraindications to makeup

○ Anyone with an allergy to makeup.
○ Any skin diseases.
○ A client with recent scar tissue.
○ Cuts or grazes on the skin.
○ Pustular acne.
○ Immediately after electrolysis.
○ Temporary disorders, for example, herpes simplex or conjunctivitis.
○ An excessively dry skin should contraindicate face powder.
○ Excessive facial hair but eyes and lips may be made up.

Corrective makeup

This is sometimes necessary to disguise prominent features or to cover blemishes on the skin and creams, powders or different shades of foundation may be used.

Facial contouring is used for correcting face shapes and the principle of most corrective work is that dark colours recede and light colours accentuate.

Common faults

Florid complexion
This can be a general redness of the skin or an abundance of dilated arterioles. To counteract this problem a green moisturizer may be applied to the area before applying a beige foundation.

Sallow complexion
This often accompanies a greasy skin or is a characteristic of certain ethnic skins. This type of complexion can be improved and brightened by applying a purple-tinted moisturizer underneath the foundation.

Dark circles under the eyes
These may be successfully disguised by using a white masking cream sparingly over the darker areas or a lighter shade of foundation.

Puffy eyes
These cause a crease underneath the 'bags' caused by the puffy tissue, which may be disguised by using a lighter shade of foundation in the crease. A darker shade of foundation should be applied to the puffy areas to diminish their size.

Protruding eyes
Dark shadow should be applied all over the lid and highlighter on the browbones, for example a plum colour on the upper lid and a pale pink on the browbone.

Deep set eyes
Use light coloured shadows all over the lid to accentuate the eyes and a slightly darker shade may be applied to the extreme outer corner blending upwards and outwards.

Wide apart eyes
To draw them together a darker shade of eyeshadow must be applied to the inner part of the eye and lighter shades used on the outer part.

Close set eyes
The eyes can look smaller because they are close together, so apply lots of highlighter to the inner corners next to the nose and then other colours applied upwards and outwards.

Nose shapes

Wide nose
It will appear narrower if shader is applied to the sides.

Long nose
This will appear shorter if shader is applied to the tip and highlighter to the sides.

Short nose
Highlight down the centre of the nose to the tip to make it appear longer.

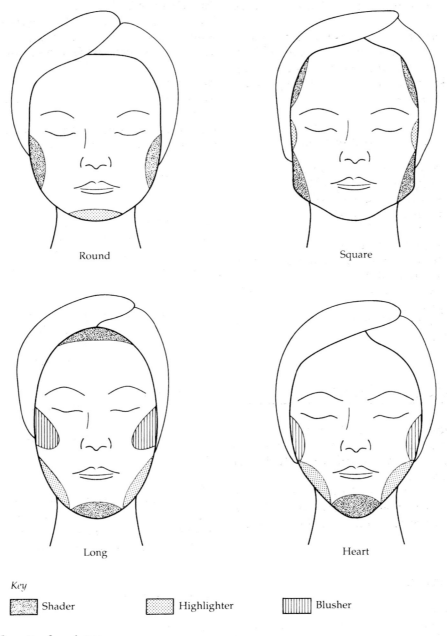

Round

Square

Long

Heart

Key

Shader

Highlighter

Blusher

Figure 8.8 *Corrective face shapes*

Nasolabial folds

These are deep creases which run from the nose down to the corners of the mouth. A lighter shade of foundation may be applied using a fine brush and then blended into the foundation to remove harsh lines.

Face shapes

See Figures 8.8 and 8.9

Round face

The cheeks are full and rounded, so a darker shade of foundation could be applied to the

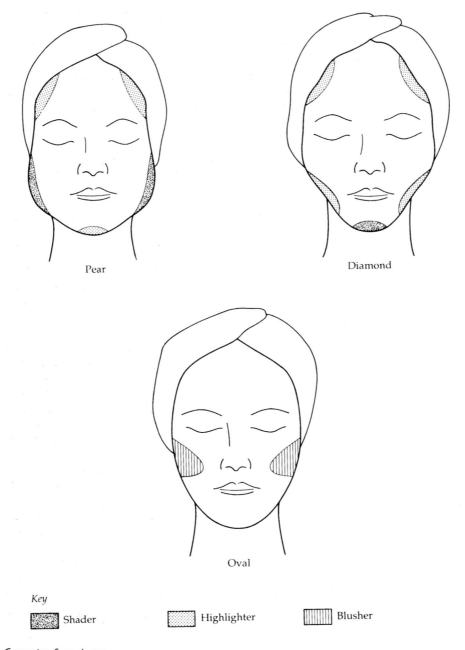

Key

Shader   Highlighter   Blusher

Figure 8.9 *Corrective face shapes*

outer edges of the lower half of the face to achieve a slimming effect and highlight applied to the chin to increase the overall length.

Square face

This shape has a broad forehead with a square jawline. Therefore, the sides of the forehead and the angles of the jaw should be shaded to soften

the angular shape and the outer part of the cheekbone highlighted to emphasize the centre of the face.

Long face

The top half of the forehead and the chin should be shaded to reduce the length of the face and the cheeks should be highlighted to create width.

Heart-shaped face

This shape is wide at the forehead and narrowing to a point at the chin. Width is needed at the cheeks and the jawline and this may be achieved by applying blusher on the cheek area and highlighting underneath at the angle of the jaw. A small amount of shader may be applied to the point of the chin.

Diamond-shaped face

This face shape has a narrow forehead and chin with wide cheekbones. The width is increased at either side of the forehead and at the angles of the jaw by applying highlighter. The point of the chin can be shaded to reduce the length.

Pear-shaped face

This face shape has a narrow forehead and a wide jawline. The forehead must be highlighted at either side to create width and the angle of the jaw must be diminished by using a small amount of shader.

Lip shapes

The problems which occur are:

○ Both lips too thin.
○ Either upper or lower lip too thin.
○ Large full lips.
○ Very small mouth.
○ Drooping mouth.
○ Asymmetrical mouth or one side smaller than the other.

Whatever the problem, it is advisable to block out the shape as much as possible with foundation and powder before applying the lipstick. Lip liners can then be used to draw in the correct shape, either just inside the natural lip line to reduce the size, or just outside the natural lip line to increase the size.

Highlighter may be applied in the cupid's bow to accentuate the lips and gloss applied over the lipstick will also highlight the mouth.

Clients who wear glasses

There are two problems which occur when clients wear glasses and they are caused by the type of lens used. For long sight the lens will make the eye more prominent so it will be necessary, therefore, to use neutral shades and avoid bright or pearly type eyeshadows.

For short sight the lens will make the eye seem smaller. To combat this light colours should be used to accentuate the eyes.

Evening makeup

When applying makeup for the evening therapists have the opportunity to apply all their artistic talents to the full. The normal everyday makeup can be adapted as follows:

○ Foundation can be lighter or darker than the normal skin colour and can be applied a little more heavily if required to create a flawless finish.
○ Face powder can have added sparkle but must not be used all over the face, just along the cheekbones to highlight them.
○ Contour cosmetics can be used with more definition, particularly under the cheekbones to create a hollow and emphasize bone structure.
○ Eyeshadows can be very bright with lots of shine and glitter, using several shades, blended together for maximum effect.
○ Eyeliners can be used more boldly and kohl pencil applied to the inside of the eye in a colour to complement the eyeshadow. Mascara may be applied in the bright shades of green, blue or violet to match eyeshadows.
○ False eyelashes can be applied either in strips, or individually to make the natural lashes appear longer and thicker.
○ Vivid shades of lipstick, with silver or gold frosting, applied to the lips in the centre will create a pouting effect, or a highlighter painted in a thin line above the cupid's bow emphasizes the shape. Gloss may be used for a gleaming finish but too much may cause it to smear.

Lighting

When applying an evening makeup a clear white light should be used and it is important to bear in mind the effects that different lighting will have on the makeup.

Lighting varies from very dark with disco lighting to very dark and candlelit, or just different coloured lights.

Pink light causes the makeup colours to look warmer, so the deeper pink shades of blusher may look red. Therefore, use a slightly lighter pink or tawny shade which contains no red. Pink light will also dull green and blue eyeshadows so if these colours are to be used try the type with added sparkle or highlight the centre of the lid over the eyeshadow.

Red light alters makeup colour drastically, particularly the yellow, gold and tawny hues which will look very much deeper. It also causes the blusher to fade away.

Rose light is flattering to all skins and will enhance any makeup.

Blue light turns makeup grey. It is a very hard colour and makes blusher or shaders look much deeper than they really are, so a lighter touch is advisable.

Black skin and makeup

There are several points to be considered when making up a black skin and the most important one is the number of different shades that there are. Black skin encompasses Afro Caribbean, Oriental, Asian and Arabic which can vary in tone from a pale brown to a deep ebony colour.

The pigmentation on the face may also be different, often darker around the eyes and lighter on the forehead. The darker the skin is, the more melanin it contains and therefore the more protection it receives from ultraviolet radiation. This will delay the ageing effect that exposure to UV radiation has on the skin.

The skin is also much oilier as there are many more sebaceous glands present. However it may still dry out when exposed to the elements and if not properly looked after and thus it may also be a combination skin.

Application of makeup

To begin with, a water-based moisturizer must be used to combat any oiliness and prepare the skin for further application.

There are now several ranges of makeup which have been developed for black skins and the colour range of foundations will suit most shades of skin. The consistency of the foundation is also important. Gels are ideal to enhance a good colour without too much cover. The foundations which provide cover contain products such as titanium dioxide which when applied to a very dark skin will have an ashy effect.

Face powder should be transparent and used very sparsely as it can dull the skin.

Blushers and shaders may be used in cream, gel or powder form and in shades strong enough to be seen and tone well with the foundation, eyeshadows and lipstick.

Eyeshadows which are more intense in colour are better as paler colours can look washed out.

Choice of colours should be selected in the normal way, in consultation with clients to suit their age, the occasion, the clothes they will be wearing and the therapist's expert advice.

Bridal makeup

Bridal packages are very popular with young and old alike, it is an occasion when even those who do not normally have beauty treatments will consider such treatments as manicure, pedicure, eyelash tinting, waxing and makeup.

It is important to ensure the finished result is suitable for clients and they are happy with the makeup as there will be photographic and video evidence to mark the occasion. There are several considerations to be made when booking a bridal makeup:

1 Discuss the requirements with the bride well in advance.
2 The time and location of the appointment must be arranged to fit in with your other clients and the bride's wishes. It also allows the bride to have her appointment at home if she wishes.
3 Consider the dress – colour, fabric and neckline. It may be necessary to use a self-tanning cream one or two days before the wedding if the neckline is low or cut out. Makeup colours should complement the dress and the bridal flowers, as well as enhancing the bride's best features.

4 It is advisable to have a trial run before the wedding. Any problems can be ironed out and changes made if necessary. This is most important if the client does not normally wear makeup or if she has requested something rather unusual which needs to be tried out first.

5 Discuss the cost and include the trial run and additional charge for a home visit.

6 Discuss any other makeup that may be required such as the bride's mother, brides-maids or other relatives. Extra time or extra therapists may be required.

The normal considerations for the application of makeup must be taken into account:

o Age.
o Face shape.
o Skin type.
o Client preference.

And:

o The dress.
o Hair style.
o Head-dress.
o Colour scheme.
o The length of time the makeup must last.
o Ensure that the client has purchased any makeup required for freshening up during the day.

In general, choose colours which suit the client's colouring and co-ordinate well with the overall colour scheme.

Use subtle shading techniques to highlight good features and detract from bad ones.

Use matt shades on the eyes and for the blusher. Pearly colours look hard and will reflect in photographs.

Apply lipstick, blot, then powder and re-apply for a longer lasting effect or apply a lip pencil in the same shade as the lipstick as the first coat and then cover with a coat of lipstick or gloss.

Powder should be applied lightly and then set with a fine mist of mineral water to set and prolong the makeup.

Use a waterproof mascara as the occasion can be very emotional for some brides.

For a very subtle effect, one shade of blusher can be used on the cheeks, on the eyes and on the lips, with a hint of gloss. This is a very natural effect ideal for the younger bride with a flawless complexion.

Semi-permanent makeup

This is a new treatment which is now being offered by many salons to correct problems and enhance looks. The procedure is known as micropigmentation and small amounts of natural pigment are placed into the skin using techniques that are more refined than tattooing and do not penetrate the skin as deeply.

The cosmetic procedures that are available are:

o Lip liner.
o Full lip colour.
o Eyebrows.
o Eyelash enhancement.
o Eyeliner.
o Beauty spots.

The corrective procedures available are:

o Areola restoration.
o Camouflage of scars, burns, cleft lip, alopecia and restoration of hairline after cosmetic surgery.

It offers effective results for those people who do not want to or cannot apply makeup on a daily basis and it may be applied to the young or old. Micropigmentation is a treatment which will benefit many people and for many reasons:

o Those people with a very busy lifestyle who would prefer not to spend time applying makeup.
o People who are allergic to conventional makeup.
o Some physical disabilities may prevent the application of makeup unless assistance is available.
o For the correction of asymmetrical features such as uneven lips.
o Partially sighted people who find it difficult to apply makeup.
o Those who wear glasses.
o Those who have an unsteady hand and wish to create a soft line around the eyes.

○ Skin disorders such as uneven pigmentation or other flaws in the skin.
○ To camouflage minor disfigurements.
○ People who live in a hot climate.
○ Sportspeople.

This treatment will last between one and three years, depending on the client's skin type and age. The colour will fade gradually over that period of time.

A topical anaesthetic cream is usually applied before treatment to minimize discomfort and the sensation the client feels should be no worse than that felt with electrolysis.

Precautions

○ Specialist training is required in these procedures.
○ Work must be carried out under sterile conditions.
○ Disposable needles must be used.
○ Machine tips that come into direct contact with the skin must be discarded after one use.
○ The local borough council must be contacted when this service is to be introduced to ensure that you are licensed to carry out the treatment.
○ Client consultation is important and a skin test will be required on the client before treatment.
○ High quality colours must be used. The ingredients are titanium oxides, alcohol, glycerine and distilled water. They are put through a process which makes them safe and remain true in colour.

This treatment is not regulated by any official body but is being investigated at the moment. Some suppliers have indicated that one outcome could be that certain areas such as the eyes may only be treated under medial supervision. Legislation is considered necessary as the procedure is similar to tattooing and thought to carry the same health risks. Standards in hygiene should be similar to the recommendations applied to tattooing:

○ The area being treated should be thoroughly cleansed first and dressed afterwards.

○ Every client should have a separate container of each pigment used.
○ Any item which comes into contact with blood must be disposed of safely and immediately.
○ Aftercare instructions must be given.
○ Sterilization of equipment should be thorough using the appropriate methods.

Three of the most popular areas for treatment are:

1 The lips.
2 Eyebrows.
3 Eyeliner.

The lips

A new lip line or full colour can appear to change the size and shape of the lips as well as adding colour. The procedure can help to balance uneven lips, prevent lipstick from bleeding and camouflage facial lines around the lips as a result of ageing, the finished look can be as natural or dramatic as the client wishes.

The eyebrows

This procedure aims to give the appearance of hair in the browline and fullness can be achieved for sparse or no eyebrows, it is especially helpful to alopecia sufferers eliminating the need for eyebrow pencil.

Eyeliner

Pigment can be applied between the lashes for a soft natural look, giving the appearance of thicker lashes. A more definite look may be achieved with a bold eyeline or a soft smudgy effect at the corners of the lid. (Some companies will not treat this area but will recommend that a doctor rather than a therapist carry out this procedure.)

Expected results after treatment

In some cases there may be some swelling after the procedure, accompanied by redness to the area, but this will subside fairly quickly. Aftercare advice will be given to the client according to the treatment procedure and the area treated.

Contraindications

o Skin disorders and diseases.
o Herpes simplex.
o Eye disorders and diseases.
o New scar tissue.
o Open cuts or abrasions.
o Moles, warts or existing beauty spots.
o Epilepsy.
o Vitiligo (sometimes companies will treat this condition).
o Abnormal discolouration.

If there is any doubt, it is advisable to obtain a doctor's note before treatment.

Photographic makeup

A much greater effort is required when applying makeup for photographic work because there are more problems created with the use of lighting techniques, than in natural daylight.

The lighting can drain colour from the face or throw it into relief. This causes unnatural effects and contours emphasizing prominent features and where overhead lighting is used the eyes are thrown into shadow.

These problems can be overcome by adapting the application of the makeup:

o Uneven skin colour or dark circles around the eyes should be blanked out using a white masking cream which is longer lasting and more effective than a concealer.
o Foundation must be even and matt, providing a good coverage without heaviness and a shade darker than usual may be used to counter the draining effect of the lighting.
o Powder is essential in photographic makeup, as an oily finish will cause a reflection.
o For a very soft effect for bridal makeup, shading and highlighting should be carried out with cream products and then set with a fine translucent powder.

o Colour blending is very important to avoid harsh lines particularly as a more obvious colour contrast can be used under artificial light.
o When applying blusher it should be placed slightly lower than usual in a more angular line because the camera has a bleaching effect on the rounded parts of the face. Therefore to accentuate the blusher, highlighter and shader must be used.
o The socket line must not be over-emphasized when applying eyeshadow because the shadow will appear deeper if there is overhead lighting.

Remedial camouflage makeup

There are many conditions of the skin that can be treated with camouflage makeup by beauty therapists but to treat the more severe cases a specialized course in remedial makeup must be undertaken.

There are several different types of camouflage makeup available to beauty therapists who should ensure that they have certain qualities to:

o Provide a good cover — enough to last a whole day and in some cases, when used on other parts of the body, for several days, providing the area is not washed with soap.
o Be waterproof to enable the client to participate in all activities including watersports and swimming. However, care must be taken when drying with a towel and a blotting action must be used to keep the makeup in place.
o Be sun proof. The skin which is being camouflaged may be quite delicate and sensitive and most products contain titanium dioxide to protect against ultraviolet rays.
o Have a good range of colours. This is essential so that all skin colours can be matched exactly and if an exact match is not available, then different shades can be mixed to the required colour.
o Be hypo-allergenic and suitable for everybody who requires camouflage makeup.

Beauty therapists may be called upon to treat the following conditions:

- ○ *Port wine stain:* A deep red birthmark which is not raised above the skin's surface and is successfully camouflaged.
- ○ *Vitiligo:* An area of skin with no natural pigment giving the appearance of white patches.
- ○ *Tatoos:* They are permanent and often in a conspicuous position.
- ○ *Chloasma:* Areas of darker pigmentation than the surrounding skin.
- ○ *Dilated arterioles:* Still show through a normal makeup.
- ○ *Burns and scar tissue:* Difficult to cover because they are non-absorbent and the creams may slip.
- ○ *Varicose veins.*

Referral from a doctor

It is very important when dealing with clients (men, women or children) who have been referred to you by their doctor to be sympathetic, reassuring and positive in your approach. Details of the problem will be included in a note from the doctor but it is also necessary to listen to the client's own requirements.

The main objective is to teach clients how to apply their own camouflage makeup as quickly and effectively as possible so that they can use it on a daily basis with total confidence. The number of visits required will be decided mutually, as the time it takes to become proficient will vary from client to client. Children will need extra special help and it may not come very easily to a male client who has had no previous experience of makeup application.

Advice to the client

Explain that they will need to allow ample time in the morning to apply the makeup but with time and practice this will take up less time as they become more proficient.

It is important to make up in a good light preferably daylight.

When applying the creams apply them sparingly, building up the layers gradually rather than using one heavy application.

Advise clients to return at any time if they feel that the results they are achieving are not satisfactory.

Application of remedial camouflage makeup

Colours should be chosen to match as closely as possible the shade of skin surrounding the blemish and if necessary use a second shade over the first for a perfect match.

The skin should be totally clean and grease free. Moisturizer must not be applied to the area of skin to be treated because any moisture on the skin will repel the cream and the application will be difficult.

The cream should be pressed onto the blemish, never rubbed, until the blemish or discoloration has disappeared. The colour should be blended beyond the edges of the blemish into the surrounding skin.

A special finishing powder should then be applied generously over the treated area. The powder should then be left for ten minutes for the cream to set, then lightly brushed with a soft powder brush to remove the excess powder.

Normal foundation may now be applied to the face but gently, without rubbing to avoid disturbing the camouflage cream. The application of makeup may now continue in the usual way.

To remove the camouflage makeup a special removing cream is normally available from the manufacturers of the makeup. This should be gently massaged in until the cream begins to dissolve, gently wipe away and then the face or area treated may be cleansed in the usual way.

Part Two   Body Treatments

9 Body treatments: an introduction

Types of treatment

The eternal quest to develop the body beautiful has led to a huge increase in the number of:

○ Salons offering slimming treatments.
○ Health clubs.
○ Fitness studios.
○ Exercise classes.
○ Toning table centres.

Many people are now also aware of the need for a fit and healthy body, to combat the stresses and strains of everyday life, and the benefits of relaxation in the forms of heat therapy, body massage and aromatherapy, and physical forms of exercise.

When the body is not fit and healthy it will become more susceptible to illness, premature ageing, fatigue and poor skin and hair condition. As well as exercise, therefore, a good diet is essential to rejuvenate the body and the mind.

The beauty therapist can offer all that a client needs to become fit and healthy:

○ Body massage and aromatherapy.
○ Application of electrical body treatments including heat and hydrotherapy.
○ Postural correction.
○ Exercise classes.
○ Dietary advice.
○ Supervision of fitness training.
○ Body toning.

To be competent the therapist must have a sound knowledge of:

1 The anatomy and physiology of the body.
2 Nutrition.
3 The use of electrical equipment, the effects and safety.

Effective treatment

Although there are many varied treatments on offer it is important to remember that one form of treatment alone will not usually succeed. The combination of diet, exercise and the application of treatments in the salon is essential in achieving the required results.

A trusting relationship between clients and therapists is therefore very important so that the correct combination of treatments are used to maximum effect and clients will follow the diet they are given and carry out any home care advice, such as follow-up exercises.

Therapists themselves must be fit and healthy since they are a natural advert for the results they hope to achieve. The work involved in body treatments is also very tiring and demands great stamina particularly when performing body massage either manually or mechanically.

Client consultation

Consultation is a very important first step in planning the course of treatment for clients. They may already be clients for facial therapy or electrolysis, in which case you will probably have built up a good relationship with them. If they are new to the salon, then it is important to put them completely at ease as they may feel embarrassed about their weight problem or their figure shape.

It is probably a good idea to combine a relaxing body massage with the initial consultation and in this way clients will talk more freely to you without feeling as if they are under close scrutiny.

Figure analysis is important when planning treatment and this will require the recording of clients' statistics. They probably will not feel as embarrassed being measured after the massage than if they had come straight in to be measured and had been asked to take the necessary clothing off.

Record cards

A detailed record card must be filled in for the usual reasons of efficiency, client confidence and professionalism and also to provide other necessary information:

○ Medical history.
○ Lifestyle.
○ Figure faults.

The record card provides the information on which you base your treatment.

Medical history

This should include:

○ The number and the age of any children and gynaecological operations in particular, as these are often the cause of figure faults.
○ Any recent operations or medical conditions which may require you to modify treatment.
○ Any form of medication that is being taken which may cause weight gain, for example steroids.

If the client has recently had a baby then medical approval must be given before treatment begins.

Lifestyle

It is important to:

○ Assess the client's possible eating habits which may affect diet.
○ Recognize any factors which may contribute to figure faults such as lack of exercise, or a job which entails sitting for long periods.

○ Recognize any underlying causes of stress.
○ Plan times when the client will be available for treatment and how much work must be done at home.

Recording the age of clients will indicate whether they may be suffering from problems caused by the menopause and if so it may be necessary to seek the doctor's approval before treatment.

Other information should include:

○ Weight.
○ Height.
○ Initial measurements, if clients will allow their measurements to be taken. (Some clients may be too embarrassed whilst others will find the recording of measurements an incentive to lose the excess weight.)

Measurements should be taken at regular intervals to chart the progress of clients and to motivate them.

If clients are obese then medical approval must be given before treatment commences.

Figure faults

A figure diagnosis should be carried out to provide information regarding:

○ The figure type.
○ Fat distribution.
○ Figure faults.
○ Postural faults.

A record should be made of all treatments as they are completed to:

○ Enable progress to be assessed.
○ Indicate to therapists when a change in the treatment plan is required.
○ Provide up-to-date information for other therapists.

Each client will have individual requirements depending on their particular problem. It is important to assess how many treatments are required, how long the course will take and the regularity of attendance so that clients will be aware of the cost and the time involved.

Special offers on courses of treatments make it more attractive to clients and ensure that they attend for the minimum number of treatments necessary to produce the required results.

The main reasons clients attend for body treatments are:

1 Relaxation.
2 Spot reduction.
3 Figure correction.
4 Weight loss.

10 Anatomy and physiology of the body

Anatomy is the science of the structure of the body. Physiology is the science of the normal function of the body. It is essential to have a thorough knowledge of anatomy and physiology for all beauty treatments but especially body treatments when figure analysis is so important. The technical terms used in anatomy describe anatomical positions and body movements. The 'Anatomical position' is Erect with the head facing forward, arms by the sides with the palms of the hand facing forward.

Useful terminology

Anatomical positions

Anterior/ventral: The front of the body.
Distal: Farthest away from the point of attachment of a limb.
Dorsum: Back surface or the top of the foot.
Inferior: Below.
Lateral: Away from the median line of the body.
Medial: Towards the median line of the body.
Median line: An imaginary line through the centre of the body from head to toe.
Plantar: Front surface, sole of the foot.
Posterior/dorsal: The back of the body.
Prone: Lying face down.
Proximal: Nearest to the point of attachment of a limb.
Superior: Above.
Supine: Lying face upwards.

Movement

Abduction: A movement away from the median line.

Adduction: A movement towards the median line.
Circumduction: A combined movement incorporating, flexion extension, abduction and adduction.
Depression: A downward movement.
Dorsiflexion: When the dorsum of the foot is brought upwards.
Elevation: An upward movement.
Eversion: When the plantar surface of the foot is turned laterally or outwards.
Extension: Increasing of an angle between two bones at a joint as in straightening.
Flexion: Decreasing of an angle between two bones at a joint as in bending.
Inversion: When the plantar surface of the foot is turned medially or inwards.
Lateral flexion: A sideways bending movement of the vertebral column as a whole or any part of it.
Plantarflexion: When the foot is stretched downwards.
Pronation: Movement of the palm of the hand downwards.
Rotation: Movement of a bone around its long axis.
Supination: Movement of the palm of the hand upwards.

The skeletal system

The skeletal system (Figure 10.1) consists of bones and the cartilage and ligaments which keep them together.

1 The axial skeleton which forms the centre axis of the body, is made up of the:

—Skull.
—Vertebral column.

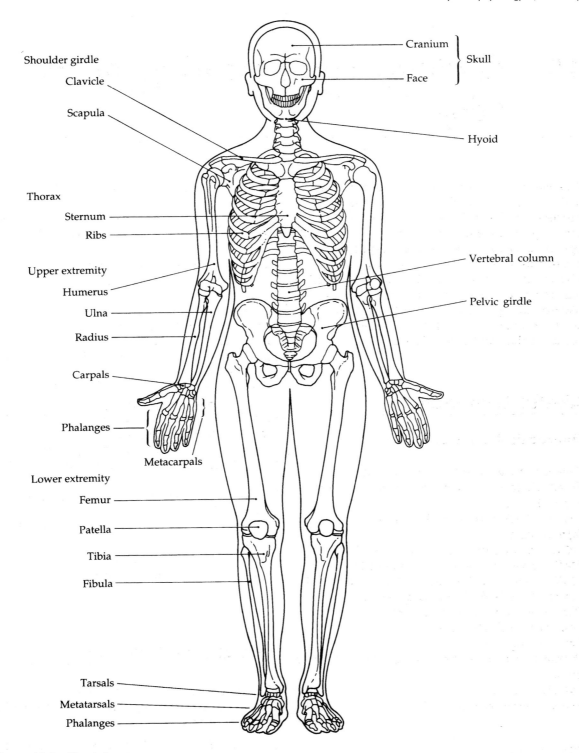

Figure 10.1 *The skeleton*

—The *ribs*.
—The *sternum*.

2 *The appendicular skeleton* or the parts which are appended to (joined on to) the axial skeleton:

—The shoulder girdle and arms.
—The pelvic girdle and legs.

Bones

The bones of the skeleton are classified as:

○ Long: Forming the limbs.
○ Short: Found in the wrists and ankles.
○ Flat: For protection, for example the skull, or for the attachment of certain muscles. They are made from a sandwich of hard bone with a spongy layer in between.
○ Irregular: The irregular shape of these bones is for the job they do, for example the vertebrae.
○ Sesamoid: A small bone which develops in the tendons around certain joints, for example the patella in the knee.

Bones are active living tissue from which they are made. *Osteoblasts* are bone-forming cells which when calcified become *osteocytes*. *Periosteum* is a tough fibrous sheet covering the surface of bones, except where the bone forms a joint and is covered by hyaline cartilage.

The blood supply is received via the periosteum on its surface and via an artery in the nutrient foramen (a hole in the bone) in the shaft of the bone.

Most of the bones of the skeleton have protuberances and ridges for the attachment of muscles and tendons.

Bone formation

The process by which bones form is called *ossification*. Osteoblasts form bone tissue and where there is a cluster of osteoblasts it is called a centre of ossification.

The osteoblasts secrete substances composed of collagenous fibres, forming a framework into which calcium salts are deposited. This process is called *calcification*.

When the osteoblasts are surrounded by this calcification it is known as a *trabecula*.

The bones develop hollow centres which contain marrow, in which the manufacture of blood cells takes place.

Bone disorders

Osteoporosis
This disorder usually affects middle-aged to elderly women. It occurs when osteoblasts become less active resulting in a decrease in bone mass. The condition affects the whole of the skeletal system especially the spine, legs and feet. Other factors which contribute to this condition are a decrease in oestrogen, calcium deficiency and poor absorption, lack of vitamin D, inactivity, high protein diets and loss of muscle mass.

Rickets
This is caused by a deficiency of vitamin D which results in an inability of the body to transport calcium and phosphorous from the digestive tract into the blood to be used by the bones. Calcification does not occur which results in bones staying soft and the weight of the body causes the bones in the leg to bow. A cure will be effected with large doses of calcium, phosphorous and vitamin D in the diet and ultraviolet light assists the body in manufacturing vitamin D.

Periostitis
This is an inflammation of the periosteum.

Arthritis
This is an inflammation of the joints and has different classifications. Osteoarthritis is a degenerative disease of the joints and it affects the hips, spine and the hands. It brings about swollen joints and pain and stiffness around the affected area, and may be caused by ageing, wear and tear on the joints or irritation. Rheumatoid arthritis is the most common form of inflammatory arthritis and it begins by affecting smaller joints and then progresses to larger joints causing inflammation, swelling, pain and, in some cases, loss of function.

Osteomyelitis

This refers to all diseases of the bone. Infections reach the bone via the bloodstream, through an injury such as a fracture or an abscess, and may destroy bones and nearby joints.

Dislocation

This is when the bone is displaced from the joint and the ligaments, tendons and articular capsules are torn in the process. It causes pain, loss of movement and swelling.

Sprain

This occurs when a joint is twisted or wrenched and its attachments are injured. Blood vessels, ligaments, tendons and nerves can be affected. It causes swelling, pain and bruising, and the most common location is the ankle.

Functions of bones
○ They make up the framework of the body.
○ They provide attachment for the muscles.
○ They allow movement with the help of muscles and joints.
○ They store calcium.
○ They contain bone marrow which forms new blood cells.
○ They protect internal organs.

The human skeleton

The skeleton has about 200 bones which vary greatly in size and shape:

○ The *skull:* Cranium, face and lower jaw.
○ The *trunk:* Spinal column, ribs and sternum.
○ The *limbs:* Which include the shoulder and pelvic girdles.

The skull

The skull is divided into the cranium and the face and is made up as follows:

1   The *cranium:*

One frontal
Two parietal
Two temporal

One ethmoid
One sphenoid
One occipital

2   The *face:*

Two maxillae
Two zygomatic
Two nasal
Two lacrimal
Two palatine
Two inferior turbinate
One vomer
One mandible

The trunk

The trunk comprises:

○   The sternum or breast bone.
○   Twelve ribs.
○   The spinal column.

The spinal column
This consists of:

○   Seven cervical vertebrae
○   Twelve thoracic vertebrae
○   Five lumbar vertebrae
○   Five sacral vertebrae, fused together to form the sacrum
○   Four coccygeal vertebrae, fused together to form the coccyx.

The spinal column provides flexibility and strength to the body. The arms are joined to the spinal column by the shoulder girdle and the legs are joined by the pelvic girdle. See Figure 10.2.

The limbs

Shoulder girdle and arm
The clavicles (collar bones) and scapulae (shoulder blades) form the bones of the shoulder girdle (Figure 10.3).
The humerus is the long bone of the upper arm (Figure 10.4).
The radius and ulna are the long bones of the forearm.

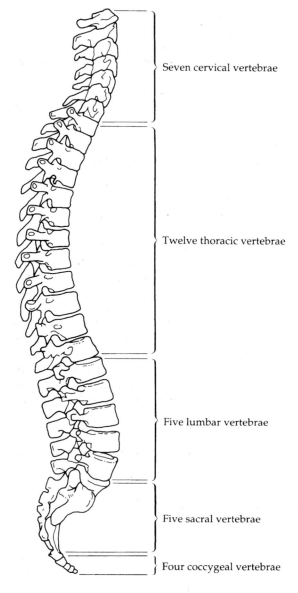

Figure 10.2 *The vertebral column*

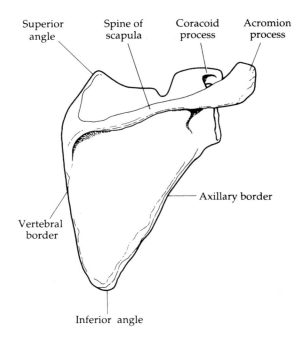

Figure 10.3 *Right scapula*

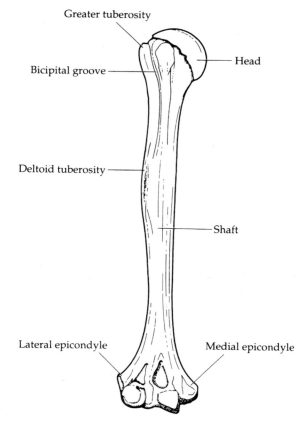

Figure 10.4 *Anterior view of the right humerus*

The bones of the wrist and hand consist of:

○ Eight carpals.
○ Five metacarpals.
○ Fourteen phalanges.

The pelvic girdle
The pelvic girdle comprises two innominate bones. The ilium is the upper part, the pubis is the anterior part and the ischium is the posterior part.

The leg

The leg consists of the *femur*, which is the thigh bone. It is the longest and strongest bone in the body.

The *patella* is a small flat bone which protects the knee joint. The *tibia* and *fibula* are the bones of the lower leg beneath the knee.

The foot

The foot consists of:

○ Seven tarsals.
○ Five metatarsals.
○ Fourteen phalanges.

Joints in the body

A joint is the point at which two or more bones meet. There are three types of joint in the body:

1 Fibrous. Fixed or immovable joints which have fibrous tissue between the bones.
2 Cartilaginous. Slightly movable with cartilage between the ends of the bones.
3 Synovial. Freely movable joints (Figure 10.5) which have particular characteristics:

—The articulating surfaces of the bones are covered with hyaline cartilage.

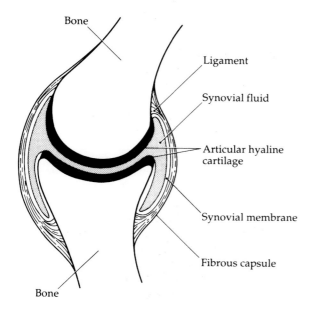

Figure 10.5 *A synovial joint*

—A fibrous capsule supported by ligaments surrounds the joint to provide protection while allowing freedom of movement.
—A synovial membrane lines the capsule of the joint.
—The capsule of the joint contains synovial fluid which is a lubricant and provides nutrients for the living cells.

Synovial joints are classified depending on their range of movement and structure:

○ *Plane (gliding):* Movement is limited to short gliding movements.
○ *Hinge:* Movement is in one plane only as the name implies. It will flex and extend.
○ *Ball and socket:* These joints allow the widest range of movement to include flexion and extension, abduction and adduction, circumduction and rotation.
○ *Pivot:* Rotation movement only.
○ *Condyloid:* Allows movement in two planes – flexion and extension; abduction and adduction, and limited circumduction.
○ *Saddle:* Similar to condyloid this joint permits movement in two planes. Movements include flexion, extension, abduction, adduction and circumduction.

Main synovial joints of the limbs

Shoulder joint: Ball and socket.
Elbow joint: Hinge.
Wrist joint: Condyloid.
Hip joint: Ball and socket.
Knee joint: Hinge.
Ankle joint: Hinge.

The muscular system

Bones and joints form the framework of the body, but they require help to produce movement which is an essential body function and this is achieved by the contraction and relaxation of muscles.

Muscle tissue

Muscle tissue is composed of highly specialized cells and makes up about 40 to 50 per cent of the body's total weight.

Characteristics

The characteristics of muscle tissue are important in maintaining homeostasis, the condition in which the body's internal environment remains relatively constant within limits, under ever changing conditions. These characteristics are:

○ *Excitability* – the ability of muscle tissue to receive messages and respond to stimuli.
○ *Contractability* – the ability to shorten and thicken (contract) in response to a stimulus.
○ *Extensibility* – the ability of muscle tissue to stretch.
○ *Elasticity* – the ability of the muscle to return to its original shape after contraction or extension.

Functions

○ Motion involves the *usual movements* of the whole body such as walking, running, swimming, and *localized movements* such as, nodding the head, waving a hand, drawing a picture. The less obvious types of motion are the beating of the heart, peristalsis, the movement of food along the digestive tract and the contraction of the bladder.
○ Maintaining posture, the contraction of the skeletal muscles enables the body to sit and stand.
○ Heat production, when skeletal muscles are contracting, helps to maintain the normal body temperature.

Types of muscle

There are different kinds of muscle in the body:

○ Skeletal – attached to bones it is *striated*, *voluntary* muscle tissue (Figure 10.6).
○ Visceral – smooth or *non-striated involuntary* muscle located in the walls of hollow internal structures, for example the blood vessels, bladder and stomach.
○ Cardiac – forms the walls of the heart, is *striated, involuntary* muscle.

Skeletal muscle

Skeletal muscle is protected by fascia, a layer of connective tissue. Deep fascia holds muscles

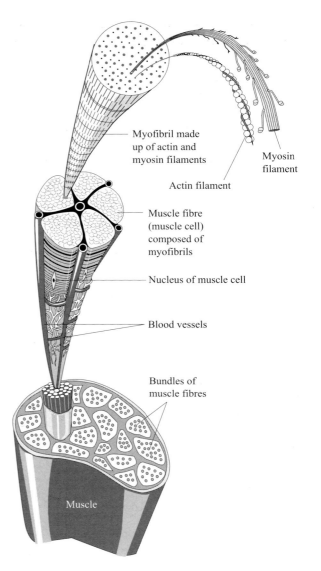

Figure 10.6   *The structure of voluntary muscle*

together, separating them into functioning groups, allowing free movement of the muscles, and carrying nerves and blood vessels. The epymisium is an extension of deep fascia and covers the entire muscle.

Skeletal muscle tissue looks like a series of parallel fibre bundles, the smallest of which are called actin and myosin filaments. Made of protein, they are sometimes known as the contractile proteins. These filaments are gathered into bundles called *myofibrils*, which are gathered into further bundles called *muscle fibres*, which are gathered into further bundles called *fasiculi*.

Actin and myosin filaments gathered into bundles make
↓
Myofibrils gathered into bundles make
↓
Muscle fibres or cells containing nuclei, nerve fibres and blood supply
↓
Muscle fibres are surrounded by a membrane called endomysium
↓
Muscle fibres gathered into bundles are called fasiculi
↓
Fasiculi are surrounded by perimysium
↓
Muscle is made up of bundles of fasiculi wrapped in epimysium, an extension of deep fascia

The skeletal muscles are well supplied with nerves and blood vessels essential for motion (Figure 10.7). They are stimulated by an impulse from a nerve cell to produce movement and muscle action depends on blood supply providing nutrients and oxygen for energy and to remove the waste products in the muscle which are the result of exercise.

Visceral muscle

This muscle is smooth, non-striated and usually involuntary. The cells are spindle-shaped with one central nucleus, and are bound together in sheets by areolar connective tissue. It is not under the control of the will and is found in the walls of blood and lymph vessels, the stomach, the alimentary canal, the respiratory tract, the bladder and the uterus. These muscles do not become fatigued.

Cardiac muscle

This muscle is only found in the heart and is striated in appearance like skeletal muscle with fibres that are short and thick, forming a dense mass, but it is involuntary muscle tissue, not under the control of the will. The cardiac muscle cells have one nucleus and very little connective tissue. Cardiac muscle contracts rhythmically even without nervous stimulation and it does not tire easily but could if the heartbeat was raised considerably for a long period of time without enough rest between contractions.

Muscle tone

This is when the muscle is in a state of partial contraction with some of the muscle fibres

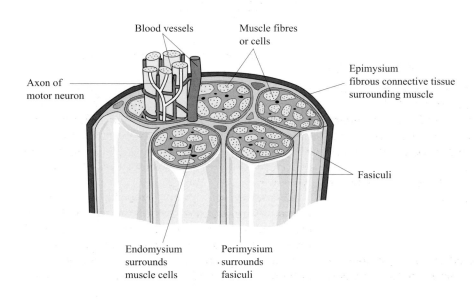

Blood vessels

Muscle fibres or cells

Axon of motor neuron

Epimysium fibrous connective tissue surrounding muscle

Fasiculi

Endomysium surrounds muscle cells

Perimysium surrounds fasiculi

Figure 10.7 *Cross and longitudinal section of a skeletal muscle*

contracted and some relaxed. Partial contraction tightens a muscle without actually producing movement. Tone is essential in maintaining posture.

Muscle fatigue

This is when the skeletal muscle has been contracted for a long period of time and it becomes tired and weaker in response until it stops responding altogether, usually as a result of inadequate blood supply and lack of oxygen and a build-up of lactic acid and carbon dioxide which accumulates in the muscle during exercise.

Over-activity of skeletal muscle
↓
Accumulation of lactic acid and carbon dioxide in the muscles
↓
An insufficient supply of glucose and energy required for contraction
↓
Impairment of delivery of nutritional substances and the removal of waste products
↓
Disturbance of the respiratory system reducing oxygen supply and increasing the oxygen debt

Skeletal muscles

These muscles are voluntary and striated, and make up approximately 40 per cent of the total body weight.

Muscle tissue is elastic and contracts to produce movement. To maintain a position such as standing or sitting the muscles are in a state of partial contraction. Muscles have their own blood supply and lymphatic system and consist of muscle fibres strengthened by connective tissue.

Tendons attach muscle to the bones and they vary in length and size. Some tendons are broad and flat and are called an *aponeurosis*, for example the epicranial aponeurosis, which joins the occipitalis and frontalis muscles of the scalp.

Ligaments are bands of strong fibrous tissue which run between the ends of bones forming the joint. They hold the surface of the joint together and prevent it from moving excessively. Cartilage provides stability in the joints, reducing friction and absorbing shock.

Skeletal muscles in general are attached to bones although some facial muscles are attached to soft tissue in the face or ligaments and cartilage.

The fixed point of muscle attachment is *the origin* and the movable point of attachment is *the insertion.*

Flexor muscles
These muscles bend the limbs at a joint.

Extensor muscles
They straighten the limbs at a joint.

Adductors
These are muscles which move a limb towards the median line.

Abductors
These are muscles which move a limb away from the median line of the body.

Supinators
Supinators turn the palm of the hand upwards.

Pronators
Pronators turn the palm of the hand downwards.

Muscle groups

Muscles of the back (Figure 10.8)

Trapezius
Origin: Occipital bone and thoracic vertebrae.
Insertion: Clavicle and spine of scapula.
Action: Elevates the clavicle and rotates the arm.

Latissimus dorsi
Origin: Lower thoracic vertebrae, lumbar vertebrae, iliac crest and inferior angle of scapula.
Insertion: Bicipital groove of humerus.
Action: Adducts and rotates the arm inwards and draws it backwards.

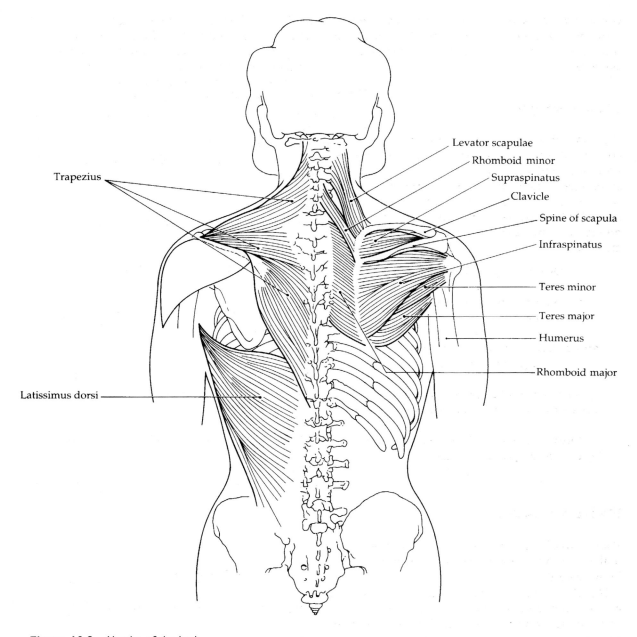

Figure 10.8 *Muscles of the back*

Levator scapulae
Origin: The upper four cervical vertebrae.
Insertion: Vertebral border of scapula.
Action: Elevates the scapula.

Rhomboid minor
Origin: The seventh cervical and the first thoracic vertebrae.

Insertion: The superior border of scapula.
Action: Braces shoulder and adducts scapula.

Rhomboid major
Origin: The second to the fifth thoracic vertebrae.
Insertion: The medial border of the scapula below spine.

Action: Adducts scapula and slightly rotates it upward.

Infraspinatus
Origin: Infraspinous fossa of scapula.
Insertion: Greater tuberosity of humerus.
Action: Rotates the arm outwards.

Supraspinatus
Origin: Supraspinous fossa of scapula.
Insertion: Greater tuberosity of humerus.
Action: Abducts the arm.

Teres major
Origin: Inferior angle of scapula.
Insertion: Bicipital groove of humerus.
Action: Adducts and inwardly rotates the arm.

Teres minor
Origin: Lateral border of scapula.
Insertion: Greater tuberosity of humerus.
Action: Rotates the arm laterally.

Muscles of the thoracic wall (Figure 10.9)

Pectoralis major
Origin: Clavicle, sternum and upper six ribs.
Insertion: Bicipital groove of humerus.
Action: Adducts and rotates the arm inwards.

Pectoralis minor
Origin: Third to fifth ribs.

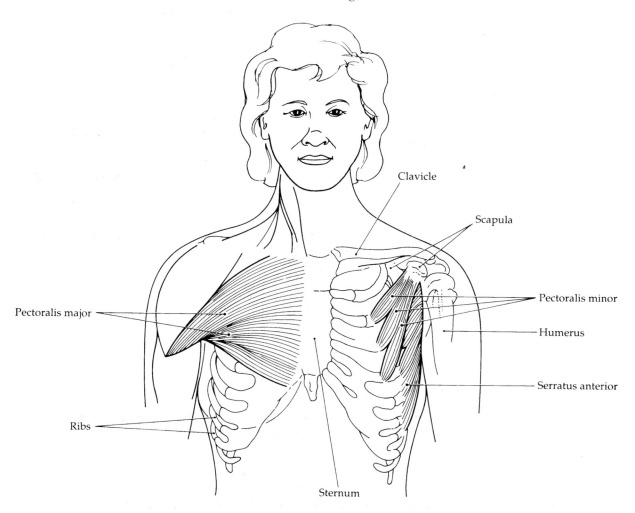

Figure 10.9 *Muscles of the thoracic wall*

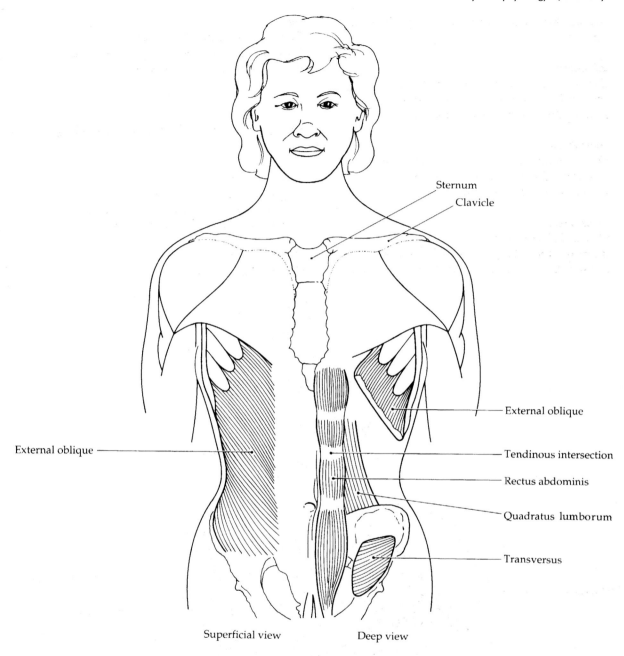

Sternum

Clavicle

External oblique

External oblique

Tendinous intersection

Rectus abdominis

Quadratus lumborum

Transversus

Superficial view   Deep view

Figure 10.10   *Muscles of the abdomen*

Insertion: Coracoid process of scapula.
Action: Moves scapula down and forwards.

Serratus anterior
Origin: Upper eight ribs.
Insertion: Vertebral border of scapula.
Action: Draws the shoulder forwards and rotates scapula.

Muscles of the abdomen (Figure 10.10)

Rectus abdominis
Origin: Pubis.
Insertion: Sternum and lower ribs.
Action: Flexes the vertebral column.

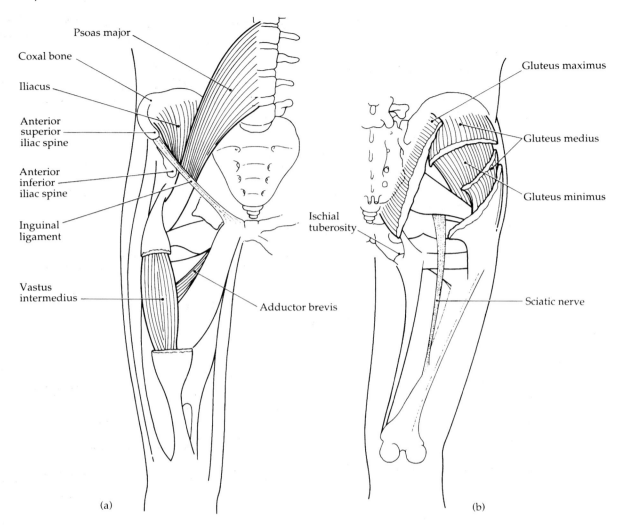

Figure 10.11 *(a) Muscles of the thigh and (b) the gluteal muscles*

External oblique
Origin: Lower eight ribs.
Insertion: Iliac crest and pubic bone.
Action: Flexes the trunk laterally.

Internal oblique
Origin: Iliac crest.
Insertion: Lower three ribs and rectus sheath.
Action: Flexes the trunk laterally.

Transversus
Origin: The lower ribs, iliac crest and inguinal ligament.
Insertion: Linea alba and pubic bone.
Action: Aids the outer abdominal muscles in their actions and functions.

Quadratus lumborum
Origin: Iliac crest.
Insertion: Twelfth rib and upper four lumbar vertebrae.
Action: Laterally flexes the trunk.

The gluteal muscles (Figure 10.11)

Gluteus maximus
Origin: Iliac crest and sacral fascia.
Insertion: Fascia lata and gluteal tuberosity of femur.
Action: Extends the hip and laterally rotates the thigh and hip joint.

Gluteus medius
Origin: Ilium.
Insertion: Greater trochanter of femur.
Action: Abducts femur and medially rotates the thigh.

Gluteus minimus
Origin: Ilium.
Insertion: Greater trochanter of femur.
Action: Abducts femur and laterally rotates the thigh.

Iliacus and psoas major (Figure 10.11)

These muscles act on the thigh and together are known as *iliopsoas*.

Psoas
Origin: Lower lumbar vertebrae.
Insertion: Femur.
Action: Flexes and rotates the thigh.

Iliacus
Origin: Iliac fossa.
Insertion: Tendon of psoas.
Action: Flexes and rotates the thigh.

Muscles of the thigh (Figure 10.12)

The anterior muscles

Rectus femoris (quadriceps)
Origin: Above acetabulum.
Insertion: Patella.
Action: Extends knee and flexes the thigh.

Vastus medialis (quadriceps)
Origin: Greater trochanter of femur.
Insertion: Patella and tubercle of tibia.
Action: Extension of the knee joint.

Vastus intermedius
Origin: Shaft of femur.
Insertion: Patella and tubercle of tibia.
Action: Extension of the knee joint.

Vastus lateralis (quadriceps)
Origin: Greater trochanter of femur.
Insertion: Patella and tubercle of tibia.

Action: Extension of the knee joint.

Sartorius
Origin: Superior spine of ilium.
Insertion: Medial surface of the body of tibia.
Action: Flexes the leg and rotates the thigh laterally.

Adductor longus
Origin: Pubic crest.
Insertion: Linea aspera of femur.
Action: Adducts rotates and flexes the thigh.

Adductor brevis
Origin: Pubis.
Insertion: Linea aspera of femur.
Action: Adducts rotates and flexes the thigh.

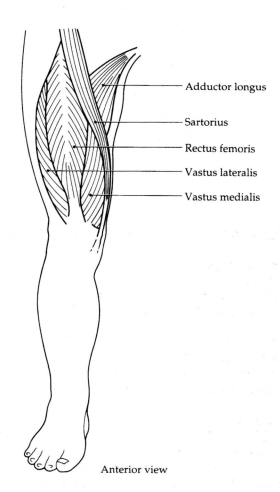

Adductor longus

Sartorius

Rectus femoris

Vastus lateralis

Vastus medialis

Anterior view

Figure 10.12 *Muscles of the thigh (anterior view)*

Adductor magnus
Origin: Pubis and ischium.
Insertion: Linea aspera of femur.
Action: Adducts and flexes the thigh (anterior part). Extends the thigh (posterior part).

Tensor fascia lata
Origin: Iliac crest.
Insertion: Tibia.
Action: Flexes and abducts the thigh.

The posterior muscles (Figure 10.13)

Hamstrings
Collective name for three muscles.

Biceps femoris (hamstrings)
Origin: Tuberosity of ischium and femur.
Insertion: Head of fibula and lateral condyle of tibia.
Action: Extends the thigh and flexes the leg.

Semimembranosus (hamstrings)
Origin: Tuberosity of ischium.
Insertion: Medial condyle of tibia.
Action: Flexes the leg and extends the thigh.

Semitendinosus (hamstrings)
Origin: Tuberosity of ischium.
Insertion: Medial condyle of tibia.
Action: Flexes the leg and extends the thigh.

Gracilis
Origin: Pubic symphysis and pubic arch.
Insertion: Medial surface of the body of tibia.
Action: Flexes the leg and adducts the thigh.

Female breasts or mammary glands (Figure 10.14)

The breasts lie over the pectoralis major muscles. They are attached to them by connective tissue. Inside, each breast consists of fifteen to twenty *lobes* separated by adipose tissue and

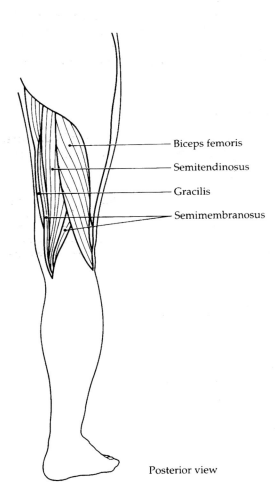

Figure 10.13 *Muscles of the thigh (posterior view)*

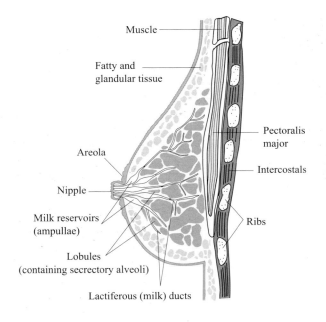

Figure 10.14 *Cross-section of mammary gland*

the amount of adipose tissue will determine the size of the breasts. Each lobe has several smaller *lobules* which are composed of connective tissue. Embedded in this connective tissue are milk secreting cells called *alveoli* which are arranged in clusters. The alveoli carry the milk into a series of tubules, to the mammary ducts and the *ampullae*, where it is stored before moving along the lactiferous ducts to the nipple.

The area of pigmented skin around the nipple is called the *areola* and it contains modified sebaceous glands.

The female breasts develop at puberty because of the increased output of oestrogen and their main function is *lactation*, the secretion and ejection of milk.

The cardiovascular system

The cardiovascular system consists of:

1 The heart.
2 Blood.
3 Blood vessels.

The heart provides the power to pump the blood around the body through the blood vessels. The blood is the vehicle by which the circulatory system conveys oxygen, nutrients, hormones and other substances to the tissues, carbon dioxide to the lungs and other waste products to the kidneys.

Functions of blood

Blood has many functions: It:

o Transports oxygen from the lungs to the cells of the body.
o Transports nutrients from the digestive tract to the cells of the body.
o Transports carbon dioxide from the cells to the lungs.
o Transports waste products from the cells to kidneys, lungs and sweat glands.
o Transports hormones from the endocrine glands to the cells.
o Transports enzymes to the appropriate cells.
o Helps in the regulation of body temperature.
o Protects the body against foreign substances.

The heart

The heart is the centre of the cardiovascular system. It is a large muscular organ and it beats

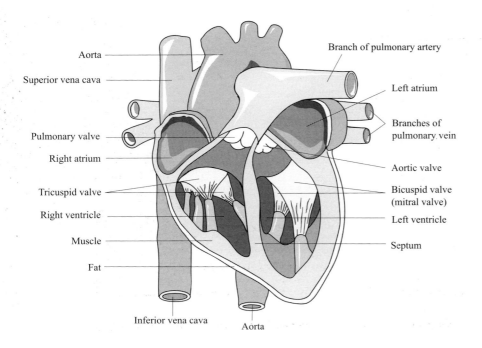

Aorta
Superior vena cava
Pulmonary valve
Right atrium
Tricuspid valve
Right ventricle
Muscle
Fat
Inferior vena cava
Aorta

Branch of pulmonary artery
Left atrium
Branches of pulmonary vein
Aortic valve
Bicuspid valve (mitral valve)
Left ventricle
Septum

Figure 10.15 *Cross-section of the heart showing the aorta and its branches and the major valves, veins and chambers*

over 100,000 times a day to pump the blood through the blood vessels. The blood vessels are a network of tubes that transport blood from the heart to the tissues and then back to the heart again. See Figure 10.15.

It is located between the lungs in the thoracic cavity with about two-thirds lying to the left of the body's midline. It is enclosed in a loose-fitting serous membrane called the *pericardial sac*.

The wall of the heart is divided into:

○ The epicardium or external layer which is thin and transparent.
○ The myocardium or middle layer which is composed of specialized cardiac muscle which makes up the bulk of the heart and is responsible for the heart contraction.
○ The endocardium or inner layer which lines the inside of the myocardium and covers the valves of the heart and tendons that hold them open. It is made up of a thin layer of endothelium which lies over a thin layer of connective tissue.

The heart is divided into four chambers or cavities and each chamber is a muscular bag with walls that contract and push the blood through:

○ The two upper chambers are called *atria* (atrium – one).
○ The two lower chambers are called *ventricles*.

Each atrium has an appendage called an *auricle* which increases its surface area.

The right and left sides of the heart are separated by the *septum*, a solid wall which prevents venous blood from the right side coming into contact with the arterial blood from the left side of the heart.

The passage of blood through the heart

Blood circulates from the heart, through the organs and tissues, delivering food and oxygen. The blood then returns to the heart in the veins having had all the oxygen absorbed from it. The heart then pumps blood on its second circuit to the lungs to replace oxygen, returning with its oxygen supply renewed.

The heart receives blood via *the right atrium* from all parts of the body except the lungs, through three veins:

1 *The superior vena cava* which transports blood from parts of the body that are superior to the heart.
2 *The inferior vena cava* which transports blood from parts of the body that are inferior to the heart.
3 *The coronary sinus* which drains blood from most of the vessels which supply the walls of the heart.

The blood from the right atrium is delivered to the *right* ventricle through the *tricuspid valve*.

Blood is then pumped into the *right and left pulmonary arteries* and transported to the lungs where it has its oxygen renewed and releases carbon dioxide.

It returns to the heart via four *pulmonary veins* which empty into the *left atrium* and then pass through to the *left ventricle*.

The blood is then pumped into the *ascending aorta* and then passed into the *coronary arteries, arch of the aorta, thoracic aorta* and *abdominal aorta* which transport the blood to all parts of the body but the lungs.

Valves of the heart

The heart depends on a series of valves to function efficiently. They open and close automatically to receive and send out blood to and from the four chambers of the heart, ensuring the bloodflow is in one direction only and preventing it from flowing backwards. These valves are:

○ The *pulmonary* and *tricuspid* valves on the right-hand side.
○ The *aortic* and *mitral* valves on the left-hand side.

The tricuspid valve is situated between the right atrium and the right ventricle and consists of three cusps or flaps.

The pulmonary semilunar valve lies where the pulmonary trunk leaves the right ventricle. It consists of three semilunar (half moon-shaped) cusps.

The mitral or bicuspid valve is situated between the left atrium and left ventricle and it consists of two cusps or flaps.

The aortic semilunar valve lies at the opening between the left ventricle and the aorta. This is also made up of three semilunar cusps.

Blood vessels

These are the channels along which the blood flows.

Arteries

These are thick-walled blood vessels which convey blood from the heart to the capillaries. They are under the control of the autonomic nervous system and they help to maintain blood pressure.

The thick elastic walls are important in that most of the force of each heartbeat is taken up in the elastic walls of the large arteries, they continue pushing the blood forward in the pause between each heartbeat.

Arterioles

These are small arteries which convey blood to the capillaries.

Capillaries

These are microscopic blood vessels composed of a single layer of cells, which connect arterioles and venules. Their main function is to allow the passage of nutrients and waste products between the blood and the tissue cells.

In addition to the change of substances they have an important function in helping to regulate body temperature. The capillaries widen when the body heats up and this allows more blood to reach the surface of the skin where it is cooled.

Veins

These have much thinner walls than the arteries and they convey blood back to the heart from the capillaries. They contain valves to prevent backflow allowing blood to move towards the heart.

The arteries and veins are similarly distributed throughout the body and those associated with a particular organ or tissue often run together.

Venules

These are found when groups of capillaries join together. They collect blood from the capillaries and drain it into veins.

Circulation of blood

Arteries carry blood from the heart to all parts of the body. They branch out and become smaller *arterioles* which in turn carry blood to the *capillaries*, microscopic blood vessels in the tissues. See Figure 10.16.

Interchange of tissue fluids (interstitial fluid) takes place, oxygen and nutrients are received by the tissue and carbon dioxide and other waste products (the result of cell metabolism) are removed.

The capillaries then drain into *venules* which form *veins* to carry the deoxygenated blood back to the heart.

Blood pressure

Blood pressure is the force exerted by the blood on the walls of any blood vessels, in particular arteries. The factors which affect blood pressure are:

○ The force of the heartbeat.
○ The volume of blood in the cardiovascular system.
○ The resistance to the flow of blood in the arteries.

A decrease in volume due to blood loss causes blood pressure to drop. An increase in blood volume, for example, excessive salt intake leading to water retention, will cause blood pressure to increase. The blood pressure also varies depending on the activity of the body.

Blood pressure is measured using a *sphygmomanometer*.

Systolic blood pressure is the force exerted by the blood on the arterial walls during ventricular contraction. It is the highest pressure measured in the arteries.

Diastolic blood pressure is the force exerted on the arterial walls during ventricular relaxation. It is the lowest blood pressure measured in the arteries.

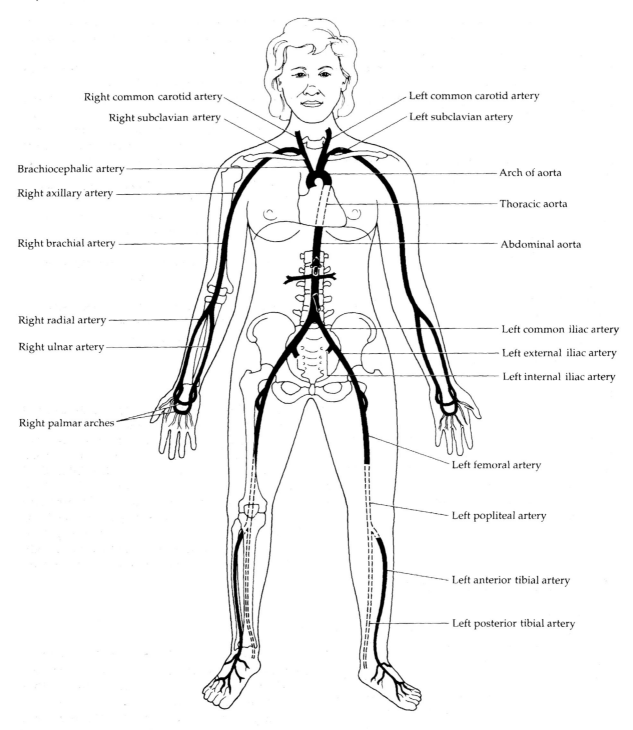

Right common carotid artery

Right subclavian artery

Brachiocephalic artery

Right axillary artery

Right brachial artery

Right radial artery

Right ulnar artery

Right palmar arches

Left common carotid artery

Left subclavian artery

Arch of aorta

Thoracic aorta

Abdominal aorta

Left common iliac artery

Left external iliac artery

Left internal iliac artery

Left femoral artery

Left popliteal artery

Left anterior tibial artery

Left posterior tibial artery

Figure 10.16   *The aorta and main arteries of the limbs*

The difference between systolic and diastolic pressure is called *pulse pressure.*

The average healthy adult male will have a blood pressure of 120 over 80. This would be a systolic press of 120 mm Hg (millimetres of mercury) and a distolic pressure of 80 mm Hg (millimetres of mercury).

Nervous control of the blood vessels

Most arteries in the body are under the control of the autonomic nervous system and the centres of control are in the hypothalamus and medulla oblongata. There are two sets of nerves – vasoconstrictor and vasodilator.

Vasoconstrictor nerves
These narrow the blood vessels reducing the amount of blood to the area of the body they supply. When impulses are sent from all the vasoconstrictor nerves then the blood vessels of the whole of the arterial system will become narrower, thus raising the blood pressure.

Vasodilator nerves
The action of these nerves is to dilate the blood vessels, allowing a greater amount of blood to reach the area. For example, during very strenuous exercise the blood vessels which supply the muscles dilate allowing more blood to reach the area.

The lymphatic system

This is a subsidiary circulatory system and is composed of lymph vessels and highly specialized lymphoid organs and tissues including the thymus, spleen and tonsils. Lymph vessels are found in all parts of the body except the central nervous system, bone, cartilage and teeth. The functions of the lymphatic system are:

○ To convey excess fluid, foreign particles and other materials from the body's tissues and cells.
○ To transport fats from the digestive tract to the blood.
○ To produce lymphocytes to deal with the waste and toxins which build up in the tissues.
○ To develop antibodies which help the body to defend itself against disease.

Antigens are substances that when introduced into the body, cause the body to produce specific antibodies, which react with the antigen.

Antibodies are proteins produced by the body to protect it against an invasion by an antigen.

Lymph vessels carry fluid to the lymph node
↓
Bacteria and foreign particles are filtered off and destroyed
↓
Lymphocytes circulate around the body in the lymph and blood vessels
↓
Lymph leaving the node picks up antibodies which together with the lymphocytes inactivate foreign particles

Lymph

Blood itself does not flow into the tissues but remains inside the blood vessels. Certain parts of the blood permeate through the capillary walls and into the tissue spaces. It is then called interstitial fluid. When this interstitial fluid enters the lymphatic vessels it is then called lymph. It consists mainly of water and substances found in blood plasma such as fibrinogen, serum albumin and serum globulin, as well as lymphocytes which aid the body in its defence against infection. See Figure 10.17.

Lymph vessels

There are *lymph capillaries* into which tissue fluid passes from tissue spaces running along side the body's arteries and veins. Their walls are thin and permeable, allowing larger molecules including bacteria, which cannot enter the blood capillaries, to be carried away. There are larger vessels called *lymphatics* which are the size of small veins and are provided with valves to prevent backflow. The larger vessels eventually converge into two large ducts – *the thoracic duct*

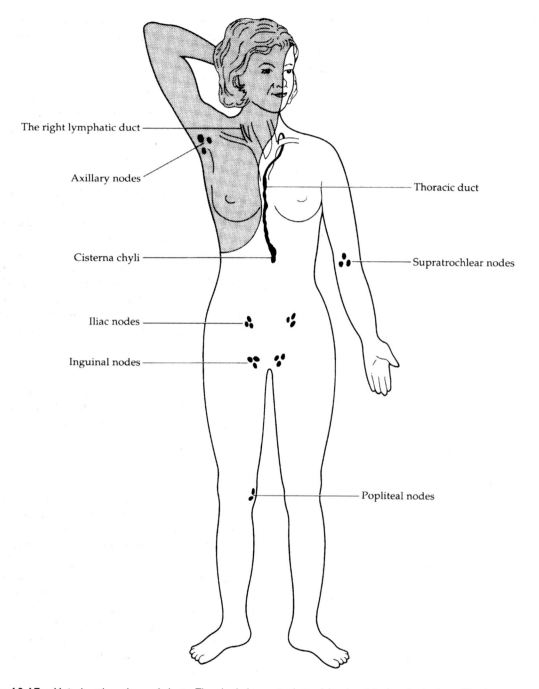

Figure 10.17   *Main lymph nodes and ducts. The shaded area is drained by the right lymphatic duct. All other areas of the body are drained by the thoracic duct*

and *the right lymphatic duct* – which drain into the innominate veins, returning the lymph into the blood. So there is a constant circulation of lymph to the tissues, via the capillaries and back again into the bloodstream.

Lymph nodes

These are situated around the body. They are usually small groups of oval or bean-shaped structures found around major arteries and these groups are arranged in two sets: *superficial* and *deep*. The outer region of the lymph node (cortex) contains densely packed lymphocytes which are arranged in masses called lymph nodules. The inner region (medulla) contains lymphocytes arranged in strands, these are called medullary cords.

The lymphatic vessels carry lymph to the node in afferent (convey towards a centre) vessels and once the lymph has been filtered it is taken from the node in efferent (convey away from a centre) vessels.

From the lymph nodes the lymphatic vessels combine to form lymph trunks and they empty into the two main ducts:

1 The thoracic duct.
2 The right lymphatic duct.

The ducts drain into the innominate veins near the heart.

The thoracic duct

This is the main collecting duct of the lymphatic system beginning as a dilation called the cisterna chyli and receiving lymph from:

○ The left side of the head.
○ Neck and chest.
○ The left upper extremity.
○ The entire body below the ribs.

The right lymphatic duct

This receives lymph from:

○ The right side of the head and neck.
○ The thorax.
○ The right arm.

From these two ducts the lymph returns to the blood circulation via the subclavian veins.

The thymus

This is a mass of lymphatic tissue situated in the upper thoracic cavity and its function is to produce antibodies to destroy foreign particles.

The spleen

This is the largest mass of lymphatic tissue in the body and is situated between the fundus of the stomach and diaphragm. It is one of the main filters of blood, removing worn out red blood cells and abnormal cells, with white cells and platelets filtered selectively. It makes antibodies which immobilize foreign particles, stores blood and releases it into the circulatory system in times of need, for example when there is a heavy blood loss during haemorrhage.

The tonsils

They are part of a ring of lymphoid tissue which encircles the entrance to the food and air passages in the throat and they are:

○ The adenoid or pharyngeal tonsil.
○ The palatine tonsil.
○ The lingual tonsil.

They play a part in the body's defence against disease, reacting to ingested material which poses a threat to health. This immunity is provided by the lymphocytes that are processed in the tonsils and the production of antibodies in the tonsils which deal with local infection. Infected tonsils are enlarged and inflamed with spots of pus exuding from the surface.

The adenoid is situated at the back of the nose and any infection breathed in is filtered by them and destroyed. Adenoids are present at birth but usually disappear by puberty.

The nervous system

The function of the nervous system is to conduct messages from one part of the body to another, helping to coordinate different activities.

The nervous system consists of:

○ *The central nervous system:* The brain and spinal cord.
○ *The peripheral nervous system:* The spinal and cranial nerves.
○ *The autonomic nervous system:* Sympathetic and parasympathetic.

The cells which make up the nervous system are called *neurones* and they come in various shapes and sizes. Each neurone is a nerve cell of grey matter with projections of white matter called *dendrites* and *axons* (Figure 10.18).

The long fibrous axon has a delicate covering called a *neurilemma* and most axons have a *myelin sheath* which acts as an insulator protecting the axon from injury and speeding the flow of nerve impulses along its length. These impulses are then carried to the nerve cell via the *dendrites*.

Neurones may be classified by the direction in which they transmit impulses:

○ *Afferent or sensory:* Transmit impulses to the brain and spinal cord from the sense organs and receptors.
○ *Efferent or motor:* Transmit impulses away from the brain and spinal cord to the muscles and glands.
○ *Association:* Are located in the spinal cord and they carry impulses from sensory to motor neurons.

The brain

The brain is one of the largest organs in the body and it consists of:

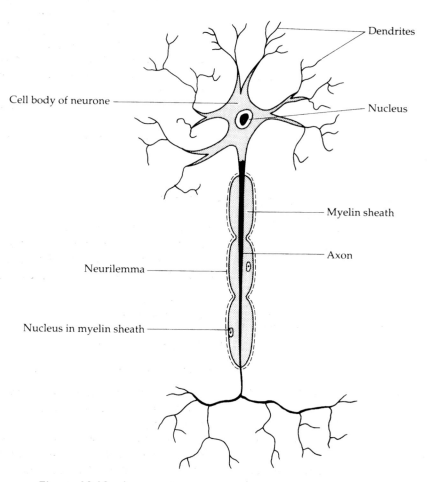

Figure 10.18 *A neurone*

o The brain stem which comprises the medulla oblongata, pons varolii and the midbrain.
o The cerebrum which makes up about seven-eighths of the weight of the brain and occupies most of the cranium.
o The thalamus and hypothalamus above the brain stem.
o The cerebellum which lies below the cerebrum and behind the brain stem.

It is protected by the cranial bones and the cranial meninges composed of dense fibrous connective tissue. The cerebrospinal fluid also acts as a protection against injury circulating around the brain and through the ventricles in the brain serving as a shock absorber for the central nervous system. See Figure 10.19.

It has a good supply of blood vessels which provide oxygen and nutrients.

The brain stem

The medulla oblongata
This is a continuation of the upper part of the spinal cord and the lowest part of the brain stem. It contains centres which help to control the heart rate, the depth and rate of breathing and other non-vital autonomic reflexes such as swallowing, sneezing and coughing.

Pons varolli
This is situated just above the medulla oblongata and in front of the cerebellum. As the name implies, it is a bridge connecting the spinal cord with the brain and parts of the brain with each other.

The midbrain
This part of the brain stem is the highest and is situated centrally under the cerebrum just below the hypothalamus.

The thalamus and hypothalamus

The thalamus is the main relay station for sensory impulses sent to the cerebral cortex from the spinal cord, brain stem, cerebellum and parts of the cerebrum and it interprets sensory messages to the brain. It is also concerned with memory and certain emotions. It is situated above the midbrain and is approximately 3 cm in length.

The hypothalamus is a small but important area under the thalamus and just above the pituitary gland (the main endocrine gland), responsible for controlling many body activities and most of them related to homeostasis:

o It helps to control the autonomic nervous system, regulating the heartbeat, controlling the secretion of many glands, the movement of food through the digestive tract and contraction of the urinary bladder.
o It receives sensory impulses.
o It is the principal intermediary between the nervous system and the endocrine system. When it detects certain changes occurring in the body it releases chemicals that stimulate or inhibit the anterior pituitary gland.
o It produces two hormones – ADH and oxytocin – which are transported and stored in the posterior pituitary gland.
o It controls normal body temperature.
o It stimulates hunger and inhibits food intake when full.
o It produces a sensation of thirst when fluid is reduced in the body.
o It helps to maintain waking and sleeping patterns.

Cerebrum

Often referred to as the cerebral cortex, it forms a large part of the brain and is divided into four lobes, each of which takes its name from the bone under which it lies and they are:

1 The frontal lobe.
2 The parietal lobe.
3 The occipital lobe.
4 The temporal lobe.

Functions of the cerebrum are:

o Mental activities involving memory, intelligence, sense of responsibility, thinking and reasoning.
o Sensory perception of pain, temperature, touch, sight, hearing, taste and smell.
o Initiation and control of voluntary muscle contraction.

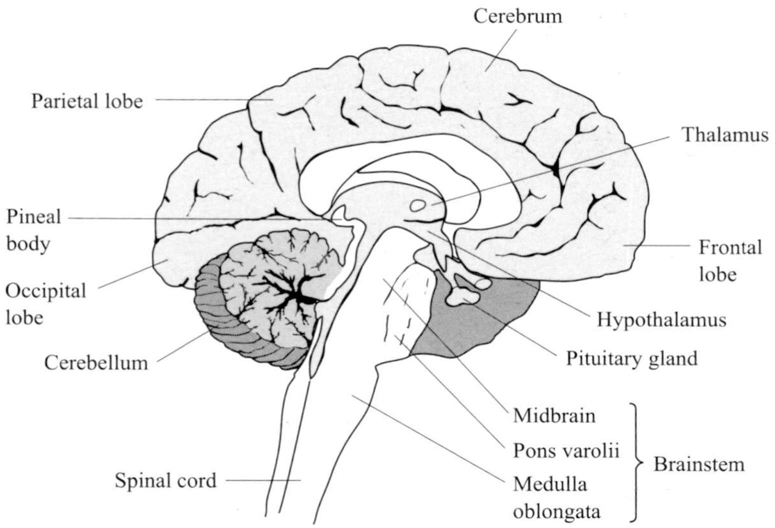

Figure 10.19 *Section through the brain*

Cerebellum

The second largest area in the brain occupying the posterior/inferior aspect of the cranial cavity. It is a motor area of the brain controlling subconscious movements of the skeletal muscles, movements required for posture co-ordination, balance and delicate movements, for example playing the piano or typing a letter. Messages are transmitted from the inner ear to the cerebellum which responds by sending impulses to the muscles necessary for maintaining balance.

The spinal cord

The spinal cord begins as a continuation of the medulla oblongata extending down the vertebral column (Figure 10.20). Its main function is conveying impulses to and from the brain and the peripheral nervous system. Its second function is to provide reflexes which are fast responses to internal or external stimuli, helping to maintain the body's internal balance.

There are thirty-one spinal nerves which are named according to the region from which they emerge. They are as follows:

○ Eight pairs of cervical nerves.
○ Twelve pairs of thoracic.
○ Five pairs of lumbar.
○ Five pairs of sacral.
○ One pair of coccygeal.

Each spinal nerve splits into branches which in turn split into smaller branches to form a network which radiates all over the body.

Note: The cranial nerves have been dealt with on pages 15–16.

The autonomic nervous system

This is the part of the nervous system that supplies involuntary muscle tissue in the body controlling movements of internal organs and secretions from glands.

It is divided into:

1 The sympathetic nervous system.
2 The parasympathetic nervous system.

The two parts have opposing effects on the body in stressful situations:

○ Sympathetic nerves speed up body activity.
○ Parasympathetic nerves slow down body activity.

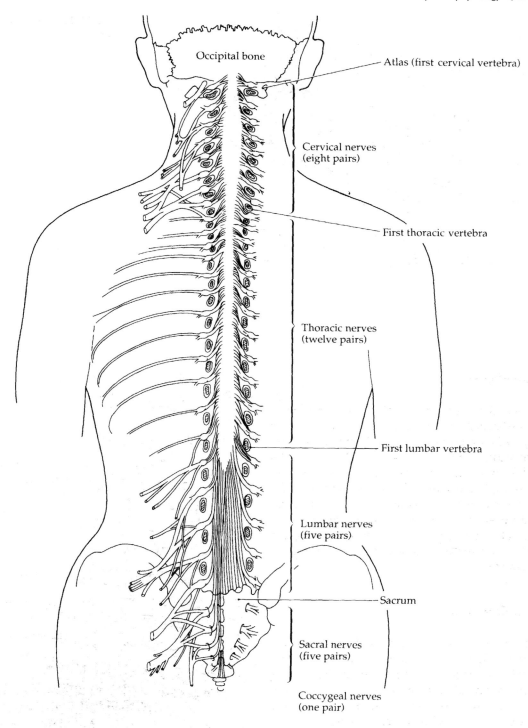

Occipital bone

Atlas (first cervical vertebra)

Cervical nerves
(eight pairs)

First thoracic vertebra

Thoracic nerves
(twelve pairs)

First lumbar vertebra

Lumbar nerves
(five pairs)

Sacrum

Sacral nerves
(five pairs)

Coccygeal nerves
(one pair)

Figure 10.20 *The spinal cord and spinal nerves*

The sympathetic impulses become stronger as a reaction to stress: the heart beats faster; blood vessels dilate; the liver produces more glucose; the pupils of the eyes dilate; hair stands on end; the sweat glands produce more sweat; and blood pressure rises due to the constriction of small arterioles in the skin. The body is now prepared to cope.

When the stressful situation passes the parasympathetic nerves take over and help the function of the organs to return to normal.

The respiratory system

Oxygen is essential for cells to survive and it is brought into the body every time we inhale and carbon dioxide is released when we exhale. This process is called respiration. The cardiovascular system and the respiratory system are both responsible for supplying oxygen to the tissues and eliminating carbon dioxide.

Respiration

This is the process by which oxygen is taken into the body and used for the oxidation of food materials, to liberate the energy necessary to support life, and carbon dioxide and water are released as waste.

External respiration is the physical means by which the oxygen is obtained and the carbon dioxide is removed from the body.

Internal respiration is a chain of chemical processes which take place in every living cell to free the energy required for its vital activities.

The respiratory system consists of the:

○ Nose.
○ Pharynx.
○ Larynx.
○ Trachea.
○ Lungs.
○ Bronchi.
○ Bronchioles.
○ Intercostal muscles.
○ Diaphragm.

The nose

The nose is the natural pathway of air entering the body and it also acts as protection against irritants such as dust which the nose will expel by sneezing so that the foreign bodies do not enter the lungs.

The nose is divided into two narrow cavities called nasal fossae, by the nasal septum, which is made up of bone and cartilage and covered with a soft delicate membrane called a mucous membrane that is continuous with the lining of the nostrils.

The nostrils are lined with coarse hairs which protect the entrance to the nose. Air entering the nose is warmed to body temperature and moistened by contact with the mucous membrane and then filtered by the tiny hairs or cilia and the mucous, from the mucous membrane. The cilia then moves the mucous gradually into the pharynx where it is swallowed. In the upper part of the nasal cavities the olfactory nerve endings detect smells in the air.

The pharynx and larynx

The throat is the area which leads into the respiratory and digestive tracts from the oral and nasal cavities to the oesophagus and trachea. It is made up of the pharynx and larynx which, together with the trachea, nose and mouth, form the *upper respiratory tract*.

The pharynx (throat) and larynx (voice box) have two main functions:

1   To channel food and liquid into the digestive tract.
2   To transport air into the lungs.
    The pharynx is made up of:
○   The nasopharynx which lies above the soft palate and forms the back of the nose.
○   The oropharynx at the back of the mouth is part of the airway between the mouth and lungs.
○   The laryngopharynx is the lowest part of the pharynx which is involved entirely with swallowing.

The movements of the pharynx are carefully co-ordinated to ensure that respiratory gases end up in the lungs and food ends up in the oesophagus.

The larynx is situated between the pharynx and the trachea and it is the body's voice box containing the vocal chords which vibrate to produce speech.

The function of the larynx in respiration is its secondary function. The opening from the pharynx into the larynx is called the glottis and is closed by the epiglottis. When we breathe in or out the epiglottis is opened to allow air into the lungs.

The trachea

The trachea or windpipe as it is more commonly called, is a tubular passageway for air approximately 12 cm in length and 2.5 cm in diameter. It extends from the larynx to the right and left bronchi. The wall of the trachea is made up of smooth muscle and elastic connective tissue with hoops of cartilage that hold open the elastic tissue. It is lined with mucous membrane and cilia which waft invading germs and foreign particles back up into the throat to be swallowed.

The lungs

The two lungs fill most of the thorax and each one is divided into lobes containing a dense network of tubes (Figure 10.21). The right lung is larger and is divided into three lobes – the upper, middle and lower lobes. The left lung is slightly smaller, as the heart takes up more room on the left-side of the thorax and it is divided into two lobes – the upper and lower.

The largest of the tubes in the lungs are the bronchi and the smallest are the bronchioles which terminate in air sacs called alveoli where the exchange of oxygen and carbon dioxide takes place. The second system of tubes is formed by the pulmonary arteries which enter the lungs alongside the right and left bronchi. These tubes branch into smaller blood vessels running alongside the bronchioles and at the alveoli they form small capillaries.

The pleural membrane encloses and protects each lung and they are held open by the surface tension created by the fluid produced by the pleural membrane.

The bronchi and bronchioles

Where the trachea terminates in the chest it divides into the right bronchus which enters the right lung and the left bronchus which enters

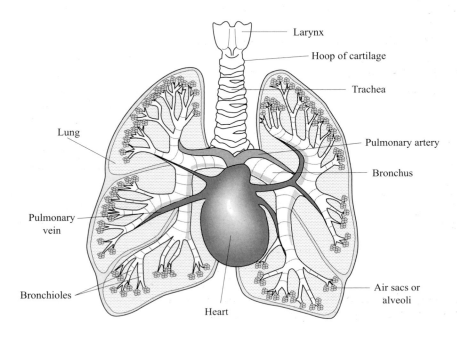

Figure 10.21 *Cross-section of the lungs*

Larynx

Hoop of cartilage

Trachea

Pulmonary artery

Bronchus

Air sacs or alveoli

Lung

Pulmonary vein

Bronchioles

Heart

the left lung. Inside the lungs the bronchi further divide into secondary and tertiary (third) bronchi which become smaller tubes called bronchioles. These bronchioles terminate in air sacs called alveoli.

The intercostal muscles

The external and internal intercostal muscles are situated between the ribs. When the external muscles are contracted they move the ribcage upwards helping to increase lung volume during inspiration (breathing in). When the internal muscles are contracted they force air out of the lungs during expiration (breathing out).

The diaphragm

This is a sheet of muscle which forms the floor of the thoracic cavity. When it contracts it flattens increasing the vertical space in the thoracic cavity, allowing the lungs to expand and fill with air during inspiration. When this muscle is relaxed it increases in size becoming dome-shaped, this reduces the space in the thoracic cavity and this helps to squeeze air out of the lungs during expiration.

Breathing

We breathe on average twelve times per minute. This rate will increase considerably during physical exercise up to eighty times per minute. In a 24-hour period we breathe in and breathe out more than 8000 litres of air. Oxygen is carried to the body's tissues to produce the energy required for life via the lungs, the heart and the blood vessels.

Oxygen enters through the mouth, nose, trachea into the lungs where it travels to the alveoli, via the bronchioles and the exchange of oxygen and carbon dioxide takes place. Oxygen is taken up by the haemoglobin in the blood and the red blood cells discharge carbon dioxide back into the lungs to be exhaled.

The process of breathing

Oxygen is taken in through the mouth and nose
↓
Oxygen passes through the trachea into the lungs
↓
The diaphragm contracts increasing the depth of the thorax
↓
The intercostal muscles contract moving the ribs upwards and outwards
↓
The diameter of the thorax increases
↓
The lungs fill with oxygen
↓
Oxygen travels to the alveoli via the bronchi and bronchioles
↓
Exchange of oxygen and carbon dioxide takes place between the alveoli and capillary network

The digestive system

Food is vital to life. The food we eat is too large to pass through to the cells that require it, so it has to be broken down for use by the body's cells during *digestion*. The organs which perform this function make up the *digestive system*.

Digestion is the process which breaks down food into molecules which are small enough to be absorbed by the cells and used by the body for energy, growth and repair.

Digestion occurs in the alimentary canal which consists of the:

○ Mouth.
○ Pharynx.
○ Oesophagus.
○ Stomach.
○ Small intestine – duodenum, jejunum, ileum.
○ Large intestine – caecum, appendix, colon and rectum.

The digestive process

Food is prepared for consumption by five basic activities of the digestive system:

1 *Ingestion* – taking food into the body through the mouth.
2 *Peristalsis* – movement of food along the digestive tract.
3 *Digestion* – the breakdown of food by both mechanical and chemical processes.
4 *Absorption* – the passage of digested food from the digestive tract into the cardiovascular and lymphatic systems for distribution to cells.
5 *Excretion* – the elimination of indigestible substances from the body.

Mechanical digestion

This consists of various movements that will aid chemical digestion:

Food is prepared by the teeth
↓
Food is then swallowed
↓
Muscles of the stomach and the small intestine churn up the food
↓
This allows food to be thoroughly mixed with enzymes that catalyse reactions

Chemical digestion

This is a series of catabolic reactions that break down the large carbohydrate, lipid and protein molecules into smaller molecules which are used by body cells. These products of digestion are small enough to pass through the walls of the digestive organs into the blood and lymph capillaries and eventually into the body cells.

The alimentary canal

Digestion and absorption take place during the passage of food through the alimentary canal. This is a continuous tube, approximately 9 metres (30 feet) long, from the mouth to the anus, most of its length is coiled up in the abdominal cavity.

The mouth or buccal cavity
Food is chewed in the mouth by teeth. It is turned over and tasted by the tongue and mixed with saliva from the salivary glands. The saliva contains the enzyme *ptyalin* which starts breaking down some of the carbohydrates into smaller molecules known as maltose and glucose. The food mass or *bolus* produced is then swallowed.

The pharynx and oesophagus
This is divided into the naso-pharynx at the back of the nose and the oro-pharynx at the back of the mouth. During swallowing these two regions are separated by the soft palate and the opening from the pharynx into the larynx is closed by the raising and pulling of the larynx forward. After swallowing the food, by contraction of the muscles of the walls in the pharynx, digestion continues automatically as we now have no control over its movement. The food is carried down the oesophagus by muscular contraction termed *peristalsis*.

The stomach
The food reaches the stomach and is acted upon chemically by the digestive juices, secreted from the glands of the mucous membrane and mechanically by the muscles of the stomach wall. Mucous, hydrochloric acid and the enzyme *pepsin* are poured on to the food and a new series of chemical reactions begin. The amount of stomach juices released is governed by nerve impulses, the presence of food and the secretion of hormones.

The hormone *gastrin* stimulates the stomach cells to release *hydrochloric acid* and *pepsin* to break the food down into peptones.

The mucous secretion prevents the stomach lining from becoming damaged by acid and gastrin production ceases when the acidity reaches a certain point. The food is broken down into a semi-fluid called *chyme*, which is then forced into the duodenum, part of the small intestine.

The small intestine
The small intestine is approximately 8 metres (23 feet) long, the first 25 cm (10 in) form the *duodenum* into which the bile duct and pancreatic duct open. The rest of the small intestine forms the *jejunum* and *ileum*.

The digestion of the food is completed in the small intestine, the acidity of the chyme is neutralized in the duodenum by the bile poured in from the gall bladder where it is stored after being produced in the liver and pancreatic juice from the pancreas.

Pancreatic enzymes help the digestion of carbohydrates and proteins as well as fats:

○ Trypsin breaks up carbohydrates and proteins as well as fats into smaller units called peptides.
○ Lipase breaks down fats into glycerol and fatty acids.
○ Amylase breaks down carbohydrates into maltose.

The digested food then enters the jejunum and ileum. The jejunum provides the site where the useful nutritional elements of food are absorbed and the absorption process is then completed in the ileum which contains millions of minute projections called villi on its inner wall. Each villus contains a capillary and a blind ended lymphatic vessel called a lacteal.

Glycerol, fatty acids and dissolved vitamins are carried via the lacteal in the villus into the lymphatic system and are then poured into the bloodstream. This fat containing lymph fluid which drains from the intestine is called *chyle*.

Amino acids from protein digestion and sugars from carbohydrates plus vitamins and minerals such as calcium, iron and iodine are absorbed directly into the capillaries in the villi.

The capillaries lead into the hepatic portal vein which then transports the food into the liver for processing before it goes into the rest of the body or stores it for its own use.

The large intestine

This is about 1.3 metres (4.5 feet) long and is divided into the caecum, colon, rectum and anal canal:

○ The caecum is a small pouch to which the appendix is attached and into which the ileum opens.
○ The colon is divided into three parts: the ascending, the transverse and the descending colon.
○ The rectum is a small muscular tube which is a continuation of the descending colon and runs directly through the pelvis to the anal canal, the opening through which the body's solid waste products are excreted.

The functions of the large intestine are:

○ Movement of solid material to the anus by the process of peristalsis.
○ Production of mucous to lubricate the passage of the faeces.
○ Absorption of the small amounts of digested food still present among the waste.
○ Absorption of most of the water to dry the faeces and conserve moisture in the body.
○ Storage of faeces and defecation.

Homeostasis

Homeostasis is the condition in which the body's internal environment remains relatively constant, within certain limits. In simple terms the body is balanced and all systems are working effectively.

Homeo means same.
Stasis means standing still.

Homeostasis is disturbed by stress which creates an imbalance in the internal environment of the body. Stress comes from different sources:

○ External, such as excessive heat or cold, lack of oxygen or persistent loud noise.
○ Internal, such as high blood pressure, pain, anxiety, fear or bereavement.

Severe stress may be caused by such things as surgical operations, systemic illness or poisoning.

The body is normally able to cope with these problems and helps itself to re-balance internally. These coping mechanisms are called homeostatic functions, keeping the internal environment of the body within normal limits.

Some examples of homeostatic functions include:

○ The cardiovascular system keeps fluids constantly moving, changing pace to cope with activity and bringing the increased amounts of nutrients required for the body to cope with the increase in activity.
○ The respiratory system works faster during increased activity to prevent oxygen falling below normal limits and to prevent excessive amounts of carbon dioxide from accumulating.

o The nervous system regulates homeostasis by detecting when the body is deviating from its balanced state. It then sends messages to the organs concerned to counteract the problem.

Homeostasis of blood pressure

If the heartbeat speeds up due to some sort of physical or mental stress the following occurs:

o More blood is pushed into the arteries.
o Blood pressure is increased.
o Nerve cells in the walls of some arteries detect the change.
o Nerve impulses are sent to the brain.
o The brain responds by sending messages to the heart to slow down.
o Therefore blood pressure is decreased.
o Homeostasis is maintained.

Homeostasis of blood sugar

Hormones are responsible for maintaining homeostasis of blood sugar levels:

o Glucose, a principal source of energy, is found in blood.
o Sugar levels are maintained by insulin and glucagon secreted by the pancreas.
o After eating food high in sugar it is digested and enters the blood.
o Stress is caused because the blood sugar level is raised above normal.
o In response the pancreas secretes insulin.
o In the blood insulin increases sugar uptake by cells.
o Blood sugar levels are lowered.
o Insulin also accelerates the process by which sugar is stored in the liver and muscles.
o More sugar is removed from the blood.
o Homeostasis is maintained.

Medical conditions that may contraindicate treatment

Diabetes

There are two types of diabetes:

1 *Diabetes insipidus,* a condition caused by the hyposecretion of the antidiuretic hormone (ADH) and it is characterized by the excretion of large amounts of urine and extreme thirst.
2 *Diabetes mellitus,* a condition caused by hyposecretion of insulin and characterized by hyperglycaemia (an elevated blood sugar level), increased urine production, excessive thirst and excessive eating. There are two major types:

o *Maturity onset diabetes* which often occurs in people who are overweight and over 50 when the level of insulin can be just above or just below the normal level and it may be controlled by diet alone. It is referred to as *non-insulin dependent diabetes.*
o *Juvenile onset diabetes* is a condition which develops in children and young adults. It is a more severe condition caused by a marked decline of islet cells in the pancreas which causes insufficient insulin production and an elevation of the glucose level in the blood. It is referred to as *insulin dependent diabetes.* This deficiency of insulin causes an accelerated breakdown of the body's fat reserves which result in the production of organic acids called ketones. As the fat is transported in the blood, particles are deposited on the walls of the blood vessels. This can lead to atherosclerosis and other cardiovascular conditions even when the condition is controlled by diet and insulin.

Diabetics are also highly susceptible to infection because phagocyte activity is depressed by insufficient intracellular glucose and they suffer from poor skin sensitivity and slow skin healing. Infection may lead to complications in areas affected by changes in blood vessels, for example the feet when sensation and blood supply are impaired.

Because of the varied complications caused by diabetes, the condition may contraindicate some forms of beauty treatment and it will be necessary to seek permission from your client's doctor before proceeding with any treatment.

Epilepsy

This is a neurological disorder and it causes short recurrent attacks of sensory, motor or psychological malfunction and those who suffer from the condition normally carry an identification card or wear a bracelet. These attacks are known as epileptic seizures and they are caused by abnormal and irregular discharges of electricity from neurones in the brain, many of which can be stimulated, sending out impulses. During seizure an individual will contract skeletal muscles involuntarily. Some brain centres may be depressed, for example the waking centre, causing a loss of consciousness and noises and smells can sometimes be sensed even when the ears and nose have not been stimulated.

The attacks can be small, *petit mal*, when the person loses contact for only 5 to 30 seconds, giving the appearance of daydreaming and without losing motor control. Large seizures known as *grand mal* are caused by electrical charges travelling throughout the motor areas of the brain and they cause the person to lose consciousness, have muscular spasms and even lose urinary and bowel control. This may sometimes be preceded by a funny taste in the mouth, the appearance of flashing lights and imagined smells. This is referred to as an aura and the sufferer may realize that an attack is imminent and be able to lie down to avoid injury.

Epilepsy may be caused by many things including:

○ Head injuries.
○ Abscesses of the brain.
○ Tumours of the brain.
○ Infections in childhood such as mumps, measles and whooping cough.

The condition may be controlled by drugs but it is not advisable to use electrical equipment on a client who suffers from epilepsy and medical permission must be sought if other treatments are requested. All members of staff should be aware of the first aid treatment for anyone suffering an epileptic attack:

○ Protect them from any danger or hazard.
○ Keep others away.
○ Speak quietly to the client.

In the case of grand mal:

○ Support or try to ease the fall.
○ Clear a space around the person.
○ Carefully loosen clothing around the neck if possible.
○ Place a soft support under the head.
○ When the attack ceases, place the client in the recovery position.

Multiple sclerosis

This is a condition which affects the central nervous system. It is the progressive destruction of the myeline sheaths in the neurones. Because of the destruction there is an interference with the transmission of messages from one neurone to another and the first symptoms of this disorder often occur between the ages of 20 and 40. The myelin sheaths deteriorate to scleroses (hardened scar tissue or plaques with a loss of elasticity) and this happens in multiple areas. Initially only a few of these plaques are formed so the symptoms are mild, periods of remission are interspersed with periods of damage and after each attack more neurones are damaged by the hardening of their sheaths, causing the progressive loss of function.

The symptoms shown will depend upon the area of the nervous system which is most affected by the formation of these plaques and may include:

○ Lack of co-ordination.
○ Partial paralysis of muscles.
○ Facial neuralgia.
○ Double vision.
○ Urinary tract infections.
○ Loss of ability to contract skeletal muscles.
○ Numbness.
○ Destruction of spinal cord reflexes.

11 Body massage

Body massage is a treatment which may be provided on its own or after some other form of treatment. It is used as a treatment to maintain physical health and well-being as well as inducing relaxation. It has become increasingly more popular in recent years as more and more people are becoming aware of the need to counteract stress in their lives and help eliminate the resulting problems.

Some of the more common problems caused by stress are:

○ Insomnia.
○ Migraine.
○ Asthma.
○ Gastric ulcers.
○ High blood pressure.
○ Lowering of resistance to disease.
○ Premature ageing.

Prolonged bouts of stress causes tension in all parts of the body but particularly in the muscles. The ability to perform a relaxing massage, therefore, is an essential key to success for therapists who provide body treatments.

General effects of body massage

○ Increases the circulation thereby increasing the interchange of tissue fluids which relieves fatigue in the muscles.
○ Removes physical tension in the muscles.
○ The lymphatic system is stimulated to remove waste products more efficiently.
○ The increase in circulation causes a hyperaemia thus improving skin colour.
○ The increased circulation also brings nourishment to the skin so improving its functions.
○ Softens and breaks down fatty tissue.

○ Stimulates or soothes nerve endings in the skin.
○ Texture of the skin is improved through desquamation.
○ Improves skin elasticity.
○ Induces relaxation.
○ Rejuvenating.
○ Promotes a sense of well-being.
○ Encourages some clients to adhere to their diet.
○ Softens and moisturizes the skin.

Massage can be beneficial to most people even if it has to be adapted in some way. If clients are attending regularly for other treatments then there will be a record of their medical history. If not, this information must be recorded and if necessary clients should be advised to seek medical approval before starting any form of treatment.

Contraindications

It is important that therapists can assess each client's suitability for treatment and understand that some contraindications are temporary and others just local so that only a small area needs to be omitted from the procedure, for example varicose veins, hairy skin.

○ Any condition that would require medical supervision.
○ Any recent operations or injuries such as a fracture.
○ Skin diseases.
○ Undiagnosed lumps.
○ Heart disorders.
○ High and low blood pressure.
○ Neuritis – inflammation of the nerves.
○ Lung disease.
○ Haemophilia – danger of bleeding if bruised.

○ High fever.
○ Sunburn.
○ Later stages of pregnancy.

When the client appears to be in extreme muscular pain the doctor must be consulted as this may mask a more serious problem, for example a slipped disc.

Classification of massage manipulations

Massage is the manipulation of body tissues either manually or mechanically to produce beneficial effects on the muscular, vascular and nervous systems of the body. The manipulations used are termed:

○ Effleurage and stroking.
○ Petrissage.
○ Tapotement.
○ Vibrations.

Effleurage and stroking

Are soothing, smooth stroking movements which are divided into:

1 Deep and superficial effleurage.
2 Deep and superficial stroking.

The technique is exactly the same for the deep movement as the superficial, the only difference being the pressure applied.

Effleurage
Effleurage starts and concludes any massage sequence and is interspersed with other movements during the massage to provide continuity and ensure that the massage is as relaxing as possible, keeping the hands constantly in touch with the client.

Effleurage is performed with the whole palmar surface of the hand following the direction of the blood flow back to the heart (commonly termed venous return) and the lymphatic flow, ending in a group of lymph glands.

The movement should be slow, smooth and rhythmical, with the hand moulded to the area being treated, ending in slight pressure and returning to the point of origin without breaking contact but exerting no pressure. The hands may perform the movement alternately or together. See Figure 11.1.

Effects
○ Improves general circulation.
○ Increases the flow of lymph, removing waste products more efficiently.
○ Soothes the sensory nerve endings so inducing relaxation.
○ Provides continuity of movement which promotes relaxation and allows the client to become accustomed to the massage.
○ Aids desquamation.

Stroking
Soothing stroking is a slow rhythmical movement performed in any direction very gently with the hand moulded lightly to the part. One hand may follow alternately from the other or both hands may be used together. It stimulates the superficial nerve endings in the skin and revitalizes lethargic clients.

Effects
○ Soothes the superficial nerve endings in the skin.
○ Relieves tension.
○ Cools down a hot area of skin.
○ Promotes relaxation.
○ Stimulating stroking is performed much more vigorously and again in any direction.

Petrissage

These are pressure manipulations and include the following movements:

○ Kneading.
○ Picking up.
○ Wringing.
○ Rolling.
○ Friction.

Pressure is applied to the muscle and then it is released systematically working over a muscle or group of muscles. The amount of pressure exerted on the muscle will depend upon the area being worked and the purpose of the massage.

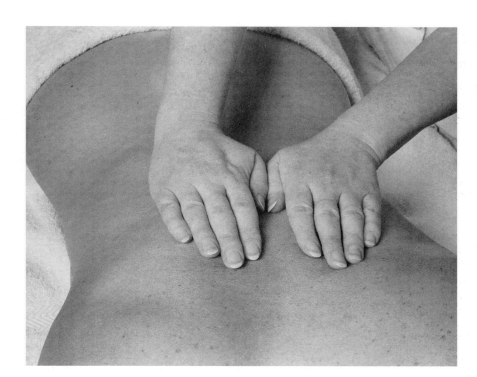

Figure 11.1 *Effleurage to the back*

A greater degree of pressure may be used on a large muscle area, for example the gluteal muscles and reduced on a smaller area, for example biceps and triceps.

Whichever movement is employed it will follow the shape of the muscle and normally towards the heart. The pressure may be applied by pressing the muscles down on to the underlying structures or lifting tissue away from the underlying structures.

Kneading

Kneading can be adapted for different parts of the body to cope with the difference in size and shape of the muscles. The tissues are pressed down on to the underlying structures and there are several types of kneading performed either with one or both hands:

1 *Flat-handed kneading:* This can be single-, double-handed or alternate. It is usually performed on the back as the muscles are large thin sheets.
2 *Squeezing kneading.*
3 *Circular kneading:* This is a deep movement when the muscles are pressed against the bone in a circular motion.

4 *Finger kneading:* This is a circular movement but this time performed with the padded palmar surfaces of the thumb or first and second fingers. It is normally performed on small areas such as the feet and around the shoulders or down either side of the spine.
5 *Ironing:* Also known as reinforced kneading, the hands are placed one on top of each other to obtain greater depth (Figure 11.2).

Effects

o Increased blood supply to nourish and remove waste products.
o To promote relaxation and remove tension from the muscles.
o Prevents fatigue by removing lactic acid from the muscles.
o Relieves aches and pains.
o Aids joint mobility.

Picking up

Double-handed picking up is when the muscle is lifted, squeezed and relaxed with both hands working alternately along the length of the muscle (Figure 11.3).

Single handed picking up is performed with one hand on a small muscle area, for example

Figure 11.2 *Ironing or reinforced kneading to the back*

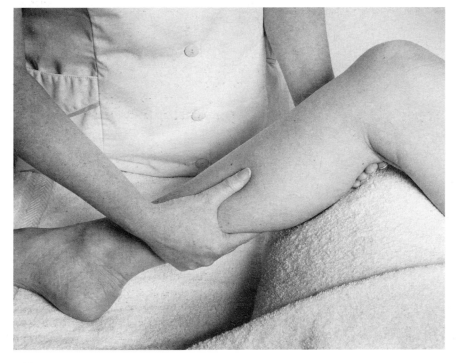

Figure 11.3 *Single handed picking up to gastrocnemius*

the deltoid and in this case the muscle is lifted and squeezed with the thumb on one side and the fingers on the other.

Effects
○ A deep movement effective on stubborn areas of fatty tissue.
○ Increases the circulation and lymphatic flow.

Wringing
This is a picking up of the muscle and then wringing it from side-to-side using both hands and pressing the tissue between the thumb of one hand and the fingers of the other, again working along the length of the muscle (Figure 11.4).

Effects
○ Increases the circulation.
○ Warmth is produced quickly in the tissues.
○ Effective on fatty areas.

Rolling
The fingers of both hands grasp the superficial tissues over underlying bone and the thumbs roll them gently against the fingers (Figure 11.5).

Effects
○ Apart from the normal increase in circulation with its accompanying benefits this manipulation can be used to loosen skin over tight areas.

Frictions
These movements are performed with the thumb or finger tips. They are deep pressure movements and can be performed in a small circular movement or transversely, across the muscle, pressing down on the underlying structures.

Effects
○ Breaks down adhesions in muscle.
○ Loosens scar tissue.
○ Joint mobility is increased.

Tapotement

These are also known as percussion movements. They are all stimulating and come in several different forms:

○ Hacking.
○ Clapping or cupping.
○ Beating.
○ Pounding.

Hacking
When performing this movement the hands should be totally relaxed and at right angles to the wrists with the elbows bent and the arms away from the body.

The hacking is performed across the muscle fibres with both hands working alternately and the fingers should strike the area rapidly leaving the area as soon as they make contact, to produce light flicking movements (Figure 11.6).

Effects
○ Has a stimulating effect on the nerve endings.
○ Has a revitalizing effect on tired muscles.
○ The increase in circulation warms the area.

Clapping or cupping
This movement is performed with the hands in a cupped position and the wrists relaxed. By flexing and extending the wrist, the hands are lifted and dropped in quick succession rapidly but with a light touch (Figure 11.7). When performed correctly there will be a hollow cupping sound.

Effects
○ Increases circulation bringing nourishment and removing waste.
○ Increases warmth in the area.
○ Helps in breaking up fatty tissue.

Beating
Loosely clenched fists are used to perform this movement and it is slightly heavier than clapping but performed in a similar manner dropping the fists from just below shoulder level, alternately and rhythmically.

Pounding
With loosely clenched fists and the elbows abducted the ulnar side of the fist will strike the area, moving towards the body rapidly alternating with both hands and moving away from the area as soon as it is struck.

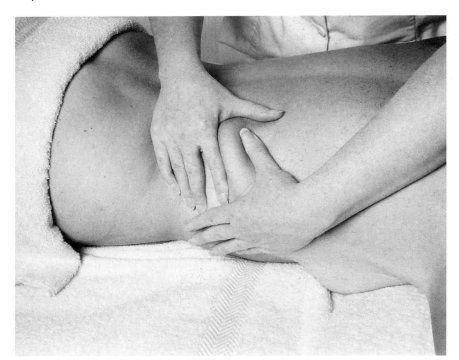

Figure 11.4 *Wringing to the back*

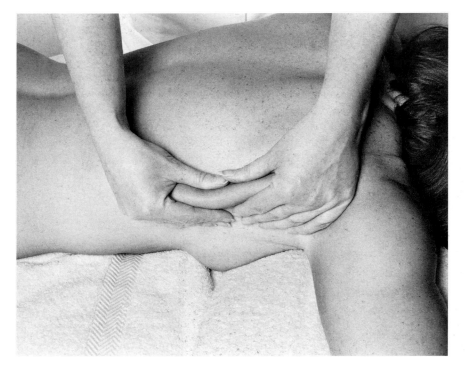

Figure 11.5 *Skin rolling on the back*

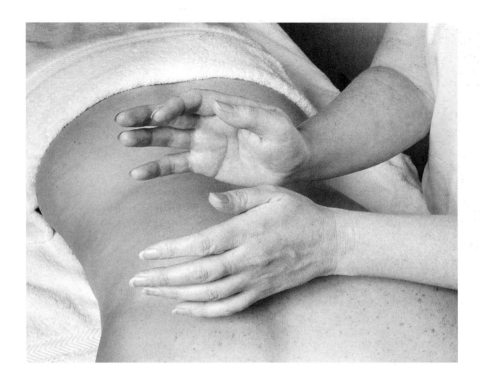

Figure 11.6 *Hacking on the back*

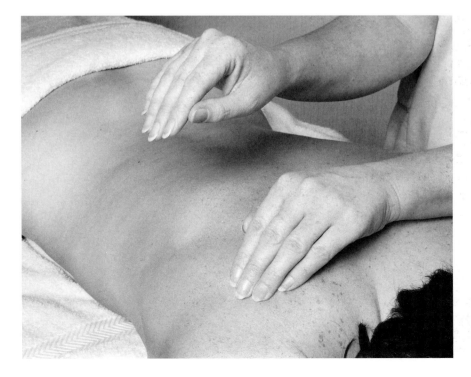

Figure 11.7 *Cupping on the back*

Effects
- The effects of these last two movements are stimulating.
- They will help to soften adipose tissue.
- Increases circulation.
- Warm the area.
- Toning.

Vibrations

These are fine trembling movements using the whole palmar surface of the hand or with the fingertips only. By contracting and relaxing the muscles in the forearm the fine trembling movement or vibration occurs.

The movements can be:

- Fine.
- Coarse.
- Static (in one place).
- Running (moving over an area while vibrating the hands).

Effects
- Stimulating to the nerve endings when the vibrations are coarse.
- Can induce relaxation when the vibrations are fine.

The effects of massage on the body

The circulation

The circulation of blood carries food and oxygen to all parts of the body and provides a defence against infection. It also carries away waste products via the lymphatic circulation. Therefore, an increase in circulation as a result of massage is going to:

1. Improve nutrition in the tissues and remove waste products more effectively.
2. Increase cellular regeneration.

The tissues are warmed because of the increased circulation. However, some massage movements will cause the surface capillaries to contract and this will have a cooling effect on the body.

The skin

A massage will have the following effects on the skin:

- The colour of the skin is improved because of the increase in circulation which causes the capillaries to dilate.
- Removal of waste products is speeded up through the lymphatic system and the sweat glands, therefore cleansing the skin.
- Skin texture is improved as the dead skin cells are desquamated from the surface.
- The activity of the sebaceous glands is increased therefore more sebum is produced to make the skin soft and supple. This helps to keep it intact preventing bacteria from entering.
- The skin is also nourished externally by the application of the special oils or creams applied as a massage medium. Different skin conditions may be treated with the appropriate product.
- The skin functions more efficiently helping to maintain its elasticity.

The muscles

When muscles have been working hard or exercising they require more oxygen, which in turn produces more waste or lactic acid, causing the muscles to stiffen.

Massage increases the circulation bringing more oxygen and removing the build-up of lactic acid leaving the muscles feeling refreshed. The increased circulation also provides the muscles with nourishment. The muscles are relaxed and elasticity is improved.

Massage also helps weak muscles to improve in tone, and aids joint mobility which helps in movement of muscles attached to the joints. Tension nodules in the muscles can be eased away gently.

The nerves

The nervous system is soothed when the massage is slow and rhythmical. Some massage movements, particularly tapotement, can be stimulating to the nerves.

Adipose tissue

This is the fatty tissue of the body and is very difficult to remove with massage alone. Therefore, for maximum effect, massage should be accompanied by a good diet and regular exercise.

Poor circulation and fat deposits together may be treated effectively with massage by moving the tissue fluids and allowing absorption of the adipose tissue through increased metabolism.

Metabolism

Metabolism is the process by which the body converts food and other substances into energy for its own use, growth, repair and maintenance of a fit and healthy body. Part of this process is the digestion of food which when broken down is absorbed and used in the metabolic process, providing energy.

Incorrect metabolism can cause minor health problems, that is, sluggish skin, over-weight, greasy or spotty skin. Massage can help to stimulate the metabolism improving the general health of the body.

12 *Aromatherapy*

This is a form of massage which is not only relaxing in its application but with the careful use of essential oils has other beneficial effects on the body. It is the most effective way of introducing essential oils into the body and it is known to benefit both physical and psychological problems (Figure 12.1). As the word suggests *aromatherapy* means:

○ A pleasant sweet smell or fragrance (aroma).
○ Healing treatment serving to improve or maintain health (therapy).

Aromatherapy is a holistic treatment using essential oils to promote balance and harmony within mind and body. Essential oils are found in:

Herbs such as rosemary and thyme.
Flowers such as rose, geranium and lavender.
Leaves such as basil, sage and clary sage.
Fruits such as tangerine, lemon and grapefruit.
Berries such as juniper and cypress.
Bark like cinnamon.
Resin which may be made into incense, for example myrrh and benzoin.
Wood such as sandalwood or rosewood.
Seeds such as anise and caraway.
Roots such as angelica.
Nuts such as nutmeg.
Grasses such as lemon grass.

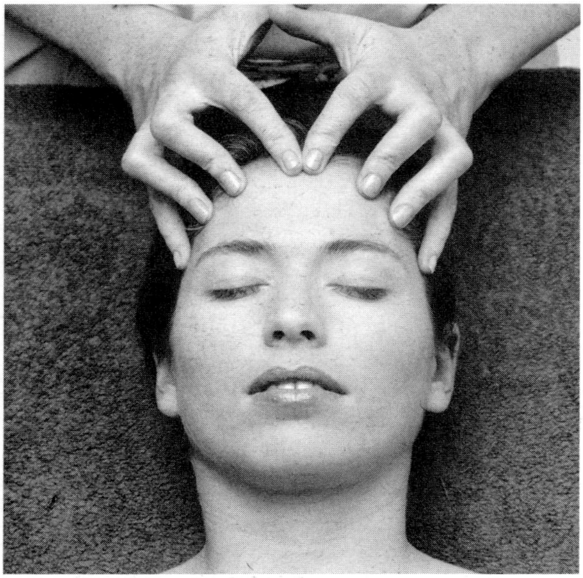

These essential oils provide not only the aroma of a plant but also many complex chemicals that treat the body in many ways. The beneficial properties of essential oils, which are sometimes referred to as the life force of a plant, are far more effective than the aroma produced from the flower or plant as they are more concentrated.

Together the use of essential oils and massage helps to maintain optimum health. They will work on the autonomic nervous system and the central nervous system, affecting the energy fields of the body. Stress causes suppression of the immune system and this treatment is an excellent antidote helping to establish and maintain balance between the nervous systems and organs of the body.

Figure 12.1 *Pressure point massage to the face. Courtesy Elemis Limited*

Extraction methods

Steam distillation

The raw materials are collected and placed in large vats with water and then heated. The steam extracts the oil from the plant and the vapour produced passes into a condenser and is then cooled with the essential oil separating from the flower water. This is the most commonly used method.

Figure 12.2 *Lemon essential oil. Courtesy Elemis Limited*

and when the alcohol is evaporated off an aromatic absolute remains.

Enfleurage

This is one of the earliest methods used to extract essential oils from flowers. A pure, odourless, cold fat is placed in a thin layer on a glass frame and the flower petals are placed in layers on top. After 30 hours the fat will have absorbed the essential oils. The glass frame is turned and new flowers take their place. Once the fat is saturated with the essential oils it is washed with alcohol which absorbs the essential oils and finally the alcohol is evaporated off leaving pure essential oil. This is an expensive method of extraction which is not in common use.

Maceration

The flowers or petals are slightly ruptured and placed in warm fat. This is repeated many times until the fat becomes saturated with essential oil and is then bathed in alcohol which evaporates leaving essential oil.

Expression

This method is used for citrus oils and the essential oil is expressed by squeezing them from the rind or peel of the fruit. This method is referred to as the cold press method and the best source of raw material would be organically grown fruit which has not been sprayed with pesticides. See Figure 12.2.

Solvent extraction

The raw materials are covered by a solvent such as ether, benzene, petroleum, hexane or acetone and then heated to extract the essential oil. This is then filtered which leaves a paste called concrete made up of wax and fragrance which is then mixed with alcohol and distilled at low temperatures, the alcohol absorbs the fragrance

Quality in essential oils

For the best results the highest quality oils should be used and there are certain considerations to be made when choosing oils:

o Choose a supplier who buys raw materials from areas with the best growing conditions, such things as altitude, soil, climate and time of harvesting affects the quality.
o Organically grown plants yield the highest quality essential oils.
o The more expensive oils are usually of the highest quality.
o Watch for blended oils that mix high quality oils with less expensive ones as the result will be to produce an inferior product which reduces the healing properties of the oil.
o Always buy oils which have the Latin name on the bottle as well as the common name.

Absorption of oils

Oils may be absorbed into the body:

o Orally.
o Manually.
o By inhalation.

Essential oils enter the body as a liquid or vapour. The liquid may be taken orally and absorbed through the mouth into the stomach and intestines where it will enter the bloodstream and reach all the body tissues and organs. Essential oils applied manually should be sufficient and oral application must be under the supervision of an experienced aromatherapist, as improper use orally may be dangerous, affecting the organs of the body in an adverse way. It is not common practice in this country but is a method used in France.

When applied to the skin manually, the oils will be absorbed into the skin, muscular tissue, the joints and the bloodstream where it will reach all the body tissues and organs.

As vapour, oils will be inhaled through the nose and into the lungs. From the lungs it will enter the bloodstream and from the nose it will reach the brain effecting hormonal and neurochemical release which has emotional and psychological effects.

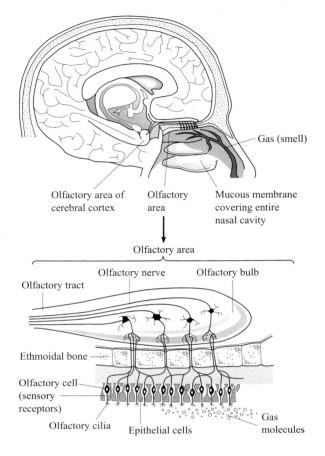

Figure 12.3   *The olfactory system*

The olfactory sensations

Special senses allow us to detect changes in the environment and the sense of smell has a connection with the part of the brain that has grown to be the sorting house for emotional responses. Our sense of smell provides us with a warning system giving us valuable information about the environment and it is closely linked with our sense of taste.

Structure and function of the olfactory system (Figure 12.3)

The sensory receptors for smell are found in the roof of the nasal cavity just below the frontal lobes of the brain. It is known as the *olfactory area* and it contains millions of *olfactory cells*. Each of these cells has about a dozen fine hairs called cilia which are surrounded by mucus to keep the *cilia* moist and trap odorous substances and these cilia help to increase our sensitivity to smell.

Most substances that have a smell are *chemically complex* and particles of these chemicals are given off into the air and then inhaled into the nostrils and to the mucus which surrounds the cilia. These chemicals must then dissolve in the mucus before they can be detected. In order that a substance can be smelled it must be *volatile*, that is, capable of entering a gaseous state so that it can enter the nostrils. The chemicals in gas form are far more efficient as high concentrations will reach the olfactory cells through the air. Wetness also heightens smell because when the water evaporates from a substance it will carry particles with it into the air. A good example is perfume which is chemically complex and gives off gas easily. A substance to be smelled must therefore be:

○ Volatile, entering into a gaseous state to be inhaled.
○ Water soluble so that it can dissolve in the mucus and make contact with the olfactory cells.
○ Lipid soluble, as the plasma membranes of the cilia are largely lipid, so the substance must be able to dissolve in this lipid covering to make contact with the hair in order to initiate a response.

The limbic system

This is the part of the brain which deals with emotions, moods, our motivation, memory and creativity. It is sometimes referred to as the primitive brain. It is closely connected with the part of the brain which receives the messages from the olfactory cells in the nose.

This connection explains why smells evoke particular memories and feelings and smells are so richly endowed with emotional significance:

○ The smell of a mother's scent can provide instant comfort to a child. A perfume may remind us instantly of a loved one we may not have seen for many years or a place where we may have first worn a new fragrance.
○ The smell of freshly baked bread may make us feel instantly hungry.
○ The smell of a new born baby can stimulate maternal feelings long after the children have left home.

Some smells will bring back memories of special occasions because we remember those things which have emotional significance and the areas of the brain which processes memories and recalls events are closely linked to the limbic system and this in turn is linked to the centres in the brain for the sense of smell.

The sense of smell

Gaseous substances are inhaled
↓
They are dissolved in mucus surrounding the cilia
↓
A chemical reaction takes place
↓
The olfactory cells are stimulated into electrical activity
↓
Messages are passed to the olfactory bulb via the sensory nerve fibres
↓
The information is processed
↓
Passed along the olfactory nerves to the cerebral cortex
↓
We then become aware of smell

Odour stimulates the release of neurotransmitters which in turn have a beneficial effect on the body, for example:

○ *Encephaline* and *endorphins* which help to reduce pain and create a feeling of well being.
○ Serotonin *which helps to relax and have a calming effect.*
○ Noradrenaline *which will stimulate and wake up.*

Essential oils are divided into top, middle and base notes:

Top notes

○ Have a sharp and immediate aroma.
○ Evaporation rate is very quick.
○ They are absorbed into the skin quickly.
○ Last for about 10 hours in the body.
○ Originate from citrus plants and herbs.
○ Generally stimulating.
○ Thinnest of the oils.

Middle notes

○ Aroma is more flowery and slower to register.
○ Evaporation is moderately quick.
○ Absorbed into the skin moderately quickly.

○ Last for 24 hours in the body.
○ Originate from herbs and flowers.
○ Generally balancing oils.
○ Affect the body organs.
○ Slightly sedative.

Base notes

○ Aroma is heavier, spicy, woody and floral.
○ Evaporation is slow.
○ Absorbed into the skin very slowly.
○ Lasts up to five days in the body.
○ Originate from woods, resins and flowers.
○ Generally relaxing to mind and body.
○ Some are sedative and aphrodisiac.
○ Fix the top and middle notes.
○ Thickest of the oils.

Classification of top, middle and base notes

Top	Middle	Base
Basil	Aniseed	Benzoin
Bergamot	Black pepper	Cedar wood
Eucalyptus	Camphor	Cinnamon
Lemon	Caraway	Clove
Cajuput	Camomile	Frankincense
Clary sage	Cypress	Ginger
Coriander	Fennel	Jasmine
Lemon grass	Geranium	Marigold
Niaouli	Hyssop	Myrrh
Orange	Juniper	Neroli
Petitgrain	Lavender	Nutmeg
Sage	Marjoram	Origanum
Tea tree	Melissa	Patchouli
Thyme	Peppermint	Rose
	Pine	Sandalwood
	Rosemary	Savory
	Tarragon	Ylang ylang

Top notes are fresh and light, the middle notes are the heart of the fragrance and the base notes are rich and heavy in their aroma.

Properties of essential oils

Essential oils:

○ Are volatile as they evaporate when exposed to air.
○ Are sensitive to heat and light.
○ Are not greasy or oily as the name suggests.
○ Are not lubricating.
○ Mix well with alcohol, vegetable and mineral oils.
○ Do not mix with water.
○ Have a fragrance.

Characteristics of essential oils

○ Essential oils come in many shades, from pale yellow to straw-coloured, and some more vibrant colours, such as camomile which is blue, sage which is pale lime and patchouli which is orange.
○ The viscosity is thin like water rather than thick like an oil.
○ They are volatile and evaporate quickly when exposed to the air. Top notes evaporate quicker than base, therefore they need to be stored in a dark glass bottle which is tightly stoppered. Plastic containers cannot be used as essential oils will corrode plastic. The evaporation rate is quickest with the top notes and slowest with the base notes.
○ They are inflammable so will catch fire easily. Therefore care must be taken when using oils in a burner.
○ They are soluble in vegetable oils and alcohol
○ They mix well with soap and honey.

Synergy

All essential oils work more effectively in a synergistic blend, the oils interacting with each other for greater effect than if they were used alone. Some essential oils when used together have a mutually enhancing effect, for example the anti-inflammatory effect of camomile is more effective when mixed with lavender. When creating a synergistic blend there are certain considerations:

○ The symptom to be treated.
○ The underlying cause.
○ Psychological or emotional factors.

Floral	Citrus	Herbs	Trees	Spices	Resins	Exotic
Camomile	Bergamot	Basil	Bay	Aniseed	Amyris	Patchouli
Geranium	Grapefruit	Bay laurel	Birch	Black pepper	Benzoin	Sandal wood
Jasmine	Lemon	Coriander	Cedar wood	Cinnamon	Camphor	Ylang ylang
Lavender	Lime	Fennel	Eucalyptus	Cloves	Frankincense	
Mimosa	Mandarin	Lovage	Juniper	Nutmeg	Myrrh	
Neroli	Melissa	Rosemary	Niaouli			
Rose	Neroli	Tarragon	Petitgrain			
Violet	Orange	Tea tree	Pine			
	Petitgrain	Thyme	Rosewood			

Creating a synergistic blend

Oils which belong to the same botanical family or share the same constituents generally blend well together.

Oils can be divided into the following families with a few examples (see above).

Oils from these families blend well together and they also blend well with the adjacent groups.

For example:

○ Exotic → Floral → Citrus
○ Floral → Citrus → Herbs
○ Citrus → Herbs → Trees
○ Herbs → Trees → Spices
○ Trees → Spices → Resins
○ Spice → Resin → Exotic
○ Resin → Exotic → Floral

○ Ointment.
○ Pot pourri.
○ Sauna.
○ Skin care products.
○ Tea infusions.

Aromatherapy massage combines the use of the relaxing effects of the massage itself with the therapeutic effect of the oils and the sense of smell. The mind and body is soothed and the body's natural energy flow is stimulated.

As an aromatherapist, using massage to apply essential oils to the body will be the principal form of treatment. You may also wish to use a burner, humidifier or fragrance bowl in the treatment room and you can give your client advice in using oils for homecare. The methods listed above are all useful to clients particularly when you choose and blend the essential oils for their own specific needs.

Methods of use

○ Aromatherapy burners (Figure 12.4).
○ Candles.
○ Ceramic ring.
○ Compress.
○ Directly on to the skin.
○ Dry inhalation on a handkerchief.
○ Facial steamer.
○ Foot spa.
○ Fragrance bowl.
○ Hair care products.
○ Humidifier.
○ In the bath.
○ In the car.
○ Inhalation.
○ Massage.

Figure 12.4 *An oil burner with a selection of essential oils. Courtesy Elemis Limited*

When recommending oils to be used at home in the bath do not forget that they can be mixed with an appropriate carrier oil, full fat milk or specially formulated bath products. Resins or absolutes must not be used in the bath as they will stain it.

Precautions

○ Always check for contraindications.
○ Do not use undiluted oils.
○ Do not administer essential oils internally.
○ Ensure the client likes the fragrance of the oils.

Carrier oils

Essential oils may not be applied directly on to the skin but should be diluted in a base oil. When choosing a carrier oil to mix with essential oils for aromatherapy massage, the best quality vegetable oils should be used. They are obtained from the seeds of plants from around the world and extracted by 'cold pressing' to ensure they are in their purest form.

Benefits of a carrier oil

○ Dilutes the essential oil to make them safe.
○ Helps to spread the essential oils evenly.
○ Slows down the evaporation rate of the essential oil.
○ Increases the absorption of the essential oils into the skin.

There are a selection of carrier oils some of which may be used for a particular purpose:

○ Aloe vera.
○ Apricot kernel.*
○ Avocado.
○ Calendula.
○ Coconut.*
○ Evening primrose.
○ Grapeseed.
○ Hazelnut.*
○ Jojoba.*
○ Olive.

○ Peach kernel.*
○ Peanut.*
○ Soya bean.
○ St John's wort.
○ Sweet almond.*
○ Vitamin E.
○ Wheatgerm.†

*Avoid the use of these oils for those with an allergy to nuts.
†Avoid the use of this oil for those with an allergy to gluten. Use Vitamin E or soya bean instead.

Specific effects and uses of carrier oils

The best oils for the body are:

○ Grapeseed.
○ Peanut.
○ Sesame.
○ Soya.
○ Sunflower.
○ Sweet almond.

The best oils for the face are:

○ Aloe vera.
○ Apricot kernel.
○ Avocado.
○ Evening primrose.
○ Jojoba.
○ Peach kernel.
○ Sweet almond.

Healing oils are:

○ Almond.
○ Calendula.
○ Jojoba.
○ Olive.
○ St John's wort.

Effects of individual oils

Aloe vera oil contains enzymes, vitamins, proteins and minerals that support all skin functions and it activates the skin's own healing powers. It will help in skin rejuvenation and is soothing to a sunburned skin. It will be useful when mixed with essential oils for the treatment of psoriasis, eczema and skin allergies.

Apricot kernel oil is especially good for prematurely aged, dry and sensitive skin.

Avocado pear oil contains vitamins, protein and fatty acids and is useful for all skin types but especially dry, dehydrated and eczema.

Calendula oil is excellent for healing and may be used on irritated skin, muscle pain and children.

Evening primrose oil is used for PMT, menopausal problems, eczema, psoriasis and helps in preventing premature ageing. It contains a high level of gamma-lanolin acid, a substance much like the body's own chemical metabolism regulator.

Grapeseed oil is a commonly used oil and may be used on all skin types.

Hazelnut oil is good for dry or damaged skin, blends well with, sandalwood, rosewood, ylang ylang.

Jojoba oil contains vitamin E. It is highly penetrative, having healing and anti-inflammatory properties, and is good for eczema and psoriasis, and is nourishing to the skin.

Olive oil has disinfecting and wound-healing properties and is soothing to rheumatic joints but it has a strong odour which some people do not like.

Peanut, safflower, soya bean and sunflower oil can be used for all skin types.

Sesame oil is useful for all skin types, in particular psoriasis, eczema, rheumatism and arthritis.

Sweet almond oil is nourishing and penetrating, and is excellent for a dry sensitive skin.

Wheatgerm oil aids regeneration of the skin, is soothing and healing and is particularly good for dry and ageing skin.

Terminology – effects of essential oils

Analgesic	Relieves pain
Antidepressant	Alleviates depression
Antiphlogistic	Reduces inflammation
Antiseptic	Helps to stop bacterial growth
Antisudorific	Reduces perspiration
Antitoxic	Counteracts poisons
Astringent	Local constriction of tissues
Bechic	Relieves coughing
Carminative	Helps flatulence and colic
Cephalic	Stimulates the brain
Cicatrisant	Helps formation of scar tissue
Cytophylacitc	Helps cell growth
Decongestant	Relieves catarrh
Diuretic	Stimulates urine excretion
Emmanagogic	Induces menstruation*
Febrifuge	Reduces fever
Galactagogic	Stimulates milk production
Haemostatic	Stops bleeding
Hepatic	Liver tonic
Hypertensive	Raises blood pressure
Hypotensive	Lowers blood pressure
Nervine	Nerve tonic
Rubefacient	Stimulates local circulation
Sedative	Induces sleep
Stimulant	Increases general activity
Sudorific	Promotes perspiration
Tonic	Generally or locally stimulating
Vasoconstrictor	Constricts blood vessels
Vulnerary	Can help heal external cuts etc.

*May also be abortifacient.

Effects on the body

Depending on the blend of oils chosen they can have different effects on the body. They:

o Penetrate into the dermis in approximately 6–10 seconds
o Stimulate or soothe the nervous system.
o Promote healthy cell growth.
o Can relieve aches and pains.
o Can soothe aching muscles.
o Can refresh the mind and increase concentration.
o Can relieve headaches.
o Can be antiseptic in effect.
o Can be anti-inflammatory in effect.
o Can be uplifting.
o Can be balancing.
o May have anti-viral properties.
o Help to stimulate the body's immune system.
o Can be sedative in effect.

The composition of essential oils

The basic chemical constituents of essential oils are:

Carbon (C).
Hydrogen (H).
Oxygen (O).

Essential oils are made up of many different organic molecules and the aroma and properties of each oil is dependent on the combination and concentration of these molecules which may vary from harvest to harvest and plant to plant. The constituents belong to different chemical families:

Acids: They are quite rare, occurring in minute quantities and usually found in a combination with esters.

Alcohols: They are the largest group found in essential oils. Germicidal in effect, they may be subdivided into:

○ *Monoterpenol*, which are anti-bacterial and anti-viral. They are stimulating with a tonic effect and can be used on all ages as they are non-irritating.

○ *Sesquiterpenol*, which have a decongestant effect on the circulatory system, have a tonic effect and are also non-irritating.

○ *Diterpenol*, which have a similar structure to human hormones so have a balancing effect on the hormonal system.

Aldehydes: They are anti-inflammatory, calming to the nervous system and they often have a powerful aroma. Some aldehydes are skin sensitizers.

Esters: They are balancing and anti-inflammatory and therefore effective for skin problems. They are also calming and uplifting, therefore beneficial to the nervous system.

Ethers: They occur rarely in essential oils and the properties are anti-depressant, anti-spasmodic and sedative.

Ketones: They have a calming and sedative effect and help to break down mucus and fat, and they promote healing in scar tissue. Some may be toxic so oils containing ketones should be well diluted and not used too often or for too long.

Lactones: They occur mostly in expressed oils such as lemon, orange, grapefruit and are generally regarded as non-toxic but are responsible for skin photosensitization.

Oxides: They are rare in essential oils apart from cineole (eucalyptol) which has mucolyptic properties and is found in oils such as eucalyptus, peppermint, camphor, marjoram. They are used to help with colds and infections of the respiratory tract but may be irritating if used in large quantities and should therefore be used with care.

Phenols: They are very strong in action so should be used in low concentrations for short periods of time. They make powerful antiseptics and are stimulating to the nervous system and the immune system.

Terpenes: They are hydrocarbons made up solely of hydrogen and carbon atoms and may be classified as:

○ *Monoterpenes*, which occur in most essential oils. Although weak in effect they are antiseptic, anti-inflammatory, stimulating, expectorant and slightly analgesic.

○ *Sesquiterpenes*, which have similar properties to monoterpenes, are calming.

○ *Diterpenes*, which are not found in many essential oils as the molecule is heavy and may not always be extracted in the distillation process.

The more that essential oils are interfered with chemically, the less effective they are. It is also important to use the correct strength of oil, as excessive use may have the reverse effect of that which is wanted.

Physiological effects of essential oils

Essential oils are non-invasive and when used correctly are non-toxic. They stimulate the body's own natural healing processes. The body absorbs the oils very quickly and they remain in the body for between 10 hours and several days when they are secreted or excreted in the normal way via the excretory system, respiratory system and the skin. It may take less time in a fit and healthy person than in someone who is obese or unhealthy for the oils to be excreted, depending on the 'note' of the oil.

The cardiovascular system

The cardiovascular system consists of the heart and the circulatory system. A healthy heart and circulatory system is essential to the normal functioning of all the body organs and tissues. Some common problems of the cardiovascular systems are:

o *Anaemia*, caused by a lack of red blood cells or haemoglobin. Symptoms may include tiredness, dizziness, headaches and general debility. Anaemia may occur suddenly after an operation or accident or it could occur over a longer period of time because of excessively heavy menstrual bleeding, lack of iron in the diet or poor absorption of iron from the digestive tract.
o *Arterial disease* such as arteriosclerosis, the thickening and hardening of the arterial walls and atheroma, the deposit of cholesterol in the lining of the artery, and coronary thrombosis, a clot in the arteries which supply the heart.
o *High* or *low blood pressure*.
o *Angina*.
o *Heart palpitations*, which may occur as a result of heart disease. It is often a symptom related to stress or anxiety.
o *Varicose veins*, dilated veins in the legs.
o *Poor circulation*.

Some of the recommended oils for the circulatory system are:

o Lavender, geranium, marjoram, camomile, ylang ylang, clary sage to *reduce blood pressure*.
o Rosemary, thyme, camphor to *raise blood pressure*.
o Black pepper, rosemary, peppermint, marjoram, ginger, rose to *improve blood circulation*.
o Rose, melissa, orange, neroli for *antispasmodic action on the heart*.
o Cypress, lemon, geranium for *varicose veins*.

The digestive system

Problems of the digestive system include:

o Indigestion.
o Constipation.
o Heartburn.
o Flatulence.
o Diarrhoea.
o Irritable bowel.
o Stomach pains.
o Loss of appetite.
o Gall stones.
o Food poisoning.
o Nausea.

Recommended oils include:

o Marjoram, rosemary, ginger, fennel, camphor, black pepper, peppermint for *laxative effects*.
o Sandalwood, rosemary, camomile for *antispasmodic action*.
o Basil, bergamot, sage, coriander, cardamon, peppermint, fennel, lavender, aniseed, melissa for *indigestion* and *flatulence*.
o Eucalyptus, sage, camomile, peppermint, cypress, sandalwood for *diarrhoea*.
o Lemon, sage, peppermint, rose for the *liver*.
o Coriander, ginger, tarragon, nutmeg, myrrh to *stimulate digestion*.
o Eucalyptus, lemon, camomile, camphor, ylang ylang for *gall stones*.

The respiratory system

The respiratory system, which includes the nose, throat and lungs, is prone to infection and essential oils can be inhaled for effective results as well as massaged into the back and chest. The effects are *antiseptic*, helping to control bacterial growth; *expectorant*, to increase the output of respiratory fluids; and *antispasmodic*, to lessen the spasm in smooth muscle fibres.

Antiseptic oils – angelica, cinnamon, thyme, tea tree, eucalyptus, pine, camphor, clove, lemon, peppermint and cajeput.
Expectorant oils – eucalyptus, camphor, pine, thyme, rosemary, hyssop, lemon, myrrh, cajeput and benzoin which all help to clear the respiratory tract of mucus.
Antispasmodic oils – clary sage, aniseed, hyssop, cypress, frankincense, rosemary and basil, which will help to alleviate and soothe coughs.

The following conditions will benefit from specific oils:

○ Basil, lemon, thyme, cypress, pine, clove for *asthma*.
○ Basil, bergamot, cajuput, eucalyptus, tea tree, lavender, pine, peppermint, benzoin, clove for *bronchitis*.
○ Eucalyptus, lemon, sage, thyme, camomile, camphor, lavender, pine, benzoin, sandalwood for *flu*.
○ Hyssop for *hayfever*.

The lymphatic system

This system is responsible for draining and removing waste from the body as well as removing excess fluid. A poor lymphatic system will result in a build-up of toxins and fluids which results in fluid retention or oedema and cellulite. Therefore stimulating oils and those with antiseptic properties are used for a sluggish lymphatic system.

Stimulating – fennel, geranium, juniper, lavender, rosemary and sage.
Antiseptic – eucalyptus, lemon, thyme and tea tree.

Urinary system

The urinary system consists of two kidneys, ureters and the bladder. An efficient urinary system is essential to help with excreting waste fluid and detoxifying the body and regulating the fluid balance. Essential oils are used to maintain an efficient system and have an antiseptic effect on the urinary tract to help deal with infections such as cystitis.

Fluid retention is improved by using diuretic essential oils such as, eucalyptus, sage, juniper, cypress, fennel, lavender, rosemary, patchouli and sandalwood.

Urinary tract infections would benefit from essential oils such as bergamot, cajuput, eucalyptus, niaouli, fennel, juniper, pine, sandalwood, benzoin, frankincense and tea tree.

Kidneys benefit from eucalyptus, lemon, sage , thyme, juniper, fennel and sandalwood.

The immune system

The immune system is responsible for fighting infection and produces white blood cells and antibodies. Essential oils are effective in stimulating the immune system to help the body destroy invading bacteria and viruses and to strengthen the immune system so that it works more efficiently.

Strengthening the immune system – bergamot, eucalyptus, ginger, lavender, lemongrass, rosemary and tea tree.
Stimulating the immune system – eucalyptus, lavender, tea tree, pine, camomile and sandalwood.
Antibacterial and antiviral – camphor, clove, cajuput, eucalyptus, niaouli and tea tree.

The nervous system

This system is the link between the mind and the body and the pace of life today is such that we overwork our nervous system causing many physical and psychological problems. The use of essential oils will help as they have many different properties. They will soothe or stimulate, regulate or balance the nervous system. Oils will be chosen for their specific effects, stimulating oils will be chosen for depression or nervous fatigue whereas soothing oils will be chosen for insomnia, hysteria, nervousness or anxiety:

○ Basil, bergamot, thyme, clary sage, camomile, juniper, lavender, geranium, marjoram, patchouli, melissa for *anxiety* and *tension*.
○ Camomile, clary sage, lavender, neroli and sandalwood are sedating antidepressant oils. Jasmine, geranium, rose, melissa, basil, bergamot are uplifting antidepressant oils. Both can be used for *depression*.
○ Camomile, camphor, juniper, marjoram, neroli, thyme, rose, ylang ylang for *insomnia*.
○ Basil, bergamot, camomile, cedarwood, geranium, jasmine, juniper, lavender, neroli, rose for *stress*.
○ Basil, bergamot, clary sage, camomile, lavender, geranium, jasmine, neroli, rose, sandalwood, ylang ylang for *nervous tension*.

The reproductive system

Treatment with essential oils will help with problems caused by hormonal changes or infection. Essential oils can be used for heavy, irregular and painful menstruation or absence of menstruation altogether. Some oils will have a regulating or strengthening effect while others have aphrodisiac qualities:

○ Basil, clary sage, thyme, camomile, lavender, melissa, peppermint and rose for *irregular menstruation*.
○ Cajuput, sage, camomile, aniseed, juniper, marjoram, melissa, rosemary, jasmine, tarragon for *painful menstruation*.
○ Clary sage, sage and thyme, camomile, fennel, melissa, rose for *absence of menstruation*.
○ Juniper, fennel, parsley, angelica, cypress, myrrh, marjoram to *induce menstruation*.
○ Clary sage, camomile, lavender, geranium, neroli, rose otto for *PMT*.
○ Clary sage, sage, camomile, cypress, fennel, geranium for *menopause*.
○ Jasmine, ylang ylang, neroli, rose, sandalwood, patchouli, vetivert, clary sage for *aphrodisiac*.

Muscular and skeletal system

This system receives a great deal of wear and tear and to maintain a good balance between the structure and flexibility of the two requires a healthy diet, moderate exercise, relaxation, good posture and the minimum of stress. Apart from minor aches and pains problems such as rheumatism, arthritis, backache and osteoporosis can affect these systems.

Muscular aches and pains will benefit from cajuput, caraway, eucalyptus, sage, thyme, black pepper, camphor, marjoram, camomile, lavender, clove and nutmeg.

Arthritis will benefit from caraway, lemon, sage, thyme, camphor, camomile, juniper, cypress and benzoin.

Rheumatism benefits from cajuput, coriander, eucalyptus, lemon, sage, thyme, camomile, juniper, lavender, marjoram and rosemary.

Sprains benefit from eucalyptus, camphor, lavender, marjoram and rosemary.

Cramp will benefit from basil, cypress and marjoram.

Lack of muscle tone will benefit from lemongrass, black pepper, lavender and rosemary.

Stiffness will benefit from thyme and rosemary.

The skin

Skin is protective and semi-permeable. It absorbs, secretes and excretes substances from the body as well as maintaining normal body temperature. The skin may become imbalanced, due to internal and external factors, or inflamed or infected. It can be helped with the use of essential oils (Figure 12.5). Essential oils will nourish, cleanse, detoxify, tighten and calm the skin and there are many conditions which may be improved such as:

○ Acne.
○ Psoriasis.
○ Eczema.
○ Dermatitis.
○ Mature skin.
○ Sensitive skin.
○ Oily skin.
○ Dry skin.
○ Broken capillaries.

Figure 12.5 *Skin care products containing essential oils. Courtesy Elemis Limited*

o Sunburn.
o Inflammation.
o Bruises.
o Burns.

Essential oils may be applied topically and can include the following:

o Lavender, eucalyptus, tea tree, thyme, lemon, camomile, sandalwood, bergamot, mint, juniper, rosemary, geranium, cypress for *acne*.
o Camomile, jasmine, lavender, myrrh, neroli, frankincense, rose are *anti-inflammatory*.
o Camomile, lavender, tea tree, lemon, pine, thyme, eucalyptus, clove, cinnamon, bergamot, lemon are *antiseptic*.
o Lemon, patchouli, tea tree are *antiviral*.
o Lemon, camomile, cypress, lavender, neroli, rose for *broken capillaries*.
o Sage, camphor, fennel, marjoram for *bruises*.
o Eucalyptus, sage, camomile, camphor, geranium, lavender, rosemary for *burns*.
o Camomile, geranium, lavender, neroli, rose, ylang ylang for *dry skin*.
o Camomile, lavender, geranium, sage, melissa for *eczema*.
o Lavender, marigold, myrrh, tea tree for *fungal infection*.
o Lavender, camomile, geranium, frankincense, myrrh, benzoin for *healing*.
o Clary sage, cypress, lavender for *mature skin*.
o Bergamot, lemon, cypress, geranium, camphor, lavender, cedarwood, ylang ylang for *oily skin*.
o Bergamot, lavender for *psoriasis*.
o Jasmine, neroli, rose for *sensitive skin*.
o Lavender for *sunburn*.

Contraindications to essential oils

Essential oils used in the correct way produce no side effects. They actually stimulate the body's own self-healing powers and work holistically treating mind and body. There are very few contraindications but care must be taken in certain circumstances:

o Pregnancy – it is advisable not to use essential oils in the first five months of pregnancy.

Care must be taken to use only the safest oils in the latter stages.
o Cancer – unless with doctor's permission.
o Heart disease – unless with doctor's permission.
o Migraine.
o Do not massage directly over skin infections, inflamed bites and stings, varicose veins, scar tissue, bruises or acute inflammations.
o Fever or high temperature.
o Recent inoculations – treatment must not be within 24 hours or 36 hours after typhoid.
o Client receiving homeopathic treatment as essential oils can cancel out the effects of the homeopathic remedies.
o After major surgery. The doctor's advice should be sought but treatment should be delayed for 6 weeks to 3 months depending on the surgery.
o Conditions requiring medical attention. The doctor's permission must be sought for asthma, diabetes, multiple sclerosis, thyroid conditions and any other condition receiving medical attention.
o Strong drugs or medication. Effects of drugs may be magnified by treatment. The doctor's permission must be sought with medication.
o Sensitization. When the skin becomes intolerant to essential oils. This may happen suddenly or over a long period of time and it may be characterized by some of the following – itching, rash appearing, runny eyes, blotches on the skin, coughing, wheezing, sneezing or shortage of breath. To ensure the client will not have an allergic reaction to an oil, it is advisable to carry out a patch test and apply the oil, leaving it for 24 hours.

The following oils are contraindicated for certain conditions:

o *High blood pressure*. Do not use hyssop, rosemary, sage and thyme.
o *Epilepsy*. Do not use fennel, hyssop, rosemary and sage.
o *Babies*. Do not use aniseed, camphor, cinnamon leaf, clove, eucalyptus, fennel, hyssop, lemongrass, marjoram, nutmeg, origanum, parsley seed, peppermint, sage and thyme (red).

○ *Pregnancy* (first five months). Do not use aniseed, basil, camphor, cedarwood, cinnamon leaf, clove, cypress, fennel, hyssop, juniper berry, marjoram, myrrh, nutmeg, origanum, parsley seed, peppermint, rosemary, savory, sage. For 6 to 9 months the following oils may be used in weak dilutions – cedarwood, cinnamon leaf, cypress, marjoram, nutmeg, origanum, parsley seed, rosemary, savory.

○ *Exposure to ultraviolet light.* Do not use angelica, bergamot, lemon, lime, orange, verbena.

Essential oils must never be given:

○ In too high a proportion to carrier oil.
○ For too long.
○ Too frequently.

Contraindications to general massage

○ Circulatory disorders.
○ Heart disease.
○ Lung disease.
○ Haemophilia.
○ Neuritis and neuralgia.
○ Infectious skin diseases and disorders.
○ Recent scar tissue.
○ Over varicose veins.
○ Around painful joints.
○ Very thin bony clients.
○ Very thin overstretched skin.

Problems with use

Irritation

If certain oils are applied in too high a percentage, too frequently or for too long, irritation of the skin or mucous membrane may occur causing inflammation in the area treated. Therefore dosage must be very carefully measured. When decanting essential oils it is important to wear protective gloves and work in a well-ventilated room. If the oil comes into contact with the skin wash off immediately.

Sensitization

Sensitization occurs when there is an allergic reaction to an essential oil. When this occurs test other oils on the client that have similar therapeutic effects. It would be exceptional if a client had an allergic response to all essential oils.

Toxicity

This is a term used to describe a level of poisoning. There may be an occasion when an oil causes toxicity so great care must be taken in the use of essential oils. Avoid those that are known to be toxic and use the correct dilutions so there is not a build-up in the body and do not treat too often. The effect of an oil's toxicity will vary from individual to individual depending on their size and age. However toxicity is dose dependent and essential oils should be administered in much smaller doses in children than in adults and the duration of treatment should be shorter and less frequent. Aniseed and hyssop are thought to damage the nervous system if used for long periods of time.

Essential oils which should never be used

○ Bitter almond.
○ Boldo leaf.
○ Calamus.
○ Camphor – yellow and brown.
○ Horseradish.
○ Jaborandi leaf.
○ Mugwort.
○ Mustard.
○ Pennyroyal.
○ Rue.
○ Sassafras.
○ Savin.
○ Southernwood.
○ Tansy.
○ Thuja.
○ Wintergreen.
○ Wormseed.
○ Wormwood.

Storage of essential oils

Pure essential oils should be stored:

○ In a cool, dry place.
○ In dark glass bottles.
○ In an airtight container.
○ Out of direct sunshine.
○ Out of reach of children.

The average shelf life of essential oils is six months to two years. The therapeutic effect of the oils diminishes with age. When exposed to the air the oxygen combining with some of the constituents of the oil will cause it to oxidize and deteriorate.

Do not store ready-mixed essential oils in a carrier oil as the essential oils have a much longer shelf life when they are stored in their pure state. When using the oil for aromatherapy massage, mix only the amount you require for the treatment.

Blending essential oils

Massage is the most common way of using essential oils, blending them with a suitable carrier oil, combining to great effect the senses of smell and touch. It is a therapeutic treatment providing benefits to both mind and body:

○ Circulation is stimulated allowing the oils to be dispersed more rapidly around the body.
○ The warmth of the skin makes the oils smell stronger.
○ The carrier oil prevents the essential oil from evaporating too quickly.
○ The carrier oil allows the essential oils to be dispersed evenly.
○ Essential oils can be chosen to meet the individual needs of each client.

Because of their potency essential oils should not be used undiluted but should be mixed with a carrier oil in specific proportions. Using double the dose of essential oils does not mean that the client will receive twice the benefit. On the contrary, some oils will have the opposite effect than that stated. They may make the client feel nauseous and some are highly toxic.

Essential oils are always measured in drops because of their potency and concentration and the general rule is to add half the number of drops of essential oils to the number of millilitres of carrier oil.

For example:

25 drops of essential oil will be added to 50 ml of carrier oil.
5 drops of essential oil will be added to 10 ml of carrier oil.

For a full body massage you will need about 20 ml of carrier oil and 10 drops of essential oil. For massaging a smaller area, reduce the amount of oils accordingly, for example 6 ml of carrier oil with 3 drops of essential oil.

Essential oils are normally sold in dark glass bottles fitted with a dropper for accurate measurement. Because they are volatile and evaporate fairly rapidly the drops should be measured quickly and accurately in small quantities enough for the particular treatment being carried out.

Considerations when blending

○ Use the most appropriate essential oils for the client.
○ Use essential oils that complement each other. Some oils may inhibit each other's effects.
○ Blend together a top, a middle and a base note oil as they work together synergistically.
○ Base notes last longer so may be used in smaller quantities.
○ Top notes evaporate quicker so may be used in slightly higher quantities.
○ Ensure the client likes the aroma of the blend.
○ Look at plant families.
○ Look at chemical constituents.
○ Choose the carrier oil for its effectiveness, lack of smell, penetrative qualities or price.
○ Mix the carrier oils when required, for example wheatgerm oil is rarely used alone as it is so rich but added to another oil will help to preserve it because of its anti-oxidant quality.

Essential equipment

10 ml (½ fl oz) dark glass bottles with a dropper for storing pure essential oils.

Pipettes or eye droppers for testing or measuring.

Strips of blotting paper to test oils.

Small funnel for pouring carrier oils into small bottles.

Small bowl or measuring beaker to hold blend for massage.

Glass rod for mixing.

Index of essential oils with botanical names

Angelica	Angelica archangelica
Basil	Ocimum basilium
Bergamot	Citrus bergamia
Birch	Betula alba
Black pepper	Piper nigrum
Cajuput	Melaleuca leuco-dendron
Calendula (marigold)	Calendula officinalis
Camphor	Cinnamomum camphora
Cedarwood atlas	Cedrus atlantica
Camomile (Roman)	Anthemis nobilis
Cypress	Cypressa sempervirens
Eucalyptus	Eucalyptus globulus
Fennel	Foeniculum vulgare
Frankincense	Boswellia thurifera
Geranium	Pelargonium grave-olens
Ginger	Zingiber officinale
Hyssop	Hyssopus officianalis
Jasmine	Jasminum officinale
Juniper	Juniperus communis
Laurel	Lauarus nobilis
Lavender	Lavendula augustifolia or officinalis
Lemon	Citrus limonum
Lemongrass	Cymbopogon citratus
Lime	Citrus limetta
Mandarin	Citrus reticulata
Marjoram	Origanum marjorana
Mimosa	Acacia dealbata
Myrrh	Commiphora myrrha
Neroli	Citrus aurantium

Niaouli	Melaleuca viridiflora
Orange	Citrus sinesis
Patchouli	Pogostemom cablin
Peppermint	Mentha piperita
Petitgrain	Citrus aurantium
Pine	Pinus sylvestris
Rose	Rosa damascena and centifolia
Rosemary	Rosmarinus officinalis
Rosewood	Aniba rosadora
Sage	Salvia officinalis
Sage (clary)	Salvia sclarea
Sandalwood	Santalum album
Spruce	Tsuga canadensis
Tarragon	Artemisia dracunculus
Tea tree	Melaleuca alternifolia
Thyme	Thymus vulgaris
Valerian	Valeriana fauriei
Vetiver	Vetivera zizanoides
Violet	Viola odorata
Yarrow	Achillea millefolium
Ylang ylang	Cananga odorata

Client consultation (Figure 12.6)

The initial consultation with your client will take quite a long time as it is important to elicit as much information as possible about:

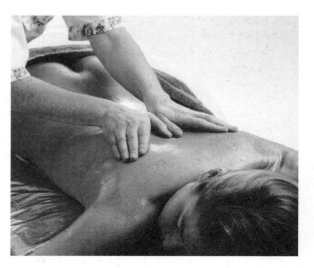

Figure 12.6 *An aromatherapy back massage. Courtesy Elemis Limited*

○ Medical history.
○ Lifestyle.
○ Client's requirements.
○ Physical condition.
○ Mental condition.
○ Personality.

A detailed record card must be filled in with the following information:

Personal details

○ Name, address and telephone number.
○ Date of birth.
○ Doctor's name and address.
○ Client's height and weight.
○ Client's objectives.
○ Indication of the state of the client's general health.

Medical history

○ Illnesses the client may have had.
○ Operations, with details.
○ Accidents and injuries sustained.
○ Reoccurring problems.
○ Muscular or skeletal problems.
○ Digestive problems.
○ Circulation (heart, blood, fluid, cellulite, kidneys, bruises, etc.).
○ Gynaecological problems.
○ Nervous problems.
○ Immune problems.
○ Other (allergy, asthma, hayfever, epilepsy, diabetes etc.).
○ Is the client currently undergoing any form of medical treatment?
○ Is the client taking any medication or drugs?
○ Does the client smoke?

Lifestyle

○ Marital status.
○ Professional capacity.
○ Description of work.
○ Time management.
○ Personal time.
○ Hobbies or interests.
○ Exercise taken.
○ Energy level.
○ Ability to relax.
○ Sleeping pattern.

○ Degree of stress (1–10).
○ Diet: what is eaten; how it is eaten; drinks daily.
○ Food allergies or problems.
○ Condition of the skin.
○ General comments.
○ Yin or yang qualities.

Postural analysis

○ Standing – posterior, anterior and lateral views.
○ Look at specific points – from the back, the shoulders should be level, the scapulae should not protrude on either or both sides, the spine should be straight with no sign of scoliosis and the hips should be level. Check the knees and ankles that they are level and there is no swelling present.
○ From the side check that the chin does not lean forward, there is no stooping or dowager's hump present at the top of the back, the abdominal muscles are not protruding and weak, there is no pelvic tilt and the feet are not flat.
○ From the front check that the shoulders are not curving inwards indicating poor posture and that waist, hips and knees are level.
○ Sitting down again check the shoulder level and the spine

Connective tissue test

With the client in a prone position on the couch, using your index finger and starting at the base of the spine, move gently upwards rolling the skin and it should ripple naturally if there is no tension present. If there is tension it will show up as a tight area with little or no rippling.

Flare reaction test

Run the sides of your thumb nail slowly down either side of the spine and note the pink areas which will indicate a good circulation and those areas where it looks white or the redness fades away quickly. This will indicate poor circulation and tension.

Reflexology diagnosis

Reflexology may be used for diagnostic purposes and will be used in conjunction with the medical history of the client and your visual and verbal assessment. There are certain points on the feet which when pressed will tell the therapist where there may be a blockage, indicating a disorder in a particular part of the body. If the correct pressure is applied on the right pressure point, then a blockage will be felt if there is one present either as a sharp sensation to the client, or a gritty feeling in the area is felt by the therapist. This should be noted and the client questioned further. Information gleaned at this stage will reinforce the information you will already have been given by the client.

Aftercare advice

Once clients have had their aromatherapy massage you may give them advice about homecare. This will reinforce the treatment and encourage clients to continue benefiting from the effects of the aromatherapy.

○ The client should relax after treatment and, if possible, not drive.
○ Do not take a bath or shower for eight hours.
○ Drink plenty of water or herbal teas.
○ Do not drink alcohol for 24 hours.
○ Do not eat straight away.
○ Do not use a sunbed or go sunbathing for 24 hours.
○ Recommend essential oils to use at home.
○ Advise clients about the different methods of application available to them.
○ Instruct clients in their use, measure in drops, don't use undiluted on the skin and do not take internally.

Effects of essential oils

Aniseed

Antiseptic, antispasmodic, carminative, diuretic, expectorant, galactagogic, stimulant, stomachic used to treat, bronchitis, whooping cough, catarrh, flatulence, colic, painful periods and stimulating breast milk.

Basil

Anti-depressant, antiseptic, antispasmodic, carminative, cephalic, digestive, emanagogic, expectorant, galactagogic, nervine, used to treat, anxiety, depression, melancholy, fatigue, insomnia. migraine, to clear the mind, muscular aches, pains, rheumatism, bronchitis, coughs, sinusitis, flatulence, stimulates menstruation.

Benzoin

Anti-inflammatory, antioxidant, antiseptic, astringent, carminative, diuretic, expectorant, sedative, vulnerary used to treat asthma, bronchitis, coughs, laryngitis, flu, arthritis, poor circulation, rheumatism, cuts, inflamed skin, stress and nervous tension.

Bergamot

Uplifting, antidepressant, refreshing, appetite and digestive stimulant and antiseptic, used to treat depression, stress, tiredness, irritability, cystitis, urinary tract infections, fever, anorexia, colic, flatulence, indigestion, sore throat and bad breath (photosensitive).

Black pepper

Stimulating, anti toxic and gently analgesic, used to treat aches and pains, to warm up before sport, nausea, cold, cough, fever, cystitis, constipation, loss of appetite and digestion.

Cajeput

Analgesic, antispasmodic, antiseptic, diaphoretic, carminative, expectorant, tonic used to treat colds, flu, bronchitis, throat infections, urinary tract infections, diarrhoea, stomach cramps, rheumatism, neuralgia, oily skin, insect bites, arthritis, rheumatism.

Camomile

Anti-inflammatory, healing, calming, sedative, relaxing, antiseptic, digestive stimulant used to treat stress, anxiety, hysteria, irritability, insomnia, headaches, rashes, inflammation, bites, burns, cuts, toothache, earache, indigestion, liver disorders, loss of appetite, aches and pains, menstrual and menopausal problems.

Clary sage

Antidepressant, antiseptic, astringent, carminative, digestive, emmenagogic, nervine, euphoric, antispasmodic, aphrodisiac, relaxing, revitalizing used to treat, high blood pressure, sore throat, painful or irregular periods, depression, nervous anxiety, stress, dyspepsia, flatulence, PMS, amenorrhea, frigidity, impotence, asthma and night sweats.

Cypress

Antispasmodic, antiseptic, astringent, deodorizing, diuretic, expectorant hepatic, sudorific, tonic used to treat asthma, bronchitis, dysmenorrhea, menopausal problems, nervous tension, stress, greasy skin, hyperhidrosis, varicose veins and wounds.

Eucalyptus

Stimulating, antiseptic, antispasmodic, diuretic, expectorant, anti-viral, aids concentration used to treat bronchitis, asthma, catarrh, fever, flu, sinusitis, throat infections, kidney infection, measles, muscular aches and pains, neuralgia, rheumatism, herpes cuts, burns, insect bites, wounds and ulcers.

Fennel

Anti-inflammatory, antiseptic, antispasmodic, carminative, diuretic, emmenagogic, expectorant, galactagogic, laxative, stimulant, stomachic, tonic used to treat, cellulite, odema, obesity, rheumatism, asthma, bronchitis, anorexia, colic, constipation, dyspepsia, flatulence, nausea, amenorrhea, menopausal problems and insufficient milk in nursing mothers.

Frankincense

Relaxing, sedative, calming, uplifting, mildly antiseptic used to treat, chest infections, catarrh, bronchitis, hay fever, insomnia, depression, bereavement, immune deficiency, wounds, scars ulcers, dry, damaged and wrinkled skin.

Geranium

Sedative, relaxing, balancing, anti-inflammatory, tonic, antiseptic, mildly diuretic used to treat cellulite, fluid retention, poor circulation, hormone imbalance, mood swings, wounds, bruises, burns broken capillaries, endometriosis, haemorrhage, throat and mouth infections, eczema, acne and mature skin.

Hyssop

Astringent, antiseptic, antispasmodic, anti-viral, carminative, cephalic, cicatrisant, digestive, diuretic, emenagogic, expectorant, febrifuge, nervine, sedative, tonic, vulnerary used to treat, anxiety, fatigue, lack of concentration, stress, amenorrhea, leucorrhea, indigestion, asthma, bronchitis, coughs, sore throat, tonsillitis, rheumatism, low or high blood pressure, bruises, cuts, inflamed skin and eczema.

Jasmine

Analgesic, antidepressant, anti-inflammatory, antiseptic, antispasmodic, aphrodisiac, carminative, cicatrisant, expectorant, galactagogic, balancing, sedative, tonic used to treat dry, irritated or sensitive skin, eczema, catarrh, coughs, laryngitis, insomnia, low esteem, depression, nervous exhaustion, stress, frigidity, impotence, joint and muscular pains and sprains.

Juniper

Diuretic, antiseptic, uplifting, relaxing, used to treat cystitis, fluid retention, cellulite, colic, indigestion, cramps, gout, circulatory problems, menstrual problems, anxiety, stress, eczema, acne and oily skin.

Lavender

Relaxing, antiseptic, antispasmodic, diuretic, healing, calming, uplifting, stimulating used to treat high blood pressure, lymphatic congestion, cellulite, fluid retention, colic, flatulence, indigestion, nausea, cystitis, conjunctivitis, headache, migraine, nose and throat infections, flu, catarrh, bronchitis, asthma, irregular or scanty periods, anxiety, depression, irritability, insomnia, acne rosacea, eczema, insect bites, burns, inflammation and sunburn.

Lime

Antiseptic, antiviral, antibacterial, stimulating, carminative, diuretic, tonic used to treat warts, verrucae, varicose veins, poor circulation, arthritis, rheumatism, flatulence, colds, flu, fever, infection asthma, greasy skin (photosensitive).

Lemon

Stimulating, invigorating, astringent, deodorizing, diuretic and antiseptic used to treat, acne, anaemia, greasy skin, poor circulation, rheumatism, hypertension, migraines, sore throat, loss of appetite, regulate stomach acidity, liver complaints asthma, colds, flu, warts and verrucae, scabies, bites and stings.

Melissa

Antidepressant, antihistaminic, antispasmodic, carminative, emmenagogic, nervine, sedative, tonic used to treat, allergies, insect bites, eczema, asthma, bronchitis and dry coughs, colic, indigestion, nausea, menstrual problems, anxiety, depression, insomnia, migraine, shock.

Marigold

Anti-inflammatory, antiseptic, antispasmodic, astringent, emmenagogic, tonic, vulnerary used to treat, burns, cuts, insect bites, wounds, eczema, menstrual irregularities, varicose veins, haemorrhoids, conjunctivitis.

Myrrh

Anti-inflammatory, antiseptic, astringent, carminative, emmenagogic, expectorant, fungicidal, revitalizing, sedative, stimulant, tonic, vulnerary used to treat colds, asthma, bronchitis, catarrh, coughs, gingivitis, mouth ulcers, sore throats, laryngitis, arthritis, amenorrhea, thrush, athletes foot, ringworm, chapped skin, mature skin, eczema, wounds and wrinkles.

Neroli

Antidepressant, antiseptic, antispasmodic, carminative cicatrisant, deodorant, digestive, fungicidal, stimulant, tonic used to treat anxiety, depression, PMT, shock, stress, palpitations, poor circulation, diarrhoea, colic, flatulence, dyspepsia, scars, stretch marks, mature, sensitive skins, wrinkles.

Niaouli

Antiseptic, analgesic, relaxing, uplifting, healing used to treat insect bites, wounds, burns, poor circulation, flu, fever, sore throat, sinus, bronchitis, cystitis, oily skin, indigestion, gastro-enteritis and rheumatism.

Peppermint

Analgesic, anti-inflammatory, antiseptic, antispasmodic, antiviral, astringent, carminative, emmenagogic, expectorant, hepatic, nervine, vasoconstrictor used to treat fainting, headache, fatigue, migraine, stress, colds, flu, fever, cramp, colic, flatulence, nausea, indigestion, asthma, bronchitis, sinusitis, halitosis, neuralgia, muscular pain, acne, ringworm and scabies.

Petitgrain

Relaxing and stimulating, antiseptic, tonic used to treat stress, nervousness, tiredness, tension, insomnia, fatigue, dyspepsia, flatulence, backache and muscular tension.

Rose

Uplifting, balancing, relaxing, soothing, antiseptic, tonic, cooling, healing, aphrodisiac used to treat, stress, depression, headaches, hangover, migraine, insomnia, irregular menstruation, frigidity, sterility, vaginitis, constipation, nausea, conjunctivitis, fever, wounds, shingles, gingivitis, eczema, herpes simplex, sorrow, disappointment, sadness and post partum depression, all skin types especially, dry, mature, inflamed, allergy prone and baby skin care.

Rosemary

Antiseptic, diuretic, stimulating, cleansing, astringent, tonic is used to treat, headaches, migraine, mental fatigue, breathing problems, fluid retention, lymphatic congestion, poor circulation, lack of periods, colitis, constipation, diarrhoea, flatulence, gall stones, gastro-enteritis, stomach pains, aches and pains, arthritis, asthma, coughs and flu, alopecia and dandruff.

Sandalwood

Antiseptic, astringent, relaxing, sedative, aphrodisiac, antidepressant, expectorant used to treat cystitis, colic, diarrhoea, gastritis, hiccups, vomiting, depression, tension, insomnia, frigidity, impotence, aggression, bronchitis, catarrh, coughs, sore throat, dry, inflamed or cracked skin.

Tea tree

Anti-inflammatory, antiseptic, antiviral, antibacterial, expectorant, fungicidal, immuno-stimulant, vulnerary used to treat, asthma, bronchitis, catarrh, colds, coughs, fever, flu, sinusitis, tuberculosis, whooping cough, cystitis, thrush, abscess, acne, oily skin, athlete's foot, verrucae, warts, cold sores, burns, insect bites and wounds.

Thyme

Anti-oxidant, antiseptic, antispasmodic, antitoxic, astringent, aphrodisiac, carminative, cicatrisant, diuretic, emmenagogic, nervine, rubefacient, immuno-stimulant, sudorific, tonic used to treat, headaches, insomnia, stress, colds, flu, cystitis, dyspepsia, flatulence, diarrhoea, asthma, bronchitis, catarrh, sinusitis, sore throat, cellulite, arthritis, muscular aches and pains, poor circulation, sprains, burns, bruises, cuts, oily skin acne, eczema and dermatitis.

Ylang ylang

Aphrodisiac, antidepressant, antiseborrheic, antiseptic, euphoric, hypotensive, nervine, sedative, stimulant, tonic used to treat, depression, frigidity, impotence, insomnia, nervous tension stress, high blood pressure, palpitations, acne, insect bites, irritated and oily skin, skin care in general.

Massage treatment

Client consideration

Performing a relaxing and enjoyable massage is very important in ensuring a successful treatment. However, the salon atmosphere and the attitude of the therapist are both factors to be considered in providing a truly effective treatment. If clients are not in a relaxed frame of mind before the massage it will take therapists longer to achieve this effect, so client care and consideration is vital.

The salon

The treatment room should be warm and well-ventilated as the clients will have to remove most of their clothing for a general body massage. The room or treatment area should be private, so curtains are essential if a separate room is not used.

Ideally, the light should be natural but if not, it should be indirect or dimmed, so that it does not shine brightly into the client's eyes.

The treatment couch should be covered with a sheet and blanket so that either or both may be used. In the summer months clients may only need to be covered with a large bath towel to maintain their modesty as a heavier covering may be too warm.

There should be a quiet atmosphere with soothing music being quietly played in the background.

The equipment

A comfortable massage couch at the correct height is essential. It must be positioned to allow therapists to work without getting backache and it must be positioned to allow clients to change position with ease.

The bedding should be warm and clean. Protective paper towelling may be used to protect the bedding, maintaining hygienic conditions and reducing laundry bills.

Pillows for client comfort should be provided and spare pillows to support the client's limbs during the massage should be kept nearby.

Spare towels should be readily available to be used when uncovering different parts of the body for treatment.

A trolley should be set up with all the necessary equipment for the treatment so that therapists do not have to leave clients during the massage. A massage medium should be chosen according to the client's skin type and treatment. These should include:

○ *Talcum powder.* Used mainly on the therapist's own hands rather than on the client, to provide ease of movement.
○ *Oils.* There are many different types of oils which may be chosen to suit a particularly dry skin type or the client's own preference.
○ *Creams.* Are more readily absorbed into the skin than the oils but some clients have a preference for a particular cream.
○ *Essential oils.* These are now in common use in aromatherapy treatment and are mixed especially for each client to suit particular needs.

Whichever lubricant is chosen, it should be applied on to the therapist's hands and not placed directly on to the client's skin. Some essential oils may be sprinkled on to the client's skin or mixed with a carrier oil.

The therapist

The appearance of therapists must be impeccable. Because of the close proximity to their clients during a body massage, which can last up to one hour, personal hygiene is very important.

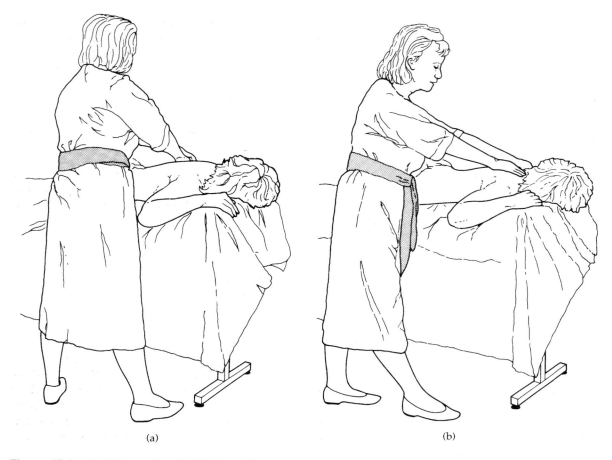

Figure 13.1 *(a) Stride standing; (b) Walk standing*

A clean white overall must be worn. It is often quite difficult to keep a white overall clean as the oil used for massage easily marks the fabric, making it look grubby. Aprons made in the same fabric may be used when performing body massage and then removed for other treatments.

Hair must be tied up if it is below chin level to prevent it falling over the therapist's face during treatment.

Therapists' hands must be clean and nails must be kept short so that they do not dig into clients, particularly when performing finger kneading or frictions.

Low-heeled comfortable shoes must be worn to prevent poor posture and backache.

To be able to relax clients completely, therapists themselves must be quiet, calm and reassuring. They must know when to listen attentively and when to discourage clients from talking, allowing them to gain maximum benefit from the massage.

Therapists should stand in an upright position and use their body weight to increase pressure in a movement when necessary. The correct working position must be assumed to allow freedom of movement and good massage technique while preventing backache.

Walk standing

This is the position assumed when the therapist is working longitudinally down the length of the muscle, with one foot in front of the other and the therapist facing the client's head. The front knee can then be bent slightly when moving forward rather than bending the back.

Stride standing

This is the position assumed when working transversely across the muscles. The therapist's feet should be slightly apart and the therapist facing the side of the massage plinth. See Figure 13.1.

The client

The working area must be prepared in advance of clients arriving so that the therapist may concentrate solely on their needs.

Allow clients to remove their clothing in private, providing them with a suitable gown to retain their modesty and then help them on to the couch making sure they are comfortable and warm.

When a client is visiting the salon for the first time, a record card must be filled in. This is an ideal opportunity to get to know clients and put them at their ease. It is at this point that therapists will note if there is any condition which will prevent them carrying on with the massage or having to adapt it in some way. If there is any doubt about a possible medical condition then therapists should ensure that clients speak to their doctor before treatment commences. Alternatively, therapists can contact their client's doctor and seek professional advice themselves.

It is common practice to have some form of heating treatment prior to massage, such as a sauna or steam and therapists should accompany clients and instruct them about the procedure as well as ensuring their safety.

When clients are wrapped in blankets for their massage, towels may be placed strategically underneath them so that different areas can be massaged without disturbing the client unduly to rearrange the bedding.

At the conclusion of the massage clients should be allowed to sit up slowly and placed in a semi-reclining position to regain their balance.

If there is an excess of oil or cream remaining on the client's skin then it may be removed with a cologne if the client wishes. However, this can feel very cold and the client may prefer the oils or cream to be left on to nourish their skin.

The general massage routine

Body massage must always be tailored to suit the needs of the clients but in general a full body massage, excluding the face and head, should last for approximately sixty minutes and should include:

○ Both arms.
○ Neck and chest.
○ Both legs.
○ Abdomen.
○ Buttocks.
○ Back, neck and shoulders.

There are many different schools of thought concerning the specific order of work to follow, but it is entirely up to therapists to decide since they alone will know the requirements of their clients. Whichever order is adopted the back should always be the last area to be treated as it is the most relaxing part of the general body massage.

It is also important to maintain continuity, keeping one hand in contact with the client at all times and the rate of movement should be moderate unless the condition requires movements to be speeded up. The flow of movement should be even and consistent with the hands moulded gently to the part being worked on.

The amount of pressure exerted will vary on different parts of the body and on different clients. With practice therapists will develop a sense of touch enabling them to treat each client more effectively.

When working on a specific area only, for example, the back, twenty to thirty minutes should be allowed.

14　*Modification of massage*

There are several reasons why a client will want a body massage and the most common ones are:

1　Relaxation.
2　To lose weight.
3　To loosen stiffness in the joints.
4　To remove aches and pains.
5　To tone up slack flabby muscles.
6　To relax contracted or tight muscles.

Relaxation

The client must be discouraged from talking and a relaxation tape could be played in the background.

All stimulating movements such as hacking, clapping, etc. must be omitted and the number of effleurage strokes can be increased accordingly. The rate of movement should be slow and the depth of pressure increased slightly, particularly when performing petrissage movements.

More time should be spent on the back working especially on the areas of tension normally found in the trapezius muscle and down the sides of the spine.

Soothing stroking could be incorporated into the massage interspersed with effleurage.

Weight problems

Many clients believe in the popular misconception that massage will help them to lose weight. In fact massage alone will not cause weight loss but as part of a carefully controlled treatment plan which includes diet, exercise and use of electrical equipment, it can be effective.

The fact that clients have approached therapists for body massage shows that they are keen to work on their weight problem and if therapists can find out the cause they can then offer a treatment plan which will include massage.

The most common cause is over-eating the wrong types of food and taking insufficient exercise. This can be easily rectified by therapists who can teach clients to eat more sensibly, take more exercise and have regular body massage, when progress will be monitored.

The problem may be hereditary and therefore results may take longer to achieve but regular body massage will maintain contact with clients allowing therapists to provide encouragement and support as well as working out a long-term treatment plan.

Hormonal imbalance

This can be responsible for a client who is obese, for example under-active thyroid gland or possibly medication such as steroids which the client is taking for a medical condition. The menopause may also cause water retention and fat storage which often settles in the area of the abdomen and hips creating the typical pear-shaped figure. In these cases the benefits of relaxation through massage will be most effective.

Whatever the cause before treatment it is important that the general health of the client is good and the doctor confirms that treatment may go ahead.

Ideally, massage should be combined with diet and gentle exercise possibly increasing as the weight problem improves. The areas which have the most excess fat should be worked on, using the more stimulating movements, wringing, picking up, skin rolling, hacking, clapping, beating and pounding. Depth of pressure must be increased considerably. If appropriate to the client a heavy-duty gyratory vibrator may be used instead of or in addition to manual massage.

Joint stiffness

It is always advisable to obtain the permission of the client's doctor before treating joint stiffness.

Massage should be applied to all muscles which act on the particular joint in question. Frictions and finger kneading may be applied to the joint itself. Plenty of effleurage movements should be interspersed during the massage.

Mobility exercises and passive movements could be done during treatment and then strengthening exercises which can also be carried out at the client's home.

It could prove effective if some form of heat treatment was applied before treating the joints, to help with mobility. Paraffin wax is a gentle form of heat and has a soothing effect.

Muscular aches and pains

First of all it is important to eliminate a medical condition as the cause of the aches and pains. Therefore, clients must consult their doctor.

Before performing massage the muscles may be warmed by applying heat in the form of a sauna or steam.

The pain may be caused by knots of tension in the muscles and deep kneading particularly with the thumbs and fingers will help to relax the tension in the muscle. These movements should then be interspersed with lots of soothing relaxing effleurage.

More time should be spent on the areas which are particularly affected, and these areas must be pointed out by the client.

Slack muscles

This can occur for several reasons:

○ After pregnancy.
○ Rapid weight loss.
○ Natural ageing process.

The elasticity of the muscles has been lost and massage must be combined with gentle exercise which can be increased as the muscles regain some strength. Nourishment will be increased to the muscles because of the increase in circulation.

The massage should be more stimulating using deep kneading and tapotement. As the muscles' tone improves some of the petrissage movements may be incorporated.

Tight or contracted muscles

Muscles can be tight due to excessive exercise or to a postural problem. Many sports men and women suffer from this problem.

The movements performed must be slow and rhythmical, in particular kneading and effleurage, to help in stretching the muscles.

Tapotement must be eliminated as this could prove painful.

Massage for men

The muscle bulk in men is larger and stronger than in women. Their muscles are firmer, there is less fatty tissue and their skin is far thicker and tougher and normally quite hairy.

The depth of pressure will have to be increased and more body weight used. A good massage cream or oil must be used to allow ease of movement. The movements should consist mainly of kneading, picking up, wringing and tapotement interspersed with deep effleurage. Excess cream must be removed with cologne or astringent.

15 Heat therapy

There are several different forms of heat treatment which may be used either for their own beneficial effects or to increase the benefits of other forms of body therapy.

Most treatments are available in beauty salons, health clubs, health farms and fitness centres and include:

○ Steam baths.
○ Sauna baths.
○ Foam and aerated baths.
○ Hydro-oxygen baths.
○ Whirlpool or spa baths.

These forms of heat therapy all have similar effects although they differ in application. In general, because they are heating the body they:

1 Relax tense muscles.
2 Have an overall soothing effect.

The effects of heat on the body

Heat therapy can have the following effects:

○ The circulation is increased warming the body.
○ An erythema is produced which improves the overall skin colour.
○ The surface capillaries dilate helping to control body temperature.
○ The sweat glands are stimulated to produce sweat which also helps in controlling body temperature, and waste products are removed.
○ The lactic acid accumulated in the muscles through exercise is dispersed with the increase in circulation.
○ The body temperature rises slowly causing the heartbeat to quicken in the same way as in taking exercise.

○ Tense muscles are relaxed.
○ It promotes a sense of well-being in the client.
○ The tissues are softened preparing them for subsequent treatments such as body massage, vacuum suction, G5 and faradic.

Blood shunting

There are occasions when the body has to make adjustments to blood flow, re-routing blood to various parts of the body and sending it to where it is most needed. At rest approximately 40 per cent of the entire output from the heart goes to the liver and kidneys but with the onset of a vascular shunt this may be reduced to as little as 5 per cent.

Just after exercise begins blood shunting occurs when blood is re-routed to the muscles to cope with the increased demand. It is also shunted away from abdominal organs and the skin as well as the liver and kidneys. For those people who are not very fit the blood shunt away from the liver often causes a 'stitch'.

During heat treatment such as sauna or steam, blood is shunted to the skin and away from the vital organs to help the body maintain a normal temperature.

After eating a large meal, blood is shunted to the intestines to help with digestion. It is important therefore that heat treatment and exercise are not taken after eating a heavy meal or consuming alcohol.

The uses of heat

The application of heat prior to body massage or electrical body treatment will improve the effectiveness of the treatment. If no heat treatment is available even a warm shower can be effective. Clients will feel refreshed and warm.

Figure 15.1 *A steam bath*
Courtesy Depilex Limited

Tension in the muscles is reduced allowing treatment such as electrical muscle stimulation to be carried out more comfortably.

Contraindications to heat

If clients are taking any medication or are having treatment for a medical condition it would be advisable for them to obtain their doctor's permission before having heat treatment. Reasons to avoid heat treatment:

○ High or low blood pressure.
○ History of thrombosis.
○ History of coronary thrombosis.
○ Angina pectoris.
○ Lung conditions – bronchitis, asthma.
○ Skin diseases.
○ Diabetics unless they have the doctor's approval.
○ Epilepsy.
○ Immediately after a heavy meal.
○ After alcohol consumption.
○ Those on a strict diet as the heat will cause them to become light headed and possibly faint.

○ During the heavy days of a period.
○ The later stages of pregnancy.

Steam baths

The original steam baths were Turkish or Roman baths and they were very large buildings with many different rooms all of varying temperatures. The principle of this type of treatment was to progress through the different rooms from the lowest temperatures to the highest and, according to personal taste, a plunge into a pool of cold water at the end. Then there would be a room for relaxation where the participant would also be able to benefit from a relaxing body massage. It was a very sociable and leisurely form of treatment enjoyed by many.

There are very few baths in existence today although they are more common in spa towns and particularly in some European countries. There are, however, smaller scale versions of steam rooms at health hydros, leisure centres, etc.

The modern, more private, equivalent is the small steam bath made from metal or fibreglass and this type of bath may be fitted into even the smallest of beauty salons. It uses moist heat caused by hot water vapour (steam is produced when the water is heated).

Metal steam baths are extremely durable and are good value for money but are harder to keep clean. They also require a lot of towels to be used to protect the client, as well as being more cumbersome than the fibreglass model.

Fibreglass looks more attractive but costs more to buy, less towels are required for client protection and they are far easier to keep clean.

The steam bath is constructed like a cabinet with a solid hinged door or a zippered plastic covering each with an opening for the head. It has an adjustable seat to accommodate all different sizes, with a tank underneath to hold the water which is heated by an electrical element (Figure 15.1).

The size of the tank must be adequate for the number of times it is to be used, for example a large capacity tank would provide approximately eight treatments without being refilled and a smaller tank would provide approximately five treatments. If the steam cabinet was in constant use, therefore, the larger tank would be essential but in a small salon which may only use the bath occasionally the smaller model will suffice.

Clients must be supervised while in the steam bath just in case they are overcome by the heat. This time may be used most effectively by discussing their personal treatment plan and their progress so far.

Effects of steam treatment

○ The circulation increases to allow the body to disperse the heat, this brings nourishment to the skin and hastens the removal of waste products via the lymphatic system as well as causing a hyperaemia.
○ The blood pressure falls and the pulse rate increases.
○ The sudoriferous glands are stimulated to produce more sweat, ridding the body of waste products and cleansing the skin.
○ The body relaxes and the nerve endings are soothed relieving aches and pains.
○ The metabolic rate is increased.
○ The skin is softened.
○ Sebaceous gland activity is increased.

Precautions

The steam bath must be checked prior to the client's arrival, to ensure that it is filled with the necessary amount of water.

The seat must be prepared by covering it with towels or disposable tissue. Although it is more economical to use paper towels it is more comfortable for the client if proper towels are used.

The temperature of a steam bath should be 50–55°C.

The client should shower before taking a steam bath.

Demonstrate to clients how they may leave the steam bath if they feel unable to continue with the treatment. It will also dispel any worries they may have about being confined in a small space.

Once the steam bath has reached the required temperature the client should be seated to the correct level. A towel must then be tucked around the client's neck to prevent steam escaping.

Treatment time will depend on the individual client but it can vary from ten to twenty-five minutes. It is important not to allow the client to remain in the steam bath longer than is necessary.

A warm shower should be taken after the steam bath and if clients are not having further treatment they must rest for at least fifteen minutes. A relaxing massage is an ideal accompaniment to any form of heat therapy.

The steam bath must be cleaned and dried thoroughly after use because the warm moist conditions are an ideal breeding ground for germs. A disinfectant solution must be used. When all treatments for the day have finished the steam bath must be left open to allow it to dry thoroughly.

Sauna baths

The sauna is another form of heat treatment but whereas the steam bath uses hot water vapour (moist heat), the sauna uses dry hot air (dry heat) to achieve similar effects (Figure 15.2).

The traditional Finnish sauna would have been made from pine logs and situated on the

Figure 15.2 *A sauna*

side of a lake so that after sitting in the sauna for the required length of time, participants could then take a plunge into the cold lake.

The saunas in common use today are made from log pines or panels of pine with a space in between filled with an insulating material to keep all of the heat within the sauna. All the internal fittings, the resting benches, the guard rail for the stove, the duck boards, bucket and ladle as well as the flooring are also made of pine as any metal used within the sauna would become too hot and burn the occupants.

Pine material is ideal because it absorbs any condensation produced thus remaining dry. The sauna can be built into a space or be free-standing, as long as there is enough room around the sauna to allow the air to circulate freely. The wood also absorbs the heat produced and then radiates it back into the sauna increasing the temperature within the cabin.

The heat is produced by an electric stove which has a small tray on top containing special stones. This heater is controlled by a thermostat which should be situated out of reach of the clients who may alter the temperature. There should be a thermometer placed as near to the ceiling of the sauna as possible to give the most accurate reading.

Effects of sauna baths

The effects are the same as the steam bath but although the sweat produced is profuse it quickly evaporates leaving the skin fairly dry.

- The skin is deep cleansed and feels refreshed.
- The body is relaxed by alternating the sauna with warm showers and rest periods and allowing the body time to return to its normal temperature slowly.
- The body is prepared for further treatment.
- Depending on the fitness of a client, a plunge pool may be used alternately with the sauna, which will have the effect of raising and lowering the temperature rapidly, providing a more stimulating treatment but placing a greater strain on the heart. This method is more popular among male clients, however.

Precautions

To reach the required temperature the sauna bath must be switched on at least one hour before use for a larger model and thirty minutes for an average-sized sauna.

The pine bucket must be filled with water ready for use and towels placed on the resting benches.

A pine fragrance or eucalyptus oil may be added to the water used in the sauna to provide a fresh smell when poured over the coals.

The time taken for a complete sauna treatment is usually between ten and twenty-five minutes with the average time being twenty minutes.

The temperature of the sauna bath is normally set at 70°C and in the larger model which has more air circulating it may be set at a higher temperature. Male clients often have the sauna at a much higher temperature, for example 95°C and female clients who are used to the heat can take the temperature as high as 85°C.

The air vents in the walls of the sauna should be opened to allow movement of air through the sauna.

It is important to ensure that the client is fit to participate before taking a sauna. The sauna routine must be explained to each new client and there should be ample supervision available during treatment.

Clients are advised to start on the lower benches to acclimatize themselves to the heat and then move up where it is hotter when they are ready. Tepid showers or rest periods outside the sauna may be taken to maximize the relaxation effects of the treatment.

Water should occasionally be poured on to the coals which will produce steam and increase the humidity, which will in turn reduce the evaporation of sweat from the body so less water is lost reducing the risk of dehydration.

The sauna should be regularly scrubbed with disinfectant and clients could be provided with disposable sauna slippers to prevent the spread of infection such as verrucas or athlete's foot.

At the end of the day the doors should be left open to allow the fresh air to enter the sauna, ensuring that there is no stale odour and it is always pleasantly smelling.

The vibratory sauna machine

The sauna has been incorporated in a body-conditioning machine as part of a special combination treatment to alleviate stress and to condition the body. The machine provides:

- *Heat:* Dry heat which helps to deep cleanse the skin, improve the circulation, ease muscular aches and pains and detoxify the body.
- *Detoxification:* Toxins are eliminated from the body through perspiration improving skin tone and helping to combat the problems associated with water retention.
- *Massage:* Simulates the effect of exercise and massage (provided by the gentle vibration, set to a frequency to reduce stress) thus promoting mental and physical relaxation.
- *Sound:* Has a built-in stereo system allowing the client to listen to a selection of music or therapeutic tapes, again to promote mental relaxation.
- *Smell:* Aromatic oils are used for their beneficial effects and the benefits are obtained through inhalation and absorption.

How it works

The vibration relaxes the muscles while the introduction of heat dilates the blood vessels, thereby increasing the heart and pulse rate. This in turn increases the blood flow and intake of oxygen. The body cells use oxygen to burn up carbohydrates, such as starches, etc.; and then they burn up the fat cells. It also accelerates the kidney function in the removal of lactic acids and body wastes.

Benefits

- Relieves muscular aches and pains.
- Relieves backache.
- Increases the circulation.
- Therapeutic for sufferers of arthritis and rheumatism.
- Helps with weight control.
- Helps eliminate body wastes and stimulates kidney function.
- Helps in the treatment of cellulite.
- Provides a soothing and relaxing environment which helps relieve tension and stress.

The machine

The machine consists of a comfortable couch (with a built in head rest) with its own fan to supply cool, fresh air. It has a hinged lid which when closed over the couch, reaches the client's neck to form a heating chamber. There is an aperture similar to that in a steam bath so that

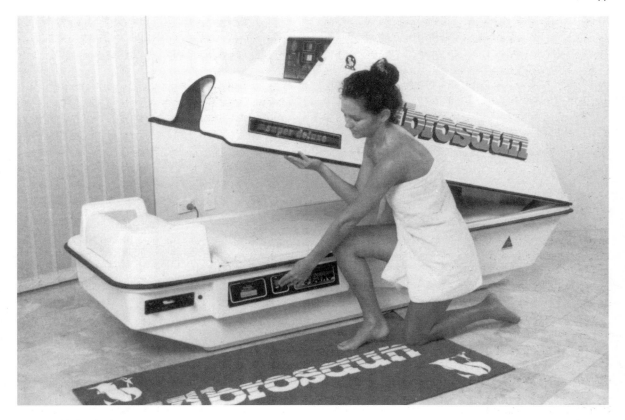

Figure 15.3   *A vibratory sauna*
Courtesy Frevila Limited

the client's head is not enclosed during treatment. There is a control panel on the outside for the therapist to preset the heat, vibration, time, fan and stereo cassette. There is also a panel inside the unit so that the client may adjust the heat, fan and volume of the stereo cassette. The display panel to show the settings is positioned for the client to monitor easily. See Figure 15.3.

The advantages over an ordinary sauna
- It is a complete model, compact and transportable.
- It can be fitted into relatively small areas.
- No pre-heating is necessary.
- It is private.
- It is a personal treatment because the temperature can be adjusted to individual needs whereas with a sauna the temperature is the same for everyone.
- It is more comfortable for those who have difficulty breathing in hot air because it

protects the nasal and bronchial passages.
- It is cooler because the head is outside the heating chamber.
- The pleasantly vibrating couch is more comfortable than wooden benches.

Foam baths

The foam bath is a very efficient way to heat the body but it is an expensive item for a beauty salon and is more likely to be used in a health hydro or on a health farm. A foam bath, however, can be made in an ordinary bath using accessories to fit.

A plastic 'duckboard' which is perforated with hundreds of holes is placed in the bath and an air compressor forces air through the holes in the duckboard. Only a small amount of water is required (about 10 cm), just enough to cover the duckboard, and it is heated to a temperature of 38–43°C. Some concentrated foam essence such as seaweed or pine may be added to the water.

The air compressor is switched on to aerate the water and left until the foam reaches the top of the bath. Clients are then helped into the bath where they will rest, with only their head above the foam, in a semi-reclining position.

The foam provides excellent insulation, generating heat in the client's body which cannot escape so that it builds up and induces more perspiration.

Aerated bath

This is a bath filled with the normal amount of water used when taking a bath but with an essence added. The compressor then aerates the water. Clients sit or recline in a comfortable position allowing the water which is suffused with bubbles, from the increased oxygen, to gently massage the body.

Treatment time is normally fifteen minutes for either type of bath.

Effects

The effects are the same as those produced by a steam bath.

Hydro-oxygen baths

The client reclines in this bath, which is in the form of a cabinet, and is bombarded with hot water jets as the cabinet is diffused with oxygen. The heat created is refreshing and invigorating.

Safety precautions

All baths should be well-maintained and regularly serviced.

All electrical precautions should be taken before treatment and the manufacturers' instructions should be strictly adhered to.

The client must be checked for contraindications and given a thermal skin test. A record card should be filled in.

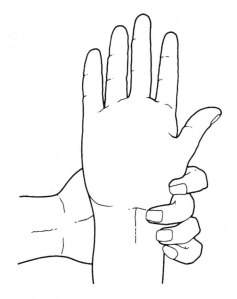

Figure 15.4   *How to take a pulse*

The shower must be cleaned regularly and a shower mat should be provided to prevent slipping.

Towels should be placed in an easily reached position. Clean towels should be provided for each client and paper towels, if used, must be discarded and replaced after use.

Soap must be placed in a soap dish or liquid soap in a dispenser.

Water on the floor in wet areas must be regularly mopped up to prevent accidents.

Do not allow the client to have infrared or ultraviolet treatment after a hydro-oxygen bath because the skin will be sensitive.

The client's pulse may be taken before treatment to ensure that it is normal and after treatment to ensure that it returns to normal.

Pulse
This is a wave of pressure which passes along the arteries indicating the pumping action of the heart. The pulse is normally taken at the wrist just under the thumb on the palmar surface of the hand and is called the radial pulse (Figure 15.4). The finger tips should be placed into the hollow at the base of the metacarpal of the thumb and pressed lightly over the artery. The number of beats in a minute should be counted, using a watch with a second hand count.

The average pulse rate in an adult is 72 beats per minute, but varies between 60 and 80 beats. The pulse rate may increase due to stress, exercise, illness, as a result of injury and while consuming alcohol. A normal pulse will feel regular and strong.

Whirlpool or spa baths

The whirlpool spa was invented twenty-five years ago in America and is becoming increasingly more popular. It is an essential element in all new health hydros, spas and health clubs. The larger baths can accommodate up to eight people at a time.

The weight of the spa is quite considerable so the floor must be tanked, drained and reinforced sufficiently to take the full weight of the spa when filled with water.

The plant room should not be sited more than five metres from the spa itself in a well-ventilated area with sufficient power to supply it. The wet area around the spa itself must have a non-slip surface to prevent accidents and good drainage facilities are required.

A good whirlpool (Figure 15.5) should have the following features:

○ An efficient filtration system.
○ An automated level deck system with overflow channel so that as clients enter or leave the pool there are no unsightly marks around the sides.
○ A heavy-duty control panel.
○ Two types of massage system which can be used separately or together.

For the soothing spa effect, air channels underneath the pool are pressurized by an air compressor and forced up through tiny apertures to produce a gentle massage.

The more stimulating whirlpool massage is produced by jets of water that are positioned around the sides of the bath to work on specific parts of the body and the jet nozzles can be angled to suit the requirements of individual needs.

Figure 15.5 *A whirlpool spa*

When the two systems are combined they produce a turbulent stream of bubbling aerated water which provides an all-over massage from every angle.

Effects of whirlpool spas

○ Increased blood flow removes waste products and increases nourishment to the body.
○ Relieves pain and eases tension in the muscles and joints.
○ The massage stimulates the skin.
○ It speeds up the body's metabolism.
○ The body becomes weightless in the water so exercising muscles against water resistance is easier.
○ Prepares the body for massage or other forms of body therapy when the gentle spa method is used.
○ The whirlpool is quite exhausting to the body as it provides resistance to the stimulating pressure of the water jets.

16 *Infrared and ultraviolet ray and radiant heat treatments*

Infrared and ultraviolet ray treatment

The infrared and ultraviolet ray treatments are available in most health and beauty establishments and are used for both therapeutic and cosmetic purposes.

The different pieces of equipment available are many and varied and the application of these treatments must be carried out safely, carefully following the manufacturers' instructions otherwise there is a risk of over-treatment and burning if carelessly applied.

The rays used are ultraviolet visible light and infrared rays which all form part of the electromagnetic spectrum.

The electromagnetic spectrum

Energy is transmitted from the sun as radiation of different wavelengths through space. This radiation consists of an enormous range of wavelengths and collectively they are known as the electromagnetic spectrum (Figure 16.1), which includes:

- X-rays
- Gamma rays.
- Radio waves.
- Microwave radiation.
- Ultraviolet radiation.
- Visible light.
- Infrared radiation.

They are all electromagnetic rays/waves which transfer energy from one point to another and they consist of varying electric and magnetic fields, which vibrate at a given frequency.

Each type of ray has a particular *wavelength* and *frequency* but they all travel at the same speed. These wavelengths are like the wave in a rope when it is shaken across the floor.

The wavelength is an important characteristic of any type of radiation, it is the distance travelled by the wave in one complete cycle, the distance from the point on one wave to the same point on the next wave.

The frequency is the number of cycles that occur in a unit of time, it is measured in cycles per second or *hertz.*

As the wavelength increases, the frequency decreases and as wavelength decreases, the frequency increases. See Figure 16.2.

Ultraviolet rays have shorter wavelengths and infrared rays have longer wavelengths than visible light. The ultraviolet ray therefore requires more cycles to cover the same distance as infrared rays and has a higher frequency and more energy.

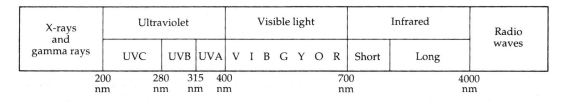

Figure 16.1 *The electromagnetic spectrum*

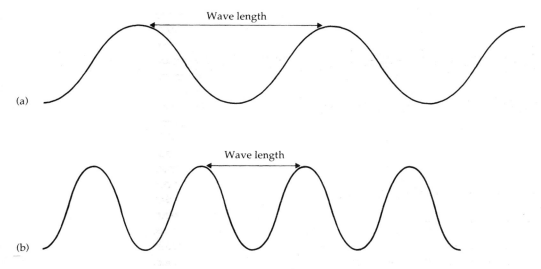

Figure 16.2 *(a) Infrared rays are longer in wavelength therefore lower in energy; (b) Ultraviolet rays are shorter in wavelength with a higher frequency, therefore higher in energy*

The waves of radiation used in beauty therapy are:

1 Ultraviolet.
2 Visible light.
3 Infrared.

Ultraviolet rays

They are used to produce a tan but they are not visible to the naked eye and cannot be felt so some light from the visible spectrum and infrared range is added to give blue warm rays. Ultraviolet ray treatments are discussed fully in Chapter 17.

Visible light

This is white light split up into a band of colours — red, orange, yellow, green, blue, indigo and violet. It lies in the middle of the electromagnetic spectrum and the wavelengths are longer than those of ultraviolet.

Infrared rays

They have a longer wavelength than visible light and can be felt as heat but are not visible. They can be made visible by the addition of some visible light to give radiant heat.

Measuring wavelength

The *nanometre* is the unit of measurement of the wavelength of rays and is equal to one-millionth of a millimetre.

Ultraviolet rays are between 200 and 390 nanometres.

Visible light is between 400 and 700 nanometres with 400 being the blue end and 700 being the red end of the spectrum of light.

Infrared rays are between 700 and 4000 nanometres.

Infrared and radiant heat treatment

There are two types of heat radiation:

1 Infrared.
2 Radiant heat.

Infrared is divided into *near infrared* which is nearest to the visible part of the electromagnetic spectrum and *far infrared* which is further away from the visible light.

Radiant heat is near infrared mixed with red light.

They both produce infrared radiation and are similar in effect, producing heat in the part of the body being treated. Infrared rays are, however, longer than radiant heat rays.

Skin penetration

Infrared rays penetrate into the superficial epidermis only and heat is produced, warming and soothing the skin.

Radiant heat rays are more intense and penetrate deep into the dermis, producing heat, affecting the nerve endings of pain. This irritant effect makes this a more stimulating form of heat treatment.

Heat lamps

The lamps available are many and varied but the principles of application are the same. There are two types of heat lamp available to the beauty therapist and these are:

1 The infrared or non-luminous lamp which provides no visible light but produces heat. It can be used for a longer period of time as it is less irritating.
2 The radiant heat or luminous lamp which combines near infrared rays and visible light to produce heat.

When giving treatment with heat lamps the characteristics of each lamp need to be considered before choosing which one to use.

Characteristics of lamps

Infrared
The infrared lamp has to be switched on at least ten to fifteen minutes before it is required to reach its maximum intensity.

The infrared generator should be mounted in a reflector which is perfectly designed without any dents which may cause the tissues to be heated unevenly. A defective reflector would cause the rays to concentrate in certain areas and create a 'hot spot'.

The radiation is of a longer wavelength and is less irritating so therefore may be used for longer periods.

Radiant heat
The radiant heat lamp will not need time to warm up as it reaches its peak thirty seconds after being switched on. The heat is also more evenly dispersed as it has its own built-in reflector system.

A red glow is given out with this type of lamp and this has a psychologically soothing effect on clients as they lie bathed in the warm red light. This treatment is ideal when treating muscular aches and pains.

The radiation from this lamp is of shorter wavelengths and the heat is quite deep so treatment time has to be kept shorter.

Effects of heat lamps

Increase in circulation
An increase in circulation is caused by the application of heat. The blood vessels dilate and the increased blood flow brings nourishment to the area being heated and increases the lymph flow thus removing waste products.

A hyperaemia or reddening of the skin is produced due to the increased circulation and it begins to fade soon after the conclusion of treatment.

Pain relief
With mild heating, the rays have an analgesic effect on the superficial sensory nerve endings in the skin. More intense heating actually irritates the superficial sensory nerve endings and pain is relieved due to counter irritation.

Mild heating is helpful in easing pain caused by an accumulation of waste products in the tissues. The increased flow of lymph helps in the speedier removal of these waste products.

Increase in body temperature
The increase in temperature usually occurs locally, just in the area being treated. This stimulates the sweat glands to produce more sweat, aiding the elimination of waste products and deep cleansing the skin.

The warmth produced also allows creams to be absorbed more readily into the skin.

Relaxation
Muscles relax making them more responsive to further treatment. The soothing effect on the

nerve endings relieves pain, so relieving tension in the body, helping the muscles to relax.

Uses of heat lamp treatment

○ As a preparatory treatment, it will relax the muscles before electrical muscle stimulation or body massage and allow easier penetration of creams and oils into the epidermis.
○ To relax a tense nervous client.
○ To relieve muscular pain or tension.
○ To relieve pain in the joints.
○ To replace other forms of heat treatment such as sauna or steam.
○ To promote healing.

Contraindications

○ Heart or circulatory problems.
○ Hyper-sensitive skin.
○ Skin disorders.
○ Diabetes because of the inefficient circulation and poor skin sensitivity.
○ Any loss of skin sensation.
○ High or low blood pressure.
○ Sunburn.
○ Metal pins or plates.

Dangers of infrared radiation

○ Burning of the skin caused by overheating or contact with the lamp.
○ Fainting, particularly if the client rises quickly from a lying position.
○ Headache may follow treatment particularly in hot weather. The back of the head should be protected if it is exposed during treatment.
○ Injury to the eyes.

Safety

The client

When applying any form of heat to the skin a thermal skin test must be carried out prior to treatment, to avoid burning the skin and to ensure that the client's skin sensitivity is not impaired:

1 Two test tubes should be filled, one with hot water and the other with cold water.
2 The client should close their eyes and the test tubes are applied alternately to the areas which will be exposed to the heat.
3 If clients can distinguish between the hot and cold test tubes then their skin sensation is normal and the treatment may proceed.
4 Check the client has no contraindications.
5 Check that clients have removed all their jewellery.
6 The skin must be free from grease so the client should take a shower before the treatment commences. Alternatively the skin can be wiped over with witch hazel or skin tonic.
7 The client's eyes must be protected if they are likely to be exposed to the rays. Damp cotton wool pads can be used to protect them – the water will absorb the rays.
8 Maintain contact with the client during treatment.

The heat lamp

Always follow the manufacturers' instructions. The heat lamp must be checked before treatment to see that it is in good working order.

The plug should not have any loose connections. The flex should not be frayed and it should be positioned so that it will not be tripped over. The switches should be in good working order.

Bulbs should be screwed firmly in place. All reflective surfaces should be clean and free from dents.

The joints in a free-standing model should be tightened sufficiently to prevent any movement once the lamp has been correctly positioned.

The lamp should be warmed up away from clients to prevent accidents.

The lamp must be positioned at the correct distance and angle from the client. This may be between eighteen inches and two feet according to the output from the generator. At the conclusion of treatment the lamp should be positioned safely away from clients to cool down.

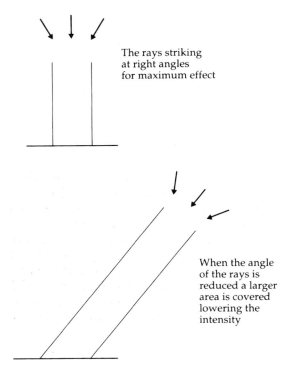

The rays striking at right angles for maximum effect

When the angle of the rays is reduced a larger area is covered lowering the intensity

Figure 16.3   *The cosine law for radiation*

The cosine law

This compares the intensity of the rays with the angle at which the rays contact the skin.

The lamp should be placed perpendicular to the area being treated so that the rays are at right angles to the body for maximum intensity.

If the angle is reduced then the rays cover a larger area and the intensity will be lowered (Figure 16.3).

Timing of treatment

Normal treatment time varies from ten to thirty minutes depending on the size of the area to be treated and the distance the lamp is placed from the client.

The more sensitive the client is to the heat the farther away the lamp must be positioned and the longer the treatment time should be to compensate for the lower intensity of the rays.

17 *Ultraviolet radiation*

Ultraviolet rays

Ultraviolet rays are situated at the violet end of the light spectrum and although they produce little heat they do have a strong reaction on the skin, causing erythema and tanning. There are three bands of ultraviolet rays and they are classified as:

1 Ultraviolet A (UVA) rays.
2 Ultraviolet B (UVB) rays.
3 Ultraviolet C (UVC) rays.

Ultraviolet A rays

These rays are a lower energy ultraviolet which penetrate deep into the dermis where they cause fragmentation of the collagen and elastin fibres which provide the skin with support.

Many sunbed manufacturers claim that tanning occurs without burning because the output is almost entirely UVA with minute amounts of UVB added. The absence of UVB means that the normal protective response of thickening of the epidermis does not occur thus

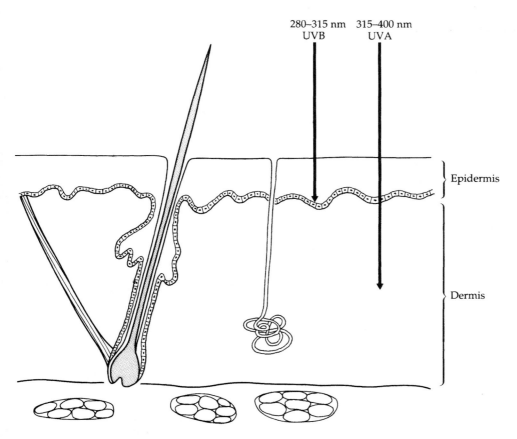

Figure 17.1 *The penetration of ultraviolet rays into the skin*

allowing excessive amounts of UVA to penetrate into the dermis and eventually causing ageing of the skin.

UVA rays produce a tan in a skin which tans easily, by stimulating the existing melanin in the skin, but it is not a long-lasting tan. They alone do not cause cancer but have a predisposition to the effects of UVB in causing skin cancers.

The wavelength is 315–400 nanometres.

Ultraviolet B rays

UVB rays penetrate only into the epidermis and they are the rays responsible for sunburn. These rays stimulate the melanocytes in the basal layer of the epidermis to produce melanin resulting in a longer lasting tan and they are the rays chiefly responsible for the formation of skin cancers.

The wavelength is 280–315 nanometres.

Ultraviolet C rays

None of these rays reach the earth's surface as they are absorbed by the atmosphere. These rays are lethal to living cells.

The wavelength is 200–280 nanometres.

Ultraviolet radiation

Natural sunshine is beneficial to most people in small doses and it has certain effects:

○ It warms the body.
○ It stimulates chemical activity in the skin increasing cellular regeneration.
○ It stimulates the production of vitamin D in the skin which is important in the development and maintenance of healthy bones.
○ It promotes a feeling of well-being giving a psychological boost.
○ It is cosmetic in effect as it produces a tan giving the appearance of good health.
○ It has a beneficial effect on some skin disorders, for example psoriasis and acne.

The amount of ultraviolet exposure that we receive depends upon several factors:

1 The part of the world in which we live.
2 The season of the year.
3 The thickness of the ozone layer, which prevents a large proportion of rays from reaching the earth.

The effects of ultraviolet radiation

The skin's physiological response to the application of ultraviolet light is a protective one, to prevent more harm coming to the skin and the body.

Beneficial effects
○ Produces a tan.
○ Stimulates the production of vitamin D.
○ Stimulates the metabolism.
○ Has a tonic effect.
○ Ultraviolet rays kill some bacteria on the skin.
○ The shedding of dead skin cells is accelerated and this will vary depending upon the amount of exposure.

Damaging effects
○ Thickens the stratum corneum, when the ultraviolet rays stimulate the cells in the basal layer of the epidermis to produce more rapidly. This creates additional protection for the skin against the ultraviolet radiation.
○ Can cause sunburn.
○ In the long-term, over-exposure to UVA will cause ageing of the skin and UVB may cause skin cancer.

The physiological process involved in the production of a tan

The technical term for tanning is *melanogenesis*. As the UV rays are absorbed by the skin, they stimulate into action the enzyme *tyrosinase*, which is present in the *melanocytes*, the pigment forming cells in the basal layer of the epidermis.

This chemical process causes the transformation of *tyrosin*, a colourless amino acid, into *melanin*, a colourful molecule which migrates upwards to the surface of the skin. *Melanin* gives skin its characteristic golden or bronze tan and helps to filter out the harmful ultraviolet rays protecting the skin from further radiation.

UVA and UVB rays
↓
Absorbed by the skin
↓
Tyrosinase is activated in melanocytes
↓
Transforms tyrosin into melanin
↓
Melanin migrates up to the skin's surface
↓
Tan is produced

Exposure to ultraviolet light should be limited to times when the sun is not high in the sky. It is at its strongest between the hours of 11 a.m. and 4 p.m.

The rays also increase in strength if they are reflected off another surface, for example sand, snow or water. On winter skiing holidays there is a high incidence of sunburn on the fairly sensitive and usually unexposed area underneath the chin, from ultraviolet radiation, which is reflected off the snow.

Many people will burn when exposed to ultraviolet radiation before they tan and some unfortunate people burn without producing a tan. The skin's reaction will normally depend upon the skin type. There are many different skin types which have developed to suit different climatic conditions.

In Africa the negroid skin is heavily pigmented and usually thicker and more greasy. This skin, however, will still become darker when exposed to ultraviolet light and lighter if protected from it.

In countries situated in Northern Europe the skin is normally thin, fair and dry and would require maximum protection.

No matter which skin type a person has, the skin will burn if there is over-exposure. The sensitive skins will only be safe for a very short time without some form of protection and the darker skins are safe only if they are not over-exposed.

Skin types

Skin types may be classified as:

Group 1: Sensitive skin which burns easily and does not develop a tan.
Group 2: Sensitive skin which burns but tans slightly.
Group 3: Normal skin which burns slightly and tans slowly.
Group 4: Skin which easily tans and rarely burns.
Group 5: Skin that is deeply pigmented and never burns.

Sunburn

Several hours after exposure the skin will become red and this reddening is called an *erythema*. There are four degrees of erythema and these are:

1 First degree erythema. This is a slight reddening which appears several hours after exposure and disappears within twenty-four hours without causing any irritation.
2 Second degree erythema. A marked redness with slight itching which lasts for two to three days.
3 Third degree erythema. Extremely red, hot, swollen and sore which lasts for a week.
4 Fourth degree erythema. The same as third degree erythema but the swelling leads to blistering and peeling. The skin is very hot and painful.

Physiological response to sunburn

Sunburn is an injury to the skin and the body responds by releasing histamine from the skin cells, which in turn cause the blood vessels to dilate allowing more blood to reach them.

Fluid leaks from the widened blood vessels so that the infected area becomes red from the increased blood supply and swollen from the increased fluid. This swelling causes pain and tenderness in the area.

The skin begins the normal healing process which is very efficient and exactly the same whether the injury is caused by infection, a wound or sunburn. The cells in the skin divide quickly to form new tissue but if the sunburn was severe then scarring may occur.

Burning of the skin
↓
Histamine is released
↓
Blood vessels dilate
↓
Fluid bathes the area
↓
Skin becomes red and swollen
↓
Pain and tenderness results

Sunscreens

There are two types of sunscreens: physical and chemical.

Physical

This type of sunscreen is an opaque film used on the skin to reflect the ultraviolet radiation and the most common example is zinc oxide cream used by winter holiday enthusiasts when skiing. It forms a dense barrier but actually blocks perspiration so its use is limited to small exposed areas such as the bridge of the nose and the cheekbones.

Chemical

This type of sunscreen can be a water- or oil-soluble chemical which absorbs ultraviolet radiation reducing its intensity. They come in the form of cream, oil, lotion or milk and some are waterproof. Sunscreens are now being included in skin care products and makeup.

The best type of sunscreen product is a *broad spectrum* sunscreen which will filter out both the ultraviolet A and B rays. These sunscreens are graded by their *sun protection factor* (SPF). The SPF is determined by the amount of time the sunscreen can extend the time a person can spend in the sun without burning. For example, a person who could stay in the sun for 10 minutes before burning could extend that period of time to 60 minutes without burning by using a sunscreen with an SPF of 6.

SPF numbers vary but some manufacturers produce them as high as 30 as well as total sunblocks.

The most sensitive skin types, that is, fair skins, babies and anyone who has not previously been exposed to ultraviolet radiation, should use the highest factor available.

One of the most common constituents of sunscreens which filter out UVB rays is *para aminobenzoic acid*. New sunscreens have been developed to absorb the A and B rays, the broad spectrum absorbers, *dioxybenzone* and *oxybenzophenone*.

For maximum benefit:

○ Apply before going into the sun.
○ Reapply regularly during the day.
○ Water-resistant sunscreens should be reapplied approximately half-an-hour before going into the water.

Fake tan treatment

A popular salon treatment for those who are photosensitive is the application of a false tan. There are also a small number of people who prefer not to expose themselves to the effects of ultraviolet radiation but still want a tan and this is an ideal solution.

The self-tanning creams are made from dihydroxy acetone and rich moisturizing creams which when applied to the skin can produce a golden tan. A chemical reaction occurs when the cream is applied to the skin causing superficial staining of the top layer of the epidermis.

Advantages

○ The client may have an all year round tan.
○ It can help to prolong the life of an existing tan.
○ It can be used for special occasions when a low cut or backless dress is worn.
○ Those who are allergic to natural sunlight can achieve a tanned look.
○ It produces a tan without ageing the skin.

Disadvantages

○ The colours of different self-tanning creams can vary greatly.

○ They may leave a streaky effect on the skin.
○ The dry areas of skin tend to absorb more colour, therefore may produce a blotchy effect, in particular elbows, knees and ankles.
○ They have to be re-applied regularly to maintain the colour.

Precautions

○ Use the correct product for face and body as the facial creams contain more moisturizer and less of the tanning ingredient to produce a more natural tan.
○ An exfoliation treatment must be applied first; brush massage or special exfoliating creams may be used. This will prevent the self tan over-staining areas of dry skin.
○ Moisturize the skin well to provide a good base for application of the cream, to give a perfect finish with no streaking.
○ A small patch test may be applied prior to treatment to ensure that the client is not allergic to the product and the colour is compatible with her own skin.

Ultraviolet lamp treatment

The application of ultraviolet by artificial means has become very popular in recent years with specialist salons opening and most beauty salons and health clubs promoting their use.

Sunbeds to be used at home are advertised extensively in the press, unfortunately allowing untrained people to apply ultraviolet radiation without knowing the rules of safe use which they should apply.

The Association of Sun Tanning Operators have agreed to a code of practice based on guidelines from the Health and Safety Executive. If a salon is a member of this association then it will have a badge prominently displayed on the premises.

Reasons for the use of ultraviolet lamps

○ For tanning purposes, to produce or maintain a tan.

○ To promote healing and increase desquamation in an acne skin condition.
○ To stimulate a sluggish skin.
○ To improve some skin conditions, for example psoriasis if the client is not on medication for the condition.

Ultraviolet lamps

The modern ultraviolet lamps are:

○ Mercury vapour which can be either high or low pressure and are designed to produce UVA only.
○ Fluorescent tubes similar to the fluorescent lighting tubes but they emit ultraviolet rays as well as visible blue light.

The lamps come in various forms:

A small sun lamp which is portable and easily packed away but only used to treat small areas and is not as efficient for general treatment.

A sunbench which is a modified couch with a transparent, concave surface on which the client lies, receiving the treatment from below.

A solarium which is a combination of several units allowing the whole body to be treated at once.

The glass used in sun beds and solaria is made of a special type which allows the penetration of ultraviolet rays. The heat produced from the lamps is caused by a small amount of infrared being added.

Safety

Patch test

Before applying any ultraviolet treatment the client's skin must be assessed first using a patch test, which shows how long it will take to cause a minimal erythema.

An area of skin not previously exposed to ultraviolet rays must be chosen, for example inside of the arm. The area must be clean and grease free so the skin is not sensitized by anything which has been applied and there is no barrier to the rays.

Use a sheet of opaque paper and cut out three different shapes and position them securely over the area to be treated. The surrounding area must be protected with towels, the lamp carefully positioned and the distance recorded.

The three shapes should then be exposed to the ultraviolet rays for one minute.

The first shape should then be covered with a towel and the two remaining shapes exposed for a second minute.

The second shape should then be covered with a towel and the last shape exposed for another minute.

A record of each shape and the time they were exposed to the ultraviolet rays should be kept. The client must then return after 24 hours to have the patches checked for any signs of reaction.

If the results of the test are negative then the client should have another test and the time exposed to the ultraviolet rays should be increased.

The time it took to produce a minimal erythema is the time the therapist will use for the first treatment, using the distance recorded from the patch test.

Inverse square law

Ultraviolet rays cannot be felt so it is vitally important that the lamp is not placed too close to the client. The closer the rays are to the body, the higher the intensity of radiation and the more likely they are to burn the skin.

The rays travelling from a lamp actually spread out, so the further away they are from the point of contact the weaker they will become. By increasing the distance away from the point of contact the rays will spread over a larger area and become weaker in effect.

The inverse square law (Figure 17.2) states:

The intensity of rays from a point source varies inversely with the square of the distance from the source.

This means that if the distance from the lamp to the area treated is doubled, the intensity of the rays is quartered. For example, if ultraviolet treatment is given for one minute, at a distance of one foot and the lamp is then moved to two feet away (doubling the distance), the time of

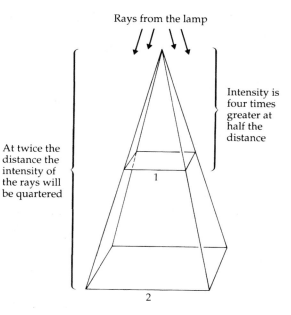

Figure 17.2 *Inverse square law for radiation*

treatment would be increased to four minutes because the intensity of the rays has quartered. Therefore, at half the distance, the intensity is four times *greater* and at *twice* the distance, the intensity is four times *weaker*.

Formula
To work out the distance and the time to obtain the same intensity:

Halve the distance – divide the time by 4
Double the distance – multiply the time by 4.

Client consultation

Client consultation is important because it provides the opportunity to discuss with clients anything which may affect the treatment they are undertaking.

A record card should be filled in with all the details of the clients and, in particular, any form of medication they are taking. Many drugs are photosensitizers which make the body extra sensitive to ultraviolet.

Check with clients if they have recently been in the sun and if there have been any adverse reactions.

Assess the sensitivity of the skin and carry out a patch test.

Check for contraindications:

o Extra sensitive skin.
o Photosensitive skin.
o Vitiligo, skin with a total absence of melanin.
o Sun allergy.
o History of skin cancer.
o Immediately after heat treatment.
o Skin disease.

During treatment

Therapists and clients must wear goggles when exposed to the ultraviolet rays and the importance of this procedure must be stressed to the clients, so that when left unattended they will not be tempted to remove them and leave eyes open to damage.

The distance of the lamp from the client must be measured accurately. The ultraviolet rays must strike the body at an angle of 90° for maximum effect and the treatment must be accurately timed.

When the treatment is purely cosmetic (that is, to produce a tan) then exposure will need to be twice a week. The aim will be to produce a first degree erythema (a tan without burning or peeling).

As the pigmentation increases and the epidermis thickens, the dosage must be increased at each treatment to be effective. This will be achieved by increasing the dose by 25 per cent at each session.

The client's skin reaction and colouring must be taken into consideration before each treatment.

Records must be kept of the:

o Date.
o Lamp used.
o Area treated.
o Distance of the lamp from the body.
o Time of treatment.
o The general effects.
o Erythema reaction.
o Therapist's name.
o Any other relevant information.

Health and Safety at Work Act 1974

This law states that the owner of a business is legally responsible for the safety of his/her employees and clients. Therefore, the following points must be considered:

1　Understand the equipment being used.
2　Train all members of staff in their safe use.
3　Follow the manufacturers' instructions to the letter.
4　Have the equipment serviced once a year and make sure it is mechanically safe.
5　Always ensure client safety.
6　There should be ease of access to the sunbed.
7　There should be adequate ventilation particularly with the 'high pressure' solaria because ultraviolet produces ozone and in excess can be irritating.
8　There should be a notice in the sunbed room stating the correct procedures, safety factors and hygiene precautions to be followed.
9　There should be a notice prominently displayed which warns the clients of the effects of UV radiation.
10　There must be some means by which a client can summon help, for example a bell.
11　There must be a timer fitted to the machine for accuracy.
12　The overhead canopies must be made of a suitable material so that lamps will not fall out or explode.
13　When new lamps have been fitted to an existing solarium a notice to this effect must be prominently displayed, to inform the clients, as the general effect is more marked with new lamps.

18 *Effects of heat and ultraviolet radiation*

The effects of extreme heat and over-exposure to ultraviolet radiation

Exhaustion

Anything which causes the body to produce excessive perspiration will deplete the body of necessary minerals and salt. Low levels of potassium and calcium will result in fatigue and cramps. There will be a feeling of lethargy accompanied by headaches and dizziness and in severe cases a feeling of nausea and collapse.

To counteract these symptoms the sufferer should lie down quietly and drink plenty of fluids, preferably water. Levels of potassium can be increased by eating foods high in the mineral such as bananas, nuts and avocados.

Sunstroke

This is a dangerous condition and occurs when the body's normal protection against overheating fails. The body is unable to cope with the excessive heat and the body's temperature rises to unacceptable levels.

The symptoms are rapid rise in temperature, severe headaches, vomiting, collapse and, in extreme cases, unconsciousness. This condition requires medical help and immediate cooling of the body with cold water. When the body begins to return to normal rest and plenty of fluids are required.

Miliaria

This is a condition which affects the sweat glands and it comes in two forms:

Miliaria crystallina (sudamina)
This occurs when the skin around the sweat ducts becomes swollen resulting in a blockage of the sweat gland. As the sweat gland continues to work the end of the duct becomes distended causing a clear fluid filled vesicle. There may be an accompanying itchiness of the skin but the condition soon subsides if the body is kept cool.

Miliaria rubra (prickly heat)
This is a reaction to heat and in particular exposure to ultraviolet radiation. It is also a blockage of the sweat ducts but in this case the duct ruptures allowing the sweat to escape into the epidermis. This causes the formation of itchy red pimples on inflamed skin. Loose clothing must be worn in natural fabrics to allow the skin to perspire freely. Cool the body by taking cool showers and if infection occurs consult a doctor.

Swelling

This normally occurs in the lower limbs because the blood vessels dilate as a response to heat and the walls of the superficial blood vessels become stretched and fluid leaks into the surrounding tissue. To treat this problem it is advisable to lie down and rest with the legs slightly elevated and to take cool showers.

Exposure to ultraviolet radiation only

Wrinkling

The name given to the changes that occur in the skin due to exposure to ultraviolet radiation is *solar elastosis*. The skin loses its normal strength and elasticity. The collagen and elastin fibres in the dermis are affected causing the breakdown of the support in the skin as well as a loss of fluid as the skin becomes much drier with constant exposure.

Areas of pigmentation

Brown patches occur on exposed areas of skin which are larger and more irregular in shape than the smaller freckles or lentigo.

Broken veins

Tissue affected by ultraviolet radiation is not as tough as normal connective tissue. The blood vessels widen and become more visible on the surface of the skin. The technical term for these visible blood vessels is *telangiectasia*.

Reduction of skin immunity

The *Langerhans cells* in the skin are part of the immune system. They locate dangerous substances in the skin and initiate an immune response. Exposure to UVB rays reduces the numbers and function of these cells, adversely affecting the body's immune system by preventing it from recognizing and dealing with foreign bodies. Therefore, cancer cells that appear may be allowed to flourish.

19 *Figure analysis*

Initial assessment

It is important to analyse the figure and posture of clients before beginning any course of body treatments for weight reduction or body shaping because:

○ It will ensure that the treatments recommended will be the most effective for clients and their particular requirements.
○ It will ensure that the treatment chosen will not cause any harm or discomfort.
○ It will help therapists to recognize any faults which are not to be treated by them and may need to be referred to a doctor.
○ When using more than one form of treatment it will influence the therapist's decision about which treatments to use.
○ It will ensure that treatment is not given unnecessarily if figure faults are caused by some simple postural problem.

The initial figure assessment of clients is a visual one. This will show any problems they may have with their range of movement and even when they are fully dressed it is easy to assess figure shape.

The next part of the assessment will require clients to remove their clothes as far as their underwear. Check for postural and figure faults in front of a full length mirror. The clients can then see how their posture may be corrected, while the therapist explains the treatments which may help any problems of excess weight, cellulite or poor muscle tone.

Correct posture

Good posture depends a great deal on muscle tone. By observing the client from the front, back and side the therapist should note any deviation from the norm as far as posture is concerned, as this will be a good indicator of the problems the client has to overcome.

A client who has good posture will stand tall and straight without strain and without having to hold in any part of the body with any effort.

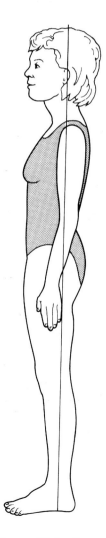

Figure 19.1 *Correct posture*

Weight must be evenly distributed on both legs and carried on the arches of the feet (Figure 19.1).

For good posture:

o   The head and shoulders should be level.
o   The scapulae should be an even distance from the spine.
o   The vertebral column should be straight down the back and not curved in either direction.
o   The abdomen should be flat and the buttocks not protruding.
o   The waist should be evenly curved with the hips level.
o   The arms should be in a relaxed position at the side and hang evenly.
o   The legs and knees should be straight with the feet together or just slightly apart and facing forward.

The benefits of good posture

o   Breathing may be full and deep as the chest is not contracted.
o   The digestive organs function more efficiently if they are not compressed.
o   An even distribution of body weight ensures that the body does not become too tired with certain muscles working overtime.
o   Postural defects will not occur if the bones are held in their correct positions.
o   The figure looks its best when the posture is correct.

The maintenance of good posture

To maintain the correct posture and allow the body to remain standing it relies on the *antigravity muscles* (Figures 19.2 and 19.3). These muscles are in a state of partial contraction all the time except when we sleep or lose consciousness.

The antigravity muscles are:

o   The *pectorals* on the chest.
o   *Biceps* on the upper arms.
o   The *trapezius* on the back.
o   The *gluteals* or buttocks.
o   The *quadriceps* on the thigh.
o   *Gastrocnemius* on the calf.

Body types (Figure 19.4)

Posture, exercise and diet can change the overall shape of the body. However, the one consistent factor is the body type. This is hereditary and is determined by the genes. The therapist can recognize the body type by its characteristics and can help clients with figure faults or help them to come to terms with their problems.

There are three classifications of body type:

Endomorph

Round in shape with a higher proportion of fat to muscle, this body type tends to put on weight easily and fat is deposited around the hips, abdomen, thighs and shoulders. The limbs and neck are short and hands and feet are small.

Ectomorph

This body type is lean and angular with long limbs and small joints. There is very little body fat with none of the usual female curves and a lack of muscle bulk.

Mesomorph

Usually strong with an even distribution of weight, this body type normally has broad shoulders and well-toned muscles. This body type is characteristic of an athletic person who normally has no weight problems while active.

Figure faults

The most common figure faults (particularly in female clients) are the pear shape with heavy hips, thighs and buttocks, round shoulders, protruding abdomen and a large bust, which can lead to round shoulders.

Many of these faults are due to slack muscles or excess fat. Slack muscles may be caused by:

o   The client's sedentary life style.
o   Lack of physical exercise.
o   The normal ageing process.
o   Pregnancy.
o   Illness.
o   Stress.

Excess fat is caused by a higher intake of calories than are burned off through normal exercise.

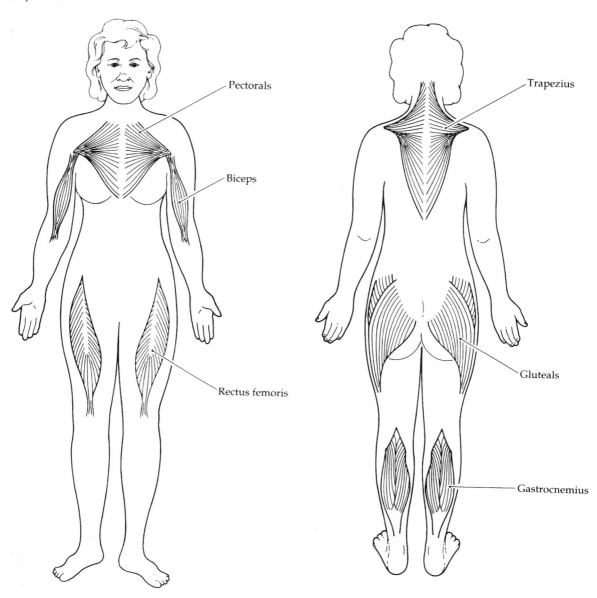

Figure 19.2 *Antigravity muscles anterior view*

Figure 19.3 *Antigravity muscles posterior view*

Body fat

Women have a higher ratio of fat to muscle than men, a large proportion of which lies just beneath the skin. This provides support and insulation, contouring the body and keeping the skin firm and supple.

If there is fat in excess the skin loses its shape by becoming dimpled and more solid. If a large amount of fat is lost the body will lose its shape as the skin sags when the underlying support shrinks away.

Spinal curvature

There are figure faults which require medical attention but are easily recognized by the

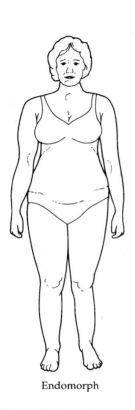

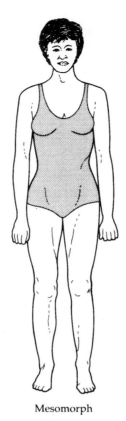

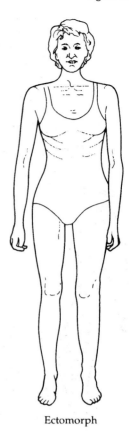

| Endomorph | Mesomorph | Ectomorph |

Figure 19.4 *Body types*

therapist when carrying out her visual assessment. In these cases medical approval must be sought before planning any exercises or treatments.

Kyphosis

This condition causes the thoracic part of the spine to curve outwards. Round shoulders and tightness of the pectoral muscles often accompanies this figure fault.

Lordosis

This condition is an inward curve of the spine in the lumbar region and is commonly referred to as a *hollow back.* It is sometimes associated with the forward tilting of the pelvis.

Scoliosis

This is a fault which shows itself as a lateral curve and rotation of the spine, either to the right or the left. This fault causes changes in the muscles, ligaments, bones and joints which may lead to further faults such as:

○ One leg longer than the other.
○ One shoulder slightly higher than the other.
○ Uneven scapulae.
○ Pelvic tilt.

Dowager's hump

This figure fault often affects women as they grow older. The head is tilted forward slightly and with age fatty deposits accumulate at the back of the neck over the spine and when established it is very difficult to correct.

Many figure problems can be alleviated to some degree just by teaching the client about good posture and then exercises can be given to the client to carry out at home which will complement the treatments and exercises in the salon.

Manual assessment

This is something the therapist can do quite easily when performing a massage. The condition of the muscles as well as the skin can be noted and contraindications to some forms of electrical treatment may be apparent.

Manipulation of the muscles allows the therapist to determine their tone and strength, indicating the client's physical condition. Tension in the muscles also shows how much stress clients are feeling, or whether they are suffering discomfort from an injury or a figure fault.

The skin condition may affect the form body treatment will take and manual assessment will show the elasticity of the skin and how different skin conditions may affect treatment, for example severe stretch marks from pregnancy or rapid weight loss. With age, whether it is natural or premature, the skin becomes loose and crepey and this will cause treatment to be modified or contraindicated.

Testing for mobility and muscle strength

There are several simple tests which may be carried out by the therapist on the client, particularly before recommending any form of exercise or applying electrical muscle stimulation treatment.

Determining the strength of the client's muscles will allow the therapist to judge the intensity of current to be used with electrical muscle stimulation for the first few treatments until the muscle reaction can be seen after several applications.

It is important to determine how flexible or mobile a client is before recommending any type of exercise. The general fitness and strength of

clients varies considerably and the tests given must not be too difficult or rigorous.

There are three different types of movement:

1 *Passive* movements are performed by the therapist on the client who takes no active part in the exercise.
2 *Active* movements are those which the client performs with or without assistance from the therapist.
3 *Resisted* movements are those performed against a resistance.

Mobility

Mobility can be inherited or acquired and it can be determined by the ease with which the joints can move through their full range of movement. Most people, with age, begin to lose mobility. Therefore, some form of exercise plays an important role as we get older. There are some simple exercises to test for mobility and these are:

Shoulder
The client should place the left arm along the back and bring the right arm over the shoulder to meet it. If the client is able to clasp fingers then mobility is good at the shoulder but if they fail to touch it is poor. There could be a difference when both sides are tested as quite often there is more mobility in one side than the other.

Spine
The client should kneel down on hands and knees, drop the forehead down and bring the knee up to meet it. If this is achieved without discomfort then mobility of the spine is good.

Finally, the client could be asked to perform a few simple exercises such as, side bends, touching the toes and arm rotations to indicate how supple and mobile they are.

Strength

Physical strength is determined by the strength of the muscles. Strong muscles are firm and allow the body to perform all movement easily. Muscle strength is tested by asking the client to perform certain movements for different areas of the body.

20 *Body electrical treatments*

Electrical equipment

Most body electrical treatments are used as part of a programme designed specifically for clients to allow them to lose weight or re-contour their body.

Electrical equipment may be introduced:

o When the client is on a weight reducing diet. The use of electrical equipment can increase the effectiveness of the diet.
o To provide variety of treatment motivating and maintaining the client's interest.
o When specific areas only need to be treated, to effect a localized reduction.

It must be stressed to the client that use of electrical equipment alone is not enough to lose weight or re-contour the body. The essential ingredients in an effective body treatment programme are:

o To follow a well-balanced, weight-reducing diet.
o To increase the amount of physical exercise taken.
o The application of appropriate body treatments by a beauty therapist.

The electrical treatments offered by the beauty therapist include:

1 Vibratory treatment.
2 Vacuum massage treatment.
3 Electrotherapy, which includes high frequency treatment, galvanic treatment and electrical muscle stimulation.

Vibratory treatment

Vibratory treatment is a form of mechanical massage and there are three types:

1 *Percussion.* Machines which work only on a vertical plane, which means that the movements they make are only up and down and physiologically are equivalent to tapotement or hacking. The percussion vibrator is used mainly in facial therapy.
2 *Gyrators.* Machines which work on a vertical and horizontal plane. The movements are up and down as well as circular, simulating the actions of effleurage, petrissage and kneading, and are used in body therapy.
3 *Audio sonic.* Machines use sound wave vibrations to achieve their effects and may be used when other types of vibratory treatment are contraindicated.

Gyratory vibrator (G5)

This machine was designed by M. Henri Cuinier and is commonly termed the G5. G5 was the original model number and this model is still used today.

The gyratory vibrator is the most commonly used type of mechanical massage machine and the models used for body work are normally free-standing, on a pedestal, with castors for ease of movement. The motor is heavy-duty with an air-cooling system so that it does not over heat with prolonged use. From the motor comes a flexible insulated arm, to which the applicator heads are attached to perform the treatment. All the applicators are kept in an accessory tray on the pedestal base. See Figure 20.1.

The machine has several different applicator heads, made from polyurethane or rubber, and they come in various shapes and sizes. They are all used during treatment to achieve similar effects to those of manual massage:

o The sponge heads are used for effleurage.
o The hard rubber heads are used for petrissage.

Sitting up from a lying position with the knees slightly bent will test the strength of the abdominal muscles.

From a lying position ask the client to lift one leg at a time and hold for several seconds. The ease with which this position can be held indicates the strength in the muscles of the leg.

Supported in a sitting position with the arm extended out to the side and then against the resistance of the therapist's hand, the client should try to bring the arm back towards the shoulder. This exercise will test the strength of the muscles in the arm.

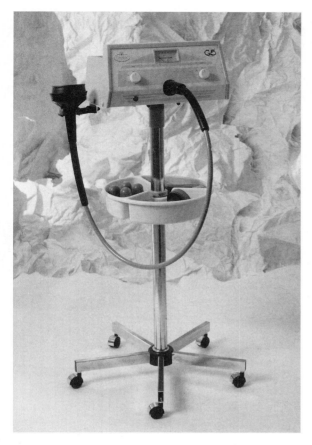

Figure 20.1 *G5 machine*
Courtesy Depilex Limited

○ The spiky and brush heads are used to simulate similar effects to those produced by tapotement.

The selection of the applicator head used depends upon the area being treated and the depth may be controlled by varying:

○ The pressure applied.
○ The type of applicator used.

Applicator heads

The round sponge applicator: This applicator is used with light pressure at the beginning and the end of treatment. It produces a hyperaemia and relaxes the client.

The curved sponge applicator: This applicator is used on those parts of the body that it moulds to, such as the limbs and shoulders. This is similar in action to effleurage in manual massage.

The pin cushion applicator: This applicator is made from rubber with many round ended protrusions and is effective in the treatment of rough skin. It produces a hyperaemia and desquamates the skin.

The heavy pronged applicator: This is a rubber applicator with larger protrusions than the pin cushion. It provides depth to the massage movements and is used in areas of solid subcutaneous fat or thick tissue.

The football applicator: Made from rubber, this applicator is used on dense areas such as the gluteals. It is also used for kneading of the colon.

The egg box applicator: This rubber applicator is used with deep pressure in dense fleshy areas such as gluteals and thighs.

The lighthouse applicator: This rubber-tipped applicator may be used on either side of the spine, but great care must be taken to avoid irritation or damage to the vertebrae.

The sucker applicator: This is a round rubber head, the surface of which is covered by small suckers. It is suitable when treating a client who has a cellulite problem.

The treatment should combine some manual massage movements with the mechanical application, thereby combining the depth of the vibratory treatment with the personal touch of the manual massage.

Effects of G5

○ It stimulates the circulatory system, increasing blood supply to the area being treated therefore providing nourishment to the skin and muscles and improving skin colour.
○ It improves lymphatic flow and aids the removal of waste products. This is particularly important for a cellulite condition.
○ It has a desquamating effect on the surface of the skin.
○ It relaxes tense muscles.
○ It eases muscular pain.
○ It penetrates deep into the subcutaneous layer helping the dispersal of fatty tissue.
○ It motivates the client by helping them to achieve the desired results in weight reduction and body shaping.

Advantages of G5

This treatment has certain advantages over manual massage and these are:

○ It is a far less personal treatment than manual massage and is therefore ideal in treating male clients.
○ It can produce a depth of massage far greater than that of manual massage.
○ It is far less tiring than manual massage, particularly for weight reducing purposes.

The client

Ideally the client should have some form of pre-heating treatment which will relax the muscles in preparation for treatment.

The movements used should be towards the heart and following the natural contours of the body.

For maximum comfort effleurage strokes should be interlinked with manual effleurage and kneading should be performed with the therapist's hand providing support and resistance.

To provide continuity, manual effleurage must be used throughout the treatment and any unnecessary changing of applicator heads should be avoided.

The machine

When this machine is in constant use it will be necessary to have several sets of applicator heads to allow enough time between treatments to clean and dry them.

Talcum powder is the only medium which should be applied to the client's skin for use with this machine because oils or cream have an adverse effect on the applicator heads and over a period of time will cause them to disintegrate.

Contraindications to vibratory treatment
○ Skin disorders and diseases.
○ History of thrombosis or phlebitis.
○ Systemic conditions.
○ Bruising or scar tissue.
○ Swelling.
○ Raised abnormalities on the skin.
○ Thin or elderly clients.
○ Varicose veins if in the area of treatment.

Varicose veins

These occur on the legs when the valves in the veins become weakened and because of this

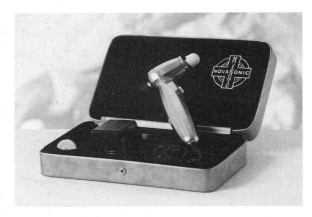

Figure 20.2 *Audio sonic machine*
Courtesy Depilex Limited

large amounts of blood are forced by gravity backwards into the vein. This has the effect of overloading the vein which then pushes the walls of the vein outwards where there is a build-up of blood. The veins closest to the surface of the legs are most susceptible to this condition.

When this happens repeatedly the walls of the veins lose some of their elasticity and become over-stretched and loose. A vein in this condition is called a varicose vein and it is often caused through pregnancy and standing for long periods of time. These swollen areas caused by the accumulation of blood forces fluid into the surrounding tissue.

This condition can be very painful and causes tiredness and aching. It will contraindicate any treatment which is stimulating to the area.

Audio sonic vibrator

This is a sound wave vibrator which is placed on the skin, vibrating smoothly up and down and gently massaging the tissues. Contact is maintained over the area being treated and the vibrations penetrate quite deep into the underlying tissues.

Sound waves are transmitted to the area requiring treatment through a sound head which is applied without pressure to the surface of the skin. There are two applicators: a round ball-shaped head which provides sound waves to a small area; and a disc-shaped head with a larger surface area for normal use. The sound

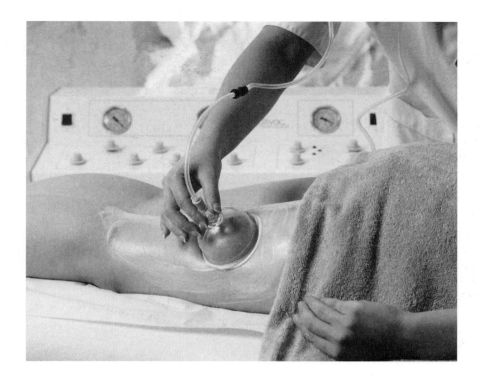

Figure 20.3 *Vacuum suction – manual method Courtesy Depilex Limited*

waves can penetrate up to 6 cm within the body, allowing the therapist to treat areas which are inaccessible to conventional manipulative techniques. When the sound wave energy produced has been absorbed by the body tissues the sound waves cease to travel further.

These are used normally for the specific effect of relieving tension in tense contracted muscles, but may also be used when the use of gyratory vibrators is contraindicated because of hypersensitivity.

The unit is quite small and is hand-held. Therefore, only small areas can be treated effectively (Figure 20.2).

The tissues are very gently stimulated and therefore this treatment is most effective on areas of soft tissue which offers little resistance. The effects achieved are deep in the tissue causing little stimulation to the surface of the skin making this an excellent treatment for sensitive skin.

Physiological effects of audio sonic
○ Massage occurs at a cellular level deep within the tissue.
○ There is an immediate tightening of cell wall membranes.

○ Cellular activity is increased and metabolism is improved.
○ Warmth is produced in the tissues.
○ The increase in circulation supplies nourishment to the area.
○ The lymphatic system is stimulated therefore waste products are removed more efficiently.
○ Tension nodules are relaxed.

Contraindications to audio sonic
○ Skin diseases.
○ Sunburn.
○ Bruises.
○ Recent scar tissue.
○ Highly vascular skin.
○ Undiagnosed pain.
○ In the chest area by wearers of cardiac pacemaker.
○ In areas with a metal plate or pin.
○ Back and abdomen during pregnancy.

Vacuum massage

The main purpose of this treatment is to increase the body's circulation and lymphatic flow to aid

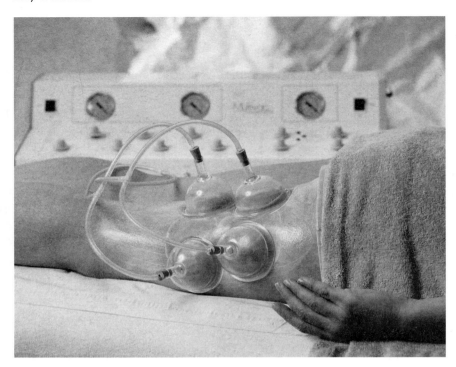

Figure 20.4 *Vacuum suction – gliding method Courtesy Depilex Limited*

in the removal of waste products and excess fluid.

It may be used on any area of the body which has sufficient fatty tissue to allow for comfortable treatment. It is normally used as part of a course of treatments combined with manual massage and diet. This treatment can be used for spot reduction on legs, back, arms, thighs and buttocks.

A thorough knowledge of the body's lymphatic system is essential as the movements used in this treatment are all related to the position of the lymph nodes in the body.

The lymphatic vessels are closely connected to the larger veins and are responsible for the interchange of tissue fluids. The lymph carries waste products along the lymph vessels towards the lymph nodes which act as filters.

The machine

Most manufacturers produce body units only and combined body and facial units.

The *body unit* can be either a basic unit which works with a single cup which glides manually over the skin, or a multi-cup unit which can operate up to six cups at a time. The application for each method is different but the effects are the same. See Figures 20.3 and 20.4.

The *combined unit* has a fine intensity control so that it is easily adjusted for use, from the delicate tissues of the face to the more dense adipose tissues of the body. The unit has a combination of small ventouses for use on small facial areas and a set of cups of varying size which are suitable for the body. The ventouses are usually made from clear perspex or plexiglass which is very tough and hard to break.

How the machine works

Whichever type of machine is chosen they all work in the same way.

They contain a vacuum pump connected by a long flexible plastic tube to a cup which is placed on the area being treated. The vacuum pump is driven by an electric motor and the amount of suction, or 'reduced pressure', is controlled by a regulating switch. There is also a vacuum gauge which indicates the amount of pressure being exerted on the tissues during treatment.

The air pressure in the cup is reduced which causes the skin tissue to be lifted up into the cup and then, with care, the cup is guided in a gliding movement over the tissues in the direction of the lymph glands. Several cups may be placed on the area to be treated statically with the multi-cup unit.

With the single cup unit the therapist glides the cup over the area, releasing the pressure by uncovering a hole in the cup or using a finger to release the vacuum at the end of each movement.

With the multi-cup unit, the cups are applied statically to a localized area and the vacuum suction is pulsed, that is, it alternates between a high level of suction and a low level of suction, just enough to keep the cup in place. This is achieved by an automatic pulsation control in the machine itself. The higher degree of suction must not be so high that it causes discomfort or bruising to the skin.

Treatment initially should have longer periods of the low-level and shorter periods of the higher level of suction. These periods can be adjusted as the client becomes used to the treatment and the therapist has assessed the skin reaction. When using static multi-cup vacuum suction it is normally preceded by the gliding method.

Effects of vacuum suction

○ Increase in circulation dilates blood vessels and causes a hyperaemia.
○ The increase in circulation nourishes skin and muscle.
○ It stimulates the lymphatic system moving tissue fluids.
○ Reduces puffiness caused by fluid retention when it is not caused by a medical condition.
○ Helps in the breakdown and removal of fatty cells particularly when used in conjunction with a diet.
○ Aids in desquamation.
○ Stimulates the metabolism.

Contraindications to vacuum suction
○ Varicose veins.
○ Bruised skin.
○ Skin diseases.
○ Recent scar tissue.
○ An area heavily stretch marked.
○ Sunburn.
○ Very thin or hyper-sensitive skin.

Mechanical lymphatic massage treatment

The lymphatic system rids the body of toxin materials and waste products before they can damage the cells, tissues and organs of the body. However, the system sometimes finds it difficult to cope with the increased demands put upon it because of the overload of toxins due to:

○ Exposure to industrial waste.
○ Exposure to chemicals and pesticides.
○ Highly processed foods.
○ Drugs.
○ Alcohol.
○ Nicotine.
○ The increasingly stressful lives we lead.

These are just a few examples and when the waste products and toxins start to build up they may require some help in their removal. This can be achieved by changing to a healthy diet, body brushing, manual massage, aromatherapy, exercise and manual or mechanical lymphatic drainage.

Manual treatment aids lymphatic drainage to improve blood circulation, skin tone and body shape. Lymphatic drainage is essential to ensure a healthy body free from toxins and mechanical methods imitate the body's muscular pumping action to move the lymph fluid around the body while at the same time giving a pleasant and relaxing massage to the legs and improving the general blood circulation.

Manual or mechanical treatment is often combined with the use of essential oils for maximum effect. The mechanical method uses boots to cover the legs and a pumping action is exerted on the legs, starting from the toes and moving rhythmically up the leg to the hips. Pure essential oils are dispersed in water to make a compress. Bandages or support stockings are then immersed to soak up the compress liquid, the excess liquid is squeezed out and they are then applied to the legs from the ankle to the knees. The oils used have different effects:

○ Stimulating.
○ Toning.
○ Relaxing.
○ Decongesting.

The legs are then encased in the massage boots which are inflated and a sequential, flowing, regulated pressure massage is applied simultaneously to both legs, starting from the feet and moving rhythmically upwards towards the inguinal lymph nodes.

Effects of treatment

○ Increases blood circulation.
○ Increases lymphatic flow.
○ Helps with the removal of excess fluids.
○ Speeds up the removal of toxins.
○ Provides a feeling a well being.
○ Relaxes the client.

Benefits of treatment

○ Detoxification leads to better toned skin.
○ Helps improve a cellulite condition by removing excess fluids and waste products.
○ Helps in the prevention and relief of varicose veins.
○ Relaxing and soothing.
○ Warms the tissues.
○ Eases aches and pains.

Contraindications to treatment

○ Client with a pacemaker.
○ Acute thrombophlebitis.
○ History of deep vein thrombosis.
○ History of pulmonary embolism.
○ Congestive cardiac failure.
○ Pitting oedema.
○ High blood pressure.
○ Open cuts or wounds.
○ New scar tissue.
○ Client under medical supervision/undergoing medical treatment.
○ Sunburn.
○ Acute infections.

A healthy lymphatic system is necessary because:

○ It assists with the absorption of nutrients required for health.
○ It carries immune cells around the body to help protect it from damage.
○ It is the body's metabolic waste disposal system.
○ It removes toxins, by-products of fatigue, stress, bacteria, dead cells and viruses.

Electrotherapy

This is the name given to treatment with electrical equipment when the electrical current actually passes through the body and the current is not just used to work a machine. This applies to:

○ *High frequency treatment*, which uses a high-frequency alternating current.
○ *Galvanic treatment*, which uses a direct current.
○ *Electrical muscle stimulation*, which uses a direct current which is surged or interrupted.

The current is used for a therapeutic purpose and the current intensities are too low to cause any serious injury but it is imperative for the therapist to understand how to use electrical equipment safely, effectively and with assurance.

How the body conducts electricity

The body is able to transmit the electrical current because the tissues of the body are made up of a large proportion of fluid which contains salt.

When salt is dissolved in water the molecules split into ions which are electrically charged particles. This turns the fluid in the tissues into an ionized solution. Therefore, the tissue fluid is an electrolyte as it is a solution which can conduct electricity.

How well the body conducts the current depends on the amount of tissue fluid in that part of the body. The epidermis is very low in body fluid therefore it will form an initial resistance to the current. This can be overcome by the use of a saline solution or other appropriate product applied to the skin.

High frequency

As in facial therapy this treatment may be applied to the body either *directly* or *indirectly*.

The high frequency current is a rapidly alternating (oscillating) current and does not have a stimulating effect on the nerve endings in the skin.

Direct method

This treatment is most appropriate to sufferers of acne as the condition often affects the upper back and the chest.

With the direct method, ozone is produced when the glass electrode is applied to the skin and this has a germicidal effect, helping to dry and cleanse the area being treated.

Talcum powder must be applied to the skin to allow the electrode ease of movement and to absorb excess sebum on the skin.

The lighter the movements over the skin the stronger the germicidal effect will be. The high frequency current mixing with oxygen produces the ozone. Therefore, the firmer the contact with the skin the less high frequency current is released through the electrodes into the air so reducing the amount of ozone produced.

Effects

○ Circulation is increased causing an erythema and warmth in the area being treated.
○ Stimulates a sluggish skin.
○ Improves the lymphatic flow and the removal of waste products.
○ Desquamates the skin, improving texture.

○ Cleanses the skin, healing pustules.

Indirect method

One of the main benefits of indirect high-frequency is the inducement of relaxation. Therefore, when used with manual body massage it will increase the relaxation effect of the treatment.

It is applied in the same way as for facial therapy with the client holding a saturator and the therapist performing the massage, remembering to maintain contact with the client at all times to keep the circuit complete and ensuring client comfort.

Effects

○ An increase in circulation warming the tissues and improving the interchange of tissue fluids and skin function.
○ Sedative, relieving tension.
○ The warm tissues absorb the nourishing products applied to the skin more easily.
○ Helps those clients who suffer from poor circulation which may cause other problems such as chilblains.
○ The massage will be more relaxing the deeper the movements are performed and more stimulating when the hands are in light contact.

Contraindications to high frequency

○ Pregnancy.
○ Epilepsy.
○ Metal plates or pins in the body.
○ High blood pressure.

21 Specialized treatments

Body galvanism

This is a very popular and successful treatment to aid in the removal of cellulite, which can occur on different parts of the body. It is applied locally on the specific areas that require treatment to help in reshaping the body contours.

To understand how this treatment works, it is important to understand what is meant by the term *cellulite*.

Cellulite

This is a condition that affects a great many women but its existence is questioned by experts in the medical field. For those women who have slim figures yet suffer with specific areas of cellulite, normally on the bottom and thighs, its existence is very real and problematic to them.

These fatty areas differ from normal fat in several ways:

1 It is very stubborn and resistant to normal forms of dieting and exercise.
2 The areas of cellulite have more water content than other areas of fatty tissue.
3 This condition does not affect men to the same extent as women and is not as noticeable because of the difference in skin structure.
4 There is a pitting of the skin in the area, which resembles orange peel and the fat feels harder than normal.
5 In more extreme cases it can be painful.

The appearance of cellulite varies in different people but the areas most affected are:

○ Thighs and inside of the knee.
○ Hips.
○ Buttocks.
○ Abdomen.
○ Upper arms and back (less commonly affected).

Cellulite is more likely to occur in areas of poor circulation due to inactivity so the hips and upper thighs of women who have a job requiring them to sit down for long periods of time are more likely to suffer from this condition than a woman who has an occupation which allows her to move about and exercise.

Poor circulation also interferes with the normal process of waste removal via the lymphatic system and prevents the tissues from receiving proper nourishment.

Tension in the muscles also restricts the circulation. Therefore poor circulation will eventually lead to congested areas forming, the interchange of tissue fluids and removal of waste products slow down, therefore there is an accumulation of fluid and waste in an area of fatty tissue which leads to the cellulite condition.

Causes of cellulite

Toxins enter the body via the air we breathe, the food we eat and the water we drink and the body normally deals with them quickly and efficiently. Sometimes, however, the body cannot deal with these toxins if they are in excess so they remain in the tissues.

Elimination problems or poor liver and kidney function causes a build-up in the body of the by-products of normal metabolism and waste products.

Eating the wrong kinds of food, an excess of sodium (salt) in the body which encourages water retention and not exercising sufficiently or doing the wrong type of exercise can all cause cellulite.

Stress can prevent the normal physiological functions of the body from working effectively:

○ It can upset the digestive system and therefore the process of elimination.
○ It affects the circulatory system, which provides the body with nourishment and removes waste products.
○ It disturbs our normal breathing process, which helps in the stimulation of lymph flow and increases the amount of oxygen that the body receives.
○ When under stress one of the first reactions is to eat. Unfortunately it is usually too much of the wrong types of food.

With age the skin becomes thinner and looser as the connective tissue loses its elasticity, allowing fat cells to migrate to the area and to enlarge.

Hormones are a contributory factor as the female body has large amounts of oestrogen which actually encourage the laying down of fat cells in the body. Therefore, it is uncommon for a girl to suffer from cellulite before puberty, even if she is overweight. Most women are predisposed to the formation of cellulite at times of hormonal change and these are:

○ Puberty.
○ When taking the oral contraceptive.
○ Pregnancy.
○ Menopause.

Treatment of cellulite

It is important when dealing with a cellulite condition that you explain to the client that there is no one treatment alone which will rid the body of the problem. It must be approached in several ways:

1 To detoxify the body by eliminating stored waste.
2 To prevent fluid retention.
3 To exercise the body more and increase the metabolism.
4 External application of treatments by the beauty therapist.
5 Eating a well-balanced diet.
6 To control stress.
7 Improve posture.

Cellulite and diet

For any treatment provided by the beauty therapist to be effective, there must be cooperation from the client as far as diet is concerned. However, it should be stressed that clients do not have to go on a deprivation diet, but just need to look at the way they eat and the types of food they are eating. A few adjustments will need to be made with guidance from the therapist.

The client may not necessarily be over-eating but may just be eating the wrong type of food.

Common faults in diet

○ Too much fat.
○ Too much salt.
○ Too much suger.
○ Eating too much processed food.
○ Eating too many sweet and salty snacks.

As a result the body has less energy, puts on weight and develops problems such as cellulite.

Dietary advice

Reduce the amount of meat especially red meat as it contains chemicals, synthetic hormones and antibiotics given to the animals for growth. Choose very lean meat, only eat it a couple of times a week and prepare it without using fat.

Reduce the intake of fat as this is a major cause of weight gain and high cholesterol levels. The body only requires 15–20 per cent of fat in a balanced diet.

Reduce the amount of sugar consumed because it depletes the body of potassium which is essential to keep the sodium balance in the body as well as causing excess weight gain.

Reduce the amount of salt in the diet. It is unnecessary to add salt to food as the amount of salt the body requires to remain healthy is contained in food naturally. When sodium and potassium levels are well-balanced they help the cells of the body to receive nutrients and remove waste products. Too much salt causes water retention and cellulite.

Advise clients to cut as much processed food out of their diet as possible. They contain large

Figure 21.1 *Galvanic machine*
Courtesy Depilex Limited

amounts of fat, sugar and salt, as well as chemicals which are of no benefit at all and will be stored in the body. In excess, processed foods are hard to eliminate.

Increase the intake of foods rich in potassium as a low potassium level can cause fluid retention and flabbiness, characteristics of cellulite. The foods which are rich in potassium are fresh fruit, fresh vegetables, pulses and whole grains.

Eat fruit and vegetables raw to receive the maximum nourishment.

Drink plenty of water as this will help to flush out all the toxins and prevent the formation of cellulite. It also aids digestion and the absorption of food. Drink a large glass of water first thing in the morning and also before and after exercise to replenish the body's supply which is lost from the body through perspiration. To ensure its purity, filter the water before drinking to remove chemicals which otherwise would deposit themselves in the tissues.

Galvanism

The two methods of galvanism have been discussed in detail in Chapter 7. For body treatment the method which is used is

iontophoresis. This method is used to allow active substances into the skin, in this case anti-cellulite substances, on a galvanic charge.

Electrophoresis is the name given to the use of the current only and in this case saline solution would be used on the pads to aid the flow of current (1 per cent saline solution on the active pad and 2 per cent saline solution on the dispersive pad. 1 per cent saline = 1 teaspoon of salt to 1 pint of water).

Aim of treatment

The aim of galvanic treatment is to soften stubborn areas of fat and disperse the fluid retained in the area, thus removing the lumps and bumps associated with a cellulite condition. This is achieved by using active substances specifically to stimulate a sluggish circulation and improve the interchange of tissue fluids in the area of cellulite, combined with the specific effect of the polarity chosen.

The substance introduced into the skin is the therapeutic part of the treatment. The galvanic current provides the transport into the skin of the therapeutic product and the polarity chosen provides the physiological response required for the breakdown and removal of cellulite.

Anti-cellulite products used with the galvanic current are based on natural substances which have a diuretic effect on the body allowing fluid to be removed naturally.

The galvanic machine

There are many different models on the market. They can be for body use only, providing eight pairs of electrodes which allow the therapist to treat large areas of the body, or they can be a combined body and facial unit with two to four pairs of pads which allows only a small area of the body to be treated (Figure 21.1).

The controls on the machine are:

○ An on/off switch.
○ Outlets for the electrodes.
○ A milliamp meter for each outlet (some models only).
○ A polarity change-over switch for each outlet.
○ An intensity control for each outlet.

Precautions

Medical history must be checked very carefully for any disorder of the nervous system which may contraindicate treatment and if necessary ask the client to seek medical advice.

Any client who suffers from kidney or urinary tract infections must ask their doctor for permission before having this treatment. The effects of the treatment will cause the client to pass more water as urine, because of the diuretic qualities of the active substances.

Clients will pass water far more often after treatment and it would be advisable to ask clients to pass water just before a full body treatment commences.

The therapist should explain to clients why they must continue to drink a normal amount of fluid but preferably in the form of water, fruit juice or other healthy drinks, rather than tea, coffee and sugary soft drinks.

The polarity

The most effective polarity for body iontophoresis is the negative pole and this is because of its specific effects which will help in the removal of cellulite.

The effects of the negative pole
○ Stimulation of the circulation.
○ Stimulation of the nerve endings in the skin.
○ Softening of the tissues.
○ Opening of the pores.
○ Production of an alkaline effect on the skin.

These stimulating effects produced by the negative pole are ideal for this treatment, therefore, because of movement of tissue fluid in the area which will help in removing or improving the cellulite condition.

The electrodes used are in pairs. The working electrode is placed over the area to be treated and the second electrode, which will be the indifferent or non-working electrode that will complete the circuit, is placed opposite, for example on opposite sides of the thigh when this area is being treated.

The active electrode which is negatively charged will have a stimulating effect on the area of cellulite, helping to increase circulation and move the fluid which is retained and causing the lumps and bumps associated with cellulite.

The anti-cellulite products which are also negatively charged are applied to the skin under the negative electrode and the negative charge will repel the negatively charged product into the skin.

Safety

Make sure the machine is in good working order with no loose wires or connections. Follow the manufacturers' instructions when using equipment. There are many different models available which are different in the way in which they work, for example some have colour-coded leads, red for positive and black for negative.

Clients must be checked for contraindications to ensure that the treatment can be carried out safely. Give clients a thermal skin test and also a test for skin sensitivity (see facial galvanism, Chapter 7).

Each electrode must be placed inside a thick viscose sponge pocket or a thick viscose sponge pad slightly larger than the electrode placed underneath it, to protect the skin from the current.

The viscose sponge must be evenly damp to aid the flow of current and must also be in firm contact with the skin. Ensure that the viscose sponges do not dry out as this will concentrate the current on a small area and this may lead to a galvanic burn.

Any scratch or abrasion on the skin must be covered as the current would be concentrated in the area causing discomfort to the client and a possible galvanic burn. The electrodes and sponge must be firmly attached to the area being treated with non-conductive straps.

Make sure that all intensity controls are at zero at the commencement of treatment. The current must be turned up slowly, keeping the intensity low to begin with until the milliamp meter registers a breakdown in the skin's resistance. This will be shown by a sudden movement of the indicator. Treatment must not exceed 2–3 milliamps per square inch of electrode.

Some models have an in-built safety feature preventing the milliampage chosen from increasing when the skin's resistance breaks down. This helps to prevent a galvanic burn.

During treatment maintain visual and verbal contact with clients to make sure that they are comfortable. Follow the manufacturers' advice when timing the treatment. When the pads are removed at the conclusion of treatment the skin should be thoroughly cleansed with warm water.

Improving the effectiveness of treatment

The more the skin is prepared for galvanic treatment, the more effective it will be in the removal of the cellulite condition, thereby improving the body shape and the skin texture.

The skin should be cleansed and if necessary a gentle peeling medium may be used. The effects are to cleanse the area of grease and desquamate the skin cells, increase the circulation and warm the tissues. This allows more efficient penetration of the products used.

Gentle heat such as infrared or massage may be applied. This will increase circulation and the interchange of tissue fluids, removing waste and at the same time relaxing the client. The therapist could perform a massage to the area while applying the heat.

If the cellulite problem is exacerbated by weak flabby muscles then faradism could be applied after the heat. The muscles will be warm and receptive to the flow of current which will exert a pumping action on the area, stimulating the interchange of tissue fluids and encouraging the elimination of waste.

Vacuum suction may also be incorporated to stimulate the flow of lymph.

Finish the whole treatment routine with the galvanic iontophoresis, which causes the penetration of the anti-cellulite products into the skin, increasing the circulation, speeding up the interchange of tissue fluids and improving elimination.

The client should be advised to have a course of ten or twelve treatments and, depending on the skin's reaction, at least twice a week. However, it is important to define the client's particular problem before planning any programme of treatment. All of the above treatments may be used in various combinations according to the client's needs.

Contraindications

○ Any skin disease.
○ Metal pins or plates.
○ Poor skin sensitivity.
○ Diabetics – impaired skin sensitivity.
○ Defective circulation.
○ Sunburn or skin inflammation.
○ Cuts or abrasions.
○ Varicose veins.
○ Oedema.
○ Hypersensitive skin.
○ Over the abdominal area in the first few days of menstruation.
○ Areas never to be treated are:
　—Kidney area.
　—Bony area.
　—Breasts.
　—Sciatic nerve.

Ultrasound

Ultrasound is the latest and most up-to-date treatment for the removal of cellulite. It has been found that over time cellulite becomes very difficult to remove because cell permeability is reduced, circulation becomes less efficient and the toxins are trapped within the tissues, forming hardened deposits around individual fat cells thus making them more difficult to remove or be utilized by the body. The treatment is sensation-free, relaxing and comfortable for the client.

Ultrasound breaks down and disperses the hardened deposits in the cellulite. The treatment is very safe to use as it is based on the same technology that doctors use to offer pregnant women the reassurance of ultrasound scans.

For the treatment of cellulite, it only penetrates a few millimetres below the skin surface to reach the adipose tissue where the cellulite is trapped. It works in the following way:

o The ultrasound is emitted at a very high frequency, sets up vibrations in the cells and breaks down the hardened fatty deposits (the same way an opera singer's high pitched voice shatters a glass).
o The ultrasound waves pass into the tissues creating a micro-massaging effect.
o Localized heat is produced helping to disperse the rigid structures formed by the hardened deposits.
o This stimulates the release of toxins and waste products out of the cells and transfers them to the lymphatic system.
o Lymphatic massage is performed to remove the toxins towards the nearest drainage point for natural elimination.
o A good homecare routine should be recommended to the client to help maintain the improved condition after treatment.

The most up-to-date systems incorporate thermographic diagnosis to help assess the areas requiring treatment. Thermographic (heat sensitive) plates display heat and cold as a series of colours and when micro-circulation is reduced areas of cellulite will show up as 'cold'. This enables therapists to determine the precise location and density of the cellulite. Because of this they will be able to tailor their treatment to the specific requirements of the client and assess the correct length of treatment required to treat the condition successfully. See Figure 21.2.

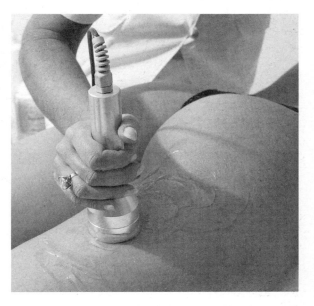

Figure 21.2 *Ultrasound treatment. Courtesy of Totally UK Ltd*

The consultation

This is important for the usual reasons of recording details, assessing the client for treatment and checking for contraindications but also lifestyle plays an important part in the recognition and treatment of cellulite. Therefore it is important to ask your clients the following questions. Do they:

o Exercise regularly.
o Smoke.
o Use anti-cellulite products.
o Have a healthy diet.
o Eat lots of spicy foods.
o Drink, tea, coffee, alcohol or carbonated drinks including sparkling water.
o Have a sedentary or active lifestyle.
o Take any medication, if so, what for.
o Have a hereditary history of circulatory related problems.
o Have they had any previous anti-cellulite treatment.

Contraindications

o Cardiovascular problems – high/low blood pressure, pacemaker.

o   Fainting spells.
o   Chest pain.
o   Varicose veins.
o   Extensive capillary damage to the area to be treated.
o   Epilepsy.
o   Diabetes.
o   Skin disorders/diseases.
o   Inflammation, infection, broken skin, bruising or tumour.
o   Joint problems.
o   Bone disorders/diseases.
o   Allergies to rubber, copper or other metals.
o   Thrombosis or phlebitis.
o   Artificial joints, metal pins or plates.
o   Back complaints.
o   Pregnancy.

Preparation

After the consultation treatment may begin, but it is important to prepare the area to be treated by brushing the skin (Figure 21.3) for about five minutes. Alternatively a G5 with the prickly head can be used. The purpose of this is to gently exfoliate the skin and stimulate the circulation. The skin should have a healthy pink glow by this time and a special gel may be applied

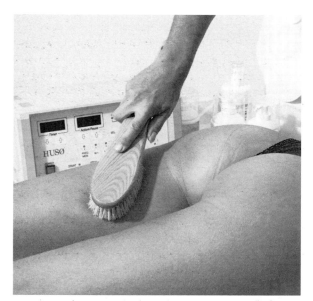

Figure 21.3   *Body brushing. Courtesy of Totally UK Ltd*

using lymphatic massage movements. This will allow the ultrasound head to glide smoothly over the treated area and ensure an even contact with the skin.

A full treatment would include :

Client preparation and assessment/body brush or G5 – 10 minutes.
Lymph massage and application of ultrasound gel – 5–10 minutes.
Ultrasound treatment – 25 minutes.
Lymph massage to aid absorption and elimination – 15 minutes.

Safety

o   Do not use ultrasound over areas which contain underlying organs, that is, the abdominal cavity.
o   Do not use on bony areas of the body, that is, elbows, knees, spinal column, shoulder blades, face and head.
o   There should be no sense of electrical stimulation, vibration or pain and if this should occur treatment must stop.
o   If the hand-piece becomes overheated due to a long working period application must be interrupted for a few minutes.

Treatment recommendation

o   A course of ten treatments is advisable for the best results – dispersing the hardened deposits and eliminating the orange peel effect of cellulite.
o   Treatments should be as close together as possible.
o   The recommended number of treatments a week is a minimum of two or three with 24 hours in between.
o   One hour should be allocated for treatment to include preparation with body brushing and massage. Application of ultrasound for twenty-five minutes and lymph drainage massage at the end.
o   The intensity of treatment varies, being set according to the relative thickness of the adipose tissue. As a guide increase the intensity as the adipose tissue increases in density:

Thin fatty layer or delicate area – lower setting.
Average thickness – medium setting.
Thick layers of adipose tissue – highest setting.

o   Always follow the manufacturer's instructions when applying the treatment.

Homecare

This plays an important part in the treatment of cellulite and each client is advised to do the following:

o   Drink plenty of water, but not carbonated water as this helps the formation of cellulite. Add lemon to the water as this helps rid the body of toxins.
o   Try not to drink while eating as this dilutes the enzymes required for efficient digestion.
o   Sip water slowly as this will help bathe the cells and take waste with it.
o   Use a body brush or loofah every day before bathing, brushing for five minutes until the skin feels warm and glowing.
o   Use a good cream or oil to massage in morning and evening directly after bathing.

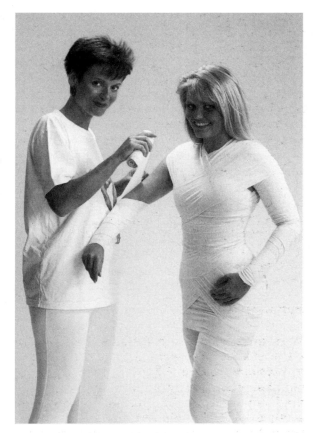

Figure 21.4   *Body wrapping. Courtesy of Totally UK Ltd*

Body wrap

There are several methods of body wrapping or inch-loss treatments using bandages, plastic or rubber (with active products applied to the skin together with heat) to increase the elimination of toxins from the body (Figure 21.4).

Choosing the right combination provides an effective treatment for clients wishing to improve their shape, texture of the skin and encourage them to diet. The active ingredient chosen will have a specific effect on the tissues:

o   *Seaweed* will act as a diuretic.
o   *Sea clay* eliminates toxins from the body.
o   *Minerals* are nourishing.

The most effective wraps are those that do not rely on water loss to achieve results as this would be temporary. Sea clay wrap is an excellent treatment which provides inch loss for clients who are trying to lose weight and improve their figure as well as removing toxins

from the body. It is a treatment which does not require a large working area – just a private room or cubicle with enough space for measuring and wrapping clients comfortably. It will benefit the following:

o   Those on a diet to provide motivation.
o   After pregnancy or weight loss to improve and firm the skin.
o   Women who have stretch marks, to tighten the skin and make them less noticeable.
o   Those who suffer from cellulite.
o   Anyone who may wish to lose inches for a special occasion.
o   Those who just wish to improve their shape even if they are not overweight.
o   To detoxify the body.
o   To improve a dry or rough skin condition.
o   To help reduce certain areas.

Consultation

At the initial consultation it is important to explain the treatment to clients, the sensation they will feel, the initial tightness of the wrap, the exercises they will do once wrapped, the time it will take (approximately 2–2½ hours) and the frequency of treatments. Also discuss the results they are likely to achieve, making no false promises as this may lead to disappointment. The benefits to the client are:

○ By tightening and toning soft tissue a few inches will be lost.
○ The skin will be deep cleansed and detoxified.
○ The cellulite condition will be improved.
○ Stretch marks will be tightened.
○ Scars and blemishes will become less noticeable.

The client's medical history must be checked as there are certain medical conditions that must be avoided and some that may require the treatment to be adapted.

Contraindications

○ Never wrap a client who is allergic to natural elements. If in doubt patch test first.
○ Pregnancy.
○ Emphysema.
○ Phlebitis.
○ Unhealed wounds in the skin.
○ Recent operations.
○ New scar tissue.

Care must be taken with the following:

○ Circulatory or respiratory problems. Do not wrap too tightly.
○ High blood pressure. Ask clients if they are on medication to control the condition and if they are, wrap as normal.
○ Skin disorders such as eczema or psoriasis usually benefit from treatment. However, if the condition is severe and there are open sores, treatment is contraindicated.
○ Breast-feeding mums. Wrap to underneath the bust. There is no medical reason for not wrapping the whole body but it could cause discomfort.
○ Epilepsy, as you could not easily get your client into the recovery position when they

are wrapped. There is nothing in the wrapping procedure or solution used that would precipitate an attack, however.
○ Heart conditions. A doctor's permission must be sought.

Treatment application

The equipment required for treatment would be:

○ Elastic contour wrap bandages about 15 cm wide.
○ The natural sea clay solution.
○ A heating tank to warm the solution and bandages prior to use.
○ A pair of tongs to handle the hot bandages after heating. They may be placed in a bowl to cool before use.
○ A large mirror and measuring tape.
○ A vinyl suit to keep the client warm while they are in the wrap.
○ Towels for clients to dry themselves after treatment.
○ A large bowl or bucket to place the dirty bandages after wrapping.
○ A laundry basket to place the clean bandages ready for rolling.

Clients must use the bathroom just before they are wrapped as they will be unable to go to the toilet for some time afterwards. Clients must then be measured and their statistics recorded. Weigh clients first to ensure they are at least maintaining their weight during the course of treatments and it will also prove to them that this is not a water loss treatment which provides only temporary weight loss.

Measure clients ensuring that they are standing correctly. They must stand straight, legs together, hands interlocked behind their head, and elbows to the side. This will provide more accurate measurements.

Wrapping begins at the lowest extremity working upwards and always wrapping towards the heart to ensure adequate blood supply to all parts of the body.

There are certain areas of the body which must be wrapped with extreme caution. They have relatively little muscle protection for underlying arteries and nerves. Therefore wraps must not be too tight in these areas as this could result in loss of blood circulation or loss of feeling in the extremities. These areas are:

○ Back of the knee joints.
○ Inside groin area.
○ Lower lumbar area of the back.
○ Inside of the elbow.

Pressure must be reduced across the back of the knee, in the groin and inside of the elbow. The edge of a bandage must not go across the joint of the knee or elbow. The middle of the wrap should always cross the joints. Clients must always be in an erect position when wrapping the lower back so there is no additional pressure to the back if they stand upright after being wrapped in a forward position.

It is important that if clients experience any tingling sensations or loss of feeling in any part of the body, they are immediately unwrapped.

Once clients have been wrapped, they are helped into the vinyl suit and they may be taken to an exercise area to stand and walk around or to do some light isometric movements. The benefits of exercise are:

○ The pores of the skin open.
○ The solution works on the toxins.
○ There is a resistance to the bandages during movement providing isometric exercises.

The last fifteen minutes of the full 60–70 should be used to cool down and then the vinyl suit is removed and the wraps are removed in the reverse order to application.

Clients are then remeasured and the results recorded.

Homecare advice

○ Shower with tepid water only to retain the solution in the pores to carry on working.
○ Limit soap to feet, underarms and groin area to prevent soap removing solution from the pores.
○ Avoid creams and lotions.
○ After 3 or 4 days have hot showers with plenty of soap to open the pores and eliminate toxins and solution.
○ Drink plenty of water (mineral and tap water only) – about three pints a day to flush out toxins.

○ Avoid, tea, coffee, sugar, salt, alcohol, fried or fatty foods and carbonated drinks.

Natural products

Therapists are responding to the increasing trend towards all things natural and holistic by using body care products which are based on natural ingredients such as essential oils and marine products such as plankton and seaweed.

Marine products

Active ingredients, for example trace elements and salts, are extracted from marine algae plants (more commonly known as seaweed) and used for their therapeutic value in body and skin care products. The three types most commonly used are:

1 Fucus.
2 Ascophyllum.
3 Laminaria.

Fucus
Deep-water brown seaweed works by activating the sweat glands, eliminating water containing toxins and fatty cells and increasing the body's temperature. Its main action is internal cleansing. Therefore, it will complement a slimming programme by helping to detoxify the system. The main components are:

○ Iodine.
○ Vitamins.
○ Amino acids.
○ Potassium.
○ Magnesium.
○ Phytin.

Ascophyllum
This is also brown and often associated with fucus. It is rich in amino acids and minerals, and it is balancing, helping to induce a sense of relaxation.

Laminaria
This is a deep water, brown seaweed which contains a high percentage of organic iodine,

vitamins, amino acids and trace elements. It helps to regulate the thyroid gland and the metabolism.

Essential oils

These oils are incorporated into products for their specific effects:

○ Improve the elimination of toxins.
○ Tones tissue.
○ Stimulates the circulation.
○ Relaxes.
○ Revitalizes.

See also effects of essential oils, Chapter 12.

Electrical muscle stimulation

Commonly known as faradism, this treatment is very popular for toning slack mucles and improving figure shapes. The client does not have to participate in this treatment although it does closely resemble natural exercise, in the effect it has on the muscles. Therefore, it may be classified as passive exercise. It is also isometric exercise as there is no movement of the joints.

It is only effective, however, if a course of treatment is undertaken so the client must attend on a regular basis for a specified length of time. The nature of the treatment is such that clients will lose inches without losing weight so they may follow a diet while having the treatment, and it may be included in a course of several different body treatments.

Most modern machines use a faradic type current which is an *interrupted* or *surged* direct current which, when applied, produces a contraction in the muscle.

The surged current is one which causes a gradual contraction of the muscle, increasing in strength and then gradually decreasing in strength. This surging is controlled by a timing device within the machine.

The interrupted current is when the current flow stops and starts again and the contraction

is only maintained while the current is flowing.

The faradic machine

The large faradic machine used for body work normally has ten outlets with an intensity control for each outlet and ten pairs of pads or electrodes made from carbon impregnated plastic in the more modern machines.

The machine has an on/off switch and a timer to regulate the length of the contraction and the relaxation period.

There is an indicator light to show that the machine is switched on and an indicator light to show the pulse or contraction period.

Depending on the treatment, there is a frequency control and an intensity control.

The frequency control indicates the impulses per second (Figure 21.5). This varies from 60 to 120 on most units. Frequency set at 60 will help to achieve comfortable contractions on large untoned muscles, areas of dense subcutaneous fat or areas with a high resistance. A frequency of 120 will stimulate superficial fascia and muscle and may be used on areas with little or no fat or well toned muscles.

The intensity control will increase the level of contraction which is chosen to suit each individual client. There is an intensity control for each set of pads therefore each muscle or muscle group can be set to an intensity that is comfortable for the client. The intensity is turned up slowly as the current is flowing and the muscle is contracting. These controls must be at zero at the beginning of treatment and returned to zero at the conclusion of treatment.

There is a phase control which can be set on monophasic or biphasic. Monophasic is when the current flows in one direction only from the negative to the positive. The negative pad will have the stronger contraction. Biphasic is when the current flows in one direction and then reverses to travel in the opposite direction. It produces strong even contractions and this setting is the one most generally used, each pad of a pair can be regarded therefore as having the same polarity.

There is often a gain control which is useful when the client has become accustomed to the

Figure 21.5 *Faradic machine*

Contraction period
Relaxation period
Frequency control
Gain control
Constant or variable control
Polarity switch

Contact
1.5
0   2.5

Relax
1.5
0   2.5

Frequency
100
65   135

Gain
min.   max.

Mode
B   U
U   B
Constant   Variable

On / off

Indicator lights for contraction and relaxation

Intensity controls

5   5   5   5   5   5   5   5   5   5
0 10 0 10 0 10 0 10 0 10 0 10 0 10 0 10 0 10 0 10
1   2   3   4   5   6   7   8   9   10

Pad outlets

contractions and the intensity of all the pads can be turned up at the same time.

A special safety feature in most modern machines is a reset button which prevents the machine from working until all the outlet intensity controls are at zero.

A variable switch allows the frequency of the contractions to be altered for those clients who are used to the treatment. See Figure 21.6.

The effects of the current

Stimulates the nerves

When the current is applied there is a slight tingling sensation caused by stimulation of the sensory nerve endings in the skin. The current is then intensified and the motor nerves respond by contracting the muscle which is being treated.

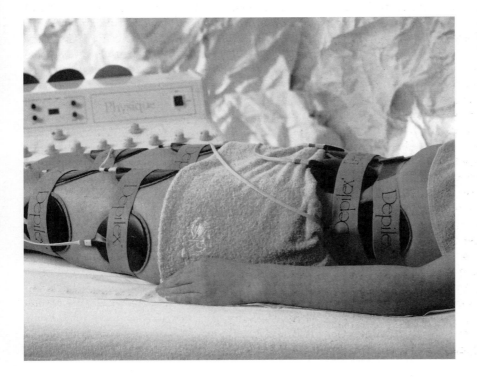

Figure 21.6 *Electrical muscle stimulation machine Courtesy Depilex Limited*

Increases the blood circulation

Blood flow is stimulated because of the muscle contracting and this also helps the lymphatic flow. The muscles are supplied with more oxygen and nutrients, and waste products are more efficiently removed.

Produces an erythema

As a result of the increased blood supply there is a reddening of the skin.

Contracts the muscle

The motor point of the muscle is where the motor nerve enters the muscle and when this point is stimulated accurately, a good contraction is obtained with the least amount of current necessary. The muscles are firmed and toned helping to re-shape body contours and retain the new shape because of an increase in strength.

Client consultation

It is important for the therapist to establish whether electrical muscle stimulation is the correct form of treatment for the client. Some clients may be overweight and others do not have this problem but have loose flabby muscles in poor tone.

The therapist should take the measurements of clients and if they are also on a diet, their weight. The measurements need only be recorded in the area being treated and they need to be taken at regular intervals during the course.

This is the time to ensure that the client is medically fit to have this treatment and a record card with all the necessary information should be completed. Information required from clients includes the number of children they have, their medical history, how much exercise they take and their family history since any problem they have could be hereditary.

Muscle contraction treatment

This treatment works by placing the electrodes in pairs, with the polarity constantly changing between them, on the muscle or muscle groups to be treated.

The contraction of the muscle caused by the application of the current should resemble natural muscle movements. The results achieved are similar to periods of active exercise.

Muscles can work *isotonically* when the contractions of the muscles cause movement of the joints and *isometrically* when the muscle contractions do not cause the joints to move. The electrical muscle stimulation treatment is generally isometric.

Giving the client some form of heat treatment first will prepare the muscles so that they are warm and more responsive to treatment. Reassure clients before and during treatment and explain to them what is happening. If they are tense then the treatment will feel more uncomfortable.

In the case of a client being allergic to the pads, small pieces of sponge or lint cut to fit and evenly soaked in saline solution may be placed under the pad. This allows the treatment to be carried out by protecting the client's skin from any irritation.

Padding layouts

Split padding: This is when the pair of pads are split and placed on corresponding muscles on either side of the body. Normally used for very small muscles, for example the pectorals.

Dual padding: This is when the pair of pads are placed on the same muscle or muscle group on either side of the body. Each side of the body is dealt with separately and different intensities of current may be used. This will compensate for differences in muscle size, shape and bulk as well as natural strength in either the right or left side.

The pads may be placed longitudinally down the length of the muscle to take greatest advantage of the muscle shortening effect of the contraction, for example on the rectus abdominis when it has been stretched after childbirth. They may also be placed diagonally either following the natural contour of the muscle or for general toning of muscle groups.

Accurate placement of the pad over the motor point is essential if it is to be effective, particularly in clients who are overweight and have slack muscles.

Antagonistic muscles, that is, those that are working eccentrically and concentrically at the same time, must not be padded up together. These movements would not occur naturally and therefore should not be applied artificially.

Pads must never be placed directly over the heart.

Before placing the pads consider carefully the effects to be achieved and the reason for using electrical muscle stimulation. Look at the way in which the muscles work naturally to help in placing the pads. The pads should be moistened with saline solution to help the current flow.

The area of treatment must be cleansed first with warm soapy water, particularly if there has been no pre-heating treatment such as sauna or steam. This will remove any oil on the skin's surface which may form a barrier to the current.

The pads should be in firm contact with the skin to provide a good contraction.

Reasons for poor muscle contractions

1 When the skin has not been sufficiently cleansed and there are oils on the skin to form a barrier.
2 A faulty machine. All connections should be checked before use.
3 Insufficient moisture in the form of saline solution on the pads or if the pads have dried out during the treatment.
4 When the pads have been positioned badly and are not directly stimulating the motor point of the muscle.
5 When the pads are strapped too lightly to the body and are therefore not in good contact with the skin.
6 When the intensity of the current is not sufficient to stimulate the muscle to contract.
7 When the subcutaneous fat in an obese client creates a barrier to the flow of current.
8 Fatigue in the muscle possibly by being overworked.

Uses of electrical muscle stimulation

o General toning treatment incorporated into a course of combined treatments which could include diet, massage and galvanic treatments.

o Strengthening weak muscles.
o After childbirth but only with the doctor's permission usually after the six-week check-up.
o Re-shaping specific areas, for example the buttocks, inside thighs or the top of the arms.
o To improve posture by exercising and strengthening muscles which are little used.
o After losing a lot of weight.
o Body maintenance.

Contraindications to electrical muscle stimulation

o Any muscular disorder.
o Any disorder of the nervous system.
o Cuts or abrasions in the skin.
o Circulatory disorders.
o Skin disease.
o After an operation unless medical permission has been given.
o Loss of skin sensation.
o Epilepsy.
o Heart conditions.
o High blood pressure.

New developments

Over the last few years there has been a gradual deviation from the normal electrical muscle stimulation (EMS) systems used in body toning and slimming and several manufacturers have produced or are now producing a variety of equipment which is purported to have a much improved action of inch reduction. However, the principles of operation of these pieces of equipment should be very carefully considered.

From the information provided by these companies it would seem that we now have something totally new in the concepts of total body therapy. However, upon close investigation of these systems the majority of them are simply modifications of normal EMS treatments. To produce the results of inch loss in short periods of time that are claimed they are relying on modifications to the normal padding layout systems that are used in conventional body therapy practice.

The conventional padding systems being taught in beauty therapy are those which the profession borrowed many years ago from medical practice. The current trends are to follow the new developments that have been proceeding over the last few years in isotonic and isometric methods of EMS.

New wave forms

There are advanced machines which use a different wave form causing the muscles to react in a different way providing a general inch and weight loss. As well as the usual effects of EMS:

○ It actually increases metabolism so utilizing fat deposits.
○ It also increases lymphatic drainage helping to eliminate waste products.

The maximum time required for each treatment is 15 minutes and a course of ten treatments, two or three a week, is recommended for the best results. However, there should be no repeat treatment within 48 hours because of the build-up of lactic acid in the muscles.

Once the required inch loss has been achieved a maintenance programme of one treatment every ten days is all that is needed.

Interferential treatment

An interferential current is a combination of two similar or dissimilar currents. It is used to combine the effects of low level muscular stimulation with the benefits of polar and interpolar effects of a galvanic current.

Forms of interferential currents are used in certain body therapy systems where they are promoting the effects of ionization and thermal increase in circulation.

The interferential treatment is soothing and warming and is an enhanced form of body galvanism.

Unlike the faradic type current used for electrical muscle stimulation treatment, interferential treatment causes very little sensation in the skin and is therefore more pleasant for the client.

Frequencies up to and not much more than 100 hertz will stimulate the muscles to produce a contraction.

The interferential current

Two currents of medium frequency are applied, one of 3900 hertz and the other 4000 hertz. When they cross in the area being treated another frequency is produced, as a result of the first two frequencies interfering with one another. This is why it is called an interferential current.

This resultant frequency, therefore, is the equivalent of the difference between the original two frequencies, for example:

First frequency = 4000 hertz
Second frequency = 3900 hertz
The resultant frequency = 100 hertz

This low frequency current therefore is generated in the tissues by the crossing of the two medium frequency currents through the body.

The resultant frequency, although stimulating muscular tissue, is low enough to have a soothing effect on the otherwise highly stimulated nerve endings.

It will stimulate muscle contraction but because it does not have to pass directly through the skin to achieve this effect it causes no painful sensation in the skin, normally a characteristic of a faradic treatment.

Effects of an interferential current

○ Stimulates muscle to contract.
○ Increases the flow of blood.
○ Increases lymphatic flow.
○ Increases the metabolic processes.

Application

It is necessary to use four electrodes for large areas of the body or four small electrodes incorporated into one viscose pad for small areas to ensure that the frequencies cross.

The two currents are applied independently of each other with the electrode pairs placed diagonally opposite each other to ensure the crossing of the two medium frequency currents to produce a natural smooth body treatment.

22 *Nutrition*

The importance of food

The body requires food in sufficient quantity and quality for growth, maintenance, repair and energy (Figure 22.1).

The food we eat must include:

○ Carbohydrates.
○ Protein.
○ Fats.
○ Minerals.
○ Vitamins.

Carbohydrates and fats provide heat and energy. Fat gives support to certain parts of the body, transports fat-soluble vitamins and is used in the formation of steroid hormones. The body needs sugar for muscle contraction. It is an efficient fuel because it requires less oxygen to work and therefore it is important during physical exercise. Proteins provide materials required for growth of the body and repair of the tissues. Vitamins and minerals are necessary for normal metabolism.

Carbohydrates

Carbohydrates consist of carbon, hydrogen and oxygen. They are found in bread, cereals, potatoes, sugar, fruit and vegetables. If the carbohydrate consumption is in excess of the body's requirements it will be converted into fat. There are three major groups:

1 Sugars.
2 Starches.
3 Cellulose

Sugars
There are two types of sugar – simple sugars or *monosaccharides* and double sugars or *disaccharides*.

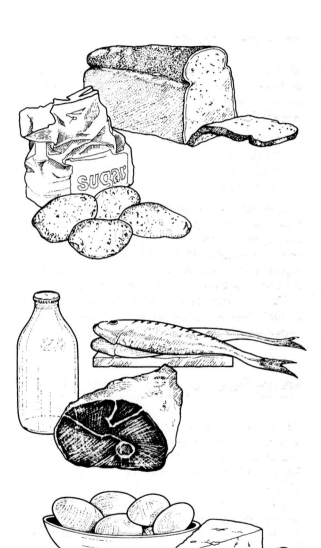

Figure 22.1 *Carbohydrates, proteins and fats*

Monosaccharides are:

○ *Glucose:* Found naturally in fruit, plant juices and animal blood.
○ *Fructose:* Found naturally in fruit and vegetables and honey.
○ *Galactose:* Which is part of milk sugar (lactose).

Disaccharides are:

○ *Sucrose:* Found naturally in sugar cane and beet sugar, small amounts in fruit and root vegetables.
○ *Maltose:* Which is a product of starch digestion.
○ *Lactose:* Which is part of milk sugar.

Starches

Starches are another major group of carbohydrates called *polysaccharides*. They consist of three or more monosaccharides but they lack the characteristic sweetness of monosaccharides and disaccharides. One of the chief polysaccharides is *glycogen* which is stored in the liver and skeletal muscles. When the body requires quick energy, liver cells break down the glycogen into glucose and release it for use.

Cellulose (other related materials)

Polysaccharides provide the rigid and fibrous structure of fruit, vegetables and cereals and they are the main component of dietary fibre.

Cellulose consists of many thousands of glucose units and it cannot be digested by humans.

Proteins

Proteins are made up of amino acids which are composed of hydrogen, oxygen, nitrogen, phosphorous and sulphur. There are different proteins which consist of certain numbers of different amino acids. First class proteins are those that contain all essential amino acids in the correct proportion and these are meat, fish, milk, eggs and soya beans.

Second class proteins are those that do not contain all the essential amino acids in the correct proportions and these are mainly found in vegetables, namely peas, beans and pulses.

Fats

Fats also consist of carbon, hydrogen and oxygen but the proportion of the hydrogen and oxygen is different than those in carbohydrates. The fats we eat are animal or saturated fat which is usually solid at room temperature, and vegetable fat which is mainly unsaturated fat and is soft or liquid at room temperature.

The fat from animals comes from meat, milk, cheese, butter and eggs. This type of fat is known to raise cholesterol levels.

Vegetable fat is found in margarine and vegetable oils.

The function of fat is to provide energy and warmth, because of the adipose layer. It protects vital organs such as the heart and liver and it provides shape and contour to the body. Essential fatty acids are important as they make up the largest part of the protective membrane surrounding all our body cells and the most common sources of fats are fish and vegetable oils.

There are four different types of fat to consider:

1 Saturated and trans fats.
2 Monounsaturated fats.
3 Polyunsaturated fats.
4 Cholesterol.

Saturated and trans fats

A diet high in these types of fat increase the level of blood cholesterol which in time will increase the risk of heart disease. Therefore we should be reducing the amount we eat.

Saturated fats are found in high quantities in animal products like fatty cuts of beef, pork, and lamb as well as in hard margarine and lard. They are also in dairy products like full fat milk, cheese and butter.

Trans fatty acids are artificially created during food processing when liquid vegetable oil is hardened to make a solid fat.

Most cakes, biscuits, pies and pastries contain a lot of hidden saturated and trans fats.

Monounsaturated fats

These are found in high proportions in olives, olive oil, almond oil and avocados. They do not increase blood cholesterol levels and some experts believe it may help to reduce them. In

Mediterranean countries where these types of food are eaten, there are much lower rates of coronary heart disease and cancer, and it is thought that this is due to the monounsaturated fats that are found in their diet.

Polyunsaturated fats

These are beneficial to health and can help to lower cholesterol levels. Oily fish such as mackerel, sardines and pilchards are an excellent source. They are also found in vegetable seeds and polyunsaturated margarines. Polyunsaturates contain 'essential' fatty acids which are vital to health.

Cholesterol

This is a soft waxy substance found in the food we eat and in our blood and it is known to contribute to heart disease when it reaches a high level. Blood cholesterol is made in the liver and carried in the blood, where it can be deposited on the walls of the blood vessels. It can lead to a narrowing of the arteries which supply blood to the heart, thus increasing the chance of heart disease. This is known as lipoprotein cholesterol or LDL. The liver makes another type of cholesterol – high density lipoprotein cholesterol (HDL) which helps clear up surplus cholesterol from our bloodstream.

Minerals

Minerals are only required in small quantities but they are necessary for the normal functioning of the body. Minerals are found in soil and are absorbed by plants as they grow. We receive the minerals from the plants, as well as the animals which have eaten the plants.

Calcium

Is essential for healthy teeth and bones and coagulation of the blood. It is found in milk, eggs, cheese, vegetables and some fish.

Phosphorous

Is important in bone and teeth formation, maintenance of body fluids and the transportation of energy inside the cells. Phosphorous can be found in cheese, liver, kidney, eggs, green vegetables and oatmeal.

Sodium

This maintains the fluid balance in the body and is associated with the transmission of nerve impulses in nerve fibres and contraction of muscles. It is found in most foods, especially meat, fish, eggs, milk and salt. Any excess is secreted by the body in urine.

Potassium

Like sodium, the functions of potassium are maintaining the fluid balance, the transmission of nerve impulses and muscular contraction. In addition, it is necessary for the chemical activities of the cells. It is found in most foods but cereals are particularly rich in potassium.

Magnesium

This is important to the composition of bones and is found in vegetables and other plant products.

Iron

This is essential for the manufacture of haemoglobin in the red blood cells and is necessary to all the body cells in a small amount. Foods rich in iron are liver, kidney, green vegetables, carrots and bread. A diet deficient in iron will cause anaemia.

Iodine

Although needed only in minute quantities, it is an essential mineral in the formation of thyroid hormones which in turn are essential for normal metabolism. It is found in seafood, watercress and added to table salt.

Zinc

This is necessary for a healthy skin and is found in nuts and fish.

Fluoride

This helps maintain healthy teeth by fighting tooth decay and protecting enamel. It is added to drinking water by some water authorities.

Chromium

This is necessary for fat and carbohydrate metabolism and is involved in the production of insulin. It is found in egg yolk, liver, wheatgerm, cheese and wholegrain cereal.

Copper

An essential component of many enzymes, it helps the formation of red blood cells. It has antioxidant effects combating free radicals and is found in liver, crab, oysters, carrots, olives, nuts, lentils and wholegrain cereal.

Manganese

This is essential for normal growth and development. It helps regulate blood sugar levels, is required for the body to be able to use vitamin C and is an antioxidant. It is found in beans, beetroot, dark lettuce, oats, pineapples, plums, almonds, hazelnuts and wheatgerm.

Selenium

This is a vital antioxidant working in conjunction with vitamin E. It is also necessary to keep the liver functioning healthily and boosts the immune system. It is found in eggs, fish, garlic, liver and yeast.

Silicon

Silicon is vital to the health of bones, cartilage blood vessels and connective tissue. It helps the body utilize calcium in the bones, and strengthens skin, nails and hair because it helps in the production of collagen and keratin.

Vitamins

Vitamins are chemical compounds which are essential to nerve, muscle and brain function and vital to normal metabolism. They are divided into two groups:

1 *Fat soluble*, vitamins A, D, E and K.
2 *Water soluble*, vitamins B complex and C.

Fat soluble vitamins

Vitamin A: Important for healthy eyes and the normal growth of most cells in the body. A lack of this vitamin can cause very dry scaly skin and difficulty in seeing in the dark.

Foods rich in vitamin A are cream, milk, eggs, cheese, butter, fish oils, and liver. Carotene can be converted by the liver into vitamin A, the source of which is carrot, spinach, cabbage and watercress.

Vitamin D: This is essential for the formation of strong bones and teeth as it helps phosphorous and calcium to be deposited in the bones. It is a very important vitamin, therefore, for pregnant women and young children.

Foods rich in vitamin D are eggs, cheese, butter, liver, sardines and fatty fish. The action of ultraviolet rays on a substance under the skin forms vitamin D. Therefore, sunlight is also a source of vitamin D.

Vitamin E: The function of this vitamin is not understood but it is thought to prevent normal growth when there is a deficiency. Vitamin E is found in peanuts, wheatgerm, milk, butter and eggs.

Vitamin K: Is essential for clotting of the blood. The sources of vitamin K are green vegetables, liver and fruit.

Water soluble vitamins

Vitamin B complex: This is a group of water soluble vitamins which include:

Vitamin B1 (thiamine): This helps to control the water balance in the body, carbohydrate metabolism and maintains a healthy nervous system. It is found in nuts, egg yolk, yeast and wholemeal bread.

Vitamin B2 (riboflavin): It helps to keep the skin healthy and it helps with the oxidation of foods to provide energy. It is found in liver, milk, cheese, eggs, leaf vegetables and beef.

Nicotinic acid: It influences the normal activities of the skin, the digestive system and the nervous system. It is found in liver, whole wheat, cheese, eggs and yeast.

Folic acid: This has an influence on the formation of red blood cells and a deficiency would cause anaemia. It is found in liver, kidney, yeast and fresh leafy vegetables.

Vitamin B6 (pyridoxine): This is necessary for fat and protein metabolism. It is found in egg yolk, meat, liver, peas and beans.

Vitamin B12: Essential for the maturation of red blood cells. It is found in meat, liver, eggs and milk.

Pantothenic acid: This influences the metabolism of fats and carbohydrates and is found in many foods, in particular liver, meat and eggs.

Vitamin C: This has several functions, helping in the formation of connective tissue, the development and maintenance of healthy bones, the absorption of iron and strengthening the walls of the blood capillaries. It also aids healing and aids the metabolism.

All of these essential nutrients are present in food in different quantities and for a well-balanced diet suitable to maintain a healthy body there must be adequate proportions from each group.

A nutrient is a substance essential for the well-being of the human body. The two other essential ingredients for a healthy body are:

○ Water.
○ Roughage.

A well-balanced diet will avoid vitamin deficiency but there are other factors which can influence vitamin deficiency:

○ Taking aspirin leads to some reduction in the amount of vitamin C in the blood.
○ Smoking is associated with low levels of vitamins C and B12.
○ The oral contraceptive pill may cause a deficiency of vitamin B6 (pyridoxine) which can result in depression.
○ Laxatives taken regularly could lead to a vitamin deficiency as well as a potassium deficiency which effects the fluid balance in the body.

Water

Water is essential to maintain the body's fluid balance as the body loses approximately two litres per day through perspiration and urine. The human body could survive a lot longer without food than it could without water because:

○ It is necessary to maintain the health of most of the body cells.
○ It aids digestion.
○ It makes up a large part of blood and tissue fluid, so aiding the transportation of substances around the body.
○ It dilutes waste products and aids elimination.
○ It is essential for maintaining body temperature.

Roughage

More popularly termed fibre, roughage is a carbohydrate found in all vegetable matter. It is undigestible but it is important as it helps the process of digestion and keeps the bowels working normally.

Roughage provides bulk so helping to satisfy the appetite and is found in pulses, peas, beans, brown rice, wholemeal bread, flour and pasta, sweetcorn, jacket potatoes, green leafy vegetables and dried fruit.

Food high in fibre contains fewer calories but more bulk and it has to be chewed more, therefore creating a feeling of fullness and reducing the appetite which is helpful when dieting.

Metabolism

The food we eat is digested and absorbed by the body and then it is converted into the energy the body needs by a chemical process called *metabolism*. Metabolism describes the chemical processes which occur in the body:

Catabolism

Catabolism is the process by which substances (food) are broken down to release energy or are excreted as waste.

The energy which is produced is then consumed by the body for cell reproduction, growth and repair, as well as the manufacture of new compounds essential to the body. This process is known as anabolism.

Anabolism

Anabolism is the building up and manufacture of new products.

The body needs food to supply it with calories which supply the energy required for every day activities and to maintain the basic metabolic rate. The metabolic rate is the speed at which energy is released into the body.

Calories
The method of estimating the energy requirements of the body is to measure it in terms of heat. The unit of heat used is the *calorie* (or kilocalorie).

A calorie is the amount of heat required to raise 1 ml of water through 1°C.

The energy value of food is also measured in calories:

1 gram of carbohydrate = 4 calories.
1 gram of protein = 4 calories.
1 gram of fat = 9 calories.

Energy may also be measured in terms of units of work called joules but calories are used far more extensively.

Basal metabolism

Basal metabolism is the minimum quantity of energy needed by the body to keep it alive throughout the day and night.

This function may be affected by age because the basic metabolic rate slows down as we grow older. Therefore, a smaller proportion of the food absorbed will be converted into energy and there may be weight gain because of the slower metabolic rate.

If, however, the amount of physical exercise taken is increased, then the basal metabolic rate will also be increased to provide the body with the energy required for the physical exertion.

An increase in body temperature will also increase the basal metabolic rate, as will certain drugs such as amphetamines and caffeine.

An adult requires approximately 25 calories per kilo of body weight every 24 hours to maintain the basal metabolic rate. To cope with normal daily activities, additional calories are required and this varies, depending on the occupation and physical activity undertaken.

Women have a lower basal metabolic rate than men and therefore need less calories per day to provide energy.

Each person's energy requirements vary depending upon:

○ Their sex.
○ Their age.
○ Their size.
○ The amount of physical activity.

The calories required by an active man will be between *2700 and 3600* per day, depending on the physical activity undertaken.

The calories required by an active women will be between *2200 and 2500* per day, depending on the physical activity undertaken.

Digestion

This is the process by which food is broken down into molecules small enough to be absorbed by the cells. Digestion occurs in the alimentary canal (Figure 22.2) which consists of:

○ The mouth.
○ The pharynx.
○ The oesophagus.
○ The stomach.
○ The small intestine.
○ The large intestine.

Digestion occurs in several stages:

1 *Ingestion* of food through the mouth.
2 *Digestion* starts in the mouth but takes place mainly in the stomach and small intestine. It is both mechanical and chemical.
3 *Absorption* is the passage of the small molecules into the blood.
4 *Excretion*. The indigestible food substances or those which have no value to the body are eliminated.

Digestion is a chemical process which begins in the mouth. The food is mechanically broken down by the teeth and mixed with saliva produced by the salivary glands which makes the food easier to swallow.

The saliva actually begins the chemical process as it contains enzymes which start to break down the food into smaller molecules.

After swallowing the food, by contraction of the muscles in the walls of the pharynx, digestion continues automatically as we now have no control over its movement. The food is carried down the oesophagus by muscular contraction termed *peristalsis*.

The food reaches the stomach and is acted on chemically by the digestive juices, secreted from the glands of the mucous membrane and mechanically by the muscles of the stomach wall. The food is broken down into a semi-fluid called *chyme*, which is then forced into the duodenum, part of the small intestine.

The digestion of the food is completed in the small intestine. Bile from liver neutralizes the acid chyme and the enzymes from the pancreas process the food further.

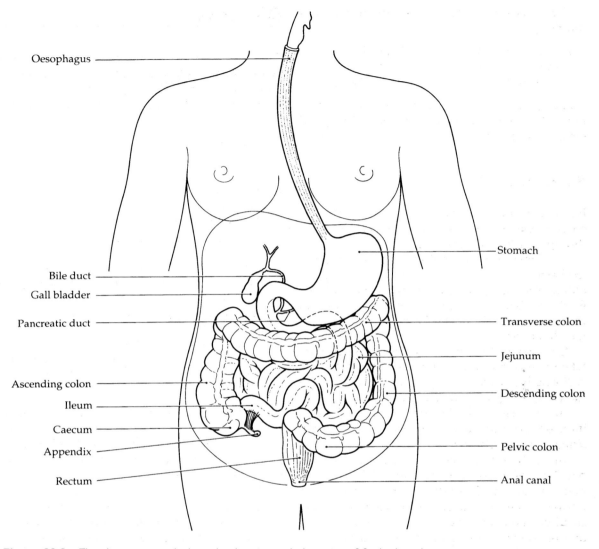

Figure 22.2 *The alimentary canal where the digestion and absorption of food takes place*

The *ileum,* which is the other part of the small intestine, absorbs the food into the bloodstream and the material which is of no use to the body enters the large intestine to be excreted.

Absorption and use of nutrients in the body

Carbohydrates
↓
Carbohydrates are broken down into disaccharides during digestion

↓
In the intestinal wall they are split into monosaccharides
↓
They are carried to the liver via the bloodstream
↓
Used directly for energy as glucose
↓
Excess converted to glycogen and stored in liver and skeletal muscles to be used as required
↓
Reserve energy source converted into fatty acids and stored in adipose tissue

Proteins
↓
When proteins enter the intestinal wall they are split into amino acids
↓
They are then carried in the blood to the liver
↓
Used for growth and repair of tissue
↓
Excess converted into other amino acids which the body requires but may not be present in food
↓
Excess amino acids may be used for energy
↓
Others are excreted by the kidneys

Fats
↓
Almost all fats which enter the intestinal wall are carried to the bloodstream by lymph
↓
Fat is transformed in the liver and then deposited in the adipose tissue of the subcutaneous layer
↓
Provides insulation and is a shock absorber
↓
Available as a reserve energy source

The urinary system

The body is continuously producing by-products and waste which must be removed to prevent the body poisoning itself. It has several methods of ridding itself of these waste products through the excretory systems in the body, *excretion* is the name given to the process by which the body eliminates waste (Figure 22.3).

The urinary system is one of the main systems responsible for excretion and it consists of:

○ The kidneys.
○ The ureter.
○ The bladder.
○ The urethra.

The kidneys

The kidneys are found just above the waist on the back wall of the abdomen. They contain

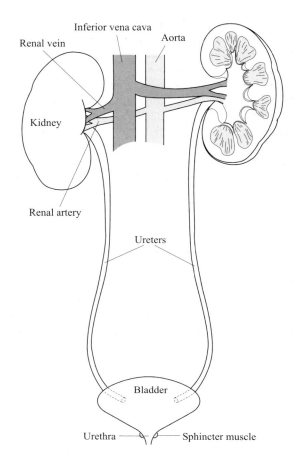

Figure 22.3 *The urinary system*

thousands of tiny filtering units called nephrons and each nephron is divided into two parts:

1 The *glomerulus* or filtering part.
2 The *tubule* where water and essential nutrients are extracted from the blood.

The glomerulus contains a knot of tiny blood capillaries which have very thin walls, water and waste pass easily across these walls into the collecting system of tubules on the other side. The tubules run between the glomerului to a collecting system which drains into the bladder. The glomerulus is surrounded by a *Bowman's capsule* and it is here that most of the filtered water and salt is reabsorbed.

The kidneys are responsible for filtering nitrogen containing waste, the most common compound of which is urea out of the bloodstream and regulating the amount of water passed out of the body maintaining the correct balance of salt in the body.

The kidneys receive about one litre of blood every minute through a renal artery, which is then filtered, separating the watery element (plasma) of blood which passes into the tubule, from the rest, water, salt and other valuable substances (glucose, amino acids, minerals and vitamins) which are absorbed back into the bloodstream. Some water, urea and other waste substances, are then passed in the form of urine, down two tubes, *ureters*, to the bladder for excretion.

The ureters and urethra

These are two tubes through which urine passes from the kidneys to the bladder. They have one-way valves in the opening to the bladder to prevent urine from flowing back to the kidneys when the bladder is full.

The urine passes out of the bladder through the urethra which is situated at the lowest point in the bladder, the opening of which is kept closed by a sphincter, a circular muscle which contracts to seal the passageway. During urination this sphincter muscle relaxes at the same time as the bladder walls contracts to expel the urine.

The bladder

This is a hollow, thick walled, muscular organ lying in the lower part of the pelvic basin between the pubic bones and the rectum. The bladder walls are composed of a number of muscular layers which stretch when the bladder is filling and then contract when it is emptying. There is an almost continuous trickle of urine from the kidneys to the bladder and when the bladder starts to resist, the need to pass urine is felt.

23 Diet

Weight problems

There are many reasons for being overweight, one of the most common being poor eating habits that have developed over the years, which probably begin in early childhood. Other reasons include:

Over-eating in infancy can lead to a large number of fat cells being produced which increase in size as more weight is gained.

Eating too much refined and processed foods which contain hidden fats and sugar.

Leading a sedentary life style with very little exercise. In fact many women can lead very busy and active lives but do not take sufficient exercise to burn off the excess calories.

A disturbance of normal metabolism can be a problem for a small percentage of women and they will need medical advice to deal with the cause.

There are several reasons why people wish to diet:

○ Because they are obese, that is, more than 20 per cent over their ideal weight.
○ To reduce the risks of heart disease or high blood pressure.
○ To reach an ideal weight.
○ After childbirth to regain their figure.
○ To lose weight in specific areas, for example thighs and hips.
○ To ease the pressure on arthritic joints.
○ For self-esteem.
○ To feel fit and healthy.

Whatever the reason, dieting must be approached in a sensible manner and it is more a case of eating a healthy, well-balanced diet. This may be achieved by cutting out all the unncessary foods while eating plenty of the foods that are allowed.

Body mass index

Being overweight must be taken seriously if it becomes excessive because:

○ The heart has to work harder.
○ There will probably be more fat in the blood increasing the risk of heart attack or stroke. Joints will suffer and in the long term may cause arthritis.
○ There will be a decrease in mobility.
○ Increases susceptibility to high blood pressure, diabetes, and gallstones.
○ Backache.
○ Varicose veins.

Being underweight is also undesirable, therefore it is important to control your weight.

Underweight	All right	Overweight	Fat	Very fat
You may need to consult your doctor, or start to eat more	This is the right weight range for good health	Try to lose the excess	It is important to lose weight	This is serious and you really need to do something about losing weight
BMI of less than 20	BMI between 20 and 24.9	BMI between 25 and 29.9	BMI between 30 and 39.9	BMI greater than 40

One way of looking at body weight is by calculating the *body mass index* (BMI). This is calculated as:

$$\frac{\text{weight (kg)}}{\text{height (m)} \times \text{height (m)}}$$

For example, if someone weighs 92 kg and they have a height of 1.6 metres, to work out their body mass index you will have:

$$\frac{92}{1.6 \times 1.6}$$

$$= \frac{92}{2.56}$$

This makes their body mass index 36, which puts them into the fat category.

How to lose weight

Excess weight is stored under the skin in the form of fat and the fat cells increase in size as more weight is put on.

To lose body fat the energy expended by the body must be more than the energy intake as food. This will cause the body to use some of its stored energy, most of which is fat.

The most sensible thing to do, therefore, is to cut out of the diet those foods which are very high in calories and eat a lot more of those which are not high in calories.

There are three rules to follow which will help:

1 Eat less fat.
2 Eat less sugar.
3 Eat more fibre.

In this way weight loss may be achieved slowly but effectively without feeling starved, deprived, or tired.

A balanced diet

This is a diet which contains a large variety of food so that there is an adequate intake of nutrients to maintain health and for the body to function efficiently. This is made easier by choosing food from each of the four main food groups:

1 Starchy foods.
2 Dairy products.
3 Meat, poultry, fish and alternatives.
4 Vegetables and fruit.

Meals should be made up mainly from starchy foods with the addition of some foods from the other groups to make a well-balanced meal. Starchy food is filling, it is not high in calories but provides other essential nutrients.

Some examples from the four main food groups:

Starchy foods	Dairy products	Meat, poultry, fish and alternatives	Vegetables and fruit
Bread	Cheese	Beans and	All vegetables:
Breakfast	Fromage	lentils	Cabbage,
cereal	frais	Cheese	carrots
Chapattis	Milk	Eggs	Peppers, leeks
Noodles	Yoghurt	Fish	Potatoes, spinach
Pasta		Meat	Turnips, broccoli, etc
Potatoes		Meat products	Salad vegetables:
Rice		Nuts	Cucumber, lettuce
Sweet		Offal	Radish, tomato, etc.
potatoes		Poultry	Fresh fruit:
		Texturized	Apples, bananas,
		vegetable	pears
		protein	Mangoes, oranges
			Kiwi, grapefruit, etc.

Food labelling

Food Labelling Regulations 1984 specify that the presentation of food must be such that there is no likelihood that a consumer would be misled to a material degree as to the nature, substance or quality of the food. The law aims to protect the consumer and provide information. This is particularly important for anyone with a food allergy or intolerance. The regulations require food for sale or supply to be labelled with:

○ Name of food.
○ List of ingredients in weight order.
○ Best before date/use by date.
○ Special storage instructions.
○ The manufacturer's name.

In addition, nutritional information will be provided.

The role of the therapist

The therapist may often suggest to clients that they follow a weight reducing diet as part of a course of treatments. It is important, therefore, that therapists have a good understanding of nutrition so that they know their recommendations are healthy, well-balanced and appropriate to the needs of each of their clients.

The relationship between the client and therapist is important as it is necessary to find out as much as possible about the client's eating habits, life style and family history. This will enable the therapist to pinpoint the cause of the problem and recommend the appropriate diet and treatment. This will not be a problem if the client has been attending regularly for treatment and a trusting relationship already exists.

The client may, however, be new and feel a little shy and embarrassed, particularly if the therapist is young, slim and looks fit and healthy. The ability of the therapist to put the client at ease, be sympathetic and reassuring is of paramount importance and ensures that the client will return and persevere in the quest to lose weight.

Provide advice on dietary control

Client consultation

It is important when advising a client about their diet that you complete a detailed record card with as much relevant information as possible to help you devise a healthy and nutritious diet taking into account:

○ Their lifestyle.
○ Their age.
○ Current eating habits.
○ General health.
○ Any food allergies.
○ Any food restrictions.
○ Specific likes and dislikes.
○ Any special needs.

This will enable you to establish their current diet, recommend a healthy well-balanced diet tailored to their requirements and then monitor their progress.

Information to be included on the record card would be:

○ Name and age.
○ Height and weight.
○ Occupation.

○ Lifestyle to include the following:
—Do they smoke and how much?
—Do they drink alcohol and how much?
—Do they take exercise and how much?
—Do they have any leisure pursuits or hobbies?
—Do they have children and what are their ages?
○ Dietary history to include the following:
—Any food allergies?
—Any nutritional deficiencies now or previously?
—Do they cook for themselves?
—Do they cook for other people?
—What is their average daily eating pattern?
○ Medical history to include:
—Current medication.
—Heart condition.
—High blood pressure.
—Pregnancy.
—Diabetic.
—Recent operations.
—Any long-term illness.

To assist clients in recording how much food they do eat in a day, it would be helpful to provide them with a chart or diary which they should complete for a week. It is useful to include a weekend in the diary, as eating habits are often different at the weekend.

The therapist will then assess how much weight the client has to lose. This can be done by working out the ideal weight for the height and build of the client, as well as taking into consideration the client's own wishes, as long as they are not unreasonable. (See Figure 23.1.)

Using all the information provided by the client, the therapist can also recommend some form of exercise. This could be a suitable exercise class or a sporting activity which will fit in with the client's taste and life style.

A combined diet and exercise programme will show results more quickly than either diet or exercise alone. It will serve to increase the metabolic rate and burn up the reduced calorie intake, thus resulting in a loss of weight.

The goals that are set for clients must be realistic to prevent them from becoming disheartened and giving up.

The three rules to follow – eating less fat, eating less sugar and increasing fibre consumption – can

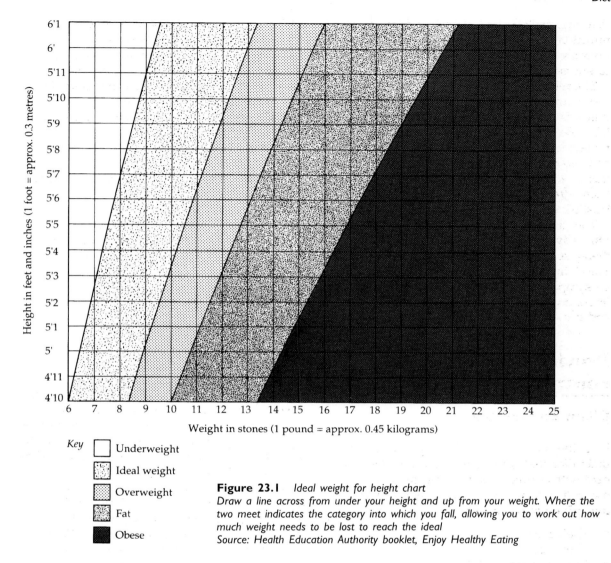

Figure 23.1 *Ideal weight for height chart*
Draw a line across from under your height and up from your weight. Where the two meet indicates the category into which you fall, allowing you to work out how much weight needs to be lost to reach the ideal
Source: Health Education Authority booklet, Enjoy Healthy Eating

Key:
- Underweight
- Ideal weight
- Overweight
- Fat
- Obese

be written into a flexible eating plan for the client to follow. The eating plan can be used by the therapist to create a personal day-by-day diet plan for those clients who need the discipline of being told exactly when and what to eat.

The flexible eating plan

Eat less fat

Eat only lean meat and chicken or turkey without the skin. Meat may not be eaten in any other form, for example sausages, pâté, pasties or pies since they all contain fat. The method of cooking should be without the addition of fat, flour or thick sauces which will contain a large number of calories. Mince may be fried using no added fat and the fat from the mince should then be poured away.

Eat fresh fish as it is low in fat and it may be poached, steamed or microwaved. Tinned fish is only permitted if it is in brine, *not* in oil. Oily fish such as mackerel or herrings should be avoided but if this is not possible, they should be grilled to remove excess fat.

Cut butter and margarine out of the diet altogether but if absolutely essential low fat spread in minute quantities can be used.

When using a cooking oil it should be high in polyunsaturates and used only when absolutely necessary, again in minute quantities.

Substitute salad dressings with a low-fat yoghurt flavoured with wine or herb vinegar.

Drink only skimmed milk or semi-skimmed milk when skimmed is totally unacceptable. Try to restrict the amount consumed to half a pint a day.

Eliminate cream altogether and substitute with low-fat yoghurt or low-fat fromage frais.

Avoid eating biscuits, cakes or pastries which are very high in fat.

Cheese is high in fat so it should not be eaten at all. The only acceptable type of cheese is cottage cheese which has a low fat content.

Completely cut out snack foods such as nuts and crisps as they are high in fat.

Eat less sugar

Eliminate any sugar that is added to the food, for example in tea and coffee or on cereal.

Drink only unsweetened drinks such as mineral water or natural fruit juices.

Eat only fresh fruit as tinned or bottled fruit does contain added sugar.

Eliminate processed food which usually contains added sugar.

Eat more fibre

The foods which are high in fibre are:

○ Wholemeal bread.
○ Wholemeal cereals.
○ Brown rice.
○ Potatoes cooked in their jackets.
○ Vegetables such as peas, beans, sweetcorn and the green leaf variety, for example spinach or spring cabbage.
○ Lentils.
○ Dried fruits.

Fruit and other vegetables contain fibre but not in such high amounts.

Salad foods contain small amounts of fibre and can be eaten in unlimited quantities as they contain few calories. It is the dressing on a salad which contains the calories so this must not be used.

Following these three simple rules, eating moderate quantities of wholesome food and taking some form of exercise three times a week for twenty minutes, should allow the client to lose weight steadily, while still eating a sensible well-balanced diet.

Eat more vitamins and minerals

By eating a healthy well-balanced diet you should obtain all the required vitamins and minerals as they are present in food in the form and proportions that the body needs. To make sure that the fresh foods you eat are as nutritious as possible food should be fresh and stored correctly as prolonged or inadequate storage can lead to a reduction in the nutrient content. 'Convenience' chilled, frozen, dried or pre-packaged foods can be as good a source of vitamins and minerals as fresh food only if they are stored correctly and cooking instructions followed.

Include more fresh fruit and vegetables on a daily basis but to preserve their vitamin values you must:

○ Avoid storing them for too long as the vitamin content of fresh food diminishes with age.
○ Chop vegetables just before cooking them.
○ Avoid overcooking vegetables. Use a steamer, microwave or stir fry because water soluble vitamins such as vitamin C and the B complex are lost in boiling liquid when cooked in the conventional way.
○ Eat fruit and vegetables raw whenever possible.
○ Large amounts of minerals are lost from food when they are refined, for example during flour milling and rice polishing, so eat wholewheat flour and brown rice whenever possible.

Eat less salt

Use less in cooking. Do not add salt but use other flavourings. Cut down on snacks and all salty foods.

Reduce alcohol intake

Alcoholic drinks contain a lot of calories so eliminate alcohol from your diet or reduce the amount per week. Drink low alcohol or no alcohol drinks, use low calorie mixers or carbonated water to make a longer drink.

Factors affecting diet

Food allergies

There are many people who are intolerant to some food in their diet which means they may have an unusual reaction when they eat certain foods. The reaction can be a simple rash but in some cases it can be severe and life threatening but more often it will cause headaches, diarrhoea or vomiting. A doctor must be consulted about food intolerance as certain foods may need to be eliminated from a diet and this must be controlled by a qualified dietician. Some allergies are hereditary and run in families. Children often grow out of allergies but some people are particularly sensitive to food additives, for example colours which can produce symptoms of hyperactivity.

Food intolerance can be caused by:

○ The lack of a certain enzyme which normally helps to digest food, for example people with milk intolerance are lacking in lactose which helps in the digestion of milk.
○ Certain substances taken in large quantities which act in a similar way to drugs, caffeine can produce symptoms such as sweating or migraine.
○ Some highly spicy foods have an irritant effect on the lining of the gut.
○ There are some substances that are allergens and cause an allergic reaction.

Types of food allergies

Coeliac disease

This is a sensitivity to the protein gluten which is found in barley, oats, rye and wheat. It is controlled by eating a gluten-free diet and there are specially prepared gluten-free products available. If this condition is not properly controlled it may cause poor growth and weight loss.

Egg allergy

This may produce eczema or other forms of rash and the only answer is to avoid eggs and any products which contain eggs.

Fish and shellfish

Allergy to shellfish often produces a rash but in severe cases it can cause anaphylactic shock which is a massive allergic reaction in the body.

Milk intolerance

A sensitivity to protein from the milk of cows can cause eczema and because of the lack of an essential enzyme some people cannot digest the lactose present in it. A soya-based milk substitute may be prescribed for babies and children but adults can drink goats' milk when there is an intolerance to milk from cows.

Peanut allergy

This is an anaphylactic food allergy because it produces such severe reactions in the body. It is a serious and potentially fatal condition which may develop in particularly sensitive individuals within a few seconds or minutes. Sufferers may also be allergic to other types of nut.

Wheat allergy

An allergy to wheat can cause symptoms of asthma, itchy skin and in some cases diarrhoea. Sufferers are sensitive to the whole grain including wheat starch, unlike coeliacs who are only allergic to the wheat protein.

It is important to look closely at the list of ingredients on food labelling to ensure that the food does not contain an ingredient which may cause an allergic reaction.

Pregnancy

It is vitally important to eat a healthy well-balanced diet during pregnancy as the placenta passes nourishment from the mother's bloodstream to the developing baby. There are several recommendations from the department of health for pregnant mothers as far as diet is concerned:

○ Avoid eating liver and products containing liver, for example paté or sausages, because they are high in vitamin A and if taken in large amounts may be harmful to the baby.
○ Folic acid intake should be increased before conception and for the first three months of a pregnancy to help prevent conditions such as spina bifida occurring. Folic acid also helps to prevent anaemia. It is found in potatoes, green vegetables, pulses, fortified breakfast cereal, bread, fruit, nuts and yeast extract.
○ Avoid eating foods which are associated with the salmonella and listeria bacteria, for example soft cheeses, mould-ripened cheeses, raw or lightly cooked eggs, food containing raw egg, paté, raw or lightly cooked meat.

After the birth new mums often want to lose weight and regain their figure. However, if they are breast feeding, energy requirements will be high and they will increase as milk production increases to satisfy the growing baby. It is important to follow a healthy eating plan and eat when hungry to prevent tiredness and to drink plenty of bland fluids such as water, milk or diluted fruit juices. Avoid foods which may upset the baby's tummy and alcohol while breast feeding.

High blood pressure

Having high blood pressure is one factor which increases the risk of heart disease, kidney disease and having a stroke. In susceptible people it is thought that too much salt in the diet may contribute to high blood pressure. Salt is required to help maintain the fluid balance in our body, the amount of salt required by the body has been estimated to be just over 1.5 grams per day (¾ teaspoon of salt). This amount is consumed easily from salt which occurs naturally in food, therefore we need no added salt. To help cut down salt intake you could recommend your client to:

○ Gradually reduce the amount of salt added to food. Taste buds will quickly adjust as the natural flavour of the food starts to come through.
○ Eat reduced salt versions of food products.
○ Use substitutes to provide flavour (ask a doctor's advice if you have a kidney complaint or are under medical supervision).
○ Avoid high sodium foods: table salt, smoked fish, dried packet soup, baked beans in tomato, canned soup, bread, breakfast cereal, pickles, salad dressing, dry roasted peanuts, very low fat spread, cured or canned meats, prawns, stock cubes, sausages, tomato ketchup, hard cheeses, milk, crisps, fish fingers, salted butter, margarine.

Coronary heart disease

A Government publication (COMA Report) based on population research has advised that those at risk of coronary heart disease should:

○ Decrease their fat intake to 30 per cent of calories from food.
○ Saturated fat should be decreased to 10 per cent of calories from food.
○ Cholesterol should be below 100 mg/1000 Kcal.
○ Avoid excess alcohol.
○ Increase starch/fibre rich food.
○ Avoid obesity.
○ Balance food intake.
○ Take regular exercise.

Vegetarian diet

Many people now follow a vegetarian diet or have excluded red meat altogether. There are those who have adopted a vegan diet which excludes all food of animal origin including dairy products and eggs. It is important that no matter which diet is followed it must be well balanced and include the correct amount of vitamins, minerals, proteins, fats and fibre for good health.

Recent research has shown that vegetarian diet reduces the risk of heart disease and cancer but there are other risks involved if the diet is not well planned to include all the requirements for health.

Eliminating animal foods from the diet can lead to health risks usually a deficiency in:

○ Iron.
○ Vitamin B12.
○ Vitamin D.
○ Calcium.
○ Zinc.

To counteract this a vegetarian must:

○ Eat plenty of green vegetables such as spinach, broccoli, seeds, nuts, wholemeal cereals and fortified breakfast cereals. It is also recommended to increase vitamin C intake as this will help the absorption of iron into the body.
○ Increase the foods which contain vitamin B12 such as yeast extract, soya milk and fortified breakfast cereals.
○ Increase vitamin D by eating egg yolk, dairy products, fortified breakfast cereals and some fish.
○ Calcium intake is dependent on vitamin D and only 30–40 per cent of calcium in the diet

is absorbed. Therefore vegans must eat more peanuts, walnuts, sunflower seeds and green vegetables in their diet and in addition vegetarians may eat, milk and cheese.

○ Zinc is required to transport vitamin A and is also involved in red blood cell production, natural sources include, mushrooms, wheatgerm, brewers' yeast and eggs.

It is also important to look at the amount of fat eaten as some vegetarians base their diet around dairy products which are high in saturated fat and cholesterol. Therefore they must limit the amount of saturated fatty foods and replace with vegetable oils such as olive or sunflower.

Diabetes

This is a metabolic disorder and is caused by a lack of the hormone insulin which reduces the ability of the body to convert food into energy and control the amount of glucose in the blood. There are two types of diabetes:

1 *Insulin dependent*, when the body stops producing insulin and injections of insulin must be given regularly and a healthy diet with regular meals must be followed.

2 *Non-insulin dependent*. People with this type produce small amounts of insulin but not enough to control glucose levels in the blood. They control their diabetes by watching what they eat and some may also take tablets. Often they suffer with weight problems.

The British Diabetic Association does not recommend a special diet but a healthy well-balanced diet similar to that of any other adult.

Age

It does not matter what age we are, a balanced diet is the very important. Sometimes poor nutrition is a problem for several reasons:

○ Low income.
○ Illness.
○ Loss of appetite.
○ Mental lethargy.
○ Disinterest in preparing food.

○ Over-indulging in the wrong type of food such as sweets, cakes etc.
○ Eating too many processed foods.

People are living longer and enjoying an active life. However dietary requirements do change in later years so they must:

○ Eat a wide variety of food from the four main food groups.
○ Maintain body weight as being underweight can increase the risk of disease and being overweight may restrict mobility and health.
○ Fats such as omega-3 polyunsaturates which may have a beneficial effect on blood clotting, arthritis and healthy eyes should be increased. Sources are oily fish such as mackerel, herrings, sardines, trout and salmon.
○ Watch salt intake particularly if high blood pressure is a problem. Eat more fibre in the form of fresh fruit, vegetables and cereals.
○ Ensure that the diet has plenty of dairy foods for calcium to keep bones strong and healthy. Increase vitamin D intake as this is required to absorb and utilize calcium in the bones, oily fish, margarine and cod liver oil are sources of vitamin D.
○ Eat plenty of vitamin C, obtained from fresh fruit, vegetables and fruit juice, which helps with wound healing.
○ Drink plenty of fluid to help the fibre in the diet work.

Fluid balance in the body

The fluid in the body refers to water and dissolved substances and it makes up 45 to 75 per cent of the body weight depending on age and the amount of fat present. The body's need for water is second only to its need for air. Water moves within the body by osmosis and the concentration of solutes (electrolytes) in the fluid will determine the fluid balance. One of the functions of electrolytes is to control the osmosis of water between body compartments. The balance of water is normally regulated by the kidneys and as a result of excessive loss dehydration occurs.

The body fluid contains sodium and potassium which together play a significant role in fluid balance and if this balance is upset it can cause problems. Sodium is also essential for muscle and nerve activity.

If water is lost from the body through excessive perspiration, using diuretics may result in a lower than normal sodium level which will be characterized by headaches, hypotension and muscular weakness. Severe sodium loss can result in mental confusion, stupor and coma. The sodium level is regulated by the hormone aldosterone from the adrenal cortex.

Loss of potassium may result from vomiting, diarrhoea, kidney disease or high sodium intake. Symptoms may include cramps, fatigue, increased urine output, shallow respiration and mental confusion. The level of potassium in the blood is under the control of the mineralocorticoids but mainly the hormone aldosterone.

It is important therefore to ensure that sufficient fluid is drunk to maintain a healthy balance and prevent dehydration.

Calorie controlled diet

There are those people who like to eat their favourite foods and still diet. A calorie chart would be helpful to them in choosing their own meals while staying within a calorie limit.

Calorie charts may be provided by some slimming clubs, dieticians, nutritionists or health centres. As all charts vary slightly it is advisable to choose one and use it to compile a calorie controlled diet to suit personal taste.

Calorie values of some common foods

	Calorie per	
Food	oz	100 g
Fresh fruit		
Apple	10	35
Apricot	8	28
Banana (peeled)	22	79
Cherries	12	41
Dates (stoned)	70	248
Gooseberries	10	37
Grapefruit	6	22
Mango	17	59
Nectarine	14	50

	Calorie per	
Food	oz	100 g
Orange	10	35
Peach	10	37
Pear	8	29
Pineapple	13	46
Raspberries	7	25
Rhubarb	1.5	6
Strawberries	7	26
Tangerines	7	23
Tomato	4	14
Fresh vegetables		
Artichoke (boiled)	5	18
Asparagus (boiled)	3	9
Aubergine	4	14
Avocado	62	223
Beans:		
broad (boiled)	14	48
french (boiled)	2	7
green (boiled)	2	7
runner (boiled)	5	19
Beansprouts	2.5	9
Beetroot (boiled)	10	35
Broccoli (boiled)	5	18
Brussels sprouts (boiled)	5	18
Spring cabbage (boiled)	2	7
Carrots (boiled)	6	20
Cauliflower (boiled)	2.5	9
Celery (raw)	2	8
Courgette	4	13
Cress	3	10
Cucumber	3	10
Endive	3	11
Leek (boiled)	7	24
Lettuce	3	12
Marrow	2	7
Mushrooms	4	13
Okra	5	17
Onion	7	23
Parsnip (boiled)	16	56
Peas (boiled)	15	52
Peppers	4	15
Potato:		
baked	30	105
boiled	22	78
chips	75	265
crisps	151	533
roast	44	155

Food	Calorie per oz	Calorie per 100 g
Radish	4	14
Swede	5	18
Sweetcorn	32	112
Turnip	4	14
Watercress	4	14
Meat		
Bacon:		
grilled	117	414
fried	136	480
Beef:		
braised	76	267
bourgignon	99	349
curried	34	120
goulash	23	80
minced/stewed	65	229
roast sirloin	80	284
rump steak	56	198
Beefburgers	93	330
Chicken:		
boiled	52	183
roast	44	155
Chicken curry	35	125
Chicken casserole	22	78
Duck (roast)	54	191
Goose (roast)	90	319
Ham:		
boiled	35	122
honey roast	44	155
Hot dog sausage	55	194
Lamb:		
grilled chop	78	277
roast leg	90	316
Pork:		
grilled chop	73	258
kebab	50	175
roast leg	81	286
Sausage (medium beef grilled)	76	269
Sausage (medium pork grilled)	90	317
Turkey (roast)	40	140
Veal (cutlets)	61	215
Cooked meats		
Chicken	52	183
Corned beef	62	218
Salami	123	435
Tongue	82	293
Turkey breast	36	127

Food	Calorie per oz	Calorie per 100 g
Fish		
Clams (steamed/canned)	29	102
Cod:		
steamed	24	85
butter sauce	26	93
breadcrumbs	32	113
fried in batter	56	198
Cod fish fingers	51	181
Crab	36	127
Haddock (fried and breaded)	30	107
Hake (poached)	30	106
Halibut fillet (steamed)	37	131
Herring (grilled)	56	199
Kipper fillet (baked)	58	205
Lobster (boiled/filleted)	34	119
Mackerel:		
fried/fillet	53	188
smoked	65	232
Mussels (boiled/shelled)	25	87
Oysters	2	6
Plaice fillets:		
steamed	26	92
breadcrumbs/fried	64	225
Prawns (peeled/boiled)	30	106
Salmon (fresh or smoked)	40	142
Sardines (tinned)	57	204
Scallops (steamed)	30	105
Scampi fried in breadcrumbs	90	316
Shrimps (boiled)	33	117
Sole fillet (steamed)	26	91
Trout fillet (steamed)	38	135
Tuna:		
oil	82	289
brine	35	123
Whitebait (fried)	148	525
Whiting fillet (steamed)	26	92
Dairy produce		
Butter	210	740
Cheese:		
natural (cottage)	29	102
half fat hard	76	270
Cheddar	114	403
Cheshire	105	372
Stilton	131	462
Brie	85	300
Camembert	88	312

Food	Calorie per oz	100 g
Cream:		
fresh single	57	200
fresh double	127	450
fresh whipping	108	381
Egg:		
boiled/poached	42	147
fried	66	232
omelette/plain	54	191
scrambled	66	232
Ice cream	47	166
Margarine	207	730
Mayonnaise	210	741
Milk:		
whole fresh	19	67
skimmed	10	35
Yoghurt:		
natural/low fat	18	64
flavoured	28	100
Sundries		
Bread (1 slice = 1 oz):		
brown	63	223
white	70	247
wholemeal	61	216
Cornflakes	101	354
Branflakes	94	332
Rice Crispies	99	349
Weetabix	95	335
Sugar	110	388
Spirits (70% proof)	63	222
Cider	11	39
Tonic water	10	35
Ginger ale	10	35
Beer:		
draught	20	71
bottled	10	35
Wine (dry white)	25	88

Exercise and diet

It is important when exercising to drink fluids as sweating causes fluid loss from the body which must be replaced by drinking plenty of water afterwards.

If the body consumes more calories than it expends in energy there will be weight gain. To lose weight more energy must be spent exercising than is consumed in calories. Regular exercise will:

○ Improve the balance of fats in the blood.
○ Strengthen the heart muscle.
○ Lower your resting blood pressure levels.
○ Use up calories to help weight control.
○ Make you feel and look good.
○ Help to relieve stress.
○ Be enjoyable.

The aim of those who want to lose weight is to lose stored fat. *Adipose tissue* is the body's long-term store of pure, concentrated fat but fat is also stored in the short term, in the muscles. *Metabolism* is in simple terms the way the body converts food into energy.

Basal metabolic rate (BMR) is the rate at which the body burns up energy to keep it alive when resting. Factors which affect the BMR are:

○ Eating, after a meal energy is required for digestion.
○ With extreme cold the body uses more energy to maintain normal body temperature.
○ Emotional stress can alter our BMR as can prolonged anxiety.
○ Regular exercise will increase the basal metabolic rate.
○ Thyroid hormones control the rate of metabolism. Too much hormone speeds up metabolism and too little slows it down.

Exercise therefore is important and choosing the right type to suit age, health and lifestyle will ensure success. *Any calorie expenditure which exceeds calorie intake will result in the extra calories coming from the fat stores.* Combining aerobic exercise with cardiovascular training is an ideal combination and a good target to aim for is three periods of exercise for up to 30 minutes every week. As fitness levels increase the amount and type of exercise can be reassessed.

In conclusion, if the amount of fat in the diet is reduced, a healthy well balanced diet is followed, choosing a good selection of food from all four food groups, in particular carbohydrates and a regular amount of exercise is taken then weight loss will result.

Contraindications to diet and exercise

A diet and exercise programme should not be started without consulting a doctor in the following circumstances if:

○ You are under 18.
○ You are pregnant or breast feeding.
○ You have a medical condition for which you are receiving treatment.
○ You are suffering from or have previously suffered from an eating disorder such as anorexia nervosa, bulimia nervosa or compulsive eating disorder.
○ You are clinically obese.
○ You are clinically underweight.

Helpful tips

To make sure that a diet or healthy eating programme works, there are several things that can be done:

○ Start a diet on a convenient day which fits in with your routine.
○ Plan a week ahead so you have a shopping list of essentials and meals are planned.
○ Stock up on healthy low fat foods.
○ Eat regular meals without snacking.
○ Take time over meals, enjoy them and do not eat in a hurry.

Wonder diets

There are many different 'fad' diets on the market which guarantee massive weight loss but they tend to concentrate on eating a small selection of food instead of eating a well-balanced and healthy diet. They may achieve rapid results as they are usually 'starvation' diets, cutting the calorie intake so drastically that you are bound to lose weight. In the long term, however, the weight is soon put back on and the body may be deprived of essential nutrients in the process.

There are disadvantages to most of these diets:

High protein diet

A diet high in protein, for example meat, milk and cheese also contains saturated fat and this is known to increase the cholesterol level in the blood, which is bad for the health.

These foods are also low in fibre which is essential to a healthy diet as fibre provides bulk and satisfies the appetite, as well as being low in calories and aiding elimination.

High fat diet/low carbohydrate

This diet normally suggests that weight is lost through the cutting out of carbohydrates, this leaves proteins and fats only to be eaten, making the diet quite high in fat. This increase in fat consumption will increase the level of cholesterol in the blood, which is bad for health and well-being.

Fats contain more calories weight for weight than other foods.

Low calorie powders

These are chemical substitutes for meals and when mixed with water, provide a very low-calorie intake per day. This is usually in the region of 350–400 calories a day, far below the normal requirements of the body and should only be used on a doctor's advice.

Special diet foods

These are usually over-refined and over-processed foods which contain artificial chemicals. It is far better for the general health of the body to eat natural wholesome foods in the correct proportions.

Alternative methods of losing weight

Tablets

These are freely available to buy over the counter and it is recommended that they are taken a short period before eating. They are made from methyl-cellulose or glucose. The former swells up in the stomach and takes the edge off the appetite. This may be achieved in a far more natural way by eating food with a high fibre content. The latter is also said to reduce the appetite but a piece of fruit eaten before a meal would have a similar effect.

Drugs

Doctors may prescribe drugs to suppress the appetite but they often have side effects which outweigh the benefits. These would only be recommended by a doctor if being overweight was a risk to the person's health.

Slimming clubs

The advantage of a club is the motivation that is received from other members who all have the same problem. In some cases when enthusiasm is waning it can be motivating to chat to others and the support, advice and encouragement they can give can help achieve targets.

The club may also provide advice about maintaining the weight loss when the target figure has been reached. Having weight loss monitored weekly provides the incentive to persevere as it can be embarrassing to admit defeat in front of others.

The disadvantage of a slimming club is that the diet may not always be the best one for the individual.

Eating disorders

Anorexia nervosa

This is a disorder which is characterized by a loss of appetite as well as some bizarre eating habits. It is self-imposed starvation, usually subconscious. It is thought to be an emotional response to conflicts of self-identity and a reluctance to accept becoming an adult. It is a problem which seems to affect mainly young females but there is increasing evidence that it is also affecting adolescent boys. The effects of this condition are:

○ Progressive starvation.
○ Massive weight loss.
○ Absence of menstruation.
○ Lowered basal metabolic rate.
○ Depression.

The result of this condition is emaciation of the body through starvation which can in some cases cause death.

Treatment of this condition is usually psychotherapy and the re-education in eating habits, with additional nutritional advice.

Bulimia

Bulimia may also be referred to as *binge-purge syndrome*. It is characterized by over-eating on a grand scale and then forced vomiting or overuse of strong laxatives. The problem often occurs because of a fear of being overweight, during periods of depression and stress, or because of physiological disorders such as hypothalamic tumours. The effects of this condition can be:

○ Electrolyte imbalance.
○ Hormone imbalance.
○ Dry skin.
○ Acne.
○ Muscle spasms.
○ Loss of hair.
○ Tooth decay.
○ Ulcers and hernias.
○ An increased susceptibility to flu and salivary gland infections.
○ Constipation.

Treatment will include psychotherapy, medical treatment and nutritional advice.

Obesity

This may be defined as a body weight 10 to 20 per cent above a desirable standard as a result of an excessive accumulation of fat. The problems related to obesity are:

○ Increased mortality.
○ High blood pressure.
○ High levels of cholesterol in the blood.
○ Increased risk of coronary heart disease.
○ Stress on joints.
○ Varicose veins.
○ Difficulties with movement.
○ Difficulties in seating, for example planes.
○ Feelings of unhappiness and inadequacy.

The causes of obesity may be metabolic, resulting from a disorder that reduces the catabolism of fats and carbohydrates, or quite simply eating far more food than the body requires, and inactivity. The treatment would be to lose body fat without the breakdown of lean tissue, maintaining some sort of exercise regime and establishing healthy eating habits.

24 Exercise

Exercising the body

Figure shapes may be improved by diet, which will help in removing fatty deposits stored in the subcutaneous layer of the skin, and by using forms of electrical treatment to tone and firm muscles or improve a cellulite condition. However, exercise also helps to re-shape the body by firming and toning muscles, as well as having other benefits which will contribute to the overall health and well-being of the client.

Benefits of exercise

○ It increases the circulation.
○ It increases the oxygen intake.
○ It firms, tones and strengthens the muscles.
○ It increases joint mobility.
○ It increases flexibility and suppleness.
○ It aids in relaxation.
○ It improves posture.

Exercise is therefore an excellent way in which to tone all the systems of the body and is most effective when used in conjunction with diet and salon treatments.

To ensure that the exercise recommended is appropriate for the client, it is important initially to choose the correct type of exercise. The points to consider are:

○ The age of the client.
○ The temperament of the client.
○ The client's figure and weight.
○ What skills the client may have.
○ The client's own particular preference.
○ The client's overall fitness.

Maintaining client interest

To encourage the client to participate fully in some form of exercise the therapist must:

○ Make sure the form of exercise chosen is effective, producing results and maintaining the client's interest.
○ Make the exercise routine easy to understand and follow.
○ Make sure that it is within the client's capabilities as asking clients to do something which is too difficult for them will result in their giving up, or possibly cause them an injury.
○ Start and finish a routine with easy exercises.
○ Change routines or forms of exercise as clients progress, again to maintain their interest and to accommodate their increasing strength, fitness and endurance.
○ When objectives have been achieved, change to a maintenance plan to prevent problems recurring.

Safety when exercising

If clients are overweight or have any medical problems such as high blood pressure, diabetes or heart condition it is advisable for them to have a medical check first.

After consuming a meal or a snack, allow at least two hours after eating before starting any exercise.

Wear the correct clothing. Clothes should be loose-fitting and comfortable, with supportive shoes.

Always warm up before exercising to improve performance. Warm muscles respond more quickly, increasing the speed at which they contract and relax, as well as being able to increase the force of the contraction. Failure to do this may lead to a torn muscle. The muscles most likely to tear are the antagonists, the opposing muscles to the agonists, the group that produces the movement. To be most effective warming up exercises must include movements for all muscle groups and all parts of the body.

Do not perform exercises using the same muscle group repeatedly as this could over-work an area. Build up gradually and slowly without pushing the body beyond its limit and trying to achieve too much too soon.

Always cool down after exercising and stretch the muscles gently to prevent stiffness. This will keep extra blood flowing through the muscles, helping to disperse waste products such as lactic acid, a by-product of exercise which can cause stiffness.

Stop exercising if there is any pain or giddiness.

The effects of exercise on the body

The overall effect when exercising regularly is a feeling of well-being that is achieved after a very short time. It will also increase energy levels, stamina and strength.

Energy is improved by the increase of physical activity dispersing adrenalin, which causes tiredness and lethargy and is produced by the body as a result of physical and emotional stress. Exercise burns off the excess adrenalin and increases energy levels.

Circulation is improved because of the increased activity having a pumping action on the blood vessels and pushing the blood towards the heart. The lymphatic circulation is also improved, removing waste products more efficiently.

The *heart* is a muscle and through regular exercise it becomes stronger as it is made to work harder, faster and more efficiently.

Muscles increase in tone and strength, as regular exercise causes the muscle fibres to increase in size. The blood supply to the muscles is increased which provides nourishment and oxygen. The elasticity and suppleness of the muscles is also improved.

Bones are nourished and fed through exercise and mobility in the joints is increased.

Respiration is increased allowing more oxygen in and carbon dioxide to be expelled.

Metabolism is increased which will help those clients who wish to lose weight.

Tension is relieved, promoting general relaxation and improving the ability to sleep.

Muscle action

The action of the muscle is by contraction. The muscle fibres contract to exert a force when they are stimulated to do so by the central nervous system. The more fibres that are stimulated the shorter the muscle will become and the stronger the contraction will be.

The muscle cells contain thousands of mitochondria which receive the oxygen coming to the muscle and it is then released to help keep the muscle working.

Prime movers
These are the muscles in a group which make the greatest contribution to the movement.

Antagonists
These are the opposite muscles which relax to allow the movement of the prime movers.

Stabilizers
These are muscles which work to stabilize the ends of other muscles so that they can work effectively.

Range of movement

When muscles contract they produce movement and the extent of each movement is called the range of movement. The full range of movements is divided into three:

1 *Inner range.* From the middle of a contraction to its most contracted point.
2 *Middle range.* From almost fully stretched to almost fully contracted.
3 *Outer range.* From the middle of a contraction to its most stretched point.

Normal everyday exercises are performed in the middle range. Strengthening exercises are given in the full range with emphasis placed on the outer range.

Types of contraction

Concentric contraction
This is when the muscle actively shortens and thickens and the origin and insertion moves closer together causing the angle at the joint to

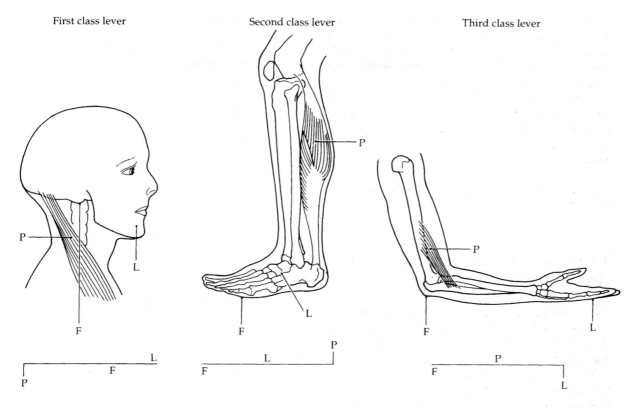

First class lever   Second class lever   Third class lever

Figure 24.1 *Levers*

decrease. It produces heat in the muscles and can be used in all ranges of movement.

Eccentric contraction
This is when the muscle lengthens and the origin and insertion move further away from each other, playing out against a resistance (gravity). Heat is produced in the muscle and it can also be used in all ranges of movement.

Isometric contraction
This is when the muscle contracts becoming harder but does not lengthen or shorten. The tension in the muscle exactly balances the opposing force. This contraction is also called a static contraction. Isometric contraction may be used to begin with when strengthening very weak muscles.

Muscles and leverage

Movement of muscles pulls on the bones to make them move, the muscles using the bones

as levers. The joint which allows the bone to move is called the *fulcrum:*

Power   →   muscles
Lever   →   bones
Fulcrum →   joint
Load   →   weight of the moving part of the body or the combined weight of the body part plus a weight.

There are three classes of lever system in the body (Figure 24.1):

1. When the fulcrum lies between the power and the load.
2. When the load lies between the power and the fulcrum.
3. When the power lies between the fulcrum and the load.

Most levers of the body are in the third class.

Breathing

Whatever the type of exercise undertaken it is important to breathe properly to provide plenty of oxygen for the active muscles.

249

Respiration

The function of the respiratory system is to exchange oxygen and carbon dioxide between the atmosphere and the body. Oxygen is inhaled from the atmosphere to the tissues and carbon dioxide is removed from the tissues and expelled into the atmosphere. This interchange of gases takes place through the walls of the capillaries. Interchange of gases is:

Oxygen absorbed from the air
↓
Into the blood
↓
Oxygen transferred from the blood to the tissues
↓
The tissues give up carbon dioxide to the blood
↓
Carbon dioxide is expelled

The client should be encouraged to breathe deeply throughout the exercise routine. If a particularly energetic routine is carried out which leaves the client breathless then a quiet period should be incorporated into the routine to allow the client to regain her normal breathing pattern.

Benefits of correct breathing

There are three types of breathing:

1 *Apical* or shallow breathing only uses the upper lobe of the lungs and occurs in times of stress, fear or excitement, if the client is asthmatic or has a respiratory disorder.
2 *Lateral* costal uses the upper and middle lobes of the lung. It is deeper and slower and is the type of breathing which occurs naturally interspersed with apical.
3 *Diaphragmatic* uses all the lobes of the lung (the upper, middle and lower). It is deep breathing and used to calm and relax, using the respiratory system effectively.

The main benefits of breathing correctly and using breathing exercises are:

○ Provides oxygen to the tissues.
○ Aids metabolism.

○ Increases resistance to infection of the lungs.
○ Maintains elasticity and strength of the lungs.
○ Improves posture.
○ Reduces stress level, aids relaxation.
○ Increases circulation.
○ Fat is oxidized.
○ Muscles are fed.

Reasons for exercise routines

Exercise routines can be given for different reasons:

○ To increase fitness.
○ To increase mobility.
○ To strengthen the muscles.
○ To correct figure faults.
○ For relaxation.

Fitness

For general fitness a scheme of exercises must be devised to work all muscle groups in the body, without overworking any one area. Explain clearly and demonstrate how to perform each exercise.

Make sure that the client has assumed the correct posture before commencing the exercise routine and start with some simple breathing exercises.

The general routine should follow a set sequence to include:

1 Warming up.
2 Breathing.
3 Head.
4 Shoulders.
5 Arms.
6 Waist.
7 Trunk and spine.
8 Abdominal muscles.
9 Legs.
10 Buttocks.
11 Breathing.
12 Cooling down.

Mobility

Mobility exercises are incorporated into most general exercise routines but are often required for an older client to gently stretch and mobilize the muscles before progressing to different types of exercise. The effects of these exercises are to loosen the body and make it more supple enabling the client to progress further. Mobility exercises should be performed fairly quickly in a relaxed manner, without static contractions and the parts being exercised should be moved through as full a range as possible.

Strength

Strengthening exercises are used to build up muscle strength, or to correct figure faults and weakness. The muscles are contracted against a resistance, increasing muscle fibres. Isometric exercises can be used with contractions being held for several seconds and the time increased as the muscle strengthens. The resistance may be increased by using weights while performing the exercises. It is essential to warm up before strength training and also to breathe correctly. The resistance to the contraction must not be extreme, it is more sensible to build up slowly and prevent injury occurring. Sessions should be three times a week and the duration will depend on the physical fitness of the client. Once the required muscle strength has been achieved exercise sessions are only necessary once a week for maintenance.

Large muscle groups should be exercised first as the smaller groups become fatigued far more quickly. The sequence should not include exercising the same muscle group consecutively as this will cause muscle fatigue.

Correction of figure faults

These problems can be caused by some muscles becoming very weak or too strong. Corrective exercises to shorten and strengthen the weak muscles, and mobilizing exercises for the stronger over-contracted muscles should be given. Static muscle contractions can often improve generally poor posture quite quickly.

Correction of figure faults with exercise

Figure fault	Aim of exercise
Lordosis	Strengthen abdominal muscles and hip extensors. Stretch erector spinae and quadratus lumborum.
Kyphosis	Strengthen middle fibres of trapezius, rhomboids and erector spinae. Stretch pectoralis major.
Scoliosis	Strengthen the muscles on the outside of the curve. Stretch the muscles on the inside of the curve and balance between the two.
Flat back	Strengthen the erector spinae muscles, abdominals and gluteus maximus. Stretch the hamstrings.
Flabby upper arms	Strengthen triceps and reduce fat through aerobic exercise.
Winged scapula	Strengthen serratus anterior and lower fibres of trapezius.
Flabby gluteals	Strengthen gluteus maximus, hamstrings and abductors. Stretch the hip flexors.
Flat feet	Increase mobility and strength.

Contraindications to exercise

○ Heart conditions or history of heart disease.
○ High blood pressure. If the condition is controlled by medication, seek a doctor's approval.
○ Arteriosclerosis.
○ Respiratory conditions.
○ Embolism.
○ Obesity.
○ Recent injury – sprains, strains, fractures, torn or ruptured ligaments.
○ Infections of any kind, for example chicken pox, tonsillitis, measles.
○ Inflamed joints, for example rheumatoid arthritis.
○ Acute fevers such as glandular fever, flu or a bad cold.
○ Neurological disorders, for example multiple sclerosis.
○ Painful joints or muscles.
○ Pregnancy exercise should be controlled and gentle.

○ After a heavy meal or consumption of alcohol.

If in doubt the client must seek advice from their doctor. It is advisable to have a medical check before embarking on a course of exercise if there is any family medical history, if the client is over 40, diabetic, asthmatic, or a heavy smoker.

Preparation of exercise area

Providing individual exercise advice will normally be carried out in the privacy of a treatment room or an exercise room. The client must be informed of the correct clothing to wear and all the equipment required should be close at hand.

○ Ensure the room is warm and there is adequate ventilation.
○ Ensure there is sufficient lighting.
○ Flooring should be non-slip and if possible sprung to prevent impact on the joints.
○ Ensure there is adequate space for movement.
○ Provide an exercise mat for client comfort.
○ Provide water for the client after exercise to replenish lost fluid.

Providing advice

A consultation must be carried out to discuss the client's requirements, assess the client's posture, body shape and problem areas, complete a record card and evaluate treatment.

A scheme of exercises can then be planned to suit the requirements of the client, this may be a general keep fit programme, an aid to weight reduction or exercises for specific problems. A general exercise plan will include:

○ A warm up.
○ Breathing exercise.
○ Arm mobility.
○ Leg mobility.
○ Head and neck mobility.
○ Trunk mobility.
○ Abdominal exercise.
○ Waist exercise.

○ Back exercise.
○ Arm exercise.
○ Leg exercise.
○ Postural correction.
○ Breathing exercise.
○ A cool down.

Demonstration and performance

It is important that clients understand what is expected of them and that each exercise is performed correctly for maximum benefit. Therefore, instructions and demonstration must be accurate and easy to follow:

○ Demonstrate each exercise and give clear instructions to clients as they attempt the exercise themselves.
○ Help them to position themselves correctly.
○ Observe and correct the exercise.
○ Increase or decrease the difficulty if necessary.
○ When clients are familiar with the exercise, brief commands only are necessary.

Progression of exercises

As clients become fitter, or find the exercises too easy then the exercise routine can be altered or made more difficult by:

○ Changing the starting position or making it smaller.
○ Increasing the repetition of each exercise.
○ Increasing the resistance by using weights, pulleys or manual resistance.
○ Increasing the duration of the whole exercise routine.
○ Lengthening the lever, for example straightening an arm or leg or holding a weight.
○ Altering the speed of the exercise.

Starting positions

The position of the client for each exercise is important for good posture. It is also important in achieving maximum effect from the exercise and to suit the capabilities of each client (Figure 24.2).

Prone lying   Crook lying   Side lying

Long sitting   Crook sitting   Astride sitting   Side sitting

Stride standing   Walk standing   Step standing   Toe standing

Stoop standing   Lax stoop standing   Prone kneeling   Inclined prone kneeling

Half kneeling   Stride hanging   Knee bend hanging

Figure 24.2   *Starting positions*

There are five starting positions which will be stated at the beginning of each exercise and they may be modified to increase or decrease the difficulty of an exercise.

Starting position	Modification
Lying	Prone
	Crook with knees bent
	Side
Sitting	Long
	Crook
	Astride
	Side
Standing	Stride
	Walk
	Step
	Stoop
	Lax stoop
	Toe
Kneeling	Prone
	Half
	Inclined prone
Hanging	Stride
	Knee bend

Stress

Stress is a psychological pressure and tension is the body's response to this pressure, an increasingly common problem as the pace of life increases. In small amounts stress is a normal part of life and it can be stimulating, but when stress changes to distress it becomes a negative and destructive force. It is bad when:

○ It seems to be continuous with no relapse.
○ It makes you feel out of control.
○ It disrupts normal everyday living.
○ It has an effect on personal relationships.

Factors causing pressure will not lead to stress for everyone but it will depend on:

○ The amount of pressure involved.
○ How each particular individual deals with the pressure.
○ How long the stress lasts for.
○ The personality of the individual.
○ The amount of support they are receiving.

Effects of stress

The damaging effects of stress are not just psychological but also physiological because stress causes the release of the hormone adrenaline into the bloodstream which prepares the body for 'fight or flight'. When this is happening over a period of time the adrenaline released into the body has an adverse reaction causing physical problems to occur. Emotional trauma, anger and anxiety caused by stress can be transformed into physical ailments with symptoms such as:

○ Fatigue.
○ Depression.
○ Insomnia.
○ Dizziness.
○ Feeling flushed.
○ Pins and needles.
○ Pounding heart.
○ Heart palpitations.
○ Tight feeling in the chest.
○ Dry mouth.
○ Abdominal pain.
○ Nausea.

○ Diarrhoea.
○ Headaches.
○ Backache.
○ Neck pain.

Physiological response to stress

Stress affects several systems of the body.

Body system	Physiological response
Circulatory	The heart rate is increased. Body temperature increases. Sweating occurs.
Respiratory	Breathing becomes more rapid and more shallow.
Digestive	Production of saliva slows down. Butterflies in the stomach. Bowel stimulation.
Muscular	Tension is increased and nodules form.

Coping with stress

Chronic stress can be linked to heart disease, high blood pressure, disorders of the immune system, allergies, asthma, eczema, irritable bowel syndrome and it can also have an ageing effect on the skin.

Stress must be recognized and dealt with effectively to maintain a healthy body and mind.

The realization that stress is adversely affecting the body is the first step in coping with the problem, then a plan must be drawn up to minimize the effects or eliminate the causes.

○ Assess your current lifestyle and identify the causes of stress.
○ List the causes that you can control.
○ Deal with each one and decide how to overcome the problem.
○ List the causes that are out of your control.
○ Look at the best way to reduce these problems and therefore reduce the stress.
○ Take time to relax. This can be time to sleep, rest and do nothing or a hobby or favourite sport.
○ Take some form of exercise as this will eliminate pent-up energy, oxygenate the blood and burn up excess adrenaline. It also makes you feel good as endorphins are released into the body.

○ Delegate responsibility to others, at work and at home.

Relaxation

Many clients will suffer from stress to a certain degree which causes problems such as tension in the muscles. This in turn leads to aches, pains and headaches. Some clients will eat more when under stress, putting on extra weight. This can adversely affect the joints and reduce energy levels. They may also find it difficult to sleep and become lethargic and generally feel unfit.

The adrenaline produced when under stress has adverse effects on the body, increasing the heartbeat and stimulating the nerves. Excess adrenaline causes a feeling of tiredness and irritability.

It is very important to teach a client how to relax as an antidote to stress, to remove the tension and reduce the anxiety will help in eliminating the harmful side effects of too much stress. Relaxation also helps to conserve energy which is required for important issues. It will also help to concentrate the mind and improve quality of life.

The therapist may use heat therapy, body massage or aromatherapy, physical exercise and teaching relaxation techniques to help the client relax.

To promote relaxation you will need:

○ A warm environment which helps promote physical relaxation.
○ A quiet room with no distractions.
○ Low lighting.
○ Comfortable position suited to the client, supported by pillows.
○ Loose warm cover if required.
○ Relaxation tape playing quietly in the background.

During client consultation you will evaluate the client's stress level and explain what options she will have for relaxation treatment. You may suggest a combination of different forms of relaxation therapy but it must be agreed with the client.

Your manner must be conducive to relaxation and your approach must be calm and relaxed.

Speak quietly with assurance, smile and do not rush the client.

Relaxation techniques

You need to make the client aware of the difference in the feeling of tension and relaxation in the muscles and this may be achieved by teaching the client how to contract and relax the muscles, feeling the tension and then slowly releasing it.

The client will be instructed to contract, tighten and relax individual muscles and muscle groups, working in a sequence from the feet up to the head. Clients will soon learn how to do this themselves with practice.

Procedure

1 Find a suitable location.
2 Prepare clients with suitable clothing, towels or cover.
3 Ensure clients are comfortable, warm and well-supported.
4 Encourage clients to close their eyes and relax.
5 Start with some slow, relaxed, even breathing to calm and reduce adrenaline secretion.
6 Focus the mind on a special place or single thing to slow thoughts down and empty the mind. It could be a quiet beach in an exotic location, lying in a warm snug bed or anywhere or time which has happy memories.
7 Beginning with the feet ask clients to repeat each movement three times.

Breathe in when tightening muscles and out when relaxing them:

○ Pull toes up towards the head (dorsi flexion) and release.
○ Push toes down to the floor (plantar flexion) and release.
○ Push legs into the floor and release.
○ Tighten the gluteal muscles and release.
○ Tighten the abdominal muscles and release.
○ Push the back into the floor and release.
○ Clench the fists and release.
○ Tighten the arm muscles and release.

○ Lift and tighten the shoulders towards the head and release.
○ Press the head into the floor and release.
○ Screw up the eyes and tighten the whole face and release.
○ Tighten all muscles and release.

Allow clients to lie quietly for ten to fifteen minutes. Ask them to practise these techniques at home and suggest further treatment.

Stretching exercise

Stretching the muscles exerts a squeezing effect on the blood, compressing veins and capillaries and moving blood back in the direction of the heart. At the same time waste products are removed more efficiently. Fresh blood enters the muscle bringing with it oxygen and nutrients. Stretching also relieves the tension in the muscles and must be performed slowly and gently while breathing normally. Sessions need only last about twenty minutes and ideally three to five times per week.

Walking

Walking briskly or using an active exercise routine particularly suited to the client can aid relaxation.

Types of exercise

Aerobics

These are exercises that require the efficient use of oxygen by the body throughout the whole exercise routine. The word aerobic means literally 'with air'. This form of exercise works the cardiovascular system (heart, blood vessels and lungs) making it stronger and less vulnerable to heart attack and strokes. See Figure 24.3.

Aerobic activities include:

Swimming
This is an excellent exercise for everybody as it places no strain on any part of the body. It

Figure 24.3 *Types of exercise: aerobics; swimming; skipping*

increases the circulation and lung ventilation, muscles are stretched and firmed as most strokes use all the muscle groups. It is a form of exercise which can be undertaken by people suffering from bad backs, arthritis and even high blood pressure, because the water supports the body, and has a relaxing effect when carried out at the client's own pace. The aerobic effect is achieved when swimming at a fast speed for as long as possible giving the body a very efficient cardiovascular workout.

Jogging

This is a very popular form of exercise, particularly when used as a group exercise. As well as toning and strengthening the muscles, this form of aerobic exercise increases energy levels and the client feels invigorated and healthier. It works the heart and lungs, increasing the stamina of the cardiorespiratory system. This is also an ideal exercise for firming the legs and the gluteal muscles which can be a problem area.

To prevent injury a good pair of running shoes must be worn and it is not advisable to jog on cement as this may cause injury to the foot and leg. A softer surface such as clay is far easier and kinder on the joints. The warm-up exercise period is essential to loosen the muscles. Allow a five-minute cooling down period for the body to slowly return to normal. This prevents lactic acid remaining in the muscles and causing discomfort.

Cycling

This also provides an excellent cardiovascular workout and strengthens the muscles of the back and legs.

Skipping

This benefits the heart and lungs and improves the figure as it tones the muscles of the arms, buttocks, thighs, hips and calfs as well as firming the pectorals. Skipping to music makes it more interesting. To prevent wear and tear on the joints wear a supportive pair of running shoes.

Brisk walking

This is often a preferred form of exercise for the older client as it is an exercise which can be sustained for fairly long periods even when unfit. It provides a gentle cardiovascular workout. There are many muscles used for walking and these include the foot, leg, back, abdominal and rib, arm, shoulder and neck muscles.

These are all forms of exercise which have a sustained rhythm of movement that puts constant demand on the heart, raising the pulse rate to between 120 and 160 beats a minute. This will help to increase the vigour and stamina of the heart, blood vessels and lungs. The general effects of aerobics are:

○   Improves the circulation.
○   Tones the muscles.
○   Strengthens bone ligaments and joints.
○   Strengthens the chest wall increasing lung capacity.
○   Increases the efficiency of the heart and blood vessels.
○   Increases overall fitness.
○   Increases energy levels.

Isotonics

These exercises produce movement in muscles and joints causing lengthening and shortening of the muscles. They are free active exercises and make up a large part of a general exercise routine.

The general effects are:

○   Development of muscle strength.
○   Toning of muscles.
○   Joint mobility.
○   Development of flexibility and suppleness.
○   Improvement in respiration.
○   Increased circulation.
○   Energy is utilized.

Isometrics

These are exercises which contract the muscle without producing movement in the joints. This increases the tone without increasing the length of the muscle. These exercises are more suited to people with a mobility problem who are obese or disabled. The muscles contract against a resistance and these exercises can be performed easily anywhere at any time.

The effects are:

○   Increased muscle tone.
○   Muscles are built up.
○   Particular muscles are shaped.
○   Improved muscle stamina.

Aquarobics

This form of exercise is becoming more popular with many people but in particular, older people, pregnant women, those suffering from an arthritic or rheumatic condition or who are unable to participate in other more rigorous forms of exercise. An instructor takes an exercise class with all the participants in the water.

Exercising in the water has several benefits:

○   Strengthens and tones the muscles.
○   Exercises the whole body.
○   Promotes flexibility and balance.
○   Increases cardiovascular fitness.

This provides a safe and invigorating way to work out without putting a strain on the joints.

Yoga

This is a form of exercise which calms the mind as well as improving the suppleness of the body.

Physical or hatha yoga is a series of positions that move all parts of the body improving the general condition. The finished positions should be achieved without causing discomfort. Therefore, the client must stop when it feels natural and comfortable in each position. The movement into the position should be performed slowly and smoothly and then held for several seconds. Each time the movement is repeated the stretch will be slightly greater.

The extreme gentleness of yoga makes this form of exercise ideal for someone who cannot take active exercise or older people who want to increase suppleness of the body.

This type of exercise is in fact suited to most people and it can have many uses:

○   To improve the general condition.
○   To learn how to relax.
○   To remove muscular tension.
○   To improve figure shape.

○ To strengthen the body.
○ To improve concentration.
○ To improve circulation.
○ To improve balance and posture.
○ To improve mobility.
○ To create a feeling of well-being.

Other forms of exercise

Multigym

This is a set of scientifically designed exercise equipment to exercise different parts of the body. The client will move from one piece of the equipment to the next, following a personalized exercise programme.

The adjustable weights and resistance factors of each piece of equipment make the multigym ideal for clients with varying degrees of fitness.

The multigym offers several pieces of exercise equipment fitted into a relatively small space. Therefore, it is an ideal addition to a salon that wishes to offer this service.

Toning tables

These have become popular in recent years in beauty salons as an addition to the body treatment range already on offer.

They are fitness machines in the form of a table that exercises different parts of the body. Tables may be used as a set, with each table performing one particular exercise on one part of the body. Alternatively, one table can combine up to twelve exercises in one table. This is ideal for a small salon lacking in space.

The exercises are isometric, toning the body and increasing flexibility. They are suitable for all age groups and levels of fitness as the body is supported by the table and exercise can be taken without causing fatigue.

25 *Floatation tank therapy*

Floatation therapy treatment

This is a relatively new form of treatment which is used for total relaxation of the body and the mind. It could have been included in the section on heat and hydrotherapy but this treatment is quite different in application and effect from the more well-known forms of heat or hydrotherapy. It should therefore be in a category of its own, as the chief aim is to relax the client and provide an antidote to the stresses and strains of a busy life.

The tank was pioneered in America in the 1950s by Doctor John Lilly, an American neuroscientist who was then based at the National Institute of Mental Health in Maryland. It is now a very popular form of relaxation in America and there are also hundreds of floatation tank centres in France and Japan.

There are several outlets in this country which offer floatation tank therapy but they are mostly natural health centres rather than health and beauty establishments. The value of this form of relaxation is now being seriously considered by the more informed members of the beauty profession.

The floatation tank

It is made of fibreglass, rectangular in structure with sides, a roof and a door, and it is about the size of a bed. The tank contains approximately twelve inches of concentrated salt water that is heated to body temperature, which allows the body to float effortlessly.

To ensure privacy, each floatation tank should be in its own room with a shower. A quiet room or area should be available for the use of the client after using the tank.

All first time floaters are given clear and thorough instructions in the use of the tank, with particular reference to any fears the client may have which may prevent the treatment being totally relaxing. See Figure 25.1.

Before treatment

It is necessary to take a shower before treatment for hygiene reasons. Earplugs need to be used to protect the ear canals from filling with water. These are the only preparations required before entering the tank and floating effortlessly on the surface of the water.

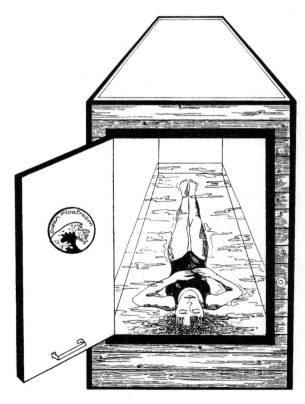

Figure 25.1 *A floatation tank*
Courtesy Float System International of London

Sometimes quite soothing music is played for several minutes at the beginning of the treatment, providing time to acclimatize to the total darkness and losing all sense of space and time.

Treatment time

This is normally one hour, time enough for the body to relax completely. Most people emerge feeling as though they have had a good night's sleep and others do fall asleep. The end of the treatment may be indicated gently to the client, who has probably lost all track of time, by the music being played again for several minutes.

After treatment

A shower should be taken to remove all the salt from the body and the client may then sit or lie in the quiet area before leaving.

Benefits of floating

Easing pain

The dense salt solution provides the body with bouyancy and eliminates the body's specific gravity. This allows the floater to experience almost total weightlessness and provides relief from bad backs, aching feet, painful joints and muscular tension.

Relaxation

The brain produces slower brain waves during a float and these are known as *theta waves*, normally only experienced during deep meditation or while under hypnosis. This is total relaxation and is almost immediate. As floating frees the brain, muscular system and the skeletal system from gravity, vast amounts of energy are available to deal with matters of the mind.

An increased sense of well-being

It has been indicated by research that floating can reduce blood pressure and heart rate. It can also reduce the levels of stress-related chemicals in the body such as adrenalin and cortisol which cause tension, irritability and anxiety. Conversely, the body produces more beta endorphins, the body's natural opiates, which have a soothing effect and create a sense of well-being which can last for some time after floating. Therefore the more regularly you float the more cumulative the effect.

Contraindications

It is not advisable for anyone who is claustrophobic to enter a float tank because of the confined space. However, the door does not have to be shut but may be left open during treatment, which may help some sufferers.

Epileptics will not be allowed the use of a float tank unless they are under medication and have permission from their doctor.

Anyone who has consumed alcohol should not use a float tank.

Sanitation

○ The tank rooms and shower facilities must be cleaned between uses.

○ The complete volume of water must be filtered between uses and the level of the water must be checked daily.

○ The condition of the water and the tank must be monitored between uses. The water must at all times be free from scum, oils and hair etc.

○ The temperature of the water must be checked between uses.

○ The pH of the water must be checked daily – the correct pH being 7.6.

○ The inside of the tank above the solution line must be cleaned weekly or more often if necessary.

○ The specific gravity of the water must be checked at least once a week – the acceptable range is 1.22 to 1.28.

○ The bromine level of the water must be checked daily – the reading should be no higher than 2 ppm.

o The tank will be tested for purity on a regular basis either by the local Environmental Health Department or by an outside laboratory.

The Floatation Tank Association

The Floatation Tank Association provide full training in floatation tank therapy to include:

o Client care.

o Equipment care.
o Marketing.
o Day-to-day running of a floatation tank centre.

Certain standards have to be maintained in the quality of equipment and the service offered by the manufacturers of the float tank. The Floatation Tank Association will provide this information and they may be contacted at 3A Elms Crescent, London SW4 8QE.

Part Three   Epilation and the Hair

26 *Electrolysis*

Hair removal methods

Electrolysis is a common term used to describe the permanent removal of unwanted hair. There are several treatments currently available.

The *electrolysis method* of hair removal uses a direct galvanic current (negatively charged) to produce a chemical action which destroys the hair follicle. The chemical process occurs when the galvanic current is applied to tissue salts and moisture contained inside the hair follicle and skin tissue, resulting in the root of the hair being destroyed.

Short-wave diathermy is a method of epilation which has largely superseded the electrolysis method of hair removal. The principle of this method is the application of heat produced by a high frequency short-wave diathermy current to the active hair-producing part of the follicle. This heat is the destructive force used to coagulate or cauterize the cell producing part of the follicle, inhibiting or preventing the growth of a new hair.

The blend method is more commonly used because it combines the more thorough galvanic current with the speed of the short-wave diathermy to produce a most effective method of epilation.

These treatments are discussed fully in Chapters 32 and 33.

The aim of treatment

Whichever method is employed the aim of the treatment is to permanently remove unwanted, superfluous hair without causing damage to the surrounding tissue while maintaining normal skin texture and appearance.

It is important to explain to the client that these results will not be achieved immediately but with regular treatment, the growth of the superfluous hair can be greatly reduced and

hopefully eliminated, depending on the cause of the problem.

Most of the cases which the electrologist has to treat are normal or cosmetic problems which may have only occurred during those times in a woman's life, when her body is changing physiologically and these are:

○ Puberty.
○ Pregnancy.
○ Menopause.

Types of hair

The hair itself is a dead structure composed of a hard durable protein called *keratin*. There are two types of hair and these are:

Lanugo or vellus

This is very soft downy type hair which is hardly visible because it is normally non-pigmented and it is found on most areas of the body. The vellus hair emanates from a lobe of the sebaceous gland which is situated at a shallow depth. Lanugo hair is hair formed on the foetus and then shed soon after birth. The growth rate is very slow, having quite an ineffective papilla and matrix and only if it is stimulated by a topical or systemic condition will it develop into a terminal hair.

Terminal

This is more deep rooted and is coarse, visible hair with well-developed roots, found on such areas as the scalp, the axillae and pubic region.

During puberty terminal hairs develop because of the hormonal changes in the body. In males this will include beard and chest hair as well as hair growth in the axillae and pubic areas. In females this occurs in the axillae and pubic area.

The hair growing on the body is classified as:

Capilli: The head.
Barba: The face.
Supercilia: The eyebrows.
Cilia: The eyelashes.
Vibrissae: The nostrils.
Tragi: The ears.
Hirci: The armpit.
Pubes: Pubic region.

Superfluous hair

An excess of hair which is not abnormal for the age, sex and race of the person involved.

Hypertrichosis

This is a condition when the growth of terminal hair is abnormal and excessive on any area of the body, for the age, sex and race of the person involved.

Hirsutism

This is when the growth of excessive terminal hair appears in the 'adult male sexual pattern' normally caused by the androgens (male hormones) when there is a hormonal imbalance.

The target areas

There are certain areas on the body known as target areas where there will be a growth of hair when stimulated by the androgens, which are male hormones.

As a woman's body produces these hormones in much smaller quantities, under normal circumstances, she does not develop hair in all the target areas, unlike the male.

There are occasions, however, during puberty, pregnancy and menopause, when there may be an increase in androgens which will result in the production of excess hair in these target areas.

The hair development in each individual will vary according to the hereditary sensitivity of the hair germ cells to the androgens (Figure 26.1).

Causes of superfluous hair

○ An increase in blood supply to the existing hair will provide nourishment and encourage growth of the already established hair, turning a vellus hair into a terminal hair.
○ Hormones also have the capacity to stimulate existing hair growth and also to create new growth, depending on the sensitivity of the hair germ cells in a particular area.

Normal congenital

The type and amount of hair growth could be hereditary or racial as problems with superfluous hair can be passed on genetically from the parents.

There are also some races who tend to be naturally more hairy than others, for example Italians, Spaniards, Greeks, Syrians or Hebrews tend to be more hairy than Scandinavians or the British, and the Orientals and American Indians are the least hairy of all.

Abnormal congenital

Congenital hypertrichosis is rare and results from an abnormality in the genes. It may be present at birth or appear later in life. The excess hair can sometimes cover the person from head to toe.

Topical causes

Sustained irritation to the epidermis is seen as a potential threat because it will cause a defensive reaction by the body. The blood supply to the area is increased, therefore the hairs growing in the follicles will receive increased nourishment accelerating their growth.

The hairs in the area of irritation will be stimulated to grow coarser and deeper, creating a protective covering on the skin, against further irritation.

Plucking the hairs with tweezers removes the hair from the follicle and re-growth takes longer than with other methods of removal, such as shaving or depilatory creams. However, blood supply is stimulated, which will eventually cause accelerated growth of the plucked hair.

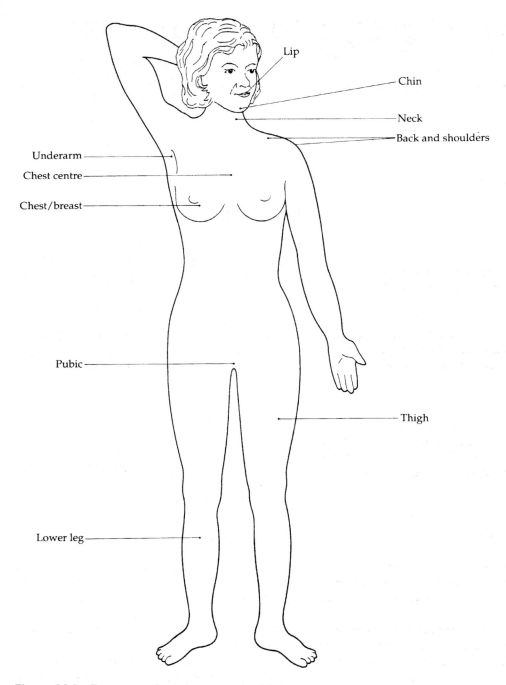

Figure 26.1 *Target areas for androgen stimulated hair growth*

Drugs

Hair growth can be stimulated when a client is taking steroids for treatment of a medical condition.

Systemic causes

The endocrine system produces hormones which control the growth, development and the metabolic functions of the body. An excess of certain hormones may result in the production of superfluous hair.

During puberty, pregnancy and menopause, normal systemic changes take place which may result in the production of superfluous hair but there are also abnormal causes.

Abnormal causes

Hysterectomy
One or both of the ovaries are removed during this operation, which results in a drop in oestrogen level. This causes an artificial menopause producing exactly the same symptoms which occur with the natural onset of the menopause. One of these symptoms can be the appearance of superfluous hair.

Polycystic ovaries (Stein Leventhal syndrome)
This is a condition where there are multiple cysts in the ovaries producing symptoms which include lack of menstruation, abnormal uterine bleeding, weight gain and, sometimes, infertility and hirsutism.

Treatment for this condition is a surgical operation and drug therapy.

Anorexia nervosa
This condition usually affects younger women when they starve themselves of food because of a desire to lose weight. This results in a hormonal imbalance. The symptoms include cessation of periods and hirsutism mainly of the downy type although some coarse hairs may appear on the face.

Stress
A severe nervous breakdown may cause the body to be suffering extreme stress. During times of crisis the adrenal glands produce large amounts of adrenalin from the adrenal medulla. This increase in activity has an effect on the adrenal cortex which then produces large amounts of androgens which will give rise to an excessive hair growth in target areas.

27   *The endocrine system*

The nervous system of the body controls many of its activities, responding rapidly to various stimuli. Working in conjunction with the nervous system is the endocrine system, which also exercises control in a different way by providing the driving force behind the mental and physical activity, growth and reproduction of humans.

It consists of endocrine or ductless glands which are also referred to as organs of internal secretion as they secrete chemical substances called hormones directly into the bloodstream.

The endocrine glands are composed of millions of cells, each of which makes hormones or chemical messengers which are then transported by the blood to the target cells in the body.

The endocrine system (Figure 27.1) consists of:

○   One pineal gland.
○   One pituitary gland.
○   One thyroid gland.
○   Four parathyroid glands.
○   One thymus gland.
○   Two adrenal glands.
○   Islets of Langerhans in the pancreas.
○   Two ovaries in the female.
○   Two testes in the male.

Some hormones affect most parts of the body and increase the rate of chemical reaction in all of the body's cells, for example growth hormone.

Some hormones only affect certain tissues called 'target' tissues and only these tissues respond to the hormone. This is because these tissues have specific receptors which receive a hormone and so initiate a response.

The endocrine glands

The pineal gland

This is situated in front of the cerebellum and is thought to produce a hormone which inhibits the growth and maturation of the gonads or sex glands until puberty.

The pituitary gland

Also known as the *hypophisis*, this gland is situated at the base of the brain and is often called the master gland because its hormones help to control so many of the other endocrine glands in the body. However, it is known that the *hypothalamus* produces secretions which regulate the pituitary gland.

The gland has two parts, the anterior and posterior lobes. The anterior lobe produces the following hormones:

○   Thyroid stimulating hormone (TSH).
○   Adrenocorticotrophic hormone (ACTH).
○   Somatotrophin or growth hormone (GH).
○   Follicle stimulating hormone (FSH).
○   Luteinising hormone (LH).
○   Prolactin (PRL).

The posterior lobe stores the following hormones produced by the hypothalamus:

○   Vasopressin, antidiuretic hormone (ADH).
○   Oxytocin.

The hypothalamus

This is an area of the brain near the pituitary gland and is the link between the nervous system and the endocrine glands. It has special nerve cells which make releasing factors which act on cells of the anterior pituitary before they can send out their hormones.

The thyroid gland

The thyroid gland has two lobes situated on either side of the windpipe and joined together

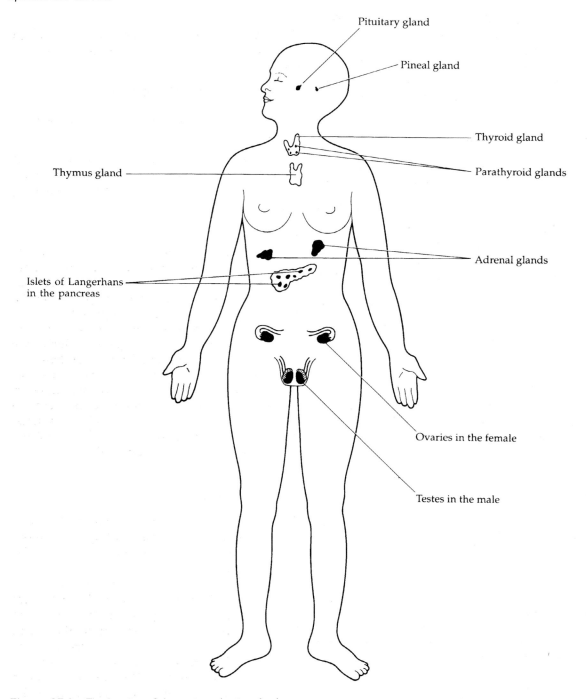

Figure 27.1 *The location of the main endocrine glands*

by a narrow strip of tissue. The thyroid gland is responsible for regulating the body's metabolic rate and influencing the growth of the body. It secretes *thyroxine* which if over secreted (hyper-secretion) causes *hyperthyroidism* or *exophthalmic goitre*. This causes an enlarged thyroid, bulging eyes, rapid pulse, excessive sweating and restlessness.

If there is an under secretion (hyposecretion) it causes *cretinism*, poor mental and physical development in children or *myxoedema* in middle age. The characteristics of the latter condition are a slowing down of metabolism, puffy tissues and a slowness of speech and movement.

The parathyroid glands

There are two pairs situated on the posterior surface of the thyroid gland. These glands together with the thyroid gland regulate the levels of calcium in the blood. The thyroid lowers the amount of calcium and the parathyroid controls calcium metabolism.

When blood calcium levels are high *calcitonin* is released by the thyroid gland and excess calcium is then deposited in the bones.

When blood calcium levels become too low *parathormone* is released by the parathyroids and calcium is reabsorbed.

Thymus gland

This gland lies behind the sternum in front of the heart. It is thought to be important in helping the process of cellular immunity.

The adrenal glands (suprarenal glands)

These glands are situated immediately above the kidneys and each gland consists of two distinct parts, the outer part or *cortex* and the inner core or *medulla*.

The cortex

Secretes hormones called steroids. The most important fall into three main groups:

Mineralocorticoids

The most important of these is *aldosterone* and its functions are:

○ Sodium and chloride retention.
○ Potassium excretion.

The water and electrolyte balance in the body are maintained by these functions.

Glucocorticoids

Cortisone and *hydrocortisone* (cortisol) which assist in the conversion of carbohydrate into glycogen. They:

○ Increase the blood sugar level.
○ Help utilize fat.
○ Suppress the natural reaction to inflammation.

A deficiency in cortisone production can cause the pituitary to stimulate an over-production of adrenal androgens, thereby creating hypertrichosis.

Sex hormones

A small number of both *androgens* (male hormones) and *oestrogens* (female hormones) are secreted. They are influential in sexual development and growth but are not as important as the sex hormones produced by the gonads.

In females, however, the adrenals are the principal source of androgens, which are capable of stimulating facial and body hair.

Under-secretion of adrenal cortex hormones causes *Addison's disease*. The characteristics of this disease are low blood pressure, an excessive loss of salt, dehydration, muscle weakness, increased pigmentation of the skin, menstrual disturbances and loss of body hair.

The medulla

The medulla secretes *adrenalin* and *noradrenalin*. They are known as the 'fight or flight' hormones because they prepare the body to cope with danger or stress.

A surge of adrenalin when the body faces danger or excitement causes the heart to beat faster and more strongly, which then raises the blood pressure. At the same time the blood vessels constrict and blood is diverted to the muscles and heart where it is most needed.

The liver is stimulated to convert glycogen into glucose supplying the muscles with the necessary fuel to provide extra energy.

The pancreas

This gland is in the abdomen and is attached to the duodenum by the pancreatic duct. It is an endocrine gland secreting insulin and also an exocrine gland as the pancreatic juice is secreted directly into the intestine to aid digestion and not into the bloodstream.

The islets of Langerhans are cells in the pancreas which secrete *insulin* necessary for controlling the sugar level in the body. A deficiency of insulin results in *diabetes mellitus*.

The gonads

These are the sex glands which in males are testes and in females are ovaries.

The testes secrete androgens, the most important one being *testosterone* and *oestrogen* in small amounts. Testosterone is the hormone responsible for the development of the secondary sexual characteristics of the male, such as the distribution of hair, deepening of the voice and enlargement of genitalia.

The ovaries produce ova and secrete the hormones *oestrogen* and *progesterone* and small amounts of androgens. They regulate menstruation and play an important part in the development of secondary sexual characteristics.

Progesterone's principal function is to initiate changes in the endometrium, the lining of the womb in preparation for pregnancy.

Many glands in the endocrine system can affect the stimulation of facial and body hair directly or indirectly.

Only androgens have the ability to stimulate hair growth on the face or body directly, therefore any appearances of hair in these areas can be traced to a systemic imbalance where there is an increase in the production of androgens.

Hormones and their actions

Hormones	Actions
Pituitary gland (AL)	
Thyroid stimulating hormone (TSH)	Controls the growth of the thyroid gland and stimulates hormones including the secretion of thyroxine. Secretion is controlled by the hypothalamus and it affects the body's metabolism.
Adrenocorticotrophic hormone (ACTH)	Stimulates the adrenal gland to produce cortisol, provides

Hormones	Actions
	negative feedback to the hypothalamus when hormone levels drop, stimulates the production of other steroids, excess causes overproduction of androgens.
Somatotrophin or growth hormone (GH)	Causes cells to grow and multiply, increases the rate of protein synthesis and fat and carbohydrate metabolism.
Follicle stimulating hormone (FSH)	Initiates the development of the ova in the female and stimulates the secretion of female sex hormones. In the male it stimulates the testes to produce sperm.
Luteinizing hormone (LH)	Stimulates the ovary to release the ovum in the female and prepares the uterus to receive the fertilized egg, stimulates formation of the corpus luteum in the ovary and secretion of oestrogen and progesterone. In the male it stimulates the testes to produce testosterone.
Prolactin (PRL)	Initiates and maintains milk production in the mammary glands.
Melanocyte stimulating hormone (MSH)	Stimulates the dispersal of melanin in the melanocytes
Pituitary gland (PL)	
Oxytocin	Stimulates the contraction of the uterus and milk flow after birth.
Vasopressin (ADH)	This is an antidiuretic hormone which decreases urine volume.
Thyroid gland	
Thyroxine	Regulates metabolism, growth and development and activity of the nervous system.
Triiodothyronine	Regulates metabolism, growth and development and activity of the nervous system.
Calcitonin	Lowers levels of calcium in the blood by accelerating the absorption of calcium by the bones.
Parathyroid	
Parathormone	Controls the balance of calcium and phosphate in the blood, increases the rate of calcium absorption into the blood from the gastro-intestinal tract and activates vitamin D.

Hormones	Actions
Adrenal cortex	
Mineralocorticoids (aldosterone)	Increases the levels of sodium and water in the blood and decreases the levels of potassium, maintaining water balance in the body.
Glucocorticoids (cortisol)	Help promote normal metabolism, resistance to stress and counter inflammatory response.
Sex hormones	Influential in sexual development, insignificant in the adult, only small quantities of oestrogens and androgens are produced.
Adrenal medulla	
Adrenaline (epinephrine)	Helps the body resist stress, increases blood pressure by increasing heart rate and constricting blood vessels, accelerates respiration, decreases the rate of digestion, increases blood sugar level and makes the muscles work more efficiently.
Noradrenalin (norepinephrine)	Less potent in action than adrenaline but the effects are the same.
Pancreas	
Insulin	Lowers blood sugar levels by transporting glucose (sugar) into the body cells converting it into glycogen. Stimulates protein synthesis and inhibits the breakdown of fats.
Glucagon	Raises blood sugar levels converts glycogen in the liver into glucose which is then released into the bloodstream.
The ovaries	
Oestrogen	Develops and maintains female sexual characteristics and fat distribution. Regulates the menstrual cycle, maintains pregnancy and prepares the mammary glands for lactation
Progesterone	Prepares the lining of the uterus for pregnancy, develops the placenta and prepares mammary glands for lactation.
The testes	
Testosterone	Stimulates the development and maintenance of the male sexual characteristics, hair growth on the body, enlargement of the larynx, production of sperm etc.

Normal systemic causes of superfluous hair

Puberty

When puberty is reached, and this varies greatly from person to person, large amounts of hormones are secreted into the bloodstream.

The hypothalamus sends a releasing factor to the anterior lobe of the pituitary gland. The pituitary gland responds by:

○ Secreting gonadotrophic hormones which stimulate the ovaries to produce oestrogen.
○ Secreting adrenocorticotrophic hormones which stimulate the adrenal cortex to produce androgens.

The oestrogens and androgens are balanced and the secondary sexual characteristics develop.

The androgens are responsible for the production of hair in the target areas. If there is an excess of androgens and a hereditary sensitivity to the androgens then excess hair may develop.

If the correct balance of oestrogens and androgens is restored after puberty then the superfluous hair will probably disappear.

Pregnancy

Large amounts of oestrogen are secreted by the ovaries during pregnancy and there will be an increase in androgens to maintain the balance. Any excessive hair growth usually affects the upper lip, chin and sides of the face and it is only accelerated vellus hair which if it is not tampered with will probably disappear after childbirth.

Menopause

This is when menstruation ceases completely but there are several years leading up to this when the functions of the ovaries slow down. The fall in oestrogen secretion can cause many physiological changes:

○ Hot flushes.
○ Palpitations.

○ Anxiety.
○ Irritability.
○ Fatigue.
○ Lack of concentration.
○ Osteoporosis.

Some women may find superfluous hair appearing mainly in the area of the upper chin and lip. This occurs when functions of the ovaries slow down and they are less responsive to the gonadotrophic hormone, therefore there is a decrease in the amount of oestrogens being secreted.

The drop in oestrogen causes the hypothalamus to respond by secreting the releasing factor to the anterior lobe of the pituitary gland.

The pituitary gland then secretes the gonadotrophic hormones which stimulate the ovaries to produce more oestrogen but there is a reduced response from the ovaries because of the slowing down of the functions. The pituitary gland also secretes the adrenocorticotrophic hormone which in turn stimulates the adrenal cortex to secrete more androgens.

The normal balance has been lost and there is the possibility of excessive hair growth depending on the amount of androgens that are produced and the hereditary sensitivity of the hair germ cells.

Endocrine disorders which cause excessive hair growth

There are occasions when an endocrine imbalance resulting from a disease or disorder, which will require medical treatment, produces hypertrichosis.

Once the problem has been medically diagnosed and treatment has begun to remove the underlying cause, the electrologist may begin to treat the hair problem with the permission of the doctor.

An endocrine disorder usually occurs from:

○ A defect of the endocrine system inherited from either parent.
○ A disease or an infection.
○ A tumour.
○ An injury.

Cushing's syndrome

The word syndrome refers to a combination of several symptoms or characteristics of a disease. Cushing's syndrome is a collection of symptoms caused by adrenal over-activity as a response to:

○ Excessive cell development of the adrenal cortex.
○ A tumour of the adrenal cortex.
○ A tumour of the anterior pituitary.
○ Administration of steroids, cortisone or hydrocortisone.

If the adrenal cortex is over-active it will produce excessive amounts of hormones, including androgens.

An excessive amount of mineralocorticoids, in particular aldosterone, results in water retention.

An excessive amount of glucocorticoids, cortisol can result in obesity in the face, neck and trunk, thin slender limbs which fracture easily, muscle weakness and thin easily bruised skin with purple striae (stretch marks) over the abdomen and thighs.

An excessive amount of sex hormones, in particular androgens, causes cessation of menstruation and hair growth on the face.

Adrenogenital syndrome

This condition arises from the over-production of androgens by the adrenal cortex. It may be congenital, appearing from birth, or it may occur in childhood or in adult life.

Congenital characteristics
These include:

Enlargement of the external genitalia. In girls the genitalia is outwardly masculine but the internal sex organs are normal. This condition may be treated successfully with plastic surgery.

Girls in early childhood may develop beard and moustache growth, a deep voice and other male secondary sexual characteristics.

In boys premature puberty may occur.

The characteristics of the female at puberty are delayed or absent menstruation, delayed breast development, an enlargement of external genitalia and hirsutism.

The characteristics of the female adult are:

○ Virilism.
○ Hirsutism.
○ Breast atrophy.
○ Enlargement of external genitalia.
○ Deepening of the voice.
○ Masculine appearance in build.
○ Infertility.
○ Frontal hair loss.

Acromegaly

This condition is usually caused by a tumour on the pituitary gland which causes an excessive secretion of growth hormone. When this occurs in an adult and the bones have stopped growing, the excess of growth hormone produced causes a thickening of the bones, an enlargement of the feet, hands, jaw and front of the skull. Goitre and menstrual abnormalities often accompany this condition.

If this condition occurs before the bones are fully formed the condition is termed *gigantism* because an individual grows to excessively large proportions due to the overgrowth of the long bones in the body.

Adrenocorticotrophic hormone (ACTH) may also be produced in excess and this affects the adrenal cortex, stimulating the production of androgens in excess which may lead to hirsutism.

28 Structure of the hair follicle and the hair

The hair follicle

The follicle is an indentation of the epidermis into the dermis. It consists, therefore, of layers relative to those of the epidermis, except for the stratum corneum which is constantly desquamating.

The base of the follicle is shaped like a bulb and it contains the loose connective tissue of the dermal papilla which also contains blood vessels, nerve endings and melanocytes.

The stratum germinativum cells of the epidermis cover the dermal papilla and all the cells in this area are mitotically active. As these cells reproduce and move further up into the area of keratinization they are invaded by the protein keratin and the hair becomes a horny dead structure.

Each hair follicle has a sebaceous gland, opening into the follicle to form a pilosebaceous unit. The sebum secreted from the sebaceous gland keeps the hair in the follicle supple.

A bundle of smooth muscle fibres, called the arrector pilorum, is inserted into the wall of the follicle below the sebaceous gland. When it is stimulated by nerve fibres, the muscle contracts causing the hair to stand on end.

The follicle consists of (Figures 28.1–28.3):

○   The inner root sheath.
○   The outer root sheath.
○   A connective tissue sheath.

Inner root sheath

This has three layers of cells:

1   Henle's layer, which is one cell thick.
2   Huxley's layer, which is two or more cells thick.

3   The cuticle layer on the inside which points downwards interlocks with the cuticle of the hair which points upwards.

The inner root sheath grows from the dermal papilla, growing upwards with the hair until it reaches the level of the sebaceous gland, where it dissipates leaving the hair to continue growing upwards.

The outer root sheath

The thickness of the outer root sheath, which surrounds the inner root sheath, varies depending on the size of the follicle. It is normally thicker in the follicles of larger hairs. This thickness is uneven causing the hair to be slightly off centre (eccentric) in the follicle.

Just above the bulb, the outer sheath changes from two to three layers and is at its thickest about a third of the way up the follicle. It is a static structure which does not grow up with the hair.

Above the sebaceous gland the outer sheath is indistinguishable from the surface epidermis. This upper part of the outer sheath forms a keratinized surface layer which is constantly being desquamated.

New follicles are formed from the outer root sheath as it is a source of new 'hair germ cells'.

Connective tissue sheath

The connective tissue sheath is a continuous extension of the papillary layer and the dermal papilla. This layer covers the follicle and the sebaceous gland providing the same function that the papillary layer provides for the epidermis, that is, providing nerve endings and blood supply.

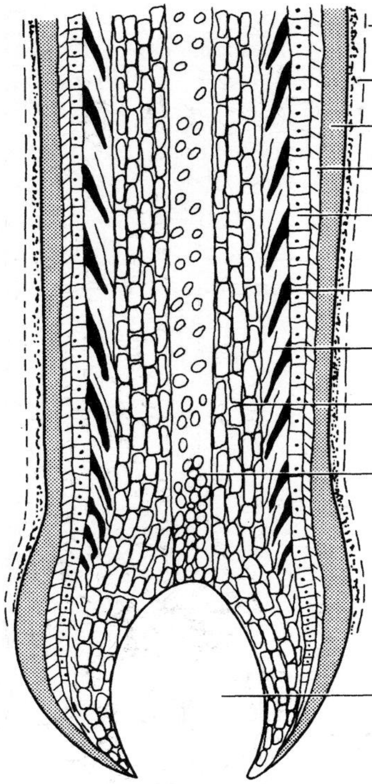

Figure 28.1 *Longitudinal cross-section of hair in the follicle*

Connective tissue

Vitreous membrane

Outer root sheath

Henle's layer

Huxley's layer

Cuticle of inner root sheath

Cuticle of the hair

Cortex of the hair

Medulla of the hair

Dermal papilla

Vitreous membrane

This separates the connective tissue sheath from the outer root sheath and varies in thickness (see Figure 28.1).

The blood supply to the follicle

The follicle receives the nourishment required for growth from the blood supplied via the network of vessels, in the dermis, known as the *hypodermal plexus*.

This network of blood vessels supplies the dermal papilla, the follicle and sebaceous gland with all its necessary nutrients.

The nerve supply

There are many nerve endings in the skin and surrounding the follicle. Some converge to form a meshwork of nerves called a *nerve plexus*. The nerves encircle and enter the connective tissue sheath just below the sebaceous gland. This is important to electrologists when probing as the base of the follicle is below the nerve plexus. Therefore, they may have to apply more current before the sensory nerves respond.

The nerve endings in the skin are dealt with in the facial treatment section. See Chapter 1.

The hair

The hair grows out of the follicle at an angle to the surface of the skin, following the natural contours of the body.

A terminal hair consists of two main portions.

The root

The root is below the surface of the skin at the base of the follicle. It includes the bulb and the dermal papilla, an area of active cells which multiply and move forward to form a column of tightly packed cells, which will form the shaft.

At its base the hair root expands into a bulbous shape called the dermal papilla. This papilla is the crucial source of nourishment for

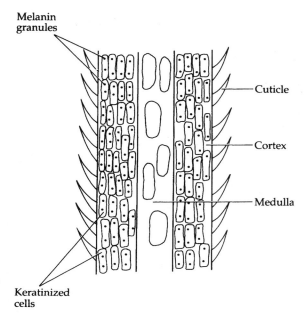

Figure 28.2 *Cross-section of hair*

the entire follicle structure and it derives its blood supply from the capillary loop adjacent to it and this determines the growth and health of the hair.

The lower part of the bulb is called the matrix. Here the cells are mitotically active and undifferentiated. There is a point called the *critical level* at which the cells differentiate. This is a process where they undergo change in growth and development, to become either the inner root sheath or the hair (Figure 28.4).

The shaft

The shaft is the part which extends above the skin surface and is made of dead keratinized cells.

It is made up of three parts: the cuticle; the cortex; and the medulla (see Figure 28.2).

The cuticle
This is the outer layer of the shaft comprising cells which are overlapping, rather like roof

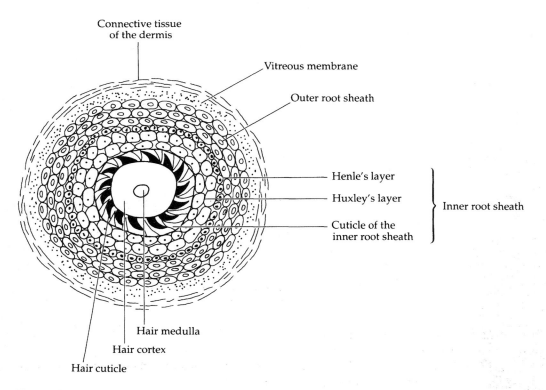

Figure 28.3 *Transverse cross-section of the hair and follicle*

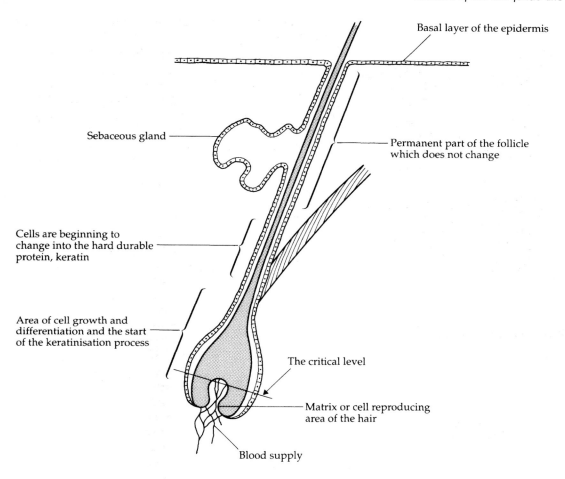

Figure 28.4 *Different areas of cell growth and keratinization*

tiles. These scale-like cells lie very tightly over each other. Heat and chemicals can damage the hair however, causing the scales to open and the hair becomes more porous.

The cells are translucent and contain no pigment thus relfecting the light and giving the hair its shine.

The scaly cells of the cuticle point upwards and interlock with those of the inner root sheath and this anchors the hair firmly in the follicle.

The cortex

This layer makes up the largest portion of the hair and consists of elongated keratinized cells. There are granules of melanin found in pigmented hairs. There are air spaces between the cells in the cortex.

The medulla

This is the centre of the hair but it may be absent in fine vellus hair.

The cells are large, loosely connected and keratinized. There are large air spaces in and between the cells which help to reflect the light and give the hair its sheen (see Figure 28.3).

Stages of hair growth

Hair growth is divided into three stages:

1. Anagen, the growing stage.
2. Catagen, the transitory stage between anagen and telogen.
3. Telogen, the resting stage.

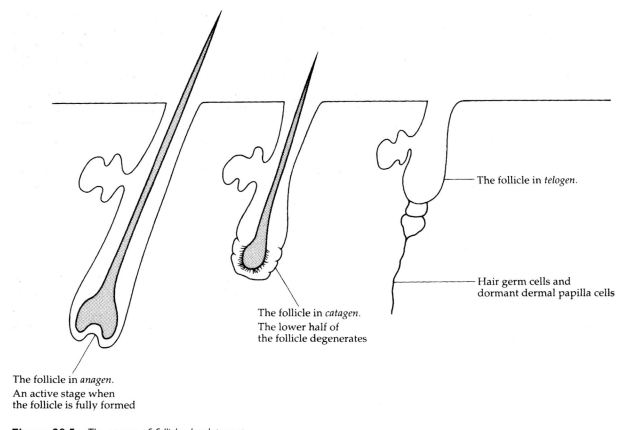

The follicle in *telogen*.

The follicle in *catagen*.
The lower half of
the follicle degenerates

Hair germ cells and
dormant dermal papilla cells

The follicle in *anagen*.
An active stage when
the follicle is fully formed

Figure 28.5 *The stages of follicle development*

The hair's normal lifetime is different from one area of the body to another. It also varies from one person to another. For example, eyelashes and brows last four to five months. Hair on the scalp lasts two to four years and, in some cases, can last up to seven years.

Each follicle has its own life cycle and at a particular point in this cycle the terminal hair separates from the papilla and moves upward while remaining attached to the follicle wall. It is called a *club hair* at this stage.

The lower half of the follicle degenerates and shrinks upwards and the club hair continues to rise until it falls out, after becoming disengaged from the follicle wall. The lower half of the follicle therefore changes with the hair growth cycle but the upper half remains stable.

A collection of *hair germ cells* from the outer root sheath and the dormant dermal papilla cells is all that remains attached to the base of the shrunken follicle. It is from these cells that a new

follicle will eventually form and this may be regarded as the beginning of the hair growth cycle (Figure 28.5).

Anagen

This starts with the total rebuilding of the lower follicle. The cells which remain attached to the base of the follicle are known as the *dermal cord* and these begin to multiply by mitosis, increasing in width and depth and moving down to form the new follicle.

The papilla cells develop into the life giving papilla. The lower part of the dermal cord develops into the bulb which surrounds the dermal papilla.

Before the new follicle has reached its final depth the mitotic cells in the matrix or lower part of the bulb move upwards, differentiating into hair and inner root sheath in the upper part of the bulb and for some short distance beyond.

The cells increase in size and elongate in the upper bulb past the critical level and keratinization occurs. These keratinized cells push their way through the dermal cord in the form of the inner root sheath.

The keratinized hair then follows, breaking through the inner root sheath approximately two thirds of the way up the follicle, to enter the permanent upper part producing the hair visible above the skin's surface.

Meanwhile, the follicle has continued growing down into the dermis. This downward growth stops when the hair has grown approximately half an inch above the skin's surface.

A hair treated in the early anagen stage produces the best results.

Catagen

The hair grows constantly for a certain period and then the catagen stage begins.

The papilla separates and withdraws from the matrix. The hair rises up and is still attached to the follicle wall, receiving nourishment to a small degree. The papilla collapses and the follicle degenerates in the lower half.

Undifferentiated cells present in the lower half of the follicle form the dermal cord. The inner root sheath disintegrates. The hair becomes detached from the surrounding tissue. It has lost the bulb-like root and is termed a club hair.

This stage of the cycle is very short and sometimes a new hair emerges before the club hair is shed.

Telogen

This is the resting stage for the upper half of the follicle until it is stimulated to begin a new cycle. The length of this stage varies and in some cases this stage does not occur as a new hair grows immediately.

29 *Contraindications to treatment*

A contraindication to treatment is any indication or reason why treatment may not be carried out. There are specific reasons why treatment must not be carried out but there are also conditions which will prevent treatment only in the affected area.

There are also occasions when the electrologist may feel that treatment is contraindicated and consultation with the client's doctor is necessary, to ascertain whether treatment may be carried out.

Contraindications

o Any diseases of the skin which may be infectious as there will be a high risk of cross infection.

o *Acne vulgaris* is a condition which affects adolescents and is caused by a hormonal imbalance. This may also cause the growth of superfluous hair. If the infected area is treated the infection would spread and further aggravate an already inflamed skin.

o *Herpes simplex* is contraindicated in the immediate area because the virus may be spread to other areas.

o *Sunburned skin* is normally inflamed and sensitive and there will be a risk of hyper pigmentation with treatment.

o A *heart condition* or the presence of a pacemaker in the heart. Doctors' permission must be sought in the case of some heart conditions as the decision must be made by them, whether treatment is advisable in relation to the severity of the problem. In the case of high blood pressure the anxiety may cause problems.

o *Epilepsy* can vary in severity so doctors' permission must be sought. The stress of the treatment could bring on an attack.

o *Diabetes* requires doctors' permission as this condition affects the skin's ability to heal itself. Once permission has been given the treatment itself must be modified, by making treatment time shorter, spacing out the needle insertions and having longer periods between treatments.

o During *pregnancy* the stomach and breasts should not be treated, as the breasts become tender and swollen and the stomach stretches, causing the skin to become taut.

o The *hairs in moles* should not be treated without doctors' permission as moles are potentially pre-malignant.

o With girls under the age of sixteen, unwanted superfluous hair may be racial or hereditary and after puberty may not go away. This can be easily treated but before treatment it is advisable to seek the opinion of a doctor in case there is a hormonal abnormality which is causing the problem.

There are certain conditions which although not contraindicating treatment special care and consideration may be required:

o *Negroid skin* is prone to keloid scarring which is an overgrowth of scar tissue and pitted scarring may form more easily due to sensitivity. The follicles are curved causing a curly hair. Therefore, insertion of the needle has to be adapted. There is also a greater risk of ingrowing hairs and hyper pigmentation as a result of treatment.

o *Hairs in the scar tissue* may be treated if the scar is more than twelve months old.

o *Mucous membranes* should not be treated, for example the nose and ears because of the high moisture content in the area.

o *Skin infections* or any areas of inflammation.

o *Bruising* of the skin.

Hepatitis B

In view of the seriousness of the Hepatitis B and the AIDS virus, treatment may be at the discretion of the electrologist. A vaccine is available for all those practising electrolysis, against the hepatitis virus.

Hepatitis B is caused by a virus and is an infection of the liver with an incubation period of two to six months. It is transmitted by means of body fluid and may be passed on through treatments administered with a needle, drug injections, acupuncture, tattooing, or electrolysis.

Contaminated blood or tissue fluid on the electrolysis needle is sufficient to transmit the disease.

AIDS

This disease is caused by a virus which is called HIV or human immunodeficiency virus.

It is a condition which develops when the body's immune system is not functioning normally. This leaves the body susceptible to illness and infection which may prove fatal. This occurs because the AIDS virus attacks the white blood cells that are responsible for fighting off infection. AIDS stands for acquired immune deficiency syndrome:

Acquired: The disease is caught from outside the body.
Immune deficiency: The impaired ability of the body to fight disease.
Syndrome: A group of symptoms occurring together, characterizing a particular disease.

This virus is also transmitted via body fluids, therefore special care must be taken when using any device that punctures the skin. This will include electrolysis needles and ear-piercing equipment.

The most efficient method for the electrologist of preventing the spread of AIDS is to use disposable needles and an autoclave to sterilize metal implements such as tweezers.

30 *Client consultation*

Because of the nature of the problem a great many clients who come for treatment will feel embarrassed and a little apprehensive. Care and consideration therefore are of paramount importance. A sympathetic approach will help to put clients at ease and a good relationship will ensue, making the treatment procedure a little more relaxing and hopefully more successful.

The initial consultation not necessarily at the time of the first treatment is important to gain the client's confidence and to elicit all the necessary information which will help to plan the course of treatment.

This could be the first impression clients will have of the salon and the electrologist as they may not have attended before. To make sure that they return and hopefully become a regular client the consultation is an important first step in establishing a rapport and promoting confidence in the client, of the electrologist's ability to solve their problem.

Points to consider

- Appearance must be professional. A clean white overall should be worn, nails short and clean, and hair neat and tidy, with makeup well applied.
- Professional badges should be worn as this is an indication to the client of the standard of training.
- The client should be greeted in a friendly but assured manner.
- The client should be taken to a private room or cubicle where she may speak in confidence.

Points for discussion

Encourage clients to talk about their problem as this will have the beneficial effect of a problem shared. It may also indicate the cause of the superfluous hair without having to question them closely and allow them to point out the area requiring treatment. Never assume from their appearance or they may be offended.

The benefits of electrolysis as a permanent method of hair removal must be explained as well as the expected results and limitations of treatment. Information regarding frequency and duration of treatment as well as the procedure can be given to the client at this stage.

Ascertain which methods of temporary hair removal if any have been used previously and the bearing this may have on the progress of the treatment and the effect it will have on regrowth. These methods may have caused certain problems, for example:

- Waxing or plucking may have caused a distortion in the follicles and results will be far slower on hairs that have been regularly waxed or plucked.
- Depilatory creams work by dissolving the hair but at the same time they attack the skin and this makes it more sensitive and possibly slow to heal.

It should be explained to clients that if they feel the need to use a temporary method of hair removal in between treatments then cutting is the best alternative.

Hair growth will diminish with each successive treatment depending on the stage of hair growth until it is permanently removed, with complete destruction of the follicle, but the treatment will probably be long term as the follicle is not usually destroyed at the first treatment and a weakened hair will regrow.

There can also be hair which is lying below the surface of the skin which may become visible after treatment. This may cause the client to become despondent. Therefore, it is important to explain that these are not the hairs that have been treated, but new hairs.

The client will also need to know that initially the visits for treatment must be quite frequent, to assess the hair growth rate and to allow time for the skin to heal, until the initial growth has been treated and then appointments to treat the regrowth will be less often, therefore becoming less expensive.

The cost of the treatment should be discussed to allow the client to budget for the visits.

How the equipment works, what the treatment entails, the sensations they will feel and the appearance of the skin after treatment, should be explained in a language that will not alarm the clients.

The opportunity to try out the treatment by removing one or two hairs from the affected area should be taken. This would be an ideal time to explain the after-care instructions for clients to carry out at home.

The record card

During this initial consultation a record card must be filled in to provide necessary information about the client which will help to determine the course of treatment, inspire confidence in the client and promote efficiency in the salon by providing all the necessary information for another member of staff to take over treatment of the client should the need arise.

Details to be recorded

These should include personal and medical history details, and treatment record.

Name, address and telephone number
Useful for filing record cards in alphabetical order.

The client may be contacted in case of a change in appointment.

It will provide a ready-made mailing list and allow the electrologist to contact clients if they so wish, to inform them of new treatments or special offers.

A note should be made of how the client was recommended to the salon as this will help to assess a salon's future advertising.

Doctor's name and address and telephone number
It may be necessary to contact the client's doctor, with their permission, about their medical history. Additionally, if clients are taken ill during treatment it may be necessary to call their doctor.

Date of birth
This information helps the electrologist determine the client's suitability for treatment and indicates whether the client is suffering from superfluous hair because of the menopause, pregnancy or puberty.

The hormonal imbalance at these times is a common cause of superfluous hair.

Medical history
Recording details of the client's medical history may help determine the cause of the problem and whether epilation is contraindicated.

Pregnancies or miscarriages and recent operations must be recorded and if the appearance of the superfluous hair coincided with any of these occurrences.

It is important to record any medical conditions clients may suffer from and are receiving medication for, for example some drugs cause superfluous hair. The contraceptive pill or steroids may also be the cause of superfluous hair.

Menstrual problems may indicate an underlying hormonal imbalance.

Hepatitis will require stringent hygiene precautions.

Hair and skin condition
The position of superfluous hair and how strong the growth is should be noted to help in establishing the intensity of the current to be used and to establish approximately how long it will take to clear.

Skin sensitivity will indicate how treatment must be adapted to suit the skin type.

Skin blemishes and disorders which may contraindicate treatment should be checked.

It is important to note any scarring to the skin or discoloration as this could be the result of previous treatment. It should be noted to protect the electrologist's professional reputation.

Details of each treatment

This section of the record card will be filled in after each treatment session and should include:

○ Date.
○ Area treated.
○ Treatment time.
○ Current intensity used.
○ Machine used as intensity can vary in action on different machines.
○ Spacing of the probes.
○ Signature of the electrologist.

The purpose of recording these details is to:

○ Provide a case history which allows another electrologist to take over.
○ The progress of the treatment can be evaluated.
○ In case of complaint the electrologist who has performed the treatment can be easily located and the details of the treatment are readily available.
○ Problems are recorded which may require future treatment to be adapted or modified.

Signature of the client

This will act as verification that the details recorded on the record card are accurate.

31 *The skin*

Skin types

Each client treated has a skin type which is specific to them, with different degrees of skin sensitivity and powers of healing.

Treatment needs to be adapted for different skin types and it is important, therefore, to analyse the skin before commencing treatment. This will help the electrologist determine what course of treatment will be most suitable for the client, the most suitable method of epilation to be used and the frequency of treatment.

The reaction of the skin to treatment is unique to each client and can in fact change from one treatment to the next, depending on the general state of health and well-being of the client or it may react differently on different parts of the body. It is important, therefore, to understand the factors present in the skin which will affect treatment.

Sensitive skin

Some clients are highly sensitive to pain while others have what is termed a high pain threshold. This means that they will be able to tolerate a higher intensity of current for longer periods of time without feeling too much discomfort.

The advantage of this is that the superfluous hair can be successfully removed over a shorter period of time. The disadvantage is that the area may be over-treated because of the client's tolerance to pain.

The skill of electrologists is important in this case as they can determine with each treatment, and by keeping scrupulous records, exactly how long and at what intensity treatments may be given.

The degree of sensitivity will determine the amount of hair which can be treated in one session. There are varying degrees of sensitivity on different areas of the body:

The face
Highly sensitive: The centre of the face to include the centre of the lip, under the nose and the centre of the forehead. The eyebrow area.
Less sensitive: The sides of the lip, the sides of the face under the chin and the neck.
Least sensitive: The chin itself.

Other parts of the body
Most sensitive: The area surrounding the nipple.
Less sensitive: The centre line, spine, chest and inside of the thigh. The axilla.
Least sensitive: The lower legs and the arms.

The sensitivity depends on two things:

1 The location of the nerves.
2 The depth of the follicle.

The skin has an abundance of sensory nerves which pass messages to the brain. These nerves have sensory receptors or fibrils in the lower layers of the epidermis which respond to cold, heat, touch, pressure and pain.

The more sensitive areas are caused because these nerve fibrils are close together or in some cases overlapping causing an intense response to a stimulant such as epilation.

The accuracy of the probe at the lowest point in the follicle is important in reducing pain, as the pain receptors are situated in the epidermis, so the deeper the follicle and the further from the surface of the skin the electrologist works, the more current may be applied, before response from the sensory receptors in the nerves.

Soft skin

When the skin is very soft or loose it will be more difficult to insert the needle into the hair follicle. On the face the firm areas of skin are found on the forehead and chin while the under

(a)

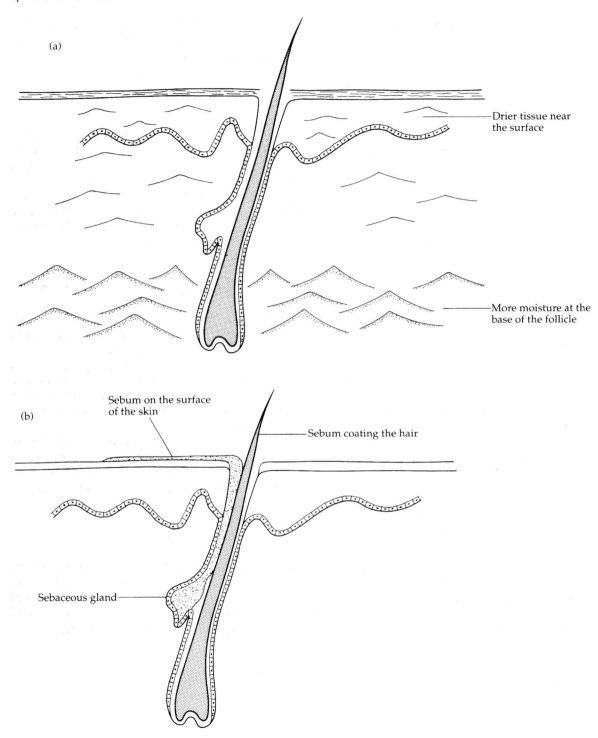

Drier tissue near the surface

More moisture at the base of the follicle

Sebum on the surface of the skin

Sebum coating the hair

(b)

Sebaceous gland

Figure 31.1 *(a) The moisture gradient; (b) Sebum insulation*

chin area and the neck are areas of soft or loose skin of varying degrees.

Thin skin

If the epidermis is very thin and translucent, as in fine sensitive skin types, the area will become red very quickly as the blood can be seen quite easily.

Thick skin

If the epidermis is thick then the follicles are probably deeper therefore insertions will be deeper. The skin reaction is not so marked on this skin type.

Moist skin

Both short-wave diathermy and galvanic electrolysis rely on the moisture level in the tissues for their effectiveness, as the diathermy heats the moisture content and the galvanic method produces a chemical reaction when combined with the salty body fluids.

There is more water content in the lower, more active layers of the epidermis and dermis. A natural part of keratinization (the change of living cells with a nucleus, to dead flat horny cells with no nucleus) is loss of fluid in the skin cells, the moisture content of the skin decreases towards the surface layers.

The skin becomes less moist with age as the epidermal cells are much flatter and without water. On the face there are varying degrees of moisture and the electrologist will have to adapt treatment by changing the intensity of the current. The area at the corners of the mouth is moist in most people and the chin area is normally less moist.

Oily skin

This is a skin which has a shiny surface due to the activity of the sebaceous glands. The layer of oil on the skin acts as an insulating layer preventing loss of moisture from the skin.

Naturally oily skins are usually moist skins also, unless clients have been using harsh products on their skin to combat the oil production and have a drying effect on the skin.

The moisture gradient of the skin

The moisture in the epidermis decreases as the cells reach the surface of the skin and this is known as the moisture gradient.

This gradient varies in different people but in everyone there is a difference in the amount of moisture at the base of the follicle compared to the epidermal tissue on the surface of the skin (Figure 31.1).

Water is an effective conductor of electricity and as a current flow takes the path of least resistance, it will be at its most destructive in the moist area of the follicle which is the dermal papilla.

Sebum insulation

The sebum coats the hair from the point where the sebaceous gland opens into the follicle, up and onto the surface of the skin. This coating of sebum insulates the epidermis from the action of the high frequency or galvanic current.

Short-wave diathermy is the most commonly used method of permanent hair removal in salons today. It may also be called *thermolysis* as this is a term which means heat destruction.

Short-wave diathermy uses a *high-frequency, short-wave alternating current* to produce heat as its destructive force. The current is applied through a fine metal needle inserted into the hair follicle and discharged for a very short time, producing heat in the tissues to cauterize and coagulate the papilla.

The heat is produced because a high-frequency current is an oscillating current, 3 million to 30 million cycles per second, with high voltage and low amperage. In simpler terms, it is a rapidly alternating current of high pressure and low power. This continuous electrostatic attraction and repulsion (oscillation) produces friction which then results in heat.

A high-frequency current has an influence on the area around the conductor (the needle) and this is referred to as the high frequency field.

Therefore heat is produced in the area of the follicle which is affected by the high frequency field, in this case the area around the papilla, cauterizing this mitotically active area and retarding growth of a new hair.

Accurate placement of the needle is essential for the treatment to be effective.

The equipment

The epilation machine

There are many different types of epilation machines available but the majority use short-wave diathermy and contain the following elements:

○ An on/off switch.
○ An intensity control which is normally graduated from 1 to 10 and indicates the intensity of the current flow.

○ Some machines have a milliamp metre which displays how much current is flowing.
○ A connection point for the needle holder.
○ A needle holder with a finger button to control the application of the current or without the button to be used in connection with the foot switch.
○ A foot switch connection.
○ A foot switch with lead to control the application of the current.
○ Some have an automatic timing device for applying the current.

Requirements
The epilation machine should be:

○ Well-constructed and long lasting.
○ Reliable in use and performance.
○ A simple design with easy-to-use controls.
○ Small in size and clinical in appearance (Figure 32.1).

The following are also required:

○ Selection of needles of various sizes.
○ A comfortable adjustable couch is essential to ensure client comfort throughout the treatment and allow all areas to be treated without causing tension in clients because they are seated uncomfortably.
○ An adjustable stool for electrologists to sit on in the most comfortable position to allow them to work effectively, reaching all areas of the client which require treatment, without causing back ache as a result of bad positioning.
○ An illuminated magnifying lamp, to allow electrologists to inspect the area to be worked upon more closely and provide a good source of light. The use of a magnifier allows more accurate work for longer, without causing eye strain and is an excellent substitute for good natural daylight, which is not consistent enough to be relied

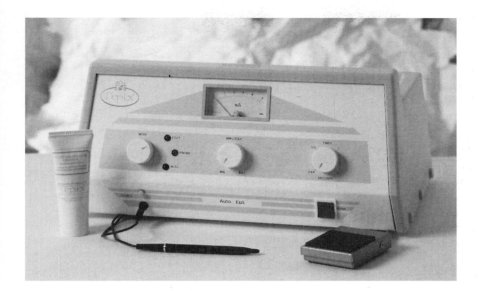

Figure 32.1 *Short-wave diathermy machine*
Courtesy Depilex Limited

upon. It may be free-standing, wall-mounted or attached to the trolley.

○ A trolley, preferably with storage space such as drawers and shelves to hold equipment which should include the following:

○ Tweezers or forceps which should be used only for the purpose of epilation.

○ Cotton wool and tissues with suitable containers.

○ Appropriate cleansing preparations for areas to be treated.

○ A sterilizing solution and medicated swabs.

○ A covered container for the disposal of used needles.

○ A small sterilizing unit.

○ Aftercare preparations.

○ A bin with a lid for waste material.

Hygiene precautions

Stringent precautions must be taken to maintain an environment free from bacteria. The electrologist is bound by law to take any steps necessary in preventing the spread of disease.

It is important to contact the environmental health officer (EHO), to obtain information about local byelaws relating to the setting up of an electrolysis clinic, or when adding this treatment to the list of services offered in an established salon.

The EHO will also provide advice on matters of hygiene and safety in the salon that are necessary to protect both the clients attending for treatment and the electrologists themselves.

Insufficient or incorrect hygiene measures may adversely affect the health of the electrologist and client, in particular the risk of contracting Hepatitis B (viral hepatitis) and from coming into contact with AIDS.

To avoid cross-infection there are many points to be considered.

Workplace

The internal aspect of the clinic or treatment room must be well-maintained and scrupulously clean. It is inadvisable to use wallpaper unless it is durable and washable.

The floor surface should be smooth and impenetrable.

The surfaces of all table tops and work surfaces should also be smooth and impenetrable. They should be kept clean and wiped with a suitable disinfectant before each treatment.

The store cupboards and shelves must be used only for equipment and materials required for electrolysis.

Chairs and treatment couches should be in good repair and kept clean by washing regularly with detergent; the surface should be in an easy-to-clean material.

There must be adequate ventilation and good lighting.

There must be a sink unit, with hot and cold running water, which is connected to the drainage system, in the electrologist's treatment room or cubicle.

The electrologist

The personal hygiene of electrologists must be of the highest standards, because the nature of the work is such that they are working in close proximity to clients most of the time. Their nails must be kept short and clean and their hair must be tied back away from their face.

In the event of an electrologist having a cut or wound, it must be cleaned and covered with a waterproof dressing immediately. This should be obtainable from a first aid box, which should be readily available for the use of the electrologist.

An electrologist should not treat a client when suffering from an infectious illness or disease as this may be easily transmitted during treatment.

Equipment and materials

Disposable needles must be used so that each client has their own needle which is then discarded after each use. The only effective methods of sterilizing needles are the autoclave and the glass bead sterilizer.

Autoclave moist heat
Once the required temperature has been reached the items will be sterilized after 15 minutes at 120°C, after 10 minutes at 126°C and after 3 minutes at 134°C.

The glass bead sterilizer
Once the required temperature has been achieved, the items will take 10 minutes to sterilize at a temperature of 190°C.

Disposable paper tissues and towels should be used and changed for each client, then placed in a lidded bin, lined with a leak-proof sealable plastic bag.

Stainless steel bowls are needed in which to place small items and cotton wool.

Stainless steel tweezers.

Pre-packed swabs impregnated with alcohol.

A 'sharps' disposable box for used needles clearly marked with the words DANGER CONTAMINATED NEEDLES which, when required, may be disposed of on the advice of the environmental health officer.

Needles for disposal should be sterilized or placed in a solution of hypochlorite before being discarded.

Appropriate disinfectants should be used such as hypochlorite and glutaraldehyde which will neutralize most viruses, especially the hepatitis ones.

Hypochlorite used for work surfaces, etc. must be made up daily according to instructions. Glutaraldehyde needs only to be made up weekly and can be used for cleaning metal instruments as well as work surfaces.

Electrologists must comply with the provisions laid down in the Health and Safety at Work Act 1974 which is discussed in detail in the business section of this book. See Chapter 50.

Care and comfort of the client

The client must always be lying or sitting in a comfortable position, which also allows the electrologist to work efficiently and comfortably.

The client's clothing in the area to be worked upon must be protected with clean towels. This helps to prevent possible cross-infection and also protects the client's clothing during treatment.

The client's eyes should be covered with dry cotton wool or goggles if she is irritated by bright light.

The client should be talked to in a reassuring and professional manner during treatment to put her at ease.

If the electrologist has a cold then a surgical mask should be worn.

The electrologist should work as quickly and efficiently as possible.

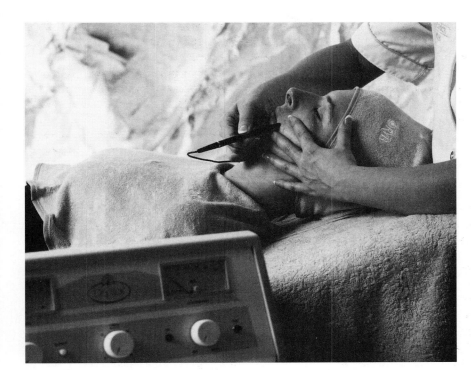

Figure 32.2 *Probing
Courtesy Depilex Limited*

Preparation of the client's skin for treatment

Even the removal of makeup prior to epilation can stimulate the skin and cause increased skin reaction during treatment. It is advisable therefore to ask the client whenever possible not to wear makeup when attending for treatment.

A soothing cooling lotion such as witch hazel is applied to the skin to gently cleanse and soothe during treatment.

Probing

Skilled electrologists will have a highly developed sense of touch enabling them to probe to the correct depth on each insertion and will also be able to manipulate the needle holder and the tweezers with great dexterity. Resistance will be felt in most cases when the base of the follicle has been reached. This does take a lot of practice and perseverance is required to be successful (Figure 32.2).

The effectiveness of treatment is determined by the heating pattern created by the application of the high-frequency current.

The heating pattern is affected by:

○ The intensity of the current applied.
○ The length of time the current is applied.
○ The depth of the follicle.
○ The diameter of the needle.
○ The moisture gradient.

A needle of the same diameter as the hair being treated will be the ideal size to use as it will slide easily into the follicle. Needles vary in size and the most commonly used are 004 and 005. 006 can be used on very coarse hair and 003 on very fine hair. The finer the needle the quicker the heat will rise up towards the surface.

The skin should be held taut around the base to allow the opening of the follicle to be seen more easily. The needle should then enter the follicle at the same angle as the hair leaves it. This is different on particular areas:

Front of the chin 60° angle.
Most body hair and the side of the face 45° angle.
Front of the neck and throat 30° angle.

The needle must then be held steady in the follicle and sufficient current applied to cauterize the papilla and allow the removal of the epilated hair.

Not being positive or precise when pressing the button on the needle holder or when pressing the foot switch to apply the current results in no current being applied and therefore the hair resists being removed by the tweezers.

Hair depth

When a hair is in the anagen or active stage of growth it is at its strongest and deepest, therefore the insertion will have to be deep. The epilated hair will have a fully formed root structure and tissue sheath.

The hair in the catagen stage is shorter in the follicle and the tissue sheath and root structure are not so well defined therefore probing should be slightly more superficial.

Hairs in the telogen stage require very little current but special care must be taken to avoid burning the surface of the skin as the hairs are quite high in the follicle. The hair will have no root sheath and will have a club-like end because of the disintegration of the hair bulb.

Current used

Current intensity should be chosen to suit the strength of the hair being treated, the skin sensitivity, the area to be epilated and the client's tolerance to pain. There should be the minimum amount of current used to remove the hair successfully. The timing of the application of the current can be altered to suit the requirements of each client.

Different machines use different levels of high frequency currents and it is up to the electrologist to decide the way in which to work: a low current for a longer application time; or a high current for a short application time.

Both methods achieve the same results but greater accuracy and competence is required when using the high current for a short length of time to prevent skin damage. It is advisable, therefore, while perfecting the skills required for epilation, that the lower current for a longer

application time is used to produce the required results without causing too much discomfort to the client.

A highly skilled electrologist will be able to use the high current with short application. This will allow her to treat more of the superfluous hair in the time allocated for treatment while minimizing pain and the adverse skin reaction which can occur.

The expected appearance of the skin after treatment

As a result of treatment and the heat produced, there is an increase in blood supply to the area and this will cause an erythema. This reddening of the skin will vary in intensity depending on the client's skin sensitivity and the intensity of the current which has been used.

The flow of lymph to the area is also stimulated because of the increase in blood supply and this will cause a slight swelling because of the excess fluid. In areas of extreme sensitivity such as bikini line, breats and abdomen as well as extremely sensitive skins, this effect can be more marked.

Care of the skin after treatment

To reduce the redness and the heat in the skin tissues it is important to apply a soothing lotion immediately after treatment. When treating several areas at once a very fine piece of cotton wool soaked in the appropriate lotion can be applied to a previously treated area while treatment is performed elsewhere. This allows the healing process to begin and skin appearance to improve.

Any lotion or cream applied to the skin after treatment must have the following properties:

○ Antibacterial.
○ Protective.
○ Soothing.
○ Camouflaging if required.

Some after-care preparations have an antihistamine and when applied to the skin it helps to reduce the inflammation.

After each treatment a small amount of epidermal tissue will be destroyed, therefore the area around the treated follicle will be susceptible to infection until the skin heals itself. It is important, therefore, to advise clients on the care they must give their own skin at home and stress the importance of adhering to these instructions strictly. The client must:

○ Follow the aftercare instructions for 48 hours after treatment.
○ Avoid the use of soap, makeup or any perfumed products which could cause an irritation.
○ Cleanse twice a day with one of the following:
  –Witch hazel which is also soothing.
  –Mild unscented toning lotion.
  –Product recommended by the electrologist.
○ Apply a medicated soothing lotion after cleansing.
○ If there is any soreness in the area treated after 48 hours, then the aftercare instructions must be continued until the skin is clear.
○ After 48 hours use only unperfumed cleanser and toning lotion.
○ Tiny scabs may form as these are part of the skin's natural healing process and must be left untouched to prevent secondary infection or scarring.
○ The client must be told to contact the electrologist if there are any problems.
○ The client should avoid heat treatment or exposure to ultraviolet radiation.

Appearance of the skin when damaged by incorrect techniques

○ Raised bumps may appear because of an excessive amount of lymph fluid in the area caused by an application of current which was too high, or had been applied for too long or in too small an area.
○ Blisters or tiny lymph vesicles may form on the surface of the skin, again caused by over-treatment and these will normally crust over and heal naturally if not touched by the client and all aftercare instructions are followed.
○ Burning of the skin shows up as small white marks on the skin's surface which can be flat or raised and do not fade away.

They normally take between two and four weeks to disappear and the skin's natural healing process provides a lymph or blood crust over the lesion to aid in healing and if this is knocked off or removed, can cause a pitted scar or small depression in the skin. The causes are:
  –Application of current which is too high or for too long.
  –Passing the current when insertion or removal of the needle has not been completed.
  –Moving the needle while it is in the follicle and the current is being applied.
  –Incorrect insertion.
○ A blue–black mark or lump may appear, caused by an incorrect insertion or using a needle which is too large. It may appear immediately as a well-defined blue mark because the tiny blood capillaries have been ruptured or later as a widespread area of discoloration. Immediate pressure to the area and the application of cold compresses will help reduce the effect.
○ Permanent scars may be a result of persistently poor techniques causing severe burning or picked crusts over healing lesions. They are tiny indentations in the skin which have the appearance of orange peel when there are many situated in a small area.

Conditions which may result from epilation

Infection

This is characterized by the formation of pustules and occurs when there are poor hygiene methods used by the electrologist or homecare advice given to the client has not been adhered to.

Ingrowing hair

This is a hair which grows horizontally along and just under the surface of the skin when it emerges from the follicle. Sometimes it will turn back on itself into the follicle opening and become compacted. Occasionally infection will set in but they can be easily removed using a sterile needle to release the trapped hair and then left to heal. Ingrowing hairs may occur as a result of waxing or plucking, or the client may be predisposed to this problem, for example negroid skin.

Absence of root sheath

This sometimes occurs when the hair is epilated quite easily but the root sheath is left behind in the follicle. The root sheath has been skimmed off before reaching the mouth of the follicle and this ball of tissue could become a breeding ground for bacteria and cause the formation of pustules.

33 *Galvanic electrolysis*

Electrolysis

Although this method of epilation is not in common use on its own it is an essential part of the blend method which utilizes the effectiveness of this method with the speed of diathermy.

Electrolysis is the term used to describe the electrolytic action of the galvanic current for the removal of superfluous hair. When a direct current is applied to a salt water solution it causes the salt and the water to break up into their chemical elements, which then rearrange themselves to form entirely new substances (Figure 33.1).

Acids form at the positive pole and alkalis form at the negative pole.

This process is called electrolysis and the new substances that are formed are sodium hydroxide or lye, hydrogen and chlorine gas.

NaCl and H_2O + direct current
= NaOH and H and Cl

Sodium chloride and water (salt) + direct current = sodium hydroxide, hydrogen gas and chlorine gas

An electrolyte is a solution which has the ability to conduct electricity and can be ionized. The tissues of the body are made up of a strong salt solution therefore making it an efficient electrolyte.

Galvanic electrolysis is a chemical process which produces the caustic lye that is used as

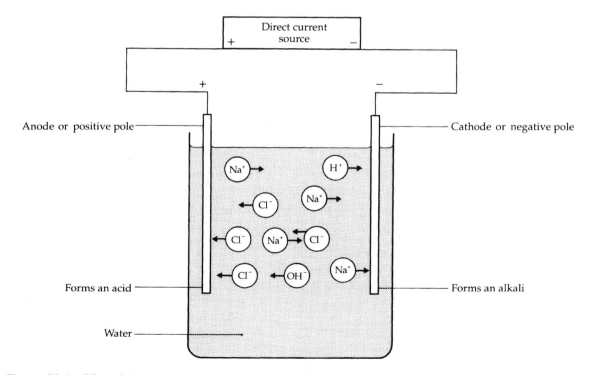

Figure 33.1 *Effect of direct current passed through a salt solution. The positive ions move towards the cathode (negative pole). The negative ions move towards the anode (positive pole). This is because unlike poles attract and like poles repel*

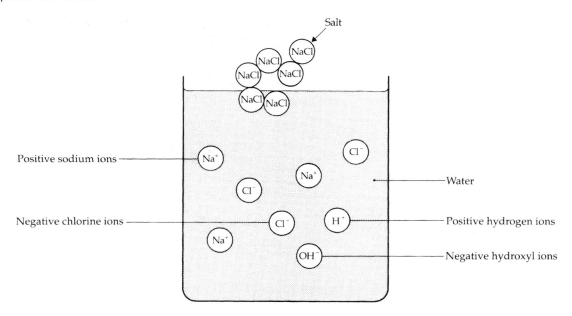

Figure 33.2 *Ionization of sodium chloride. Sodium chloride (NaCl) dissolved in water produces positive sodium ions (Na+), negative chlorine ions (Cl-), positive hydrogen ions (H+) and negative hydroxyl ions (OH-)*

the destructive force in this method of superfluous hair removal.

A galvanic current is a constant direct current and as in facial treatment the client must hold an indifferent electrode to complete the circuit.

The active electrode in galvanic epilation is the needle and it will be used on the negative pole only. The client will hold the indifferent electrode to complete the circuit and this will be positively charged.

The needle is inserted into the follicle and the direct current is applied.

When using a galvanic current it has to be applied for approximately 10–15 seconds so that enough lye is formed to decompose the tissue.

The area around the base of the follicle is moist with tissue fluid containing body salts (moisture gradient). The current only affects the tissue where it encounters moisture, therefore the galvanic current converts tissue moisture and body salts in the follicle into lye, causing hydrogen and chlorine gas to escape from the follicle mouth.

There are two factors to be taken into consideration which aid in the effectiveness of this treatment, as well as protecting the epidermis, particularly as the current has to be applied for a fairly long period. These are as follows:

1   The moisture gradient of the skin ensures the largest amount of galvanic action is concentrated on the moist area of the lower follicle, causing decomposition of this vital active area without causing damage to the surface of the skin.

2   The insulating effect of the sebum, which helps to protect the skin as the sebum secreted by the sebaceous gland attached to the follicle forms a layer over the part of the hair above the sebaceous gland and the surface of the skin, insulating it from the galvanic current.

The polarity

The alkali effects of the negative pole and the acid effect of the positive pole both destroy tissue. However, the positive pole must never be used as the hydrochloric acid produced also causes most metals to disintegrate. In the case of the positive pole being used accidentally, a hard lump and scar will result. It is very important therefore to only use the *negative pole* in galvanic electrolysis.

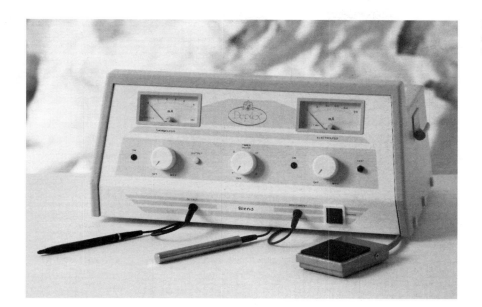

Figure 33.3 *The blend machine*
Courtesy Depilex

The blend method

This method of superfluous hair removal incorporates both the galvanic current used in electrolysis and the high-frequency current used in short-wave diathermy. Most machines allow the currents to be used separately or together.

The combination of the speed of diathermy and the efficiency of the galvanic method is utilized for maximum effect. The high frequency current uses heat as its destructive force and the galvanic current produces lye which is used as its destructive force. Together the heat from the high frequency current increases the caustic effect of the lye which destroys the hair papilla (Figure 33.3).

34 *Ear piercing*

Ear piercing is an ideal service to offer your clients as:

○ It requires little capital outlay.
○ The equipment required needs very little storage space.
○ The procedure can be carried out anywhere that a client can sit down.
○ The procedure is very quick and therefore it is not occupying a great deal of staff time.
○ Profits are good.

Equipment required

○ Ear piercing gun.
○ Pre-packed sterile studs.
○ A marker pen.
○ Antiseptic or pre-packed sterile wipes.
○ List of after-care instructions.
○ Mirror.
○ Wash bowl.
○ Towel.
○ Hair clips.

Contraindications

○ Skin infections.
○ Ear infections.
○ Cuts or abrasions.
○ An excessively nervous client.
○ Ear lobes which are too small.
○ Lumps, bumps or swellings.

As the tissue is being pierced stringent hygiene precautions should be followed to ensure that the client is treated safely and without risk of infection.

There are several ear piercing systems on the market which are designed to conform to certain safety standards laid down by the Government and a list of these is available from the DoH.

Safety and hygiene

The work area to be used for ear piercing must be clean and work surfaces wiped down with disinfectant.

The client must be checked for contraindications before piercing the ear.

The client's hair must be clipped back from the face. The client's ears must be wiped over with the medicated wipe to cleanse the area.

The therapist's hands must be washed.

The ears must be pierced according to the manufacturer's instructions.

The client should be seated in an upright position level with the therapist so the earring does not enter the ear at an abnormal angle.

Clients should be issued with a printed set of after-care instructions to follow at home and each point must be explained in full so that they are quite aware of how to look after their ears for the required length of time after they have been pierced.

After-care advice

The studs should be left in for six weeks to allow the ears to heal and they should be turned twice a day.

Clients should wash their hands before touching their ears.

The back and the front of the studs and the ears should be wiped with the recommended antiseptic or, alternatively, with surgical spirit.

After washing their hair clients should ensure that all traces of shampoo have been rinsed thoroughly from around the ear lobes.

When using hair spray or spray perfume the ears should always be covered. If any irritation occurs bathe with saline solution.

Remove the studs after six weeks.

It is advisable to use only gold or silver studs in case of an allergic reaction to some metals.

Precautions

The therapist must not:

○ Pierce through or near a cyst, which is a hard lump near the skin surface.
○ Pierce through a mole.
○ Pierce if the ear is infected internally.
○ Pierce through the cartilage because it can be sore and uncomfortable.

The therapist must also explain to diabetic clients that their skin may be slow to heal.

If in doubt do not pierce

Records should be kept with the name and address of the client and the date of treatment.

These records may prove invaluable if there is any question of an infection problem at a later date as this can happen if the after-care instructions are not followed to the letter.

Dangers

Fainting: The client should be seated safely with no sharp edges nearby.

Tearing the ear lobe: The client should be informed what will happen at each stage of the procedure in case they jump unexpectedly.

Keloid formation: The client should be asked if she is prone to keloid scarring, an overgrowth of normal scar tissue. This is a problem which occurs more commonly in a black skin.

Skin burns: Burns can occur if the client cleanses the ears with undiluted antiseptic. They should be advised to flush the area with cold water.

Infections: This would appear as redness and irritation of the ear. The client should be advised to clean the ear and the earring thoroughly and consult a doctor if the ear lobe begins to swell.

Closed holes: This can occur in some cases and re-piercing may be carried out when the skin is fully healed.

Part Four Manicure, Pedicure and Depilation

35 *Manicure*

The word manicure means care of the hands and the purpose of this treatment is to improve the appearance of the hands and nails by cleansing, nourishing and beautifying them.

A manicure is also an ideal opportunity for the therapist to gain the client's confidence, by giving a professional treatment and talking about any beauty needs and explaining what other treatments are available in the salon.

There are many very common nail disorders such as flaking, brittle and bitten nails which may be improved with regular manicures. Professional advice may also be proffered to the client regarding the care of hands and nails.

A manicure consists of the following:

○　Filing and shaping of the nails.
○　Care of the cuticles.
○　Hand and arm massage.
○　Enamelling or buffing.

Once the therapist has become proficient the manicure should take no longer than thirty minutes.

Manicure equipment

○　A tray or small trolley with compartments for all manicure preparations.
○　A container in which to place jewellery.
○　A finger bowl for warm water, in which clients immerse their hands during the manicure.
○　Two bowls, one for clean cotton wool and one for waste.
○　Nail clippers or scissors for reducing the length of the nail.
○　Emery boards for filing and shaping the nails (Figure 35.1).

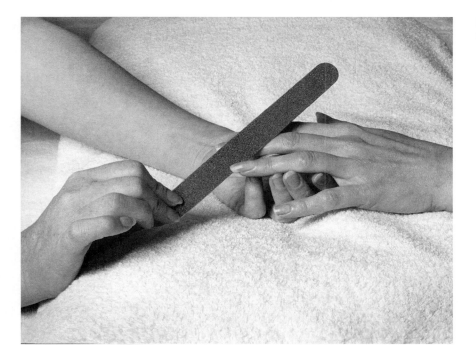

Figure 35.1　*Filing the nail*

○ Orange sticks for treating the cuticles and removing some preparations, for example cuticle massage cream, from their containers.
○ A cuticle knife to remove traces of cuticle adhering to the nail plate.
○ Cuticle nippers to trim torn or ragged cuticle.
○ A nail brush for removing any grease or debris on the nail plate.
○ A nail buffer to buff and polish the nail.
○ A spatula for removing hand cream from the container.

Manicure preparations

Nail enamel remover

Nail enamel remover is used to remove the enamel gently but effectively. It contains acetone or ethyl acetate, which is a solvent necessary to dissolve the enamel, and oil, such as glycerol, to counteract the drying effect of the solvent.

Cuticle cream

Cuticle massage cream is used to soften and nourish the cuticle, allowing it to be pushed back with ease and replacing natural oils lost, due to exposure to drying elements.

It is a mixture of fats and waxes such as:

○ Beeswax.
○ Cocoa butter.
○ White soft paraffin.

Cuticle remover

Cuticle remover is an alkaline lotion applied to the cuticles to help in its removal from the nail plate. It does have an irritating effect on the skin because of its alkalinity and may dry out the nail plate. Therefore, it must be applied and removed quickly.

The constituents are:

○ Potassium hydroxide which is alkaline.
○ Glycerol to counteract the drying effect of the potassium hydroxide.

○ Oleic acid to make it into a milky lotion.
○ Water.

Handcreams

Handcreams or lotions are used to supplement the natural moisture of the skin without leaving a greasy film and should be rich and creamy and easily absorbed by the skin.

They contain such ingredients as:

○ Lanolin.
○ Mineral oil or cetyl alcohol.
○ Perfume.
○ Preservatives.
○ Water.

Paste polish

Paste polish is used when buffing the nails is indicated, as opposed to enamelling them. Powdered silica or powdered pumice may be combined with a wax polish, made from a base of mineral oil, soft paraffin and paraffin wax mixed together to form a smooth paste.

Nail enamels

Nail enamels include:

○ Base coat.
○ Top coat.
○ Coloured cream or frosted enamels.

They are all made from:

○ A plastic film such as nitrocellulose.
○ A plasticizer to provide flexibility.
○ A solvent to allow the enamel to dry.
○ A plastic resin to create a gloss.
○ Pigments to provide colour.

The pearl or frosted enamels contain guanine or bismuth oxychloride.

An ideal coloured enamel should have a good consistency, not too thick or thin and be easy to apply. It should also be long-lasting and protective.

Allergy to nail enamel does occasionally occur and the ingredient which causes this is

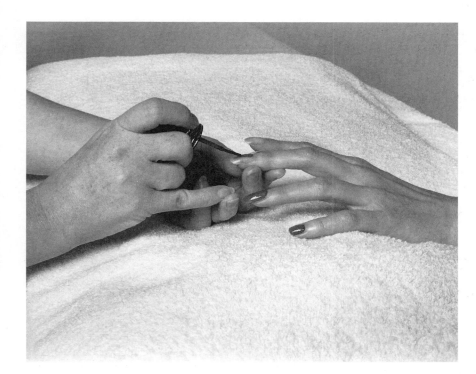

Figure 35.2 *Enamelling the nail*

formaldehyde. However, many enamels are now produced formaldehyde free, to combat this problem. See Figure 35.2.

Contraindications to manicure

It is highly unlikely that clients will request a manicure if they have any condition that would contraindicate treatment. However, they may be unaware that a problem exists so it is left to the therapist to recognize any possible contraindication. In the case of a client wearing nail enamel it may not be evident that there is a nail disorder until the nail enamel has been removed.

Any skin disease which affects the hands or nails would be a contraindication to manicure:

○ *Tinea unguium* or ringworm of the nail is highly contagious, it usually spreads from the free edge (the top of the nail) to the matrix (the root of the nail) and is caused by a fungus which can be of human or animal origin. The nail plate becomes discoloured and opaque with a rough horny appearance.

○ *Scabies* caused by the female itch mite burrowing into the epidermis, where she lays her eggs and they then hatch causing extreme itching. This condition is characterized by tiny red papules and irregular lines on the skin, particularly between the fingers.

○ *Verruca vulgaris* or common warts are due to a viral infection and are very contagious. They occur frequently on the hands, sometimes in groups and often around the nail. There are treatments available from the chemist but they can disappear spontaneously.

○ *Bruising.*

○ *New scar tissue.*

○ *Undiagnosed lumps and bumps.*

○ *Skin disorders* such as eczema, psoriasis or dermatitis are contraindicated only when the condition is at its worst and it may cause the client discomfort. Mild cases of eczema and psoriasis actually benefit from manicures especially if they include a special moisturizing treatment.

Natural nail cultivation

There has been a revolution in nail care in recent years, with many therapists questioning the practices employed in caring for their clients' nails. Many of their clients were having regular manicures, quite often on a weekly basis and yet a common complaint was that their nails did not appear to be growing. In response, many therapists are now employing different methods, following different procedures and eliminating harmful products to ensure the client is satisfied and the end result of regular manicures is strong, healthy nails.

Manicure has now become more of a treatment and more thought has gone into the development of products used, the practical procedures followed and in treating each client individually.

Principles of natural nail cultivation

○ Treat each client as an individual and analyse their nail type accurately.
○ Assess the condition of their hands and nails and devise a treatment plan.
○ Choose the most appropriate products for their nail type.
○ Use techniques which are not damaging to the nail.
○ Advise the client on a good home care routine.
○ Regularly review the nail condition.

Nail types

The nails are made up of the protein keratin, just as the skin and hair are. Therapists are accustomed to analysing skin types and using the appropriate treatment products and hairdressers are accustomed to analysing their clients' hair type and recommending the appropriate treatment products. It is a natural step therefore for therapists to analyse clients' nail type before carrying out any treatment.

There are five different nail types:

1 Dry.
2 Brittle.
3 Dehydrated/ageing.
4 Normal.
5 Damaged.

Characteristics of nail types

Dry nails

○ Are dull in appearance.
○ Have a dragging feeling to the touch.
○ Often have a flaking free edge.
○ May peel easily.
○ May have superficial ridges.
○ The cuticles are normally very dry.

The dry nail type is one of the most common and a large proportion of clients will have this condition. The causes are many:

○ The hands may be exposed to detergents and chemicals. These may include washing and cleaning products, some of which are very harsh, hair treatment products, chlorine in the swimming baths or products which have to be used in a normal day at work or home.
○ Cold weather conditions which will dehydrate the skin and nails if they are not well protected.
○ Dietary deficiency, in particular lack of fats. Many clients will be following a no fat or low fat diet to help them lose weight and low levels of fat in the diet cause a dry skin condition and the nails will also be affected as they require a certain amount of fat for the layers of the nail plate to bond together. The small amount of fat which is obtained from natural sources will be required by the body for the essential functions, for example the uptake of fat soluble vitamins.
○ Illness from a common cold through to more serious conditions will affect the nails and cause a dry flaky condition.
○ Overusing nail enamel remover, particularly one which contains acetone will dry out the nail plate, causing it to flake and peel.
○ Excessive or over-zealous buffing will contribute to a dry nail condition as the friction which occurs, when buffing the nail, produces heat, which will dehydrate and cause the nails to flake even more and the nail plate to become thinner and weaker.

○ The client's profession may mean that they have to perform some sort of task which will cause the nails to dry out or use products which will have the same effect.

Brittle nails

○ Are very hard.
○ Are usually inflexible, with little movement.
○ Often break or crack very easily.
○ Have a thicker nail plate.
○ May become curved as they grow longer.
  The causes of this nail type are:
○ Age because of the natural moisture loss which occurs as we get older.
○ Over-using nail enamel remover which strips the nail plate of natural moisture affecting flexibility.
○ Over-using nail strengtheners. A nail strengthener is a product which contains ingredients to make the nails hard. Therefore when used on a regular basis they will achieve this result. However once this has been achieved if the strengthener is used continuously the nails will become so hard that they are brittle.
○ Poor diet, particularly a lack of fats which are necessary to maintain flexibility and to prevent breakage.

Dehydrated nails

○ Dull in appearance.
○ Flaky and peeling.
○ Often have superficial ridges.
○ Sometimes have a thickened nail plate.
○ May be discoloured.
○ Have a dragging feeling to the touch.

These nails are often a combination of dry and brittle but the condition is more extreme. The external causes will therefore be similar to those of the dry and brittle nail types but there are other causes which are more age related, so this nail type is more common to the older, more mature client.

○ Cell renewal slows down as we age therefore new cells are being formed more slowly and old cells are not shed so rapidly.

○ Circulation slows down as we age therefore nutrients and oxygen will not be so readily available to feed and generate the new cells.
○ The menopause will often have an adverse effect on the nails.
○ Causes of the dry and brittle nail types will also apply.

Normal nails

○ Have a healthy pink colour.
○ Are flexible.
○ Have a smooth surface with no ridges.
○ Are very strong.
○ There are no blemishes present.

Normal nails are very much like normal skin. Not many people have normal nails as there are many external factors which conspire to prevent nails remaining in a normal condition. If a client has normal nails it is often pure luck, hereditary or because the client works very hard to maintain them. The reasons therefore for normal nails are:

○ The client has inherited good healthy nails.
○ The client is probably eating a very healthy and well-balanced diet with all the necessary vitamins, minerals, nutrients and fat required for healthy nail growth.
○ The nails are very well cared for, well-moisturized and manicured.
○ The client may be in a profession which requires constant movement of the hands, stimulating circulation and promoting healthy growth.

Damaged nails

○ Extremely soft.
○ Very thin.
○ Very weak.
○ May peel easily.
○ The free edge disintegrates when filed.
○ There is evidence of bruising.
○ They are slow to grow or do not appear to grow at all.
○ They are sensitive to the touch.

One of the reasons the popularity of natural nail cultivation has increased in the last few years is because of the rise in the number of clients with damaged nails. There are several causes:

○ The poor application of nail extensions.
○ Over zealous buffing.
○ Consistent nail biting over a long period of time.
○ Systemic illness.
○ After a major operation.
○ With prolonged drug use.

Quite often the last three causes are inextricably linked because someone who has a serious illness will probably be taking some form of medication and may require an operation at some point. The body will use all its resources to aid recovery and therefore the nails are the last to receive all the necessary nourishment required for healthy growth.

Aim of treating nail types

Dry	To replace lost moisture
	To bond the layers together
	To prevent flaking
Dehydrated	As above
Brittle	To replace lost moisture
	To promote flexibility
	To prevent breakage
Normal	To maintain the healthy
	condition and pH balance
Damaged	To provide strength
	To improve condition
	To replace lost moisture
	To promote growth

Techniques

Nails are prepared in the usual way by removing existing nail enamel and checking for contraindications. The order of work for the rest of the manicure is different for the following reasons:

○ The hands and nails are moisturized at the beginning of the manicure to hydrate and nourish the nails, bonding the layers of the nail plate together. This will prevent flaking of the free edge when it is filed later. The cream used will have time to penetrate into the nail plate before enamelling, thus eliminating the need to 'squeak' clean with nail enamel remover if the cream is used at the end of the manicure.
○ Oil and cream are used to help soften and shrink back the cuticle naturally. This eliminates the need to use caustic cuticle removers which are harmful to the nails because of the bleaching and drying effect. The oil contains jojoba and vitamin E which have healing properties.
○ Cuticle knives and orange sticks are replaced by a cuticle care machine which is far more gentle in effect, helping to remove dead skin adhering to the nail plate which will become hard, thickened cuticle if left unattended.
○ Nails are degreased by using a wet brush or towel and not nail enamel remover which will strip the nails of oil and moisture.
○ Base coats, top coats and enamels are painted over and under the free edge to build up a protective covering on the whole nail.

36 Anatomy and physiology of the arm and hand

Bones of the forearm, wrist and hand

The forearm consists of two long bones namely the *radius* and the *ulna*, the radius being on the outer side when the palm of the hand is facing forward (see Figure 36.1).

The wrist consists of eight irregularly-shaped bones called the *carpal bones* which are arranged in two rows of four.

scaphoid lunate triquetral pisiform
trapezium trapezoid capitate hamate

The bones of the palm of the hand are long bones and are called the *metacarpal bones*.

The bones of the fingers are also long bones and are called the *phalanges*. The thumb has two phalanges while the fingers each have three. See Figure 36.2

Joints in the forearm and hand

A joint is formed where two bones meet and all joints are classified according to the amount of

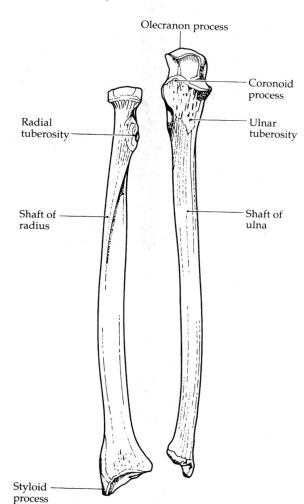

Figure 36.1 *Anterior view of the right radius and ulna*

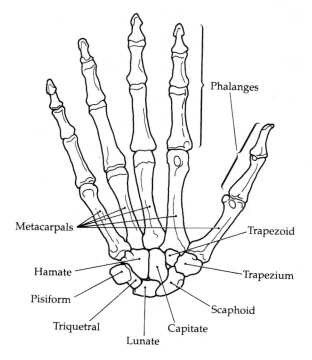

Figure 36.2 *Bones of the wrist and hand*

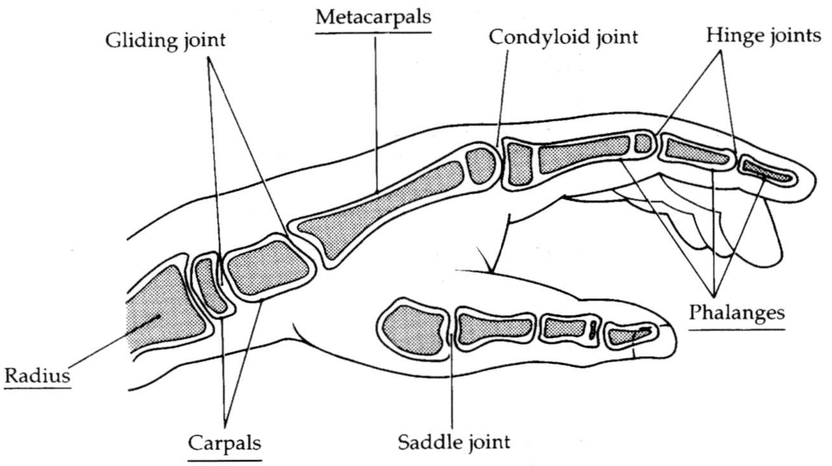

Figure 36.3 *The joints of the hand*

movement possible between the two articulating surfaces.

The joints of the hand and arm are synovial joints as they are all freely movable. These joints have cavities filled with synovial fluid, a form of lymph, which acts as a lubricant and provides nutrition for the living cells of the cartilage, which covers the ends of the bones in the joint. This fluid is produced by the synovial membrane which lines the cavity.

Terminology

Abduction: Movement of a part away from the body.
Adduction: Moving towards the body.
Circumduction: A combination of all movements in some degree.
Extension: Straightening.
Flexion: Bending.
Rotation: Movement around a centre point.

The joints of the forearm and hand are capable of different movements and can be classified as:

Condyloid: Capable of flexion, extension, abduction, adduction and limited circumduction.
Gliding: A gliding of one plane surface across another.
Hinge: Capable of flexion and extension.
Saddle: Capable of flexion, extension, abduction, adduction and circumduction.

Joint classification (Figure 36.3)

o   The elbow is a hinge joint.
o   The wrist is a condyloid joint.
o   The intercarpal joints form gliding joints.
o   The carpometacarpal joints are gliding joints.
o   The metacarpal of the thumb and the trapezium is a saddle joint.
o   The metacarpals and phalanges form condyloid joints.
o   The interphalangeal joints are hinge joints.

Muscles of the arm and hand

The muscles of the arm are shown in Figures 36.4 and 36.5.

Muscles of the upper arm and shoulder

Deltoid
Origin: Clavicle and spine of scapula.
Insertion: Deltoid tuberosity of humerus.
Action: Lifts and abducts the arm.

Biceps
Origin: Scapula.
Insertion: Tuberosity of radius.
Action: Flexes elbow and supinates forearm and hand.

Muscles of the forearm

Brachioradialis
Origin: Humerus.
Insertion: Radius.
Action: Flexes the forearm.

Pronator teres
Origin: Humerus and coranoid process of ulna.
Insertion: Radius.
Action: Pronates the forearm so the palm faces downwards.

Supinator
Origin: Humerus.
Insertion: Radius.
Action: Supinates the forearm so the palm faces upwards.

Superficial flexors

Palmaris longus
Origin: Humerus.
Insertion: Palmar aponeurosis.
Action: Flexes the wrist.

Flexor carpi radialis
Origin: Humerus.
Insertion: Second and third metacarpals.
Action: Flexes the wrist and abducts the hand.

Flexor carpi ulnaris
Origin: Humerus.
Insertion: Carpals and fifth metacarpal.
Action: Flexes the wrist and adducts the hand.

Flexor digitorum sublimis
Origin: Ulna and radius.
Insertion: Tendons of palm of the hand.
Action: Flexes the fingers.

Superficial extensors

Extensor carpi radialis longus
Origin: Humerus.
Insertion: Second metacarpal.
Action: Extends and abducts the wrist.

Extensor carpi radialis brevis
Origin: Humerus.

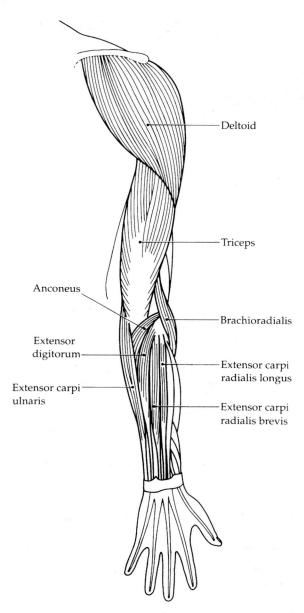

Deltoid

Triceps

Anconeus

Extensor digitorum

Extensor carpi ulnaris

Brachioradialis

Extensor carpi radialis longus

Extensor carpi radialis brevis

Figure 36.4 *Posterior view of the main muscles of the arm*

Triceps
Origin: Scapula and humerus.
Insertion: Olecranon process of ulna.
Action: Extends the forearm.

Brachialis
Origin: Humerus.
Insertion: Ulna.
Action: Flexes the forearm

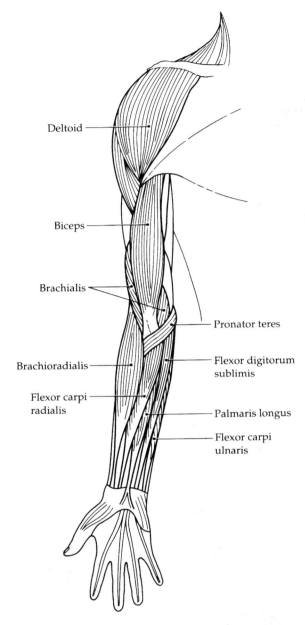

Figure 36.5 *Anterior view of the main muscles of the arm*

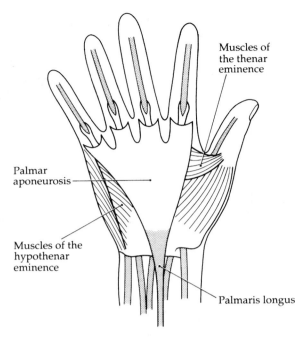

Figure 36.6 *Muscles of the palm of the hand*

Anconeus
Origin: Humerus.
Insertion: Ulna.
Action: Extends the forearm at the elbow joint.

Muscles of the hand (Figure 36.6)

Thenar eminence
The thenar eminence is situated at the base of the thumb and consists of short muscles which move the thumb:

o   Abductor policis brevis.
o   Opponens pollicis.
o   Flexor pollicis brevis.

Hypothenar eminence
The hypothenar eminence is the prominence on the ulnar side of the palm situated at the base of the little finger:

o   Opponens digiti minimi.
o   Flexor digiti minimi brevis.
o   Abductor digiti minimi.
o   Abductor pollicis.

Insertion: Second and third metacarpals.
Action: Extends and abducts the hand.

Extensor digitorum
Origin: Humerus.
Insertion: Proximal phalanx of the little finger.
Action: Extends the fingers.

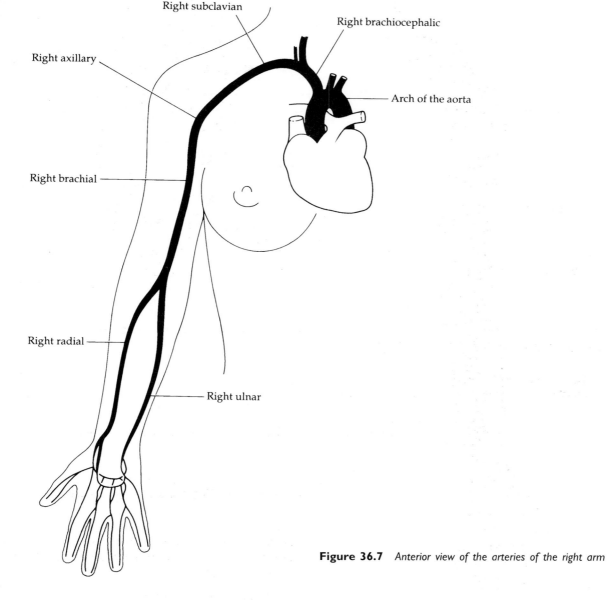

Figure 36.7 *Anterior view of the arteries of the right arm*

Lumbricals

The lumbricals in the hand originate between the metacarpals and insert into the phalanges and they move the fingers.

Interosseous muscles

The interosseous muscles are in the palm of the hand and also originate between the metacarpals and they are also responsible for moving the fingers.

Circulation of blood to the arm and hand

The aorta is the largest artery in the body and gives rise to the left subclavian artery. The right subclavian artery arises from the brachiocephalic artery.

The subclavian arteries then pass into the axillae where they become the axillary arteries.

315

The axillary artery is quite deep but is more superficial as it becomes the brachial artery which extends past the elbow joint and branches into the radial and ulnar arteries.

The radial artery passes down the lateral (outside) part of the forearm passing between the first and second metacarpal bones.

The ulnar artery passes down the medial (inside) part of the forearm, past the wrist and into the hand.

Between the radial and ulnar arteries are two connecting arteries, the deep and superficial palmar arches. From these come the palmar metacarpal arteries and the palmar digital arteries which supply the hands and fingers. See Figure 36.7.

The structure of the nail

The technical term for a nail is *onyx* and it consists of three main parts:

1   The nail root or matrix.
2   The nail plate.
3   The free edge.

The nail is an appendage of the skin which forms a protective covering for the ends of the fingers.

The chemical composition of the nail is:

○   Carbon.
○   Hydrogen.
○   Oxygen.
○   Sulphur.
○   Nitrogen.

A healthy nail is pink in colour with a smooth, slightly curved surface and clear of any mark or defect. A new nail will always grow in place of an injured or lost nail. However, if the matrix is damaged, a deformed nail may grow in its place.

See Figure 36.8.

The matrix

This is situated immediately below the cuticle and is the only living reproducing part of the nail. It contains nerves and blood vessels and cell production occurs here. When the new cells are formed they are continually pushing forward to form the nail plate. A healthy matrix will produce a healthy nail but if injury occurs in this area the nail may grow with a deformity which may be temporary or permanent. The cells receive their nourishment from the blood supply.

The lunula

This is the point where the matrix and the nail bed meet. It is crescent shaped and pearly in colour because the cells are pushed so closely together that the blood capillaries in the nail bed, which provide the pink glow, cannot be seen.

The nail bed

This is a continuation of the matrix and is abundantly supplied with nerves and blood vessels. It is the part of the finger upon which the nail plate rests. It has numerous parallel ridges that dovetail exactly with ridges on the undersurface of the nail plate.

The nail plate

This is the visible portion of the nail which rests upon the nail bed and terminates at the free edge. It consists of dead cells held together with a minimum amount of moisture and it is semi-transparent allowing the colour of the blood supply of the dermis to show through.

The free edge

This is an extension of the nail plate which overlaps the hyponichium and is the part of the nail filed to form its shape.

The hyponichium

This is the portion of skin at the end of the finger underneath the free edge.

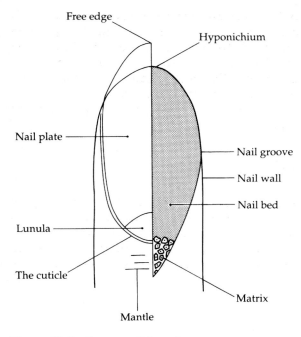

Figure 36.8 *Structure of the nail*

The cuticle

This is the overlapping epidermis surrounding the nail, the function of which is to protect the matrix from invading bacteria and physical damage.

The *eponychium* is the cuticle at the base of the nail.

The *peronychium* is the cuticle at the sides of the nail.

The nail walls

These are the folds of the skin overlapping the sides of the nails.

The nail grooves

These are the grooves or furrows at the sides of the nail upon which the nail moves and acts as a guideline for the nail to follow.

The mantle

This is the deep fold of skin over the matrix and around the base of the nail plate.

Keratinization of the nail

Keratinization is the change of living cells containing a nucleus into flat, dead, horny cells with no nucleus. The process starts in the basal

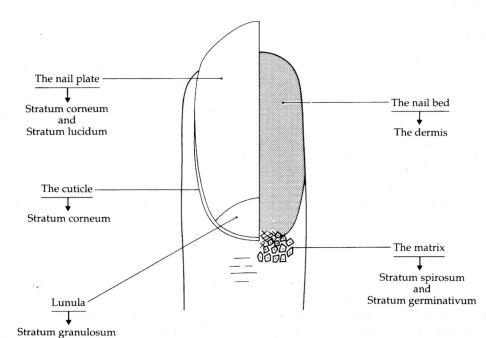

Figure 36.9
Structure of the nail in relation to the layers of the skin

layer of the epidermis and ends in the horny layer.

The nail plate lies on the nail bed (the dermis) which contains nerves and blood vessels. It is made up of cells which are pushed forwards from the matrix and they go through a process of keratinization causing the nail plate to grow in thickness and length.

New cells are formed in the matrix – *stratum germinativum*. These cells divide to produce new cells in the matrix – *stratum spinosum*.

Partly keratinized cells which are losing fluid and contain a nucleus which is beginning to disintegrate form the nail in the area of the lunula – *stratum granulosum*.

Dead horny keratinized cells make up the nail plate – *stratum lucidum* and *stratum corneum*. See Figure 36.9.

Growth of the nail

The growth of the nail can be affected by age, ill health and diet but on average it takes between five and six months to grow from the matrix to the free edge.

The nail grows more quickly:

○   In the summer than in the winter.
○   In younger people than in older.
○   On hands rather than feet.
○   During pregnancy.

There are many disorders of the nail which are irregularities in growth, or blemishes, which can actually be treated by the beauty therapist and in some cases can be improved with professional treatment in the salon and through professional advice on care.

Nail diseases are normally characterized by the presence of infection, soreness or irritation but can also be caused by a health disorder.

Most of these disorders and diseases have unusual names and are quite difficult to pronounce.

Pronunciation chart

Disorder/disease	Pronunciation
Corrugations	cor-oo-ga-shuns
Hangnails	hang-ney-els
Koilonychia	coy-lo-nic-ee-ah
Leuconychia	lu-co-nic-ee-ah
Onychatrophia	on-ee-cat-row-fee-ah
Onychauxis	on-ee-kawk-sis
Onychocryptosis	on-ee-co-crip-to-sis
Onychogryphosis	on-ee-co-gri-fo-sis
Onycholisis	on-ee-co-li-sis
Onychomycosis	on-ee-com-ee-co-sis
Onychophagy	on-ee-co-fa-jee
Onychophyma	on-ee-co-fee-mah
Onychoptosis	on-ee-cop-to-sis
Onychorrhexis	on-ee-co-rex-is
Onychosis	on-ee-co-sis
Paronychia	pa-ro-nic-ee-ah
Pterygium	te-rij-ee-um

Disorders and diseases of the nail

Corrugations

These are superficial ridges in the nails which are caused by uneven growth and may be the result of an illness. Buffing should be included in regular manicures to eliminate this problem.

Furrows

These are deep ridges in the nail which may be caused by a nutritional problem, injury to the matrix or illness. Constant rubbing of the cuticle can cause friction in the area of the matrix and cause a deep ridge which will continue up the nail plate until it reaches the free edge. If, however, this nervous habit is removed, the problem will not recur.

Leuconychia

This is a common condition of the nails and is usually referred to as white spots, a problem caused by injury to the base of the nail whereby a tiny air pocket forms between the nail bed and nail plate. To prevent an occurrence of this problem, injury to the nail must be avoided by treating them gently.

Pterygium

This is a thick hardened growth of dry cuticle which sticks to the nail plate as it grows. The treatment for this problem is to soften the cuticle by using oil or paraffin wax, the cuticle may then be gently pushed back and any remaining cuticle gently removed with cuticle nippers. The nails should be regularly manicured to prevent the problem recurring.

Hangnail

This is caused when the cuticle splits and can be as a result of pterygium when the cuticle has stretched so much it begins to split or because the cuticle is very dry. Moisturizing treatments are advisable and any torn or ragged cuticle should be removed with cuticle nippers. It is important to improve this condition as the torn cuticle could become infected.

Onychauxis

This is an excessive thickening of the nail plate and it may also change colour. The thickening may occur in response to a constant irritation, for example a badly fitting shoe rubbing on the nail. It may also be caused by internal disorders, infection or neglect. This condition is sometimes referred to as hypertrophy and may only be treated by filing the nails smooth and buffing if there is no infection present.

Onychatrophia

This condition is when the nail becomes smaller and smaller and in some cases wastes away completely. The nail loses its lustre, becoming opaque and ridged. It may be caused by injury to the matrix, nervous disorder or disease and should be treated very gently. Manicures would be inadvisable until the problem had been solved but the nails must be protected from harsh products, for example household detergents.

Onychophagy

This is the technical term for bitten nails and in some cases the cuticle around the nail. Nail biting is a nervous habit which results in exposure of the hyponichium and can cause very weak or even deformed nails. Regular manicures with oil treatments to soften the cuticles will help but the best cure is to stop the nail biting.

Onychorrhexis

This is a very common condition when the nails become brittle and split. It is caused by over-exposure to harsh detergents or over-use

of nail cosmetics. In fact, anything which dries out the nail plate. A bout of illness can leave the nails as well as the hair and skin in a very dry condition. Regular manicures, moisturizing treatments and a good diet should be recommended.

Onychosis

This is the technical term for a nail disease.

Onychomycosis

This condition is also known as ringworm of the nails, a highly infectious disease caused by a vegetable parasite which enters the nail at the free edge and spreads towards the matrix, causing the nail to become thickened and discoloured. The degree of the disease can vary from barely negligible to almost complete disintegration of the nail plate.

Paronychia

This is a bacterial infection of the skin surrounding the nail which looks red and inflamed and sometimes swollen. It may occur when the skin is broken, for example hangnails.

Onychocryptosis

This condition affects the fingers or toes but is most common on the big toe. Its common term is an ingrown nail whereby the side of the nail plate actually grows into the flesh of the nail wall. The cause can be incorrect cutting or filing too far down the sides, pressure from ill-fitting shoes or just neglect. This condition may become infected and should be treated by a doctor if it is.

Onychoptosis

This can affect one or several nails and it is the periodic shedding of either the whole nail or part of it.

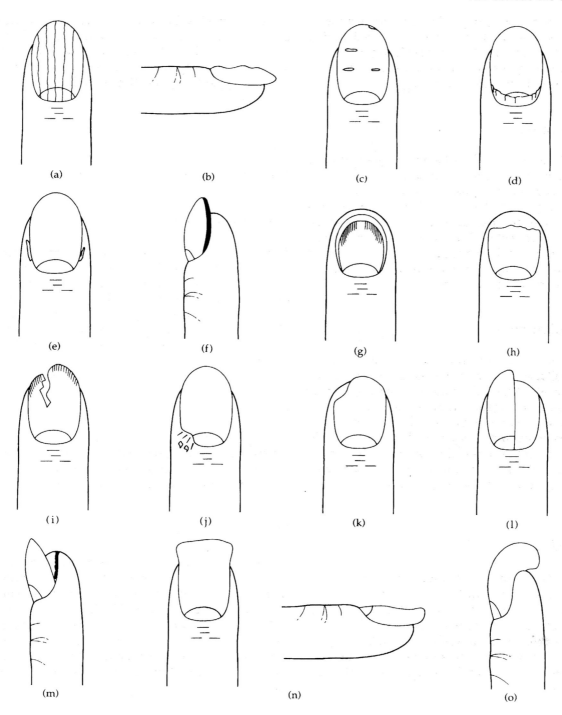

Figure 37.1 *Nail disorders*

(a) Corrugations	*(f) Onychauxis*	*(k) Onychocryptosis*
(b) Furrows	*(g) Onychatrophia*	*(l) Onychoptosis*
(c) Leuconychia	*(h) Onychophagy*	*(m) Onycholysis*
(d) Pterygium	*(i) Onychorrhexis*	*(n) Koilonychia (front and side view)*
(e) Hangnails	*(j) Paronychial*	*(o) Onychogryphosis*

Onycholisis

This is a gradual separation of the nail plate from the nail bed whereby the nail loosens without coming away completely. There are several possible causes such as an internal disorder, psoriasis, eczema or rough treatment of the nails, for example cleaning too far down the nail under the free edge, particularly with a pointed object.

Onychophyma

This condition is a swelling of the nails.

Onychogryphosis

This is an enlarged nail with an increased curve. The enlargement is caused by an increase in the production of the horny cells of the nail plate and this leads to a curvature of the nail resembling a ram's horn. It is more common in older people and the big toe is most frequently affected. The most common causes are age, neglect or ill-fitting shoes. This condition must be treated by a chiropodist or removed surgically if it causes pain.

Koilonychia

This condition may be caused by an accumulation of horny cells at the sides of the nail plate, under the nail wall or an abnormal growth stemming from the matrix. This abnormal growth gives the nail a spoon shape. This condition can be temporary or permanent depending upon the cause which can be an inherited abnormality, a side effect of a certain type of anaemia or an overactive thyroid condition.

Psoriasis

Although not an infectious condition, psoriasis has different degrees of severity and as well as affecting the skin it can affect the nails. The mildest form it takes is when it just causes a pitting of the nail plate. The next stage is when it causes a separation of the nail from the nail bed and there is a noticeable discoloration in the area.

The most severe form causes thickening of the nail plate which at first becomes opaque and then turns yellowish brown in colour and the surface can become rough and atrophied.

Lamella dystrophy

This is a very common nail disorder with many causes. It is characterized by flaking, peeling and breaking of the nail plate and it can affect one or all of the nails. The causes are:

○ Nail disease.
○ Exposure to harsh detergents or chemicals.
○ Dietary deficiency.
○ Over-use of caustic nail products, for example nail enamel remover and cuticle remover.
○ Over-use of false or acrylic nails.
○ General ill health.
○ Having the hands immersed in water for long periods.
○ Incorrect filing.
○ Incorrect buffing, produces heat and dries out the nail plate.
○ A hereditary factor.
○ The habit of nail biting.
○ Wearing nail enamel for long periods of time.
○ Using the nails as a tool.
○ Poor circulation.
○ Neglect.

In the majority of cases this condition is easily treated by the therapist with regular manicures, moisturizing treatments and good homecare advice to the client.

Blue nails

This is a characteristic of poor circulation, but in some cases may be attributed to a heart disorder.

Black/blue spots

These spots appear on the nail plate and are normally caused by injury to the nail bed which produces bleeding. The mark will disappear as the nail grows. Treatment should be gentle avoiding pressure. When the nail suffers a severe blow from a heavy object it may turn completely blue and usually falls off. It will be replaced by a new nail in due course unless the matrix has been damaged.

For a manicure, the manicure trolley should always be prepared well in advance, with all equipment positioned in a convenient order to save time and to allow the therapist to work comfortably. All working areas should be clean and new towels used for each client.

The full manicure consists of several different procedures which must be carried out quickly and efficiently to produce a polished end result.

Filing

When filing the nails, the finger must always be supported and the emery board should be used carefully, filing from the outside inwards along the free edge, working each side alternately and quickly. It is important not to use a sawing action as this will disturb the layers of the nail plate causing split nails and may cause possible damage to the matrix due to the rocking movement. It will also produce heat in the nail plate which will dry out the natural oils causing flakiness. The nails should not be filed down into the sides as this causes a weak point in the nail which will easily break. The shape of the nail is chosen for various reasons:

○ The client's preference.
○ Fashion.
○ The shape of the hands.
○ The state of the nail.

The ideal shape is oval, the strongest shape is square and the weakest shape is pointed.

Buffing

This is often used instead of enamelling the nails for the following reasons:

1 The client may be allergic to the enamel.
2 The occupation of the client may require her not to wear enamel.
3 For a manicure on a male client.
4 For a client who bites her nails, to stimulate circulation and improve the appearance.
5 To remove superficial ridges on the nail plate.
6 To remove stains from the nail plate.

Only the tiniest amount of buffing paste should be applied to each nail because it spreads very easily and this will prevent it spreading to the skin tissue at the sides of the nail. Buffing should be performed in one direction only, from the matrix to the free edge until the nail appears shiny. This will prevent damage to the matrix which would be caused if the nail was buffed from side to side. The movements should be of a moderate speed and in one direction to prevent heat building up in the nail, thus drying it out. See Figure 38.1.

Cuticle work

Cuticle remover is slightly caustic so it should be left on the nails for the shortest length of time necessary to complete the work and then it should be removed either with a nail brush or damp cotton wool.

Cuticle or orange sticks must always be tipped with cotton wool and when pushing the cuticle back, the stick should be used in small circular movements to prevent causing damage to the matrix.

The cuticle knife must only be used to remove excess cuticle adhering to the nail plate. The blade must be wet at all times as this provides a protective cushion to the nail plate and it should be held at an angle of 45° to prevent scratching the surface of the nail plate.

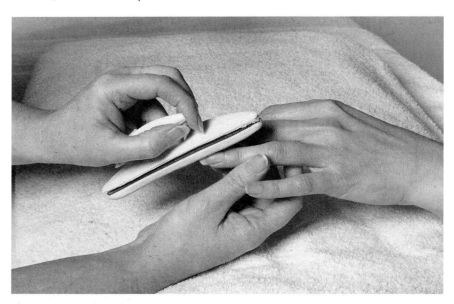

Figure 38.1 *Buffing the nail*

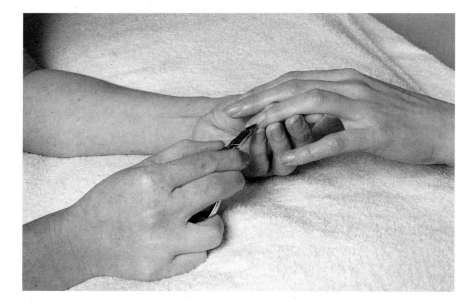

Figure 38.2 *Using cuticle nippers*

Cuticle nippers must only be used to remove hangnails and they must be held firmly, cutting the hangnail cleanly, without pulling and tearing the tissue. See Figure 38.2.

Hand and arm massage

There are several reasons why massage is incorporated into the manicure, normally after the cuticle work and immediately prior to the enamelling:

1 It is relaxing to the client and if performed well it may encourage the client to book further treatments such as facial or body massage.

2 It also relaxes tense, tired and aching muscles.

3 The blood circulation to the area is stimulated bringing essential nutrients to the area

and removing waste products as well as improving skin colour.

4 It helps with joint mobility and keeps the hands supple.

5 As rich creams may be used the skin's natural moisture content is replenished and the skin is softened.

6 It aids desquamation, the removal of dead skin cells, from the surface of the skin leaving it brighter looking.

To ensure comfort throughout:

o The client's arm must be well supported to ensure that the muscles are totally relaxed and the massage strokes should flow smoothly and continuously.

o The hand cream should be warmed in the palm of the hands before applying it to the skin, as it can sometimes feel cold on application.

o A fast-absorbing cream should be used which does not leave a sticky feeling on the skin.

o The cream used must have a pleasant smell.

o The client's clothing must be protected from the cream used.

Massage manipulations

Effleurage

The massage movements should begin and end with light stroking effleurage, a soothing, relaxing movement always performed in an upward direction, following the blood and lymph flow.

Petrissage

Finger and palmar kneading are both relaxing and soothing to the muscles. Slight pressure is added on each movement and these movements also follow the blood and lymph flow.

Rotations

Circular movements to the joints to aid joint mobility.

Contraindications

All contraindications which apply to manicure also apply to massage of the hand and arm but there are also some reasons for omitting the massage only from the manicure and these are:

o Extremely hairy arms as the massage movements would be uncomfortable.

o Recent sunburn to the arms.

o Recent scar tissue.

o Over-stretched, very thin skin.

Nail enamelling

Before the nails are enamelled, it is important to ensure that there is no grease left on the nail plate to create a barrier and prevent the enamel adhering to the nail. This is most easily achieved by wiping over the nail with a piece of cotton wool soaked in nail enamel remover.

A base coat must be applied first:

o To prevent pigments in the nail enamel from staining the nail plate.

o To fill in any grooves and ridges which may be on the nail plate.

o To provide a smooth base for the enamel, making the application easier.

o To help in prolonging the life of the enamel.

o To protect the nail plate by hardening it.

There are two different types of enamel:

1 Cream.
2 Frosted.

When using the cream variety two applications should be used. When using a frosted enamel three coats should be applied.

A top coat is then applied to the cream enamel only; a frosted enamel does not require the added lustre of the top coat. The top coat is applied:

o To protect the enamel from chipping.

o To prolong the life of the cream enamel.

o To add a high gloss to cream enamel.

A quick-dry liquid may then be applied to speed up the process but the best way to ensure the nails dry quickly is to have a pause in between the application of each coat of enamel. However, this is not always practical in a busy salon so clients must sit for a short period after the manicure to allow their nails to dry.

Certain problems may occur if the enamelling technique is less than perfect.

Enamel will peel away if:

○   An oily residue is left on the nail plate.

○   The enamel is applied too thickly.
○   Inferior enamel is used.

Enamel will chip if:

○   There is a flaking nail condition present.
○   The enamel is forced dried.
○   There are ridges present on the nail plate.
○   The enamel has been thinned with too much solvent.

39 Hand and nail treatments

There are occasions when the client will benefit from the incorporation of a special treatment into the manicure routine at the appropriate time. The most common treatments are:

Paraffin wax

The aims of this treatment are:

○ To nourish and moisturize the skin.
○ To improve a flaking nail condition.
○ To improve the skin colour.
○ To increase joint mobility.

The manicure should be performed in the usual manner and a rich nourishing cream applied after the cuticle work has been completed. The hand and arm should then be completely covered in the wax, heated to 48°C, either by immersing it in the wax or by painting the wax directly on to the hand and arm building up several layers until the coating is quite thick.

The whole area treated must then be wrapped in foil before being covered by towels. This maintains the heat for a short period allowing the treatment to take effect.

Encased in the warm paraffin wax the following actions occur:

○ The circulation increases.
○ Skin temperature rises.
○ The pores open.
○ Sebaceous gland activity increases.
○ The activity of the sudoriferous glands also increases.

These actions result in:

○ The absorption of the nourishing cream which has been applied.
○ An improvement in skin colour due to the increase in circulation.

○ A softening of the skin texture from the application of the cream and paraffin wax and the increase in sebaceous gland activity.
○ A soothing effect on the joints due to the increased warmth in the area.

Oil

The aims of this treatment are:

○ To moisturize dry cuticles.
○ To return lost moisture to flaking nails.
○ To soothe and moisturize a dry skin condition.

This treatment will also be carried out after the cuticle work has been completed and before the hand and arm massage. The oil used should be heated to a comfortable temperature and the nails or whole hands, depending upon the reason for the treatment, should be immersed in the warmed oil. They should be left to soak for 10–15 minutes and then the oil on the hands may be used to perform the massage. This treatment may

Figure 39.1 *Paraffin wax heater*
Courtesy Depilex Limited

be performed as often as required. The client may also be advised to follow the same routine at home until the condition has improved.

Salt rub

The aims of this treatment are:

○ To improve skin colour.
○ To desquamate the dead skin cells.
○ To improve circulation.
○ To even out a fading suntan.

Again this treatment will be carried out after cuticle work and before the hand massage. The salt should be moistened with a small amount of water, the massage cream to be used, or a moisturizing lotion and then rubbed well into the hands, until there is a noticeable improvement in skin colour. This improvement is due to the increase in circulation.

The salt must then be rinsed off and after the therapist's hands have been dried, more hand cream should be applied and massaged well in.

The actions on the skin are:

○ Stimulating.
○ Nourishing.
○ Refining.

Thermal mitten treatment

A special nourishing treatment combining heat and moisture to:

○ Nourish and hydrate the skin.
○ Improve skin texture and colour.
○ Add moisture to the nail plate bending the layers.

○ Increase the circulation bringing fresh nutrients.
○ Increase lymph flow, removing waste products.
○ Soothe aching joints and improve mobility.

The moisturizing products are applied generously to the hands and nails which are wrapped in clingfilm and placed in a pair of lined thermal mittens. The mittens are thermostatically controlled, therefore, the temperature may be adjusted to suit the client.

Homecare advice

To maintain healthy nails clients must be responsible for their own nail care when they are not attending the salon for treatment. The condition of their nails will not improve if they do not attempt to remove the cause of their problems, so the advice given is very important.

1 A well-balanced diet should be eaten.
2 The hands should be protected from detergents and household chemicals.
3 Hand cream should be applied after immersing the hands in water, and last thing at night.
4 The nails should not be used as tools.
5 Metal files must never be used because they cause the nails to flake.
6 An oily enamel remover should always be used to prevent too much moisture loss from the nail.
7 A base coat should always be used to protect the nail.
8 Nail hardeners should be used when the nails are weak.
9 The nails should not be bitten and the cuticles should not be picked.
10 Gloves should be worn in the winter to prevent chapping.

Several different types of artificial nails are available which make it possible to have long, strong and beautiful nails. There are several reasons why artificial nails are worn:

○ To conceal broken or damaged nails.
○ To improve the appearance of very short nails.
○ To help overcome the habit of nail biting.
○ To protect weak nails against splitting or breaking.
○ For special occasions e.g. a wedding.

There are three different techniques which may be used, namely false nails, nail extensions and nail sculptures.

False nails

These are plastic nails which fit snugly over any nail and they come in all shapes and sizes to suit all different hand and nail shapes. They are attached to the nail plate with a strong adhesive, although they are quite easy to remove. They are ideal, therefore, as a temporary answer to short nails.

Once the appropriate nail size has been chosen, the length is filed to the correct shape at the free edge, and then adhesive applied to the nail and the false nail carefully positioned to fit as close to the cuticle as possible. The false nail should be held firmly in place for 30 seconds to ensure that both nails are well bonded.

It is necessary to follow the manufacturers' instructions when applying false nails but here are some general points which apply to all makes:

○ Check the client for contraindications, for example:
   —Infected nails.
   —Damaged cuticles.
   —An allergy to the adhesive.
   —Skin disorders of the hand.
○ The nails must be clean and grease free to allow the glue to work efficiently, as any grease on the nail plate will create a barrier between the nail plate and the false nail.
○ The base of the false nail should be placed lightly under the cuticle, which should be free from the nail plate, if this procedure is carried out during the manicure.
○ The false nails should not be immersed in water for too long as this can loosen them.
○ Care should be taken when wearing false nails as they are inflammable.

Advantages of false nails

These include:

○ Very little equipment is required.
○ The cost is not very high to the client.
○ The application time is between 20 and 30 minutes.
○ The technique is not difficult to perfect.
○ The nails may be removed quite easily when required.
○ Instant precoloured nails are available, thus eliminating the need to enamel the new nails.

Nail extensions

A nail extension is a method used quite extensively to produce a natural-looking nail which does not require the application of nail enamel because once applied it closely resembles the natural nail.

A nail tip is applied to the nail plate which will extend the nail to the length required. The width should fit perfectly between the nail grooves. Because this is not just a false nail, the tip is stuck to the nail using a very strong adhesive no more than two-thirds of the length of the nail plate.

The nail tip then has to be filed at the join, blending the nail and tip together. A special gel should then be painted over the whole nail and then left to set under an ultraviolet light. Three applications of the gel are required to produce the desired effect.

Advantages of nail extensions

These include:

o   They do not harm the natural nail.
o   They are odourless.
o   Once in place they are flexible and will not lift away from the nail plate if they have been applied correctly.
o   They will not peel or shatter.
o   The new nail will not change colour.
o   The gel is self-levelling which makes it easy to apply.
o   It is not necessary to file the nail after application as it applies thinly and evenly just like nail enamel.
o   Moisture is not trapped during the process thus eliminating the possibility of fungal infections.
o   It is an efficient method of nail repair on a broken nail.

Disadvantages of nail extensions

These include:

o   The nail plate has to be filed before applying the nail tip.
o   As the nails grow there will be a gap at the base of the nail which will have to be filled in regularly to maintain the natural look.
o   It is expensive to have a complete set.
o   The application of a full set of nail extensions is time consuming.
o   Removal of nail extensions can also be a lengthy procedure.
o   Once removed the nail underneath can look dull and lifeless and possibly ridged.
o   Special care must be taken when using the ultraviolet light to harden the gel:

—The light must be positioned so that it is out of the client's and therapist's eyesight.
—The dosage of ultraviolet light must not exceed 6 minutes in any one day.
—Some drugs can cause a temporary photo-sensitivity so clients should be asked if they are taking any medication.

Nail sculptures

These are semi-permanent nails made from a mixture of powder and liquid acrylic applied to the complete nail plate which extends its length. The mixture is very tough and can withstand abrasive drills filing them to the desired shape.

There are many different nail systems available to the beauty therapist and it is important to follow the manufacturers' instructions, as each system differs slightly from the next.

Once this nail addition has been applied the client will be required to return approximately every three weeks to infill, where the natural nail has grown.

The client's nails must be checked for any contraindications and the nail plate should then be roughened slightly with an abrasive file. A nail form is then placed under the free edge, around the nail to be treated, allowing the artificial nail to be formed over the free edge, fitting firmly around the cuticle without overlapping the nail plate.

The powder and liquid acrylics are then placed in separate bowls and, using a sable brush, the bristles should be saturated in the liquid and then dipped into the powder. This mixture forms into a small ball which is applied to the nail at the centre close to the free edge. It should then be brushed smoothly and evenly over the whole nail plate. The new sculptured nail may be shaped by dipping the brush into the liquid and brushing smoothly over the whole nail.

The whole hand is completed and left to harden while the second hand is treated in the same way. Once the liquid and powder compound has set hard the nail forms may be gently removed. The shaping procedure is now carried out using a special file or an abrasive drill. This is important as the shaping of the nail if performed skilfully can make the sculptured nail look very natural.

Removal

Special removing solution recommended by the manufacturers should be used and removal should be done with the nail immersed in the removing solution. The dissolving material can be pushed off using a cuticle stick. If the nail is removed from the solution too quickly the chemical process will stop, leaving some of the acrylic nail in place.

Precautions

There should be adequate ventilation in the salon to prevent an accumulation of vapours.

Do not leave the products in direct sunlight. Never use on:

○   Infected nails.
○   Weak or damaged nails.
○   Badly bitten nails deep into the nail bed.
○   Nails with sore or inflamed cuticles.

Most manufacturers provide a disinfectant which should be used to clean the nail and left to dry before applying the acrylic nail sculpture.

41 Pedicure

The feet take a lot of stress and strain every day and although they are not on show, like the hands, the client will benefit greatly from the pedicure treatment.

Most clients will book a pedicure during the summer months because their feet are on display. However, feet need to be looked after all year round as most of the time they are enclosed in shoes and tights, often becoming very hot and swollen because of the pressure put upon them.

Although a pedicure is basically a manicure of the feet, it usually requires more time as there are a few differences in procedure.

It should be explained to the client that the therapist is not going to treat the feet in the same way as a chiropodist and such problems as ingrowing nails, corns, bunions and callouses should be treated by a chiropodist.

Equipment

The same equipment used for a manicure is required for a pedicure but with the following pieces of equipment added:

○ A large bowl in which to soak the feet.
○ A refreshing and cleansing foot soak.
○ Nail clippers.
○ Hoof stick.
○ An implement or cream for removing hard skin.
○ Foot powder.
○ Extra towels.
○ Toe separators.

Chapter 35 lists the manicure equipment.

Preparation of the work area

The client should be seated in a comfortable position with her back well supported. Easily adjustable multi-position beauty couches are ideal but if there is not one available, and pedicures are carried out in a small area away from treatment cubicles, a comfortable chair with a back support must be used.

A towel should be placed under the foot bowl in case of spillage and spare towels must be easily accessible to cover the client's foot which is not being worked upon, to keep it warm.

Pedicure techniques

Most clients who have a pedicure will come to the salon already having washed their feet, but the pedicure should begin by soaking the feet in warm water to which has been added an antiseptic or a refreshing foot soak such as peppermint.

Contraindications should be looked for before starting the treatment and if there are any signs of infection or abnormality then the client should be advised to seek the advice of a doctor or a chiropodist.

Work should begin on one foot, keeping the other one well wrapped and warm.

Filing

After removing the enamel, the nails should be cut first with clippers, to reduce the length, and then filed straight across. The toe nails must not be shaped into the sides as this could cause ingrowing toe nails, a condition which can be very painful.

Hard skin removal

Hard skin tends to build up on the foot in those areas which receive the greatest pressure and these are the balls of the feet and the heels. The hard skin may be removed after the filing has been completed using the implement for hard skin removal. Alternatively, a cream specially formulated for hard skin removal can be massaged well into the problem areas. After applying cuticle massage cream to the cuticles the foot may then be soaked in the warm water.

Cuticle work

The cuticles on the toes are often quite hard and thick unless the client has been having regular pedicures. The hoof stick, which is a rubber tipped orange stick, is used to gently push back the cuticles and any tissue adhering to the nail plate can be removed with the cuticle knife and nippers. Care should be taken not to tear the cuticle leaving it open to infection.

Leg massage

It is very soothing and relaxing for the client to have a leg massage to the knee, as well as massage to the foot. The leg must be well supported making sure the knee joint is not hypo-extended.

Oil, body lotion or massage cream may be used as appropriate. Foot or talcum powder could be applied after the massage to absorb any excess cream or oil and allow the client to feel comfortable in her shoes after the pedicure. Talcum powder will also keep the client's feet fresh and dry in the summer.

Enamelling

The foot must be flat when enamelling the toe nails or the enamel tends to run down towards the cuticles giving an uneven application. Toe separators must be used so that the wet enamel on the toe does not touch the next one and smudge.

Contraindications

Any infectious diseases of the skin or nails would contraindicate pedicure treatment. Some of the most common conditions are:

Tinea pedis

The more common name for this condition is athletes' foot. It is a fungal infection which affects the spaces between the toes causing a sodden, white appearance often with deep splits at the base of the tissue.

The foot is a common site for fungal infections because fungi grow better in moist conditions and the feet being enclosed in shoes provide ideal conditions. It is an extremely infectious condition and is usually acquired by contact with objects which have already been in contact with the disease. The sources of infection are communal areas such as swimming baths and residential schools.

Verruca plantaris

This is a viral infection causing warts on the soles of the feet, which become flattened with pressure. The most common sites are the ball or heel of the foot. They do become painful, so to avoid discomfort they should be treated as soon as possible by a doctor or chiropodist. See Figure 41.1.

There are several conditions of the feet which do not contraindicate pedicure treatment by a beauty therapist but for specific treatment of the condition itself, a chiropodist or doctor must be consulted.

Corns

These are thickened dense areas of skin, forming a raised appearance and situated on pressure areas, such as the toes. They are most commonly

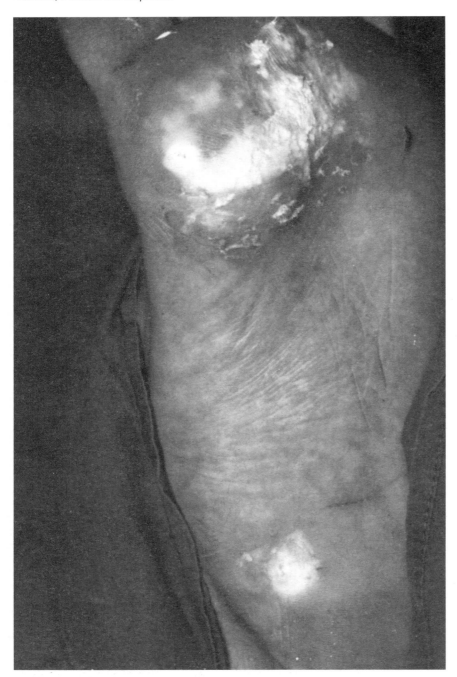

Figure 41.1 *Verruca plantaris*
Courtesy Leeds Foundation for Dermatological Research

caused by ill-fitting shoes and if they become sore or painful it is advisable to consult a doctor. Seed corns are usually found on the heel or under the arch of the foot and are given their name because they have a small nucleus, which resembles a millet seed. This type of corn is not usually painful.

Callus

This is a patch of hard thickened skin which accumulates as a result of pressure on the foot and the most common sites are the heel and the ball of the foot.

Bunions

This is another condition which can be caused by wearing badly fitted shoes and is the result of displacing the toe joint. The toe may be forced into an unnatural position by pressure from ill-fitting shoes over a period of time. A lump then forms on the inside of the foot at the base of the big toe.

At first the lump will be sore and tender but will begin to harden as the bone itself begins to grow into the deformed shape. Bunions are permanent and may only be removed surgically.

Chilblains

These are painful itchy areas on the feet, varying in colour from dull blue to red. The cause is an inadequate blood supply but the condition is aggravated by cold and damp. Those more susceptible to the condition are the elderly and anyone who works in hot, cold or damp conditions. To cure the problem, the affected parts must be kept warm and dry and an ointment may be applied, which will act as a vasodilator, dilating the blood vessels and improving circulation.

Onychogryphosis

This is more common in older people and it is an enlarged curvature of the nail caused by an increase in growth of the horny cells of the nail plate which then causes the formation of an irregular horn shaped nail. If it becomes painful it should be cut by a chiropodist or removed completely.

Onychocryptosis

A common condition of the big toe, it is an ingrowing nail caused by incorrect trimming or filing, or pressure from ill-fitting shoes. The nail plate itself penetrates the tissue of the nail wall at the sides of the nail. It can become very red, sore and painful. If the condition becomes uncomfortable a chiropodist should be consulted.

Flat feet

This is a condition due to partial or total collapse of one or both arches of the feet. There are several causes and these are:

1 Hereditary.
2 Weak muscles.
3 Injury.
4 Being very overweight.
5 Ill-fitting shoes.

Corrective measures
○ Keep the feet mobile by exercising them. A good strengthening exercise is to pick up a pencil or a marble with the toes and pass it from one foot to the other.
○ One of the best exercises for the feet generally is to walk barefoot in the sand as this will tone every muscle and ligament.
○ Walking around the house barefoot as often as possible.
○ Lose weight if this is a contributory factor.
○ Make sure that shoes are a correct fit.

Hyperhidrosis

This term refers to the overactivity of the sweat glands. This is a common foot problem and can lead to other conditions of the feet.

General foot care

Because tight-fitting shoes are the cause of many foot problems, shoes should be purchased later in the day when the feet are their largest as feet tend to swell slightly when they become warm.

High heels are very bad for the posture as they throw the body out of alignment, so if they are worn often they will eventually contribute to a bad back.

The same pair of shoes must not be worn constantly. It is better to alternate between different pairs.

A stock of products especially for the feet should be kept, for example foot powders, anti-perspirant or foot refreshing spray, all designed to keep the foot healthy.

Foot salts are a useful antidote to swollen and aching feet as they draw out the moisture. Epsom salts or sea salt in lukewarm water can be used to soak the feet.

Massage the feet often as this is very therapeutic, not just for the feet but for the whole body.

Anatomy of the leg and foot

The bones of the leg

The lower leg consists of the tibia and fibula bones.

The tibia or shin bone
The medial of the two bones which forms the lower leg. It is a long bone and the stronger of the two.

The fibula
Also a long but slender bone and it is the lateral of the two bones in the lower leg (Figure 41.3).

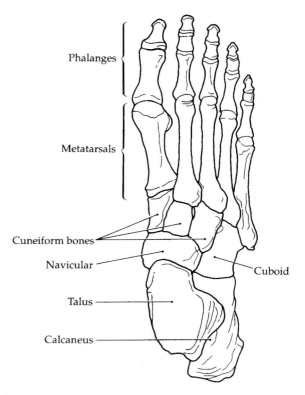

Figure 41.2 *Dorsal view of the right foot*

The bones of the foot

The foot is made up of a complicated arrangement of bones which help us to stand firmly with ease and to walk and run while keeping our balance. Another factor in maintaining balance is that the bones of the toes are broader and flatter than our fingers.

The bones of the foot consist of the following:

The tarsal or ankle bones
○ One talus.
○ One calcaneus.
○ One navicular.
○ Three cuneiform.
○ One cuboid.

The metatarsal bones
There are five metatarsals which are long bones and they connect the tarsal bones to the phalanges.

The phalanges
There are fourteen phalanges altogether, two in the big toe and three in the other four toes (Figure 41.2).

The bones of the feet are supported by muscles and ligaments which form four arches:

○ The medial longitudinal arch.
○ The lateral longitudinal arch.
○ Two transverse arches.

Muscles and ligaments

Posterior tibialis
This muscle originates from the middle of the tibia and fibula and inserts into the navicular, cuneiform, cuboid and metatarsal bones. It provides essential support for the medial longitudinal arch.

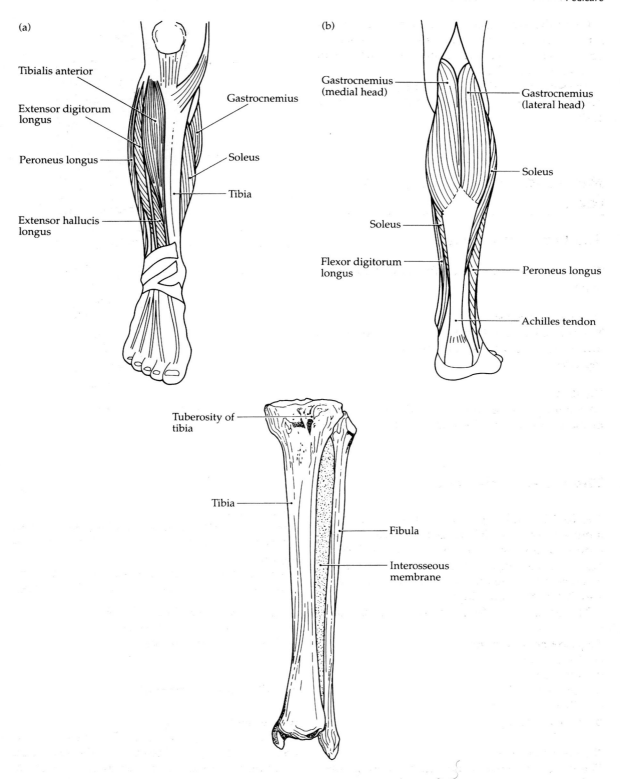

(a)

Tibialis anterior

Extensor digitorum longus

Peroneus longus

Extensor hallucis longus

Gastrocnemius

Soleus

Tibia

(b)

Gastrocnemius (medial head)

Gastrocnemius (lateral head)

Soleus

Soleus

Flexor digitorum longus

Peroneus longus

Achilles tendon

Tuberosity of tibia

Tibia

Fibula

Interosseous membrane

Figure 41.3 *Muscles and bones of the lower leg. (a) Anterior muscles of the lower leg; (b) Posterior muscles of the lower leg; (c) The bones of the lower leg*

Short muscles of the foot

These form the fleshy part of the sole of the foot and provide support for the lateral longitudinal and the transverse arches.

Plantar calcaneonavicular ligament (spring)

This ligament is essential to the support of the medial longitudinal arch. It is strong and thick and stretches from the calcaneus to the navicular bone.

Muscles of the lower leg

Gastrocnemius

Origin: lateral and medial condyles of femur.
Insertion: through the Achilles tendon on the calcaneum.
Action: flexes the knee and plantar flexes the foot.

Soleus

Origin: tibia and fibula.
Insertion: through Achilles tendon on the calcaneum.
Action: plantar flexes the foot.

Peroneus longus

Origin: fibula.
Insertion: first metatarsal and first cuneiform bone.
Action: plantar flexes and everts the foot.

Tibialis anterior

Origin: tibia.
Insertion: first metatarsal and first cuneiform bone.
Action: inverts and dorsiflexes the foot.

Extensor digitorum longus

Origin: tibia and fibula.
Insertion: second and third phalanges of four lateral toes.
Action: extends the toes and dorsiflexes the foot.

Extensor hallucis

Origin: fibula.
Insertion: base of distal phalanx.
Action: extends the toes and dorsiflexes the foot.

Achilles tendon

Origin: attached to the gastrocnemius and soleus.
Insertion: calcaneum.
Action: raises the foot.

Muscles of the foot and ankle

Flexor digitorum longus

Origin: calcaneum.
Insertion: phalanges of four lateral toes.
Action: flexes the foot.

Flexor hallucis longus

Origin: calcaneum.
Insertion: base of big toe.
Action: flexes the foot.

Lumbricals

Origin: tendons of long flexor muscles of the toes.
Insertion: base of phalanges of four lateral toes.
Action: help to flex the proximal phalanges.

42 *Depilation*

Depilation is any method of temporary hair removal:

○ Waxing.
○ Tweezing and plucking.
○ Shaving.
○ Depilatory creams.

Waxing

The most commonly used method in the beauty salon is depilatory waxing. There are two methods of waxing:

1 Hot wax.
2 Cool wax.

The hot wax method of depilation is long established but has been superseded by the cool wax method which is now used more extensively.

Hot wax

The basic ingredients in hot wax are beeswax and resins plus a soothing agent such as azulene.

Beeswax is a true wax from the honeycomb and is solid in appearance. Resin is added to the beeswax to give it some flexibility. Depending upon the manufacturer the wax varies in colour. It may be pale yellow, deep brown, rusty brown or green.

The melting point of hot wax is approximately 50°C and the working temperature is approximately 68°C.

The modern hot wax machine has enclosed heating elements and is thermostatically controlled to prevent overheating (Figure 42.1).

Because of stringent hygiene regulations the hot wax should not be re-used. Therefore, it is not as necessary to have the larger wax machines with two pots, one in use and the other for filtering the used wax. However, they are still readily available.

The modern machines are much smaller and easier to keep clean and should comply with British Standard regulations.

Cool wax

The ingredients in cool wax vary and they are not really waxes at all. They can be a mixture of

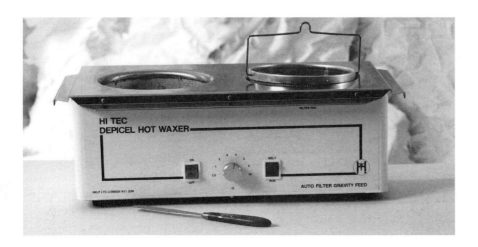

Figure 42.1 *Hot wax machine*
Courtesy Depilex Limited

rubber latex solution and solvents or organic substance such as honey which is used more often.

Some of these mixtures need warming and others may be applied cold and they never set hard on the skin, making it far easier to treat larger areas quickly.

The working temperature of cool wax is approximately 43°C. The wax is heated in a compact, thermostatically-controlled unit to a fairly low temperature. The cool wax is thrown away once it has been used and is therefore very hygienic (Figure 42.2).

The most recent model of cool wax machine comes in the form of a cartridge with a roller applicator head which attaches to a handle. All parts are disposable except the handle, making this method totally hygienic to the client.

Figure 42.2 *Cool wax machine*
Courtesy Depilex Limited

New waxing system

One of the major problems with waxing is to be totally hygienic in application and treatment. The industry requires very high standards and a system has been developed which is said to be the most hygienic method of depilation available.

This revolutionary new method uses disposable applicator heads for applying the wax and this means that clients have their own applicator which is not inserted into the wax, but is screwed on to a tube instead. It is then discarded after use and this minimizes the risk of cross-infection during waxing treatments.

The system consists of:

○ A compact unit which has a compartment for all the items required, a double-heater for the wax and a booster for use when required.
○ Pre-depilatory cleansing gel containing aloe vera and witch hazel for their soothing and antiseptic properties.
○ Wax which comes in tubes.
○ Pre-sealed, disposable applicator heads to be attached to the tubes for each treatment.
○ Wax removal strips.
○ Post-depilatory lotion for hydrating and conditioning the skin. It contains witch hazel and allantoin for their antiseptic and healing properties and lemongrass oil for its refreshing smell.

The special applicator dispenses the wax evenly, cleanly and quickly. The wax does not smell as strongly in the tubes as it does in a wax heater.

A comparison of the two methods

Preparation of the client
Whichever method is employed a thermal skin test should be carried out to test the client's sensitivity to heat so that there is no risk of burning the skin, particularly with the hot method. Contraindications to waxing should also be checked.

Equipment required for hot wax treatment
○ Hot wax machine.
○ Witch hazel.
○ Talcum powder.
○ Cotton wool.
○ Spatulas.
○ Soothing lotion.
○ Waste bowl.

The area to be treated must first be wiped over with witch hazel to remove any grease. Talcum powder should then be applied against the hair growth. This will lift the hairs away from the surface of the skin ensuring good adherence to the wax.

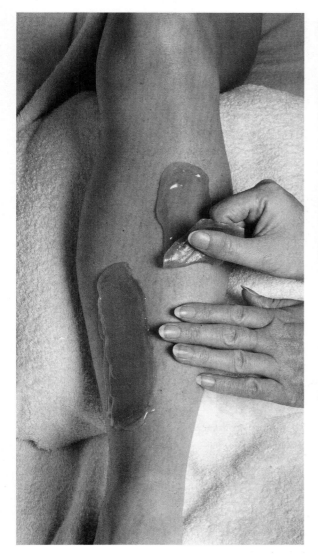

Figure 42.3 *Removal of hot wax*

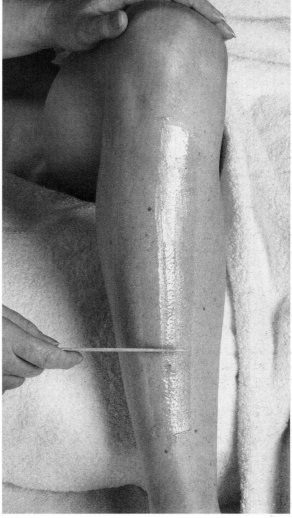

Figure 42.4 *Application of cool wax*

The temperature of the wax must then be tested on the inside of the therapist's wrist and then tested on a small patch of the client's skin.

Application and removal for hot wax treatment
Wax is applied with a spatula against the hair growth so that as the wax hardens it grips and contracts around the hair. The strips should be approximately two inches wide by any length which may be easily removed by the therapist, usually between four and six inches and several layers are built up until the strip is quite thick.

On a large area such as the leg as many strips as possible should be applied leaving a similarly sized gap between each strip.

A second set of strips may then be applied to the gaps after removal of the first, being very careful not to overlap the previously treated area with the hot wax, as this will be painful to the client.

As the wax is beginning to set and is still flexible the edge of the strip should be very quickly flicked up. When it is set sufficiently the raised edge allows the therapist to grip the wax and pull the strip off decisively, following through with a soothing rub to the area to relieve the stinging sensation (Figure 42.3).

After care for hot wax treatment

Cotton wool saturated with witch hazel may be applied over the treated area to remove any traces of wax and to soothe the skin. A special soothing lotion may be applied if there is a strong reaction.

Equipment required for cool wax treatment

○ Cool wax machine.
○ Witch hazel.
○ Spatulas.
○ Muslin strips.
○ Cotton wool.
○ Soothing lotion.
○ Waste bowl.

Again the area to be treated should be wiped over with witch hazel to remove surface grease. Nothing else should be applied as this will form a barrier between the cool wax and the skin and could prevent the wax adhering, causing the treatment to be ineffective.

The temperature of the wax is tested in the same way as hot wax, by applying a small test strip to the therapist's wrist and then on the client.

Application and removal for cool wax treatment

When the wax is at the correct working temperature it is applied with a spatula to the whole area to be treated. The wax should be applied with the direction of hair growth and as thinly as possible, using the spatula at an angle of 90° (Figure 42.4).

A muslin strip is then placed on to the wax, smoothed down to bond firmly with the wax and then pulled back against the hair growth, almost parallel to the skin, to remove the hairs cleanly and efficiently (Figure 42.5).

There is less reaction on the skin to this method and wax may be re-applied over areas already treated. However, a skilled therapist will complete the treatment efficiently without the need to re-apply the wax.

After care for cool wax treatment

Any remaining traces of wax may be removed by applying an after-wax oil or lotion.

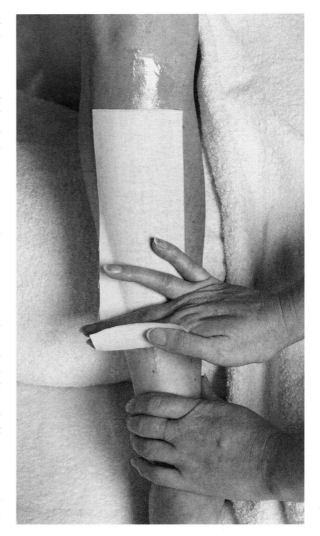

Figure 42.5 *Removal of cool wax*

Contraindications to waxing

○ Any disease of the skin.
○ Varicose veins.
○ Broken skin.
○ Bruising.
○ After exposure to ultraviolet rays.
○ Hypersensitive skin.
○ Warts and moles.
○ Recent scar tissue.

Preparation of work area and client

The wax machine should be placed on a stable surface which is not made of glass as it could shatter, and it should be placed in such a position to allow ease of movement during treatment.

All other equipment and materials should be placed within easy reach.

The couch should be protected with a plastic sheet and a towel placed on the area where the client will be sitting.

All clothing should be removed from the area to be treated and the client's clothes should be protected with towels or paper roll.

The client should be positioned comfortably on the couch.

Precautions for safe use

All wax machines must be wired correctly. The heating elements must be enclosed and all machines should comply with the British Standard of safety.

The wax must be left to heat up in a safe position away from anything inflammable. The wax machine must not be moved while hot.

The wax should not be overheated and the temperature should be regularly checked even on the thermostatically controlled units.

The machine must be cleaned immediately after use to prevent drips of wax burning and to maintain high professional standards. Special equipment cleaner or surgical spirit should be used.

The covers provided with the machine must be left in place while it is not in use.

Advantages of hot wax

○ The higher working temperature of this wax allows strong hair growth such as underarm or bikini line to be removed more easily.
○ Hair re-growth is tapered and soft and takes up to six weeks to grow back.

Disadvantages of hot wax

○ The wax takes longer to heat up.
○ Application and removal takes longer. A half leg wax will take approximately thirty minutes.

○ The wax may not be re-applied if all the hairs do not come out.
○ The reaction of the skin to this wax is more severe. An increased reddening and blotchy effect can take several hours to subside.
○ The wax often becomes brittle with over-use or over-heating.
○ This method is not permanent.
○ Hairs must be at least 2 cm long to be effectively removed.
○ Can be painful to the client.
○ Can be messy to use.

Advantages of cool wax

○ The lower working temperature makes this wax suitable for the more sensitive skins.
○ The application and removal procedure is very quick. A half leg wax should take approximately fifteen minutes.
○ Re-growth is tapered and soft, taking up to six weeks to grow back.
○ Shorter hairs may be treated.
○ It is clean and easy to use.

Disadvantages of cool wax

○ It is not as efficient in the removal of coarse dark hair as the hot method.
○ If the therapist is not as proficient in its use, removal can be very sticky.
○ Can be painful.
○ This method is not permanent.
○ It may cause ingrowing hairs.

Areas to be treated

Legs
The treatment can be either half leg or full.

The fronts of the legs should be completed before turning the client over and treating the backs of the legs.

The knee must always be in a bent position when applying and removing the wax.

The hair growth on the backs of the legs and the thighs can vary in direction and it is important to bear this in mind when applying and removing the wax.

It is also important when removing the wax from the thigh area to support and tighten the skin when removing the wax to make the treatment more comfortable.

Bikini line

The bikini line is normally a separate treatment and the price of this area should be in addition to the full leg treatment.

Client consultation is important to ascertain how much of the area is to be waxed. This will probably depend upon the sports or swim wear to be worn.

The client's leg should be bent in a figure of four position and supported by a cushion to make the treatment more comfortable and the muscles less tense. The skin around the area being treated must be held firmly when removing the strips to prevent too much discomfort.

The hair growth pattern in this area is quite erratic, so small strips should be applied in the direction of the hair growth.

Skin may react more to waxing of this sensitive area and tiny blood spots may occur. This is due to the fact that the hair in this area is often much stronger than other areas and the skin more sensitive. Regular waxing should be advised to prevent this problem as less hair will be present at each treatment.

The client should be advised to avoid friction from tight fitting underwear after treatment and to use a soothing, antiseptic lotion if necessary.

Underarm

This is a popular salon treatment because once depilated the hairs do not regrow very quickly and there is rarely a shadow left, even in very dark haired clients, as there is with some of the other methods used.

The client must again be positioned comfortably, with her hand behind her head in such a position that the area is flat and easier to treat, with the back of the couch slightly elevated for client comfort.

Perspiration which may be present could affect the efficient application of the wax. Therefore, the area needs to be cleansed first and then dried before applying the wax.

The hair growth pattern is again erratic in this area.

Small strips must be used and the direction of growth must be carefully followed: cool wax application with the growth and hot wax application against the growth.

The client should be advised not to wear antiperspirant or deodorant for twenty-four hours after treatment and to avoid friction from clothing.

Arms

This is a relatively easy area to treat as the hairs grow in the same direction. This is particularly effective on clients who have a very dark hair growth even if it is not particularly thick. Cool wax is probably the best method to employ and because of the size of the area, the muslin strips should be cut into smaller pieces to aid removal.

Lip waxing

The area must be thoroughly cleansed first, particularly if makeup is worn. Either type of wax may be used.

The area although small should be treated in three sections (either side of the upper lip and then a small section in the middle). Strips must be cut to size to fit the area.

Soothing lotion must be applied immediately after removal and if the area reacts and becomes very red or even slightly swollen a cold compress should be applied.

Advice to the client

After a wax depilatory treatment it is necessary to advise the client how to prevent an adverse reaction on the skin:

○ Wash or shower in lukewarm water.
○ Do not use soap as this could irritate the skin.
○ Do not use any perfumed body lotions.
○ Do not expose the area to ultraviolet light.

Other methods of depilation

There are several methods of hair removal which may be used but these methods are not usually performed in the salon.

Tweezing or plucking

This method is used in a salon but only for shaping the eyebrows. The hair is completely removed from the follicle.

There is a depilation machine, which is available to the general public, which allows mass plucking of the hairs. It can be used on the legs and arms.

Shaving

With this method an electrical shaver or a wet razor used with soap or cream may be used. The hair itself is cut off at skin level and the hair then grows with a coarse blunt ended tip and re-growth is usually apparent twenty-four to forty-eight hours afterwards.

Depilatory creams

Although these creams are not in general use in beauty salons, they are, however, an alternative treatment which can be provided in cases of varicose veins when leg waxing would be contraindicated over an area.

Due to the chemical constituents in depilatory creams, it is important to test first on a small area of skin to see that the client is not allergic to the product.

The active ingredient in a depilatory cream is a *keratolytic*, which is a keratin dissolving substance. Therefore, it will cause the skin to become very sensitive if used on a regular basis as it will attack the skin as well as the hair, because it also contains the protein keratin.

Before applying the cream the area to be treated must be thoroughly cleansed. It is then applied using a spatula and left on for the required amount of time.

The removal of the depilatory cream should be completed with a spatula before rinsing the area with lukewarm water. Removing all the cream first before applying water should reduce the nasty smell which often occurs with the use of these products.

Soap or deodorant must not be used for several hours afterwards.

The hair is only removed from the surface of the skin and blunt re-growth is apparent after only a few days.

Composition of depilatory creams

Manufacturers are careful with the composition of these creams so that they do not irritate the skin. They should also be pleasant smelling, clean and easy to apply, and remove the hair quickly.

There are two chemical compounds which are effective in this type of preparation.

Strontium sulphide

This is very effective in removing hair in three to five minutes. The strength, however, may irritate certain skins. The main fault is the strong smell when they are washed away. This can be alleviated by removing most of the cream with a spatula before applying water. Severe reaction on the skin will occur if all traces are not removed.

Calcium thioglycollate

This type will take longer to act but the action is far more gentle and this may be used on facial hair. The other advantage is the smell, which is barely noticeable.

Formulations
Strontium sulphide

Strontium sulphide	20%	Depilatory.
Talc	20%	Harmless powder in which the depilatory is dispersed.
Methyl cellulose	3%	Forms the mixture into a paste.
Water	42%	
Glycerine	15%	Preservative

Calcium thioglycollate

Calcium thioglycollate	7%	Depilatory.
Calcium hydroxide	7%	Alkali to help the depilatory.
Calcium carbonate	20%	Chalk in which the depilatory is dispersed.
Cetyl alcohol	5%	Makes a smooth cream.
Sodium lauryl sulphate	1%	Soapless detergent.
Sodium silicate	2.5%	Abrasive.
Water and perfume	55%	Provides the liquid base.

Part Five   Business Management

43 *Career opportunities*

Beauty therapists today have a variety of career opportunities after they have completed a recognized course in beauty therapy and received the necessary qualifications to put their skills into practice.

Types of work

Beauty salons

Therapists will have the opportunity to practise facial and body treatments (manual and electrical, electrolysis and makeup) in a good beauty salon and this provides a sound base for going on to other more specialized jobs and even to consider starting their own business. The experience gained here is varied and they will learn how to sell products, keep records, supervise other members of staff, manage the salon and, most importantly, to please the client and promote the business.

Health farms

The type of work encountered on a health farm is similar to that of a beauty salon but the hours can be much longer and there is more emphasis on body treatments and weight reduction. The therapist will also work closely with the dietician and will take exercise classes which can include yoga, aerobics, jogging or pool exercise and work in the gym providing fitness training.

Leisure centres

The work here will involve taking exercise classes and fitness training and supervising treatments such as sauna, steam and sunbeds.

Cruise liners

All treatments are now available on cruise liners but therapists are normally required to gain at least two years' experience before they are accepted. The hours are long and it is essential that the therapist is competent to work with initiative and without the need for close supervision.

Makeup artist

The areas for a makeup artist besides a salon are with a professional photographer, in a model agency or freelance. Television or film work is highly competitive and quite often the therapist will be required to serve a long apprenticeship but the work is interesting even though the hours are long. Theatres may employ makeup artists but probably on a part-time basis or in a self-employed capacity.

Makeup and skin care consultant

Cosmetic companies are pleased to employ beauty therapists as their background knowledge is an asset when selling makeup and skin care ranges within a store. There is also the opportunity then to work up through the ranks and become an area representative for the company, responsible for many retail outlets.

Remedial makeup practitioner

Working in conjunction with a dermatologist or in a hospital, teaching people how to apply camouflage makeup skilfully, to conceal scars and blemishes and skin care maintenance and makeup application after plastic surgery.

Public relations

There are now many treatments offered in cosmetic surgery clinics which do not require surgery. Because of the extensive knowledge therapists have concerning the skin and beauty requirements of most women, they are an ideal person to present the services available to other therapists and to the general public. They may also help with post-operative advice to clients who may never have worn or shown an interest in makeup before because of a problem which has now been corrected.

Beauty journalism

Producing articles or columns for magazines and newspapers. With a knowledge of the beauty industry and the ability to write, information booklets and brochures may be produced for manufacturers.

Teaching

It is important to gain as much industrial experience as possible before embarking upon a teacher-training course. Teaching can then be full-time or part-time while still pursuing other interests within the beauty field.

Franchising

Taking out a franchise to sell products such as skin care, gives therapists a well-known name to trade under, the training and continuing guidance of a large organization, with the advantage of independence and self-employment. The risks are not quite as great when selling a tried and tested product and the franchise operator is providing technical help and in some cases national advertising.

Technical representative

There are many companies producing beauty therapy equipment, professional skin and body care ranges as well as makeup. They employ qualified beauty therapists to demonstrate all their products to colleges and potential buyers. They also provide a follow-up service presenting new equipment and products and giving specialist training when necessary.

Mobile therapist

This is an ideal way of providing beauty therapy services without the overheads of business premises and many people prefer treatments in the comfort of their home. The largest capital outlay would be a car but there are limitations in the services you may offer as it would be difficult to carry a great deal of equipment. It is important to gain experience first in an established business and choose carefully the treatments you will offer. Sometimes specializing in a particular area, for example aromatherapy, is the answer as this only entails carrying a portable couch, towels and oils.

44 *Starting your own business*

Running a business is not easy. It provides job satisfaction and independence but means longer working hours, fewer holidays and, to begin with, lower earnings. Commitment is essential and those who produce a good business plan are more likely to succeed. The initial steps to success include the following:

Finding the right location for a new business

There must be a demand for the services in the area for your business to be successful.

If there are already established businesses in the chosen location find out about the type of treatments on offer and check out their strengths and weaknesses. There is little point setting up an identical business in opposition to an already thriving one. It may be better to research other locations until a more suitable one is found.

Buying an existing business

It is important to find out exactly why a business is up for sale. There are many reasons why businesses are sold but the owner of the business you are interested in may feel that it is under threat or not a viable business and is cutting his/her losses and running. When you are completely satisfied that everything is above board then it is time to examine all aspects of the business.

A thriving beauty business is reliant on the continuing patronage of the existing clientele. Therefore, it is important to obtain an undertaking from the present owner that he/she will not be opening up elsewhere in competition with you and the clients will be remaining with the salon.

The sale price may include equipment which will only be of use to you if it is in good working order and has a long working life ahead of it. It would be worthwhile, therefore, to have everything checked by an expert.

Retail stock must be up-to-date and preferably of products which will be easy to sell.

Have the accounts for the last few years checked by an accountant to ensure the business is profitable.

A business from home

The idea of working from home is very appealing as there would be no travelling to and from work and the hours worked could fit in with your normal daily routine.

Such a business is only viable if there is the room available to use for the salon. Space such as a loft or an integral garage could be converted but first it is necessary to determine what equipment and furniture will be required and this will indicate how much space will be needed.

Since many beauty therapy equipment manufacturers now make combined self-standing units, it is possible to offer a variety of different face and body treatments in a limited space.

Before making any decisions it is important to ascertain if you are legally entitled to use your home for business. Planning permission must be sought if the business will materially change the use of your home. This is open to interpretation by different local authorities.

Check the deeds of the house to ensure there are no clauses to prevent part of the house being used for business purposes. In the case of your home being mortgaged it is important to check the documents to ensure there is no breach of contract.

The insurance cover may need to be changed on your home when using it for business so check with your insurance company for advice.

Mobile beauty business

A mobile business is an increasingly popular option for the many fully trained beauty therapists who want to specialize in one particular treatment. There are also many more individuals who are training in just one specialized subject. These specialisms include:

o Aromatherapy.
o Reflexology.
o Body massage.
o Sports therapy.
o Electrolysis.
o Makeup artist.
o Nail technician.

Advantages

o There is a captive market as there are many prospective clients who cannot leave home because they are disabled or elderly, are a carer looking after a relative, are without transport, or even agoraphobic. In rural areas there may not be a beauty salon and travelling to the nearest large town or city may be time-consuming, inconvenient and expensive.
o There is a relatively small capital outlay particularly when specializing in one particular treatment as the mode of transport is the largest expense.
o Overheads are low as the location for business is the client's own premises which could be a home or workplace.
o It is easier to offer a specialized service, for example aromatherapy.
o A choice of working hours and flexibility is available to the mobile therapist allowing other commitments to be accommodated without having to consult with colleagues or superiors.
o The service is more personal and a good client therapist relationship is easily established and maintained.

o There are increased benefits to clients because they will not have to travel and treatments will be far more relaxing.

Disadvantages

o A limited number of treatments may be achieved in a day because of the time needed to travel. Planning of appointments will be essential to prevent unnecessary time wasted.
o It is necessary to carry all equipment and products required to ensure an efficient service so good planning and organization are essential
o Equipment may get damaged.
o Setting up equipment may be difficult depending on the location to be used for the treatment.
o Business expansion is difficult.
o There are risks involved when attending new clients. It is important, therefore, to vet any prospective clients or rely on personal recommendation.

Considerations

o The local authority bylaws should be checked before offering a mobile service to ensure that all regulations are complied with.
o Registration will be required for electrolysis and ear piercing.
o Many suppliers of equipment will supply special mobile units in a protective carrying case which will reduce the risk of damage occurring in transit.
o Some product suppliers also provide cushioned carrying cases to prevent accidents.
o Lightweight sturdy equipment is a must for mobile businesses to prevent therapists suffering from back strain or injury when loading or unloading.
o Team up with a mobile hairdresser and share client lists. It will help to increase business and ensure clients are recommended.

Franchising

Franchise: Is a licence to operate a business in a particular area, given by a business with an established name and reputation.

Franchisee: This is the person who buys the franchise.

Franchiser: This is the person who sells the franchise.

The basic principle involved in franchising is when a successful company that manufactures, retails products or provides a service decides to expand its business by becoming a franchiser instead of opening up other branches which are owned by its parent company.

The company is selling its already established reputation and valuable expertise to a franchisee. In effect, the franchisee is buying a complete business system or way of trading.

The franchisee enters into a contract to sell the product or provide the service under the franchiser's name, following strict guidelines laid down by the franchiser.

The legal form the franchise will take will be the same as any other business, that is, sole trader, partnership or limited company.

Advantages

The chief advantage of starting a business by buying a franchise is that all the problems normally encountered when running a business from scratch will already have been analysed and solved and, with a reputable franchiser, there is a greater chance of success:

o The business is your own.
o There are reduced risks in the setting up of the business as the problems have been solved by the franchiser.
o There is continuing support provided by the franchiser which is particularly good for those inexperienced in business.
o The product or service bought has a recognizable name with an established reputation.
o The business will benefit from the advertising and promotion carried out by the franchiser.

o Previous experience is not necessary in most cases, for example retail sales, as training is normally given by the franchiser.

Disadvantages

o There will be restrictions on how the business is run as all business transactions must be in the best interest of the franchiser and the other franchisees.
o There is usually a large initial fee to be paid for the franchise.
o Subsequent payments must then be paid each year usually as a percentage of turnover.
o The franchiser has the right to come to the business premises to inspect records, and sales statistics have to be sent on a regular basis.
o Operating methods laid down by the franchiser have to be strictly adhered to which may prevent franchisees using their own initiative and expertise.
o All stock may have to be purchased from the franchiser, not allowing the franchisee freedom to seek competitive alternatives.
o If the franchisee wants to sell the business before the end of the contract the franchiser has to agree.
o The franchise runs for a set number of years with an option to renew 'if the franchisee's performance is satisfactory'. This may mean a commitment to spending more on refurbishment.
o If the franchisee cannot renew there may be little to sell as the franchisee cannot sell the name and goodwill.

Precautions

o An accountant should examine the forecasts given by the franchiser.
o A solicitor should go through any contract before it is signed to see how the franchiser is making money and to analyse the restrictions they may impose.
o The franchisee should find out how many franchises have already been sold and how long they have been trading.

o The franchisee should talk to existing franchisees.

Expert advice

It is most important to consult experts who have the knowledge to help you turn an idea into a thriving business and by consulting the right people you will ensure the advice you are given is both relevant and professional.

Enterprise agencies

Many local authorities, supported by private industry, central and local government, provide training courses in starting and running your own business. The aim of these agencies is to promote economic growth and employment opportunities in local communities. Specialists from the area in which you hope to work are available to offer expert advice and they come from:

o Supporting businesses.
o The professions such as solicitors and accountants.
o Financial institutions.
o Local authorities.
o Government departments.

The help they provide includes the following:

o How to start up your business.
o Financial and legal considerations.
o Marketing.
o Finding premises.
o Business planning.
o Obtaining grants.
o Accounts, budgets and cash flow.
o Developing an existing business.

There are courses run by the Manpower Services Commission which vary from one week to sixteen and details of these can be obtained from your local job centre.

There are various government agencies whose existence is specifically for providing assistance to new business ventures. These agencies provide schemes which give free business advice, counselling and training. The schemes may provide an allowance for a short time which provides financial assistance through the difficult start-up period. Certain conditions have to be met to receive the allowance and these relate to:

o Benefits received.
o Your employment situation.
o Your age.
o The hours you have to work in the business.
o Your own financial commitment.
o The business must also be approved by the Department of Employment.

As specific conditions and requirements are subject to change, current up-to-date information may be obtained from:

The Manpower Services Commission,
Moorfoot,
Sheffield S1 4PQ.
Telephone number: 0114 275 3275.

Banks

Most of the major banks have a business adviser who will offer advice to anybody starting their own business and can help in planning sensibly for the future. The bank is there not only to lend money but also to create successful businesses. Therefore, they are pleased to help even if they do not provide the capital.

The bank manager may decide to lend you money for your business after you have presented him/her with a viable business plan and the bank will advise you of the full range of services available and provide support and advice to prevent problems occurring.

Accountants

An accountant can be of great help to you. In presenting your case to your bank manager, when you are trying to raise capital for your business, an accountant will have the experience to present your case in the most acceptable form, increasing your chances of approval.

Once the business is assured the accountant can help set up an efficient accounting system which will allow you to find out quickly and easily how your business is doing.

Accountants can also prepare salary structures and provide advice on the company formation and the legal structure of the business.

They will explain the tax laws and advise you on how to obtain the maximum tax relief (the reduction you can make in your tax bill by deducting legitimate expenses, which can be many and varied, from the overall tax liability).

It is important to ensure that your accountant is properly qualified, so choose an accountant in your area from:

The Institute of Chartered Accountants,
PO Box 433,
Chartered Accountants Hall,
Moorgate Place,
London EC2P 2BJ.

The Chartered Association of Certified Accountants,
29 Lincoln's Inn Fields,
London WC2.

Solicitors

Choose a solicitor who specializes in commercial law and provide him/her with copies of all relevant documentation including your business plan.

A solicitor will help in various ways:

o   Advising you on any business contracts.
o   Helping you to understand employment laws and draw up contracts of employment.
o   Negotiating leases and conveyancing on business premises.
o   Drafting company rules and partnership agreements.

Solicitors' fees are quite high, so if you need free legal advice contact the Citizens Advice Bureau who will provide you with all the necessary details.

Insurance broker

The best way to ensure you have adequate insurance cover is through a broker. To obtain a list of insurance brokers in your area contact:

The British Insurers Association,
Fountain House,
14 Bevis Marks,
London EC3A 7NT.

Telephone number: 0171 623 9043

45 *Finding the right location and premises*

For your business to be successful you must have the right premises, in the right area and at the right price. This may prove to be quite difficult but it is important not to compromise and accept premises which you consider to be second best.

Because you are providing a service the business should:

○ Be centrally situated in a well-populated area.
○ Provide the services the area requires, a fact which should already have been gleaned from your market research.
○ Provide services which either differ from, or are better than your competitors.
○ Be close to other businesses which have a brisk trade, for example a bank or post office, as there will be people constantly passing.
○ Be near to other businesses which may complement your own and bring in new clients, for example a hairdresser or a chemist.
○ Be easily accessible to drivers and those using public transport.

There is a current trend for beauty therapists to share premises with aromatherapists, reflexologists and other alternative therapists as well as chiropodists, the main advantages being the sharing of costs and the gaining of clients from the other practices.

The premises

The options when you have found the ideal premises are to lease or to buy.

Leasing

Leasing has the advantage that any existing capital will be available for use within the business rather than being tied up in buying a property, with mortgage repayments that could be a burden.

When negotiating the lease it may be advisable to go for as short a lease as possible with the option to renew the lease for a longer period when you feel sure that the business is going to be a success.

It is important, however, to allow your solicitor to advise you as he/she is the expert in these matters.

The disadvantages are that over a long period of time the lease will cost as much if not more than buying the premises.

Although you have the right to agree new terms for the lease when the present one expires, landlords can refuse if you have not been a good tenant or if they require the premises for their own occupation then they may be able to take possession but they will have to pay you compensation.

You must seek the landlord's permission for any alterations you may wish to make.

Before signing a lease it is important to check the following:

○ That the premises can be used for a beauty salon or the purpose you require.
○ Who is responsible for the repair and maintenance of the premises.
○ What is the length of the lease (the length can vary considerably).
○ Is subletting part or all of the premises permitted.
○ How often is the rent reviewed.

- Are there any major works planned to improve the area which may affect your business?

The Landlord and Tenant Act 1954

The purpose of this act is to give the tenant some security in remaining in the premises after the lease has expired and to be compensated for improvements which add to the value of business premises.

The landlord has to give six months' notice if the lease is to be terminated. This will give the tenant the opportunity to apply to the court to have the lease renewed. The court may refuse the application if the landlord can show the following:

- The rent is in arrears.
- The property has been allowed to fall into disrepair.
- The landlord has found alternative premises for the tenant.
- The premises are to be demolished or reconstructed.
- The landlord needs the premises for his/her own occupation.

If the court orders termination of the lease and the tenant is not at fault then the tenant has the right to compensation from the landlord.

The tenant has the right to compensation for improvements to a lease if the work was undertaken:

- After the landlord has been given notice of the tenant's intention to make the improvements.
- The improvements were undertaken with the approval of the landlord.

Buying

Buying has the advantage of being a sound investment, if a good property is bought at the right price and then sold at a profit after some years.

The disadvantages are that it may be difficult to obtain a commercial mortgage for a new business so the problem lies in raising the money to purchase the property.

The money you have available to invest may be more profitably invested in the business rather than the property itself.

The salon

The image a beauty salon presents is very important especially with competition close by. Therefore, the appearance must be attractive to the type of client you hope to draw. The correct image must be achieved at a reasonable cost which still allows you to work profitably.

The salon should provide adequate space for the staff you hope to employ, to work comfortably and efficiently. Look for premises which have the following services and facilities installed:

- Telephone system.
- Burglar alarm.
- Heating.
- Adequate lighting.
- Electricity points.
- Air conditioning and ventilation.

The name

Choosing a name is not something to rush into because once it has been chosen and placed in a prominent position above the business it will probably remain, and a mistake could adversely affect the business.

Creating the right image is important and the image of the salon will be reflected in the name. It should also identify the services you are selling to the client and convey a message to both new and existing clients.

Try the name out on people first, asking them to describe the picture it conjures up in the mind.

Make sure the name you have chosen is original. If the business is to be entered in *Yellow Pages* then it may be advisable to choose a name which begins with a letter from the beginning of the alphabet so the client will ring your number first.

The choice of name must conform to the rules laid down by The Companies Act 1985 and The Business Names Act 1985. The main purpose of these acts is to enable anyone dealing with a business to know the owner's name and address.

According to the act the owner of the business must disclose his/her surname as a sole trader, all surnames in a partnership and the full corporate name if it is a limited company and in each case the address. This information must appear on all stationery if trading under a name other than the surname or corporate name.

One of the most important decisions to make when opening a business is the legal form the business will take. There are three options:

1   Sole trader.
2   Partnership.
3   Limited company.

Each one of these options has its advantages and disadvantages.

Sole trader

To start up as a sole trader all you have to do is inform your local tax inspector and DSS office with little effort and few formalities. Being a sole trader means that you are solely responsible for the business and liable for all the money the business owes. When there is not enough money in the business, all personal possessions, including your home, could be taken to settle debts. All the profits, however, belong solely to you.

Accounts do not have to be submitted to Companies House but annual accounts do have to be submitted to HM Inspector of Taxes.

As a sole trader income tax is paid at the normal rate and is paid on a preceding year basis. This means that tax may be paid on profits up to two years afterwards and this helps a small business with cash flow.

You are not answerable to anyone else for decisions you make regarding the business.

When using a trade name you must put your name and address as proprietor on all business stationery and on a notice displayed on the business premises.

Partnership

This is where there are a minimum of two people or a maximum of twenty people who will provide the start-up cash and share the workload in a business.

In a business partnership there may be either a full partner who will participate fully and share both the profits and losses or a sleeping partner who takes no active part in the running of the business but who provides working capital and does take responsibility for any debts but only up to the amount they have put in the business.

As each partner is responsible for the debts of the others it is advisable for a partnership agreement to be drawn up by a solicitor so that each partner has some sort of protection.

The partners should agree on certain things:

o   The name of the business.
o   The date the partnership will start and how long it will last.
o   The amount of capital to be provided by each partner.
o   Who is authorized to operate bank accounts.
o   How the business will be managed and what each partner's responsibilities will be.
o   How the profits will be divided.
o   What provision will be made for holidays and other time off.
o   What will happen in the event of a partner withdrawing from the partnership for whatever reason, for example retirement or leaving.
o   What provision will be made in the event of the death of a partner.
o   Arrangements for admitting new partners.
o   The conditions under which the partnership may be terminated in case of a dispute.
o   The arrangements to be made for the dissolving of the partnership.

If there is no agreement then any of the partners can pull out of the partnership at any time, leaving the other partners to find the money to buy out their share of the business.

Limited company

Forming a limited company is more complicated than a partnership and advice must be sought from a solicitor. When a limited company is set up a new legal entity is being created. A company must have at least two shareholders, one director and a company secretary who may also be a director.

The company must be registered with the Registrar of Companies and the following should be provided:

o   Memorandum of association.
o   Articles of association.
o   Various forms.
o   A registration fee.

The Certificate of Incorporation should be on public display. There is also certain information which must be displayed on all stationery and letterheads:

o   The registered name and address in full.
o   The place of registration.
o   The registration number.
o   Either all or none of the directors' names.

The advantages of a limited company

The main advantage of a limited company is that the shareholders have a limited liability for debts. They are not personally responsible for the company's debts and creditors may only claim on the assets of the company and not on personal assets.

Other advantages are that a limited company may lend credibility to your business and investors and creditors may have greater confidence.

There is a lower tax rate payable on profits under £200,000.

The disadvantages of a limited company

It can cost up to £200 to register if you use an agent.

Annual accounts have to be submitted to Companies House.

The details of the company are open to public scrutiny.

An annual meeting of members is compulsory.

The directors are subject to company law and have responsibilities to act in the best interests of the company and its shareholders, answering personally for failure to do so.

Naming the business

A sole trader is not obliged to register the name of the business if it is not their own name, but it must not be too much like a name already in existence, as this may be construed as misleading the public.

Their own name, however, must figure prominently on:

o   Business letters.
o   Written orders for goods.
o   Invoices.
o   Written demands for payment of debts.

When a limited company is formed the name must be registered with Companies House and it must not be identical to any other company's name.

The name must not be considered illegal or offensive and it must not contain the word 'limited' anywhere in the name but at the end.

There are two leaflets produced by the Department of Trade and Industry and may be obtained from:

Companies House,
Crown Way,
Cardiff CF4 3UZ.

They are entitled *Disclosure of Business Ownership* and *Control of Business Names*.

47 The business plan

An essential ingredient in a successful business is to have *a business plan*, a document which details the business you hope to start and the expectations you have for its success for at least the first year (Figure 47.1).

This is helpful to yourself in establishing your business as it is valuable for reference when so many day-to-day problems are diverting your attention from your long-term business objectives.

The business plan lays down these objectives allowing you to follow your plan closely and keep it on course. The plan is also helpful in presenting your case when applying for a loan.

The plan should be divided into two parts:

1   A section about the business itself which will allow the reader to assess instantly whether this business venture has the potential for success.
2   A financial section to present your case to the bank or possible investors in such a way that you will secure the capital you require to start up.

INTRODUCTION

DETAILS OF THE BUSINESS

Name of business

Business address

Business status

Type of business

Telephone

Date business began (if you have already started trading)

Business activities

PERSONAL DETAILS

Name

Address

Telephone (home)   Telephone (work)

Qualifications

      Date of birth

Relevant work experience

Business experience

Course attended

Details of key management personnel (if any)

Name	Name
Position	Position
Address	Address
Date of birth	Date of birth
Qualifications	Qualifications
Relevant work experience	Relevant work experience
Present income	Present income

What skills will you need to buy in during the first two years?

PERSONNEL

Estimate the cost of employing any people or buying any services you may need in the first two years

Number of people	Job function	Monthly cost	Annual cost

(Remember to include your own salary and those of any partners you may have in this calculation)

PRODUCT/SERVICE

Description

continued

Figure 47.1 *The business plan*

Contribution of individual products or services to total turnover

Product	% Contribution
	(the figures in this column should add up to 100)

Break down the cost of materials (if any)

PRODUCT A

Materials (including packaging, labelling etc.)	Cost

*Selling price for Product A:

PRODUCT B

*Selling price for Product B:

PRODUCT C

*Selling price for Product C:

(*These are assumptions)

Where did you get your estimate from?

Material	Source

MARKET

Describe your market

Where is your market?

Who are your customers?

Is your market growing, static or in decline?

Itemise the competitive products or services

Competitor's name

Competitor's product/service A

Name	Price
Strengths	Weakness

Competitor's name

Competitor's product/service B

Name	Price
Strengths	Weakness

Competitor's name

Competitor's product/service C

Name	Price
Strengths	Weakness

What is special about your own product or service?

Advantages of your product or service over
Competitor A

continued

The business plan — continued

Competitor B

Competitor C

What is your sales forecast for the
*1st three months?

Treatments/products	Total value

*2nd three months?

Treatments/products	Total value

*3rd three months?

Treatments/products	Total value

*4th three months?

Treatments/products	Total value

(*These are assumptions)

Explain how you have arrived at these estimates

Give details of any firm orders you already have

MARKETING

What sort of marketing do your competitors do?

Competitor A

Competitor B

Competitor C

What sort of marketing or advertising do you intend to do?

Method	Cost

Why do you think that these methods are appropriate for your particular market?

Where did you get your estimates from?

Method	Source

PREMISES/EQUIPMENT/PRODUCT

PREMISES:

Where do you intend to locate the business and why?

What sort and size of premises will you need?

What are the details of any lease, licence, rent, rates and when is the next rent review due?

What equipment & products do you require?

Is equipment bought or leased and how long is their life span?

On what terms will the products be purchased?

continued

The business plan — continued

RECORD SYSTEM
Describe records to be kept and how they are to be kept up to to date?

_____
_____
_____
_____

OBJECTIVES
What are your personal objectives in running the business?
Short-term
_____
_____

Medium-term
_____
_____

How do you intend to achieve them?
_____
_____

What objectives do you have for the business itself?
Short-term
_____
_____

Medium-term
_____
_____

How do you intend to achieve them?
_____
_____

What are your long-term objectives (if any)
1. _____

2. _____

3. _____

4. _____

5. _____

How do you intend to achieve them?
_____
_____
_____

FINANCE
Give details of your known orders and sales (if any)

Date	Orders/sales	Details	Delivery date
1			
2			
3			
4			

Give details of your current business assets (if any)

Item	Value	Life expectancy

What will you need to buy to start up and then throughout your first year?
Start up

Item	Value

Year 1

Item	Value

continued

The business plan — continued

365

How will you pay for these? Grants	Value	Date
Own resources		
Loans		
Creditors		

What credit is available from your suppliers? Supplier	Estimated value of monthly order	Number of days credit

What are your loan or overdraft requirements?

What are you putting in yourself?

What security will you be able to put up?

OTHER
Accountant
Address

Telephone
Solicitor
Address

Telephone

VAT registration
Insurance arrangements

The business plan – continued

Plan contents

Introduction

This could be a brief summary of your business but made as interesting as possible to gain the attention of the reader and stating what you hope to achieve in the next twelve months or more.

Business details

This must include:

o The name and address of the business.
o The telephone number.
o The legal status (sole trader, partnership, limited company).

o The type of business (beauty salon, fitness centre, diet clinic etc.).
o The business activities and services.
o The date the business began or is to begin if not already running.

Personal details

These would be of yourself as a sole trader or of the partners in a partnership or limited company.

o Name, address and home telephone numbers.
o Telephone numbers at work.
o The qualifications held.
o Work experience relevant to the business.
o Previous business experience.
o Any courses attended in relation to the setting up of the business.

○   The present or planned role in the business.

Staff details

Those you may be employing immediately.

○   Name, address.
○   Position in the business.
○   Qualifications.
○   Relevant work experience.

New staff
Any other skills needed by the business which will be required within the next year or two.

Staff costs

An estimate of the cost of employing staff and buying in new skills, to include your own salary and any partners in the business.

○   Number of staff.
○   Role in the business.
○   Cost per month.
○   Annual cost.

Services

Details of all the services on offer emphasizing anything that is different or special about the various treatments and why this business will succeed.

What percentage of the turnover will each treatment contribute, why the treatment is special and what the key selling points are.

Estimate the prices for the treatments on offer and explain how the estimates were produced. Give an approximate breakdown of the cost of providing each treatment or service.

Explain what competition there is and how your services compare with theirs.

State whether you are carrying out research into new areas which may be added to the business's list of services available in the foreseeable future.

What product lines you will be selling and how relevant they are to the treatments you are offering. State the selling price and the original cost.

The market

It is important to demonstrate that you have a positive idea of the market you are aiming your business at and you are sure that the services you are offering will sell. Therefore, the following information should be given:

○   Where is the market and does it have the potential for growth, or is it static or in decline.
○   How large is your market.
○   Identify the potential customers.
○   State the possibility of tailoring the services to meet the demands of other sectors within the market.

Make a list of:

○   Your competitors' services.
○   The price they charge.
○   Their strengths and weaknesses.

Then state why your own are better and the advantages of your treatments and services over theirs.

State your advertising methods and how appropriate they are.

Operating the business

The information required here would encompass premises, equipment and suppliers.

Have business premises been found or are there plans to buy or lease? In the case of premises already acquired details should be given of the location, size and type of premises and whether there are any plans for future development or change.

State how much equipment will be needed and if it is to be bought or leased. Who will be supplying your goods and what the alternatives are if they fail to supply.

If the premises are leasehold, state:

○   The term of the lease.
○   What period of the lease is outstanding.
○   If there is an option to renew.
○   The present rent and when it is paid.
○   When the next rent review will be.
○   Who is responsible for all repairs.

CASHFLOW FORECAST FOR: MONTH   TO

	MONTH		MONTH		MONTH		MONTH		MONTH		MONTH		MONTH		TOTALS	
RECEIPTS	BUDGET	ACTUAL	BUDGET	ACTUAL	BUDGET	ACTUAL	BUDGET	ACTUAL	BUDGET	ACTUAL	BUDGET	ACTUAL	BUDGET	ACTUAL	BUDGET	ACTUAL
Cash Sales																
Cash from Debtors																
Capital Introduced																
TOTAL RECEIPTS (a)																
PAYMENTS																
Payments to Creditors																
Salaries/Wages																
Rent/Rates/Water																
Insurance																
Repairs/Renewals																
Heat/Light/Power																
Advertising																
Printing/Stationery/Postage																
Cash Purchases																
Telephone																
Professional Fees																
Capital Payments																
Interest Charges																
Other																
VAT Payable (refund)																
TOTAL PAYMENTS (b)																
NET CASHFLOW (a–b)																
OPENING BANK BALANCE																
CLOSING BANK BALANCE																

Figure 47.2 An example of a cash flow forecast

Future prospects

What plans you may have to cope with the growth of the business or any changes you may wish to make.

Financial details

This will provide the information required by a bank manager or investor when you wish to borrow money. There is a risk involved when lending money therefore it is important to show what assets you have available as insurance against anything going wrong along with the following information:

○ When you hope to repay the capital.
○ What funds of your own you have available.
○ Will there be any other source of funds open to you, if so who will provide them, how much will it be and when will it be available.
○ A cash flow forecast which analyses expenditure and receipts over a period of time, usually one year.

Receipts or money coming into the business would include:

○ Cash from sales.
○ Loans received.
○ Capital invested.
○ Other income (for example slimming club).

Expenditure or money paid out of the business would include:

○ Payments to suppliers.
○ Purchases.
○ Wages.
○ Insurance.
○ Rent, rates and water.
○ Services – heat, light, power, telephone.
○ Loan repayments.
○ Interest.
○ Leasing repayments.
○ Capital expenditure.
○ Advertising.
○ Professional fees.
○ Bank charges.
○ Other.

Closing bank balance is ascertained by adding the opening bank balance to the total receipts and taking away the total expenditure.

Because the cash flow forecast will be based on assumptions which form a vital part of the financial forecast, it is important to be realistic and note the assumptions made. It provides a picture to any possible investors of when you envisage money flowing in and out of your bank account over a set period of time.

From the forecast it will be evident when your need for cash is the greatest and what your funding requirements may be (Figure 47.2).

Useful terminology

Asset: Something of value owned by the business, for example property or equipment which may be sold to pay debts.

Balance sheet: A statement which shows the assets and liabilities of the business.

Capital: The amount of money in the business belonging to the owner or shareholders.

Cash book: This provides a daily record of financial transactions.

Credit: When a period of time elapses before payment is made for goods or services.

Creditor: One to whom debt is due.

Debtor: One who owes money to the business.

Depreciation: A reduction of the value of an asset over a period of time.

Facility: Bank loan or overdraft offered to a business by the bank.

Fixed costs: Overheads of the business.

Income: Money received for goods and services.

Liability: A debt within the business or a future commitment.

Liquid asset: An asset of the business which may be easily converted into cash.

Overdraft: An extension of credit given by the bank on a current account.

Statement of account: A record of all transactions over a period of time sent by a bank or a company to the business.

Stock: Goods stored for sale or use.

Trading account: A record of sales for a period plus the cost of the sales for the same period which shows the gross profit.

Working capital: The money which is used for the day to day running of the business.

48 *Business insurance*

Insurance cover

One of the priorities for a new business is to provide insurance cover against all risks. Some insurance is required by law and there is general insurance, some of which is relevant only to your own business. Being under-insured, or failing to insure, could cause serious financial problems by using cash resources to meet uninsured losses.

When taking out insurance it is important to ensure that the cover is adequate otherwise it is a waste of money. Insurance may be obtained from:

○ The insurance company directly.
○ An insurance broker.
○ A solicitor or accountant.
○ The bank.

Insurance companies

Companies who sell insurance, sell directly to the public or through insurance brokers or agents. Some companies specialize in certain types of insurance and others will provide a comprehensive range of insurance.

Insurance broker

A broker is an impartial adviser who deals with all the insurance companies, providing every type of policy. Brokers are required by their code of conduct to put your interests as a client above all others so they will probably be the best source of insurance. Professional advice is usually given free and without obligation.

Solicitor or accountant

There are solicitors and accountants who may work full time with insurance and may have the title agent, consultant or financial adviser.

It may be convenient to consult a professional that you already work with. However, the solicitor or the accountant may deal with a limited number of insurance companies and there is a chance that you may not receive the best quote, or know that you are dealing with a company that has a good record in paying claims.

Bank

The bank manager or insurance adviser will explain the type of insurance your business will require and the probable cost. Most banks will provide insurance. However, they may only deal with a limited number of insurance companies unless they specifically act as an insurance broker themselves, then they will have to follow the code of conduct, putting your interests before all other considerations.

Types of insurance

There is a large range of insurance policies available for small businesses and package policies can be arranged which will provide all the insurance required for your business. The following are the most frequently used types of insurance protection:

Fire

Buildings and their contents can be insured against fire damage.

Special perils

If it is thought necessary 'special perils' may be added. These can include explosion, impact by aircraft, riot and malicious damage, impact by vehicles, storm, flood, bursting or overflowing of water tanks and pipes. It would be advisable to insure against storm and flood damage if the premises are located in a coastal area.

All risks

This is a much wider cover. In addition to the above it also includes any accidental damage or loss not specifically excluded by the insurance company. The exclusions which will be stated in the policy are things such as:

o Wear and tear.
o Electrical breakdown.
o Gradual deterioration.

Theft

Providing there has been forcible entry to, or exit from the premises, contents are usually insured against loss from theft. Policies should include damage to the building as a result of the theft. Theft by employees or shoplifters is not normally included in this policy.

Fidelity

This type of insurance compensates the employer for loss of money or goods as a result of an act of dishonesty by an employee.

Money

Cover will apply to the theft of cash, cheques and certain other negotiable documents. There are different limits which apply to:

o Money on the premises.
o In and out of business hours.
o In safes.
o At the homes of directors or employees.
o In transit.

Consequential loss

Business may be interrupted or come to a complete standstill as a result of any of the above. This will lead to a loss of income and possibly other expenses incurred in trying to maintain the business. This policy will compensate for the loss of income so that ongoing business expenses can be met.

Liability

There are three different types of liability:

Employers' liability
This insurance is required by law so that you are insured against injury to employees or illness as a result of the work undertaken.

You are also required by law to exhibit a certificate of employers' liability insurance at your place of work. The premium you will pay for this type of insurance will be related to the size of the payroll and the risks attached to the jobs.

Public liability
This provides insurance cover against injury or illness caused by your business to any member of the public. It also covers legal fees and costs that may be incurred as a result of a claim against you.

Product liability
If the business manufactures or sells products, as a beauty salon most probably will, then you could be held legally liable for any injury which may occur arising from product defects. Product liability insurance provides the necessary cover.

Credit

Credit insurance will protect your business against clients failing to pay but this insurance is not easily available unless you have a well established business.

Legal expenses

In the event of a contractual or employment dispute these policies will provide cover for the legal expenses.

Life insurance

If the death of a member of your staff would actually cost the business money, as that person's expertise and knowledge was crucial to the running of the business, it would be worthwhile arranging 'key personnel' insurance to cover the cost of replacing the employee.

Permanent health insurance

This insurance provides for a continuation of income in the event of ill health or accident preventing you or an employee from working for a period of time or permanently.

Personal accident and sickness

These policies are renewable annually and provide cover for incapacity caused by accident or ill health.

Buying insurance

The insurance company will probably carry out a survey of the premises before providing cover and will draw attention to any potential hazards and advise on ways to reduce the risk.

The proposal form

This must be filled in to provide the insurance company with all the information they require. This will include:

- The name and address of the proposer.
- The type of business.
- Details of previous losses.
- Insurance history.
- Details of the risk to be insured.

Duty of disclosure

Any person applying for insurance is obliged to disclose to the insurer all the relevant facts which might affect the risk insured or the terms of acceptance, for example the premium. Failure to comply could entitle the insurer to treat the policy as invalid.

The policy

The insurance policy is a document which sets out all the details of the contract.

Premium

The premium is the payment for insurance which may be paid annually or by instalments during the period for which insurance cover is provided.

When operating a beauty business, finding the right staff is extremely important as constant changes will adversely affect the business.

Clients who attend regularly for beauty treatments usually return to the same therapist each time, once a professional client–therapist relationship has developed.

A good therapist soon gains the confidence of the client and will therefore generate a great deal of business for the salon owner.

When looking for staff it is important to make sure that the right person for the job is chosen first time because hiring the wrong staff and then having to re-advertise will be disruptive to the business.

To begin with a job description, which provides details of the purpose of the job and the specific tasks and duties, will be helpful and should contain the following points:

o   Job title.
o   Aim of the job.
o   Accountability – the person to whom the employee is responsible.
o   Who the employee will be responsible for.
o   The specific duties listed in order of importance.
o   Special tasks which may be required of the employee.

Title: Salon manager.

Aim: Increase the clientele and help to expand the business. To be responsible for four members of staff.

Accountability: Liaise with the salon owner.

Staff responsibility: Four fully-trained but inexperienced beauty therapists.

Duties: Organizing staff rotas.
Training staff in new techniques.
Stock controller.

Special tasks: Assisting the owner in marketing the salon and its products.

Once this has been set down you will have a clear picture of the position to be filled. It is now important to form a picture of the person you want by drawing up a job specification, which is a detailed statement of the physical and mental activities in a job.

The details required would be:

o   Education.
o   Specific training.
o   Previous experience.
o   Specialized skills.
o   Personal attributes.
o   Communication skills.
o   Fitness and health.

Example of a job description

The salon is relatively new and there are four therapists, all with little industrial experience, currently working with the owner. The owner now requires a manager to help in the plans to increase business and motivate existing staff. The job description for a salon manager would include the following details:

Example of a job specification

Education: Nationally recognized qualifications.

Training: A certificate in business management or a willingness to attend a recommended course.

Experience: Three years' industrial experience in all areas.

Specialized skills: Aromatherapy.

Personal attributes: Confident and outgoing with a sense of humour.

Communication: The ability to work as part of a team.

Under normal circumstances the employee will become a full-time, permanent salaried member of staff. The beauty business, however, depending upon the treatments offered does have very busy periods when more staff are required and quiet periods when employees have little to do. It may be worthwhile therefore to look at the alternatives.

Part-time staff

When a business is new, the financial commitment of permanent, full-time members of staff may be too big a burden or the work available may not add up to a full working week. Sometimes the employees do not wish to work full-time due to other commitments and to accommodate them it may be the best course of action to offer part-time work rather than lose a competent member of the workforce.

Commission only

Working on a commission only basis will be an incentive for the therapist to increase the number of treatments per week and the amount of sales on complementary products, thus increasing the takings along with the wages. Salaried staff with a regular wage each week may only carry out the minimum amount of work required.

The two can in fact be combined quite efficiently by the employer guaranteeing a basic wage and when the employee reaches a set target figure a commission is earned on any sales above that figure.

Freelance

There may be a time such as the pre-summer period or pre-Christmas period which are heavily booked and a therapist may be very happy to work for that period for a set fee. National insurance contributions, holiday or sick pay are the responsibility of the freelance not the therapist. The terms must be agreed at the outset that the work is temporary and for a certain period of time.

Attracting staff

There are several different avenues open to you when looking for staff:

1. Advertising.
2. Recruitment agency.
3. Local college.
4. Asking colleagues, business contacts or clients.

Advertising

The main purpose of advertising is to attract the largest number of candidates with the right qualifications thereby ensuring a reasonable chance of finding the most appropriate person for the job.

This can be done locally or nationally and the response is usually fairly quick. The advertisement needs to attract the ideal candidate for your business therefore:

○ It should be appropriately placed to reach the target audience.
○ It should stimulate their interest and hold their attention.
○ It should be clear to the job applicants if they are suitable candidates for the job and that it is worth applying for.

The advertisement (see Figure 49.1) should contain:

○ The job title.
○ The salary.
○ The location.
○ The work involved.
○ The requirements.
○ Closing date for application.
○ Application contact.

Figure 49.1 *Job advertisement*

PORTERS BEAUTY SALON
require a
SALON MANAGER

The successful candidate must hold nationally recognizable qualifications and have a minimum of 3 years experience in the industry.

Dedication and ambition is required to expand this new, modern health and beauty centre.

The ability to organize staff and take responsibility for stock control as well as patience and a sense of humour are essential.

In return we offer excellent working conditions and salary is negotiable.

Apply in writing with full curriculum vitae to:
Mrs Stewart, Porters Beauty Salon, Ashley Road, Hale, Cheshire.

Recruitment agency

This is a costly method of staff recruitment and there are few specializing in jobs within the beauty industry. The main advantage is that the agency will sift through all prospective candidates, leaving you time to run your business. The agency may also have people with special skills on their books.

Local colleges

Recruiting direct from colleges in your area would save advertising costs and hopefully the college tutors could recommend a student with the qualities and expertise that you require.

Their industrial experience would however be minimal. Therefore, it could be some time before the student would be working to full potential and contributing effectively to the business profits. It would be advisable to accept students on industrial release from college and see them working first hand before employing them full-time.

Colleagues/business contacts

This has the advantage of personal recommendations but it would be advisable to ask for a CV and carry out an interview in the normal way.

The disadvantage is that there is a possibility of missing out on a more suitable candidate by not advertising the job.

Selecting staff

When the prospective candidates reply to the advertisement it is now time to collect all the information together about each application in such a way that the unsuitable candidates will be easily eliminated.

The most efficient way to do this is to ask each candidate to fill in an application form (Figure 49.2) and from this you can choose a certain number of candidates who match up with your requirements and arrange an interview with them.

The interview

An interview provides the opportunity to give all the necessary information about the job to the applicants and ask any questions which will help you decide which of them will be successful. There are certain considerations to be made when conducting an interview:

○ Decide in advance where the interview will be held. This is particularly important if you

APPLICATION FOR EMPLOYMENT

Thank you for applying to Top to Toe Health and Beauty Salon.
Please complete the application form in your own handwriting.

POST APPLIED FOR:

Title:_____   Surname:_____

First Name(s):_____

Address:

Telephone No.:

Date of Birth:_____

Nationality:_____

How did you hear about the vacancy?

EDUCATION AND TRAINING:- SECONDARY, FURTHER AND PART-TIME

SCHOOL/COLLEGE ADDRESS	FROM-TO	QUALIFICATIONS	GRADE	DATE

EMPLOYMENT - PLEASE GIVE DETAILS OF THE LAST TWO EMPLOYERS

NAME & ADDRESS	FROM-TO	BRIEF JOB DESCRIPTION
1		
2		

Figure 49.2 *An example of an application form*

RELEVANT ADDITIONAL INFORMATION:	DO YOU HAVE A HEALTH PROBLEM/ DISABILITY?
	_____ (Yes/No)
	IF YES, PLEASE DESCRIBE:
	ARE YOU REGISTERED DISABLED?
	_____ (Yes/No)

HOBBIES AND INTERESTS:

REFERENCES - Please give the name of two referees we can contact to support the information in this application.

Name:_____   Name:_____

Address_____   Address:_____

_____   _____

_____   _____

_____   _____

Occupation:_____   Occupation:_____

I declare that the statements in this form are correct to the best of my knowledge. I understand that my engagement will be conditional upon satisfactory references and medical clearance.

Signature:_____   Date:_____

wish the applicant to demonstrate practical skills. The salon or treatment area will then be the ideal location. To promote a relaxed atmosphere it would be advisable to make sure the salon is not too busy at the time of the interview so that the applicant will not be overlooked or overheard.

- Always begin by putting the applicant at ease to bring out the best in them.
- Ensure the questions you ask will elicit the required information. Asking open questions which require more than a yes or no answer will provide you with a good idea of their communication skills and competence.
- Specific questions should also be asked to test the applicant's knowledge of the subject.
- When interviewing several people in a short space of time it would be useful to take notes as a source of reference when assessing all the applicants afterwards.
- Provide interviewees with some information about the job and show them where they may be working.
- Answer any questions interviewees might ask and provide the opportunity for them to bring out any points which may prove their suitability for the job and may not already have been covered.
- Inform interviewees when and how they will be contacted to give them the result of the interview.

As a courtesy to those people who have responded to the job advertisement who have had an interview but have not been selected, an acknowledgement in the form of a letter is appropriate. A short letter, to the point is all that is required, for example:

Dear Miss Jones,

Re: Vacancy for salon manager

Further to your interview on Friday, 20 September 1991, with regard to the above vacancy, I regret to inform you that on this occasion your application has not been successful.

I would like to take this opportunity to thank you for your interest shown in our salon and wish you every success in your future career.

Yours sincerely,

After the interview

Once you have decided which applicant matches up to the criteria you originally set out, by assessing all their strengths and weaknesses, their references must be checked, before finally making an offer of a job.

It can be more fruitful speaking to a referee by phone rather than contacting them by letter and trying to interpret what has been written.

The job offer should be put in writing and it should be on the condition that the references are satisfactory. This is important because once the offer has been accepted there is a contract and if references are then deemed unsatisfactory it is very difficult to remove the employee from the job.

The employer should secure the permission of the prospective employee before applying for references.

When the new employee joins your workforce set out your plans for induction and training and this will increase motivation and provide a positive start to the new job.

Induction

An induction programme will help a new employee settle in to a new job and will provide them with information about how the business works. The management should provide information about some or all of the following:

- The business – history, activity development and plans for the future.
- Policies, rules and regulations.
- Terms of employment to include disciplinary rules.
- Employee benefits and services.
- The roles of supervisors.
- Familiarization with the establishment, procedures and systems.

Induction should take place as soon as new employees start work, allowing time for them to adjust to the new social and work environment.

An experienced member of staff may be enlisted to help guide the new employee through the induction process and pass on valuable experience and knowledge, introducing the new member of staff to fellow employees and generally making them feel comfortable in their new job.

Factors which motivate staff

- A fair and equitable pay system.
- When there are opportunities for promotion.
- Varied work experience and training to develop further skills.
- To be given responsibility with a certain amount of independence.
- Praise for good work.
- Generous holidays.
- Job security.
- Flexibility in working hours.
- Being part of a successful team.

Discrimination

To help eliminate discrimination at work there are several acts which attempt to remove any inequality in the workplace.

The Equal Pay Act 1970

The main aim of this act is to eliminate discrimination on grounds of sex and to give all employees equal treatment. This should guarantee a woman:

- Equal pay for doing the same or broadly similar work as a man.
- Equality in all benefits laid down in the contract of employment.

The Sex Discrimination Act 1975

This act requires the employer not to discriminate between men and women in employment recruitment, training and all areas of employment other than pay:

- In the job advertisement.
- In the interview.
- In opportunities for promotion.

There are qualifications an employer may ask for that may indicate that a certain sex is being discriminated against but if it can be shown that these qualifications are genuinely necessary for the job there would be no case.

It is illegal to victimize any person who may take you to an industrial tribunal over sex discrimination, who has helped another person to do so or that you suspect might do so.

The Race Relations Act 1976

This act makes it unlawful to discriminate against anyone simply on the grounds of race in recruitment, training, employment and promotion.

The Commission for Racial Equality has produced a code of conduct to help eliminate racial discrimination.

Employment procedures

Once an employee starts work a contract of employment exists as the employee has accepted the employer's terms and conditions of employment. A written contract of employment must be given to the employee by the employer within eight weeks of starting the job. This is basically a written statement laying down the terms and conditions agreed by both parties. The items for inclusion on the statement would be:

Employer's name.
Employee's name.
The job title.
The date employment commences.
The rate of pay and how it is calculated.
When payment will be made.
Working hours.
Holiday entitlement including public holidays and holiday pay.
Arrangements for absences due to sickness or injury and provisions for sick pay.
Details of pensions and pension schemes.
The period for notice of termination the employer and employee must give.
Provision for maternity leave.
Disciplinary rules and grievance procedures.

Change in terms

The employer is obliged to inform the employee, in a further written statement, of any change in terms of employment within a month of its introduction. The employer may also meet this obligation by updating reference material which is readily accessible to the employee, as long as the reference documents are updated within one month of the change.

In the event of no written statement being given, the employee may refer the matter to an industrial tribunal. The terms which it may lay down will be as binding as those of the employer.

Example of a written statement

Terms and conditions of employment

I *Sally Hart* of *Face Facts* beauty salon, Westhampton.

am employing

Rachel Walker of 25 Clarendon Place, Norcliffe.

On:

20 June 1992

In the position of *salon manager*.

The basic weekly wage is £120. In addition 10% commission will be paid on all sales above £500.

The working hours will be:

Tuesday–Thursday 9 a.m.–5 p.m.
Friday 9 a.m.–7 p.m.
Saturday 9 a.m.–3 p.m.

Holiday entitlement will be 4 weeks per annum and all public holidays.

Payment will be made in full for any time lost through sickness or injury other than the first three days. All claims must be accompanied by a sick note.

There is no company pension scheme.

The amount of notice of termination of employment to be given by:

The employer is – two weeks.
The employee is – two weeks.

The disciplinary rules of the salon can be found in Document no. 001.

You may appeal to the *staff manager, Jenny Roberts*, to discuss any disciplinary decision.

The procedure for making your appeal is laid down in Document no. 002.

Grievances concerning employment should be made to *Sally Hart* in person.

Your solicitor could draw up a standard contract of employment and may be able to advise you on additional items to be included which are of relevance to your business, for example a radius clause.

Radius clause

This clause is to prevent a member of staff who leaves to set up in opposition, or to work for an already established salon, from taking any of your clientele.

The clause should state that the employee may not work within a specific distance for a specified length of time. The distance and time stated must not be deemed unreasonable.

Written statements need not be given to:

○ Someone who is working freelance.
○ Employees who work less than sixteen hours a week unless they have been employed for five years continuously for at least eight hours a week.

It is advisable to keep a duplicate of the written statement together with the employee's application form, a copy of your letter of offer and any notes you may have made at the interview.

The terms set out in the statement cannot be changed without the consent of both parties. In the case of promotion or a change of role, the job is not the same and therefore the employee may need a new written statement.

It is also necessary when taking on a new employee to inform your local tax office.

Payment of wages

Most employees have the right to an itemized pay statement. The details to be included are laid down by law and these briefly are:

1 *The gross pay.* The total amount earned by an employee before any deductions have been taken. It will include the basic pay, plus additional payments, for example commission, which is a percentage of the sales the employee has made, and overtime.
2 Any *fixed deductions* and the reason they are made itemized separately on the pay slip with a reason for each deduction.
3 The amount of *variable deductions* and the reason they are made.
4 *The net pay.* The total amount received by an employee after any deductions have been taken.

When wages are paid in cash the employee should be asked to sign your copy, as a receipt of payment.

Deductions

The deductions from the employee's wages are either laid down by law or are with the agreement of the employee.

Tax and national insurance must be deducted.

In some cases money may be deducted to enforce a court order, for example non-payment of council tax. This is called an *attachment of earnings*.

Voluntary deductions
These could be any of the following:

○ Private pension schemes, to supplement their state pension.
○ Savings.
○ Private medical scheme.

PAYE
Once you have registered with the tax office that you have become an employer, they will send you tax and national insurance contribution tables which will show you how much tax and national insurance must be deducted from the employee's wages.

A deductions working sheet is then made up for each employee. This is filled in for each pay day.

Tax and national insurance contributions are sent to the accounts office within fourteen days of the end of the month.

An end of year summary for each employee must be filled in at the end of each tax year. All details are then recorded on one statement and sent to the tax office.

Each employee should receive a copy of form P60 at the end of each tax year. This is a summary of gross and net pay during the year.

These procedures will not have to be carried out if the employee earns less than a minimum amount, which is laid down by the tax office but they must still be informed.

When a new employee commences work they should provide a copy of the P45 which has been given by the previous employer. This is a statement of earnings and tax deducted by the previous employer. In the case of an employee not providing a P45, you must then fill in a P46 and send it to the tax office. When the employee leaves, you must provide a P45 and send a copy to the tax office.

Income tax

People of working age must fill in a tax form stating the name of their employer. Any other information relating to income, earned or unearned, must be included. A claim may be made for expenses incurred as part of the job to be set against the tax they pay. The amount of income tax paid will depend upon:

○ Income.
○ Allowances.

A tax allowance is given depending upon their status, married or single, whether they have dependent relatives living at home, the size of a mortgage, etc.

The Inland Revenue will give each employee a tax code which will inform the employer how much tax to deduct from their wages.

National insurance

National insurance contributions are paid to the Government jointly by the employer and the employee. These contributions go to:

○ The national insurance fund.
○ The national health service.
○ The redundancy fund.

Contributions pay for the following:

○ Sickness and unemployment benefit.
○ Old age pensions.
○ The national health service.

The contributions are deducted as a percentage of the employee's wage and the employer's contribution is the larger part of the overall contribution.

Maternity entitlements

The employer has certain duties towards an employee who becomes pregnant:

○ To allow paid time off work to attend antenatal classes.
○ The employee may not be dismissed due to pregnancy except in certain circumstances.
○ To give the employee statutory maternity pay.
○ To allow the employee to return to work after maternity leave.

The employee may be fairly dismissed due to pregnancy if her condition prevents her from doing her job properly or if she could not legally carry out her work.

If there is no other work suitable for the employee she is still entitled to statutory maternity pay and has the right to return to work.

The employee has the right to return to work in the same or a similar position if she has stated in writing that she does intend to. The employee may lose her right to return to work if:

○ The job no longer exists and there is not a suitable alternative.
○ If a suitable alternative is offered and refused.

Sickness entitlements

Sick pay must be paid to an employee if this has been agreed and laid down in the contract of employment.

To obtain statutory sick pay the employee must provide evidence of the illness lasting more than four consecutive days or up to 28 weeks and the employer's obligation ceases after this period when state benefit takes over.

The amount to be paid in statutory sick pay is laid down by the Government and this is then claimed back by the employer, by deducting it from the national insurance contributions for that month. Statutory sick pay does not have to be paid for the first three days of sickness.

Employees are not entitled to receive sick pay if their earnings are below the weekly earnings limit for national insurance contributions or if your employee is 60 years or over (65 in the case of men).

There is a detailed booklet explaining the rules called *Employer's Guide to Statutory Sick Pay* which is available from the local office of the DSS.

Redundancy

It may become necessary to make an employee redundant if the employer needs to cut the workforce, move the business or close it down completely. When an employee is dismissed from a job because of redundancy, he/she is entitled to a lump sum payment as long as the employee has at least two years' service in the business, working for 16 or more hours a week, or five years or more service, working between 8 and 15 hours a week.

Redundancy payments depend upon:

o Age.
o The length of continuous service after the age of eighteen (work before the age of eighteen does not count).
o Weekly pay.

The employee is entitled to receive a written statement confirming the amount of redundancy pay and how it has been calculated. The Department of Employment will refund a percentage of the redundancy pay when the payment has been made, if there are fewer than ten employees on the date the dismissal took effect.

The employee is entitled to a week's notice if he/she has been in your employ for less than two years but more than a month. More than two years and he/she is entitled to two weeks'

notice. For each additional year the employee has been in your employ he/she is entitled to an extra week's notice up to a maximum of twelve weeks.

An employee who is to be made redundant, who has two years' continuous employment or five years' part-time is entitled to time off with pay to look for employment.

Dismissal of an employee

There may be very good reasons for dismissing an employee and it is important to behave in a reasonable manner and give the correct notice to prevent the employee accusing you of unfair dismissal.

Notice

The following notice should be given:

o One week's notice or one week's salary in lieu of notice if the employee has worked for you for four weeks.
o One week's notice for each year worked up to a maximum of twelve weeks if the employee has worked for you for over two years.

It would be advisable to follow a set procedure so that if necessary you could prove to an industrial tribunal that you have behaved in a fair and reasonable manner.

Disciplinary procedure

o Investigate any suspicion of misconduct.
o Inform the employee of your dissatisfaction preferably in writing.
o Allow your employee to respond and discuss ways of resolving the problems.
o Allow a reasonable amount of time for the employee to show improvement.
o If there is no improvement then give the employee a second written warning.
o Allow a certain period of time for the employee to show an improvement and monitor their progress.

○ If, after all this, the employee has not responded, you will be safe in giving correct notice of dismissal in the knowledge that you have behaved reasonably and fairly throughout the whole procedure.

A policy statement from the employer concerning disciplinary procedures could include the following:

○ In all matters of alleged employee misconduct the management will investigate, thoroughly and fairly, each case before any action may be taken.
○ The employee will be provided with every opportunity to state his or her case.
○ Disciplinary action that might be taken will be applied fairly and consistently in accordance with the company's disciplinary procedure.

There is a booklet published by ACAS entitled *Discipline at Work* which includes the Code of Practice on dismissals and is available from:

ACAS,
Clifton House,
83–117 Euston Road,
London NW1 2RB

The Trade Union and Employment Rights Act 1993

This recent act provides part-time employees with an improvement in their employment rights. Some relevant issues are:

○ All pregnant women regardless of length of service or hours of work are given the right to 14 weeks maternity leave and are protected against dismissal on maternity-related grounds.
○ All employees are entitled to written terms and conditions of employment after 8 weeks.
○ All employees have the right to complain to an industrial tribunal.

Because of this new law protecting the rights of part-time workers it is important to comply with employment law for all employees full- or part-time.

Unfair dismissal

Providing employees have worked for an employer for two years or more they have the right to complain to an industrial tribunal if they feel they have been unfairly dismissed.

Fair dismissal is when:

○ The employee was made redundant.
○ The employer can prove that the employee was not qualified or unable to do the job required.
○ The employee's conduct had been unacceptable, for example:
—Wilful destruction of equipment or property.
—Poor attendance record.
—Continual bad time-keeping.
—Theft.
○ The employer has acted reasonably when dismissing the employee.

Unfair dismissal is when:

○ The employee is dismissed because she is pregnant or not allowed to return to work after maternity leave when a suitable job is available, unless the employer has five or less employees and it would not be practicable to take the employee back.
○ When the reason for dismissal is because of trade union membership or activities.
○ When the business has been transferred to a new owner and the new owner wishes to replace an employee.
○ When an employee has been improperly selected for redundancy, for example on the grounds of sex, race, religion, a married woman or a trade unionist.

When employees have a case for unfair dismissal they can take their case to *an industrial tribunal.*

An industrial tribunal is a body appointed to investigate grievances at work. The decision of the tribunal is binding on both parties. It will normally have:

○ A legally qualified chairperson.
○ An employer's representative.
○ An employee's representative.

Constructive dismissal

This is when employees resign from their job because of the unreasonable actions of their employer.

For example, if the working hours are increased without increasing the pay or expecting employees to do something that was outside the contract of employment and which they may feel to be illegal. On these grounds a tribunal may judge an employee to be unfairly dismissed.

Advisory, Conciliation and Arbitration Service (ACAS)

An employer can obtain advice from ACAS on employment practice and there are offices in most large UK cities. The conciliation service is provided to help in solving problems between employers and employees, through informal discussion.

The cases most often dealt with are of dismissed employees seeking compensation. ACAS also deals with collective issues such as pay claims or other disputes.

Conciliation is the process of trying to get each side in a dispute to appreciate the other's point of view.

Arbitration is a process through which both parties in a dispute allow a third party to reach a decision.

Employee grievance procedures

Each employee has the right to seek redress for any grievance relating to conditions of employment.

○ The matter should be raised with the employee's immediate superior and they may be accompanied by a fellow employee.
○ The matter should be dealt with without delay.
○ If the response is not satisfactory to the employee the matter may be referred higher.
○ Results of all meetings should be recorded in writing and copies given to all parties concerned.

Dealing with a grievance interview

When dealing with a grievance interview the manager is usually unable to prepare for it in advance and the employee may have been storing up the grievance for weeks so a structured framework is therefore advisable. The format for the interview should include:

Objectives
○ To obtain the facts.
○ To arrive at an acceptable solution.

Strategy
○ Aim for a mutually beneficial result.

Tactics
○ Listen to the employee's story.
○ Ask probing questions to elicit the facts.
○ Summarize from time to time to ensure mutual understanding.
○ Attempt to unravel the cause of the grievance.
○ Check the facts and meet the other parties involved.
○ Consider actions that could be taken and assess their consequences.
○ Reply to the aggrieved employee and record the actions to be taken.

Results
○ The employee should go away feeling reassured that there is no problem or that the problem has been tackled constructively.
○ The manager should feel that the grievance has been handled correctly and that both parties are satisfied.

Health and safety management

It is an important task for any manager to devise a health and safety policy and promote it within the business. Employees should be involved in this process and contribute by making suggestions for improvement. This should prevent accidents occurring and provide a safe environment for all members of staff and clients.

The health and safety policy

The purpose of a health and safety policy is to provide concise information for all employees about the organization's health and safety aims, objectives and how these may be achieved. In written form it is a clear guideline and will provide a record of the standards set by the management.

The following points should be included in a health and safety policy:

○ The designated responsibility of the manager.
○ The designated responsibility of supervisors.
○ The duties of employees to include statutory and the organization's own rules.
○ Systems used to monitor health and safety performance.
○ Health and safety training provided.
○ Identification of hazards and risks.
○ Fire precautions.
○ Facilities for dealing with accidents.
○ Methods of recording accidents and contravention of health and safety rules.
○ Facility for consultation with management regarding health and safety.

TOP TO TOE HEALTH AND BEAUTY SALON
Policy on Health and Safety at Work

It is the policy of this establishment to make every reasonable and practicable effort to maintain a safe and healthy working environment for all employees and members of the public.

The establishment recognizes that the responsibility for enforcing this policy lies with the management. However, all employees must accept a joint responsibility for the safety of themselves, their colleagues and members of the public.

The co-ordination and monitoring of the safety at work policy and effective safety communication with the establishment will be the responsibility of Joan McLouglin, the elected safety representative. The management will ensure that every effort is made to meet the statutory requirements and codes of practice relating to the activities of the salon and any relevant recommendations from bodies dealing with health and safety.

To achieve this we will:
Provide training in safety procedures.
Appoint a safety representative.
Implement safe systems of work.
Provide information about specific hazards.
Issue protective clothing where possible.
Monitor safety procedures.
Provide training in fire and evacuation procedures.
Check all electrical equipment once a year.
Provide training in first aid.
Record all accidents.
Provide adequate rest facilities.
Provide a healthy environment.

Since employees are under a legal obligation to co-operate in matters of health, safety and welfare, all must accept personal responsibility for the prevention of accidents.

All employees will be informed of any revision of this policy.

A copy of the health and safety rules of the establishment are displayed in the staff room.

Karon Holmes
Proprietor

Figure 50.1 *An example of a health and safety policy*

Statute law

This is the written law of the land and consists of Acts of Parliament and the rules and regulations which are made relating to the Acts. An Act of Parliament itself sets out the principles and objectives while the regulations are made to help in achieving these objectives. Regulations are often written into an Act of Parliament years later.

The laws relating to health and safety at work with relevance to the health and beauty salon are:

- ○ The Health and Safety at Work Act 1974.
- ○ The Management of Health and Safety at Work Regulations 1992.
- ○ The Offices, Shops and Railway Premises Act 1963.
- ○ Local Government (Miscellaneous Provisions) Act 1982.
- ○ The Fire Precautions Act 1971.
- ○ The Control of Substances Hazardous to Health Regulations 1988.
- ○ The Electricity at Work Regulations 1989.
- ○ The Health and Safety (First Aid) Regulations 1981.
- ○ The Reporting of Injuries, Disease and Dangerous Occurrences Regulations 1985.
- ○ The Safety Representatives and Safety Committees Regulations 1977.
- ○ Classification, Packaging and Labelling of Dangerous Substances Regulations 1984.

Bylaws

These are laws which are made at a local rather than national level and are made by the local council. A business may have to consider some of the following.

Planning permission must be sought from the local council if the present use has changed and this will include changing a shop window. The planning department and the public highways department will decide if the business or proposed changes will not cause aggravation to local residents or greatly affect the flow of traffic and that parking facilities are adequate.

Building regulations administered by building control officers working for the local council must be strictly adhered to, to ensure the good health and safety of the public.

Fire regulations are important and must be followed when making any structural alterations particularly if it involves a second floor or an area below ground level. A local fire officer will provide necessary advice to ensure safety, the provision of fire-fighting equipment and procedures for evacuation.

A **certification of registration** will be required when a business provides certain treatments, that is, electrical epilation, ear and body piercing and tattooing. Any person carrying out these treatments must be registered with the local authority.

Licensing is required by some local councils for certain treatment such as body massage. Licences are usually valid for one year and are granted with a set of standards and conditions for a set fee. These standards must be met or the licence may be revoked.

The Management of Health and Safety at Work Regulations 1992

The employee has certain duties according to these regulations. To:

- ○ Assess adequate health and safety risks to employees, clients and other members of the public who enter the premises.
- ○ Plan, organize and control preventative measures.
- ○ Monitor the preventative measures.
- ○ Regularly review these measures.
- ○ Record the results of regular services.
- ○ Appoint a competent person to implement evacuation procedures and to provide the necessary training.
- ○ Provide employees with comprehensive and relevant information regarding health and safety.
- ○ Provide adequate health and safety training.

The regulations also require an employer to consult with the elected safety representative (the Safety Representatives and Safety Committees Regulations 1977) in sufficient time, with issues relating to the employees represented.

These issues will include:

- ○ The introduction of new procedures, equipment or substances which may affect the health and safety of the employees.
- ○ The appointment by the employer of 'competent persons', employees who will help in assisting the employer to comply with regulations.
- ○ Health and safety information the employer wishes to pass on to employees.
- ○ Health and safety training.
- ○ New rulings concerning health and safety.

The Safety Representatives and Safety Committees Regulations 1977

The main objective of the regulations is to allow the appointment of a safety representative, from a trade union recognized by the employer, who will consult with the employers in matters relating to health and safety.

The number of these representatives would be in relation to:

- ○ The total number of employees.
- ○ The variety of occupations.
- ○ The different work activity.

A union wishing to make an appointment must apply in writing to the employer with the name of the appointed person. The safety representative may only qualify if he/she has been employed for the proceeding two years by the employer or has been employed for two years with 'similar' work experience.

The representative has the right to time off for training and to carry out the required functions of the position. The representative has the right to be consulted in sufficient time by the employer when introducing new information concerning health and safety.

Health and safety and the employee

It is of vital importance that every single employee in the business is aware of the importance of health and safety procedures and the identification of all risks and hazards.

Risk: Is the probability that harm may result from an action, situation or circumstance.

Hazard: Is the possible potential for harm to occur in a given situation.

The manager could implement a system for employees to communicate information they feel would be helpful in maintaining standards of health and safety. This could be done in three ways:

1 Regular staff meetings when health and safety matters may be discussed.
2 The facility for employees to forward any suggestions through the correct channels to the manager or owner of the business.
3 Delegate the job of monitoring health and safety in the workplace, to one member of staff, who will pass recommendations to the appropriate person.

Health and Safety at Work Act 1974

The Health and Safety at Work Act 1974 protects self-employed people and employees, with the exception of those in domestic employment in private households. The employer is responsible for ensuring that the workplace is a safe and healthy place in which to work.

If you employ five or more people you must prepare a written statement setting down the arrangements and policy you have adopted to ensure their health and safety and procedures for carrying out that policy. When employing people, therefore, it may be advisable to contact the Health and Safety Executive office in your particular area and they will advise you about your duties to your employees.

There are Inspectors of the Health and Safety Executive who have extensive powers and may enter your business premises at any reasonable time or if there is a dangerous situation. If the inspector finds a fault he/she will serve an *improvement notice.* This will state the fault and also the time which will be given to put it right. This is usually within 21 days.

A *prohibition notice* may be served, which requires the employer to stop any activity which carries risk of personal injury. If there is failure to comply with this notice then it is a criminal offence and it could lead to prosecution.

Health: Includes mental as well as physical health.

Safety: Is the freedom from foreseeable injury.
Welfare: Are the facilities available for the employee's comfort.

Employer's duties

o   To provide and maintain the place of work and systems of work that are safe and without risk to health.
o   To ensure safety when storing and using equipment and substances.
o   To provide the necessary information, instruction, training and supervision to ensure health and safety.
o   To maintain the place of work in a safe condition and without risk to health.
o   To provide and maintain the access to the place of work and all exits.
o   To provide and maintain a safe and healthy working environment.

These are the duties of the employer, so far as it is reasonably practicable. Failure to implement these duties may give rise to criminal liability and to a claim for damages.

Employees' duties

To ensure health and safety at work there must be cooperation between the employee and the employer. Employees must therefore be responsible for the health and safety of:

o   Themselves.
o   Other employees.
o   The general public.

There must be cooperation with the employer to enable the duties and requirements of the act to be carried out.

Accidents

When accidents occur they may be human or environmental.
Human error may occur through careless work, improper behaviour, lack of necessary training, unsupervised work, inexperience or fatigue.

Environmental causes of accidents may include faulty equipment, poor ventilation or poor lighting.

How to prevent accidents

The employer must be aware of any potential hazards and the possible effects on the health and safety of the workers. These hazards must then be removed:

o   Entrances and exits to the premises must be kept clear.
o   The premises should be well lit.
o   All members of staff must be trained in the use of equipment.
o   There should be no trailing leads.
o   All electrical equipment should be correctly wired and well maintained.
o   Power points must not be overloaded.
o   Checks should be made regularly for cracked plugs and frayed wires.
o   All electrical equipment must be switched off before being cleaned or repaired.
o   Electrical equipment should never be touched with wet hands.
o   Ensure that all containers which contain chemicals are clearly marked.

The Office, Shops and Railway Premises Act 1963

This act contains legislation which aims to provide certain minimum standards relating to the health, safety and welfare of those people working in offices, shops and railway premises. The first two categories may apply to a health and beauty therapist who is working in a salon because:

o   An office can be defined as a building or part of a building which is used for administration, handling money, operating telephones and all forms of clerical work or similar activity.
o   A shop will include any place of work where retail or wholesale trade is carried out. The act deals with the working environment and welfare provisions for employees.

Working environment

o   The premises and all fixtures and fittings must be kept clean.

○ Dirt and refuse must be removed daily.

○ There must be adequate drainage.

○ The number of people employed in the business must not cause a risk of injury or risk to health.

○ A reasonable working temperature must be maintained not less than 16° C after the first hour.

○ Effective ventilation must be provided.

○ Humidity levels should be maintained.

○ Fumes and dust must be controlled.

○ Suitable lighting in all work areas with windows and skylights being kept clean.

○ Floors passageways and stairs should be kept clear of obstruction.

○ Handrails must be provided on stairs with open sides.

Ventilation

Good ventilation is essential in a salon to provide a healthy environment for employees and clients. It is a process which allows stale air to be replaced by fresh air.

Ventilation may be produced naturally through open windows or doors, the disadvantage of this method is the noise which may be evident and also lack of privacy for the client.

Artificial ventilation may be provided in several ways:

○ Free-standing fans which are portable and may be utilized when and where they are required. This produces air movement but is not an efficient method of ventilation.

○ A supply system which supplies fresh air from outside and filtered to remove dust.

○ An exhaust system which literally pushes air outside from the salon.

○ The ideal combination is the supply and exhaust system together with an air-conditioning unit.

Air conditioning

An air conditioning unit filters out particles of dust and either cools or warms the air depending on what is required and moistens or dries the air to maintain the correct humidity level.

Humidity

When humidity is high it may be uncomfortable for the client as well as the therapist. It is most important to control the humidity levels particularly when sauna, steam and other heat treatments are in use, to prevent problems occurring such as headache, fatigue and irritability.

Welfare provision

There must be a sufficient number of toilets, easily accessible, kept clean and tidy with good lighting and ventilation:

○ Up to five employees of either sex – one toilet.

○ Over five employees – one for each sex.

○ Over ten employees and if the public have access extra toilet facilities must be provided.

Other provisions to be provided include:

○ Washing facilities must be suitable and include a supply of clean hot and cold running water, soap and clean towels or another means of drying.

○ There must be a supply of clean drinking water and cups, unless provided by a water jet.

○ Facilities for rest and eating must be provided when meals are taken on the premises.

○ There must be provision for clothing particularly when the employee has to wear a uniform.

○ There must be adequate first aid facilities.

○ Adequate provision for fire prevention must be provided.

This Act has been superseded by the Health and Safety at Work Act 1994, which covers all employees.

All accidents must be recorded in an accident book, giving details of how, where and when the accident occurred, the names and addresses of the staff and clients involved and the first aid procedures carried out. Details will be required if a claim for injury benefit is made from the DSS.

Training and supervision of employees must be maintained.

Employers should prepare a written statement of their general policies concerning the health and safety of the employees if there are more than five employed.

Local Government (Miscellaneous Provisions) Act 1982

This is an important Act to any therapist who is providing electrical epilation treatments or ear-piercing. Each individual should be registered with the local authority before providing these services.

The environmental health department of the local authority will send an inspector to check that the premises are hygienic, the correct methods of sterilization are employed and the procedure to be followed in the disposal of needles is safe. When the inspector is satisfied he/she will issue a certificate.

Safe systems at work

Accidents involving members of staff and clients will be eliminated or greatly reduced if safe systems of work are put into practice. A safe system of work is the way a procedure is carried out to ensure maximum safety.

The manager can devise a safe system by:

○ Assessing the task.
○ Identifying the hazards and risk.
○ Defining a safe system.
○ Implementing the system.
○ Monitoring the system.

Task assessment

1 Write down the procedure.
2 List what equipment and products are used.
3 Look at where the procedure is carried out.
4 Look for possible sources or errors.

No....*60*..

LOCAL GOVERNMENT (MISCELLANEOUS PROVISIONS) ACT 1982

Certificate of registration to carry on the [Business of [Ear-Piercing] [Electrolysis]]

THIS IS TO CERTIFY that   *KARON CHRISTINE HOLMES*

of   *14 CAPESTHORNE ROAD, TIMPERLEY*

carrying on the [business of [ear-piercing] [electrolysis]] on the premises situated at

208 MOSS LANE, ALTRINCHAM

is duly registered in respect of such premises by the*

TRAFFORD BOROUGH COUNCIL

in accordance with the provisions of the above Act.

DATED *3rd OCTOBER*   19 *94*

(Signed) ..... *M S Jasper* ....†

PRINCIPAL ENVIRONMENTAL HEALTH OFFICER

The officer appointed for this purpose.

* Insert name of local authority.   †Insert designation of proper officer

NOTE: This certificate, together with a copy of any byelaws made under the Act relating to the practice or business, must be prominently displayed on the premises. Failure to do so is an offence.

Figure 50.2 *A certificate of registration issued by a local authority*

5   Look at how the procedure is carried out.
6   Carry out the procedure with an employee.

Identifying the hazards and risks

For each individual element of the procedure identify and record any possible hazard or risk to the client or therapist.

Defining a safe system

Once a procedure has been agreed upon and is deemed safe the information is then passed on to other members of staff, orally and in written form, with a copy safely filed away for reference.

Implementing the system

All members of staff must follow the set procedures, therefore training must be given when required and the manager is responsible for ensuring all information has been communicated to and understood by the employees.

Monitoring the system

Regular checks and staff appraisal must be made to maintain standards and information must be revised when necessary. Have regular meetings with employees to check that the systems in place are safe and working effectively.

The Health and Safety (First Aid) Regulations 1981

These regulations came into force in 1981 and they stipulate the minimum requirements for the provision of first aid at a place of work. The requirements vary depending upon the number of staff employed and the type of work which is carried out.

The following list is based on five members of staff being employed. The first aid box should be clearly labelled and contain the following:

○   One guidance card.
○   Ten individually wrapped sterile adhesive dressings.
○   One sterile eye pad with attachment.
○   One extra large sterile unmedicated dressing.
○   One triangular bandage.
○   One sterile covering for serious wounds.
○   Six safety pins.
○   Three medium-sized sterile unmedicated dressings.
○   One large sterile unmedicated dressing.

There should be at least one employee who has been adequately trained in first aid. This must be brought to the attention of all members of staff as this person should be responsible for carrying out all first aid procedures and replacing any items which have been used. In the absence of that person there must be an equally qualified person to take charge of all first aid duties.

Emergency phone numbers should be listed and stored in the first aid box; for example doctor, fire service, ambulance service.

The box should be stored in a dust-proof and damp-free atmosphere to keep the contents in good condition.

The employer must inform employees of all first aid arrangements including the location of equipment, facilities and the person in charge of it.

When an accident occurs the person responsible for first aid should:

○   Assess the situation.
○   Identify the problem.
○   Provide the appropriate treatment.
○   Arrange transport to the doctor or hospital if the condition so requires.

It is inevitable that even in the most safety conscious establishments accidents may occur which will require attention from a qualified member of staff. These may include:

Fainting

A temporary loss of consciousness caused by a reduced flow of blood to the brain.

Treatment

Lie the client down with legs raised slightly to stimulate the flow of blood to the brain or place in the recovery position if there is any difficulty in breathing, to maintain an open airway (see Figure 50.3). If clients only feel faint sit them down and assist them in leaning forward with their head between their knees. Loosen tight clothing, keep warm and supply fresh air.

Figure 50.3 *The recovery position*

Burns and scalds

Injuries to skin tissue, burns are caused by dry heat and scalds are caused by wet heat. A superficial burn causes redness, swelling and tenderness of the epidermis. Intermediate burns affect the dermis and in addition to redness and swelling will be painful and blistered.

Treatment
Cool the area immediately, preferably with cold water by immersion or holding the part under running water. Cover the area with a sterile dressing and seek medical attention if seriously burnt. Always remove rings, watches or constricting clothes from the injured area before any swelling occurs.

Blisters which occur are protective, preventing infection entering the wound therefore they must not be broken.

Chemical burns

May be caused by the acids and alkalis found in dyes, bleaches or antiseptics and disinfectants which have not been diluted. Some cleaning products may also cause a chemical burn when they come into the skin. If all safety precautions are not adhered to during galvanic treatment the concentration of acids and alkaline formed may cause a burn which penetrates deeply into the skin.

Treatment
Flush with lots of cold water, remove any clothing which may have chemicals on it and cover the area with a sterile dressing. Seek medical attention if necessary.

Electric shock

Electrical injuries may result from faulty equipment, loose wires, switches or frayed cables. Handling appliances with wet hands will increase the risk of injury

Treatment
Switch off the current at the mains or unplug the equipment. If this is not possible stand on an insulator, for example clothing, paper or rubber mat and using a wooden broom handle or chair to push the equipment or cable away from the injured person or remove their limbs from contact with the source.

If breathing is normal place the injured person in the recovery position, send for medical help and treat for shock.

Shock

May vary from a feeling of faintness to complete collapse. It may be caused by blood or fluid loss, heart attack, extreme pain, fear or electrical injury.

Treatment
Reassure and comfort the client, keep warm and loosen their clothing. Treat the cause of shock when possible and lie the client in the recovery position if there is a possibility of vomiting.

Seek immediate medical help in severe cases.

Cuts or wounds

A cut is a break in the skin which allows blood to escape, and germs or bacteria may enter and cause infection.

Treatment
For a minor cut, clean around the wound with warm water and a mild antiseptic. Apply slight

pressure over a pad of dry sterile gauze for 2–4 minutes and the bleeding should stop. Apply a clean adhesive dressing. For deep cuts seek medical assistance and try to control the bleeding by applying pressure at either side and cover with a sterile dressing once the bleeding has stopped. Use disposable plastic gloves if possible.

Eye injuries

These include a foreign body or chemicals in the eye.

Treatment
Chemicals may be washed out with a large amount of cold water. A foreign body may be removed by using a twisted, moistened corner of a sterile dressing or bathing the eye using an eyebath and lukewarm water. Seek medical attention in more severe cases.

Asthmatic attack

Caused by the muscles of the air passages going into spasm making breathing very difficult. Asthma may be triggered by an allergy or nervous tension and the condition is controlled by the sufferer with medication.

Treatment
Reassure and calm the client, sit them up in a comfortable position leaning on the back of a chair or table. Loosen the clothing and ensure a good supply of fresh air. Make sure clients take their medication if it is available.

Seek medical attention in severe cases.

Fire regulations

The Fire Precautions Act 1971 is concerned with fire prevention and the provision of fire escapes. A fire certificate is required if:

○ There are more than twenty people employed at any time.
○ There are more than ten people working anywhere other than the ground floor.
○ When the total number of people working in the building, including the salon, exceeds twenty.

Employers have a duty to provide a means of escape in case of fire for both their employees and any members of the public on the premises at the time.

Once a certificate has been granted it must be kept on the premises as long as it is in force and it will state:

○ The greatest number of people who can safely be employed at any one time on the premises.
○ The means of escape to be used.
○ The exits to be marked as fire escapes.
○ Any special risks in the structure of the premises.

Employers must ensure that any means of escape will be kept clear of obstruction at all times, kept in good working order and doors must be unlocked. All employees must be made aware of the means of escape and the procedures to be followed in case of fire.

The fire-fighting equipment suitable for all types of fire including chemical and electrical must be easily reached and kept in good working order.

Any breach of the fire regulations could make you liable for a fine or imprisonment.

Fire extinguishers

Fire extinguishers are colour coded and there are five different types which are used for different types of fire:

Powder
Blue in colour for flammable liquids, gases and electrical equipment. This may cause sensitivity if it comes into contact with the skin.

CO_2 gas
Black in colour for flammable liquids, gases and electrical equipment.

These two extinguishers may be used in a beauty salon where electrical equipment is used. Both types of extinguisher have limited cooling properties therefore it is advisable to use a fire blanket after the extinguisher, to deprive the fire of oxygen and prevent re-ignition.

Water

Red in colour for wood, paper, textiles, fabric and similar material. It must never be used on burning liquid, electrical or flammable metal fires.

Foam

Yellow in colour and may be used on burning liquid fires. It must never be used on electrical or flammable metal fires.

Halon

Green in colour for burning liquid fires. It must not be used on flammable metal fires.

Precautions

The fire extinguisher may be used on a small fire but in the event of a serious fire, it is important to evacuate the premises as quickly as possible.

Do not attempt to retrieve personal belongings.

(a) A *water* extinguisher for use on paper, wood textiles, and fabric. It must not be used on burning liquid, electrical or flammable metal fires

RED

(b) A *foam* extinguisher for use on burning liquid fires. It must not be used on electrical or flammable metal fires

YELLOW

(c) A *powder* extinguisher for use on burning liquid and electrical fires. It must not be used on flammable metal fires

BLUE

(d) A *halon* extinguisher for use on burning liquid and electrical fires. It must not be used on flammable metal fires

GREEN

(e) A *carbon dioxide* extinguisher for use on burning liquid and electrical fires. It must not be used on flammable metal fires

BLACK

(f) A light-duty *fire* blanket for use on burning liquids and burning cloth. Heavy-duty fire blankets are available for industrial use

RED

Figure 50.4 *Types of fire extinguisher*

Guide your client or employees for whom you are responsible, to the nearest fire exit, closing the doors behind you.

Ring the emergency services by dialling 999 and provide the necessary information:

○ Location of the fire and address.
○ The nature of the fire.

The Electricity at Work Regulations 1989

These regulations are concerned with ensuring safety when using electrical equipment. The management have responsibility to ensure:

○ All electrical equipment is properly maintained and in good working order.
○ Regular tests are made by a qualified electrician on each piece of equipment – at least once a year.
○ A record of each test and the date the tests were carried out is made and provided for inspection if necessary.

It is the responsibility of all employees to co-operate with their employer in complying with the regulations. A set of rules may be devised by the manager to inform each employee of their daily responsibilities in maintaining electrical equipment in good working order:

○ Store equipment safely in its designated place with all the wires and attachments securely fixed in place.
○ Clean equipment after each use.
○ Place the equipment on a stable surface when in use.
○ Check the wires are not twisted, worn or frayed.
○ Check the plug has the correct fuse.
○ Check the plug is not cracked or loose.
○ Do not overload plug sockets by using multiple adaptors.
○ Ensure there are no trailing leads which someone could fall over.
○ Always dry your hands before touching the plug or equipment.
○ Do not place equipment on or near water.
○ Always follow the manufacturer's instructions.

○ Report faulty equipment to your superior and store it safely to be repaired.

Control of Substances Hazardous to Health Act 1989

There are products used by beauty therapists that may be hazardous to health if they are not stored and used correctly, following procedures laid down by the organization. The health and safety welfare, of all employees and members of the public with access to the premises, is the responsibility of the employer by law. The manager or delegated employee (health and safety representative) has to:

○ List all substances which may be hazardous to health.
○ Evaluate the risks to health.
○ Decide what action needs to be taken to reduce the risks.
○ Devise rules and regulations about safe storage, handling, use, transportation and disposal of hazardous substances.
○ Provide training for all staff in their use.
○ Monitor the effectiveness of the control measures.
○ Keep records up to date of all measures taken and safety checks made.

Assessment procedures
The first step is to check everything which comes into the premises, products used during practical procedures as well as products required for other services such as cleaning and sterilization.

The law requires suppliers to provide information about the safe use of the products they are selling on clearly marked labels. To recognize substances which may be hazardous it is important to read the labels carefully but do not rely solely on this information.

Check carefully what the hazards may be, do they:

○ Cause irritation.
○ Burn the skin.
○ Give off fumes.
○ Cause breathing difficulties.
○ Cause allergies.

It is also useful to research information from other sources which may be of help. These could include:

○ Other therapists.
○ Health and safety experts.
○ Company representatives.
○ Manufacturers.
○ Professional trade organizations.

Obtaining all published material concerning health and safety, available from health and safety executive public enquiry points:

Health and Safety
Executive,
Broad Lane,
Sheffield,
S3 7HQ
Tel: 0114 289 2345

Health and Safety
Executive,
Rose Court,
Southwark Bridge Road,
London SE1 9HF
Tel: 0171 717 6000

Labelling
Once the hazardous substances have been identified warning symbols should be applied in a prominent position according to the Classification, Packaging and Labelling of Dangerous Substances Regulations 1984.

These dangerous substances may be categorized in different ways. In relation to health and safety this will be according to the harm they can cause. Reaction may be immediately after exposure, this is an acute effect, but there are other substances which have long-term effects on the body only after repeated exposure, and this is known as a chronic effect.

Classification
Corrosives: These are substances which attack chemically, materials or people.
Explosive and flammable: These are dangerous because of the rapid release of energy and the harm that they cause as a result of combustion.
Harmful: These substances present a limited risk to health if inhaled, ingested or enter the body through the skin.
Irritants: These will have a detrimental affect on the skin or respiratory tract.
Oxidizing: These are substances which give off heat when they come into contact with other substances, in particular flammable ones.
Toxics: These are substances which prevent or interfere with body functions in a variety of ways.

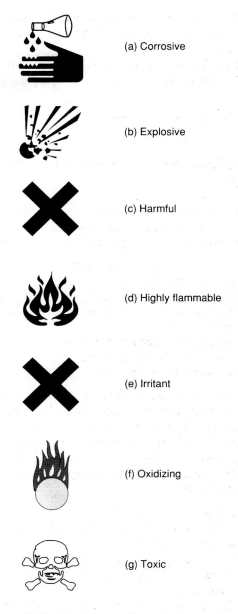

(a) Corrosive

(b) Explosive

(c) Harmful

(d) Highly flammable

(e) Irritant

(f) Oxidizing

(g) Toxic

Figure 50.5 *Classification of hazardous substances*

All therapists must be aware of the potential risk involved when handling hazardous substances in the course of their work.

Storage
Any product which has been identified as hazardous must be stored in a cool, dry place, with good ventilation away from direct sunlight.

ACCIDENT REPORT FORM

Date: Time of Accident:

Name:	**Age:**
Address:	
Relationship to salon:	
Nature of visit to salon:	**Contact Tel No:**

Brief description of Accident:

_____

Location of accident:

_____

Cause of accident (list all materials used):

_____

_____

Damage incurred to injured person:

_____

Action Taken:

_____

_____

Witnesses:

Signature of Client: Date

Signature of Witnesses: Date:

                                      Date:

Signature of Therapist: Date:

Signature of Manager: Date:

Figure 50.6 *An example of an accident report form*

A metal cupboard with adjustable shelving is ideal for flammable products and large heavy items must be stored on the low shelves and always resealed after each use.

Handling
All treatment rooms should have good ventilation to remove fumes and freshen the air.

Therapists must wear protective clothing when using substances which may cause harm. Gloves may be used to protect the hands particularly when using cleaning fluids. Masks may be worn to prevent inhalation of fine powder and goggles to protect the eyes from irritation.

Smoking must be prohibited when handling any hazardous substance.

Always ensure the manufacturer's instructions are strictly adhered to at all times, particularly in the dilution of concentrated substances.

Aerosol sprays must be kept cool and away from heat while in use and must never be sprayed near a naked flame.

The Reporting of Injuries, Diseases and Dangerous Occurrences Regulations 1985

These regulations cover all employees, clients or members of the public who suffer injury or a condition resulting from a work activity.

The purpose of these regulations is to ensure the information regarding incidents or injury arising from work activities is provided to the enforcing authority by the person responsible within the organization.

To prevent any future accidents or injury occurring the information is useful to highlight areas which require improvement or change in practice.

The procedure
○ The relevant enforcing authority should be contacted immediately regarding injury, disease or a dangerous occurrence which results from work activities. The enforcing authority will be the Health and Safety Executive or local authority.
○ The person to provide the information would be the manager or the person who has been given the responsibility within the organization for the control of health and safety.
○ Information could be transmitted immediately by telephone and then a written report with all the details should be sent within seven days.
○ Form F2508 must be used when reporting injuries and dangerous occurrences.
○ Form F2508A must be used when reporting disease only if there is written confirmation from a medical practitioner that the disease is listed and is a result of work activity.
○ Records must be kept and can be entered into the accident book, Form B1510 and photocopies of any reports sent to the enforcing authority. These records should be kept for a minimum of three years from the date they were made.

Manual Handling Operations Regulations 1992

These regulations have been introduced under the provisions of the Health and Safety at Work Act. They implement the requirements of a European directive on the manual handling of loads, to prevent injury from moving or lifting heavy objects by hand or bodily force. The most common injuries are sprains and strains, often to the back, due to incorrect methods of lifting and handling or prolonged use of body force.

Many injuries which occur are cumulative rather than being caused by one single incident. Therefore, the employer is required to assess any task which involves manual handling of loads and take into account:

○ The task to be undertaken.
○ The capabilities of the staff.
○ The limitations of the staff.
○ The type of load to be handled.
○ The working environment.

Risk of injury may be avoided
○ By eliminating the need to manually handle and any heavy load, e.g. repair heavy equipment *in situ* and arrange for heavy goods to be delivered to the point of use.
○ By handling heavy loads by other means such as automation, a power system and using trolleys for transportation.
○ By training all members of staff in correct procedures when handling heavy loads, making loads smaller, lighter or easier to grasp.

The duties of the employee are
○ To take reasonable care for their own health and safety and others who may be affected by their activities.
○ To co-operate with their employers to enable them to comply with their health and safety duties.
○ To make use of appropriate equipment provided for them for the safe handling of loads.
○ To follow appropriate safe systems of work laid down by the employer to promote safety during the handling of loads.

The Provision and Use of Work Equipment Regulations 1992

These regulations require that all equipment used in a salon must be suitable for the purpose for which it is used. It must also be properly maintained and all members of staff must be trained in its use. These regulations apply to any equipment whether it is new or has been bought second hand.

To comply with these regulations you must:

○ Have all equipment regularly serviced.
○ Keep records of when equipment has been checked or repaired.
○ Always check that equipment bought second hand is checked by your own service engineer or electrician.
○ Train all new members of staff in the use of equipment.
○ Have training days to update information or to evaluate use of equipment.
○ Provide written instructions in addition to training if and when required.

The Personal Protective Equipment at Work Regulations 1992

These regulations require every employer to provide protective equipment to any employee who may be exposed to any risk to health or injury during working hours.

To comply with these regulations:

○ Assess the need for use of personal protective equipment.
○ Supply protective clothing or equipment free of charge.
○ Train staff in use of personal protective equipment.
○ Ensure all such equipment is well maintained.
○ Ensure it is suitable for the nature of the work.

The Health and Safety (Display Screen Equipment) Regulations 1992

With the increasing use of computers in all types of business these regulations must be complied with if any employees are using equipment which may cause the following:

○ Eye strain.
○ Mental stress.
○ Muscular pain.
○ Other physical problems.

The duty of the employer is to:

○ Assess the equipment and the work station for risk of injury or strain to the employee.
○ Plan the display screen equipment so that there are breaks or changes of activity.
○ Provide training for the employees using the equipment.
○ Provide any special spectacles needed but they must be paid for by the employer.
○ Provide a properly designed desk and chair.

The Environmental Protection Act 1990

This Act is relevant to the hair and beauty industry in that some products used may contain hazardous substances which must be disposed of safely.

○ Any person disposing of 'waste' has a duty to dispose of it safely in such a way that it does not cause harm to the environment or individual.
○ There are occasions when out-of-date stock must be disposed of and it may be necessary to consult with the manufacturer for advice.

To comply with this Act:

○ Obtain the relevant information from suppliers about the safe use and disposal of products.
○ Provide training for all employees in the safe disposal of products or chemicals.
○ Never dispose of chemical products where they may be found by any unauthorized person, in particular, children.

51 Advertising the business

All business will benefit to some extent from advertising. There are many health and beauty salons in competition with each other and each one has to prove that their particular business has more to offer than the rest.

The aims of advertising

Advertising has two basic aims:

1   To inform potential clients about the nature and availability of treatments and products.
2   To persuade clients to buy the treatments and products.

Advertising may vary in that adverts convey different messages, either providing information or being persuasive. An announcement of the time and venue of a forthcoming demonstration evening is mainly providing information; the statement that 'the new non-surgical facelift machine will make you look and feel years younger' is mainly persuasive.

Advertising is successful when:

○   There is an increase in retail sales.
○   There is an increase in the number of clients.
○   There is an increase in all sales bought by existing clients.

Some forms of advertising are aimed at a long-term view being designed to create an image of the business which will appeal to a large proportion of the market.

Types of advertising

There are many different forms of advertising and it is important to choose the correct one so that the money spent is used to the best advantage.

Figure 51.1 *An example of a salon advertisement placed in a local newspaper*

○   Local/national newspapers.
○   Local radio.
○   Magazines.

○ Specialist brochures.
○ Leaflets/posters.
○ Mail shots.
○ Word of mouth.
○ Demonstrations.
○ Directory.

Which type of advertising you use will depend upon the budget allocated for the purpose, the market you are aiming at and the media involved in that particular market.

A beauty salon would benefit from advertising locally as the majority of clients will not want to travel a distance for their treatments.

Newspapers

Most areas have a free paper which is delivered to everybody in a particular area. Therefore, the paper will probably reach more of the market than an advertisement placed in a paper which is bought only by a percentage of the population in that area.

Features, contributed by experts, are gratefully welcomed by the publishers of free papers, so that they are not just full of adverts. So contact the editor and offer to write articles or an advice column related to your business. This will then give you valuable free advertising.

Although newspapers will often have the facility to design an advertisement for you, it may be advisable to use a professionally designed advert to catch the reader's eye. The only drawback to this is the cost of the services of a graphic designer.

A good advertisement should draw attention to the services or products you are trying to sell and be easily understood. It should convince the reader of the benefits and create a desire to either go and buy the product or sample the treatments advertised.

An interesting story about yourself, your business or somebody working for you, particularly if it is accompanied by an unusual photograph, may be deemed by a newspaper editor to be worth including in the publication. This sort of free advertising is often worth far more than a written advertisement because the general public find the objectivity of a journalist far more credible than an ad.

National newspapers would not be the right media to advertise treatment packages but would be ideal if you had a product to sell through mail order, for example your own brand of skin care products.

Local radio

It could prove quite expensive to advertise on local radio. However, your advisory services could be offered and when the occasion requires asking someone with beauty therapy experience to take part in a discussion or current affairs programme, you may be called upon and the resulting exposure could prove to be an invaluable free source of advertising.

Magazines

Placing an advertisement in the advertising section of a magazine which specializes in beauty will ensure that the people who are going to read the advert will be those most interested in the services you are offering. Because there will be other similar advertisements it is important to ensure that yours will be designed in such a way that it will stand out from the rest.

Specialist brochures

This can be a certain way to ensure that the target audience are all interested in the treatments advertised. An excellent example of this is the *Bridal brochure* that many large hotels produce. These brochures detail the services that they offer, as a hotel, mainly in connection with the catering and entertainment facilities they have to offer a couple who are planning a wedding. They will then invite other businesses such as florists, hairdressers and beauty salons to place advertisements in the brochure. The wedding makeup or pre-wedding beauty package could receive an excellent response, when advertised in this type of publication. Many brides who do not normally have beauty treatments will on such a special occasion. This

Figure 51.2 *An advertisement included in a travel agent's portfolio*

provides you with the opportunity of gaining new business on a permanent basis, if the bride is sufficiently impressed with your work.

Leaflets/posters

Advertising leaflets can look like a second rate form of advertising unless they are of a high quality. They can be used in several ways:

○ Picked up by established clients and passed on to potential clients.
○ Given to someone who calls in to enquire about the services offered.
○ Sent out in mail shots.
○ Posted through letter boxes.
○ Given out at exhibitions or demonstrations.
○ Leaving the leaflets at another business which complements your own, for example a hairdressing salon. This could be reciprocated and their advertising literature could be left at your salon.

Posters are effective when placed in a position where they will be read by either a captive audience or where there is a considerable amount of passing trade.

An antenatal clinic has a captive audience and there are many pregnant women who may not have considered beauty treatments previously but who may now have a great need for the services of a beauty therapist, both before and after the birth of her child. She may require pedicures, waxing treatments or even a relaxing facial before the birth and she will almost certainly require help and advice after the birth, on losing weight and regaining her figure.

A poster in a busy local shop such as a newsagents or a chemist will probably be seen by a large number of people and even if the return on this form of advertising is small the value for money is excellent as it is not an expensive form of advertising.

Mail shots

By keeping a record of the addresses of all clients and any person who may have requested information from you, or names passed on through personal contact, a mailing list can be built up. This may then be used to provide information about new products or techniques and seasonal or special offers.

Word of mouth

This is a very valuable form of advertising. Once you have established a reputation for quality, professionalism and good client care and the treatments you offer are competitively priced, clients will automatically recommend your business to friends, relatives and colleagues, enabling you to build up your client base quite quickly. Having business cards with an address and telephone number available at all times provides a form of advertising but also ensures that a prospective client will be able to contact you even after some time has elapsed.

Demonstrations

A demonstration is an ideal way to bring a new concept or technique to the notice of the general public, or to provide a means of raising money for a charity, which will in turn provide your business with publicity. It is an interesting way of educating the public about health and beauty

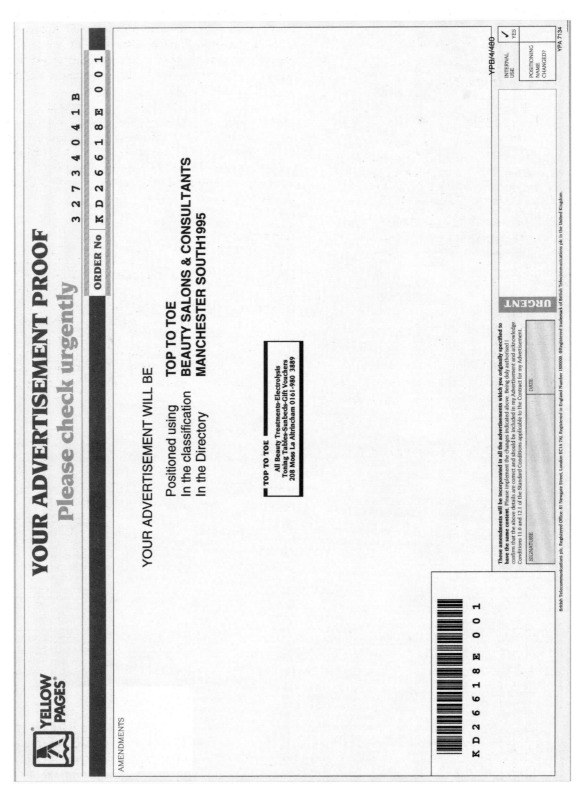

Figure 51.3 *An advertisement from Yellow Pages*

and promoting your own treatments in an entertaining way.

For a successful demonstration:

○ Find out the type of audience and the general age group that will attend.

○ Be sure of the numbers attending so that you can provide everybody with the necessary advertising literature or information leaflets, samples etc.

○ Have a basic format to follow and time the demonstration well – not too long or the audience may lose interest.

○ Prepare a set of cards with key points to ensure everything of importance is covered.

○ Know your subject well and prepare answers to questions that you think may arise.

○ Involve the audience whenever possible, in particular, encourage them to ask questions and use them as demonstration models.

○ Know the retail prices of products and treatments and the advantages they have over your competitors.

Use good judgement when choosing a model from the audience, for a makeup demonstration; choose someone who will enhance your products, for example an unmade up face will show a greater difference after the application of makeup and time will not be wasted cleansing when the purpose of the demonstration is the application of makeup.

You may feel it is advisable to provide your own model to ensure that unknown factors do not interfere with the demonstration, for example a very sensitive skin or skin blemishes.

Practise the demonstration in advance if it is your first, or the particular technique being used is a new one.

Directory

Finally entering the name, address and telephone number in a directory such as *Yellow Pages* is a useful form of advertising. Many people who are looking for a service may automatically refer to a directory. It is important, therefore, when choosing a name for the business to consider choosing one which begins with one of the first letters in the alphabet so that your name is one of the first that they call.

The keeping of records is vital to the smooth running of a business. Therefore, it is important to develop a simple yet efficient method of organization suitable for your business.

Accounts have to be prepared for the Inland Revenue and if they are not well documented it may be difficult to work out the tax and you could end up paying more than is necessary. Accounts also have to be prepared for customs and excise if the business pays VAT and possibly the bank manager who may require information on a regular basis.

If you have formed a company then the accounts must be properly prepared for the auditor.

Detailed accounts and regular stocktaking will provide you with an immediate picture of the state of the business, allowing you to plan ahead or recognize any financial problems that may exist.

Any book-keeping system must be backed up by keeping all receipts or evidence of payments made. These should include:

○ The bank paying in book.
○ The bank statements.
○ Cheque book stubs.
○ Copies of invoices, receipts and delivery notes received or given.
○ Petty cash receipts.

The books

Cash book

This will record all receipts and payments made on a daily basis. It will record what has been paid into the bank and what is taken out. At regular intervals the cash book should be added up and checked against your bank statement and this is called a bank reconciliation.

The receipts section should contain columns with the following headings:

DATE RECEIVED	INVOICE NO.	CLIENT	AMOUNT £	PAID INTO BANK

The payments column should contain columns with the following headings:

DATE PAID	CHEQUE NO.	REF	SUPPLIER	PETTY CASH	MONEY FROM BANK

There should also be a column for VAT where applicable. The more detailed the cash book is the better.

Petty cash book

This book is used to record minor transactions and would be used in conjunction with a petty cash box. A small lump sum will be drawn from the bank account, the transaction will be recorded in the cash book and placed in the petty cash box to use when necessary. When money is taken out it must be replaced with a receipt for each transaction.

Each receipt should include:

○ The date of the transaction.
○ The amount of cash taken.
○ Reason for the transaction.

Sales day book

This supplies you with a record of money owed to you for goods already issued. The invoice will have been sent and a copy retained for your records which will be used to fill in details of the transaction in the sales day book. The information required would include:

○ The date.
○ The name of client.

PORTERS BEAUTY SALON
Ashley Road
Hale
Cheshire
SR5 MJ4

Figure 52.1
Example of an order form

TEL: 0253 310717   10th April 1992

ORDER   NO: 27884

TO: ANTON COSMETICS LTD.
     5, THE GLEN
     SHREWSBURY
     JR9 AA7

CATALOGUE NO:	QUANTITY	DESCRIPTION	£	P
B20579	12	OIL OF EVENING PRIMROSE CLEANSING CREAM	24	00
B20581	12	OIL OF EVENING PRIMROSE FACE MASKS	16	00
C9362	4	EYESHADOW PALETTES	3	00
		TOTAL	43	00

SIGNED:....*Sarah Thomas*.....................

○ Invoice number.
○ Net amount.
○ VAT.
○ Invoice total.
○ Date it was paid.
○ Any remarks, for example not paid within the given time, etc.

Invoices should be filed away safely in numerical order and have separate files for paid and unpaid invoices.

Purchases day book

This records the money that you owe, when goods have been supplied to you and you have to pay for them within a given period. All details should be entered into the purchases book immediately and the invoice filed away with a note of the date on which the bill must be paid.

The documentation

Order forms

An order form is necessary to record your requirements so that your supplier knows exactly what you need and you have a copy for your records so that you may check your order when it arrives (Figure 52.1).

Advice notes

An advice note will be sent to you from your supplier when you have placed an order for goods. This will indicate that the order has been dealt with and the goods should arrive within the next few days. In case of a delay you will be able to inform the supplier and the problem can be dealt with.

Delivery notes

A delivery note is sent with the goods itemizing each article in the package. This will enable you to check immediately if the order is complete. If the goods cannot be examined at the time of delivery then this must be clearly marked on the copy and original that they have not been examined.

Invoices

An invoice outlines the details of the sale, the amount charged and the terms of the sale, as follows:

○ There will be an order number for you to check the goods received match the goods on the order form.
○ Terms of payment, for example cash discount for immediate payment or the length of time in which to pay.
○ Carriage, which is the cost of transporting the goods, it is sometimes paid by the supplier, if the order is above a certain amount and it would be indicated by the words 'Carriage paid'.
○ Errors or omissions in the order which will be corrected.
○ VAT.
○ The VAT registration number.
○ The invoice number, which will allow the supplier to identify the invoice immediately.

Proforma invoices
A proforma invoice is normally used when the customer's credit worthiness has not yet been established. It is an invoice which requires the customer to pay for the goods before they have been despatched.

Credit notes
A credit note will be sent by the supplier if:

○ The invoice price has to be reduced because of a mistake on the invoice.
○ Faulty goods have been returned.
○ The wrong goods were delivered.
○ An incomplete order.

These notes are often printed in red to make them easily distinguishable.

Debit notes
A debit note will be sent by the supplier if:

○ The price has to be increased because of a mistake on the invoice.
○ More goods have been sent than were ordered.

Statement of account

This is sent by the supplier on a regular basis, usually monthly, and is a record of all business transactions over that period.

Stock records

Stock control is very important to prevent running out of vital items or over purchasing. The stock should remain constant so that clients will not be disappointed when they are keen to buy something and then find that it is out of stock. Buying too much stock which remains in cupboards unsold is inefficient, as the money paid for the goods could have been used in other areas.

Efficient stock control requires:

○ One person to be responsible for stock, as the more people involved the higher the chance of mistakes being made. A stock control book or an index file for each item which must be kept up to date.
○ A minimum and maximum figure required should be included because when the stock level reaches the minimum figure the person in control will know when to re-order and maintain the correct level of goods. The maximum figure will prevent buying too much of any product and tying up business capital.

○ Regular reviews of stock, which will tell you immediately the products that are selling well and those that are not.

Personnel records

These are details of the members of staff you have working for you. Records should be kept of:

○ Their initial application form.
○ Any relevant details from the interview.
○ The contract of employment laying down their terms and conditions of employment.
○ Training courses completed.
○ Future plans for training.
○ Personal details which could include family, absence from work, problems at work, etc. In fact, anything which may help in promoting a harmonious working relationship between employer and employee.

Wages records

These records are very important as the employer has a duty to the employee to give an itemized pay statement and to deduct tax and national insurance from their wages.

You must have:

○ The name and address.
○ The national insurance number.
○ PAYE reference number.
○ Pension details.
○ Deductions which have been authorized by the employee.

Client records

These must be kept to provide certain information:

○ Name, address and telephone number.
○ Doctor's name, address and telephone number.
○ Medical history.
○ Body/skin analysis.

○ Treatment record.
○ Products bought.
○ The name of the therapist.

These details promote confidence in your clients, of your professional abilities, reassure them that the treatment they are receiving is appropriate, even when they are being treated by a new therapist and allows a personal relationship to develop making it easier to sell the services of the salon.

It also allows for a smooth running business particularly during times of staff absences and, more importantly, provides a ready-made mailing list of clients to use when promoting new techniques or products.

The Data Protection Act 1984

Many businesses now use computers to keep records and store information about their clients. The Data Protection Act 1984 requires all personal data to be protected, therefore even if the information is just a list of names and addresses you probably need to be registered with the Data Protection Registrar. Information is available from:

Data Protection Registrar,
Wycliffe House,
Water Lane,
Wilmslow,
Cheshire
Tel: 01625 535 777
Fax: 01625 524 510

Once registered you must comply with the principles of good information handling practice, set out in the Data Protection Act:

○ Obtain and process personal data fairly and lawfully.
○ Hold information only for the purposes specified in your register entry.
○ Use information only for those purposes and disclose it only to the people listed in your register entry.
○ Only hold data which is adequate and relevant.

BEAUTY TREATMENTS

Name: ....

Address: ....

Telephone No .... Date of birth ....

How did you hear about us? ....

Are you on a diet at the moment? ....

Does any of the following apply to you : ....

Blood pressure .... Epilepsy ....

Heart disorders .... Arthritis or rheumatism ....

Diabetes .... Recent operations ....

Under medical treatment .... Taking pain killers ....

Metal implants ....

Are you or have you been pregnant in the last three months? ....

I have been familiarised with the Top to Toe treatment and I agree to use the equipment at my own risk. Furthermore, I understand that Top to Toe makes no warranties or representation regarding medical, therapeutic or cosmetic benefits either expressed or implied.

I hereby release Top to Toe, this facility and its employees from all claims now or in the future from any injury or damages in connection with the use of the equipment.

I confirm that the information provided by me is correct as of todays date and that I will inform Top to Toe immediately of any changes in circumstances relevant to the above questions.

Signature: .... Date: ....

DATE	TREATMENT	COMMENT	THERAPIST SIGNATURE

Figure 52.2 *An example of a client record card*

- Ensure that data is accurate and kept up to date.
- Hold information for no longer than is necessary.
- Allow individuals access to information held about them.

- Take security measures to prevent unauthorized or accidental access to alteration, disclosure or loss and destruction of information.

53 Banking procedures

Banking services

Commercial banks provide different services:

○ They receive money on deposit from customers providing a safe place to keep their money.
○ They lend money to the customer.
○ They transfer money for the customer to other people.

Commercial banks use the money deposited with them to provide loans for others. The interest paid on these loans provides revenue for the bank, thus making the depositors' money work for them.

Loans

Loans which are made to industry and commerce provide much of the bank's profits but they also provide short-term working capital for many small businesses.

The loan is a specified sum borrowed from the bank and paid back over a certain period of time, for example two or three years. The business loan will only be given if the bank is certain that the business will have the cash flow to cover all the repayments and the interest charged. The business plan presented to the bank is important in this case, as this should show the expected cash flow for at least the first year of business.

Security must also be supplied, for example the deeds to the business premises or a fairly substantial amount of capital to help in setting up the business.

An overdraft

This is when the customer has made an arrangement with the bank to draw out more money than is in the account, up to an agreed figure and for a short period of time.

This is the cheapest form of loan as interest is only charged on the outstanding balance and not on the capital borrowed, which is the case with a loan.

The bank account

Managing money is made far easier with a bank account. It will allow you to make payments without having to use cash and bills can be paid on a regular basis by arranging a standing order or direct debit.

A statement of your account will be sent to you at regular intervals allowing you to keep up-to-date with your financial position.

There are two types of bank account: the current account and the deposit account.

The current account
This account stores money safely which can be withdrawn at any time and is used for paying bills and other transactions. The account does not provide any interest for the account holder so any money is not working for you and if the account becomes overdrawn, the bank will charge interest on that amount.

The deposit account
This is similar to a savings account and will earn interest on the money on deposit. A certain amount of notice has to be given before withdrawing your money. However, this will vary from bank to bank.

The bank will provide you with various means of paying and receiving money, in the form of:

Paying in book

This provides a record of all money paid into your account. It is a book of personalized credit slips and each one is divided into two: a counterfoil which the cashier will stamp and initial and retain for bank records; and a receipt left in the book for your own records. Both cash and cheques can be paid in at any branch of your own bank but a small charge will be made if paid into a branch of any other bank.

Cheque book

Each cheque is a written instruction, signed by the account holder (drawer), addressed to the bank to pay the amount indicated to the person or company named (payee).

Cheques may be crossed or open.

The crossed cheque
This is the most commonly used as it is safer than an open cheque. There are several types of crossing on a cheque:

o   A/C payee only may be written in the crossing to ensure that the money is paid into the account named on the chque. It may not be endorsed and signed over to another account.
o   The name and address of a specific branch of a bank may be written in the crossing to ensure the money may only be paid into that particular branch.

The open cheque
This has no crossing at all so the person to whom the cheque is payable could either pay the cheque into an account or take it into the bank and obtain the cash. If the cheque was stolen it could be cashed by anybody posing as the payee.

The cheque guarantee card

This is issued as a safeguard to anyone who accepts a cheque for goods or services supplied and will guarantee payment up to a certain amount. When presented with a cheque card the payee must:

o   Check that the specimen signature on the card corresponds with the signature on the cheque.

o   Ensure the cheque has been signed in their presence.
o   Write the card number on the reverse side of the cheque.

The bank statement

This is a confidential record, sent to you by the bank, detailing all transactions, payments, withdrawals, standing orders, direct debits, etc., over a set period (for example one month), which provides you with the current balance of your account.

Credit card

This is a popular method of paying for goods or services without using cash as it is a form of credit given to a person by the credit card company. Accounts will be sent out monthly and may either be paid in full, thus incurring no interest payments or paid in instalments, thus incurring interest on the balance outstanding.

Standing orders

Bills that have to be paid on a regular basis at a regular amount (for example rent, rates or hire purchase payments), can be paid by standing order. The bank will require from you, in writing, the name of the person or company to be paid, their bank details and the amount to be paid. The bank will then pay that sum of money on the same date each month until you request them to stop.

Direct debit

This works in a similar way as a standing order with written instructions being given to meet certain payments when they fall due. This time, however, it is the company or organization receiving the money which has to present the request for payment which will then be deducted from your bank account. This is very useful when the interval between payments varies.

Credit transfer

This is the transfer of money from one bank to another without cash actually changing hands. Details of the money to be transferred will be written on a bank giro transfer slip and it can be paid into a single account.

A multiple giro is when several amounts of money can be transferred using just one cheque and listing the names, account numbers and banks into which the money is to be paid.

Financial management

The purpose of any business is to make a profit by managing the financial resources effectively. Financial control is concerned with cash flow and all financial transactions should be recorded, for several reasons:

1 To provide information to the Inland Revenue.
2 To provide information to shareholders.
3 To assess business performance.
4 To help plan for the future.
5 To help improve the running of the business.
6 To control money flowing in and out of the business.
7 To prove creditworthiness to suppliers.
8 To obtain loans.

The three documents which are essential to providing an accurate plan are:

1 The balance sheet.
2 The profit and loss account.
3 The cashflow forecast.

Together these three documents provide:

○ An overview of the money in the business.
○ Where the money came from.
○ How it is invested.
○ How the business has performed.
○ How cash is managed now.
○ How cash will be managed in the future.

To prepare a balance sheet information must be provided about the following:
Funds: These may be in the form of a loan, share capital in a limited company or investment capital.

Fixed assets: These are resources acquired to help the business function, for example in a hairdressing salon they would include chairs, mirrors, back washes, dryers and other fixtures and fittings as well as the premises themselves.
Current assets: These are part of the working capital of the business and will include cash and stock.
Current liabilities: Money which is owed to creditors, bank loans and income tax.

The profit and loss account is a summary of all trading transactions in one year and it shows how financially successful the business is. It shows the net profit after tax by subtracting business expenses and taxation from the turnover.

Cashflow

Poor cashflow will cause problems for a business as cash is needed to buy resources which are used for services or goods to be bought by the client for cash.

The amount of money required to pay for the day-to-day running of the business is known as working capital.

Cashflow problems may be caused by:

Stockpiling: Money tied up in stock is unproductive and the minimum amount of stock should be maintained to provide an effective service. Stock control therefore is an important feature of cash management.

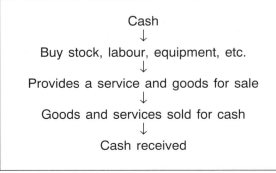

Figure 53.1 *Cashflow*

Spending: Large amounts of capital spent on equipment will stretch financial resources to the limit. Leasing instead of buying will leave more cash for working capital.

Over borrowing: Borrowing money for expansion will increase the amount of interest to be paid and place an added financial burden on the business.

Change in demand: Changes in fashion may cause a fall in demand for particular treatments which may lead to poor sales and less cash flowing into the business.

Seasonal changes: Business may be quiet at certain periods of the year, for example January and February after the Christmas rush or July and August when people are away.

There will inevitably be times when a business may run short of cash and when this happens the main aim is to cover costs rather than make a profit. The following steps may be taken to improve cash flow:

○ Stimulate sales by offering discounts.
○ Sell off stock at cost price or below if necessary.
○ Sell any fixed assets which are rarely used or not vital to the business.
○ Sell equipment and lease instead.
○ Think twice before making any purchases, ensure they are essential.
○ Adjust salon opening hours to meet demand.
○ Extend credit with suppliers.
○ Contact clients whose attendance may have lapsed.
○ Motivate staff to generate new business by offering incentives.
○ Use a supplier who will deliver stock quickly allowing you to maintain a low level of stock.
○ Ensure all members of staff are used effectively to increase productivity.
○ Train staff in new techniques and skills.

○ Make use of those members of staff who wish to work part-time employing them at busy times only.

Budgeting

A budget is a plan based on the objectives of a business, it will show what money is required and how it will be raised. A budget may be set for a twelve-month accounting period but if necessary it can be as little as one month. A flexible budget is sometimes required to change as a business changes, for example if there is a sudden increase in demand for a particular service or treatment this will result in much higher sales levels. Therefore, the sales budget may need to be altered.

Preparation of a budget
○ Determine how long the budget period will be and decide what the objectives are.
○ Information must be collected based on results previously achieved and estimates of future sales.
○ Targets for sales must be set.

The sales budget: This contains monthly sales estimates, that is, how many treatments and products will be sold.

The production budget: This shows what the required labour hours will be, the consumables required and equipment needed to provide the services.

The main objective is to make a profit so the income from sales should cover the production cost and provide a healthy profit.

The advantages of using a budget are:
○ It helps to control income and expenditure.
○ It will draw attention to waste.
○ It provides employees with an awareness of costs.
○ It ensures that capital is used effectively.

54 *Tax, national insurance and VAT*

Starting a business

The first step taken when you start a business as a sole trader or a partnership is to inform the tax office who will provide you with a form 41G which you must fill in and return. This will provide them with the necessary information about your business.

The local customs and excise department needs to be informed if your business qualifies for registration for VAT.

The local Department of Social Security must be informed for national insurance purposes.

It is also advisable to employ an accountant to provide valuable advice about records, accounting and business expenses.

Finally, a bank account needs to be opened for the business.

Tax

Setting up in business means payment of tax can be in different ways:

○ Tax on individual earnings.
○ Tax on profits as a sole trader or partnership.
○ Corporation tax on the profits of a limited company.
○ A director in a limited company pays income tax on his/her salary and also on any money withdrawn from the company.
○ Value added tax.
○ National insurance.

Accounts must be prepared at least once a year and even though an accountant may actually draw up the accounts, it is the owner of the business who is responsible for their accuracy and any declarations made about the profit must be correct.

If the turnover is below a set figure, which is subject to change, a summary of these accounts is all that is required.

Example

Turnover	£7103
Less Business expenses	£1299
Net profits	£5804

Turnover

This is the gross amount the business earns before deducting any business expenses. The accounts or the summary can be sent into the tax office:

○ On the 5 April following the date your business started.
○ The date which is twelve months after the date on which you started.
○ Any date which suits your business, for example at the end of a calendar year on the 31 December or a quiet trading time when business is slow and stocks are low. For a beauty salon this could be early in the year after Christmas and New Year or in the late summer months after the busy holiday period.

The tax which has to be paid is on the profits made from the business, less allowable business expenses. In other words, any expense incurred to enable you to run your business.

Allowable expenses

These are expenses which you incur wholly in the course of running your business and may include:

○ Goods and materials bought for use in the business.

○ Interest on business loans.
○ Hire of equipment.
○ Business insurance.
○ Subscriptions to professional associations.
○ Advertising.
○ Rent.
○ Telephone.
○ Heating and lighting.
○ Protective clothing.
○ Wages.
○ Depreciation on capital items.

Depreciation

This is allowed on any capital item, for example a car or computer. A percentage of the cost is allowed to be claimed against tax each year.

Expenditure

This is the money spent in running the business and it may be classified as:

1 Capital expenditure.
2 Revenue expenditure.

Capital expenditure is used for acquiring or altering assets for use in the business, for example extending the premises, buying a motor vehicle or machinery.

Revenue expenditure is the money spent on covering the cost of everyday items such as wages, heating, replacing stock, etc.

When an expense is claimed against the business, which also has a personal use, then only the percentage which relates to the business will be allowed.

Profit and loss account

This is a summary of all the trading transactions in one year. This can be drawn up using the accounts which have been kept during the year:

○ Sales book.
○ Purchases book.
○ Petty cash book.
○ All receipts.
○ Record of wages.

○ Money drawn from the business.
○ Capital added.

Balance sheet

This is a statement of assets and liabilities of the business which may be given to the tax office with the profit and loss account.

Based on the accounts you send to the tax inspector he/she will make an assessment of how much tax is to be paid and this is usually paid in two instalments on 1 January and 1 July.

The rules on taxation are different for a sole trader and a limited company.

If you have set up a limited company you are in effect your own employer and will pay your tax through the normal PAYE system and as both employer and employee, you will have to pay both contributions.

Income tax is not paid on every penny earned; a personal allowance on which tax is not paid is given to everyone. Your accountant will advise on any other allowable business expenses.

PAYE

Once employees earn over a certain limit, tax and Class 1 national insurance, must be deducted from their wages under the Pay As You Earn (PAYE) system. The employer also pays a national insurance contribution for each employee.

Documentation
P45: Contains the employee's code number, total pay and tax deducted to date in the financial year. It must be given to the employer when the new employee starts work. The employee must provide a P45 from the previous employer which certifies the tax which has been deducted for the year so far.
P46: Obtained from the tax office by a new employee who has not paid PAYE tax before. It is a starting certificate signed by the employee and sent to the tax office, who will then give the employee an emergency code number.
P14: At the end of each tax year, all information concerning each employee's wages, income tax

and national insurance contributions must be entered on a triplicate form. One copy goes to the tax office and one to the DSS.

P60: This is the third copy of the P14 which goes to the employee.

A new employee who has not paid PAYE tax before must have a P46.

To help work out the PAYE system there are two sets of tables which will be provided by the tax inspector:

1   Free pay table A.
2   PAYE taxable pay tables B–D.

Each employee has a code number and this can be found in the tables which then tells you how much tax to deduct.

Each employee has a deductions working sheet with spaces for each week of the tax year. The gross salary, tax deducted and other details are entered each time the employee is paid.

At the end of each tax year all the information concerning wages, income tax and national insurance must be entered on a form P14. One copy, the P60, is given to the employee and two copies must be sent to the tax office who will pass one copy on to the DSS.

National insurance

As an employer it is your responsibility to collect your employee's national insurance (NI) contributions, with their income tax and the employer's NI contribution and send them on to the Inland Revenue.

The Inland Revenue will supply you with tables to work out the contributions for all employees who are over 16 and under 60 for a woman or 65 for a man, whose earnings reach the lower earnings limit.

The contributions are classified as follows:

Class I

These are paid by the employee who is over 16 and under 60 for a woman and 65 for a man, whose earnings reach the lower earnings limit.

Class 2

These are paid if you are self-employed as a sole trader or a partner. Flat-rate class 2 national insurance contributions are paid to the DSS unless you are eligible for small earnings exemption, when you can show that your net earnings from self-employment will fall below a certain figure in a tax year. They can be paid by direct debit through the bank.

Class 4

These contributions are earnings related, on profits between certain limits, for the self-employed. They are assessed and collected by the Inland Revenue and there is an upper limit on the amount payable.

For more details the DSS will provide a set of leaflets giving updated information.

Value added tax

Value added tax (VAT) is a tax which is levied on most business transactions. Business transactions which are liable to VAT are called *taxable supplies*. A salon owner will charge VAT on:

○   The services provided.
○   The products sold.

And will pay VAT on:

○   Equipment and stock bought from VAT registered suppliers.

The tax given to the customs and excise is the difference between the tax charged to your clients and the tax you have paid to your suppliers.

When to register

When you are in business you must register for VAT when your taxable turnover reaches a certain limit. The taxable turnover is the total value of all taxable supplies. This limit is subject to change due to inflation or government intervention. The person not the business must register for VAT. Therefore, a company is treated as a person for VAT purposes.

It is possible to register for VAT if when you first start your business your costs are very high and involve paying out large amounts of VAT, so that you may reclaim the amount when you are registered. Failure to register when you should can prove expensive as the customs and excise can impose financial penalties.

There are three categories of goods and services:

Standard rate

Goods on which the current rate of VAT is charged. The present rate is 17½ per cent but this can be changed by the government.

Exempt

This is when no VAT has to be paid, for example banking, insurance, education and health services.

Zero rated

This is when tax is payable in theory but in practice none is actually paid because it is zero rated. However VAT which has been paid on purchases can be claimed back from customs and excise therefore detailed records of all transactions must still be kept. Examples of zero rated goods are:

o Books, brochures, periodicals, maps and newspapers.
o Food.
o Drugs and medicine.
o Exports.
o Children's shoes and clothing.

VAT procedure

A VAT registration form must be filled in and this is available from your local VAT office. You will then be given a registration number and an effective date of registration by customs and excise.

Detailed records must be kept and you must start to charge VAT as soon as you know that you are required to be registered for VAT. VAT may only be shown as a separate item on an invoice when you know your registration number.

Records

You must keep a record of all tax paid on purchases you have made and all tax received from sales and treatments provided. This can be recorded in the VAT column of your sales and purchases book.

Inputs are your purchases and *outputs* are your *sales* (products and treatments). Therefore, the tax you pay on goods you buy is called *input tax* and the tax you charge your client is called *output tax.*

You have to fill in a VAT tax return (form) and send it to customs and excise every three months. This period is referred to as a tax period.

Payment

Where output tax charged exceeds input tax the difference is then paid to the customs and excise. When input tax is more than output tax then it may be reclaimed from customs and excise.

Example

Hannah Macaulay makes skin care cosmetics from recipes which have been handed down to her from her grandmother. She sells her special moisturizer to Sarah Thomas, who owns a beauty salon specializing in facial treatments using natural products. Sarah also sells them to her clients.

Hannah sells £1000 worth of products to Sarah and charges her £1000 for the cosmetics and adds 17½ per cent to the invoice for VAT. The total Sarah pays her is £1175 (£1000 plus £175 VAT). Hannah then pays the £175 of tax collected (*output tax*) to customs and excise.

Sarah repackages the moisturizer into 100 special containers and sells then to her clients for £15 a jar plus VAT. She receives £1500 plus £262.50p VAT.

Sarah claims back the VAT charged by Hannah Macaulay (*input tax*) that is £175 and hands over the VAT of £262.50 the clients have paid to her for the special moisturizers (*output tax*).

This means a net payment of £262.50 – £175 = £87.50 to the customs and excise.

Therefore:

Sarah's *output tax* (tax received from sales) = £262.50p

Sarah's *input tax* (tax paid on products bought) = £175

Sarah pays customs and excise the difference. Therefore:

£262.50 – £175 = £87.50

VAT invoice

Only if you are registered for VAT can you use a VAT invoice. This is an invoice which shows the VAT registration number of the business proprietor.

When supplying goods or services direct to the public as you are in a beauty salon, it is not necessary to provide a tax invoice unless you are requested to do so.

When the value of the services or goods is less than £50 the VAT does not have to be shown separately but there must be an indication that the total is inclusive of VAT.

Always ensure that you obtain an invoice with the VAT on it, the registration number and the date so that you can claim back the VAT paid from customs and excise.

55 *Effective management*

Introduction to management

It is becoming increasingly more important for the hairdresser, beauty and holistic therapist to acquire management skills. Such skills will enable each individual to improve their position within an organization or to start a business of their own.

All managers operate by achieving goals through the co-ordinated efforts of other people. The functions of management are basically the same for any kind of organization although they may be applied differently. The principal management functions are:

1 Planning.
2 Organizing.
3 Controlling.
4 Monitoring.

Planning

Planning is the management function of setting the objectives of a business, determining how best to achieve them, and making decisions concerning:

○ Policies.
○ Strategies.
○ Systems.
○ Procedures.
○ Standards.
○ Budgets.
○ Resources.

Planning may be:

Short term: Identifying day-to-day requirements which may be communicated verbally.
Medium term: Identifying requirements which may be needed over a longer period of time.

Long term: Involving higher level management in strategic planning which may be recorded in a written format.

Good planning ensures satisfactory service and production, making the best use of the resources available. Staff should be kept to the minimum which allows the smooth running of the business while maintaining standards and quality.

Types of plan
Strategic plans: Plans that establish the nature of the organization's mission, objectives and strategies.
Standing plan: Plans which include policies, procedures, rules and regulations that are fixed for a long period of time.
Single use plans: Plans that serve a specific purpose for a short period of time.

The necessary considerations for planning are:

○ What, who, when, where.
○ To be flexible when making plans.
○ To produce plans in reasonable time to allow for consultation and familiarization before implementing them.
○ To offer clear directions in their achievement.

Plans must:

○ Provide adequate detail.
○ Be put into operation with ease.
○ Achieve the desired result.

Organizing

The management function of determining resources and activities required to achieve organizational objectives, combining them into a formal structure, assigning responsibility for achieving the objectives to capable individuals and giving them the authority needed to carry out their assignments.

Controlling

Controlling is the management function of implementing plans and ensuring the activities of the employees are achieving the set objectives.

Monitoring

Monitoring is the management function of determining methods for measuring performance, carrying out appraisal of systems, procedures and staff, comparing performance with established standards and taking the necessary corrective action.

Resources

Resources are used in a business to produce the activity and it is the responsibility of the management to use them effectively. The resources available are:

Human: The employees or personnel in a business that help to achieve its goals. It is important to provide the right type and number of employees.
Capital: Money invested in a business to set up or expand.
Equipment: Used to provide the services offered must be up-to-date, of good quality and appropriate to the requirements of the business.
Time: The manager's time and time of the employees must be used effectively. Therefore, planning and delegation are important so this valuable resource is not wasted.

The management role

Setting objectives

Objectives are the end results towards which all organizational activities are aimed.

Before establishing objectives it is important to analyse the business:

○ What it is achieving now.
○ What your goals are.

Set objectives
↓
Establish strategies, systems, procedures, policies, standards
↓
Organize work into manageable activities
↓
Set standards and implement systems of work
↓
Set targets and tasks for employees to achieve objectives
↓
Delegate tasks
↓
Communicate information to all employees
↓
Provide motivation
↓
Analyse performance
↓
Develop staff

Figure 55.1   *The process of communication*

○ How you will achieve your goals.
○ What obstacles may stand in your way.

The current position of the business may be analysed by using a SWOT analysis and it will be the start of the planning process. The analysis will provide information about the business in terms of its:

○ Strengths.
○ Weaknesses.
○ Opportunities.
○ Threats.

Strengths
Strengths are the good points which contribute to a business's success. They may include committed and highly qualified staff, excellent facilities, well-established business with a large clientele or new technology not yet available to the competition.

Weaknesses
The problems the business may have at present are called weaknesses and they may include high staff turnover, ineffective management,

limited services offered, poor facilities, lack of resources, over borrowing or high rent and rates.

Opportunities

Opportunities that may arise may include a rival salon closing down, new technology becoming available, new staff with specialist skills being employed, or an unexpected windfall.

Threats

Anything that may arise to hinder a business's plans which must be avoided at all costs can be classed as a threat.

The results of a SWOT analysis will provide useful information when making any decisions, setting objectives or business planning.

Establishing objectives for your business

The main objectives for the hairdressing, holistic and beauty manager are:

○ To provide a service efficiently and effectively.
○ To make the best use of resources.
○ To maximize profit.
○ To benefit the workforce.

The objectives should be achieved in a safe working environment to meet legal requirements.

When a business fails to provide a service which meets the requirements of its clients they will no longer patronize the establishment, and there will be no profits. The manager therefore must:

○ Establish what resources are available to achieve the objectives set and employ the appropriate number of staff with the best qualifications to ensure the highest standard of service.
○ Communicate information to employees of company policies, procedures and changes to be made at regular staff meetings or through other specified channels of communication.
○ Set targets and delegate responsibilities to individual employees, discuss methods of appraisal.

○ Establish and maintain a professional relationship with product and equipment suppliers to ensure quality of service for your clients at a reasonable cost to the business.
○ Take disciplinary action when necessary to maintain quality of service.
○ Plan and implement marketing strategies to reach the appropriate consumers for the services you offer.
○ Be prepared to change direction by keeping abreast of new innovations and treatments and develop and motivate staff to cope with change.
○ Implement efficient systems to cope with the day-to-day running of the business and ensure that quality standards are maintained.

Quality control

This is the process by which management will ensure that its services meet the expectations of clients and consumers. To maintain quality standards, all employees should be involved and the following procedures should be followed:

○ Identify any problems.
○ Discuss problems with employees.
○ Plan for improvement.
○ Implement solutions/changes.
○ Evaluate results.
○ If successful make the changes permanent.

Working as a team

Most successful businesses will have a hard working and effective team or number of teams depending upon how many employees there are. Self-managing work teams are groups that tend to operate by member consensus rather than management directions. The team can be most effective when each member understands his/her own role and fulfils that role to the best of their ability.

To be most effective there are many things that need to be considered, some of which are:

○ Meetings must be held on a regular basis for group discussion and decision making.
○ Strengths of each member should be recognized and used appropriately.
○ Work must be allocated fairly and evenly utilizing the skills available.
○ When problems occur feedback to other members of the team must be immediate, remedial action must be taken or problems must be referred upward to the line manager if nothing is resolved.
○ Flexibility is required to cope with changing circumstances.

When problems do occur a list should be made of jobs to be done in order of priority and the team must work together to determine who does what to overcome the difficulties. Staffing levels are more easily maintained when all team members are able to cover for others and work flexibly adjusting the rotas when necessary.

Useful terminology

Budget: A detailed plan or forecast, generally expressed in monetary terms, of the results expected from an officially recognized programme of operations.
Objectives: The end results, goals or targets that an organization, department or individual seeks to attain.
Marketing: The management process of identifying, anticipating and satisfying consumer requirements profitably.
Organization: Group or individuals with a common goal bound together by a set of authority/responsibility relationships needed to reach objectives.
Planning: Process of establishing objectives or goals and determining how best to attain them.
Policies: General statements that serve as guides to managerial decision-making and to supervising the activities of employees.
Procedures: Detailed plans that establish a standard or routine method or technique for handling recurring activities.
Projects: Plans for the execution of individual segments of a general programme.

Rules and regulations: Guidelines that state specifically what can and cannot be done under any given circumstances.
SWOT analysis: The process of systematically identifying and analysing an organization's strengths and weaknesses, opportunities and threats.

The manager

The manager is responsible to the employer to achieve all the objectives laid down for the success of the business, through efficient administration and creating a good working atmosphere for all the staff employed in the business, ensuring that everyone works well as a team.

The qualities of a good manager are:

○ Commitment to the job.
○ Responsibility.
○ Enthusiasm.
○ Being decisive.
○ Using initiative.
○ Being enterprising.
○ Having patience.
○ Good judgement.
○ Integrity.

The main activities of a manager are:

1 To plan how the business is run.
2 To implement the plans.
3 To direct.
4 To coordinate.
5 To train.
6 To delegate responsibility.
7 To deal with problems.
8 To counsel.

To be successful a business needs a good leader who can communicate well with the staff, clients and business associates. The task of a manager is to get things done through people for whom they are responsible, so it is important that the manager has a good relationship with the staff to bring out the best in them.

To become an effective manager there are several important areas to be considered:

Communication

Communication may be defined as the process of creating, transmitting and interpreting ideas, opinions and facts. There are many ways in which we communicate:

o Speaking to each other.
o Using a telephone and fax machine.
o Giving instructions.
o Chairing meetings.
o Holding interviews.
o Sending memos.
o Writing reports.
o Making a presentation.

Methods of communication

Verbal: Oral communication.
Non-verbal: Use of body language, gestures and facial expressions.
Written: Letters, memos, reports, etc.

Each of these methods have advantages and disadvantages.

Verbal
Advantages
o Instant communication.
o Personalized.
o May be reinforced by non-verbal communication.
o Quick.
o Provides instant feedback.
o Opportunity for clarification.

Disadvantages
o Percentage of the information will be forgotten.
o No point of reference later.
o Lacks the considered nature of written communications.

Non-verbal
Advantages
o Conveys a silent message.
o Can be used when silence is required.

Disadvantages
o Open to misinterpretation.

Written
Advantages
o Permanent.
o Less liable to be misinterpreted.
o Information may be absorbed at the reader's own pace.

Prepare the message/information

↓

Select the method of communication

↓

Send the message/information

↓

Check it has been accepted and understood

Figure 55.2 *The process of communication*

o Evidence that message has been sent.
o Ideal for important, detailed or complicated information.
o May be referred to at a later date.

Disadvantages
o Takes time to produce.
o Impersonal.
o No opportunity for questioning.
o Possibility that it may not be received.

It is important to keep staff informed about the business, how it will develop and what part each member of staff has to play in this development.

When a member of the staff is achieving good results or working particularly well, then it is important for the manager to praise their efforts as this is an important motivating factor.

Communication is a two-way thing and the manager must always be available to listen to anything a member of staff might have to say. Regular staff meetings are an ideal way to keep the staff informed and to allow them to contribute, with comments about the way the business is run and how improvements may be made or anything they want changing, to create a happier or more comfortable workplace.

The manager must then pass on these views to the owner, who may find the information useful when formulating future plans, or to other managers in the organization, as it may encourage exchange of information for mutual benefit.

Meetings

Meetings may be formal, following set procedures, with a chairperson to control the activity

Figure 55.3 *An example of an agenda*

TOP TO TOE HEALTH AND BEAUTY SALON

MEETING: Monthly
FROM: Karon
TO: All staff
VENUE: Manager's office
DATE: 14.2.96 - 2 P.M.

A G E N D A

SUBJECT	INCLUDED BY	RESULT/ACTION	BY WHOM
DETAILS OF VISIT TO HEALTH + BEAUTY SHOW	KH.		
TRAINING DATES FOR NON. SURG. FACE LIFT	SC		
SUGGESTIONS FOR COLOUR SCHEME FOR NEW REFLEXOLOGY ROOM	KH		
APPOINTMENT OF HEALTH + SAFETY REPRESENTATIVE	KH		
ORGANISATION OF PROMOTIONAL EVENING	CP		

and other elected officers with special roles. Informal meetings have unwritten rules and procedures and more self discipline is required to ensure that results are achieved. The manager will normally take on the role of chairperson or 'leader' in a staff meeting to provide direction and ensure that time is not wasted. A successful meeting will depend upon:

○ How the people present behave.
○ The atmosphere in which the meeting is held.
○ Whether the communication is effective.

○ How large the meeting is.

All employees should be encouraged to attend meetings by:

○ Holding them at the same time so that everyone is aware of when they will be held.
○ Planning the content and making it relevant.
○ Provide an agenda which goes out on time (Figure 55.3).
○ Keep to the time allocated.
○ Any other business raised must be dealt with in the time allocated or put forward to the next meeting.

○ The outcome of the meeting should be implemented as soon as possible by the individuals concerned or those enlisted to take action.

Leadership

The manager is responsible for the work of all of the staff as well as his/her own. This can be very rewarding when everything is running smoothly and the business is doing well. However, if things go wrong and staff are not achieving the objectives laid down, then the manager will receive the criticism and be responsible for putting things right.

It is important to set a good example and work to the same high standards that are set for the staff.

Delegate responsibility to those most capable but ensure that no one person is left out, by giving them a job to be responsible for, which is within their capabilities. Delegation will free the manager for other constructive work and it also helps with developing staff potential and developing further skills.

The manager is a team leader and the staff are part of that team so it is important for them to know that they can trust him/her to represent their views fairly when in any sort of dispute.

Discipline

Rules and regulations have to be laid down and strictly adhered to. If they are flouted by some members of staff and they are allowed to get away with it the manager's authority will be greatly weakened.

Whatever the problem, it is important to be seen to be fair and impartial so that the respect of the remaining members of staff is not lost. To prevent problems occurring, make sure that each member of staff pulls their weight and do not wait for other staff members to point this out, as it will already have caused dissatisfaction.

When having to discipline a member of staff do it in private to avoid embarrassment. Deal with the problem yourself unless it is deemed beyond your experience when you may confer with your superior.

When confronted with a problem there are certain things to be done to solve it:

○ Define the problem and recognize the priorities.
○ Decide on possible solutions.
○ Choose the solution which seems most appropriate.
○ Ensure the solution is practicable, if not look at the alternatives.
○ If necessary confer with any person involved, for example the owner, before suggesting the final solution.
○ Record the content of all interviews.

Training

It is assumed that when the position of manager has been reached you will have many skills which can be passed on to your staff which will benefit the business.

A good manager will recognize the potential of a member of staff, point them in the right direction and allow them to progress. The manager can therefore devise training programmes and implement them either in the salon or arrange for the training elsewhere.

Training will be carried out at all times in the workplace as all the staff should be familiar with the day-to-day running of the business and the manager will be responsible for this, unless a particular member of staff has been delegated to deal with this area.

Induction of new employees is an important part of a manager's job, as their first impressions often have an impact on their approach to their work. Induction should not be for the first day only, it should carry on until new employees are confident about the job and feel part of the team.

An employee may have certain skills when first employed and the terms of their contract may have stated that further training would be given. The manager must ensure that these terms are met.

Working

The work carried out must be of a high standard as this will set an example to the rest of the staff.

It is important to do a fair share of the practical work without doing too much so that some members of staff are sitting about idly.

Employees will learn a great deal from watching more experienced staff at work and how to treat clients to ensure their loyalty.

Counselling

Normally the manager of the business will be the first person to be approached by a member of staff with a problem. If the manager is seen to be accessible and approachable then members of staff will find it easy to come with their problems, whether they are to do with work or their personal life. The important thing to remember is to listen and make the time to listen.

Often problems can be solved by the member of staff if you, as manager, just listen and act as a sounding board. Make suggestions without actually providing a solution to the problem, as the solution you suggest may not be the correct one, then the staff member may blame you for the wrong outcome.

Anything said to you in private should remain so, as you will soon lose their confidence if you discuss their problems with others.

Organizing

Any group of people who are working together to achieve a given objective work far more effectively and efficiently if they are organized well.

The manager takes on the role of organizer so that all the resources are used most effectively. The resources available are:

- o People (human resources).
- o Money (financial).
- o Equipment/products (material).
- o Services.
- o Time.

These resources may be quite substantial depending on the size of the business. The organizing role therefore will be the full-time occupation of the manager. In a smaller business the manager's time may be divided between organizing and working with the clients. In this case delegation is important so that the manager's time may be used most efficiently.

There is a limit to the number of people a manager can effectively control, therefore the appropriate span of control – the number of subordinates directly controlled by a superior – will depend on a number of factors:

- o Are any subordinates qualified to make decisions without having constantly to refer upwards to the manager?
- o Do they have the skills required to take the right course of action and see it through?
- o Is the manager prepared to delegate authority to other employees?
- o Does the business have a well-defined agreed set of objectives?

A manager may be able to control and organize a larger number of employees when the communication systems work efficiently and quickly feeds information between employees, supervisors and management. Some businesses depend a great deal on personal contact to operate effectively particularly when dealing with the public. These businesses inevitably will have small spans of control.

The manager will delegate by giving authority to an employee to perform certain tasks and responsibilities and make their own decisions without having to refer back. Successful delegation requires:

- o Adequate authority being given to allow tasks to be carried out.
- o Specifying limits of authority.
- o Understanding by the employee of what is involved.
- o The employee to know that his/her authority and position are not duplicated elsewhere.

Advantages of delegation
- o It will highlight those employees who are suitable candidates for promotion.
- o It is useful for training purposes.
- o It develops potential.
- o It allows the most skilled person to perform a particular job.
- o It frees the manager to perform more important tasks.

Delegating tasks to employees makes good business sense as it will be more cost-effective

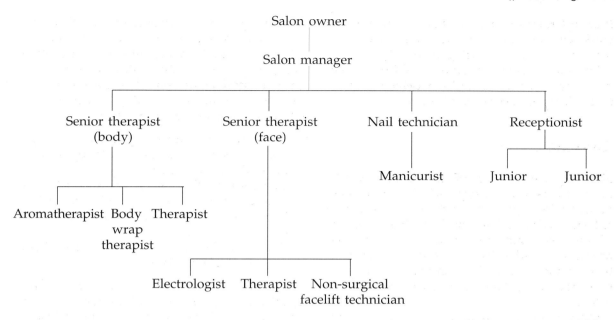

Figure 55.4 *Example of line management*

and it provides job satisfaction for the employee, leaving the manager to be more effective. The line of authority must be clear cut so that all employees will know where they stand, that is, to whom they are responsible and who they are responsible for. Where an employee has responsibility to one clearly defined superior the less likely it is that there will be conflicting instructions.

Line management refers to the direct working relationship between the vertical levels of an organization. This is the most common type of relationship where authority flows from the top level down to the most junior position.

Communication channels are clear, authority is agreed, instructions and information flows between the individual concerned.

Motivating staff

Motivation is a process of encouraging an individual or group to achieve the objectives of an organization or business while also working to achieve their own objectives and ambitions. Motivation encourages employees to perform more effectively and become more productive.

A good manager will have a good understanding of the requirements of each person working within the business, as each person's needs and objectives are different.

Motivated staff are happy staff and this will ensure that they remain with the business for a long time.

The benefits of this to any business are:

○ *Continuity* – as staff are familiar with the objectives of the business and all procedures, time is not wasted on training new staff and clients will not be lost when staff leave. Other members of staff can take over the role of another with little disruption.
○ *Efficiency* – as the business will be run smoothly with staff familiar with company procedures and policies.
○ *Teamwork* – it allows a good team to evolve who will work together and capitalize on the particular skills of each individual member of staff for the benefit of everyone.
○ It provides a familiar environment for clients who feel at ease with therapists they have known for a long time.
○ It inspires confidence in the clients.

o It allows a professional working relationship with suppliers to evolve which will contribute to the efficiency of the business in relation to stock control, retail sales and the provision of new products and treatments.

o It provides a good advertisement for the business when the staff turnover is low.

o High employee performance ensures a healthy turnover and profit.

o Plans can be made with the certainty that the staff who implement new policies and procedures will be available to carry them out.

Managers must provide the right environment to stimulate improved performance and develop the potential of each employee. Increased performance relies on a combination of ability and motivation, ability alone is not enough to improve productivity, strong motivation with improved ability achieves results.

Even when there is a climate of positive motivation provided by the management there must be motivation from within each individual to improve performance. When the abilities of each employee are used efficiently this should result in increased productivity and job satisfaction.

Theories of motivation

Content theories – needs

These are theories of motivation which deal with:

o What causes behaviour to occur and to cease.
o The internal needs and perceptions of the individual.
o The external factors such as incentives.

Maslow's hierarchy of needs is the most popular of content theories. The psychologist Abraham Maslow's concept was that human needs may be arranged in a hierarchy of importance progressing from basic needs at the bottom to higher needs at the top and that a satisfied need was no longer a prime motivator of behaviour. These needs are shown in Figure 55.5.

Self-actualization needs
|
Esteem needs
|
Social needs
|
Safety needs
|
Physiological needs

Figure 55.5 *Hierarchy of needs*

The hierarchy begins with:

Physiological needs: For example food, drink and sleep. The manager provides these needs through wages, holidays, provision of adequate staff facilities, a healthy environment, clean drinking water, lunch breaks and rests.

Safety needs: For example, protection against danger, threat or deprivation and the provision of a stable environment. The manager provides these through ensuring a safe and secure working environment, health insurance, staff development, promotion prospects, saving plans and pension schemes.

Social needs: For example, belonging, association with and acceptance by colleagues, giving and receiving love. The manager provides these by creating formal and informal teams that work well together, company sponsored activities and providing status for employees through delegation.

Esteem needs: For example, status, self-esteem, recognition and appreciation. The manager provides these through promotion, praise, commendation and reward.

Self-actualization needs: For example, achieving one's potential, achieving ambitions and self-development. The manager may help by setting targets and goals, providing challenges, setting assignments and developing skills.

Herzberg's motivation–hygiene theory

Herzberg's theory was based on information provided by employees about job satisfaction. His initial research was based on answers provided by several hundred engineers and accountants about their jobs. Further studies were then carried out with other working groups including clerical and manual workers, the results from each group were similar.

The factors which provided the employees with job satisfaction were motivators (motivating factors) and those that caused dissatisfaction were demotivators (hygiene factors).

Motivators – motivating factors
○ Achievements.
○ Recognition received.
○ The creative and challenging nature of the work.
○ The responsibility given.
○ Opportunities for personal growth.
○ Promotion.

Demotivators – hygiene factors
○ Company policy and administration which stifles enthusiasm.
○ Poor quality of supervision – technical aspects.
○ Salary.
○ Interpersonal relations.
○ Working conditions.
○ Working environment and lack of benefits.

The conclusions of his research were that motivating factors which gave job satisfaction had a positive effect on performance and morale and factors which caused job dissatisfaction had a negative effect.

Based on these theories and in simple terms the employer/manager must try to ensure that the employee has:

○ A fair and acceptable wage system.
○ Job security.
○ Generous holidays.
○ Varied work experience.
○ Flexibility of working hours.
○ Training to develop further skills.
○ To be given responsibility with a certain amount of independence.
○ The opportunity for personal growth and achievement.
○ Compatibility with colleagues.
○ An opportunity to be part of a successful team.
○ Safe and secure working conditions.
○ Good staff facilities.

○ Recognition and praise for good work.
○ Prospects of promotion.

Interviewing

An interview is communicating with someone to achieve a specific objective, which could be selecting staff, counselling, disciplining, assessment, grievance, etc.

There are certain considerations common to all interviews and these are:

The preparation

Have available all the necessary information required and any relevant documentation. Confer beforehand with other parties with an interest in the outcome of the interview, for example the salon owner may want to put some specific points to you with regard to the interview, or another member of staff who may be involved.

The objective

Know exactly what you hope to achieve by the end of the interview, this will allow you to complete the business in hand without further time being wasted.

Conducting the interview

Move the interview towards your objective and ensure that you elicit a constructive response from the interviewee while retaining control and deciding on the action to be taken, informing the interviewee of any follow-up procedures.

Appraisal

This is an evaluation of an individual member of staff in terms of their job performance or skills. It must be fair and accurate and it may be necessary for various reasons:

○ To identify standards of job performance.
○ To identify strengths and weaknesses.
○ To identify training and development needs.
○ To identify possibilities for promotion.
○ To review salary and responsibilities.
○ To provide staff motivation.
○ To formulate business plans.

Informal assessment occurs naturally on a day-to-day basis in the workplace. The formal assessment is planned and uses a standard set of criteria to evaluate performance. A systematic approach should be adopted and the following steps should be taken:

1 Design an appropriate appraisal form.
2 Conduct an appraisal interview or observe performance in practical skills.
3 Complete an appraisal form.
4 Review the appraisal with the employee.
5 Agree on a plan of action which could be further training, promotion, an increase in salary or job improvement.

The appraisal form

When designing an appraisal form, the focus of the appraisal must be clear, that is, the job or the person. When the main focus is the job, the criteria will concentrate on such things as reaching sales targets and achieving set objectives. Where the main focus is on the person, the criteria will concentrate on personal qualities, attitude and behaviour as well as practical skills. To save time the form must be as simple to use as possible. To be effective it must have relevant performance criteria and an efficient measurement system.

Figure 55.6 is an example of a general appraisal form. When practical skills are to be assessed more specific criteria must be used. For training purposes the detailed procedure must be written down and assessed. The outcome of any appraisal must be discussed with the employee as soon as possible. In fact, if this process can be tackled as a joint problem-solving exercise between management and employees it will be far more productive working together on a more equal basis.

Figure 55.7 is an example of a practical assessment form.

Training

Training may be for induction purposes, the training of new staff in the organization or the general and specialist training of existing employees. If a business is to grow and develop then the people within it must also grow and develop.

Generally speaking, the better developed employees cause fewer problems and have greater job satisfaction.

Reasons for training

○ Induction of new employees.
○ Training in health and safety procedures to comply with current legislation.
○ To introduce a new treatment or service.
○ To improve product knowledge.
○ To update existing skills.
○ To develop knowledge or skills of employees.

Methods of training

Coaching/supervision: Explaining and supervising methods of work, procedures and systems. Normally a manager or supervisor would take on a role of developing and improving a subordinates abilities.

Planned progression: Moving the employee through a well-ordered series of jobs into increasing higher levels of activity.

Job rotation: Moving the employee through a series of diverse jobs to experience all aspects of a business and improve knowledge and experience.

Demonstrations: Learning from an expert's demonstration and performing under the guidance of an experienced person or mentor. The expert could be from a company or training institution or from among your own staff.

Training centres: An employee may attend college on a part-time basis combining more structured learning with the real work situation. Open learning enables the employee to complete a training programme devised by a college or training centre using a correspondence course or

TOP TO TOE HEALTH AND BEAUTY SALON
STAFF APPRAISAL

Name of employee: Position:

Period of assessment: From: To:

Assessment criteria	1 Unsatisfactory	2 Average	3 Above average	4 Outstanding	Score
1 Organization skills					
2 Quality of work					
3 Reaching sales targets					
4 Initiative					
5 Teamwork					
6 Communication skills					
7 Adaptability					
				Total	

Score
1–12   Unsatisfactory
13–18   Average
19–25   Above average
26–28   Outstanding

Comments:

Action:

Assessor:_____

Employee:_____

Date:_____

Figure 55.6 *An appraisal form*

TOP TO TOE HEALTH AND BEAUTY SALON
PRACTICAL ASSESSMENT

Name of employee: Position:

Date of assessment:

Treatment:

Assessment criteria	Satisfactory	Above average	Excellent	Comments
Preparation of work area				
Health and safety procedures				
Client care and consideration				
Practical procedure				
Recording treatment				
Homecare advice				
Recommendations				

Action taken: Assessor signature:

_____

Employee signature:

_____

Figure 55.7 *An assessment form*

flexible learning programme to combine work and study.

Benefits of training

○ Achievement of high standards in performance.
○ Staff motivation.
○ Job satisfaction.
○ Higher quality production.
○ Reduction in staff turnover.
○ More flexible workforce with transferable skills.
○ More efficient use of human resources.
○ Improved status or salary.

Training procedure

Identify training needs
↓
Establish training objectives
↓
Plan the content
↓
Arrange a time for training
↓
Provide the training
↓
Monitor and review

Figure 55.8 *The training process*

Staff rotas

A staff rota is a plan of the working hours of each member of staff. It is required to ensure that there are sufficient numbers of staff available at any given time to accommodate all the clients booked.

The rota must include:

○ When staff are in the salon for work.
○ When staff are on holiday.
○ The times staff are out of the salon for training.
○ When staff are working overtime or involved in other activities, for example marketing or promotions.

○ Time off in lieu of overtime.

Considerations when planning a staff rota are:

○ Which days of the week are the busiest.
○ What time of the day is the busiest.
○ Seasonal fluctuations – before Christmas and before summer are very busy periods of the year
○ Staff requirements and special requests
○ What jobs and activities need to be covered
○ Which members of staff are most appropriate for the jobs

Contingency plans must be made for the unexpected:

○ Staff absence due to illness.
○ Staff leaving.
○ An unexpected increase in business.
○ An unexpected decrease in client numbers.

These problems may be overcome if:

○ A number of flexible part-time members of staff who are prepared to work more hours are employed.
○ If the full-time members of staff are prepared to work more hours or overtime when required.
○ If a floating member of staff is employed to step into any role if it is affordable to do so.

Disciplinary procedures

One of the more difficult areas of staff management is dealing with disciplinary issues. The aim of discipline is to correct behaviour and the last resort is to penalize a member of staff. Therefore the best way of dealing with problems of discipline is to prevent them occurring in the first place.

To do this the manager must:

○ Explain to each new member of staff exactly what is expected of them.
○ Set standards in job performance which have to be met.
○ Lay down a fair set of rules and regulations which all members of staff will follow.
○ Explain the reason for the rules.

Rules can cover many areas and the more important ones for the smooth running of a salon are:

Punctuality

Each member of staff must arrive for work at the designated time and ready for the first appointment. There is little point arriving for work on time and then spending half an hour changing into work clothes and applying makeup while the first client is sitting waiting as this will upset the appointment system for the rest of the day.

In the case of genuine illness, the employee must inform the manager at the earliest possible time to allow him/her to contact clients to change their appointments or for replacement members of staff to be called in.

Behaviour

A professional approach is required in dealing with clients and other members of staff. Treatment of clients is important as a friendly but respectful manner will encourage loyalty and ensure the client returns. Respect should be shown for senior members of staff and all employees should work together as a team.

Safety

Rules regarding health and safety at work include hygiene and maintenance of the salon, handling hazardous substances and being responsible for the safety of clients and other members of staff. It is the responsibility of the manager to make everyone aware of their own responsibilities in these areas.

Company property

The appearance of the salon is important as this often forms a lasting impression in the mind of a client. Staff should be responsible for their own particular work area as well as having joint responsibility for communal areas, in particular the reception area and for staff comfort, the staff room.

Company property must not be abused and telephones should not be used for personal calls as this ties up the telephone when prospective clients may be ringing. It also costs the business money.

Stock

Certain people should be responsible for care and maintenance of stock and to prevent pilferage. Special concessions may be made to staff, for example buying at cost price or at a generous discount to prevent pilferage.

Disciplinary action

The procedure to follow for breaches of discipline are dealt with in detail in Chapter 50 of this section. Disciplinary action should only be taken if there is clear evidence of a serious breach of the rules and any action must be fair and consistent with the misdemeanour.

When giving an employee a verbal warning it is advisable to do so in front of a third person and then write an account for the records. The member of staff concerned has the right to appeal against disciplinary action.

The manager must ensure that all members of staff have access to their job descriptions, a list of all rules and regulations and the disciplinary procedures set down.

To prevent industrial tribunals or other legal actions, follow strict guidelines for disciplinary procedures. Guidelines can be obtained from your local branch of ACAS.

To summarize, the guidelines propose that disciplinary procedures should be in written form; they may be included in the written terms and conditions of employment; in a staff handbook, displayed in the workplace or available to the employee in an easily accessible file.

○ They must specify to whom they apply.
○ They must be capable of dealing speedily with disciplinary matters to avoid disruption, maintain staff morale and allow the management time to concentrate on more important matters.
○ They must indicate the form of disciplinary action which may be taken.
○ They must specify who will deal with disciplinary action.
○ They must state how an individual will be informed of their misconduct.

○ They must allow for proper investigation.

○ They must state how an individual will be informed of disciplinary action.

○ They must provide for a right of appeal.

Organizing your time efficiently

There are so many jobs for a manager that it can be easy to neglect certain aspects of the work. It is important, therefore, to sit down and analyse the time being spent on each area of responsibility.

Start by making a list of each job that must be done, for example:

○ Paperwork.

○ Training.

○ Practical application of treatments.

○ Stock control.

○ Business meetings.

○ Planning.

○ Interviewing.

Then rearrange the list in order of importance to you and the approximate time you devote each week to that task.

Ask yourself the following questions

1 Are you spending enough time on the more important matters?

2 Can the time spent on less important activities be reduced?

3 Are there any activities which you can delegate?

4 Can you eliminate any activities?

Make a chart of jobs that have to be done:

○ Daily.

○ Weekly.

○ At longer intervals.

The simpler the system of recording when jobs must be done, the easier it will be and nothing should be overlooked. The options are to:

1 *Keep a large wall calendar* and record regular activities, special jobs, appointments, etc.

2 *Keep a desk diary* which has a separate page for each day and record the same information as the wall calendar but with additional room for more detail.

Work out a daily routine for:

○ *The start of the day*
  —Check the appointment book.
  —Deal with any problems regarding staff, lateness, absenteeism.
  —Check the salon and all treatment areas are prepared.
  —Switch on all necessary equipment, for example saunas.
  —Check equipment.
  —Check the stock details.
  —Carry on with any other work.

○ *The end of the day*
  —Consider problems which have arisen during the day.
  —Consider the action required to deal with the problems.
  —Look at jobs which have to be done the next day.
  —Work out an approximate timetable.
  —Anticipate problems which may arise and make arrangements to cope with them.

Marketing

The market may be defined as a group of existing clients and potential clients who will use your services and products.

A very important function in any business is to increase turnover and profits. Marketing, therefore, is a key managerial function, particularly in the health and beauty business which is so highly customer-orientated. It is essential to:

○ Assess clients' needs and wants.

○ Monitor changes in the marketplace.

○ Anticipate future trends.

○ Promote the business.

Marketing is an ongoing process or business philosophy which helps to provide what the client needs and wants and allows a business to be prepared to respond to change. Marketing activities will include:

○ Creating the right image.

○ Market research.

○ Testing products on consumers.
○ Advertising.
○ Selling.
○ Promotions.

The importance of marketing as a managerial function for beauty and hairdressing salons has increased over the last forty years for several reasons:

Economic growth: There has been an increase in the disposable income of many consumers and this has resulted in a growth in demand for products and services in a far wider range of choice.

Fashion: There has been a considerable change in fashion, taste and lifestyle of consumers. Many more women consider a visit to the hairdresser or beauty therapist a necessity rather than a luxury and men are becoming increasingly more aware of the therapeutic treatments that are available.

Technology: Firms are constantly inventing, designing and launching new or more advanced products onto the market offering increased benefits to the consumer.

Competition: The number of businesses competing for the consumer's attention is constantly increasing therefore marketing is vital to each business in maintaining its market share.

The marketing mix

To achieve marketing objectives a business must consider the 'marketing mix':

PRODUCT   PRICE   PLACE   PROMOTION

To meet consumer needs the business must produce the right product at the right price, make it available in the right place and let the consumers know about it through promotion.

Market research

To be successful, the services you offer and the product you sell must meet the requirements of your clientele. Therefore, efficient market research is vital.

There are several methods of evaluating the needs of your clients:

1 Talk to your clients when you have their initial consultation and complete their record card. They will give you a clear indication of their beauty needs and you can ask them certain pertinent questions to elicit the information you require.

2 Listen to your clients. They may have a specific request or they may casually mention a new product or service that they are interested in while they are waiting for treatment. Discussions may occur naturally during treatment as a result of a query they have made or advice you may be giving.

3 Compile a questionnaire that you can send to all existing clients with relevant questions about the services you are already offering and new services you are proposing. You may then assess the likely response to the introduction of new treatments and whether it is a worthwhile investment.

4 Attend professional health and beauty shows, held nationally or internationally, to provide you with the most up-to-date information about services, treatments, trends and products. Many companies use these exhibitions to launch their latest and most up-to-date procedures and treatments and you have the opportunity to compare different companies together.

5 Subscribe to professional health and beauty publications as they will provide addresses, telephone numbers of many companies as well as articles and information which will keep you abreast of current trends. They also provide an efficient service allowing you to receive all the information you require from the companies of your choice, by filling in one reference card and sending this to them directly to process. This saves you time and the expense of contacting individual companies yourself.

Market orientation

A market-orientated business is one which continually identifies, reviews and analyses consumer needs. This is particularly important in a highly competitive industry which is so customer-orientated. It will allow the business to:

○ Anticipate market changes.
○ Respond more quickly to these changes.

- Be in a stronger position to meet the challenge.
- Be more confident of success when launching new treatments or products.
- Ensure the requirements of the consumer are identified, can be met and are constantly reviewed.

Consumer categories

Consumers, purchasers and clients all differ in terms of income, attitude and preferences. They all have different priorities and may be categorized according to their socio-economic group:

- Young singles.
- Young marrieds with no children.
- Young marrieds with youngest child under six.
- Young marrieds with youngest child over six.
- Older marrieds with children under eighteen.
- Older marrieds with no children under eighteen.
- Older singles.
- Others.

Each of these groups will have different amounts of disposable income and different priorities. Some may be restricted by their working hours, looking after children or a lack of mobility. Conversely, they may have an abundance of time. They will all require different services, treatments and products and will therefore respond to different marketing methods.

The psychological factor is also important in marketing health and beauty therapy products as appeals may be made to conflicting motivations. Emphasis may be placed on the benefits to health, from particular treatments which provide an antidote to the stresses and strains of modern life. At the more expensive end of the market and particularly when selling skin care and makeup products, emphasis may be placed on the exclusiveness or distinctiveness of a particular line. Advertising could also be aimed at a large segment of the market, taking advantage of the need to belong to a group, the group may be associated with a particular lifestyle, concept or moral stance. Consumers may be strong supporters of 'beauty without cruelty', buying only products which are not tested on animals or contain animal by-products or treatments which imply exclusivity and wealth reflecting a lifestyle to which they aspire.

Marketing therefore takes into account people's need to fulfil their various roles and aspirations.

The product

In any health and beauty establishment the 'product' means the services offered and the retail lines available to buy. There are many different types of treatments available, covering a wide range and this is called a product mix.

In a typical salon this 'product mix' could include:

- Facial therapy.
- Body therapy.
- Hand, foot and nail treatments.
- Holistic therapy.

Within most of these product lines variety may be offered, for example:

Facial therapy
- Basic manual treatments.
- Specialized electrical treatments.
- Anti-ageing treatments.
- Eye treatments.
- Permanent makeup.

Body therapy
- Electrical slimming treatments.
- Body wrapping.
- Anti-cellulite treatment.
- Body brushing.
- Spot reduction.
- Body toning.
- Heat therapy.

Hand, foot and nail treatments
- Manicure.
- Pedicure.
- Nail extensions.
- Natural nail cultivation.
- Depilatory waxing.

Holistic therapy
- Aromatherapy.
- Reflexology.

○ Shiatsu.
○ Iridology.

Clients will buy the product which provides the greatest benefit to them, no matter what features the product has. Therefore, when promoting products, emphasis must be placed upon what the end result will be in having a particular treatment or buying a particular product.

There are many companies selling their particular treatments and products for professional and retail use. To provide the appropriate products for your own clientele there are several considerations.

Brand names

Choosing a well-known brand name has the advantage that many people will be familiar with the product. The business will benefit from any advertising, which will probably be on a national level, that the company carries out. Some brand names are synonymous with a particular image concept or quality which would be applied to the business if the branded product is used.

Packaging

The presentation of a product to clients is very important because, no matter how good the benefits of a product are, if it is unappealing to look at they will probably look for an alternative elsewhere. The look of a product particularly in retail skin care, body care and makeup reinforces the brand image, for example, the neutral colours of recycled packaging which may be used by a company who holds environmental issues as a high priority or the sophisticated black and gold packaging of the company promoting glamour. The packaging also provides point of sale attraction to a potential customer who may then consider the benefits of the product or be persuaded to buy.

Packaging must also be functional as it protects some items such as glass bottles from breakage and may be see-through to allow the customer to see the product quickly and easily while maintaining the quality of the outer packaging due to less handling.

Variety

It is necessary to provide a variety of treatments and products to maintain client interest. The variety chosen must be appropriate to the market, the treatments should be introduced only when they are required, as investing money in stock or equipment which are not used is wasted capital. When buying retail products it is advisable to buy from a company who provides variety, does not require a minimum order and will deliver quickly.

Quality

Aiming for quality of treatments, products and services is an essential ingredient in business success. Time taken to research companies is well spent if the end result produces a quality product. Make sure that equipment is tried and tested before agreeing to buy, you may then see and feel the quality for yourself. Samples of products you intend to purchase should be provided so that an informed decision can be made.

The life cycle of a product

Trends in treatments and services have changed greatly in the beauty industry over the last ten years. Emphasis has changed often from one aspect to another highlighting the life cycle of a product. Several years ago there was a boom in the use of sun beds and solaria to produce an all-year round golden tan. Research in recent years has shown that the exposure to any form of ultra-violet radiation is harmful to the skin in that it may cause cancer and premature ageing and these facts have been constantly reinforced through the media, in magazines, newspapers and on television, as well as from the medical profession.

The increased awareness of the general public to these dangers and their insistence on using a different safer method to produce a tan has provided the opportunity for therapists to offer a fake tan treatment. This service is now growing rapidly to satisfy the demand while the use of sun beds is declining. There may be many other factors which will contribute to the growth or decline in a particular product or treatment, such as:

Growth of a product
○ It is fashionable.
○ Well-promoted creating a demand.
○ High-quality product.
○ Improves the quality of life.
○ Promotes good health.
○ Has noticeable benefits.
○ Environmentally friendly.
○ Therapeutic.

Decline of a product
○ Saturation in the marketplace.
○ It is unfashionable.
○ Proved to be ineffective.
○ Does not live up to expectations.
○ Cost is prohibitive.
○ Not environmentally friendly.

A good manager will be aware of problems which arise at each stage in the product life cycle and take the necessary measures to cope.

Stages of the product life cycle

The introduction stage: When introducing a new treatment, the initial cost is high and sales are low so steps must be taken to promote the product and recoup the cost quickly. Offering discount on courses of new treatments booked and paid for in advance will bring in capital and ease the financial burden. The manufacturer may allow payment in instalments over a period but this may increase the overall cost of the product.

The growth stage: The treatment is well-established and sales rise rapidly increasing profits. Capitalize on this by ensuring that there are sufficient number of staff to cope with the demand and opening hours are flexible to accommodate all clients.

The maturity stage: Sales will continue to rise but competition within the marketplace may cause a reduction in price of the treatment thus reducing profits.

The saturation stage: The competition is extensive, prices will fall and therefore profits will be less. Consider change or improving current treatment.

The decline stage: Sales are poor and profits low or non-existent.

A good manager will predict the correct time to change direction or improve the existing product before it goes into decline.

Promoting treatments and products

Sales promotion is a form of indirect advertising which provides incentives to stimulate sales and is used for the following reasons:

○ To draw the client's attention to a new treatment or product.
○ To stimulate sales of slow-moving lines.
○ To encourage bookings during off-peak time.
○ To increase turnover.

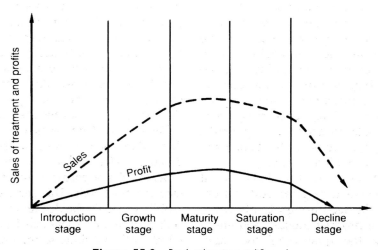

Figure 55.9 *Product/treatment life cycle*

442

FOR THE BODY

SLENDER PROGRAMME
immediate inch loss by passive
exercise to muscles

SINGLE SESSION .... £ 7.50
COURSE OF 10 .... £70.00

ACTION PROGRAMME
specific toning to the face to improve fine lines
& wrinkles £23.00
specific toning to lift bust .... £ 7.50

DEEP VIBRATORY MASSAGE
increases circulation and tones
muscles, helps reduce cellulite .... £ 7.50

SEA CLAY WRAP
detoxifying treatment with visible
inch loss

FULL BODY £35.00
PARTIAL BODY £25.00

TONING TABLES
SET OF 7 TABLES EACH ONE DESIGNED TO
PASSIVELY EXERCISE, DIFFERENT MUSCLES,
AND ALSO INCREASE CIRCULATION, WHICH
CAN HELP REDUCE FLUID RETENTION. THIS
SUITS ANY AGE & ANY PHYSICAL FITNESS
ABILITY

1 hour session .... £ 5.00
course of 10 .... £45.00
one month unlimited use £60.00

subscription available 1 year £100.00
entitles you to 1 hour session .... £ 2.50
10% off all beauty treatments

MASSAGE

FULL BODY MASSAGE £17.00
ladies only
BACK AND NECK MASSAGE £8.50
all massages are with pre-blended
aromatherapy oils

FACIALS

HALF HOUR FACIAL £10.00
includes cleanse, peel massage and mask.

GALVADERM FACIAL 1¼ hr £23.00
with the use of individually prescribed gels and mask,
treatment will suit any skin, type or problem. Includes
peel, massage.

Galvaderm facial to include chest 1½hr £35.00
Galvaderm facials for the upper back 1½hr ... £40.00

PURIFYING FACIAL 1hr £20.00
deep cleansing treatment to decongest the skin,
improves texture and skin tone. Includes peel, massage,
mask.

ELECROLYSIS

10 min £4.30
15 mins £6.25
Free consultation available

FAST TAN SUNBED WITH FACIAL BOOSTER
(shower available)
¼ hour .... £ 4.50
COURSE OF 10 .... £40.00
COURSE OF 20 .... £60.00

BEAUTY FOR THE HANDS AND FEET

MANICURE £6.75
RE-SHAPE & VARNISH £3.75
FRENCH MANICURE £9.50
RE-SHAPE & FRENCH VARNISH £6.50
NAIL REPAIRS from £1.00
PEDICURE £9.75
includes foot spa soak in aromatherapy oils, rough skin
& cuticle removal. massage & varnish

NAIL EXTENSIONS - fibre glass, gel or acrylic
full set £27.00
fill in £15.00
per nail .... £ 2.80

WAXING

FULL LEG (inc bikini line) £16.00
HALF LEG .... £ 9.00
THREE-QUARTER LEG £11.00
UNDER ARM .... £ 3.75
BIKINI LINE .... £ 3.75
UPPER LIP .... £ 3.00

BEAUTY FOR THE EYES

EYE BROW SHAPE £3.50
EYE BROW TINT £2.50
EYE LASH TINT £5.20
BROW & LASH TINT & SHAPE £9.00
(patch test required if not had tint before)

EYELASH EXTENSIONS from £8.00

Figure 55.10 *An example of a price list and promotions leaflet*

Types of promotion

○ Introducing a new treatment at a special introductory price for a limited period.
○ Booking a course of treatments at a discount.
○ Providing a free gift with a purchase.
○ Including a discount voucher in a newspaper advertisement or article.
○ Providing treatment packages, for example in the summer, after Christmas or a Mother's Day special.

Promotions may be:

○ Used on a regular basis, for example promotion of the month. This will generate sales and allow regular clients to take advantage of special offers.
○ Timed to take advantage of seasonal trends, for example a holiday package.
○ Timed to increase turnover during quiet trading periods.
○ Aimed at particular age groups to increase client numbers.
○ Used to introduce a new service or product, for example bridal service or specialist treatments such as reflexology or sports massage.

Launching a new treatment or product

The launch of a new product can be turned into an enjoyable social occasion for your clients and their friends who are potential new clients.

A ladies lunch could be arranged at a local hotel and the company from whom you are buying the new product could provide a guest speaker and demonstrate the product for your clients. A raffle prize of a free treatment or product could be offered and the proceeds could be given to a local charity.

A more informal occasion would be to have a cheese and wine open evening to which all your clients would be invited. This could also be advertised locally to encourage prospective new clients to come and see what treatments were available.

A demonstration could be arranged locally to accommodate a large number of people. A local hall or conference room in a hotel could be hired for the occasion or a visit could be made to ladies groups such as the Women's Institute, charity organizations such as the NSPCC or the Rainbow Trust. There are many informal groups such as mother and toddler groups, nursery nurses, slimming clubs and exercise groups who meet on a regular basis and are looking for interesting guest speakers.

Regular clients may be encouraged to try new treatments by sending them a special voucher on their birthday for a treatment they do not normally have. The benefits of this are two-fold:

1 They may enjoy the new treatment and book it on a regular basis.
2 It provides customer satisfaction and increases the loyalty of the client.

Controlling stock

The control of stock is a very important function as there can be a large amount of capital invested in it. For a salon that sells retail products as well as providing treatments, then there will probably be a large amount of stock in the salon to cope with the demand.

Stock items

Records must be kept of all stock in the salon and this will include such items as:

○ Equipment used to perform the treatments such as steamers, high frequency, vacuum suction, faradic and galvanic machines.
○ Tools required to perform the treatments such as, tweezers, accessories for the electrical equipment and spatulas.
○ Protective bedding and clothing such as sheets, blankets, towels and gowns.
○ Consumable items are those which are used up during treatment such as, skin care products, mask ingredients, massage oils, special gels and ampoules, cotton wool and tissues.
○ Semi-consumable items are those which may be used more than once but do need to be replaced at regular intervals due to general wear and tear, such as sponges and headbands.
○ Retail products to sell to the clients.

Stock control system

This is a necessity as it helps in the smooth running of the business, it will:

○ Ensure that stock will not run out and avoid disappointing clients because the correct products are not available.

○ Help to maintain the correct stock level required, for the smooth running of the business and allow therapists to carry out their treatments knowing that they have everything available.
○ Ensure that the salon is not over stocked and any available capital is working for the business and not tied up in excess stock.
○ Ensure that stock does not deteriorate with age.

Requirements of a stock control system

Responsibility

One member of staff should be put in charge of stock control as the more people there are involved, the more chance there is of mistakes being made. There may be times when the person in charge is absent due to illness or holidays. A suitable alternative, therefore, should be allowed to assist on these occasions.

The duties of the stock controller are:

○ To buy stock.
○ To keep records.
○ To distribute stock.
○ To carry out regular stock checks.

Records

Separate stock books or sets of stock cards should be kept for the different categories of stock. This is because electrical equipment would not have to be checked as often as retail stocks, which in a busy salon would need to be checked on a daily basis.

Manufacturers or suppliers of goods will often provide a set of stock control forms as it is

Figure 56.1 *Glass front display cabinet*
Courtesy Depilex Limited

in their best interest to help with stock control so that you are re-ordering on a regular basis.

Storage

There should be a stock room or a large stock cupboard in which to store a larger percentage of stock. The shelving should be adjustable to allow for the difference in size of containers, particularly when buying in bulk.

Everything should be easily washable for hygiene purposes and the shelves should be clearly labelled to show exactly where each item is stored.

For safety, liquids should be stored in plastic bottles to prevent breakages and large or heavy items should be stored at the bottom or on the lower shelves.

The most frequently used stock should be placed at eye level or slightly below, to prevent unnecessary bending and stretching.

Retail products should be on display in the reception area in a glass fronted cabinet which can be locked when left unattended. There is little point having the products out of sight, as the clients will not buy them if they cannot be seen (Figure 56.1).

Shelving can be used to display retail products allowing the clients easy access but this does have several disadvantages:

1. Stock may be damaged when handled.
2. Stock can become dirty and dusty on open shelving.
3. The products could be easily stolen.

Shelving can be used to display dummy products provided by the manufacturers which will then encourage the client to ask about the products on offer.

Treatment areas should have trolleys with drawers, or small cupboards with shelves, to store a small amount of treatment products so that in the event of the therapist running out of a cream or lotion, there will be a replacement in easy reach and the therapist will not have to leave the client to go to the storeroom for the replacement.

Stock control procedures

○ First of all choose a manufacturer or a supplier of goods who is competitively priced. To do this enquiries need to be made with several different companies until you are satisfied that you are buying the most appropriate products at a reasonable price.

It will also save a great deal of your valuable time if you find a company who deliver the goods for you and can do so in as short a time after placing the order as possible.

Discounts on large orders for prompt payment is also a plus point when choosing a supplier as this will enable you to cut your costs and increase your profits.

When purchasing stock use an official, numbered order form on which the date is written clearly, with a duplicate copy for reference in case the order arrives short or damaged. The problem is then easily dealt with if there is a copy filed away for inspection.

○ Retain the advice or dispatch note the supplier will send, to inform you that the order is being dealt with. If the goods ordered do not arrive within a reasonable time the stock controller can then inform the supplier and the matter can be dealt with.

○ When the goods arrive the delivery note will itemize the goods contained in the parcel, this may then be checked with the original order form and the goods in the parcel to ensure the order is complete and undamaged.

○ All purchases should then be recorded in the stock book in the 'In' column.

○ The new stock can then be dated and placed in the appropriate place in the stock room. New stock should be placed behind existing stock so that the products are used in strict rotation.

○ Any item which is below standard or incorrect should be immediately returned to the supplier with a 'returned goods' notice, a copy of which you retain for your own records.

○ If the delivery is received short of any item it is important to ring the supplier immediately if this was not noted on the delivery note and the order marked accordingly.

Displaying stock

Some care should be taken to display retail stock in the most eye-catching way to attract the attention of clients in the salon or potential clients who may be passing by.

Displays should always be placed in a prominent position such as:

○ The window.
○ The reception.
○ Waiting areas.
○ Treatment rooms.
○ Next to a work station.

Whatever the position of the display, it is essential that is well-maintained, clean and colourful.

The window

A salon situated at ground level provides an ideal opportunity to promote the business by using posters, products or different props and materials to promote an image. The type of display you have will depend upon the amount of window space available and if it is open with the interior of the salon clearly visible or completely closed in.

The disadvantage of a window display is that it will deteriorate when exposed to sunlight as the colours will begin to fade, liquids will evaporate and some products will change in consistency because of the increase in temperature. This problem may be overcome by using dummy products and empty boxes with posters and changing the display on a regular basis. Some of the larger companies will provide display materials and equipment as well as practical advice particularly when the business has a large account with them.

The reception/waiting areas

This is the ideal place to display retail stock as the client starts and finishes a visit here. Sometimes the client or guests will be sitting in the reception area for a period of time, providing the opportunity to browse. The attention of passers by may also be attracted by goods displayed in reception when the window is open to the salon beyond. Stock may be displayed in glass-fronted cabinets, on free- standing units or on shelves.

Treatment rooms

It is often during the course of treatment that retail sales are made and having a display of goods on offer may encourage the process. Also being able to give the product to the clients to take out to reception when paying their bill is more likely to ensure a sale than giving them the opportunity to change their mind or forget when they have left the treatment room.

The main disadvantage is that it will make stock control slightly more difficult and clients may forget to pay if the therapist does not accompany them to reception or inform the receptionist of the purchase.

Next to a work station

Retail products for hair care may be displayed on wall-mounted units or on shelves next to the work station. Clients will be sitting facing the products while having their treatment and this provides ample opportunity for discussion and advice on home care procedures. The disadvantages are that the products are easily accessible to anyone who passes and they may become dusty and covered in hair and lacquer.

Displays should:

- Be well balanced.
- Use lines to draw the eye in to the focal point.
- Reflect an image or theme.
- Use the correct props and materials to complement the product.
- Be colourful.
- Achieve the desired effect.
- Be clean.
- Be safe and secure.

Setting up a display

Find the right location
↓
Establish objectives for the display
↓
Draw a plan
↓
Collect fixtures, props and other materials
↓
Collect items to be displayed
↓
Assemble the display safely and effectively
↓
Check the finished display conforms with the plan
↓
Check the lighting is appropriate

Computerized stock control

This is a very efficient system of stock control, particularly in the area of retail sales as the till can be linked up to a computer system, so that levels of stock are maintained and the stock required is worked out automatically.

There are several ways to increase your profit:

1 Cutting your costs.
2 Increasing your range of treatments.
3 Increasing your prices.
4 Selling more.

Cutting costs

Shopping around

Shop around and find a supplier of the goods you need, whose prices are lower than anyone else's. The problem that may occur is that the products may be inferior to those you are already using, or you may have to buy in such large quantities, that you are over-stocked and tying up capital, as well as risking having stock which may be out of date before you have had the opportunity to use it. If, however, the products are of an acceptable quality then this may be a successful way to increase profits.

Certain suppliers will offer a reduction on price if you deal exclusively with them. The advantages of this are:

o Less work for the manager or stock controller in ordering goods.
o Establishment of a good working relationship with a supplier who will advise you of new trends and special offers as your business success is also beneficial to them.

The disadvantage is that you are offering a limited range of products to your clients and providing them with less choice.

Staff cuts

Reducing staff costs by employing part-time members of staff and ensuring that the maximum number are available at the busy times and the minimum number required at the quiet times.

Opening hours

The salon's opening times could be altered to suit the clientele. For instance, if the largest percentage of clientele is the working woman it may be beneficial to have several late nights and close for several mornings when business is slow. This will save money on fixed costs which have to be paid whether business is good or bad.

Increasing the treatment range

Introducing new treatments will increase profits if there is a demand for that particular treatment. It is important, therefore, to assess the market first of all by approaching your existing clientele. If there is a positive response then offer reductions on the new treatment if a course is booked in advance. In this way revenue from advance bookings may pay for the new treatment or equipment.

The manufacturer may allow you to lease the equipment so that there is not a large capital outlay, with an option to renew the lease, or buy outright, if you decide that the treatment is successful.

By increasing the treatment range you may need to employ more staff or extend the business premises and the added costs may not be recouped very easily creating a cash flow problem, so this course of action must be seriously considered.

Increasing prices

Prices charged for treatments or products should be set initially at a level that will give you the highest profit possible. By increasing prices you run the risk of losing some clients but there are also those clients who believe that by paying a higher price for a service then it is of a higher quality and a more expensive product must be better for them and worth the extra cost. Therefore the increase in profits may more than compensate for any clients lost.

Setting a price

There is no ideal way of setting a price for services or products but there are certain considerations:

The market
The price you set is limited by the market, you have to charge what the potential client is willing to pay. It is important, therefore, to set a price in relation to the clientele you are hoping to attract.

The product/treatment
If you have a product or new treatment which has a genuine advantage and is not provided by any other business then you can charge the highest price possible. Paying a high price also appeals to clients with high incomes or those who like to buy the most expensive products or treatments and be seen to be doing so. This is known as *price skimming*, by aiming at the cream at the top end of the market.

The competition
The services you offer and the products you sell should be looked at in relation to your competitors if their business is the same. You may be able to justify charging a higher price if your services or products are superior to those of your competitors. The areas for consideration are:

○ The quality of the service you provide.
○ The salon image.
○ The availability of products and services.
○ The reputation of your business.

○ The standard of the employees.
○ The extras you provide, for example free drinks and snacks service.

Your costs
When deciding on a price you have to take into consideration your:

○ Fixed costs.
○ Variable costs.
○ The profit you want to make.

Fixed costs are those which you have to pay whether you are actually carrying out treatments or not. So when you open up for business these are expenses which will always have to be met:

○ Rent and rates.
○ Heating and lighting.
○ Telephone.
○ Interest charges.
○ Advertising.
○ Insurance.
○ Accountancy.
○ Depreciation.
○ Wages.

Variable costs are the cost of the materials used for carrying out the treatment as these will vary with each treatment or the number of treatments carried out.

Profit is the percentage to be added to the variable and fixed costs to set your price.

Sell more

Train your staff in sales techniques and encourage them to sell products to clients that complement the range used during their beauty treatments. While performing the treatments the therapist has the ideal opportunity to discuss with the client their beauty requirements.

Give therapists commission on their sales to encourage them to sell more. Encourage the staff to use the products they are selling so that they will sell the products from personal experience.

Take advantage of training courses provided by the manufacturers whose products you sell.

Ensure that all the staff have a good technical knowledge of all treatments and products so that they may sell with confidence.

Figure 57.1 *Retail makeup display unit*
Courtesy Depilex Limited

Provide gift vouchers for clients to give as presents as this will bring in new business as well as providing revenue.

Promote specific treatments or products at the appropriate time of the year:

○ The month leading up to Christmas is an ideal time for promoting gift sets of skin care products and makeup, when many people are looking for presents to buy.

○ In the summer months you can promote the sun protection products, false tans and treatments such as waxing, eyelash tinting, pedicures and figure correction.

○ When you know that the business will be quiet, have special offers on treatments, a free gift with each booking or a reduction on the price of a treatment if the client brings along a friend at the time specified.

Retail sales

Selling retail products to clients is essential for business growth and should account for at least 40 per cent of turnover. While performing treatments there is a limit to the profit made as there are set prices for each treatment to be performed in a particular time. A specialized facial may take an hour and a half and earn £25, spend 10 minutes selling a client a set of skin care products and earn £60! The potential for increasing sales of retail products is enormous. To help there are certain considerations.

Make sure that all the selling aids they need such as testers, free samples and product leaflets are readily available (Figure 57.1).

Record all sales on your client's record card as this will be helpful to other therapists when they are treating that client and it will allow you to contact the right people when there are special offers that they may be interested in.

Make sure the products you are selling are in stock to avoid disappointing the client.

When employing new staff, sales experience could be an important point to include in the job specification.

Place an attractive display of retail products in the salon window to catch the attention of the passer-by. This could also create new business. When a prospective new client comes in to buy something on offer this will give you the opportunity to sell the beauty treatments to them.

Advertising could be worth investing more money in and also look at the type of advertising you are already using and see if it could be improved or changed.

Product knowledge

The management should ensure that all members of staff receive the relevant training from the manufacturers or distributors of all products sold. Being able to provide up to date, accurate information and explaining the features and benefits of products will inspire confidence in the client. The features describe the product and the benefits explain to the client what effects the features will achieve. Most companies provide up-to-date information through newsletters or offer a telephone helpline which salons may call for assistance.

Product display

The reception area is an ideal place for a retail display as the clients can browse when entering or leaving the salon or if they are waiting for treatment.

An eye-catching window display attracts passing trade but must be changed regularly to maintain interest and kept clean. Most companies provide display stands which show products to their best advantage. When making your own displays they must be changed regularly to maintain client interest and also to change with the season.

Each working area could have a small display of relevant products, for example skin care in a facial treatment room, aromatherapy oils in a body treatment room and sun care products in a sunbed room.

If the reception is left unattended it would be advisable to store retail products in a glass front cabinet which can be locked when unattended but the goods are on permanent display. Using a cabinet also ensures that the goods remain in good condition and do not become dusty and dirty. When products are displayed on open shelves it is a good idea to use dummy products which will be provided by some companies. This cuts down on the risk of theft as the products could be stored in a locked cupboard.

Advertising literature

Leaflets and information booklets should be available for clients to read, particularly when you are selling products which require advice in their use.

Free samples

These are not always easy to provide as not all companies have samples. When you can, provide them for the client to try particularly if the product is very expensive to buy. In this case some companies will provide 'trial size' products at a greatly reduced price for the client to buy.

Body language/communication

Always be positive and helpful and smile when making a sale but do not stare directly at the client and intimidate her into a sale. Do not rush the sale or be too persistent in your approach as this can also be very intimidating to the client. Concentrate solely on clients, answering their questions and asking your own. Open questions should be used. These are questions which may not be answered with a yes or no; they should include words such as why, how, when, what and which, to elicit information which may help to make the sale.

Involve the clients by allowing them to smell, feel, touch and test the products.

Professional approach

Always listen to your clients and ensure that you do not miss an opportunity to sell a product to the client, in particular when they are telling you about a problem they may have, sympathize with them and then assure them that you have just the product for them. You must, however, be honest and sell clients something that will be effective.

Once you have built a good client therapist relationship the client will always ask for your advice. You must also introduce clients to products you know will benefit them even when they have not asked. They will be relying on your expert opinion.

Link selling

When the client asks for a product always link it to another product which complements the one asked for, for example a toning lotion with a cleanser or a quick dry top coat nail polish with an enamel.

Closing the sale

This is when you feel that the time has come to complete the transaction, the client in your opinion is convinced that they want one or more of the products which are on offer.

The alternative close: This is when you will ask clients questions, such as 'Would you like the large or small size?' or 'Would you like the red or pink?' Clients will then make a decision.

The professional recommendation: This is when you are using your professional judgement in advising clients so you would say, 'I would strongly recommend that you use the primer for your brittle nails to give them flexibility and stop them from breaking.' This is the most effective as a regular client with whom you have a good relationship would not hesitate to buy what you have recommended.

The 'yes' technique: This is when you ask clients a series of questions to which they will answer 'yes', so the final question completing the sale will be answered with a 'yes'.

The elimination technique: Many clients like to feel in control of the sale so you must allow them to eliminate a number of products you are offering but make sure that you are left with an alternative.

The key to successful selling is to be honest with clients and ensure that the products you are selling to them are appropriate, will be effective in their use and good value for money.

Consumer protection

The consumer, any person who buys goods and services for money, is well protected by law and voluntary associations of traders and manufacturers, for example the Consumers Association. The greatest protection for the consumer is provided by legislation which gives them statutory rights, the most important statutes are:

The Sale of Goods Act 1979

The main points of the act are:

○ The goods must be of merchantable quality so, for example, if you buy a new wax machine and discover that the heater is dented and badly scratched you would be entitled to a replacement.

○ The goods must be fit for the purpose. For example, the wax machine is thermostatically controlled but the first time it is used it overheats and burns the wax when set at a low temperature. In this case you would be entitled to a full refund as the machine was not fit for the purpose.

○ The goods must correspond with the description. If, for example, the model of wax machine delivered by the suppliers was not the model agreed upon, the goods were not as described and the customer is entitled to a refund.

Faulty goods should be returned immediately if one of the above conditions has been broken. If the supplier thinks the manufacturer is to blame then they must claim for them.

This act only applies to a sale between a business and the public and does not apply to sales made through classified advertisements or private transactions.

The Trade Descriptions Act 1968

This act provides protection for the consumer who has been misled or given inaccurate descriptions of goods or services offered.

The Consumer Safety Act 1978

This act lays down legal safety standards to minimize risks to the consumer from potentially harmful or dangerous products.

The Consumer Credit Act 1974

This act requires that borrowers should be made aware of the true rate of interest charged on credit facilities.

Consumer Protection Act 1987

This act implements directives laid down by the European Community providing a safeguard from products used or sold that are not safe.

The Supply of Goods and Services Act 1982

This act was introduced to improve the rights of the consumer in relation to poor service or workmanship. The act was required to make up for the short-comings of the Sale of Goods Act 1979 which applied only to the transfer of goods to the buyer from the seller and not to a situation where goods were being provided as part of a service. The conditions are the same in that goods must be of merchantable quality, fit for purpose and fit the description, but it applies to:

○ Contracts for work and materials.
○ Free gifts – applicable to many health and beauty establishments.
○ Part exchange – a method used to update equipment.
○ Contracts for hire of goods – many companies provide equipment in this way for use by the therapist.

The act also requires the person providing a service to:

○ Act with reasonable care and skill.
○ Work within a reasonable time.
○ Charge a reasonable price.

The Prices Act 1974

Prices must be displayed in such a way that it does not give a false impression.

The Resale Prices Act 1976

Manufacturers are not allowed to enforce a price at which their goods must be sold. Many companies do have a recommended retail price which they suggest a supplier should use.

The British Standards Institution

This is an independent body which establishes voluntary standards of quality and reliability. Its now famous kitemark indicates that goods conform to the high standards set by the institution. Its main objectives are:

○ The promotion of health and safety.
○ The protection of the environment.
○ The establishment of quality standards.

It provides specifications on such things as:

○ Strength.
○ Safety.
○ Quality.
○ Ingredients.

Manufacturers may submit products voluntarily for testing. If they pass they will carry a kitemark which provides the consumer with a guarantee that they are at least of reasonable quality.

Returned goods

Any business which provides retail products will, on occasion, have to deal with a customer returning goods which have been found to be unsuitable. This could be for several reasons:

○ Product is damaged.
○ Product did not work.
○ Colour not correct.
○ Product was not appropriate.
○ Out of date stock.
○ An incorrect product was originally given.

Whatever the reason, a courteous manner must be adopted as more often than not the complaint will be genuine. Even if it is not, the situation will be resolved much more quickly and effectively if the therapist adopts a professional and concerned attitude.

It is important to follow rules laid down by the management when dealing with returned goods or complaints. Listen to what the client has to say, inspect the goods, ask the client relevant questions and decide on your course of action.

When the complaint is, in your opinion, genuine, either exchange the goods or offer an alternative. When the required goods are not in stock, provide the client with a credit note, offer a refund or order a replacement which will be given to the client as soon as it becomes available.

When in doubt about the validity of the complaint, the best course of action is to refer the problem to your immediate superior, supervisor or manager.

Always keep a record of returned goods and refunds given for stock control and accounting purposes.

Contact the supplier or manufacturer of defective goods which have been returned to you and then follow their set procedure for customer complaint.

There are occasions when you may feel that the returned goods are defective through no fault of your own or your supplier. It may be in the best interest of the business to accept the returned goods and lose a small amount of money rather than lose regular income and the goodwill of a client. This is a decision which must be made by the management and is often a company policy.

Processing the sale

The receptionist will normally be responsible for taking payment from clients but each individual therapist should be familiar with all methods of payment. A procedure laid down by the management should prevent any confusion or misunderstanding.

Procedure

1   Make a record. The use of a computerized or electronic till provides an efficient method of taking money and recording sales. Numbered bills are an alternative and should include the following:
    o   The name of the therapist.
    o   The date.
    o   All treatments.
    o   All retail sales.
    o   Other details, for example discount.
    o   Total amount.
2   Inform the client. State clearly the total amount and show the client the itemized bill.
3   Accept payment. This may be cash, cheque, credit card, debit card or gift voucher.
4   Finalize the process. Count out the change, handing it to the client and place any notes in the till. If payment is made by any other method, follow the correct procedure.

Methods of payment

Cash

Check that notes are not forgeries by checking the water-marked picture of the Queen's head, the metallic strip running through the note, or by using an ultraviolet detector machine. Always count the change into the client's hand before placing notes into the till.

Cheque

Ensure that the cheque has been signed by the client in your presence, if not ask them to sign the back of the cheque again. Make sure that all the details are correct:

o   The date.
o   The correct amount in figures and numbers.
o   To whom the cheque is payable.
o   The signature of client.

The number of the cheque guarantee card must be written by you on the back of the cheque.

Debit card

This method of payment eliminates the need for cash or cheques. Any business that provides this service will require a special terminal through which the card will be swiped. Duplicated receipts are signed and one copy is give to the client and the other copy retained by the salon. As long as there are sufficient funds in the client's account, payment will be authorized by the bank via this computerized system.

Credit card

Before accepting a credit card always check the details to make sure that it is valid and has not expired. Computerized terminals may be used to swipe cards but they are not in general use in small salons which use hand-operated machines that imprint all details on a triplicate voucher.

There are several types of credit card each with their own stationery and they should be filled in using a ball-point pen. The client must be asked to check the details before signing and after ensuring the client's signature is the same as that on the card, the top copy can be given to the client. The second copy is retained by the salon and the third is sent to the credit company. The disadvantage of accepting credit cards is the

Figure 57.2 *A example of a salon gift voucher*

charge made by the credit card company which is a percentage of the total sale.

Gift voucher
An ideal method of increasing turnover and reaching potential new clients is to offer a gift voucher scheme. Vouchers are popular particularly before Christmas or Mother's Day and can be for a particular treatment or a specific amount. When accepting a gift voucher as payment a record must be kept of the amount and serial number for accounting purposes.

The reception

This is a very important part of any business because the client has to enter through the reception or make an enquiry over the telephone, which is normally situated in the reception. Clients' first impressions are lasting ones, so they must be good to ensure that they feel comfortable and at ease when arriving for treatment.

The *decor* should be attractive, relaxing and inviting so that it will:

○ Make the new client feel at ease.
○ Make an existing client feel at home.
○ Encourage the prospective client passing by to want to come in to the salon and try the treatments which are on offer.

The *receptionist* should be:

○ Welcoming to all clients whether they have been attending the salon for years or if it is their first visit.
○ Helpful, as it is important that she attends to the client's needs but it is important to the therapists that she books appointments to suit them as well as accommodating the clients.
○ Patient, as she will probably have to deal with awkward clients who are not easy to please, therapists who may be overworked, and at the same time attend to all the day to day duties and responsibilities of the reception.
○ Pleasant and courteous as she will set the tone for the rest of the salon.

Duties of the receptionist

○ Answering the telephone.
○ Booking appointments.
○ Welcoming clients.
○ Dealing with problems when clients arrive late and appointments have to be re-arranged.
○ Using the till and making out bills.
○ Selling retail products.

Answering the telephone

The receptionist must have a thorough knowledge of all the treatments on offer and the prices charged so that she can answer any queries made over the telephone.

The telephone should be situated in a quiet place, which is not always possible in a busy combined hair and beauty salon.

There should be an up-to-date telephone book close by and the clients' record cards with their telephone numbers clearly marked.

The receptionist should speak clearly so that there is no misunderstanding and the caller must always be referred to by their name.

When answering the telephone the caller should be greeted in a friendly and courteous way at the same time being informed briefly of the business or person they are speaking to. For example, 'Good morning, Grange Health Hydro, Lorraine speaking, may I help you?'.

The enquiry should be dealt with in an interested and helpful way making sure that all the information the caller requires is given. If their query cannot be answered immediately then they should be asked politely to hold while another member of staff who may be able to help is sought. If this is not possible, the name and telephone number of the caller must be taken so that someone can ring back with the relevant information later in the day.

For those clients who have a habit of cancelling appointments at short notice or just not turning up, it may be worthwhile confirming their appointment by telephone the day before and the client will either cancel then, giving you the opportunity to re-book the appointment, or he/she will feel obliged to attend.

Booking appointments

An efficient system is advisable to make use of the therapist's time as this is how bookings are made for treatments. A certain length of time will be booked according to the treatment the client is having.

An appointment book with half hour blocks is necessary and it is advisable to book appointments in a regular order from the beginning of the day to the end.

If a therapist is busy all morning and a client rings for an appointment then it is more efficient to book the appointment in the first available slot after lunch rather than later in the afternoon.

Make sure that regular clients' appointments are put in the appointment book as the new pages for each month are put in. This will avoid any problems that will occur if their appointment slot is given away, particularly if they are having a course of treatments such as slimming or special facials.

Take the telephone number of a new client when booking the appointment in case you need to contact them for any reason, as there will not be a record card available.

Treatment room or area

In large businesses such as health farms and health hydros separate treatment rooms are an essential part of the business. This is because there are so many different types of treatment available. They can include:

- Swimming pool with sauna, steam and whirlpool facilities.
- A rest area.
- Multigym to cater for large numbers.
- Exercise rooms.
- Beauty rooms.
- Hair salon.

For privacy and total relaxation treatment rooms are ideal but there are many salons that do not have enough room to provide them. Therefore treatment areas should be available with curtains to provide a certain amount of privacy.

Whether the treatment room is a separate entity, a room within another salon such as hairdressing, or a room in your own home there are certain basic items which are a necessity and others which can be added as the business grows.

Washing and drying facilities are a must so that there are plenty of clean towels available. The need for clean towels can be reduced considerably by the use of disposable paper towelling to protect the bedding.

Facial work

- A multipurpose treatment couch which allows different treatments to be performed.
- A sink unit with storage space underneath for towels, treatment products and tools.
- A trolley to hold equipment, cosmetics, treatment materials and with a small drawer to store small implements.
- A magnifying mirror for close inspection of the skin.
- A sterilizing unit.
- Depilatory waxing unit for legs, arms and face.
- A selection of facial equipment which may be chosen according to the client's requirements, the working capital you have available and your specialist skills. They may include:
  - Facial steamer.
  - High frequency.
  - Vacuum suction.
  - Brush massage.
  - Galvanic machine.
  - Electrolysis machine.

There are combined units available with several pieces of equipment in one. The advantage of this is that little space is taken up in a small area.

The disadvantages are that all the treatments in the unit are available only to one therapist and cannot be shared. When one part of the unit is not working the whole thing will not be

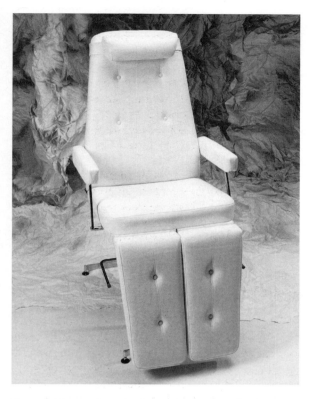

Figure 58.1 *Multipurpose treatment chair*
Courtesy Depilex Limited

available for use while the defective part is being mended.

○ Selection of materials for treatments such as eyelash tinting and makeup application.
○ Selection of facial treatment products for all skin types to include:
   –Cleansers.
   –Toners.
   –Moisturizers.
   –Massage cream.
   –Face masks.
   –Oils.
   –Specialized products, for example galvanic gels.
○ Sheets and blankets.

Body work

Many clients require figure treatments and ideally there should be plenty of space for heat treatments such as sauna and/or steam, shower facilities, rest and changing areas. It is possible, however, in a small salon to provide the basic treatments for all figure correction requirements.

○ A steam bath or small sauna.
○ A massage couch of suitable height and strength.
○ A sink unit with storage space for towels and small items required for treatment.
○ A trolley with shelves to support clinic size equipment.
○ A heavy-duty gyratory vibrator.
○ A vacuum suction unit.
○ A muscle contraction unit.
○ A galvanic unit.

The galvanic and muscle contraction treatments are now available in a combined machine to use the treatments together for maximum effect.

○ Treatment products, oil, talc, essential oils, specialized gels and ampoules for conditions such as cellulite.
○ Weighing scales.
○ Gowns, spare blankets and pillows.

Other treatments and facilities can be added at a later date as required, an ultraviolet treatment area or infrared lamps, paraffin wax and exercise equipment.

The layout of the salon

Planning the layout of any business whether it is a facial or body salon, a health and fitness club or a specialist clinic, it is advisable to use the professional expertise of a designer specializing in industrial design. This may be expensive but in the long run the efficient running of the business because of the effective use of the space available will generate more income.

When planning the layout of the salon there are certain areas for consideration and these are:

○ Space.
○ Decor.
○ Lighting.
○ Power.
○ Walls.
○ Flooring.
○ Staff facilities.

Space

There should be adequate space for the type of business that you have and this may include some or all of the following:

○   Reception area.
○   Treatment areas, cubicles or rooms.
○   Changing facilities.
○   Sauna and or steam with a rest area.
○   Staff facilities.
○   Toilet for staff and clients.
○   Laundry room.

There should be enough space to allow ease of movement for therapists to work efficiently and clients to be comfortable. Curtains could be used to partition the work areas and then when not in use can be drawn back to create the illusion of space.

In the long term it would be advantageous if the premises were easily extended to allow for the growth of the business.

Decor

This should reflect the type of client you are hoping to attract, for example elegant and luxurious for the mature client or modern and trendy for the younger working clients.

If space is limited, then pastel shades are ideal for a colour scheme as they make the salon look more spacious. Although white creates the illusion of space, it can be hard, cold and clinical so should be avoided unless this is the image you hope to achieve.

Curtains, gowns, towels, sheets and blankets could be made in complementary shades. This gives a luxurious feel to the salon.

Lighting

This is very important to both the client and the therapist. There must be sufficient light for the therapist to be able to work efficiently but the client needs a soothing and relaxing atmosphere which bright lights do not achieve.

An ideal solution to this problem is the use of track lighting. As many spotlights as are required can be fitted to the tracking, which can then be pointed in any direction. Dimmer switches may also be used, so that the lights can be put on their lowest setting while the client is having a relaxing body massage and then on the highest setting when required for work such as the application of makeup.

Special makeup mirrors can also be used which are surrounded on three sides by light bulbs to accommodate clients who are sitting in an upright position to have their makeup applied or having a makeup lesson.

Power

There must be a sufficient number of power points available in each work area to ensure that the therapist may work safely using electrical equipment without overloading the plug socket. Also it will avoid the therapist having wires trailing from other plug sockets further away causing a safety hazard.

Walls

These should be easy to clean and no materials used which may deteriorate in the warm atmosphere of the salon.

Flooring

The floor covering should be non-slip and easy to keep clean but it does not have to be the same throughout the premises. The reception could have carpet to promote a feeling of luxury when the client comes in. In the work areas the flooring should be durable, easy to clean, warm to the feet and non-slip, particularly in wet areas.

Staff facilities

There must be an area set aside for staff to change, keep their personal belongings, have their lunch breaks and retire to when necessary. This provides them with a comfortable working environment and prevents them from having to stand around in the salon when they are not busy.

Salon security

It is in the best interests of a salon owner to ensure that the property and contents of the business are well-insured to cover all risks. There will be certain steps to follow to reduce the risks of burglary or theft from the premises from any person who may enter as a client, member of staff or business contact.

Premises
○ Install a burglar alarm which will help to deter burglars – some sophisticated alarms are linked directly with the police or to a security firm who have the facility to detect movement and sound inside the premises.
○ If the salon has a large window frontage make sure it is made from toughened glass and contains an alarm in the form of a metal strip across the full length of the window.
○ Check that the locks on all the doors and windows are up to standard and if not ask for advice from the insurance company about the correct type of lock that should be fitted.
○ Key holders should be appointed to open and lock the salon daily. These people should also be known to the police in case the premises are broken into outside opening hours.
○ Provide some sort of night lighting to provide a clear view into the salon as a deterrent and to help security.

Money
○ Use an electric till, one which can be locked or a cash box kept in a drawer or cupboard which may be locked.
○ If possible appoint one person to be responsible for the handling of cash.
○ Pay money taken daily into the bank before they close.
○ Store money taken after banking hours in a safe. This may also be used for any valuables inadvertently left on the premises.
○ Leave the till drawer open at night to show that it is empty.

Stock
○ Appoint one person to be responsible for stock control.
○ Therapists should sign for stock when it is required for treatments.

○ Store consumable products in a locked store room or cupboard.
○ Check stock regularly.
○ Retail products should be displayed in a locked glass fronted cabinet.
○ Use only dummy products on open display.
○ Keep records up to date.

Clients' property
○ Place jewellery and valuables in a safe place in the treatment room. If the room is left unattended ensure that the valuables are locked away or out of sight.

Staff property
○ Provide lockers or lockable cupboard in the staff room for staff members to store their property.

The therapist

It is extremely important to present a professional, courteous and warm image to your clients, to instil confidence, provide reassurance and make them all feel welcome. This initial contact will determine whether the client becomes a loyal and regular client or takes the business elsewhere. The management will set standards of appearance, hygiene and conduct and it is the duty of the employee to maintain these standards.

Qualities

The therapist should be:

Friendly: To make people feel welcome.
Sincere: Putting the best interests of the client first.
Honest: Never mislead or provide the client with unrealistic expectations.
Cheerful: To relax the client and promote a pleasant atmosphere.
Polite: Treat all clients with equal respect no matter how difficult they may be.
Discreet: The client must feel secure in the knowledge that any personal information or anything which has been said in confidence will not be passed on.

Approachable: Allows clients to communicate their requirements.

Appearance

The therapist should:

○ Wear a clean, loose-fitting and well-pressed uniform.
○ Wear comfortable low-heeled shoes.
○ Wear the minimum amount of jewellery – small stud earrings and a wedding ring is acceptable.
○ Wear well-applied and discreet makeup which will look good even in warm working conditions.
○ Make sure hair is clean and well-groomed. If it is below chin length it should be tied back so that it does not fall in the eyes or over the client.
○ Have well-manicured, short nails which allow treatments to be performed effectively and hygienically.
○ Practice good hygiene:
  —Bathe daily.
  —Use an antiperspirant.
  —Wash hair regularly.
  —Change underwear daily.
  —Clean teeth morning and night and after eating.
  —Use breathfreshener.

Behaviour

The therapist must act in a professional manner towards clients, colleagues, suppliers and competitors:

○ When treating clients, always give them your undivided attention and ensure that treatment is appropriate.
○ Do not discuss your personal problems and avoid controversial topics of conservation.
○ Always co-operate with your colleagues and become a reliable and effective member of the team.
○ Always be hard-working and conscientious using initiative in all aspects of work.
○ Always be open and honest in communications with management and show a willing-

ness to learn and improve on skills and experience.
○ Always be ethical in your behaviour by respecting other therapists and following the code of conduct laid down by the professional association to which you are affiliated.

Code of ethics

Many professional associations and organizations will have their own code of ethics which is a set of guidelines that impose various obligations on their members, to ensure that members of the public are protected from improper practice.

The code will be implemented by the organization by issuing a set of rules and regulations which establish the required conduct expected of its members.

The code will:

○ Establish appropriate conduct.
○ Establish acceptable practices.
○ Protect clients or consumers from improper practices.
○ Maintain professional standards of behaviour towards
  —Other members of the organization.
  —Members of the public and clients.
  —Other professional therapists.
  —Members of other professional organizations.
  —Colleagues within the industry.

In general all professional therapists and hairdressers should:

○ Comply with statute law and local bylaws.
○ Apply treatments for which they are qualified.
○ Not treat a client who may be contraindicated.
○ Consult with the client's medical practitioner when necessary.
○ Maintain client confidentiality.
○ Treat colleagues with respect.
○ Not criticize other businesses.
○ Not deliberately poach clients from a competing business.

Professional associations

Association of Reflexologists
27 Old Gloucester Street
London
WC1N 3XX

British Association of Beauty Therapy and
Cosmetology
Parabola House
Parabola Road
Cheltenham
Gloucestershire
GL50 3AH

British Association of Electrolysists
18 Stokes End
Haddenham
Buckinghamshire
HP17 8DX

British Association of Skin Camouflage
25 Blackhorse Drive
Silkstone Common
Near Barnsley
South Yorkshire
S75 4SD

The Federation of Holistic Therapists
38A Portsmouth Road
Woolston
Southampton
SO19 9AD

The Guild of Professional Beauty Therapists
Ltd
Guild House
PO Box 310
Derby
DE23 9BR

Independent Professional Therapist
International
8 Ordsall Road
Retford
Nottinghamshire
DN22 7PL

International Aestheticians
Bache Hall
Bache Hall Estate
Chester
CH2 2BR

International Federation of Aromatherapists
Department of Continuing Education
Royal Masonic Hospital
Ravenscourt Park
London
W6 0TN

International Society of Professional
Aromatherapists
Hinckley and District Hospital and Health
Centre
The Annexe
Mount Road
Hinckley
Leicestershire
LE10 1AE

Bibliography

ABC of Dermatology, second edition, P. K. Buxton, BMJ Publishing, 1993.

Aromatherapy Handbook, The, Daniele Ryman, C. W. Daniel, 1989.

Art and Science of Manicuring, Alice Cimaglia, Milady Publishing, 1990.

Atlas of Anatomy, Trevor Weston, Marshall Cavendish, 1900.

Basic Anatomy and Physiology, third edition, H. G. Q. Rowett, John Murray, 1990.

Beyond Cellulite, Nicole Ronsard, Century Vermilion, 1993.

Business Studies, David Hall, Rob Jones and Carlo Raffo, Causeway Press, 1993.

Clayton's Electrotherapy, ninth edition, Forster and Palastanga, W. B. Saunders, 1985.

Complete Aromatherapy Handbook, Susanne Fischer-Rizzi, Sterling, 1991.

Dermatology: An Illustrated Guide, third edition, Lionel Fry, Butterworth-Heinemann, 1984.

First Aid Manual, seventh edition, St John's Ambulance Association, Dorling Kindersley, 1997.

Illustrated Encyclopaedia of Essential Oils, Julia Lawless, Element Books Ltd, 1995.

Lloyd's Bank Small Business Guide 1997, tenth edition, Sara Williams, Penguin Books, 1996.

Management and the Organization, Shaun Gregson and Frank Livesey, Butterworth-Heinemann, 1983.

Management: Concepts and Applications, fourth edition, L. C. Megginson, D. C. Mosley and P. H. Pietri, Addison Wesley Longman, 1991.

Manual of Nutrition, tenth edition, HMSO, 1995.

Nails in Disease, Peter D. Samman, Butterworth-Heinemann, 1995.

Physiology and Performance, National Coaching Foundation, White Line Press, 1988.

Practical Aromatherapy, third edition, Shirley Price, Thorsons, 1994.

Practical Aromatherapy, Penny Rich, Robinson Publishing, 1994.

Principles of Anatomy and Physiology, sixth edition, G. Tortora and N. Anagnostakos, Addison Wesley Longman, 1990.

Ross and Wilson's Anatomy and Physiology in Health and Illness, eighth edition, Kathleen J. W. Wilson amd Janet Ross, Churchill Livingstone, 1996.

Skin Deep, Alix Kirsta, Century Publishing, 1985.

Supervision, Mike Savedra and John Hawthorn, Macmillan, 1990.

Supervisor's Handbook, The, Julie Reay, Northwood Books, 1981.

Index